PORTRAIT AND BIOGRAPHICAL

RECORD

OF

ORANGE COUNTY
NEW YORK

Containing Portraits and Biographical Sketches of Prominent
and Representative Citizens of the County.

— Volume 3 —

NEW YORK AND CHICAGO:
CHAPMAN PUBLISHING CO.,
1895.

HERITAGE BOOKS
2011

HERITAGE BOOKS
AN IMPRINT OF HERITAGE BOOKS, INC.

Books, CDs, and more—Worldwide

For our listing of thousands of titles see our website
at
www.HeritageBooks.com

A Facsimile Reprint
Published 2011 by
HERITAGE BOOKS, INC.
Publishing Division
100 Railroad Ave. #104
Westminster, Maryland 21157

Copyright © 1994 Heritage Books, Inc.

Originally published: New York and Chicago
Chapman Publishing Co.
1895

— Publisher's Notice —

The first 110 pages of the original text, containing biographies of the presidents of the United States, have been omitted from this reprint. Also missing are pages 607–608, 821–822, 1129–1130, 1165–1166, 1273–1274, and 1279–1280; since the text is not disrupted, these pages most likely contained illustrations.

In reprints such as this, it is often not possible to remove blemishes from the original. We feel the contents of this book warrant its reissue despite these blemishes and hope you will agree and read it with pleasure.

International Standard Book Numbers
Paperbound: 978-0-7884-5353-3
Clothbound: 978-0-7884-8872-6

fidelity. Mrs. Sallie Gordon died at the age of seventy-six. She had long been a member of the Presbyterian Church and served her Master faithfully. Of the five children born to Elias and Sallie Gordon, four are yet living. Laura, who married Daniel Bedford, died in Sullivan County; Elizabeth G., now Mrs. Harry Moot, resides in Liberty; Coggswell K. is our subject; Jerusha is Mrs. Chancy Wheeler, of Youngsville, Sullivan County; and Sophia is Mrs. Luther Smith, of Cedar Falls, Iowa.

The subject of this sketch was reared in Sullivan County, and was educated in its public schools. From a boy he was very handy with tools, and learned the carpenter's trade with his father, continuing with him from the time he was fifteen until twenty-one years of age.

He then located in the Strong Settlement, where he engaged in contracting and building. In 1847, when the Erie Railroad was being constructed, he entered the employ of the company as master carpenter on the Delaware Division, having in charge the carpenters engaged in building bridges and trestles between Port Jervis and Susquehanna, Pa. He was also foreman in the shops where the bridges were constructed at Owego, and had charge of the bridges placed on the road from Corning to Jersey City, together with those on some other branches of the road. He was with the Erie Railroad from 1847 to 1874, a period of twenty-seven years, for ten years of that time being roadmaster on the Delaware Division, including the Carbondale Branch. In 1874 he resigned his position with the Erie Road and located in Middletown, where he engaged in the lumber and coal busiuess on Henry Street, buying out the yard of William G. Stanton. In this business he continued until 1889, when he sold out, and has since been living a retired life. He owns a beautiful residence at No. 28 Highland Avenue, and is there living in the enjoyment of a life well spent.

Mr. Gordon was married in the town of Thompson, Sullivan County, in January, 1843, to Phœbe Monroe, who was born in the town of Crawford, Orange County. They became the parents of four children: Albert, engaged in car-

pentering in Middletown; Alice, who married Lewis Stanton, and died at Fishkill. N. Y.; Adella, Mrs. C. W. Martin, of Middletown; and Carrie, who married Rev. George W. Downs, of the Methodist Episcopal Church, and resides in Middletown.

In politics Mr. Gordon is a stanch Republican, and while a resident of Narrowsburg, Sullivan County, he was a Trustee of schools. In 1889 he was elected Assessor of Middletown, and by reelection served six years. Religiously he is a member of the Methodist Episcopal Church, of which he is Treasurer and Trustee, and has served as Steward. Before the organization of the Republican party he was a Whig, and voted for William Henry Harrison in 1840.

━━━━━━━━❀❀❀━━━━━━━━

CHARLES C. FULLERTON, of the town of Wawayanda, was born here in 1847. His early life was spent on the farm, and his education was received in the common schools. When ten years of age he left home and began working on the farm by the month, continuing in that occupation until 1864, when he enlisted in the Seventh New York Independent Battery, being mustered into the service at Goshen. From that place he was sent to New York City, and thence to Virginia, his first engagement being at Dutch Gap Canal, where he received a flesh wound. The battery saw considerable service, during the remainder of the war, and was in the engagements at Ft. Darling, Drury's Bluff and Manchester, besides many skirmishes. Just before the final surrender of Lee, the soldiers were reduced to two hardtacks and a limited supply of coffee per day. Mr. Fullerton was in front of Manchester, on the James River, at the time of the surrender, and he received his discharge at Albany, August 22, 1865. He then went to Ulster County, where he remained until 1876, when he removed to his present place of residence.

On the 21st of December, 1869, he was united in marriage with Eliza C. Conklin, and by their union seven children were born: Augusta L., now the wife of George D. Booth; Ellen J., Sarah J., Elsie D., Annie B., Etta D. and Edna.

Politically Mr. Fullerton is a Democrat. In 1880 he was elected Justice of the Peace, and has since held the office, with the exception of the year 1893. He has been a member of the Board of Health since 1881. Socially he is a member of the Grand Army of the Republic. As a citizen he stands high in the estimation of his fellow-citizens, as is attested by his repeated election to local office.

WILLIAM F. WHEELER. Five generations of the Wheeler family have resided on the farm where the subject of this notice makes his home. The property is situated in the town of Warwick, and comprises two hundred and eighty acres, upon which first-class improvements have been made. While some attention is given to the raising of cereals, the principal industry is the dairy business, which is one of the most profitable industries in the county. Upon the place will be seen all the buildings necessary for the proper management of the farm, including substantial barns and a neat residence.

The founder of the family in this section of the country was Joel Wheeler, who settled here in 1800. His son, Col. William F., the grandfather of our subject, was a native of Orange County, and was born in a little hamlet, formerly called Wheelerville. His father bought the Wheeler homestead, which has been in the family for ninety-five years. The old house and barn are still standing, the former being occupied by tenants. The present family residence was erected in 1850, and is commodious and substantial, as are also the barns. Some years after the erection of the house, it gained the first prize as the best model farm house in the county.

The parents of our subject, Isaac V. and Phœbe (Bull) Wheeler, were born in this county, and the father followed agricultural pursuits throughout his entire life. He died in 1876, and was followed to the grave by hundreds of friends and relatives, who held him in the highest esteem.

Preferring to attend to his private affairs rather than mingle with politicians or become prominent in public life, he never sought o e. His wife, who is now sixty-five years old, still enjoys good health.

On the farm where he now resides, William F. Wheeler was born May 22, 1859. He attended the district school, and for a number of years was a student in the Warwick Institute. When he was sixteen years of age, his father died, and he was compelled to leave school and take charge of the farm. From that time until the present, he has labored early and late, and is to-day the possessor of a valuable farm, the high standard of which he maintains. He takes a special interest in dairy matters, and is serving as Secretary of the Warwick Valley Milk Association, of which he is also a Trustee.

In May, 1882, Mr. Wheeler married Miss Tillie, daughter of William P. and Mary R. (Roe) Wisner, natives of this county. Five children came to bless their home: William F., Jr., Charles V., Jesse I., Mary A. and Roe, all of whom are with their parents. Mrs. Wheeler is a member of the Reformed Church. In politics our subject is a Republican, and believes firmly in the principles of that party, but cares nothing for official positions. He is a highly respected citizen, and enjoys the confidence of friends and neighbors.

SAMUEL A. CONFORT, a well known business man of Searsville, established himself in the confidence and good-will of this locality years ago by his uniformly fair and upright dealings. He was born in this county November 26, 1828, and since that time has been closely identified with its prosperity, taking an active interest in whatever affects its welfare.

Our subject was sixth in order of birth of the children born to Samuel and Fannie (Low) Confort. Of these, Mary Jane, the eldest, died when sixty-five years old; Eve Ann was seventy years old at the time of her decease; Lawrence L., who

FARM RESIDENCE OF WILLIAM F. WHEELER,
Two Miles East of Warwick, Orange County, N. Y.

was for many years a minister of the Dutch Reformed Church in this and Ulster Counties, died at the age of sixty-five years; Emily is now living in Michigan; Elizabeth makes her home in this county; Samuel A. was the next-born; Julia died after attaining her thirtieth year; Jacob T. was accidentally killed when forty years of age; James died in his fifty-eighth year; and Alonzo is farming on the old home place in this town.

Samuel Confort, Sr., was also born in Orange County, and passed the greater part of his life in farming in the town of Crawford. He was well-to-do in this world's goods, and died when in his fifty-ninth year. In his political views he was an adherent of Democratic principles, and in the Reformed Church, of which he was a member, held the office of Elder. During the War of 1812 he won distinction as a soldier. Many generations back his parents came of good old German stock. The mother of our subject was also a native of the town of Crawford, and survived her husband many years, dying when seventy-five years of age.

The subject of this sketch remained at home until about thirty years of age, when he was married, and purchased a tract of land, on which he located. After operating this for five years he sold out and came to Searsville, where for the past thirty years he has conducted a general store. He is therefore well known, and his upright manner of dealing has secured for him the good-will and patronage of the people for miles around.

November 1, 1860, Mr. Confort and Miss Sarah Ellen Youngblood were united in marriage. The lady was born in this town, and has become the mother of two children: Fannie Jane, who married R. C. Gillespie, of this town; and Julia Ellen, at home with her parents. Mr. Confort has always taken a very active part in local politics, and never fails to vote for Democratic candidates. He has been Clerk of the town for several years and has occupied the position of Postmaster of Searsville for a quarter of a century. Our subject and his family are members of the Reformed Church, in which he has been Deacon and Elder. He is very active in church work, and gives liberally of his means toward extending the good cause throughout the county. Mr. Confort is just and considerate of the rights of all with whom he is brought in contact, and conscientious in the observance of all the proprieties of life. Thus he has made many friendships, which grow stronger with more intimate acquaintance.

SAMUEL GLASSON, D. V. S., of Middletown, has his office and veterinary hospital at No. 7 Roberts Street, and also an office in Wilkinson's livery stable. In February, 1895, he was called as expert witness in the Long and McKenzie case, and also filled a similar function in a law trial, both cases being decided in accordance with his testimony.

The Glasson family is of Scotch and French descent. Our subject's grandfather, James Glasson, was extensively engaged in buying and selling horses, having an office on Cliff Street, New York. The father of our subject, Samuel, was born in New York City, where he was employed as mechanic, electrician and inventor, having designed and patented a number of useful articles. Socially he was a Knight-Templar Mason. During the Civil War he enlisted as a private in the Eighth Connecticut Infantry, and later was promoted to the rank of Captain of Company C of that regiment, serving in that capacity until he was obliged to resign on account of rheumatism.

The mother of our subject, Emeline B., was born in Massachusetts, and was a daughter of Benjamin Loomis, at one time Postmaster of Pine Meadow, Conn., and a participant in the Civil War. He served first as Drum Major of the Thirteenth Connecticut Infantry, and later was similarly engaged with the Second Louisiana Infantry. His death occurred in Connecticut. Of the family of three children who attained years of maturity, our subject is the youngest child and only son. In New York City, where he was born, his education was obtained in the public schools and in the College of the City of New York. Four years were spent in that institution, but he left just at the commencement of the junior year, and entered the American Veterinary College, where he remained until his graduation in 1893, with the degree of D. V. S.

For six months after graduating Dr. Glasson practiced his profession in Peekskill. In January, 1894, he was appointed veterinary surgeon of a detachment of cavalry at West Point, and held the same position for the whole reservation, meantime continuing his practice at Peekskill. He became known in other places, and was frequently called to Highland Falls and Newburgh. In August, 1894, through the assistance of the Adjutant-General at Washington, he received an honorable discharge and retired from the army, after which he spent a few months in New York City. In March, 1895, he located in Middletown, where he has become well and favorably known for the thoroughness of his work.

The marriage of Dr. Glasson, which took place in New York City, united him with Miss Harriet Gray, and they are the parents of a son, Harold L. Socially Dr. Glasson is connected with the Phi Gamma Delta Society in the College of the City of New York, and he is also identified with the United States Veterinary Association, and is a fellow in the Medical Association of the American Veterinary College.

C. B. WILKES, of the firm of C. B. Wilkes & Bros., dealers in coal and wood, was born at Seven Springs Mountain House, in the town of Monroe, September 16, 1858, and is a son of George F. and Hilenda (Maroney) Wilkes, the former a native of the town of Monroe, and the latter of the town of Goshen. His grandfather, Jonathan Wilkes, was also a native of Orange County, and his great-grandfather came from England. The father was a second cousin of George Wilkes, editor of the New York *Sporting Times*, and the breeder of the original Wilkes horses. George F. Wilkes was a large farmer in the town of Monroe, and continued farming until his retirement in 1887, when he removed to Mid-

dletown, and here died at the age of seventy-three years. From the organization of the Republican party he was a strong advocate of its principles. In religion he was a devout member of the Methodist Church, of which body his wife is also a member. She is yet living and resides in Middletown. Of their eight children, seven are yet living.

C. B. Wilkes, our subject, was reared on his father's farm, and had only the advantages of a common-school education. He remained at home until 1887, and then had charge of the farm and dairy business until 1890. At that time he located in Middletown, and started in the wood and coal business on Railroad Avenue, near North Street, in company with his brother, George M. There they remained until removing to their present location, on the corner of Beattie and Railroad Avenue. Here they have a factory and tenement house of two flats, and here also they manufacture kindling-wood, having a wood-splitting machine run by steam, eighteen horsepower, with a capacity of one hundred barrels an hour. The coal-yard and office are also located at this point. Two teams are constantly engaged, and the firm does a large wholesale as well as retail business. They are popular men, and enjoy the confidence of the entire community.

Mr. Wilkes was married in Circleville to Miss Mamie Gibbs, who was there born, and they have one child, Hilda S. In politics Mr. Wilkes is a Republican, and in his religious belief is a Congregationalist. He is a member and Deacon in the North Street Congregational Church, and has been very active in building up the society. He was a member of the Ontario Hose Company, and was President of the same for one year.

BURKE PILLSBURY, M. D. During the period of nearly twenty-five years in which he has engaged in the practice of medicine, Dr. Pillsbury has gained a broad experience, which, ripened by careful study, enables him to make a successful diagnosis of the most intricate and complicated diseases, and to apply the remedial agencies calculated to bring the speediest relief to the patient. He has his office in Middletown, where he has charge of an extensive and remunerative practice, covering a large portion of the surrounding country.

It being generally believed that heredity and environment have much to do with forming the character, and that our lives are stimulated by the immediate or indirect influence of our ancestors, a short resume of the ancestral history of Mr. Pillsbury may serve as an index to the liberal impulses that mark his daily life. Through his maternal ancestors he traces his lineage to John Alden and Priscilla Molines, of Puritan fame. His paternal ancestors were equally prominent and honorable, the family being of the oldest Colonial stock.

His great-grandfather, Joshua, as shown by the Revolutionary rolls in the Massachusetts capitol, was one of the minutemen who responded to the Lexington alarm, April 19, 1775. His great-uncle, Samuel, was of the boat's crew that rowed Benedict Arnold to the British ship "Vulture," at the time of his escape, and was captured by the British and carried to New York. Another ancestor, Elijah Pillsbury, fought with General Wolfe on the Heights of Abraham, and still another went with the expedition to Louisburg. The progenitor of the family in America came to this country in the "Mayflower," upon the second trip of that historic ship, in 1641.

The name of Pillsbury is derived from "peel," meaning a tower, and "bury," a hill or mound. The name has been identified with the history of the ancient parish of Leek, in Staffordshire, England, ever since King Edward IV. commanded, in 1333, that each individual should "take upon himself a separate surname, either of his trade or faculty, or from some quality of his body or mind, or the place where he dwelt, so that everyone might be distinguished from the other." Pillsbury Grange is a quaint and ancient place, twelve miles across the moorland in the parish of Hartington, belonging to the rich Cistercian Abbey of Dieulacres. Leek was in the earldom of Algar,

son of Godiva, and was the last place in England to yield to the encroachments of William the Conqueror.

The above is an engraving of the ancient arms of the family, of which the following description is given: "Arms: Arg. on a chev. inter three crosses crosslet fitchee, sa, five ermine spots or. Crest: On a torque, arg. and sa, a felon's head couped ppr. with rope around the neck and cross on breast. Motto: *Mors janua vitæ.*

The subject of this sketch was born in Boston, Mass. In youth his educational advantages were exceptionally good, and upon completing his literary education he turned his attention to the medical profession. This science he commenced to study in 1868 and four years later he was graduated from the Harvard Medical School. To his theoretical knowledge he added practical experience gained by a year's hospital course in the Massachusetts General Hospital and at St. Mary's in Rochester. Since beginning in active practice it has always been his ambition to keep abreast with the latest discoveries in the science, and he has remained a close, thoughtful student of the profession.

For thirteen years the Doctor has been a member of the United States Pension Board, and he is also examiner for numerous insurance companies. In professional circles, both in this country and abroad, he is well known, being a member of the State Medical Society, the New York Academy of Medicine and the Tuberculosis Congress of Paris. He has met with signal success in the treatment of consumption, in which he has taken a deep interest. In addition to this he is also an expert microscopist and pathologist, holding himself in readiness to make any examination called for. There are few of the major operations in surgery that he has not performed with success. Among the physicians of this locality he ranks high, and has served with efficiency as President of the Orange County Medical Society. He has secured a substantial recognition of the genuineness of his merits in his professional capacity, and by his conscientious discharge of duty, his ability and skill, and his character as a gentleman of culture, he has won the confidence which is the crown of his manhood. While his attention has been given principally to matters connected with his profession, he is also interested in other organizations and matters of public interest, and is an active member of the New York Society, Sons of the Revolution.

REV. JAMES C. FORSYTHE, pastor of the Presbyterian Church of Montgomery, was born in Allegheny County, Pa., June 24, 1826, and is the son of George and Margaret (Henry) Forsythe. The family is of Scotch-Irish descent. James C. Forsythe, the great-grandfather, emigrated from the North of Ireland to Chester, Pa., in 1730. Accompanied by his son James, he settled in Mifflin, Pa., eight miles from Pittsburg when on the site of the latter city were no buildings save the remains of old Ft. Pitt, this being during the period between the French and Indian and Revolutionary Wars. The next in line of direct descent was also James Forsythe, and three generations of the family were buried side by side in Mifflin, Pa.

George Forsythe inherited a part of the old homestead which belonged to his grandfather. With his family he removed to Washington County, Pa., and there our subject grew to maturity

and acquired his education in Washington College, from which he was graduated in 1848. This was the year after James G. Blaine graduated from that school, and the young men were companions in college together for two years. Mr. Forsythe later entered the Associate Reformed Theological Seminary at Allegheny, Pa., and was graduated therefrom in 1852. The previous year, however, he was licensed to preach, and his first pastorate was at Cadiz, the county seat of Harrison County, Ohio, where John C. Brigham was one of his parishioners. There he was ordained in November, 1852, by the Associate Reformed Presbytery of Steubenville, Ohio. He remained at Cadiz for five years, and did a good work. During his stay there the Associate Reformed Church and the Associate Presbyterian Church were united, under the name of the United Presbyterian Church, into a strong organization.

Mr. Forsythe's next pastorate was at Salem, Washington County, N. Y., where he continued for twelve years. The church was in a disorganized condition when he took charge and required delicate management. It had been established by a band of members who emigrated together from Ireland one hundred and thirty years before, and the church celebrated the one hundredth anniversary of this emigration during the pastorate of Mr. Forsythe. His labors there were very successful. They built up a strong congregation, and in 1870 he left the church in a flourishing condition. He then accepted a call from the Reformed Church of Farmer Village, of Seneca County, where he remained for five years, when, on the 1st of July, 1875, he was established as the pastor of the Presbyterian Church of Montgomery, of which he has now had charge for twenty years. It had been formed about sixty years previous, but was then in a broken-down condition. Rev. Mr. Forsythe's work here, as in other places, soon proved beneficial; large numbers have been added to the church, societies have been organized that are now in good working order, and the whole church is flourishing.

On the 10th of November, 1857, in Braintree, Mass., Rev. Mr. Forsythe married Miss Persis

COURTLAND S. HULSE.

Maria Thayer, of that place. They had three children, but all have been called to the home beyond. Elizabeth Thayer died in infancy, Harriet Thayer at the age of two and a-half years, and James Storrs in his thirteenth year. Mrs. Forsythe is a most estimable lady, an efficient helper to her husband, extending her sympathy to the suffering, and lending a helping hand to the poor and needy.

Rev. Mr. Forsythe is a Republican, but takes no active part in politics. He is the only surviving charter member of the Phi Gamma Delta Society, the mother of all the Delta societies in the United States, and his connection with it began in the days when it was bitterly opposed by college officials; but in the years that have passed it has become very popular, and is now strongly encouraged by college professors. Rev. Mr. Forsythe is a man of large body and mind, powerful physically as well as mentally. He is possessed of clear, keen perception, is quick of comprehension, and soon notes and masters the strong points of any subject. He is a logical reasoner, a fluent and forcible speaker, and his earnest and effective words in the pulpit have been productive of a good that cannot be estimated on this side of the grave. He is pleasant and warmhearted, possessing a kindly and charitable disposition, and all recognize in him a friend on whom they may depend in the hour of need. He is loved by his own people and those of other denominations, and throughout the community no one is more highly respected than the pastor of the Presbyterian Church of Montgomery.

COURTLAND S. HULSE, who is numbered among the oldest citizens of Middletown, was born in the town of Mt. Hope, this county, April 14, 1818. He is the son of Anselm H. Hulse, a native of this county and a member of the family that came here from Long Island. His grandfather and the grandfather of G. O. Hulse were own brothers. Settling upon a tract of unimproved land, Anselm H. Hulse succeeded in redeeming it from the wilderness and converted it into a productive farm, one of the best in Mt. Hope. From there he moved to the town of Crawford, where he died at the age of more than seventy years. His wife, Catherine, was born in New Jersey, to which state her father, Thomas Cahill, had come from Ireland.

In the family of Anselm H. Hulse there were six sons and six daughters, but Courtland S. and Mrs. Ellen Jane Tice, of Cass County, Mich., are the only survivors. The former was reared in the towns of Wallkill and Crawford, and attended school at Campbell Hall. At the age of sixteen he was apprenticed to the painter's trade at Montgomery, where he remained for three years, and then came to Middletown. In 1838 he finished the trade under George S. Corwin, and soon afterward started for himself, following his chosen occupation here until 1851. He then went to Morristown, N. J., where he was employed as a contract painter for eleven years, coming back to Middletown in 1862. He purchased ten acres on what is now Cottage Street, and in 1876 built a residence at No. 47 East Main Street, where he has since made his home.

At Middletown, February 27, 1840, Mr. Hulse married Miss Susan Wood, who was born in Goshen, being a daughter of Benjamin Wood, proprietor of a tannery at Dolsontown. Mrs. Susan Hulse died at their home in Middletown March 22, 1891, aged seventy-four years. Of her four children, the only survivors are Martha and Antoinette, both at home. The latter is the wife of George Hommel, who was born in Wurtemberg, Germany, came to New York City in 1872, and to Middletown in 1887, since which time he has carried on a bakery business. He and his wife are the parents of a son, Roger Courtland.

In former years Mr. Hulse was connected with the Independent Order of Odd Fellows, belonging to the lodge at Middletown. He was a member of the pioneer fire company of this city. Politically he is a Democrat, and in his younger years took an active part in public affairs. While in New Jersey he was in partnership with his brother-in-law, George S. Corwin, the firm title being Corwin & Hulse, but Mr. Corwin died while there, and Mr. Hulse soon returned to Middletown. He has been identified with the growth of this city and a promoter of its public enterprises. He laid out Courtland Street, which was named in his honor, and erected the first house on that street, a structure that still stands. For a time he was engaged in the restaurant business on North Street, where he built a store. No man has taken a greater interest than he in the upbuilding of this place, and its prosperity is due to the efforts of such men as he. In politics he is independent.

—+–+– —◊>÷◦⊛◦÷<◦— –+–+—

APT. LEWIS S. WISNER is one of the oldest residents of Middletown, and traces his ancestry back for several generations. He was born in Middletown, August 11, 1841, and his father, Daniel Carpenter Wisner, was also born here, in 1807, his death occurring in 1871. His grandfather, Henry Barnet Wisner, was born in Orange County in 1772, and died in 1846. For many years he was a Justice of the Peace, and started the first store in Middletown, on Main Street, being a partner of Stacy Beakes. He owned the land which was later purchased by the father of our subject, and which is now part of our subject's estate. Maj. Henry Wisner, the great-grandfather of our subject, was born in Orange County, in 1740, and died April 11, 1800. He served as Captain in the Revolutionary War, and later was commissioned Major of Colonel Hathorn's Warwick and Florida Regiment. He lived on the Wallkill, on the present site of Barr's Hotel at Phillipsburg, his farm adjoining the Midway Park. In addition to farming he operated a gristmill on the place. During the Revolutionary War he was engaged in the manufacture of powder, a business started by his father at Phillipsburg. He married Sarah Barnet, who was born in 1742, and who died in 1790.

The great-great-grandfather of our subject was Hon. Henry Wisner, born in the town of Goshen in 1720. He was a delegate to the First, Second and Third Continental Congresses, and voted for the Declaration of Independence, July 4, 1776, but did not wait to sign the document, for the reason that he was sent home to manufacture powder, which was needed to enforce that measure. He was one of the four commissioners who laid out West Point, and also assisted in the selection of the site of Ft. Putnam. From 1770 to 1782 he was in the State Legislature, and was very prominent in business transactions. He died in 1790, and his remains are interred in Hopper Hill Cemetery. Over the grave, on the red sandstone slab, is recorded the following: "Sacred to the memory of Henry Wisner, who departed this life March 4, 1790, a devoted friend to the liberties of his country." On account of the extensive aid furnished his country he died in poverty. His wife was Sarah Norton, who came from the eastern end of Long Island.

The great-great-great-grandfather of our subject, Hendrick Wisner, was born in 1698, and died in 1767. He came with his father from Switzerland, and in 1719 married Mary Shaw, a native of New England. He became very wealthy, and was an extensive land-owner. His father, Johannis Wisner, the great-great-great-great-grandfather of our subject, also came from Switzerland. He was a Lieutenant in the Swiss Contingent of Queen Anne's army, and is said to have been the first settler in Orange County on the Wawayanda Patent. Our subject has deeds of every one of his ancestors, except Johannis, as far back as 1703, and signed by Queen Anne.

Daniel C. Wisner, the father of our subject, was by occupation a farmer, and followed that vocation all his life. He was an Elder in the Second Presbyterian Church of Middletown, and was one of its charter members. In politics he was originally a Whig and afterwards a Republican. He married Sarah M. Weed, who was born in 1813, at Stamford, Conn., and who was a daughter of Smith Weed. The latter was a cooper by trade, and died in Connecticut. Mrs. Wisner, who died in 1885, was a relative of Uzual Knapp, one of Washington's bodyguards. The marriage of Mr. and Mrs. Wisner occurred in

1833, and by their union four children were born: Sarah M., who died in infancy; Julia Ann, who died at twenty years of age; Henry B., who resides in Berea, Ohio; and Capt. Lewis Smith, the subject of this sketch.

Capt. Lewis S. Wisner was the youngest of the family, and grew to manhood in his native town, which has always been his home. He was educated in the public schools, and finished his course in Wallkill Academy. Until August 6, 1862, he remained at home, engaged in farming with his father, but at that time enlisted in Company K, One Hundred and Twenty-fourth New York Volunteer Infantry, as a private. Soon after he was promoted to be Second Sergeant, then First Sergeant, and in May, 1863, was commissioned Second Lieutenant. February 23, 1864, he was promoted to be First Lieutenant, and July 14, 1864, was commissioned Captain of his company. No man in the regiment received more promotions. He was in all the general engagements until his discharge, and was slightly wounded at Chancellorsville. On account of severe hernia he resigned, August 2, 1864, and returned home.

On recovering his health, Captain Wisner went to Titusville, Pa., where he purchased real estate, and for a time was engaged in speculation. Returning home, he purchased the old homestead, on which he now resides, and which consists of fifty acres. It has a beautiful location on Wisner Avenue, which was laid out and improved at his expense. He has constructed an artificial lake on the place, and has it stocked with black bass. His fine residence is provided with a porch around the entire house. Captain Wisner is an admirer of Jersey cattle, in which he has been quite an extensive dealer, and at present has a number of fine animals. On his place are fine beds of sand of the very best quality for building purposes.

June 21, 1865, Mr. Wisner was married, in Middletown, to Miss Adelaide Robertson, who was born in Centreville, and who is a daughter of George E. Robertson, a retired farmer of Middletown. The latter was born at South Centreville, while his father, David Robertson, was born in Scotland, and settled at Centreville at an early day. His wife was Catherine Swartwout, of French-Huguenot descent. Of this union were born three children, two of whom are living, Mrs. Wisner being the second-born. She was reared in Middletown, and was educated in a private seminary. To Captain and Mrs. Wisner were born four children: Mary R., a graduate of Wallkill Academy; George R., who is now in Colorado, an engineer on the Santa Fe Railway; Henry Barnet, a clerk in the Merchants' and Mechanics' Bank; and Theresa Weed, a student in Wallkill Academy.

Captain Wisner is a charter member of Capt. William A. Jackson Post No. 301, G. A. R., and he is also a member of the New York Sons of the Revolution. In politics he is a true-blue Republican, and religiously is a member of the Methodist Episcopal Church. During the past year he received a medal of honor tendered him by the United States Congress for gallantry at Spottsylvania, Va., May 12, 1864. This was given in response to a petition signed by every surviving officer of the One Hundred and Twenty-fourth Regiment.

THOMAS L. GILLSON, M. D., is a successful practicing physician of Middletown. He was born at Budd's Lake, N. J., December 31, 1862, and is a son of Hugh B. and Mary (Donohue) Gillson, both of whom are natives of Ireland. The grandfather, Hugh Gillson, was also a native of Ireland, where for many years he was Superintendent of Schools and where he died. The father was reared in his native country, and when eighteen years of age came to America, and located in Morris County, N. J., and later in Sussex County, that state. There he was engaged as a mining contractor until he removed to a farm known as the old Gillson Farm, one-half mile from Franklin Furnace, N. J., where he yet lives at the age of sixty-eight years. In politics he has always been a Democrat, and is a prominent town official. His wife, the mother of our subject, is a daughter of Michael Donohue, who was a farmer by occupation, but who is now deceased. Hugh B. and Mary Gillson are the parents of nine children: M. W., a practicing physician of Paterson, N. J.; James R., a tea merchant of Troy, N. Y.; John T., a physician at Paterson, N. J.; Thomas L., our subject; Hugh B., Jr., a merchant at Albany, N.Y.; Mary E., a teacher in Sussex County, N. J.; Theresa, a trained nurse at home; and Sarah and Anna, at home.

In his youth our subject attended Baxter's School at Franklin Furnace, N. J., and in 1881 commenced teaching school at McAfee and Stockholm, N. J. The remarkable aptitude and native energy of the young teacher led to his being appointed Principal of the well-known Bloomingdale Academy, at Passaic, N. J. During the latter years of his teaching at this academy, he had a strong inclination towards medicine, and with his brother, Dr. M. W. Gillson, a prominent physician of Paterson, N. J., he commenced its study. After leaving his brother, he went to Bellevue Medical College, New York, in 1888, taking two complete courses of study, and spending much time in the use of the scalpel, under the direction of master surgeons there. In 1891 he graduated from the Long Island College and Hospital. For some time previously he had studied under the famous Dr. Skene, of Brooklyn, and therefore had received a thorough intellectual and medical training.

In 1891 Dr. Gillson located at Middletown, where he has built up a large and well paying practice. For two years he was Health Officer of Middletown, and is at present examiner for several insurance companies. He is an honorary member of McQuaid Engine and Fire Company, and of the Orange County Medical Society. In religion he is a member of St. Joseph's Catholic Church, and is examining physician of the Catholic Benevolent Legion.

Dr. Gillson was married at Bloomingdale, Passaic County, N. J., in 1889, to Miss Elizabeth Heffernan, a native of that place, and daughter of Thomas and Margaret Heffernan, the former of whom was for years manager of the Booneton Iron Works. Mrs. Gillson was educated in Bloomingdale and at Paterson, and was leader in St. Anthony's Church Choir at the former place. Three children have been born unto our subject and wife: Marguerite Theresa, Mary Elizabeth, and Thomas L., Jr.

Besides being a well trained student and physician, Dr. Gillson has talent as a speaker. During the Cleveland campaign of 1884 he was a member of the New Jersey State Democratic Committee, and was the youngest stump speaker in that state. He canvassed the state in company with the late ex-Gov. Leon Abbett, and Hon. Thomas Noonan, of Jersey City. In his profession, Dr. Gillson is highly esteemed by the practitioners of every school of medicine.

HORATIO NELSON CASE, one the best known citizens of the town of Wawayanda, has made his home on his present farm since he was five years of age. He is a man of unostentatious and quiet life, and has made it his main business to attend to the wants of his family and to the proper management of his farm.

Our subject was born in the village of Monroe, May 31, 1824, and was the son of Gideon and Hannah (Terry) Case, the former a native of the town of Goshen, this county. The grandfather, who bore the name of Zaccheus Case, was born on Long Island. He departed this life January 9, 1822, aged eighty-one years, and was buried in the town of Goshen. He married Hannah Salmon, who died September 12, 1823, aged seventy-seven years. Gideon Case fought as a soldier in the War of 1812 one year, bearing himself honorably and bravely in that conflict. He died November 4, 1867, at the age of eighty-two years, ten months and four days. Our subject has but one sister, Hannah J., who is living in Newburgh and is the wife of William Chambers. Another sister, Jane, died in the town of Monroe when two years and a-half old.

The father of our subject, who was a farmer

REV. JOSEPH RECHTSTEINER.

through life, moved from the town of Goshen to this section about 1829, and here lived until his decease, which occurred November 4, 1867, his remains being interred in Ridgebury Cemetery. As stated above, Horatio Nelson was in his fifth year at the time the family came hither, and is therefore one of its oldest residents. Being the only son of the household, he took charge of the farm on the demise of his father, and has continued to manage it ever since. It is thirty-four acres in extent, and although not as large as many in the town, is cultivated in such a manner as to bring forth good results. Mr. Case thoroughly understands his business, and as he enjoys it is satisfied to spend the remainder of his life amidst rural scenes. He has never been active in political matters, but is always anxious during elections of every nature to vote for Democratic candidates.

◇◁++++++++++++◈++++++++++++▷◇

REV. JOSEPH RECHTSTEINER, pastor of St. Peter's German Evangelical Lutheran Church of Port Jervis, received a call from his present congregation in March, 1888, where he located and has ever since made his home. He is a native of Germany, born in Granheim, Wurtemberg, on the 9th of February, 1853, and was educated in the gymnasium at Ehingen, where he took a complete course of ten years, after which he took the theological course in the Tubingen University, and also studied Greek, French and Hebrew in a gymnasium. On account of the demands of the Government for military service, and not wishing to become a soldier, he left college at the age of twenty-one years, before completing the course, and started for the United States. Taking passage on a steamer at Liverpool, England, he landed in New York on the 27th of October, 1874, a stranger in a strange land, and unable to speak our language.

Mr. Rechtsteiner immediately proceeded to New Hampshire, where he went to work with a shovel, and for one month was thus employed; but not being able to collect his wages, he returned to New York City, using some money that he had

brought with him. For eleven months he was then engaged with an American family as a farm hand in Rockland County, and there picked up the language. At this place he received $6 per month and his board, but later began working for a German farmer. While thus employed, he met a German Presbyterian minister, Rev. Henry Lock, who took an interest in him and persuaded him to attend the prayer-meetings. This gentleman later sent him to the Presbyterian Theological Seminary at Bloomfield, N. J., where he remained for one year. He then entered the Lutheran Theological Seminary at Mt. Ayr, Philadelphia, where he pursued his studies for a year. He had paid his own tuition thus far, but as his money now gave out, he applied for a position as teacher. At a college in Nyack, N. Y., he taught Greek, French and Spanish for about six months.

On the expiration of that time, Mr. Rechtsteiner received a call from a congregation in Allegheny County, Pa., and in March, 1878, there preached his first sermon. The following August he was ordained before the Pittsburg Synod, at Greenville, Pa., and remained with his first charge for four years, leaving the church in an excellent condition. He then went to Mahanoy City, Schuylkill County, Pa., where he preached for two years, when he was called to Rochester, N. Y., where he had charge of a large congregation for three years. There he repaired the house of worship, and paid off a large part of the church debt. He was then called to the directorship of Wagner College, a church school, which had been in existence about seven years, and employed five assistant teachers. Here he taught the higher classes, but at the end of one year he resigned.

Mr. Rechtsteiner had previously preached in Port Jervis on different occasions, and in March, 1888, permanently located here. On his arrival the church was divided, and affairs were not in a very prosperous condition, but he has labored untiringly for its welfare. The present house of worship, which was formerly the Episcopal Church, is situated on the corner of Sussex and Hammond Streets, and the congregation now numbers about one hundred and twenty families.

48

Since his pastorate here he has not only gained the love and confidence of the members of his church, but by all is held in the highest respect. He devotes his entire time to the needs of the church, and as he is a great scholar, his sermons are logical and convincing. In politics he is a Republican.

In Bloomfield, N. J., on the 26th of December, 1878, Rev. Mr. Rechtsteiner was united in marriage with Paulina Rall, of that place, and to them were born three children, but Emma died at the age of two years. Those still living are Hermann and Josephine. The family holds an honored place in this community, where they are widely and favorably known.

JONATHAN FALCONER. Prominent among the capable and efficient agriculturists of Orange County stands Mr. Falconer, who follows farming and dairying in the town of Crawford. Here he is the proprietor of one hundred and seventy acres of excellent land, which he cultivates in a most intelligent and highly profitable manner.

Our subject was born March 17, 1827, and was the eldest in a family of eight children born to John and Christina J. (Jansen) Falconer. The former was born in Westchester County, N. Y., where he spent the first sixteen years of his life, when he came to Orange County, remaining for a short time in the town of Newburgh. He next returned to his native county, and in company with his father engaged in the tanning business. After continuing in this line for a few years he was married, and then removed to Herkimer County, this state, where he farmed until about the year 1829, when he went to Ulster County, at this time he purchased property of his own and lived there until his decease, which occurred in his sixty-fourth year. His father bore the name of Jonathan Falconer, and during the War of 1812 served as a soldier, being employed in the secret service of the Government. He was born in this state, while his parents were natives of France. His father was likewise a soldier in the Revolution, as were also his brothers, one of whom, John, was an aide-de-camp to General Washington.

The mother of our subject was a native of Ulster County, where her death occurred when sixty-nine years of age. Her parents were natives of Holland, and on coming to the United States her father became a Colonel in the War of 1812, acquitting himself honorably and bravely in those trying times.

The subject of this sketch remained on the home farm with his parents until their death, when he purchased the interest of the other heirs in the property and made it his home until the year 1887. That year he disposed of the estate, and with the proceeds purchased the farm on which he now resides. This he devotes to general agriculture, although he makes a specialty of dairy farming. From the first he has been successful, and he is regarded as one of the substantial residents of the town.

October 25, 1871, Mr. Falconer was married to Miss Mary A. M. McKinney, daughter of Luther McKinney, and to them have been born three children, namely: John L., at home; William B., engaged in teaching school in this town; and Maria C., also with her parents. Our subject is a Republican in his political views and takes an active interest in the success of his party. With his wife and family he is a devoted member of the United Presbyterian Church. They give liberally to the support of the same and are always ready to lend a helping hand to the needy.

WILLIAM HAMMOND, who resides at No. 73 Ball Street, Port Jervis, was born at Franklin Furnace, Sussex County, N. J., October 3, 1833, and is the son of Hosea and Huldah (Truex) Hammond, also natives of that state. The great-grandfather, Noah Hammond, is supposed to have been born in England. His son Elisha located at Franklin Furnace, where he reared a family, and died when seventy-five years old. He was born February 6, 1769, and his wife, who bore the maiden name of Phebe Wallen, was born May 30, 1775, and died in 1843.

Hosea Hammond, the father of our subject, was born January 7, 1798, and departed this life January 29, 1875. He was a drum-major in the state militia during the War of 1812. In 1848 he came to Port Jervis, where he followed the carpenter's trade until his demise. His wife was born February 12, 1798, and lived until September 19, 1881.

Our subject was a lad of fifteen years at the time the family came to this place, and after securing a good common-school education he learned the carpenter's trade under his father. Good workmen were in demand after the building of the Erie Railroad through this place, as the town grew rapidly, and our subject followed this trade for five years, when he abandoned it to become a fireman on the Erie Railroad. After four years he was made brakeman, and was later given the position of engineer with the Eastern Division, remaining in that capacity for eleven years. During that period he only met with one accident, when he ran into a washout. Although the tender and train were thrown into a ditch, the engine remained on the track.

After this experience our subject, in company with his brother Horace, rented an old planing-mill which stood on Pike Street, and was occupied in running this from 1866 to 1871. That year William again became an engineer, but only remained on the road for a short time, when he again began operating the mill, the partnership existing with his brother until April 2, 1894, when the mill was destroyed by fire. Since that time he has followed his trade, and is regarded as one of the most efficient carpenters and machinists in the city.

Prior to attaining his majority, Mr. Hammond was married, December 29, 1852, to Mary E. Smith. She died October 29, 1856, aged twenty-two years, leaving a daughter, Ella J. M., who was about two years old at the time of her decease. Our subject chose for his second companion a sister of his former wife, Miss Sarah J.

Smith, a daughter of Jacob and Jane (Dougherty) Smith, who was born in Morris County, N. J., July 2, 1837, and was married October 11, 1857. To them were granted five children, two of whom are living. George A., a dentist, is engaged in practice in Brenham, Tex. He was graduated from the New York College of Dentistry, after which he married Miss Elsie E., daughter of Charles I. Peck, of Port Jervis. Lena C. Hammond is now the wife of Dr. C. W. Banks, of this city. Mr. and Mrs. Hammond are members of the Methodist Episcopal Church, in which he has held the official position of Trustee.

NELSON KNAPP is a native of Middletown, born on the 21st of May, 1863, and is a son of Walter H. and Martha J. (Dickson) Knapp, whose sketch appears on another page of this work. He grew to manhood in his native city, and received an academical education in Wallkill Academy. When seventeen years of age, he went into the store with his father, and there continued three years. At the age of twenty, he went to New York City, and attended the Sullivan School of Embalming, from which he graduated, being the first to graduate from Orange County. Returning home, he was made a partner with his father, and the business continued under the name of W. H. Knapp & Son. This partnership continued until March, 1891, when the father retired from the business, and our subject formed a partnership with his brother-in-law, under the firm name of Knapp & Merritt. They are now located on the corner of James and West Main Street, which has been the location of the house for more than twenty years.

In October, 1883, Mr. Knapp was united in marriage with Miss Julia A. Crist, a native of Middletown, and a daughter of Lawrence J. Crist, who was a carriage manufacturer on East Main Street and East Avenue. His establishment was one of the oldest in the city, Mr. Crist being the first to engage in carriage manufacturing in this place. He died in 1886. His wife, formerly Mary Ludlom, was also a native of Middletown, and died here in June, 1893. The grandfather, John T. Ludlom, who died here at the age of ninety-two years, was one of the first settlers here, and at one time owned all the ground on which the business part of the city is now located. For years he conducted a general store here, and was also engaged in the burning of lime. To Mr. and Mrs. Knapp have been born four children: Lawrence Crist, Walter H., Harold DeWitt and John Gordon.

Fraternally Mr. Knapp is a member of the Independent Order of Odd Fellows, the Knights of Pythias, and the Legion of Honor. He is a member of the Twenty-fourth Separate Company, having been connected with it since its organization, and now holds the rank of Sergeant. With every other business man, he is interested in the fire department, and is a member of Excelsior Hook and Ladder Company No. 1. He is a member of Grace Episcopal Church, and has been Vestryman of that body. Politically he is a stanch Republican.

———————❀❀❀———————

JOHN WOOD, a contractor and builder residing at No. 4 Montgomery Street, Middletown, was born in Haverstraw, N. Y., in 1831, and is the eldest of the twelve children of Jacob Wood, of whom mention is made elsewhere in this volume. He was reared on a farm near Haverstraw, and in boyhood attended the neighboring schools. At the age of sixteen he commenced to work out on a farm and continued as a farm laborer for four years. When twenty he turned his attention to the carpenter's trade, which he learned in Haverstraw, and followed later in Blauvelt, Rockland County, being engaged there as contractor and builder.

Entering the employ of the Erie Railway Company, Mr. Wood became assistant foreman in their shops at Piermont, where he remained a short time. For four years afterward he was foreman of the Ramapo shops of the Atlantic & Great Western, but when the shops were removed to

Franklin, Pa., he resigned his position, not caring to go to that place. In 1865 he came to Middletown, where, after working at his trade for a year, he started independently as a contractor and builder. In 1872 he took charge of the machinery in Draper's hat works on Railroad Avenue, and remained in that position until 1885, when Mr. Draper retired from the business.

For two years afterward Mr. Wood, under W. M. Mitchell, erected the machinery shafts in the Ontario & Western shops in Middletown and at New Durham, N. J., and since resigning from that position he has given his attention undividedly to his work as contractor and builder. A number of substantial buildings of the city have been erected under his supervision, and he superintended the erection of the steeple of St. Joseph's Catholic Church, which is one hundred and eighty feet high.

The first wife of Mr. Wood was Jane D. Clark, who was born and married in Nanuet, N. Y., and there died, leaving two children: Edgar, who is a locomotive engineer on the Housatonic Railroad; and Mrs. Anna Grier, of Middletown. In Great Barrington, Mass., Mr. Wood married his second wife, who was Miss Sarah Kilmer, a native of that place. Five children blessed their union, namely: Stella, wife of W. D. Harding, an electrician of New York; Charles, who is in business with his father; John, who died at the age of fifteen months; Flora and Myrtle. Mrs. Wood is connected with the Methodist Episcopal Church and interested in its good works. Socially Mr. Wood is a demitted Mason, having been connected with Hoffman Lodge No. 412, F. & A. M. In politics he supports Republican principles.

———————✠✠✠❀❀✠✠✠———————

JOSEPH HAINEN, Master Mechanic on the Delaware Division of the Erie Railroad, makes his home in Port Jervis. He has had eighteen years' experience in railroading, for he began when he was a mere lad, and has thoroughly acquainted himself with every detail of the work. Our subject was born in Sandusky, Ohio, February 24, 1863, and is a son of Samuel

CHARLES T. FORD.

and Frances (Higgins) Hainen, the former a native of Belfast, Ireland, and the latter of Canada. For twenty-seven years the father was a machinist and foreman, being a resident of Meadville, Pa. In the latter place in 1877 young Hainen commenced serving an apprenticeship in the shops of the New York, Pennsylvania & Ohio Railroad, then called the Atlantic & Great Western. He finished his trade on reaching his majority, and then worked as a journeyman in the same shops until April 1, 1889. At that time he was made foreman of a gang of men who were engaged in erecting and repairing locomotives for the Meadville Works. From that time until 1892 he superintended some twenty hands, and was then offered a position as General Foreman of the Erie Railroad Shops at Salamanca, where he had over one hundred and twenty-five employes under him.

One year later Mr. Hainen was made Master Mechanic of the Delaware Division, coming to Port Jervis in March, 1893, and now he has about three hundred and forty men in the shops under his supervision. The repair department is utilized for both cars and engines, and the round-house has stalls for thirty-seven engines. Altogether there are seventy-eight engines in his division, which are manned by one hundred and one engineers and one hundred and twenty-six firemen. These, added to his other hands, make a total of five hundred and sixty-seven men under his direct management. He is a member of the American Association of Railway Master Mechanics, and belongs to the New York Railroad Club.

CHARLES T. FORD, a railroad contractor, residing at Central Valley, was born October 7, 1844, in Southfield, where he resided until ten years of age, when the family removed to Sterling. He attended the district school until twelve years of age, and subsequently went to Farmers' Hall Academy at Goshen for two years. He next attended the private school of William N. Reid, at Newburgh, for two years; then went to Claverack Institute for two years. After taking a one-year course in the Poughkeepsie Business College, he went to New York City and was employed in the wholesale and retail grocery of William S. Corwin & Co. for one year. While residing in that city the great Draft Riot, of which he has a very vivid remembrance, occurred. Tiring of city life, he went to Sterling, where he had charge of the iron works store for four years. In the spring of 1867 he went to Southfield as manager of the iron works at that place, remaining three years. In 1870, being worn out by close attention to business, he bought a farm in the town of Woodbury, where he resided one year, at the end of which time, his health being restored, he went to Bangor, Mich., built a charcoal furnace, and put it in operation.

From Bangor Mr. Ford went to Holland, that state, where he organized a furnace company, but the panic of 1873 occurring at that time, all new furnace enterprises were stopped. He lost heavily by the panic, and was appointed station agent at Turner, N. Y., to which place he had removed. He also operated a quarry at Central Valley, and leased the Lary Turner property in the village of Turner until 1880. Resigning the agency at Turner, he removed to Central Valley, where he resided for one year, and then began contracting for the West Shore Railroad, excavating along the line between South and North Streets, Newburgh, and built large walls, putting in thirteen thousand yards of masonry. From Newburgh he went to Albany, and thence to Rochester, building five miles of road. After the failure of the construction company, he connected the Genesee Valley with the West Shore Railroad, giving the latter entrance into Rochester. He next worked on the Olmstead Parallel at Stamford, Conn.; thence went to New York, where for five years he contracted for city work. He next took a contract for grading on the Port Jervis Railroad from Rhodesdale to Huguenot, and also laid the track and ballasted the entire line. His next work was building the north dam of Tuxedo Park, after which he graded eleven miles of the Baltimore & Eastern Shore Railroad. On the completion of this contract he graded ten miles of the Pittsburg, Akron &

Western Railroad, between Sterling and Clinton, Ohio, connecting with the Baltimore & Ohio at the Chicago junction. He then graded two miles of the Potomac Valley Railroad, connecting the Western Maryland with the Baltimore & Ohio at Cherry Run, and later went to Spring Brook, Lackawanna County, Pa., and graded five miles of the Wilkesbarre & Eastern Railroad; subsequently he finished twenty-one miles on the same road.

Mr. Ford is a son of Charles T. and Martha (Weyant) Ford, the former born at Woodbury Falls, and the latter near Central Valley. The father was born March 14, 1815, and was reared on the farm. In 1838 he was superintendent of the furnace of Governor Kimball at Woodbury, and in 1840 he went to Southfield as manager of a furnace for Peter and Isaac Townsend, remaining with the firm until the spring of 1870, when he retired to his farm near Woodbury. In 1861, after he had been in their employ as manager for twenty-one years, he received a fine silver service. He died August 12, 1887. His wife was born September 12, 1817, and died September 15, 1890. They were married April 13, 1840, and to them were born five children: Mary, who died in infancy; Charles T., the subject of this sketch; Edward, who died in the spring of 1867, at the age of twenty-one years; Elizabeth, now the wife of James Seaman, of Woodbury; and John, who resided between Woodbury and Highland Mills.

Charles T. Ford and Miss Josephine McKelvey were united in marriage March 26, 1868. She was born at Greenwood, now Arden, N. Y., and is a daughter of Rensselaer and Rachael (Weyant) McKelvey, both of whom were natives of Orange County, the latter's birth occurring in Central Valley. Rensselaer McKelvey was the son of John McKelvey, who at one time owned a square mile of land where the village of Turner now stands. Rachael Weyant was the daughter of John and Mary (Hazzard) Weyant, natives of Lower Cove Valley.

To our subject and wife have been born three children: J. Barlow, who married 'Miss Bessie Howeth, of Vienna, Md., and who is in business with his father; Bertha; and Harriet Louise. Mr.

and Mrs. Ford are both members of the Methodist Episcopal Church. He is a member of Standard Lodge No. 711, F. & A. M., at Monroe; of Schunnemunk Lodge No. 276, K. of P., of Highland Mills; and of Central Valley Lodge No. 502, I. O. O. F. He is an active Republican in politics, and served as Justice of the Peace four years and as Town Clerk two or three terms.

WILLIAM SHANNON, Superintendent of the Eagle File Works, at Middletown, is one of her representative American citizens of Irish birth. He is a good-hearted, generous man, and is well liked by those in his employ. He was born in 1849, in County Antrim, about thirteen miles from Belfast, and within a short distance of the Giant's Causeway. His parents, James and Sarah (Coats) Shannon, were also natives of that country. The mother died there in 1858, while the father still lives in his native country, at a ripe old age. He is a member of the Episcopal Church, of which body his wife was also a member. They were the parents of nine children, eight of whom grew to maturity, and two sons and three daughters are yet living. Only the two sons, however, reside in America. One son, Joseph, served two years in the Seventeenth New York Infantry, and was wounded at Antietam. He now resides in Middletown, and is in the employ of the Ontario & Western Railroad.

Our subject remained under the parental roof until seventeen years of age, and received but a limited education in the public schools of his native country. In 1866 he crossed the Atlantic, boarding the "Royal Standard" at Liverpool, and after a voyage of fourteen days landed in New York, from which place he came directly to Middletown. Within two weeks he secured employment with the Eagle File Works, apprenticing himself to learn the trade of file-maker under J. T. Cockayne, with whom he remained four years. He continued to work at his trade as a journeyman here until he became foreman. In February, 1889, he was made Superintendent of the works, which position he has held ever since. He has charge of the manufacturing department, and has under him from sixty to eighty men. The works have a capacity of from two hundred and fifty to three hundred and fifty dozen files a day.

At Middletown Mr. Shannon was united in marriage with Miss Maggie Miller, a native of Elmira, N. Y. Her father lost his life while in the service of his country during the late war. Four children have been born to our subject and his wife: James F., William H., Herbert H. and Harvey. The first two are at present in the academy, and the third in the high school. Fraternally Mr. Shannon is a member of the Knights of Pythias, and religiously is a member of Grace Episcopal Church. In politics he is a stanch Republican, and has voted with that party since becoming a naturalized citizen. He is a stockholder in the Co-operative Store at Middletown. The family resides in a neat residence at No. 37 Grand Avenue. In the life of Mr. Shannon is an example of what may be done by anyone who has within him a desire to better himself in life. Coming to this country a poor boy and without influence, he has worked his way up to an enviable position, and is honored and respected by all who know him.

JOSHUA HIRST, Alderman of the Third Ward, Middletown, was born in Meltham, Yorkshire, England, May 14, 1843, and is a son of James and Sarah Hirst, both of whom were natives of that country. James Hirst was a carder by trade, and in 1847 came to America and located at Glenham, N. Y. In 1848 the family, consisting of wife and three children, joined him. He was employed at his trade at Glenham, and later moved to Newark, N. J., where both he and his wife died. Of their seven children, four are now living. One son, John, was in Company E, One Hundred and Twenty-fourth New York Volunteer Infantry. He enlisted in 1862, serving until the close of the war, and now resides in Louisville, Ky.

At the time of the removal of the family to America, the subject of this sketch was but five years of age. They came over on the sailing-vessel "Queen of the West," and were twenty-nine days on the trip from Liverpool to New York. Our subject remained at Glenham until sixteen years of age, mean time attending the common schools, and then went to Matteawan and commenced work in a hat factory. When eighteen he went to Brooklyn, and was employed as an apprentice in the hat factory of Ames & Moore to learn the trade of hat-finisher, remaining there until 1861. April 22, 1861, he enlisted in Company B, Thirteenth New York State Militia, and served in Maryland three months, being mustered out and honorably discharged in Brooklyn. In May, 1862, he re-enlisted in Company A for another three months, and after serving until the expiration of his term, was again honorably discharged at Brooklyn. He then resumed his trade in that city, where he remained until 1864, and then moved to Newark, N. J. In 1870 he came to Middletown and was employed in the hat works of Fuller & Babcock. He commenced with this firm shortly after they started in business, and remained with them until they closed out, when he was employed by Fuller & Bros. in the Wallkill Hat Works. After continuing with them as hat-finisher until 1891, he resigned his position on account of ill-health, and was appointed guard at the State Prison at Sing Sing, where he remained two years.

Mr. Hirst was married, July 22, 1867, near Suffolk, Va., to Miss Ella Newman, a native of Norfolk, Va., and daughter of John B. Newman, a merchant at Portsmouth, in the same state. They have one child, Marian Civilla.

In 1887 Mr. Hirst was elected Alderman of the Third Ward on the Democratic ticket. During this term he was Chairman of the Building Committee and a member of the Fire Committee. In 1895 he was again elected to the office on the same ticket, receiving a majority of twenty-nine votes. He is on the Committees of Ways and Means, Finance, Railroads, Lights, Lamps and

Lamp Posts, and Law, and is Chairman of the Committee on Rules and Order. In 1883 he was elected City Collector, serving one year. He belongs to Middletown Lodge No. 112, I. O. O. F., of which he is Past Vice-Grand, and is a member of the Knights of Honor, being a charter member of the lodge at this place; he is also a member of General Lyon Post, G. A. R., of which he is Past Senior Vice-Commander, and is an active member of Wallkill Engine Company No. 6.

JACOB M. JOHNSON The Grand View Farm, well known as the home of Mr. Johnson, is situated in the suburbs of Middletown, a portion within, the remainder adjoining, the city limits. Upon it are two houses, the family residence being heated by steam and furnished with every modern convenience. There are also two large barns, an icehouse, workshop, wagon house and other outbuildings. The well is said to be the best in the county and the water is unexcelled. One of the most prominent features of the place is the garden, which is upon an incline, sloping gradually to the south. The farm consists of one hundred and twenty acres, and is utilized mostly for the stock business, cattle being brought here from the West, and afterward sold. Of the entire tract of one hundred and twenty acres, all but forty acres are within the corporate limits of the city.

In the town of Minisink, Mr. Johnson was born August 9, 1846. The family of which he is a member is of Scotch-Irish descent. His paternal grandfather, Capt. William Johnson, was born in the town of Shawangunk, Ulster County, whence he removed to the town of Minisink and started a blacksmith-shop at Smith's Village, then a large and prosperous place. His death occurred there when he was about eighty years of age. Through his service as Captain of the militia, he received the title by which he was familiarly known. His wife was a Miss Millspaugh, member of one of the pioneer Dutch families of Ulster County.

The father of our subject, Capt. William C.

Johnson, was born in the town of Minisink, in 1802, and there died in 1876, aged seventy-four. He was a personal friend of Dr. Cash, and for some time a neighbor of that illustrious gentleman. As a farmer he was successful, being owner of a tract of one hundred and sixty acres, forty-two acres of which belonged to the old Stewart homestead. When the Middletown, Unionville & Water Gap Railroad, now known as the New York, Susquehanna & Western, was built, the company located a station on his farm, calling the place Johnson. He married Miss Sarah Durland, who was born on the Durland homestead near Ridgebury, town of Wawayanda, and died in September, 1891, aged seventy-two. She was a daughter of Charles and Lydia (Terry) Durland, natives of Long Island, and the former a farmer by occupation.

The subject of this sketch is the survivor of two brothers. The other, Charles D., formerly a farmer near Smith's Village, went to New York City in 1887 on business, but was never heard of again. Our subject was reared on the home farm and received a common-school education. At the age of sixteen he secured a position as brakeman on the Erie Road, between Corning and Buffalo, beginning at a salary of ninety cents per day, and receiving a gradual increase in wages. He was promoted to be baggage master, then became conductor between Corning and Rochester; later his run was between Elmira and Buffalo, and in 1868 he was transferred to the Eastern Division, as conductor between Port Jervis and Jersey City. When the New York, Oswego & Midland opened in 1872, he took a position with the company as conductor on a milk and mail train, and ran the first freight train ever run on the road, now known as the New York, Susquehanna & Western.

Upon his election to the position of Sheriff, Mr. Johnson resigned from the railroad service. In 1888 he was elected to that office on the Republican ticket, and assumed the duties of the position the first of the following year, serving in that capacity until January, 1892. While employed as conductor he had resided on forty-two acres, a portion of the old homestead at Johnson,

JOHN H. THOMPSON, M. D.

but later he sold it, and in 1891 purchased his present property, upon which he settled the ensuing year. Politically he is a Republican, and has been prominent in local conventions and county affairs. He is a member of the Order of Railway Conductors, in which he is still interested, though no longer in the service. In Newburgh he married Miss Clara A. Van Evera, a native of Vernon, N. J. They have three children, Nellie G., Clara A. and Jacob M., Jr.

JOHN HUDSON THOMPSON, M. D., one of the prominent practitioners of Goshen, is a representative of one of the long established families of Orange County, some six generations having resided at the old homestead in this town. He is one of the very oldest members of the Orange County Medical Society, and has been President, and is now Treasurer, of the same. He has frequently contributed papers of great value and research to representative medical journals on various subjects. In other departments of scientific work he is well versed, having prosecuted studies along these lines with great diligence and success, and is a felicitous writer and a liberal contributor to literature. He is a member of the Goshen Scientific Association, and has been very active in promoting general educational measures, such as furthering the grading, raising the standard of the schools, etc. He was Town Inspector of Schools until the office was abolished.

William Thompson and wife, whose maiden name was Ann Jenkins, came to this section from Edgeworth, County Longford, Province of Leinster, Ireland. They were wealthy and highly respected, and among their fellow-passengers on the vessel which bore them to their future home was the father of Gens. George and James Clinton, cousins of William Thompson. The first American ancestor of our subject was George Thompson, who was an industrious farmer of the town of Goshen. His wife was a Miss Elizabeth Wells, and their son William (grandfather of our subject) was born July 29, 1756. He married Submit Hudson, daughter of John and Hannah (Coleman) Hudson, of Blooming Grove. John Hudson was a nephew of the celebrated discoverer and navigator, Henry Hudson. William Thompson served in the War of the Revolution, and took part in the defense of West Point. His son Benjamin, the Doctor's father, was no less patriotic, and enlisted in the War of 1812, being attached to one of the bands, for he was a musician of exceptional ability. By occupation he was a farmer, like his ancestors, and owned land near Circleville, in this county. For many years he was Commissioner of Highways, Justice of the Peace, and was one of the most honored and upright citizens of the vicinity. For a great number of years he was an Elder in the Presbyterian Church, and lived to reach nearly fourscore years. His wife, whose maiden name was Maria Antoinette Owen, was born in Blooming Grove, and her parents were Capt. Jonathan and Martha (Racket) Owen. Mrs. Thompson died when in her eighty-third year, leaving five children to mourn her loss, namely: J. H.; Albert G., a farmer living at Sunny Dale, in the town of Wallkill; Harrison, also a farmer, who is residing near Middletown; B. Frank, now operating the old parental farm; and Samuel R., recently deceased. William Harrison died at the age of eight years; Owen died at the age of eleven years; and Martha at the age of twenty-six years.

Dr. J. H. Thompson was born near Circleville, this county, March 8, 1827, and received a public-school education. Later he entered the Sullivan County Academy, and during 1847-48 attended the State Normal School at Albany, graduating therefrom in the spring of the latter year. After devoting himself to teaching for a time, he came to Goshen, having been offered a position in Farmers' Hall Academy. In 1849 he commenced the study of medicine, and graduated from the College of Physicians and Surgeons of New York in 1852. Among his preceptors was Dr. W. B. Thompson, with whom he entered into partnership for a year, and ultimately succeeded him in his practice here. In New York City he was a student under the distinguished Professor Lewis A. Sayre, the great American surgeon.

Immediately after graduation, Dr. Thompson was appointed as a physician in the Seaman's Retreat Hospital on Staten Island for one year. In the spring of 1853 he returned to Goshen, where he has since remained. For six or seven years he was physician of the Orange County Poorhouse, which position aided him greatly at the outset of his professional career. When the One Hundred and Twenty-fourth Regiment of New York Volunteers was organized at his home in 1862, he was commissioned Surgeon by Governor Morgan, and accompanied the regiment to the field. Later he served as Surgeon-in-Chief of the brigade and division, with the rank of Major, and did most effective service in caring for the sick and wounded. He was present at the battles of Fredericksburg, Chancellorsville, Beverly's Ford, Gettysburg, Kelly's Ford, Locust Grove, the Wilderness, and in fact was in all the engagements in which the Army of the Potomac took part from August, 1862, until late in November, 1864. He then resumed his private practice at home with increased experience and a most excellent reputation as a practitioner of medicine and surgery. At length he was obliged to retire on account of necrosis of the left arm, it becoming necessary to operate upon it in order to effect a cure. This misfortune was the result of an accident in a surgical operation, which resulted in blood poisoning, and finally in the more serious trouble mentioned. The Doctor was at one time Official Surgeon for the Erie Railroad Company. He is enthusiastic in his profession, and is faithful in his attendance at meetings of the County Society, and Tri-States Medical Association. He was sent as a delegate from the latter to the American Medical Association, which assembled in Philadelphia in 1876. The Doctor belongs to the Society of the Veterans of the One Hundred and Twenty-fourth Regiment, and helped to organize Cummings Post No. 176, G. A. R., of which he has been Surgeon. Politically he is a Democrat, and has been very active in campaign work. Religiously he is a Presbyterian, and a member of that church in Goshen.

March 15, 1853, Dr. Thompson married Emily, daughter of Enoch J. and Caroline (Aspell) Pop-pino. She died in May, 1854, leaving one son, Wilmot P., who is one of the most extensive wholesale grain and feed merchants in the vicinity. He is eligible on all sides of his kindred to membership in the Sons of the Revolution. October 6, 1858, Dr. Thompson married Adaline L. Post, by whom he had one child, Martin Post; he was born June 15, 1860, but died on the 13th of the following September. Mrs. Thompson is an only daughter, and received a fine education, having pursued her studies in Farmers' Hall Academy and in Goshen Institute. She has marked executive ability; is a leader in the best society of the place, and displays great energy in religious and benevolent enterprises. Her father, Ellis A. Post, who died December 28, 1882, built the beautiful residence on the corner of Church and East Main Streets, which is now occupied by the Doctor and his wife. Mr. Post was in the commission and produce business, and also had extensive real-estate investments. He was born in Sussex County, N. J., in 1810, and about 1843 moved to New Hampton, this county, later coming to Goshen, where he was successfully engaged in business until his death. He organized the savings bank of this place, of which he was thenceforward President, and held a like position in the Orange County Agricultural Society for several years. He was public-spirited, and in many ways advanced the prosperity of Goshen. For years, while living in New Jersey, he held county offices, among others being that of Justice of the Peace. His wife, Prudence, was a daughter of Deacon Humphrey Martin, and was born in Deckertown, N J.; she was a woman of rare gentleness and amiability of character, and her death occurred at the age of seventy-one years. Her husband, who was known as Captain Post, was an active promoter of the interests of the Presbyterian Church, and served on the Building Committee in charge of the erection of the present imposing edifice, assisting materially by time and money in the construction of the same. Mrs. Thompson's grandfather, Gabriel Post, was born at Postville, now Edenville, this county, April 9, 1765, and resided there until his death, which occurred April 9, 1820. His wife, a native of Goshen, born November 14, 1769, was Anna, daughter of Capt. John Wisner, of Revolutionary fame. For further particulars of the Wisner family, see their sketch elsewhere in the work. The parents of Gabriel Post were James and Martha (Garrison) Post.

UGH McDONALD STRUBLE, M. D. The practical knowledge of medicine which, through assiduous study, Dr. Struble has gained, supplemented by years of experience in the profession, has enabled him, though still a comparatively young man, to gain a commendable position in the medical fraternity and in the confidence of the people. His elegant and commodious residence and office at No. 8 William Street, Middletown, are fitted up in the most modern style, the latter being especially adapted to his professional work.

The Struble family is of German descent, and the ancestors in the Fatherland were among those who adopted the Protestant faith during the days of its infancy. On crossing the Atlantic the first of the name in America made settlement in New Jersey, and there our subject's grandfather, Anthony Struble, gained wealth and prominence, becoming known as a successful business man and farmer of Sussex County. At one time he owned over one thousand acres of land, and his real-estate speculations proved very profitable. During the War of 1812 he rendered loyal service in the American army. He died suddenly of heart disease, at the age of sixty-two.

In Sussex County, N. J., Leonard Struble, our subject's father, was born and reared, and there he has made his life-long home. His occupation has been that of farming, and he resides on the old homestead, where he is surrounded by every comfort. Though eighty-three years of age, he is robust and enjoys excellent health, having a physique and mental powers equal to those of most men of fifty or sixty. His political preferences are with the Democratic party. His wife, who is now seventy-two years of age, was in maidenhood Jane McDonald and was born in Sus-

sex County, her father being a merchant in La-Fayette until his death, at the age of forty years. The McDonald family is of Scotch-Irish origin.

The eight children born to the union of Leonard and Jane Struble are all living, and of these the Doctor is fourth in order of birth. He was born in Newton, Sussex County, N. J., May 9, 1852, and grew to manhood on his father's farm, receiving the rudiments of his education in the public schools. Later he attended a private seminary at Swartswood, N. J., and on completing his studies he engaged in teaching in Sussex County. Two years were devoted to that profession, after which he began the study of medicine under Dr. James Hedges, of Branchville, N. J., continuing it under Dr. James F. McCloughan, of Swartswood, N. J. His private study covered a period of two years, and then, in order to perfect himself in his theoretical knowledge of the science, he entered the University of Pennsylvania and took a thorough course of lectures in the medical department, from which he was graduated in 1875 with the degree of M. D. In 1885 he took a post-graduate course in gynecology in New York City.

Immediately after his graduation in 1875, the Doctor opened an office at Andover, within a mile of his boyhood home. After practicing there for five and one-half years he removed to Unionville, Orange County, where the six ensuing years were spent. Feeling, however, that a large city offered greater opportunities and advantages, he came to Middletown in March, 1887, and opened an office on King Street, where he remained for four years. He then purchased property and built his present residence and office on William Street.

At Andover, N. J., Dr. Struble married Miss Mary E. McConnell, a native of Sussex County, and they are the parents of one child, a daughter, Olive B. For two years the Doctor was City Physician and Health Officer of Middletown. He is a member of the Alumni Association of the University of Pennsylvania, and is connected with the Masonic order, belonging to Huffman Lodge. Interested in matters pertaining to the profession, he is identified with the Orange County and Tri-States Medical Societies, and during his residence in New Jersey belonged to the Sussex County Medical Society, of which he was Secretary for one year. In politics he supports Democratic principles.

———————

JAMES H. GLASIER, Chief Dispatcher of the Delaware Division of the Erie Railroad, resides at No. 10 Catherine Street, Port Jervis. He was born in Oriskany Falls, Oneida County, this state, July 25, 1836, and is a son of Ezekiel and Mary (Willard) Glasier.

Our subject remained at home until sixteen years of age, when he entered an office at Oriskany Falls, where he learned the art of telegraphy. For three years he operated a private line from that place to Utica, and then was transferred to Salina, a suburb of Syracuse, where he remained as operator until the completion of the Erie Road at Dunkirk, in 1856. At Cochecton, then a small station on the line, he was first given a position as operator, and afterward he went to Susquehanna, where he was residing at the outbreak of the late war.

Mr. Glasier entered the service in February, 1862, in the military telegraph department. He was first stationed in Washington City, at the north end of Long Bridge, but when MacClellan was sent to the Peninsula he was ordered to go with him, and was given a line at Savage Station, ten miles in advance of the forces. There he remained until transferred to Harrison Landing, but was soon laid off for three months on account of sickness. When able to resume his duties he was sent to Union Mill, the extreme front of the Union lines, on Bull Run Creek and the Orange & Alexandria Railroad. He was with the army all the time, operating on this line of road at Manassas, Bristow, Warrington Junction and Rappahannock. When General Grant assumed command of the forces, Mr. Glasier was sent up the James River to Jamestown Island with General Butler, for whom he operated. When wires were placed in City Point, he remained there two months longer, and was then sent to the front with Generals Burnside and Parke, of the Ninth

Army Corps. He was with the Army of the Potomac until the surrender of Lee, at which time he was with the fifth corps of Grant's main army, and had served in all a period of three years.

On the close of the war our subject was given a position on the commercial line of the United States Telegraph Company at Utica, N. Y., and later operated with the Western Union in Pithole, Pa. Sometime thereafter he was transferred to Binghamton, N. Y., in the employ of the same company, and in 1872 came to Port Jervis as dispatch operator. Two years later he was made dispatcher for the Delaware Division, which position he has since held. He has in the office three assistant dispatchers, besides seven operators. In all there are about seventy-six operators and agents along the division under his supervision.

Mr. Glasier was married, May 12, 1861, to Miss Mary White, of Binghamton. They have no children of their own, but have an adopted daughter, Bessie L., who is now twenty-one years of age, and who has been a member of their household since she was five years of age. Socially Mr. Glasier is a member of the Knights of Honor.

———————

WILLIAM VOGEL, of Middletown, proprietor of The Standard, and agent of the Beverwick Brewing Company, of Albany, N. Y., is a native of Germany, born at Neifra, Prussia, in 1869. His father, Fridolin Vogel, is also a native of that place, where he yet resides, and where he is engaged in farming. He married Annie Reiser, who is also a native of that country, and they became the parents of six children, two sons and four daughters, all of whom are living, and three of whom reside in America. The family are all members of the Catholic Church.

William Vogel passed his early life in his native country and attended the parochial schools until fourteen years of age, when he was employed on the farm, where he remained until he

JOSEPH B. HULETT, M. D.

was seventeen years old. In 1886 he bade farewell to parents and friends and sailed for New York, where in due time he landed. From there he came to Middletown, and secured employment on a farm near Otisville, in the town of Mt. Hope, where he remained two years. He then came to Middletown and entered the employ of the National Saw Works, where he remained three months, and was then for five years and two months clerk in Bastian's Hotel.

On the 1st of April, 1894, Mr. Vogel was appointed agent by the Beverwick Brewing Company. On the 7th of July, 1894, he became proprietor of The Standard, located on Wickham Avenue, near the New York, Ontario & Western Depot. In the same month he also started the bottling business, bottling only the Beverwick Lager. He employs one truck to deliver his goods, and, with his brother James as assistant, he has built up a large and lucrative trade.

Mr. Vogel was married, in Paterson, N. J., to Miss Annie Widner, who is a native of Switzerland. They have one child, Annie. Mr. Vogel is a member of the German Maennerchor, of which he was Treasurer one year. He is also an active member of Eagle Hose Company No. 2.

JOSEPH B. HULETT, M. D. The reputation enjoyed by Dr. Hulett as a physician, and his character as a man, are of the highest order, and the professional success with which he has met indicates that he possesses large ability and keen intuitive powers. After having by careful study gained a thorough theoretical knowledge of medicine, he acquired valuable experience through his work as house surgeon and physician of Manhattan Hospital. Upon retiring from that position, he came to Middletown, in 1888, and here he has since engaged in practice, having his office at No. 20 Orchard Street.

The Hulett family originated in England, and was founded in America by one of the Pilgrim Fathers. For some generations identified with the history of Connecticut, the Doctor's great-grandfather removed from there to Athens, Pa.,

and thence Grandfather Hulett came to New York, where Cyrus, our subject's father, was born. His maternal grandfather Quick was a Revolutionary soldier, and his uncle, Thomas Quick, was the noted Indian slayer of Port Jervis. Cyrus Hulett followed farming for some years, but afterward carried on business in New York City. Late in life he went back to Tioga County and settled in Waverly, where he continued to make his home until his death, in 1877.

The mother of our subject, Ruth Emily, was born in Orange County, and was a daughter of Lockwood Slawson, who engaged in farm work in the town of Wallkill, and also carried on the mercantile business at New Hampton. The family is an old established one in Orange County, and the great-grandfather Slawson lies buried in the Pine Hill Cemetery. Mrs. Ruth E. Hulett died in Middletown, in 1889, at the age of sixty-five. In religious belief she was identified with the Presbyterian Church. Her two children were Joseph B. and Cora M., the latter being the wife of Daniel B. Ryerson, of Goshen.

The subject of this sketch was born in the town of Barton, Tioga County, N. Y. His boyhood years were largely passed in Jersey City, and he was educated in the Middletown Academy. After completing his studies, he engaged in teaching school in the town of Hamptonburgh, and also in Wallkill Academy. As soon as possible, however, he turned his attention to the study of medicine, which he prosecuted under the preceptorship of Dr. Everett, and later of Dr. Mills. Turning his attention to business, he became manager of the Phillipsburg Creamery, which he ran for three years. He then went to New York City, and studied medicine under Dr. Charles H. Wilkin until 1883, when he entered the medical department of Columbia College, and after four years' study was graduated, in 1887, with the degree of M. D. While in New York City he was with his great-uncle, J. B. Slawson, well known as the inventor of the street-car-fare box, with whom he remained until his death. During this time he took special courses in histology, pathology, chemical analysis and surgery, and in 1886 he was assistant in the out surgery department of the New York Hospital. He passed a competitive examination for house surgeon and physician of Manhattan Hospital, and received both appointments, which he held for one year.

In 1888 the Doctor came to Middletown, where he has since conducted a profitable general practice. He gives especial attention to surgery, and has performed a number of difficult operations very successfully. In addition to his general practice, he is examining surgeon for the New York, Ontario & Western Railroad, and attending surgeon for Thrall Hospital. For five years he was examining surgeon for the Twenty-fourth Separate Company, and by Governor Hill was commissioned First Lieutenant. He is a stockholder in the Casino Theatre, and is interested in numerous local enterprises.

In Middletown Dr. Hulett married Miss Lottie B. Hulse, daughter of Hudson E. Hulse, a farmer of the town of Wawayanda. They are the parents of one child, a son, Leslie B. Socially Dr. Hulett is identified with the Knights of Pythias, and is an honorary member of the Excelsior Fire Company. In Masonic circles he is connected with Hoffman Lodge No. 412, F. & A. M.; Midland Chapter No. 240, R. A. M., at Middletown; Delaware Commandery No. 44, K. T., at Port Jervis; and Mecca Temple, New York City, having attained the thirty-second degree in Masonry. He is examining physician for the Brotherhood of Railway Trainmen, and for various insurance companies. In the Orange County Medical Society he is officiating as Vice-President, and he is connected with the State Medical Association. Every year for the past five years he has attended the conventions of the National Association of Railway Surgeons, of which he is a member. In the New York State Association of Railway Surgeons he served as Secretary for some time. He is an honorary member of the Association of Medical Officers of the National Guard and Naval Militia of the state of New York.

From this brief review of the life of Dr. Hulett, it will be seen that he has gained unusual prominence in his profession. He is connected with many organizations devoted to the science,

and by his personal labors has advanced the profession to which he has devoted his life. Skilled in the diagnosis of diseases, and successful in their treatment, he stands in the front ranks of the medical fraternity, not only of Middletown, but also of this part of the state.

━━━━━◆◆◆◉◆◆◆━━━━━

EVAN T. REISLER, Roadmaster of the Delaware Division of the Erie Railroad at Port Jervis, is a native of Maryland, and was born in Calvert, Cecil County, March 14, 1864. His parents were Evan and Susanna (Steele) Reisler, also natives of that state, where they were well-to-do farmers.

Our subject passed his boyhood days on his father's estate, and in 1884 entered the Lehigh University at South Bethlehem, Pa. From that institution he was graduated with the Class of '87, having taken a four-years course in three years, and received the degree of civil engineer. One year prior to entering this college he took a preparatory course in the West Chester State Normal School of Pennsylvania.

The father died when our subject was very young, but the mother continued to reside upon the old homestead until her children were reared. Mr. Reisler's first work as a civil engineer was on the Delaware Division of the Erie Railroad, after which he came to Port Jervis as transit-man, under the assistant engineer, F. W. Dalrymple. In February, 1888, that gentleman was promoted, and our subject succeeded him as assistant engineer. In September, 1890, however, he was made Roadmaster, under W. H. Starr, Superintendent, and now has about two hundred and fifty men under his superintendence. He has charge of all the railroad property, with the exception of the rolling stock and shops. He performs work on twenty-six different sections, and with J. R. Davis as assistant engineer has built several of the largest bridges on the road, among them being the one spanning the Lackawaxen River and the Callicoon Creek.

Mr. Reisler was married, February 18, 1890, to Miss Anna Paul, of Philadelphia. She was born in Cecil County, Md., and is finely educated, having attended a private school at Oxford, Pa. She is the mother of two sons, Evan Holmes and Paul Roebling. Our subject has a very pleasant home and a valuable library, filled with standard literary and scientific books. Politically he is a Republican.

JACOB WOOD, a contractor and builder residing in Middletown, is a native of Haverstraw, N. Y., born September 21, 1850. His father, Jacob, also a native of Rockland County, was a son of Joseph Wood, a farmer of Orange County, and a soldier in the War of 1812. After reaching manhood he removed from Orange to Rockland County, and settled in Haverstraw, where he died at the age of about eighty-nine years. The family is of English origin.

Upon a farm near Haverstraw the father of our subject engaged in agricultural pursuits until 1880, when he came to Middletown and retired from active labor. He died in this city at the age of eighty-five years. During the existence of the Whig party he advocated its doctrines, and after its disintegration he affiliated with the Republicans. Religiously he was connected with the Methodist Episcopal Church. His wife, Nancy, was born in this county, and died in Middletown when seventy-eight years of age. Her father, John Hill, was born in Orange County, and was a cooper by trade.

The parental family consisted of twelve children, all of whom attained mature years and were married, and eleven are still living. Jacob, who is next to the youngest, was reared near Haverstraw until nineteen years of age, meantime attending the common schools. In the fall of 1870 he came to Middletown and served a three-years apprenticeship to the carpenter's trade, under his brother, John Wood, in this city. He then spent two years in Haverstraw, working at his trade. On coming back to Middletown he worked as a journeyman until 1893, when he began contract-

ing for himself, and has since carried on the business with flattering success. He has erected many of the most elegant residences of the city, among them being those of T. W. Davy, R. N. Boak, Charles H. Smith, Jesse Bakewell and L. J. Beers. He also built his family residence at No. 5, Chestnut Street.

At Haverstraw, N. Y., occurred the marriage of Mr. Wood and Miss Mary Babcock, a native of that city. They are the parents of four children: George S., Emmett C., Irving and Cecil. Politically Mr. Wood is a Republican and religiously he is connected with the Methodist Episcopal Church.

ALFRED H. REED, a veteran of the Civil War and Superintendent of Streets in Middletown, was born in New York City May 1, 1840. His father, Alfred, and grandfather, Rev. Thomas Reed, were born in England, where the latter was a clergyman in the Presbyterian Church. For a short time he made his home in New York City, but returned from there to England and died in his native land.

The father of our subject, a farmer by occupation, moved from New York City to Ulster County, where he still lives on a farm, being now seventy-six years of age. He is identified with the Methodist Episcopal Church. Politically he adheres to the principles of the Republican party. In 1862 he volunteered in the Union service, becoming a member of the Twenty-fifth New York Cavalry, in which he served until physical disability, resulting from sunstroke, caused his honorable discharge. He is an active Grand Army man and takes considerable interest in the workings of the order. His wife, who bore the maiden name of Elizabeth White, was born in England, and died in Ulster County in 1888.

There were two sons in the parental family, of whom the younger, Edward W., served as Corporal in the Twenty-fifth New York Cavalry·

from 1862 until the close of the war. He is now a farmer in Kidderville, Hodgeman County, Kan. The elder of the sons, our subject, was reared in New York City until seventeen years of age, attending the grammar and high schools there. In 1857 he came to Middletown and secured a position as foreman in the brickyards of Wallace & Wood. In 1863 he enlisted in the Seventh New York Heavy Artillery, Battery D, and was mustered in at Albany. From there he was sent to join the Army of the Potomac, with which he took part in the defence of Petersburg. He was in garrison at Baltimore, Md., for some time, and at the close of the war he was mustered out, in June, 1865, being honorably discharged at Albany.

On returning to Middletown Mr. Reed resumed work as foreman in the brickyards, and after a time began to manufacture brick by contract. Failing health, however, obliged him to retire from the business, and afterward he traveled in this state as an insurance agent. He was also the representative of the Prudential Company in Orange County. In 1886 he was appointed Superintendent of the Streets by the Board of Trustees, under President Bailey, and served for four consecutive years. Under the Democratic council he retired, and for two years was engaged in the insurance business, but in 1892 he was again appointed Superintendent of Streets, and has been re-appointed each succeeding year. He has had entire charge of the streets, and their excellent condition is due to his watchful oversight. At times he has from forty to sixty men in his employ and superintends their work in repairing and laying sidewalks, as well as in sewer-building.

In Bloomingburg Mr. Reed married Miss Sarah McKenny, who was born in Ulster County and who is the daughter of Evenson McKenny, a farmer of Walker Valley. They are the parents of seven children, namely: Alfred E., an insurance agent with the Metropolitan Company; Daniel M., who is with the Prudential Insurance Company; James H., a grocer and dealer in fruits at New Hamburg, Dutchess County; George W., who is with the Middletown & Goshen Traction Company of Middletown; Frank; Carrie, Mrs.

Thomas E. Coyne, of this city; and Cora, who is with her parents. The family occupy a pleasant residence at No. 152 Academy Avenue.

Socially Mr. Reed is connected with Lancelot Lodge, K. of P., of which he is Financial Secretary, and with the Royal Templars of Temperance. He is a charter member of W. A. Jackson Post, G. A. R., and is serving as its Quartermaster-Sergeant. With his family he attends the Methodist Episcopal Church and contributes to the support of that organization. In politics he always gives the Republican party the support of his ballot and influence.

WILLIAM SEEHOLZER is proprietor of the New York, Ontario & Western Restaurant, at the railroad depot at Middletown. He was born in Poughkeepsie, in 1862. His father, Berthold Seeholzer, is a native of Germany, and came to this country when a young man, locating in Poughkeepsie. By trade he is a merchant tailor. In the latter place he was married, and both he and his wife are members of the Methodist Episcopal Church. Of their eight children, all are yet living, our subject being third in order of birth. The family yet reside in Poughkeepsie with the exception of two children.

William Seeholzer remained with his parents in his birthplace, and attended the public school until thirteen years of age, when he entered the employ of Johnson Brothers, with whom he remained about four years. In 1883 he was made assistant manager of the railroad restaurant at Kingston, remaining one year, and for a short time was assistant at Syracuse. Subsequently he returned to Kingston, and later went to Weehawken. In 1886 he came to Middletown as manager for W. H. Sumner, to open the New York, Ontario & Western Restaurant, which was then located in the old depot, and in 1887 he became proprietor. The dining-room is 87x32 feet, and in conducting the restaurant fourteen employes are required.

Mr. Seeholzer was married, at Poughkeepsie, to Miss Minnie Conklin, a native of that city,

DAVID L. ACKERMAN.

and a daughter of George Conklin, a ship-build-er by trade. They have one child, Helen. Mr. and Mrs. Seeholzer reside in a pleasant residence at No. 4 Albert Street. In politics he is a Re-publican, firmly believing in the principles of that party, and is an active member of Excelsior Hook and Ladder Company No. 1.

DAVID L. ACKERMAN, contractor and builder of Central Valley, is a son of David and Elizabeth (Hemma) Ackerman. He was born February 1, 1836, in New York City, where he grew to manhood, attending the public schools until seventeen years of age, when he was apprenticed to Henry Christie, a large builder and contractor. He served four years, learning the carpenter's trade in all its branches, and after finishing his apprenticeship worked at his trade as journeyman in New York City for four years and then removed to Paterson, N. J., where he learned drafting under John P. Post. He subse-quently took charge of the latter's business, and also that of Van Houten Bros., the largest build-ers in Paterson. Later he was employed in the pattern-making department of the Cook Locomo-tive Works at that place, remaining some four years. During that time he made all the patterns for the Passaic Rolling-mills, which he started in operation.

Desiring to learn car-building, in 1860 Mr. Ackerman went to the Atlantic & Great West-ern Car Shops at Ramapo, Rockland County, where he remained three years, or until the fail-ure of the company. In these shops he had en-tire charge of the interior construction of all the fine passenger and sleeping cars, including the fine wood-work, furnishings and upholstering. In 1863 he returned to the locomotive works at Paterson, where he remained two years. At this time his brother-in-law, Alfred Cooper, desired him to come to Central Valley and enter upon a mercantile life. After ten years the partnership was dissolved and Mr. Ackerman again returned

to Paterson and took charge of the works of Van Houten Bros., but after remaining with them five years he was earnestly solicited to return to Central Valley, as there was a large number of fine residences to be built. Since his return, Mr. Ackerman has been quite active and has been in-strumental in improving the architecture of this pretty village. Nearly all the fine ornamental residences of Central Valley and Highland Mills have been planned and constructed by him.

Mr. Ackerman was united in marriage, Janu-ary 30, 1860, to Miss Susan Cooper, a daughter of Peter and Mary Cooper. Seven children have blessed their union: Carrie, a teacher at Estrada Institute; Edmond Cooper, with the Union Trans-fer and Storage Company of Detroit, Mich.; Mary Augusta, wife of E. B. Anderson, of Cen-tral Valley; Lewis David, with the Tuxedo Stove Company at Tuxedo Park; Fred, who works for his father, having charge of a corps of painters; and Gertrude and Irene, at home.

In politics Mr. Ackerman is a Republican, and is a Trustee of the Union Free School. He was one of the founders of the building and loan as-sociation of Central Valley. Socially he is a mem-ber of Standard Lodge No. 711, F. & A. M., at Monroe, and is Past Prophet of Wawa Lodge No. 235, I. O. R. M., at Central Valley. Mrs. Ack-erman is a member of the Methodist Episcopal Church and quite active in all religious and be-nevolent work.

HENRY FUNNELL, Alderman from the First Ward, and foreman of the blacksmith department of the New York, Ontario & Western Railroad, is a native of Thetford, Eng-land, born February 16, 1843. His father, Will-iam Russell Funnell, was also born in England, and was a blacksmith in the employ of the South-eastern Railroad at Ashford, Kent County. About 1874 he came to America, and, going direct to Syracuse, N. Y., was employed by the Delaware, Lackawanna & Western Railroad until he retired

49

from business on account of age. He is now about seventy-four years old. Religiously he is a member of the Episcopal Church. He married Maria Mason, who was born in Ipswich, England, and who died in Syracuse in May, 1892. They had the following children: Henry, the subject of this sketch; Thomas, a coach-builder in London, England; Walter, a blacksmith in Syracuse; Alfred, foreman in the blacksmith department of the New York, Ontario & Western Railroad at Norwich, Chenango County, N. Y.; and Margaret, who also resides at that place.

The childhood days of our subject were spent in Kent County, and his education was received in the public schools of Ashford. When thirteen years of age he was apprenticed as blacksmith and boiler-maker in the Southeastern Railroad shops, where he served seven years. At the expiration of his term of apprenticeship, he worked for the company as a journeyman until 1872, when he came to America with his wife and two children. He sailed from Liverpool on the old "City of Paris," for New York City, from which place he went to Syracuse, and was employed as blacksmith for the Delaware, Lackawanna & Western Railroad for about eighteen months. In the fall of 1873 he went to Oswego, and there worked as a blacksmith until 1875, and July 3 of that year came to Middletown, in the employ of the New York, Ontario & Western Railroad. He was the only blacksmith in the company's employ at the place for some time, and in 1880, when the shops were erected, he was made foreman, which position he has since held. In 1887 the present shops were built, and he has entire supervision. There are fifteen fires in the shops, and two men are employed for each fire.

Mr. Funnell was married in Kent County, England, to Miss Harriet Hayward, a native of that country, and daughter of William Hayward, who was by occupation a farmer. Of their five children, two were born in England, and three in this country. They are as follows: William, a practical machinist, and foreman of the New York, Ontario & Western roundhouse at Middletown; Laura, Mrs. Fryover, of Norwich; Walter, a machinist in the shops with his brother; Alfred,

with the Middletown & Goshen Traction Company; and Lillie, at home.

Mr. Funnell is a member of the Knights of Honor and of Ontario Hose Company No. 5, of which he is Vice-President. In politics he is a stanch Republican, and at present is a member of the City Republican Central Committee. In the spring of 1894 he was nominated on the Republican ticket as Alderman from the First Ward, to which position he was elected. He is Chairman of the Lighting Committee, and the Committee on Rules, and a member of the Street, Fire and Auditing Committees. Religiously he is identified with Grace Episcopal Church.

MAJ. CHARLES B. WOOD was born in the village of Warwick, September 3, 1839, and is a son of Jeremiah and Frances (Patton) Wood, the former a native of Long Island, and the latter of Orange County. Solomon Wood, the grandfather of our subject, was in the War of 1812, and at Perth Amboy was killed by the British in a naval attack which occurred at night. He had three sons in the same war. Dudley and Pierson were powder-boys on one of Captain Lawrence's ships, and the eldest son, Solomon, was also killed in a night naval attack by the British off Brooklyn. The great-grandfather of our subject came from England, and was a Lieutenant-Colonel in the British service, stationed at Nova Scotia. He espoused the American cause during the Revolution, and, joining the Continental army in Connecticut, attained the rank of General. He lived in Connecticut after the close of the war, and there died. Captain Lawrence was an uncle of Major Wood, having married the eldest sister of his father, Jeremiah Wood. The three uncles of Major Wood did not receive their share of the prize-money resulting from the capture of vessels in the War of 1812 until about 1864, which shows rather tardy justice on the part of the Government.

Jeremiah Wood, the father of our subject, grew to manhood on Long Island, and after coming to Orange County was married in the town of New

Windsor. After his marriage he settled in New York City, where he remained for a time, and then returned to Orange County, locating in Warwick. He was a carpenter and builder by trade, which he followed in Warwick, and afterward in Chester, to which place he removed with his family. He died in the latter place at the age of ninety years. For some years he was Captain of the Orange County Militia. In his religious views he was a Methodist, and was very active in church work. Politically he was an old-line Whig, then a Democrat until the breaking out of the war, when he became a Republican. His two brothers, Pierson and Dudley, of whom mention has been made, each died at the age of ninety-three years. His wife, the mother of our subject, was of Scotch and French descent, her grandfather Patton coming from Edinburgh, Scotland, and locating in the town of New Windsor. The grandmother was born in France. Mrs. Wood died at the age of seventy-seven years. In the parental family were ten children, five sons and five daughters. Four of the sons served in the war for the Union. John F. was a member of the Fifty-sixth New York Infantry, and now resides on Myrtle Avenue, Middletown. William B. was bugler in the company of which our subject was a member, but was transferred to the signal corps, where he served to the close of the war; he now resides in Jersey City. Peter L. enlisted in Company A, One Hundred and Twenty-fourth New York Volunteer Infantry, and died in service in front of Fredericksburg.

The subject of this sketch was next oldest of the four sons living at the time of the war. He grew to manhood in Chester, and received his education in the public schools and at Chester Academy. Under his father he learned the carpenter's trade, and while yet a boy began studying law with Charles Winfield, of Chester. He was subsequently coaxed to accept a position on the Erie Railroad as flagman, and then as telegraph operator. On the 19th of April, 1861, he enlisted in Company I, Seventy-first New York State Militia, as a private, for a period of three months. His regiment was first sent to Annapolis, then to Washington, and was engaged in the first battle of Bull Run. After being honorably discharged at New York, July 30, he returned home and recruited part of Company A, One Hundred and Twenty-fourth New York Volunteer Infantry, under the command of Col. Charles H. Weygant, and was mustered into service as First Lieutenant. After the battle of Gettysburg he was promoted and commissioned Captain, his commission dating from July 2, 1863. At the close of the war he was breveted Major for gallant and meritorious conduct.

The military life of Major Wood was an active one, and he took part in many engagements, and had many narrow escapes. As stated, his first engagement was in the first battle of Bull Run. He was afterwards at Wapping Heights, Fredericksburg, Chancellorsville, Beverly Ford, Gettysburg, the Wilderness, Spottsylvania, besides many minor engagements. At Gettysburg he received a slight wound in the knee, and at Spottsylvania, May 12, 1864 he was wounded while leading his men. He reached the top of the rebel works, when he was shot through the right elbow, and fell into the trenches. After the battle he was taken to the hospital, and subsequently he returned home on a furlough. At the expiration of forty days he had recovered sufficiently to return to the service, and rejoined his regiment in October, 1864, in front of Petersburg. He participated in the siege of that city, but was honorably discharged in October, 1864, on account of wounds received in action.

Major Wood after his discharge returned to Chester, but soon afterward went to St. Louis, Mo., and joined the United States Telegraph Corps, where he remained until mustered out at the close of the war. He again returned home and took his place on the Erie Railroad as conductor between Port Jervis and Jersey City, and for nineteen and a-half years ran a milk train between these points. In 1892 he retired from railroad life, and is now living retired. Since 1870 he has made his home in Middletown, on Lake Avenue, the place comprising sixteen acres inside the city limits.

In 1871 Major Wood was united in marriage in Port Jervis with Miss Gussie Jones, who was born in Bridgeville, Sullivan County, N. Y. One child was born of this union, George B., now in the railroad business on the New York & New England Railroad, with headquarters at East Hartford. In political and civil affairs Major Wood takes an active interest. He has served his adopted city as Alderman from the Second Ward, and in 1873 was nominated and elected on the Democratic ticket as a Member of the General Assembly from the Second District of Orange County. While in the Assembly, he served on several important committees, and aided in securing appropriations for the asylum at Middletown. In 1888 he recruited the Twenty-fourth Separate Company, New York State Militia, being its Captain for three years. He is a member of Hoffman Lodge, F. & A. M., at Middletown; Neversink Chapter at Port Jervis, and also of the Commandery at Port Jervis, of which he has been Captain-General. He is Past Commander of Capt. William A. Jackson Post No. 301, G. A. R., and has served as Aide on the Department Commander's staff.

———⊙✸⊙———

SAMUEL H. WILCOX, architect, and formerly engaged in contracting and building, has planned and erected some of the finest buildings in Middletown. He was born in the town of Le Roy, Bradford County, Pa., June 14, 1828. His father, Samuel Wilcox, was born in the town of Minisink, as was in all probability his grandfather, Nathan Wilcox, who was engaged in farming in that town. Samuel Wilcox, the father, was a sawyer, and in early life located in Bradford County, Pa., where he died in the prime of life. He married Mary Moore, who was born near Goshen, and was a daughter of James Moore, who was also born at that place. She died in Pennsylvania, at the age of fifty years. Of their family of four boys and two girls, only three are now living. After the death of Samuel Wilcox, the mother married again, and by her second marriage had two sons.

Samuel H. Wilcox, our subject, grew to manhood in his native state, and received his education in the public schools. When fourteen years

of age, he was apprenticed for a period of four years to learn the carpenter's trade. On completing his term of service, he worked as a journeyman in various points in Pennsylvania until 1849, when he removed to Tioga County, N. Y., and two years later to Millport, Chemung County. September 2, 1851, he came to Middletown and worked for Richard Van Horn until 1853, when he commenced contracting for himself, continuing in this, in connection with building, until 1885, since which time he has given his attention exclusively to architecture. Among the buildings which he has either planned or erected may be mentioned the Methodist Episcopal Church, Moffett House, Bull's Opera House, Baptist Church, Eagle Company's Hose House, William Burke's building, and many of the finest residences in the city.

Mr. Wilcox was married, in Middletown, to Miss Catherine Overton, who was born near this city. She died in 1886, leaving five children: John O., of Newark, N. J., employed as a night watchman in a jewelry factory; J. B., a telegraph operator in Minneapolis, Minn.; Florence, who married Frank Cock, a telegraph operator at Passaic, N. J.; Frank, employed in a paper-box factory at Newark, N. J.; and Kate M., who married John I. Sliter, of Middletown, where he is engaged in the stone business.

In politics Mr. Wilcox is a stanch Republican, of which party he has been a member since its organization. In religious belief he is a Baptist, and takes an active interest in the work of the church. At the present writing, in the summer of 1895, he is visiting his sister at Saguache, Colo.

———◉———

PETER F. MILLER. Since 1855 this gentleman has been a resident of Middletown, where, as contractor and builder, he is well known. Under his supervision have been erected some of the substantial business blocks and residences of the city, among which may be named the First National Bank Building, the Masonic

WILLIAM SEELY.

Block (in which is the postoffice), the Lipfield and George B. Adams Blocks, Clemson Brothers' works, the Thrall Hospital, the Robert Houston, Wilcox and Madden residences, and many other structures. At different times he has built for himself eight residences here, and he still owns four of these, making his home at No. 40 Houston Street, where he has a planing-mill in the rear.

Born in Wurtsboro, Sullivan County, N. Y., September 15, 1835, the subject of this notice is a son of Isaac B. Miller, a native of New Jersey, and a carpenter and builder by trade. Grandfather Peter Miller, who was a soldier in the War of 1812, became one of the early settlers of Sullivan County, and there died. The mother of our subject, Eliza, was born in Dutchess County, N. Y., and died in Sullivan County in 1885. Her father, Joseph Field, was a member of a prominent Eastern family and was distantly related to Cyrus W. Field.

There were six children in the parental family, of whom Peter F. was next to the youngest, and of that number three are now living. Our subject was very young when his father died, and he was therefore obliged at an early age to become dependent upon his own exertions for a livelihood. He remained in Wurtsboro until sixteen years old, being a clerk there for two years, and later an apprentice to the carpenter's trade under his brother Ambrose, now of Barryville, N. Y., with whom he remained two years. In 1855 he came to Middletown to finish his trade under Richard Van Horn, and with him he continued for twelve years, since which time he has been in business for himself. During busy seasons he gives employment to twenty-five men in the various departments of his works. Doors and sashes are planed in his mill, which is adjacent to his residence. It is a building 40x60 feet, with two wings, each 20x60, power being furnished by a steam engine of thirty horse-power.

The first marriage of Mr. Miller took place in Middletown, and united him with Miss Nancy Tice, who was born near Newburgh. Two children were born of the union: Irene, who is at home; and Mrs. Minnie Biggen, of Middletown.

After the death of his first wife, Mr. Miller was united with Miss Mary E. Van Sciver, a native of this city, and daughter of Robert Van Sciver. Socially Mr. Miller is connected with Huffman Lodge No. 412, F. & A. M.; Midland Chapter No. 240, R. A. M.; and is a demitted member of the Knights-Templar fraternity. During the war he was a member of the Union League, and his views, politically, have always been in sympathy with the principles of the Republican party, of which he is an old and faithful member. His wife is a member of the Methodist Episcopal Church, and with him shares in the esteem and friendship of many acquaintances.

>: ⟶ ❈◉❈ ⟶ ◈ ⟵ ❈◉❈ ⟵ =:.

WILLIAM SEELY. The success which has rewarded the exertions of Mr. Seely represents much hard work on his part. From early boyhood he was self-supporting, for his parents were poor and unable to assist him in getting a start for himself. Working out on farms by the day or month, he gained habits of perseverance and industry, and saving his earnings he finally accumulated a sufficient amount to purchase a home of his own. The farm of which he is the owner and occupant comprises two hundred and ten acres of land, and is situated in the town of Greenville.

The son of Ira and Rachel (Courtright) Seely, our subject was born in Sussex County, N. J., April 25, 1819. At the age of thirteen, having previously attended the district schools for a short time, he began to work in the employ of neighboring farmers, and continued thus engaged for thirteen years. When twenty-six he rented a farm in this town, and here he made his home for five years, at the expiration of which time he purchased his present place. In general farming and the dairy business he has been quite successful, and is numbered among the efficient agriculturists of the county. On his farm he built a creamery, one of the first in the county, and this he operated for several years, the investment proving a profitable one.

September 27, 1844, occurred the marriage of

William Seely and Julia Schultz, daughter of James K. and Deborah (Reeves) Schultz, old and highly respected residents of this county, their home being situated near Middletown. Five children were born to Mr. and Mrs. Seely, one of whom died in infancy. Emily married Louis Remey, of Port Jervis, and they have seven children; Lizzie, who died at the age of forty years, was the wife of Merritt C. Manning, of New York City, and at her death left five daughters; Jessie is the widow of John Slawson; John M., who married Mary Smith and has five children, assists in the management of the home farm, and has a milk route in Port Jervis.

In his political views Mr. Seely is an old Jacksonian Democrat, but has never cared to occupy public positions, and has invariably declined nomination for office. Though not identified with any denomination, he assists in the maintenance of the Methodist Episcopal Church, to which his wife belongs. He is a man of genial personality and warm-hearted disposition, a kind and indulgent father, and one greatly loved by his family and respected by his friends. The family of which he is a member is noted for longevity. His grandmother lived to be over one hundred years old, and his parents both lived to be over fourscore and four years. His life has been a busy one, and he deserves the prosperity and comfort which he enjoys in his declining years.

DEWITT G. LIPPINCOTT, M. D., a prominent citizen of Campbell Hall, has since 1883 been one of its most skillful physicians, his marked success in the treatment of disease in its various forms placing him at the head of his profession in Orange County.

Dr. Lippincott was born April 15, 1861, in Ulster County, and was the son of Rev. Benjamin C. and Mary C. (Parker) Lippincott, the former of whom was born in New York City. In 1847 he took up his abode in Ulster County, and made that section his home for many years. The parental family included four children, of whom DeWitt G. was the youngest. His two brothers and sister were: Leonard K., a farmer of Wallkill, Ulster County; Catherine P., who is living at home with her father, at Port Ewen, Ulster County; and Harry, now in New York City.

When our subject was a lad of five years his parents removed to Rockland County, and six years later to Wallkill. From there they went to Bucks County, and after some time spent there took up their abode in Port Ewen. DeWitt G. first attended Wallkill Valley Institute, after which he spent two years in the grammar school connected with New Brunswick College, from which institution he was graduated with the Class of '79. Having decided at this time to follow a professional life, for which he was especially adapted, he began his medical studies in the Jefferson Medical College of Philadelphia, Pa., receiving his diploma therefrom in 1882, and continued for a year in the hospital of that institution. In the spring of that year he came to Campbell Hall, and has since that time given his undivided attention to the practice of his profession. He is a man of high personal standing, being well known and honored throughout this and other counties. In politics he is a Republican, but has never allowed the use of his name for office.

Dr. Lippincott and Miss Susie Ryerson were united in marriage September 23, 1885. To them were born two children, the elder of whom died in infancy. Roy is a charming lad at home. In religious matters the Doctor attends the Presbyterian Church at Campbell Hall, of which church his wife is a member.

MRS. ELIZABETH FIRNHABER, proprietor of Firnhaber's Greenhouses, was born at Frankfort-on-the-Main, in Germany, and came to this country in 1867, landing in New York City. There she soon afterwards married Herman Firnhaber, who was born near Leipsic, Prussia, in 1843, and was reared on the farm, receiving a common-school education. In his native land he learned gardening, and for a time worked in that country as a journeyman, coming to the United States in 1867. Soon after his marriage, Mr. Firnhaber located in Middletown, where, for twenty years, he was employed in the file department of the saw factory of Wheeler, Madden & Clemson. After leaving that firm, he turned his attention to his old trade of gardening, and, having purchased the place now owned by his widow, carried it on until his death, June 9, 1895. He was a highly respected man, of irreproachable character, and one who enjoyed the respect and confidence of the entire community in which he lived. As a gardener he had few superiors, as he thoroughly understood the business. At his death he was a member of the Knights of Honor, and had formerly been connected with the Independent Order of Odd Fellows, being one of the charter members of the lodge at Middletown. He was a devoted member of Grace Episcopal Church, and his political affiliations were with the Republican party.

Mrs. Elizabeth Firnhaber is a daughter of Heinrich Miller, a native of Germany, born near Frankfort-on-the-Main. By vocation he was a book-binder and fancy designer in wood-work lettering. He died near Frankfort, when about fifty-six years old. Mrs. Marie (Limpert) Miller, the mother of our subject, was born in Hesse-Darmstadt, and died in Frankfort. Eight of their ten children grew to maturity, two of whom came to this country, our subject and a sister, Mrs. Bettie Baker, who died in Middletown in 1886. Our subject's grandfather, Baldazer Miller, was born in Stuttgart, and moved to the vicinity of Frankfort in his early manhood. By trade he was a baker, but for some years ran a large laundry in Frankfort. During the war with Napoleon he served his country as a soldier. In religious belief he was a Catholic, but he married a Lutheran, and the family was reared in the latter faith.

Since the death of her husband, Mrs. Firnhaber has continued the business, and has already shown that she possesses the ability to make of it a success. The grounds on which the greenhouses are located have a frontage of one hundred and fourteen feet on Grand Avenue, and a depth of three

hundred and sixty-four feet. She has six greenhouses, each 17x70 feet, with sufficient room for garden and hotbeds, and cultivates all kinds of flowers, making a specialty of roses, carnations, violets and chrysanthemums. She makes regular shipments to New York City, and expects in the future to conduct a wholesale as well as a retail trade. The business is under the management of M. Bartholomew, an experienced florist. Table and other decorations are provided on short notice.

Five children were born to Mr. and Mrs. Firnhaber, two of whom are yet living: Emil, a machinist with the New York, Ontario & Western Railroad shops; and William, a carpenter in New York City. Mrs. Firnhaber is an active member of Grace Episcopal Church. For some years she was also a member of the Rebecca Degree of Odd Fellows. In manner she is very pleasing, and has a host of friends in and around Middletown.

—•+•+—•✥❋✥•—•+•+—

UTHER BARBER, contractor and builder at Middletown, is a native of England, born in Hailsham, Sussex County, in 1845, and is a son of John and Hannah(Frost) Barber, both of whom were natives of England, where they lived and died. They had eleven children, who grew to maturity, seven of whom are now living, our subject being the only one now in America. One brother, Herbert, came to this country and located in Middletown, where he was a successful contractor in partnership with Richard Miller, under the firm name of Barber & Miller. He died here in 1878. By occupation John Barber was a farmer.

The subject of this sketch was reared in his native county, and at the age of seven years began to help make a living for the family. He first worked at the carpenter's trade, and at the age of seventeen was apprenticed to learn the trade of a brickmason, at which he served seven years. His educational advantages were very limited, and all his schooling was received in evening schools. In 1871 he came to America, via Liverpool to New York, thence to Middletown, where he remained one year engaged at his trade. Later he removed to Franklin Furnace, Sussex County, N. J., where he worked as a journeyman two years, and then engaged in contracting and building for himself. In 1878, Herbert Barber having died, Mr. Miller went to Franklin Furnace to persuade our subject to return with him to Middletown and take the place of his brother. This he did, and business was conducted under the firm name of Miller & Barber until about 1887, when Mr. Miller died, since which time Mr. Barber has continued the business alone. Among the buildings he has erected in Middletown are the Swalm Block, Charles Dill's block, and the family residences of Wiggins, Rogers, Vail, Jones, Daugherty and George Swalm.

Mr. Barber was married, in England, to Miss Jane Longhurst, who was also a native of Sussex County. Nine children were born to them, five of whom are deceased, and those living are: William Luther, a telegraph operator; and Edith M., Bertha E. and Jennie I. The family resides at No. 67 Prospect Street. Mr. Barber is a member of the Methodist Episcopal Church, and takes an active interest in all religious and benevolent work. In politics he is a Republican, and while taking an active interest in political affairs has never aspired to official position.

A R. SARGEANT, of the town of Wawayanda, was born in the town of Monroe, September 2, 1822, and is the son of Abel and Sarah (Pilgrim) Sargeant, who were the parents of four children, three sons and one daughter, namely: James P., Abel R., Harriet and Mary A. The first and last are now deceased.

The subject of this sketch was reared on the farm, and there remained until sixteen years of age, attending the common schools in the winter months and assisting in farm work during the summer. When sixteen years of age he began

working in the mill, serving a five-years apprenticeship, at the expiration of which time he continued to work at the trade for three years. He then began working at cabinet-making, but continued in that avocation but a short time. Buying fifty-four acres of land in the town of Wawayanda, he removed to the place and there resided until 1863, when he removed to Slate Hill, where he now lives. In 1891 he opened a mercantile business in the same place, but only continued it about two years.

On the 22d of January, 1845, Mr. Sargeant was united in marriage with Mary A. Taylor, born in the town of Wallkill, and a daughter of Abraham and Mary (Newkirk) Taylor, the parents of two children, David and Mary A. To our subject and wife were born four children. David married Phœbe Mills, and resides at Woodbury Falls; Augustus married Armenia Morse, and resides in the town of Wawayanda; Mary is now the wife of K. Skinner, and resides in Slate Hill; Alonzo died in 1893.

Although Mr. Sargeant commenced life with but little means, he is now the possessor of three hundred acres of land, all in one body, his principal occupation being dairy farming. Politically he is a Democrat, and religiously he and his wife are members of the Methodist Episcopal Church.

G EORGE HENRY HADDEN has been a resident of Middletown since 1876, and as a contractor and builder has been successful, the list of the public and private structures he has erected including some of the finest buildings in the city. Among these may be mentioned the Everett, Iseman and Trust Company's buildings, the chapel connected with the State Asylum, Clemson Brothers' sawshops, the schoolhouse in February, 1881, and the Eagle Hose Company, Law, Central and Stern's buildings.

Born in County Armagh, Ireland, in 1856, the subject of this sketch is a son of John and Maggie (Duncan) Hadden, natives, respectively, of Ireland and Glasgow, Scotland. His father, who was a mason by trade, died in his native

ROSWELL C. COLEMAN.

MRS. ROSWELL C. COLEMAN.

land, and there the mother still continues to reside. The family consists of ten sons and one daughter, all of whom are living. George H., who attended school in County Armagh in early boyhood, began to learn the bricklayer's trade at the age of thirteen, and this occupation he followed as long as he remained on the Emerald Isle. At the age of sixteen, in 1872, he came to America, via Liverpool to New York City, and, going up to Wappinger's Falls. Dutchess County, he began to work at his trade. For four or five years he was in the employ of the Dutchess Print Works, erecting stonework.

In 1888 Mr. Hadden formed a partnership with R. A. Malone, which was dissolved about four years later, and since that time he has worked alone. While in Wappinger's Falls, he married Miss Effie J. Patterson, who was born in Ft. Dodge, Iowa, where her father, David Patterson, was a large contractor. Four children complete the family circle, Lizzie, Nellie, George and Frank. The family attend the Second Presbyterian Church, to which Mr. Hadden is a generous contributor. He is a member of Hoffman Lodge, F. & A. M.; Middletown Lodge No. 112, I. O. O. F.; and Eagle Hose Company No. 2. Favoring the protection of home industries, he naturally gives his allegiance to the Republican party, and in that organization he is prominent, having frequently represented it as delegate to county and congressional conventions.

ROSWELL CARPENTER COLEMAN has held the important judicial position of Surrogate of Orange County since 1883. He has in a large measure succeeded in his endeavors to elevate the office to what it should be by enforcing proper rules, and by careful decisions in cases coming before him. He is a man of recognized ability, wide information, both on matters pertaining to his profession and to the sciences and public questions of the day as well. For some years he was Trustee of the village of Goshen, and has been engaged in practice here for about thirty years. In early life he was a Jus-

tice of the Peace for eight years, and after being nominated and elected to his present responsible place on the Democratic ticket, assumed the duties of the office in January, 1884. That his services were appreciated, was shown when he was reelected in 1889, being the only one of his political faith so honored, and receiving a majority of about one thousand votes. His term runs until 1896.

The Colemans are of English descent, and after coming to America are supposed to have located first about New Haven, thence going to Southold, L. I. Our subject's great-grandfather, Benjamin, was born April 16, 1755, in Orange County, and died August 5, 1832. He married Hannah (Carpenter) Finch, who was born November 15, 1761, and who died April 8, 1846. She and her father's family were refugees from the Wyoming Massacre. Our subject's grandfather, Benjamin Carpenter Coleman, was born in this county, August 2, 1791, and was accidentally killed August 16, 1845. He was a soldier of the War of 1812. His wife, Eleanor, was a daughter of Gen. Abram Vail, who was a Member of the State Assembly and a resident of the town of Goshen. His parents, John and Mary (Alsop) Vail, lived and died in Goshen. The former was born September 22, 1744, and died February 2, 1815; and the latter was born March 21, 1742, and died May 31, 1811. Benjamin, the father of John Vail, served in the French and Indian War. Abram Vail was born November 3, 1771, and died October 4, 1851. He married Esther Rockwell, who was born March 19, 1768, and died October 21, 1811. Their daughter Eleanor, whose birth occurred August 9, 1793, died October 9, 1853.

Our subject's father, James Carpenter Coleman, was born in Orange County, March 28, 1820, and died February 1, 1882. For many years he was engaged in merchandising in New York City, but in 1860 removed to the vicinity of Goshen. His wife, Phœbe A., was born in Warwick, this county, January 15, 1821, being a daughter of Hon. Roswell Mead, who was born in Wilton, Fairfield County, Conn., July 15, 1784. His father, Col. Matthew Mead, was a native of England, his birth occurring August 20, 1736, and his death February 26, 1816. He won his title in the War of the Revolution, in which his son Thaddeus also served as powder-boy. His wife, who was a Miss Phœbe Whelpley, was born July 1, 1740, and died August 1, 1811. Hon. Roswell Mead came to this county as a school teacher, later engaged in mercantile pursuits in Newburgh, Warwick and in Smith Village, and died at Slate Hill, June 6, 1850. His wife was Hannah, daughter of Reuben Cash, a farmer of this county, and a descendant of Daniel Cash, who came from Connecticut and settled in the Wyoming Valley with a large family of children. He married Mary Tracy, a daughter of Isaac Tracy, of that place. She managed to escape the notable massacre, and, joining her husband at Rutger's Kill, in Orange County, settled there. Hannah Mead was born November 4, 1796, and died April 15, 1868. Her mother, a Miss Millicent Howell, was a daughter of John Howell, a pioneer of Neversink, who was born in 1745, and whose death occurred on Christmas Day, 1790. He married Sarah Dougherty, who was born in 1752, and died June 24, 1834.

Our subject is one of five sons. His eldest brother, Dr. James C., was a surgeon during the war, and for fifteen years served on the Board of Medical Examiners; he is now a resident of this locality. The next younger brothers, John M. and Charles W., live in Goshen, the latter being an attorney-at-law. Thaddeus V. is a clerk in the National Bank of Commerce of New York. Our subject was born in the town of Goshen, December 3, 1840, and received his primary education in the Thirteenth Street Ward School, No. 35, of New York City, after which he attended the Free Academy for a year, completing his classical course in the private school of David M. Towle, of this place. Afterward he took up the study of law in the office of Sharp & Winfield, well known attorneys of Goshen. In 1863 he graduated from the law school at Albany with the degree of Bachelor of Laws, and was admitted to the New York Bar. Later he opened an office for practice in Goshen, and here he has since been located.

In 1865 Mr. Coleman married Sara W. Wilkin, who was born in the city of New York, and who is the daughter of Samuel J. Wilkin, an attorney, who has served as a Member of the State Assembly. He has been a Member of Congress, and many years ago his name was placed on the ticket for the Lieutenant-Governorship with Millard Fillmore. He was a son of James W. Wilkin, who had held all of those positions before him, and was also a leading lawyer. The pleasant home of our subject and family is situated in a beautiful thirty-acre tract within the village limits. His wife was educated here and in Miss Green's school in New York City. She became the mother of ten children, all but two of whom are living. Catherine D., a graduate of Mt. Holyoke Seminary, is the wife of Harry E. Colwell, of New Rochelle, N. Y. Annie M. is a graduate of the Sharity Hospital, where she took a course of training as a nurse, and is now located in New York. Sarah W., who attended Mt. Holyoke Seminary, afterward took up stenography and typewriting, and is at present in Goshen. Wilkin attended the Albany Law School, later was admitted to the Bar in Kansas, and is now practicing in Goshen. Mary E. attended the Northeastern Conservatory of Music of Boston for a year and was a fine violinist, but she was claimed by death when only eighteen years of age. Eleanor C., who graduated from Miss Graham's school in New York City, is at home. Henrietta is a student in Wheaton Seminary in Massachusetts. Roswell C., Jr., was educated in Worcester, Mass., and is now clerking in a store in Goshen. Alexander W. is attending the local schools; and Charles C. died at the age of seven years. Mr. Coleman has for many years been recognized as one of the leading lawyers of the county, and is more especially noted as an authority concerning the law and practice in Surrogate courts, and the law in relation to real estate. He has occupied judicial positions for about twenty years, but has always continued to practice his profession even while holding office.

With his family Mr. Coleman attends the Presbyterian Church, and for several years was a Trustee of the same. In 1875 he went with the first American rifle team on a visit to Ireland under Captain Gildersleeve, and was gone for three months. He has always been interested in athletic sports, and has usually belonged to some amateur baseball club. He owns a permanent camp at Indian Lake, in the Adirondacks, where he and his children go from time to time in order to seek recreation and rest.

NELSON HILL, who recently came to Middletown and erected a residence on Richmond Hill, is a carpenter by trade, and follows that occupation successfully in this city and vicinity. His home was formerly in the town of Tuxedo, where he still owns a fine fruit farm of thirty acres, with large numbers of apple, pear and peach trees in bearing condition.

In the town of Tuxedo, near the Rockland County line, Nelson Hill was born in 1848, being a son of Rensselaer and Charlotte (Conkling) Hill, both natives of this county. His paternal grandfather, John Hill, was a cooper by trade, while his maternal grandfather, Jacob M. Conkling, was engaged in the manufacture of spoons, and as a worker in wood. The parents were married in this county, and for many years after their union they made their home at Long Pond, in the town of Tuxedo, where the father, though giving his attention to a small extent to agricultural pursuits, was principally engaged at the cooper's trade. After the death of our subject's mother, in 1865, the father married again. His closing years were spent in Port Jervis, where he died at the age of sixty-seven.

On the home farm in the town of Tuxedo, our subject passed the days of his youth, unmarked by any noteworthy event. His education was gained in the common schools and was practical, fitting him for an active business life. Having a liking for the carpenter's trade, he became familiar with it during leisure hours in youth, and he also learned the business of manufacturing wooden-ware. On starting out for himself, however,

he turned his attention to the fruit business. Purchasing thirty acres of his father's farm in Tuxedo, adjoining Long Lake, he set out a peach orchard, and later planted apple and pear trees. The fruit is sold to the home market, and the business has proved remunerative.

In the summer of 1895 Mr. Hill came to Middletown and erected a residence on Conkling Avenue, Richmond Hill Addition to the city, where he has since made his home. While in the town of Tuxedo, he married Sarah A. Hall, a native of that town, and they are the parents of eight children, all at home, namely: Viola, Calvin, Lizzie, Hattie, Israel, Rensselaer, Edith and Elmer. Mr. Hill is intelligently informed regarding matters of current interest, and is a stanch adherent of Republican principles, supporting the candidates of that party with his vote and influence.

JOSEPH SNIFFIN, of Middletown, was born at Thunder Hill, Ulster County, N. Y., in 1857, being the youngest child of John and Hannah (Coon) Sniffin, natives, respectively, of Sandsburg, Sullivan County, and Ellenville, Ulster County. His father, who was a soldier in the Union army during the Civil War, followed the shoemaker's trade throughout almost his entire active life, but when advanced in years he retired from that occupation and went to the Black Hills. There he engaged in mining until he was killed by the Indians, at the age of sixty-five, his death occurring about the same time as that of General Custer. The paternal grandfather, Joseph Sniffin, was a descendant of English ancestors, and was a shoemaker by trade. The maternal grandfather, Abraham Coon, was born in Dutchess County, whence he removed to Ellenville, and engaged in farming there until his death, at the age of one hundred and one years. He was a soldier in the War of 1812.

The family of John Sniffin consisted of three

daughters and two sons, of whom two daughters are deceased. Joseph, the youngest of the number, was reared in Ellenville, Ulster County, where he attended the public school. At the age of sixteen years he began an apprenticeship to the trades of mason, bricklayer and plasterer, all of which he learned during his three years' service. Later he engaged in journeyman work for eleven years, after which, in 1889, he came to Middletown and formed a partnership with Nicholas Coleman, remaining with him for three years. Since dissolving that partnership he has been alone.

During the busy season Mr. Sniffin employs from six to fifteen men. He has had the contracts for many of the best residences in the city, including the homes of Messrs. Van Keuren, Wells, George A. Green, John W. Slawson and scores of others. His residence at No. 19 Knox Avenue was built by himself, and he has had the contract for fourteen houses situated on Knox Avenue, California Avenue, West Main Street and Monhagen Avenue.

The marriage of Mr. Sniffin took place in Ellenville, N. Y., his wife being Miss Mary Edwards, a native of Putnam County, Pa. Four children comprise their family circle, Bertha, Guy, Eva and Earl. Mr. Sniffin affiliates with the Knights of Labor, and politically is a loyal adherent of Democratic principles. He is identified with the Methodist Episcopal Church, and may always be found abetting any useful scheme that will enhance the material, social or religious progress of his community.

JOSEPH NELSON TURNER, a worthy representative of the boys in blue in the late Civil War, was born in Fishkill Landing, Dutchess County, N. Y., May 8, 1847. His father, Stephen Nelson Turner, died when he was a very small child. His mother married again and located in Salisbury, Orange County, from which place she removed to Washingtonville.

Our subject was there educated in the public schools, and in 1861, although but fourteen years of age, ran away from home and enlisted in the Fifty-sixth New York Infantry, being the third person to enter his name as a soldier in that regiment. On account of his youth, his mother secured his release and took him home. In the following fall he ran away again, and was mustered into the service at Newburgh, as a member of Company C, Fifty-sixth New York Infantry, or the Tenth Legion. His regiment was ordered on board a boat in New York Harbor, for the purpose of going South, and while on the voyage a riot occurred on board the boat, and an attempt was made to set fire to it. In endeavoring to save himself and the vessel he was kicked in the mouth and stomach, and an attempt was made to throw him overboard. The riot was finally subdued, and our subject was taken to the hospital at Beaufort Island, where he remained some months, in the mean time having typhoid and brain fever. When the Fifty-sixth veteranized he enlisted again, and was mustered in at Albany, joining his regiment at South Carolina. While on John's Island he received a sunstroke, and was sent from there to Beaufort and later to Hilton Head, where for a time he was very ill. When he recovered he joined his regiment at Beaufort, and was in the Harney Hill fight. The regiment was then sent to Charleston, thence to Mt. Pleasant, then up the South Santee River to Secessionville, back to Charleston, Ridgeville, Summerville and finally to Greenville, from which place it was ordered home. In the fall of 1865 Mr. Turner was mustered out, and honorably discharged at Albany, N. Y.

After his discharge Mr. Turner came to Middletown, where he has since resided. For four years after his return he could not engage in any employment. He first tried engineering, but had to give it up. He has been twice married, first to Miss Olivia Lubert, a native of Charleston, S. C. His marriage with this lady was brought about in quite a romantic way. While in Charleston he was set upon by fifteen armed rebels, and to escape he jumped over a high board fence and sprang into a cistern, where he was up to his arm-

pits in water. Miss Lubert began pumping the water from the cistern, and persuaded the rebels that he was not there. In the mean time her brothers returned home, and with a rope drew him out of the water. No sooner was he on the street than he was again attacked, but this time was saved by Union soldiers. At the close of the war he returned to South Carolina, where he was married. His wife died in Middletown, leaving two children: Ida, wife of William Stratton, of Matteawan, N. Y.; and Eugene, also of that place. Mr. Turner subsequently married Miss Helen Platts, and by this union has one child, Ruby, at home. Mrs. Helen Turner is a daughter of John D. Platts, a native of New Hampshire, who was left an orphan when seven years old, and afterward came to New York State. On the breaking out of the Civil War he enlisted in a New York regiment and served through the entire conflict. He then went West, and after remaining in Iowa for a time again returned to New York, locating in Sullivan County. He married Sarah Barber, a native of Delaware County, and a daughter of Eli Barber. Mrs. Turner is the second of their three children, and was reared and educated at Rockland. In politics Mr. Turner is a Republican. As a matter of course he takes great interest in the past, and can never forget the adventure which came so near costing him his life.

✦✦━━━━✦✥✖✦✥✦━━━━✦✦

THOMAS P. PITTS. In this volume, while the reader's thoughts are directed principally to the deeds of men now living, considerable attention is also given to the life records of our honored dead, those who once shared our joys and sorrows, and who labored to promote the welfare of the community, but who are now gone from among us. This tribute to the memory of Thomas P. Pitts, given by her who was his devoted wife and efficient helpmate, will be perused with interest by those who were associated with him in former years.

A son of George Pitts, the subject of this notice was born in Warwick, and spent his boyhood years upon his father's farm. Arriving at man's estate, he selected for his occupation that to which he had been reared, and for some years he carried on a farm in the town of Wallkill. Later, however, he abandoned agricultural pursuits and became interested in the shoe business, being proprietor of a store in Warwick until his demise. He was energetic, judicious in his investments, and accumulated a competency. He died in September, 1890, aged seventy-six, and was buried in the cemetery at Middletown. In religious belief he was identified with the Methodist Episcopal Church, and his deep religious faith upheld him in his last hours. Politically he was a Democrat.

The first wife of Mr. Pitts was Emily J. Gardner, of Florida, this county, and they became the parents of four children, three of whom are living. His son, Dr. John W. Pitts, a young man of great ability, was graduated from the College of Physicians and Surgeons of New York City, and practiced his profession in that city. On the opening of the Civil War, he enlisted in Company E, One Hundred and Twenty-fourth New York Infantry, and though but nineteen years of age at the time, was as brave and valiant as men twice his age. At the close of the war he returned home, and studied medicine, as above stated. During his service in the army he contracted a cold that undermined his constitution, and from its effects he died at Warwick, aged thirty-five.

May 13, 1869, Miss Mariam Beakes, daughter of Joseph Beakes, and a member of one of the most prominent families of this county, became the wife of our subject. She was born on the old Beakes homestead adjoining Middletown, and now owned by her brother, Henry L. Beakes, of whom mention is made upon another page. The family of which she is a member has an honorable record, and its history, traced back through successive generations, is one of which every descendant may well be proud. Upon the death of her husband, she sold out the business in Warwick and came to Middletown, where she has since resided. Beloved by all who know her, she is "Aunt Mariam" to her hosts of friends. Her religious connections are with the Methodist Episcopal Church of this city. She is a lady of unusual ability and intelligence, maintaining herself in every position in which she may be placed with dignity, and in her social relations her genial, gentle and amiable temperament commends her most affectionately to all who are thrown in her daily pathway.

BENJAMIN HAFNER, depot master of the Erie Railroad at Port Jervis, has been an engineer for fifty-one years and six months. He has had many interesting experiences, has had many narrow escapes, and has operated all kinds of engines, from the "Grasshopper," of the old Baltimore & Ohio, to the modern one-hundred-ton "Mogul," which is used for hauling heavy freights up the mountains, or the lightning express making its seventy miles per hour. Besides having made many fast runs for the railroad officials, he eclipsed the record by covering the eighty-eight miles between this point and Jersey City, on Express No. 8, in two hours exactly, besides stopping at Turner, for dinner. He owns three good residences in this city.

Mr. Hafner was born March 24, 1821, in Baden, Germany, and came to the United States in 1832, landing at Baltimore, September 18. His father, Valentine Hafner, was one of Napoleon's soldiers, serving as First Lieutenant, and went on the march to Moscow. He died in 1862, at his home in Baltimore, when seventy-seven years old. His wife, whose maiden name was Mary Ann Murrout, departed this life in 1861. Their family numbered eight children.

Our subject worked as a broom-maker for four years, and then clerked in a store in Baltimore. For three years he served an apprenticeship to the blacksmith's trade, and in 1839 entered the railroad shops. He was soon placed on an old-style engine as fireman, and his peculiar locomotive, which had no cab, was exhibited at the World's Fair in Chicago. A year later young Hafner was placed in charge of an extra engine, and in 1840 commenced running on regular trips between Baltimore and Cumberland, Md. This road was constructed with the old slab rails, and

one night Mr. Hafner's engine and train were precipitated into the Patapsco River, below Ellicott's Mills. He and his fireman were immersed in the river, but managed to escape and no one else was injured. At another time during a heavy rain in the mountains, the tracks were washed away and the train ran into the Potomac River, but no one was hurt.

In 1845 Mr. Hafner was in charge of the train that carried Polk's message from the Reeley House to Harper's Ferry. The first telegraph was laid the same year, being placed in a trough beside the track, but later was placed on poles. M. Hafner was acquainted with many of the public men of that period, among whom were Andrew Jackson, J. C. Calhoun, Daniel Webster, Henry Clay and Thomas H. Benton. He carried all of these men as passengers, when he was fireman on the Washington road. In 1848 our subject went to Piermont and was soon given an engine running between that point and Port Jervis. Piermont was then the eastern end of the road, and from there to New York City freight had to be shipped by boat. In May, 1854, Mr. Hafner resigned and went to Yellow Springs, Ohio, to visit a brother whom he had not seen for nineteen years. In 1839 Mr. Hafner entered the Baltimore & Ohio service, running a distance of one hundred and seventy-nine miles between Baltimore and Cumberland. After a time he began working for the Illinois Central Railroad, running to East Dubuque from Amboy, and in 1855 had charge of the night express. The winter of 1854 was a very severe one and for three days Mr. Hafner and his train were stuck in the snow, before being extricated.

In 1855 our subject went to Europe, looking up business matters in his native city, and also made a trip to France. He returned in 1857, and the following year took up his permanent residence in Port Jervis. Until April, 1859, he ran a freight train from here to Piermont, after which he was given an express passenger train between Port Jervis and Jersey City, running the same for twenty-nine successive years. In March, 1892, his service as an engineer closed, and since that time he has been depot master. In 1849 Mr.

Hafner was on an engine drawing a gravel train, and when coming down hill it collided with a freight whose engineer had disregarded his flag of warning. In 1852 his engine was capsized at Paterson on account of a misplaced switch, and ten years later he was buried under his engine, but was not seriously injured. For a great many years he has been a member of the Brotherhood of Locomotive Engineers.

February 14, 1858, Mr. Hafner married Mary Catherine Goetz, of Baltimore and a native of Bavaria. They have had eleven children, of whom but five are living, namely: Mary, Anna (Mrs. Henry H. Monton, of Flushing, L. I.) Wilhelmina, Rose and Alice. The parents are members of the Catholic Church of Port Jervis. Mr. Hafner has always been a Democrat since the days of Jackson, and cast his first vote for James K. Polk.

HENRY CLINTON CUNNINGHAM is one of the oldest merchants, not only of Port Jervis, but of this portion of New York State. His business career covers some forty-eight years, and for seventeen years of this period he has managed a store at his present location, having constructed the building in 1878. He is a man of practical and methodical ways, and has been prospered in his various undertakings. Born October 30, 1828, at Butternut, Otsego County, N. Y., he is a son of John and Louisa (Farnum) Cunningham, the former a farmer by occupation.

Our subject was the eldest child and was named in honor of his uncle, Henry H. Farnum, and DeWitt Clinton. He received his early education in a log schoolhouse, and one of his comrades was Martin Van Buren, a relative of the ex-President of that name.

H. C. Cunningham came to Port Jervis in April, 1847, and served a clerkship with his uncle, H. H. Farnum, who had engaged in business here in 1843. Four months later he returned on a visit to his mother, who was very ill, and went by stage from Port Jervis to Oneonta, the trip taking two days and two nights. During the seven years in which he worked for his uncle he held various positions, being gradually promoted. They did a large business with the railroad and canal, furnishing them with supplies, and the old store, which was built of foot-boards laid flatways, is still standing on the bank of the canal, and there the collector's office is located. In 1854 our subject took a one-third interest, with Farnum & Peck as partners, the company then being styled H. H. Farnum & Co. Thus the business was carried on for five years, when, April 1, 1859, Mr. Cunningham retired.

May 1, 1859, our subject opened a store for himself in Lockwood's Building on Pike Street, which he rented for nearly nineteen years, carrying a full line of dry goods, notions, groceries, etc. In 1864 he purchased the property at the corner of Orange Square and Pike Streets, on which he erected the building he now occupies. He has advertised extensively, and has neglected no well approved and legitimate manner of increasing his business.

March 4, 1861, Mr. Cunningham and Stephen St. John, Sr., were the only citizens of Port Jervis who attended the inauguration of Lincoln. Since 1856 he has been a Republican, and at one time attended a torch-light procession to Milford, Pa., it being the first Republican campaign in 1856, for Fremont. He has served in local offices and has always taken a great interest in party matters. Acceding to the request of Rev. Dr. Samuel W. Mills, Corresponding Secretary of the Orange County Bible Society, Mr. Cunningham became agent for the society and started a repository about 1863,. He has since been the representative for the town of Deerpark, and has done much to further the interests of the organization.

March 6, 1855, occurred the marriage of Mr. Cunningham and Catherine, daughter of Mark Decker, the latter of whom died in 1894, aged about eighty-four years. Henrietta C., the only daughter of our subject, was born in 1873. She possesses great talent as a musician, having received superior advantages, and is especially accomplished as a pianiste. She has appeared before the public in concerts a great many times, and is the author of a popular composition for the piano, "Cheerfulness" (dedicated to her mother), which has been highly spoken of by talented musicians. Both parents and daughter are members of the First Presbyterian Church. Since the new edifice was constructed our subject has served as a Trustee, as a Ruling Elder, or in one or another official capacity, and in various offices has been identified with the Sabbath-school for a good many years.

JAMES E. BRAZEE. Not only as one of the oldest employes of the New York, Ontario & Western Railway Company, in point of years of service, but also as an honorable and genial gentleman, Mr. Brazee is well known to the citizens of Middletown, which city has been his headquarters since 1873. He entered the employ of the company when the road was building, and, receiving promotions at various times, now occupies the position of conductor. During the winter season he has charge of the milk train, while in summer he is conductor on the mountain express. It is worthy of note, as an unusual occurrence, that for the past fourteen years he has had the same run.

The Brazee family is of honorable descent, being of the old Puritan stock. The first of the name to settle in New York was the great-grandfather of our subject, a soldier of the Revolutionary War, who came hither from Massachusetts. Grandfather Teunis Brazee was born in Delaware County, was a farmer by occupation, and during the War of 1812 rendered valiant service. Next in line of descent was George, our subject's father, who was born in Delaware County, and in addition to farm work also engaged in the lumber business there. In 1862 he enlisted in the One Hundred and Forty-fourth New York Infantry, but afterward was transferred to the First New York Engineer Corps, and served as an officer of his company. He remained in the army until the close of the Rebellion. He now makes his home in Walton, Delaware County, and since

1873 has led a retired life. Politically he is a Republican. In the Methodist Episcopal Church he is an active and successful worker, and has officiated as one of its local ministers.

Margaret, our subject's mother, was born in Hancock, Delaware County, to which place her father, Daniel I. Weeks, had removed from Connecticut. Being one of the pioneers of that locality, he endured many hardships, and took an active part in the wars with the Indians. Our subject, who was the only child of his parents, was born in Colchester, Delaware County, September 17, 1855. After receiving the rudiments of his education in the public schools of his native town, he attended the Rochester University for a time, then taught school in this county, being engaged in that profession for three terms. In 1871, when a mere boy, he entered the employ of the New York, Ontario & Western Railway Company, when the road was building in Delaware and Sullivan Counties. His first position was on the engineer corps, and in 1873 he became a brakeman on the Northern Division of the road, his run being on a construction train. August 18 of that year he was made brakeman on the through freight train between Norwich and Middletown, with his headquarters in the latter city. In 1875 he became conductor, and in that capacity ran special trains on every branch of the road. The following year he began running the local freight between Middletown and Walton, and in 1878 he was made passenger conductor, which position he has since held. He has been very fortunate in his railroad experience, never having had any accidents on his runs.

At No. 36 Broad Street, Middletown, stands the home of Mr. Brazee, the residence being a neat structure erected by himself. He married, in this city in 1891, Miss Jennie Quinn, who was born here. By their union one child has been born, a daughter, Edna B. While on one of his runs, in 1894, Mr. Brazee was elected Supervisor of the First Ward on the Republican ticket, and his election attested his popularity, as the Ward was strongly Democratic. His many friends, however, irrespective of politics, were glad to vote for a man whom they deemed so well qualified for

DAVID McCAMLY.

the place, so he overcame the usual Democratic majority of two hundred, having instead a Republican majority of sixty-six. During his service in this office he has served on several committees, and was also on the special committee for re-districting the Second Senatorial District of the county. Socially he is connected with Walton Lodge No. 559, F. & A. M. In the local lodge of the Order of Railway Conductors he was the first Chief, which position he held for many years. He was also Representative to the Grand Division, and attended the conventions at Boston, Louisville, New Orleans, Denver, Toronto, Rochester, Toledo, Atlanta and St. Louis, having, in fact, failed to attend but three of the conventions of recent years.

DAVID McCAMLY. One of the early settlers of the town of Warwick was David McCamly, who was born in the North of Ireland, in 1704, and by his marriage to Jane Ellison, December 30, 1726, was connected with the well known Ellison family of New Windsor. He came to America with the Clinton colony, landing October 1, 1729. The following year he settled on a tract of twenty-five hundred acres, extending from near Warwick into Sussex County, N. J. On the farm, which now forms a part of the estate of W. M. Sanford, he built a dam and established a flourmill. He died December 15, 1785, and his wife passed away February 27, 1786. They and several of their descendants are buried in a secluded spot near the banks of the Wawayanda Creek, where their graves may still be distinguished.

The children of David and Jane (Ellison) McCamly were as follows: John, who was born in Ireland, October 9, 1727; William, who was born August 28, 1730, and died August 28, 1758; Mary, born July 15, 1732; Sarah, August 30, 1734; Elizabeth, Mrs. Owens, who was born September 27, 1736, and died April 17, 1801; Jane, born May 17, 1740; and David, September 9, 1743. The last-named, whose official service in

50

the Revolution won him the title of Colonel, was united in marriage, May 10. 1774, with Phœbe Sands, who was born September 11, 1759, and was a daughter of Capt. Samuel and Lavinia Sands, of Newburgh, N. Y.

Colonel McCamly settled on a tract of fifteen hundred acres at New Milford, N. Y., given him by his father, and there he built a spacious stone dwelling-house, which he occupied until his death. He also established the family cemetery, in which he and three generations of his descendants are buried. During the Revolutionary War he served first as Captain of a company belonging to Colonel Hathorn's Florida and Warwick regiment. In recognition of his courage and loyalty, he was later commissioned Colonel. In his household, as on the field, he maintained habits of military discipline and exacted unquestioning obedience from his children and his large retinue of slaves. To each of his daughters he gave a slave as a personal attendant; these slaves accompanied them to their husbands' homes and remained with them until their death. It is a noteworthy historical fact that at the home of Colonel McCamly in New Milford, in 1786, was the first appointment for religious services by a Methodist minister in Orange County. His death occurred January 16, 1817, and his wife died June 10, 1822. He was a remarkably handsome man, of dignified manners, and was noted for his horsemanship.

Of the children of Col. David and Phœbe (Sands) McCamly, we note the following: Samuel, who was born July 27, 1775, married Elizabeth Wheeler, and died May 22, 1814. Lavinia, born November 2, 1777, died January 30, 1779. Mary, Mrs. Nathaniel Blaine, born February 26, 1780, died October 26, 1836. John, born December 24, 1782, married Sarah Wheeler, and died at Battle Creek, Mich., in 1858; one of his sons, John Wheeler, settled at Matagorda, Tex., and there many of his descendants still reside. Eleazer Gedney, born February 12, 1785, married Ruth Wheeler, and died in Michigan. Jane, Mrs. Francis Price, who was born April 12, 1787, died of cholera in New York City, April 12, 1833, leaving among her children a son, Rodman McCamly Price, who became Governor of New Jersey. Mercy was born April 27, 1789, and died September 16, 1793. David was born June 14, 1791, and died July 19, 1849. Sands, born August 16, 1793, married Eliza Coleman, and became the founder and one of the most influential citizens of Battle Creek, Mich., representing his district in Congress, and being an intimate personal friend of Gen. Lewis Cass. Rodman, born March 15, 1797, first married Nancy Wheeler, and after her death was united with Catherine DeKay McCamly, and his death occurred at Vernon, N. J., December 3, 1870. The youngest son of Rodman McCamly was the late Maj. James Monroe McCamly. He was twice wounded in the War of the Rebellion, and died of yellow fever at New Orleans. R. McCamly's only surviving child is Sarah Catherine, wife of Rev. Lewis R. Dunn, of East Orange, N. J. Elizabeth Ann, the youngest of the family, was born August 21, 1802, became the wife of William Dolson, and died August 28, 1823.

David McCamly, whose portrait accompanies this sketch, was the eighth child of Col. David McCamly, and was born at the homestead at New Milford, where he resided on a tract of two hundred acres, inherited from his father, until his death in 1849. Although not a member of any denomination, yet he was deeply interested in the growth of the Methodist Episcopal Church, and gave the land on which the edifice at New Milford was built; also contributed liberally to the support of the church. On the 2d of January, 1812, he was united in marriage with Sarah Davis, daughter of Samuel and Ruth (Rumsey) Davis, of Sugar Loaf Valley, this county. This lady was born December 10, 1792, and died September 4, 1832, after having become the mother of ten children. The second union of David McCamly took place June 24, 1835, and united him with Mrs Eleanor Higgins, widow of John Higgins, of New York, and daughter of Francis and Catherine (Hepburn) Geraghty, of Warwick. Mrs Eleanor McCamly was born in New York City, July 28, 1810, and died December 3, 1888, having become the mother of six children by her second marriage.

The eldest child of David McCamly was Edmund, who was born October 22, 1812, and died April 5, 1842. Sands, the second son, was born July 11, 1814, and died at Newburgh, April 10, 1848. He married Mary Elizabeth, daughter of David Crawford, of Newburgh, and their only child is Mary E. C., wife of Charles F. Allen, of Newburgh. Jane Davis, the eldest daughter, was born June 24, 1816, became the wife of Col. Anthony Parcell Kerr, January 1, 1840, and died at Mt. Eve, August 26, 1880. Francis Price, the fourth child, was born May 5, 1818, and married Anna Augusta Turner, of New York City, May 14, 1840; after her death he was united with Mary Greene, of Illinois, and now resides with his sons and grandsons at McCamly, Sully County, S. Dak. Susan, whose birth occurred June 28, 1820, married Rev. John Goodsell Smith, of New York, November 29, 1842, and resides in Newburgh. Abigail, born April 16, 1822, was married to John Edsall McCain, January 8, 1843, and died at Goshen February 5, 1895. Harrison, who was born March 7, 1824, resides at Carson City, Nev. Caroline Adelia was born December 31, 1826, and died January 1, 1850. William Henry, who was ninth in order of birth, was born August 5, 1829, and died at Shingle Springs, Eldorado County, Cal., February 27, 1867. Frederick Louis Vulte, the youngest child of the family, was born July 14, 1832, and died October 12 of the same year.

Of the second marriage of David McCamly the following children were born: Sarah Catherine, who was born March 27, 1836, and died February 10, 1841; Marietta, who was born January 29, 1839, married M. C. Belknap, of Newburgh, May 13, 1862, and died November 27, 1873; Victoria, who was born May 2, 1841, and died January 30, 1842; Josephine, born May 2, 1841 (twin of Victoria), married John N. Crane, February 5, 1861, and died at Newburgh, April 2, 1886; Eugenia, who was born April 1, 1844, became the wife of John S. Walker, of New York, December 24, 1863, and now resides in Newburgh; and David, who was born October 29, 1848, married Anna Mary Preston, of Battle Creek, Mich., June 30, 1885, and is a resident of that city.

OL. ANTHONY PARCELL KERR was at one time intimately associated with the history of Orange County, where his life began March 6, 1809, and closed July 18, 1881. The house in which he was born, and which is now the home of his daughter, was built in 1804 and is still in a good state of preservation. The nails and shingles used in its construction were manufactured by hand; the sidings were of red cedar, and the floors and doors of hardwood. In the kitchen still hang the old crane pothooks used in the early days, and the fireplace was so large that a horse was trained to draw in the back logs.

The old homestead, which is known as Mt. Eve, takes its name from the adjoining peak, which, with a neighboring peak, Mt. Adam, rises from the edge of the drowned lands, and has been a well known landmark for two hundred years or more. Both peaks are of a peculiar formation, Mt. Eve being the higher and longer, and on it several granite quarries have been opened, from which stone is quarried similar to the celebrated Quincy granite. This property has been in the possession of the Kerr family for four generations, and in early days was frequently visited by the Indians, with whom the white settlers were on the most friendly terms.

The founder of the Kerr family in America was Walter Kerr, a native of Lanarkshire, Scotland, born in 1653, and who died June 10, 1748. He was a strict Presbyterian and was arrested as a Non-Conformist, his property seized, and himself sentenced to perpetual banishment. For this reason he sought, in 1685, a home in the New World. Settling at Freehold, N. J., he became one of the founders and ruling Elders of the famous Tennent Church, of which the brothers, Gilbert and William Tennent, were pastors for many years. He was one of the most prominent men and largest land-owners of his section, and became the progenitor of a large family, his descendants now numbering fifteen hundred. He and his wife, Annie, reared several sons and daughters, and they are buried in the old churchyard at Freehold, as are many of their descendants.

One of the grandsons of Walter Kerr was Rev.

Nathan Kerr, D. D., who was for thirty-eight years pastor of the Presbyterian Church of Goshen. Another grandson was the ancestor of the Newburgh branch of the family. Another grandson, David Kerr, was the grandfather of Col. Anthony P. Kerr, and was born in Monmouth County, N. J., where he received his education. After his marriage he settled at Ramapo, then in Orange, but now in Rockland, County, making his home on a tract of land there, where were born his six sons and one daughter, viz.: Mark, George, Anthony, Richard, James, Robert and Esther.

The six sons were men of splendid physique, being over six feet in height, and they were soldiers in the Revolution, attaining distinction through their valor in that memorable contest. Mark was a non-commissioned officer, a member of the lifeguard, and during the War of 1812 he was Captain of a company of artillery. After the war was ended he settled in Louisiana, whither he had gone on a trading expedition. Four sons died either during or shortly after the Revolution from wounds received, or as a result of exposure while in the service. They left no children. Esther married, and died in New York City, her union having been childless.

For many years David Kerr lived at Ramapo, and there his children were born. Several years before the breaking out of the Revolution he removed with his family to Mt. Eve, and from that homestead his sons marched forth to the war. He was one of the founders of the Presbyterian Church at Amity, and is buried in that churchyard. His son Robert, our subject's father, was born at Ramapo, January 19, 1756, and accompanied the other members of the family to Mt. Eve. Enlisting in the Colonial army, he joined the troops in New Jersey, and with General Washington crossed the Delaware on that memorable Christmas Eve and participated in the battle at Trenton, and that of Princeton, which followed. He continued with the army, and was at Morristown and Valley Forge, and during the winter previous to the discharge of the troops he was stationed at New Windsor. The camp was broken up in October, 1783, and in November following he witnessed the evacuation and departure of the British soldiers from New York City.

The first wife of Robert Kerr was Mary Benjamin, of Amity, by whom he had four children, namely: Samuel Benjamin, David, George and Sarah. In November, 1802, he married Mary Christina (Pitts) Parcell, widow of Anthony Parcell, a non-commissioned officer of the Revolution, who died in 1796, from the effects of exposure while in the army. Two children were born of that union, our subject and Phœbe Maria. The latter, who was born November 27, 1806, became the wife of Alvah Foster in 1822, and died in New York City in September, 1872. Our subject's mother was born at Snufftown, N. J., August 24, 1765, and died at the homestead at Mt. Eve, January 31, 1831. She was the daughter of John and Mary Magdalene Pitts, French-Huguenots, whose parents had settled in Holland after the revocation of the Edict of Nantes, and after their marriage, in 1760, they came to America, establishing their home in New Jersey, where they reared a large family. Robert Kerr died November 28, 1846. He was a stanch Jacksonian Democrat, and his granddaughter Harriet has the old cane that was sent to him by General Jackson in recognition of his fealty to the General's cause. She also has a musket, bayonet and powder-horn carried by him during the Revolutionary War, and a sword taken by him from a British officer, whom he captured and disarmed.

The subject of this sketch was educated in the schools of Amity and Edenville, and followed the occupation of a farmer throughout all his life. January 1, 1840, he married Jane Davis McCamly, the third child of David and Sarah (Davis) McCamly, of New Milford, N. Y. She was born June 24, 1816, and died August 26, 1880, having by her union with Colonel Kerr become the mother of three children. Of these, Sarah Ellen died in girlhood; Jeanie Dale married Benjamin P. DeGroot, of New York City, and died January 5, 1874, leaving no children; and Harriet, who is the only survivor, occupies the old homestead. Colonel Kerr was greatly interested in military matters and was Colonel Commandant of the Nineteenth Regiment New York State Militia

for several years, or until its disbandment. In politics he was a Democrat, and his first vote was cast for General Jackson. A man of great generosity, with a companionable disposition and upright character, he won the regard of his associates, to whom his manly qualities endeared him. For many years he and his wife were identified with the Methodist Episcopal Church at Edenville. He died July 18, 1881, and is buried in the family graveyard at Mt. Eve, where also lie the bodies of his parents, his wife and his children.

GEORGE BERGEN This prominent resident of the town of Montgomery is industriously pursuing his chosen occupation, that of a farmer, on the old homestead which was left him by his honored father. He is one of the most valued citizens of the community, and the property of which he is the owner is one of the best in the town in point of improvement.

Our subject was born August 15, 1836, in Queens County, L. I., and was the son of Henry and Cornelia (Bourum) Bergen. The father, who was also born on the same farm as his son, came with his family to Orange County in the year 1856. He was well-to-do in this world's goods, and purchased the estate in the town of Montgomery on which his son, our subject, now resides. Here he lived, taking an active interest in all enterprises in the community, and here also his death occurred when he was in his seventy-ninth year. His wife, whose birth also occurred on Long Island, lived to be eighty-two years of age. She was of Holland extraction, and her people were very much respected wherever their lot was cast. Both parents of our subject were members in excellent standing of the Reformed Church, and were active in all good works in their locality.

The subject of this sketch made his home with his parents until their decease, when he inherited the home farm on which he has since resided. This property comprises one hundred and fifty

RESIDENCE OF GEORGE BERGEN,
OMERY, Town of Montgomery, Orange County, N. Y.

acres, which Mr. Bergen cultivates in a most profitable manner. He has attained a high rank among the prosperous farmers of the town, and is highly regarded in the community where he has passed so many years of his life. In politics he is a stanch Republican and never lets an opportunity pass when he can use his influence for the good of his party.

RANK W. DENNIS, M. D., of Unionville, was born in Sussex County, N. J., July 30, 1857. The family of which he is a member is of Scotch-Irish extraction, and was represented in America at an early period in the settlement of this country. His parents, David Wilson and Sarah (Read) Dennis, were natives of Sussex County, and unto them were born eight children: David R., who was drowned while on a fishing trip; Frank W., of this sketch; Annie M., wife of Marshall Cook; John, who was drowned at the age of two years; William E., a druggist at Far Rockaway and a graduate of the College of Pharmacy, New York City; Violetta; Flora L., a professional nurse in Stillwater, N. J., and New York; and Martin R., who died in infancy.

The subject of this sketch grew to manhood near Stillwater, N. J., and received his primary education in the public schools. When fifteen years of age he entered a store at Middleville as a clerk. The next year he accepted a more remunerative position in Phillipsburg, N. J. His leisure evening hours were devoted to study in the night schools, and for one year he attended a business college at Easton, Pa. He then began teaching school in Sussex County, continuing in that profession for four years and meeting with success in it. In 1879, having resolved to enter the medical profession, he became a student in the medical department of the State University of Michigan at Ann Arbor, from which institution he was graduated in 1881.

Opening an office in Gilead, Ind., the young Doctor began the practice of his profession, continuing in that place until 1884, when he went to New York City and took a post-graduate course

in the College of Physicians and Surgeons. On leaving there, he engaged with Dr. Berlin at Chapman's Quarries, Pa., where he remained nine months, coming from there to Unionville, in the town of Minisink, He is regarded as a skilled, capable physician, one fully informed regarding the profession and successful in practice.

June 23, 1887, Dr. Dennis was united in marriage with Miss Mary Wisner, and they have one child, Edna E., who was born May 6, 1892. Since locating in Unionville, Dr. Dennis has built up a good practice, which is being continually extended. He is a great reader and keeps abreast of the times. In the winters of 1892-93 he attended the Vanderbilt clinics in New York. In 1892 he was elected Trustee of Unionville for two years, and in 1894 was chosen President of the Village Board, to which responsible position he was re-elected the following year. In politics he is a Republican. His election to various local offices attests his popularity as a man.

CHRISTIAN S. HULSHIZER, who is better known as "Charlie" in railroad circles, is one of the old and reliable employes of the Erie Railroad, his headquarters being at Port Jervis, Orange County. For the past twenty-seven years he has made his home here, and during this time has been in the Delaware Division. He now runs the Mountain Express, a local passenger train from this point to Susquehanna. For eight years he has had charge of passenger trains, and has never had a serious accident. From 1875 to 1882 he was interested in the livery business in this city, which enterprise did not interfere in the least with his regular employment. Since 1868 he has been an active member of the Brotherhood of Locomotive Engineers, and is very popular among the employes as well as the officials of the railroad.

September 9, 1842, occurred the birth of our subject in Stewartsville, Warren County, N. J., his parents being Andrew and Halana (Sharps) Hulshizer. Our subject's great-grandfather, Martin, with his three brothers, emigrated from

Germany, settling in Warren and Hunterdon Counties, N. J., prior to the Revolutionary War. This Martin Hulshizer had a son named in his honor, and who was nine years old at the time of the emigration. The parents of our subject were natives of Warren County, N. J., where many families of the name and distant relatives are still living.

C. S. Hulshizer continued to dwell with his parents until twenty years of age, receiving a good education. He then took up railroading as a brakeman and baggageman on the Lehigh Valley Railroad, and for a short time was employed by the Ohio & Mississippi Road, running to St. Louis. In the spring of 1863 he enlisted in Company C, Thirty-first New Jersey Infantry, and was assigned to the First Brigade, First Division of the First Army Corp, under Maj.-Gen. J. G. Reynolds and General Wadsworth, Division Commanders, the latter of whom was killed at Spottsylvania. Mr. Hulshizer served in the Army of the Potomac until June, 1864, when he was honorably discharged, after having participated in the battles of Fredericksburg and Chancellorsville. In the last-named engagement his regiment was held in reserve during the heaviest fighting, but was under constant fire for two days preceding. Our subject remained with his regiment all of the time, with the exception of a few weeks when he was on special duty.

Returning to the regular routine of life, Mr. Hulshizer obtained a position on the Orange & Alexandria Railway, and later ran on the Harper's Ferry & Winchester Railroad, being in the Government employ for two years. When the Lehigh & Susquehanna Railroad was completed he ran for eight months between Wilkes Barre and White Haven, and then, until July 1, 1856, he was an employe of the Delaware, Lackawanna & Western Railway. For the next two years he operated an engine on the same railroad, but since October, 1868, has been in the Delaware Division of the Erie Railroad.

In 1880 Mr. Hulshizer erected a handsome and comfortable residence on one of the leading streets of this city, and has surrounded himself with

many of the luxuries of life. He was married, October 27, 1880, to Mary Ettie Moses, of Port Jervis, and daughter of Burton and Martha Moses, well known citizens of this place. Our subject and wife have hosts of sincere friends in this community, and take great pleasure in entertaining them.

LOUIS V. BAUER, proprietor of the Wallkill River Park House, was born in Saxony, Germany, December 10, 1846. He is the son of Charles Louis and Fredericka (Jager) Bauer, natives of Germany, where they spent their entire lives, the father being engaged in the postoffice department of that country for many years. He passed away in 1861, and is survived by his wife, who continues to live in Saxony.

In the public schools of Germany the subject of this notice gained a practical education, and at the age of fourteen began a three-years apprenticeship to the machinist's trade. He served until the close of his time, and followed the trade in Germany until twenty-one years of age, when he crossed the ocean and established his permanent home in America. Going to Newark, N. J., he took charge of the machinery in the morocco factory of C. Nugent & Co., where he remained for two years. Later he embarked in business for himself. He was the first to manufacture genuine Russian leather in the United States, the secret of which he learned in Europe, and this statement is a matter of history. For a time he was in the employ of Howell, Hinchman & Co., at Middletown, and during his connection with that firm he made a trip to Europe for them in the interests of his discovery. It was through his instrumentality that the great reduction in the price of Russian leather was secured in this country.

It was in 1889 that Mr. Bauer took charge of the resort he has since successfully conducted. Bauer's Park, which adjoins Midway Park, and which contains ten acres, is situated between Goshen and Middletown, and bids fair to become one of the leading resorts in the county.

February 15, 1870, Mr. Bauer married Miss Sarah, daughter of Dr. Lambrecht, of Elizabeth Ford, N. J. Of this union two children survive, Herman and Annie, who are with their parents. When the body of General Grant lay in state in New York City, although there were more than one hundred thousand people waiting outside for the purpose of viewing the body, Mr. Bauer was the first to gain entrance. Socially he is identified with the Masonic fraternity and the Independent Order of Odd Fellows. Politically he is a Republican, but is bitterly opposed to sumptuary laws. He has served two terms as Excise Commissioner of Middletown, and was the first President of the Board of Excise under the new city charter. His majority at both elections was overwhelming, and his service in that capacity was most satisfactory to the people and creditable to himself.

GILBERT GOODGION, a contractor and builder at Middletown, was born in the village of Montgomery in 1854, and is of English descent. Two brothers of that name came to this country at a very early day, one of whom located in Orange County, and the other in the South. William Goodgion, who was a farmer by occupation, was born in Ulster County. His son, Jacob Goodgion, the father of our subject, was also born in Ulster County, near Rutsonville. The father learned the carpenter's trade in his youth, and for a short time followed it in Montgomery, and then returned to the old home farm in Ulster County. There he followed farming until his death, at the age of sixty-six years. Politically he was a Democrat. He married Susan Moore, a native of Montgomery and a daughter of Joel Moore, who was of Scotch descent and who was a farmer residing near that village. Mrs. Goodgion was a devout member of the Reformed Church, and died at the age of seventy-two years. Of her eight children, seven grew to maturity, and five are yet living.

Gilbert Goodgion was fifth in the parental family. Soon after his birth his parents removed

to Rutsonville, and on the old farm of his father and grandfather he grew to manhood. He was educated in the public schools, and in 1871 came to Middletown. Under Seth Wright he was apprenticed to learn the trade of mason and bricklayer, and after remaining with him two years returned to his old home, where for one year he was clerk in a general store. He then went to Woodbourne, Sullivan County, where he remained two years as clerk in a general store, and again came to Middletown and engaged at his trade. After working for different parties until 1882, he began contracting and building in partnership with Mr. Springstead, under the firm name of Goodgion & Springstead. This partnership was continued until 1894, when it was dissolved, since which time our subject has been in business alone. In rustic mason work he is quite experienced, and in almost every part of Middletown may be found specimens of his work.

Mr. Goodgion was married in Ellenville to Miss Serepta Edwards, a native of Woodbourne. She died December 27, 1894, leaving five children: Frank, Fred, Charles, Clarence and Jennie. In politics Mr. Goodgion is a Democrat, and has served as Committeeman from his ward. Fraternally he is a member of the Knights of Pythias, and for some years he was a member of Eagle Hose Company No. 2.

CHARLES DAVIS, of Port Jervis, is foreman of the engine-house and repair department in the Erie Railroad shops. He is a native of Bath, Somersetshire, England, but has resided in the United States for the past thirty years. A son of Joseph and Sarah (Branch) Davis, he was born March 15, 1845, and in his birthplace spent his boyhood. He received common-school advantages, and when he was fifteen years of age commenced learning the millwright's trade. Five years later he set sail for America, coming at once to Port Jervis, where he obtained a position in the shops and completed his trade. Until 1870 he was an employe in the roundhouse, and that year he went to New Orleans, La., remaining in that city and in western Mississippi for two years and eight months. In November, 1872, he returned to this city, having been offered a position as a machinist in the roundhouse. Later he was promoted to be foreman, succeeding P. J. Smith, deceased, and in his department he has some twenty men.

January 30, 1869, the marriage of Charles Davis and Sarah Whitehead was celebrated in Port Jervis. Mrs. Davis was born in Oldham, England, and had crossed the Atlantic to the United States less than a year prior to her marriage. She was called to the home beyond June 18, 1891, having been an invalid for three or four years. She was the mother of three sons and three daughters, two of whom, Mabel and Victoria, died in infancy. Florence C. is a successful school teacher; Alfred is a clerk in the car shops; Arthur J. occupies a position in a drug store; and Stanley, the youngest son, is still in school. The children are all members of the Episcopal Church and have received good home training. Mr. Davis is a member of Port Jervis Lodge No. 328, F. & A. M.; Neversink Chapter No. 186, R. A. M.; Delaware Commandery No. 44, K. T.; and Mecca Temple of the Mystic Shrine of New York City. Politically he is a Democrat. For thirteen years he has been a leader of the Erie Cornet Band of Port Jervis, which he helped to organize in 1867. Ever since boyhood he has displayed ability as a musician, and in former years was quite a vocalist. The instrument which he now plays in the band is a B flat cornet.

WILLIAM CONN is engine dispatcher for the Erie Railroad at Port Jervis, and has filled this position uninterruptedly and faithfully since 1869. His duties require his constant presence and supervision of engines, which must leave this point in good order, and he also looks after all repair work in the engine-house. There are about forty men who take orders direct from him, and altogether, counting those who are on the road, he superintends some three hundred and fifty hands. For twenty-six years he has been a member of Division No. 54, Brotherhood of Locomotive Engineers.

A native of New Jersey, Mr. Conn was born in the city of Newark, August 11, 1838, and passed the first eleven years of his life in that locality. He then removed to Piermont, N. Y., which was then the termination of the Erie Railroad, and there he attended the common schools. His parents were William and Mary (Campbell) Conn, natives of Scotland. When he was seventeen years of age, young Conn ran away from home, and going to New Bedford, Conn., shipped on a whaling-vessel, the "Analda," commanded by Capt. Smith Sarvent. The trip which ensued consumed three and a-half years, during which time the vessel touched at the Sandwich Islands and other points in the Pacific, and proceeded to the Arctic Ocean, passing the coast of California and penetrating the Arctic Ocean. The result of the voyage was three thousand barrels of oil, and was therefore considered very successful. Mr. Conn received as his payment one barrel for every two hundred barrels of oil procured, and as it was then worth about $45 a barrel, his share was $675, besides a percentage of the whalebone taken.

In 1858 our subject, having returned home, started in his railroad career on the Erie Road at Piermont, in the humble capacity of oilman, his duties being to oil the cars at points of friction. In 1860 he was made fireman on the Eastern Division, and acted as such for two years. In August, 1862, he enlisted in the United States navy as a fireman, and was assigned to the gunboat "Norwich," under Capt. James Duncan, being attached to the North Atlantic Squadron. The vessel assisted in blockading the city of Charleston and other points, helped to take St. John, Fla., and guarded Yellow Bluff. Mr. Conn was one of nine firemen on the "Norwich," and served altogether fifteen months. On his return to the ordinary pursuits of life, he was re-employed by the Erie Road, and became hostler at Port Jervis, February 22, 1864. Soon afterwards he was given the place of assistant engineer, his

WILLIAM L. CUDDEBACK, M. D.

duties being to take engines to and from the yards. Then he was made assistant engine dispatcher under W. Kimball, and was promoted to his present place in 1869.

February 10, 1864, Mr. Conn married Mary E. Travis, of this city. They have but one child, Nathaniel, who is a clerk in the road department of the railroad service. Mrs. Conn is a lady of good education, and is a faithful member of the Baptist Church. Fraternally our subject is identified with the Masonic order, belonging to Port Jervis Lodge No. 328, F. & A. M.; Neversink Chapter No. 186, R. A. M.; Delaware Commandery No. 44, K. T.; also Mecca Temple of the Mystic Shrine of New York City. In these orders he has held a number of offices, and stands high in the estimation of the brotherhood. His right of franchise is used in favor of the Republican party.

<<++++++++++++++🌑++++++++++++++>>

WILLIAM L. CUDDEBACK, M. D. This well known physician of Port Jervis is descended from the French-Huguenots, belonging to one of the oldest families in the United States, who arrived in Deerpark, Orange County, in 1690. In that year five men, Jacob Cuddeback, Thomas, Anthony and Bernardus Swartwout and Peter Gumaer, with their families, formed a settlement called Peenpack on the Neversink River, some six miles northeast of the present site of Port Jervis, which, with the exception of one small place, was the earliest settlement made in what is now Orange County. Amicable arrangements were made with the Indians, and deeds to their land obtained, as it is known they lived in peace until the French and Indian War, a period of more than sixty years.

Two of the settlers, Mr. Cuddeback and Mr. Gumaer, were from France. In 1685 the King of France, Louis XIV., revoked the Edict of Nantes, leaving the Huguenots without protection from the intolerance of the Catholics, who so oppressed them as to cause a great exodus of such families as could manage to leave the country. Caudebec was formerly the capital of Caux, situ-

ated on the Seine, in that part of France anciently called Normandy. It was a flourishing city before the revocation of that edict, but was almost ruined as a result of that measure. It would seem that the family of Cuddeback, or Caudebec, was an influential one, and when flight was decided upon it was done hastily; but circumstances indicate that Jacob, in company with Mr. Gumaer, remained for a time either in England or Holland, expecting to be joined by his sisters, who were to bring sufficient funds to enable them to become established in life elsewhere; but after weary waiting they decided to seek their fortunes as best they might, the whole world, except their own native land, being open to them. So they sailed for America, the refuge of thousands of others of the same faith. On landing in Maryland, their means were exhausted, but they soon after came to New York, where they were married, Jacob espousing Margaret, a daughter of Benjamin Prevost, a trader of Kingston on the Hudson. Their marriage occurred October 21, 1695. At the latter place they met the Swartwout families and decided to go to the wilderness for a home. Mr. Cuddeback later went to the Governor of New York to secure a patent to the land, which comprised twelve hundred acres, and was granted the same October 14, 1697. The original settlers were soon joined by John Tyse and David Jamison, but they were not left long in undisputed possession of their land, as parties from New Jersey laid claim to this valuable tract. Needing additional strength to repress the invaders, we find that Harmonas Van Inwegen, who had married a sister of the Swartwouts, and who was a bold, hardy, fearless, resolute man, and had traveled all over the world as a sailor, received part of the land and added his ability to retain the homes and property from the Jersey men.

Jacob Cuddeback said that he had been deprived of many enjoyments in having to leave France, but he had the satisfaction of leaving his posterity in a country where good land was easily acquired. Being reproached by one of his sons for not having laid claim to a large tract, he retorted, "You have the same chance as I had to provide for your family, see if you will do better."

He lived to be nearly one hundred years of age, and of his family we make the following mention: Benjamin, unmarried, died at the age of eighty years; William, who married Jemima Eltiug, died at the age of seventy-four; James, who married Neltje Decker, a daughter of Christopher Decker, had three sons, John, James and Richard, who removed to Niagara County, N. Y., and he died at the age of thirty years; Abraham, who wedded Esther Swartwout, a daughter of Maj. James Swartwout and Annie Gumaer, of Peenpack, removed late in life to Skaneateles, N. Y., where he died at the age of eighty-eight; Jacob married Jeannette Westbrook; Elsie became the wife of Harmonas Van Gordon, of Ulster County, N. Y., June 11, 1727, and died at the age of eighty years; Morice first wedded George Westfall, August 20, 1716, and later a Mr. Cole, and she lived to be nearly one hundred; Dinah became the wife of Abraham Lovis (now called Low) May 31, 1738; Eleanor married Evert Hoornbeek, and died at the age of seventy years; and Naomi was the wife of Lodiwyke Hoornbeek.

William spelled the name Caudebec, but the children changed it to Codebec. He wedded Jemima Elting on the 8th of April, 1732, and became the owner of the old homestead, where he died at the age of seventy-four years, he having been born in June, 1704. He was tall of stature, being over six feet, large-boned, muscular and lean, and was very strong in his youth. He was talkative and witty, probably the quickest at repartee of any in the neighborhood. Argument was his hobby, and he liked nothing better than to discuss the Scriptures, being familiar with all of them. He made much sport of witchcraft, in which so many believed in those days, and told many amusing stories concerning it. As a business man he was slack, but was widely beloved and respected. He had five children. James, who became deranged, died at the age of eighty years; Capt. Abraham, who married Esther Gumaer, daughter of Peter Gumaer, died at the age of eighty-two. His son Benjamin wedded Catherine Van Fleet, and died at the age of forty-five years. Roulif, who never married, died at the age of fifty years. He is spoken of in the Eagers' His-

tory as having had a hand-to-hand encounter with an Indian warrior. Both were strong, stalwart men, and unarmed, but as neither could get the advantage of the other they parted friends. Sarah was the wife of Daniel Van Fleet.

The second son of this family, Abraham, remained upon the old homestead, of which he owned half. He became Captain of a company of militia during the Revolution, and filled an important place during that exciting time. Six feet in height, he weighed over two hundred pounds, and was a strong, handsome athlete. He learned almost intuitively to do all kinds of complicated mechanical work; could weave cloth and make it into clothing; could tan skins, from which he would manufacture leather clothing or shoes; made a fanning-mill after having seen one while on a visit to Old Paltz; made wagons and other farming implements; and had the ability to use his naturally bright mind and dexterous hands for the comfort and pleasure of himself, family and friends. He was a brave soldier, always alert, and with an eye single to the safety of those in his charge. His soldiers were his old neighbors, and each thought he knew about as much as the Captain, but by using tact and patience he brought them into a fair state of military subordination. His first service was at Ft. Montgomery, and he was there with his company the day the fort was captured, after which he went home. He did good service in keeping in touch with the village settlements, especially Cohocton, forty miles distant. In 1778, when the enemy invaded the neighborhood, he commanded the men stationed at Gumaer Fort, and largely through his personal bravery and encouragement to the men and women inside the fort, the enemy were repulsed and the fort retained. His service continued until the declaration of peace, and the independence of the Colonies was recognized.

Benjamin Cuddeback, the third son of William Codebec, and the next in direct line to our subject, wedded Catherine Van Fleet, and they had six children. Benjamin died at the age of ninety-one years; Levi died of colic when a young man; Jemima became the wife of Anthony Van Etten; Henry married Esther Gumaer; Syncthe was the wife of Simon Westfall; and William, who married Annetje Van Inwegen, died at the age of ninety years. The eldest son, Benjamin, married Blandina Van Etten, a daughter of Levi and Jane (Westbrook) Van Etten, and of their children we make the following mention: Levi died when young; Catherine, the wife of James Cuddeback, died at the age of seventy-eight years; Jane, who became the wife of Alex S. Johnson, lives in Port Jervis; Asenath married S. B. Farnum, of whom see sketch elsewhere in this volume; Elting first wedded Ann Bevier Elting, and after her death Margaret Cuddeback; Hannah became the wife of Col. Peter P. Swartwout; Thomas, a doctor, married Elizabeth Thompson; Jemima married L. S. Chapin; and Lydia became the wife of W. W. Titsworth. (For further information regarding Benjamin Cuddeback see biography of Elting Cuddeback.)

The Doctor, whose name heads this sketch, was born in the town of Deerpark, on the 26th of April, 1854, and is the son of Elting and Ann Bevier (Elting) Cuddeback, who were the parents of six children. Cornelius, an attorney, married Esther Mills (see sketch elsewhere in this volume); Benjamin E., who remained upon the home farm with his father, wedded Clara Conkling, and died in 1893, at the age of forty-two years; our subject is next in order of birth; Blandina is the wife of Rev. J. L. Stilwell, pastor of the Reformed Church at Bloomingburg, N. Y.; and two children, who both bore the name of Philip, died in infancy.

The father has made agriculture his chief occupation through life, and is still living on his farm, at the age of seventy-eight years. He was married in Deerpark, his wife being a daughter of Rev. C. C. Elting, of the Reformed Church, who was stationed at Port Jervis, and there he died at the age of fifty-one years. Mrs. Cuddeback was called to her final rest in 1861. The father never cared for political preferment, though he held several minor offices, but desired to give his time and attention to his business interests.

The primary education of Dr. Cuddeback was received in the home schools, after which he took a special course of two years in Cornell University.

He then began reading medicine with Dr. Solomon Van Etten, of Port Jervis, after which he attended Bellevue College in New York City, taking the regular course, and was graduated in the Class of '76. He then became an *interne* in the Bellevue Hospital, and after his graduation, in 1878, began practice in Port Jervis, where he has remained ever since. In company with Dr. H. B. Swartwout he purchased the hospital here in 1892, which had been started three years previously. It is a general hospital, with a capacity of twenty-four beds, to which the railroad patients for about one hundred and fifty miles are brought. The Doctor is also engaged in general practice and surgery, and has ever met with excellent success.

On the 16th of October, 1880, Dr. Cuddeback was united in marriage with Miss Alice D. Malven, a daughter of George and Philenda (St. John) Malven. Her father, who was a hardware merchant, departed this life in 1894. To our subject and wife have been born five children: Frank, Edgar G., Lizzie M., Alice and Philenda.

Religiously the Doctor and his wife hold membership with the Reformed Church. He is a member of the Orange County, New York State and National Associations of Railroad Surgeons, the New York State Medical Society, and is now serving as Pension Examiner. For five years, from 1887 until 1892, he was President of the Board of Education, during which time the Main Street Schoolhouse was erected. Since the establishment of the Free Library he has been President of the board. Politically his support is given to the Democratic party.

R W. MARTIN, wholesale and retail dealer in blue and flag stone, on the corner of North Street and the Erie Railroad, Middletown, is one of the enterprising men of the city. He was born in the town of Liberty, Sullivan County, January 17, 1849, and is a son of Daniel T. and Lydia (Shaw) Martin, both of whom were natives of the same town. The first of the name came from England in the "Mayflower," first locating near Bedford, Mass., from which place they scattered to various parts of the country, one of the number settling in Connecticut. At a very early day, Lemuel Martin, the grandfather, removed from Connecticut, his native state, to Sullivan County, N. Y., in company with a Mr. Hall, and after building a log house returned to Connecticut. The next season he, his wife and a Miss Trowbridge and others went by team to Liberty and were among the first settlers in that town. The grandfather there engaged in the lumber business and in wood-turning, and also built and operated a saw and grist mill on the Beaver Kill. For some years he was a Justice of the Peace in that town. His son, Daniel T., the father of our subject, was there born and has followed the occupation of a farmer during his entire life. He resides in the old place and is about eighty years of age. In politics he is a Republican. His wife, the mother of our subject, died at the age of sixty years. The family consisted of two sons and three daughters, all of whom grew to maturity and are yet living.

The subject of this sketch was the eldest in the parental family, and remained upon the home farm until after he was eighteen years of age. He received his primary education in the public schools of his native town, and finished his course at the Normal Institute. When eighteen years of age he engaged as a clerk in a general store in Wayne County, Pa., opposite Narrowsburg, Sullivan County, where he continued four and a-half years. He then formed a partnership with a Mr. Decker and started a general merchandise store at Narrowsburg, under the firm name of Decker & Martin, which business was continued for four years. He then sold out to his partner, and bought out Stanton & Green, general merchants of Narrowsburg, and continued in business alone until 1885, when he disposed of the store, and engaged in his present business, quarrying and selling blue and flag stone. In 1888 he located in Middletown, carrying on the wholesale trade, and in 1893 he opened a retail business, and now has an extensive trade in both.

In the past ten years he has operated many quarries, and now has four that are yielding good returns.

Mr. Martin was married in Narrowsburg, September 17, 1873, to Miss Adella Gordon, daughter of C. K. Gordon, whose sketch appears on another page of this work. Three children have been born unto them: Mabel, Bernice and May. In politics Mr. Martin is a Republican, and while residing in the town of Tusten, Sullivan County, was Supervisor for two terms and School Trustee two years. He is a member of the Methodist Episcopal Church, in which he holds the office of Trustee.

JAMES C. RIDER, proprietor of the creamery at Central Valley, was born in the town of Cornwall, March 3, 1859, being a son of Charles C. and Mary A. (Cornell) Rider. At the age of seven years he accompanied his parents to Middletown, where, five years later, he began to work in a hat factory, and from that time he was practically self-supporting. June 7, 1876, he removed with other members of the family from Middletown to Brooklyn, where he and his brothers were engaged in the milk business, under the firm name of Rider Bros.

After carrying on business for some years at Brooklyn, our subject in 1884 became interested in the creamery at Turner. Two years later he came to Central Valley, where he opened a creamery, but was unfortunate in losing all by fire. Undismayed, however, by this disaster, he rebuilt the plant and is now carrying on a large and profitable business. In addition to this, he has also erected creameries at Youngs and Sidney, on the Ontario & Western, and at Bridgewater on the Delaware, Lackawanna & Western. The output has increased to such an extent that he now handles about four thousand gallons per day.

The marriage of Mr. Rider was solemnized in Brooklyn, March 16, 1881, at which time Miss Lucy A. Smith became his wife. Mrs. Rider was born in Brooklyn, being the daughter of

CAPT. CHARLES R. FULLER.

David and Lucy E. (Cross) Smith, and she made her home in the city of her birth until the time of her marriage. She is an estimable, well informed lady, and a sincere member of the Methodist Episcopal Church. Two children complete the family circle, a son, Howard E., and a daughter, Florence E.

In his political sentiments Mr. Rider is a Prohibitionist, believing that the liquor traffic is the greatest evil of the present age and that its overthrow will conduce more to the prosperity of the nation than any other issue of the day. In his religious belief he was reared in the faith of the Hicksite Friends, to which doctrine he still adheres.

⁂

APT. CHARLES R. FULLER, of Middletown, is one of the best posted men in the lumber trade in the entire country. He was born in Broome County, N. Y., in 1834, and is the son of John W. and Uraina C. (Russell) Fuller, both of whom were natives of Connecticut. The father located in Broome County in an early day and purchased a farm at Whitney's Point, where he engaged in farming and also in the manufacture of hard and soft wood lumber. He continued in these occupations until his death, at the age of sixty-three years. His wife survived him many years, dying in 1893, at the age of eighty-four years. They were both members of the Baptist Church. Of their family of two sons and six daughters, three of the latter are deceased. One son, Francis Fuller, was a member of the Eighty-sixth New York Volunteer Infantry, enlisting in 1862 and serving until the close of the war. Subsequently he went West. John W., Jr., now resides in Corning, N. Y.; Sophronia is the wife of Joseph H. Conkling, of Coldwater, Mich.; Alma is the widow of S. S. Mott, of Auburn, N. Y.; Lemira L. is the widow of James Wessels, of Middletown.

The subject of this sketch remained upon the home farm until ten years of age, when his parents removed to Union, N. Y., locating on a farm near that village. Here he remained until nineteen years of age, assisting his father in the sawmill and attending the district school as opportunity was afforded him. At that age he went to Corning, N. Y., where he was engaged as inspector of lumber for two years, and then started a commission-yard in that city; His shipments were made principally by the Erie Canal, and he continued in business there until 1862. In that year he raised a company in Corning, which became Company D, One Hundred and Forty-first New York Volunteer Infantry. He was commissioned and mustered in as Captain at Elmira, N. Y. His regiment was assigned to the Army of the Potomac and took part in the battle of Antietam, its next principal engagement being at Gettysburg. Shortly afterward it was ordered west, joining Sherman's army in front of Atlanta and assisting in the capture of that city. From Atlanta it was with Sherman in his celebrated march to the sea, and continued in that command until the close of the war. In July, 1865, Captain Fuller was mustered out and honorably discharged at Elmira. During his service he refused promotion, because of a desire to remain with his company.

On receiving his discharge, the Captain returned to Corning, but only remained there a short time, going thence to Oil City, Pa., where he became a member of the firm of Fox, Fuller & Co., wholesale and retail dealers in lumber. At this time Oil City was enjoying a boom, occasioned by the discovery of oil. He remained as manager of the firm's business for about two years, and then sold out, and located in Wilkes Barre, Pa. In three months he had a large yard started, and there ran a successful business for seven years.

On account of ill-health Captain Fuller was compelled to sell out his business in the latter place, and for the two succeeding years was engaged in traveling through the West and South. For his wife he married Mrs. Ella Beecher, of Middletown, the daughter of J. H. Weed, from Raysville, Pa. Four children were born unto them, three of whom, Blanche, Grace and Claire, died of diphtheria within two weeks. The surviving child is Helene.

In the fall of 1876 Captain Fuller located in Middletown, and in May, 1877, bought the lumber-yard of S. S. Conkling, which he yet conducts. It is situated on the corner of Depot and Foundry Streets, and is well supplied with sheds and buildings for sash, doors and blinds, and also for the storage of lumber and coal, both of which he sells at wholesale and retail. His business has assumed large proportions, and he sells carload lots to other dealers in lumber on the line of the Erie and other railroads centering in Middletown. He buys his lumber direct from manufacturers. At one time he was largely interested in timber-land in Michigan. He was one of the original stockholders and is a Director and a member of the executive committee of the glass company, and since its organization has been a member and Director of the Board of Trade. In Corning he was connected with the Alliance Hook and Ladder Company for ten years, now being an honorary member, and is a member of General Lyon Post, G. A. R. In politics he is a Republican. His wife is a member of the Methodist Episcopal Church.

Captain Fuller and wife spent considerable time at the World's Fair at Chicago. He is regarded as one of the most enterprising men in Middletown, and to every enterprise calculated to advance its interest he is ever ready to lend a helping hand. In his own private business he shows energy and zeal, and is accommodating to all his friends and customers.

～ ==⊗⊃～ ※ ⋘～——→—

GEORGE E. BEAKES is a successful business man in Middletown, and is the proprietor of three creameries. He was born in the town of Wallkill, two and a-half miles from Middletown, December 1, 1842, and is a son of Mahlon Stacey and Emeline (Carpenter) Beakes, the former born near Middletown, on the old Beakes homestead, and the latter about four miles from this city. His grandfather, Joseph Beakes, was also a native of Orange County. (For the ancestry of the Beakes family, see sketch of Henry L. Beakes.) The father of our subject was a

farmer, and owned and operated a farm of one hundred acres near Middletown. He was an active member of the old-school Baptist Church, and in politics was a Republican. His death occurred in 1891. Our subject's maternal grandfather, William Carpenter, who was of Scotch-Irish ancestry, was a well-to-do farmer of Orange County. Mrs. Beakes died in 1870. Of the eleven children in the parental family, ten are yet living: James A., who was a member of Company E, One Hundred and Twenty-fourth New York Volunteer Infantry, and who is now a farmer residing in Middletown; George E., our subject; C. H. C., at Orr's Mills; Fanny, of Cornwall; William B., now engaged in the milk business at Newburgh; J. E., Abbie J. and Albert S., of New York City; Annie M. and Emma, at home in Cornwall.

The subject of this sketch was reared on the home farm, commenced his education in the public schools, and completed the course at Wallkill Academy. In October, 1861, he enlisted in the Fifty-sixth New York Infantry. At Washington he was transferred to the First New York Mounted Rifles, Troop C, and was stationed at Fortress Monroe, becoming a part of General Wool's bodyguard, while he was in command, and afterward that of Benjamin F. Butler. After MacClellan's advance he went into more active service, and as orderly conveyed dispatches from one post of the army to another. Near the close of his three-years term of service with the rank of Sergeant, he was detailed to the Adjutant-General's headquarters in charge of the orderlies.

In October, 1864, Mr. Beakes was mustered out and honorably discharged at Point of Rocks, Va., immediately returning home, where he secured employment in the Rockville Creamery. The second year he took charge of the Circleville Creamery, which he operated one year, and then again had charge of the Rockville Creamery for the same length of time. In Wallkill, in 1867, he married Miss Hannah Jordan, a native of that town, and daughter of I. C. and a sister of J. V. Jordan, of Newburgh. Mr. Beakes purchased the old Horton homestead, consisting of one hundred and twenty acres, and located three miles from Middletown, and there engaged in farming for six years. Renting the farm, he accepted a position with Brown & Bailey, as manager of the Glenwood Creamery, where he remained three years. In company with his brother-in-law, J. V. Jordan, he then purchased the Pleasant Valley Creamery, and business was conducted under the firm name of Beakes & Jordan. For one year they engaged in the manufacture of butter and cheese, and also in the shipment of cream and milk. The Shawangunk Creamery was then purchased of Jeff Post, and in partnership with his brother, Mr. Beakes conducted business under the name of C. H. C. Beakes & Co. Later they purchased the Montgomery Creamery, and the following year built the Coldenham Creamery, near Orange Lake. The firm now had three creameries, but the next year they sold the Shawangunk Creamery and continued the other two. On account of ill-health, however, Mr. Beakes was compelled to abandon the creamery business and retire to his farm, where he remained two years. He then went to Sidney Centre, Delaware County, where he built a large creamery, and the second year sold the others to J. V. Jordan. He then bought the Merrickville Creamery and took his brother, C. H. C. Beakes, into partnership. After operating the two creameries for eight years the firm was dissolved, and our subject continued the Sidney Centre Creamery. At this time he purchased a milk business in New York City, which he placed in charge of his son, Charles H. Beakes, the milk being supplied from the Glen Farm daily, and from Sidney Centre. In 1893 he purchased a half-interest in the East Masonville Creamery, which was run under the name of Beakes & Gifford. The firm owned the property and manufactured the cream for farmers. In 1894 Beakes & Gifford purchased the Tacoma Creamery, in Delaware County, which they ran on the same plan. The Sidney Centre Creamery is the largest one with which Mr. Beakes has been connected, and he operates that alone, as well as the New York City milk business, located at No. 210 East Fifty-first Street. The East Masonville Creamery has a capacity of eleven thousand pounds a day, while the capacity of the

Tacoma Creamery is nearly as large. Mr. Beakes gives his personal attention to the disposal of the products.

In addition to the property already mentioned, Mr. Beakes owns a farm of two hundred and forty-two acres near Sidney Centre, which he operates himself, and on which he keeps about fifty head of cows. He also owns his old home of one hundred and twenty acres and runs it as a dairy farm, keeping thirty head of cows. From 1883 to 1893 he resided with his family at Sidney Centre, but is now located at No. 16 Highland Avenue, Middletown, where he has a very comfortable residence. His family consists of his wife and three children: Charles H., a graduate of Eastman's Business College, and now in charge of the New York business; Crosby J., a student in Hamilton College, of the Class of '97; and Edna. In army matters Mr. Beakes retains a deep interest, and is a member of Capt. William A. Jackson Post No. 301, G. A. R., at Middletown. He is a Ruling Elder in the Presbyterian Church at Middletown, and in politics is a staunch Republican, taking an active interest in local politics. He is a stockholder in the New York Consolidated Milk Exchange.

WSCOTT COOK has been interested in railroading since 1862, and has been a conductor since 1864. He was born in Otisville, October 24, 1841, and is a son of Dr. Avery and Pamela (Loomis) Cook, the former a native of Beechertown, Mass., and the latter of Otisville, N. Y. Dr. Avery Cook comes of an old Congregational family, who long resided in his native state. In 1827 he came to Orange County, where he taught school for a time, and while so engaged studied medicine. He then entered Fairfield Seminary, in Otsego County, N. Y., and in 1834 graduated with the degree of M. D.

The Doctor then located at Otisville, where he practiced with his father-in-law, Dr. Loomis, who was an old physician at that point. After death of Dr. Loomis, he had charge of his entire practice, and it is estimated that he rode seventy-five thousand miles on horseback in the practice of his profession. He had patients for many miles around, and the old saddlebags which he carried are now in the possession of our subject. For many years the Doctor was proprietor of a drug store at Otisville, which he continued until his death, March 30, 1891, at the age of eighty-three years and eleven months. In early life he was a Whig, but in later years a Republican. His wife, Pamela Loomis, died in 1889, at the age of seventy-nine years. She was a member of the Presbyterian Church, and took an active interest in all matters of a religious and benevolent nature. To Dr. Avery and Pamela Cook were born seven sons and one daughter, our subject being the only one now living. One son, Virgil C., was in an Illinois regiment during the late war, and died in Chicago in 1864.

W. Scott Cook was reared in his native village, where he received his literary education; his business education was obtained in Eastman's Business College at Poughkeepsie, from which he graduated when nineteen years of age. In 1862 he entered the employ of the Erie Railroad as brakeman between Port Jervis and Jersey City. Eighteen months later he was made conductor on a freight train, where he remained for two years, and was then in charge of a passenger train until 1873. In that year he left the service of the Erie Railroad, and came to the Oswego & Midland Railroad, now the Ontario & Western, as conductor between Bloomingburg and Jersey City. In 1883, the road having been completed from Middletown to Weehawken, he was transferred to that line, and has now charge of a milk train. In 1894 he built his present residence at No. 9 Albert Street. For some years he resided at Otisville, but on the death of his father sold out and removed with his family to this city.

At Port Jervis Mr. Cook was married to Miss Catherine J. Wood, who was born in Mongaup Valley, Sullivan County, and they have one child, Lelah M., who is at home. Socially Mr. Cook is a member of Port Jervis Lodge, F. & A. M., and is a demitted member of Neversink Chapter No. 186, R. A. M., and of Delaware Commandery, K. T., both of Port Jervis. He is also a member of Orange Railroad Conductors' Association, Division No. 104, of the Legion of Honor, and is a stockholder in the Co-operative Store. In politics he is a stanch Republican.

THOMAS H. DESMOND, superintendent of the rolling-mill of the National Saw Works at Middletown, was born December 6, 1855, in Coatesville, Chester County, Pa., and is the son of John and Catherine (David) Desmond, the former born near Philadelphia, and the latter in London, England. She died in Coatesville, some years ago, leaving three children, of whom our subject is the only one living. The name Desmond is of Norman origin. John Desmond, the father, has always been connected with the rolling-mills, and has been boss roller and foreman of the rolling-mill at Coatesville since 1850. However, he is now living a retired life.

Thomas H. Desmond was reared in his native town, and was educated in the high schools of that place. From early boyhood he has worked at the iron and steel business, which he learned under the instruction of his father, in the works at Coatesville. From that place he went to Chester, Pa., with John Roach, the great ship-builder, and for seven years was foreman in his establishment. He then went to Philadelphia, and entered the employ of S. Robbins & Sons, of the Philadelphia Rolling-mill, as superintendent for two years, when, in 1883, he accepted his present position as superintendent of the rolling-mill of the National Saw Works. They manufacture sheet steel for saws only, and for their own use exclusively. They also manufacture the best grade of crucible steel, and give employment to seventy-five men.

Mr. Desmond was married in Philadelphia, Pa., to Miss Kate Safried, a native of that city. Five children were born unto them, four of whom are living, viz.: Ella, Charles, Catherine and Kenneth. Josephine died at the age of six and one-

JAMES PORRITT.

half years. Fraternally Mr. Desmond is a member of Hoffman Lodge, F. & A. M.; Midland Chapter, R. A. M.; the Consistory of Middletown; and Lancelot Lodge, K. of P. In politics he is a Republican and a strong advocate of the principles of that party.

~~~~~~✦~~~~~~

JAMES PORRITT, of Port Jervis, is foreman of the machine-shops of the Erie Railroad. He is an efficient manager and enjoys the high regard of his superiors, at the same time being in pleasant relations with the men under his supervision. He superintends every detail of the work done in the shops, and is a practical mechanic of long experience.

Our subject's father, George Porritt, was a machinist and was an engineer on the Paterson Railway prior to 1842, later having charge of the Swinburne locomotive works south of Paterson. At another time he had charge of the machine-shops of the Rogers works, and subsequently was with the Beckwith Rolling-mills at Paterson. He married Miss Betsey Nichols, by whom he had four children, as follows: our subject; Nancy, deceased; Sarah Ann, wife of J. D. Campbell, Master Mechanic of the Buffalo & Susquehanna Railroad; and an infant.

James Porritt was born in Paterson, N. J., September 22, 1832, and when he was fourteen years of age entered the Swinburne & Smith shops to learn the machinist's trade. His father was then engaged in the construction of cotton-mills for the Mexican trade. The boy served for seven years, receiving fifty cents per day, and became proficient in all lines of mechanical work, giving particular attention to overhauling engines and making repairs on the same. After completing the business he entered the employ of the Erie Railroad at Susquehanna in 1853, and from that time until the present he has remained with this corporation, with the exception of the time from 1855 to 1857, when he worked in the Lake Shore shops at Cleveland, Ohio. For two years he was employed in the Susquehanna Railway shops, becoming accustomed to the finest kind of loco-

motive repairs. When in Cleveland he overhauled the first engine relegated to the shops of the then new Lake Shore Road.

August 5, 1857, Mr. Porritt came to this city, entering the old Erie shops, which were burned in October, 1862. The present shops were opened for business February 1, 1863, since which time our subject has filled his present position. He usually has in his department thirty men, though at times he has upwards of eighty men under his orders. For the past thirty-one years he has been identified with the Masonic order, and is also a member of the Legion of Honor. At Presidential elections he deposits his ballot in favor of the principles advocated by the Republican party.

October 18, 1859, occurred the marriage of Mr. Porritt and Bessie Richardson. They have become the parents of a son and two daughters, namely: George, a locomotive engineer and machinist, who is now in California; Aletta, the wife of A. Parsons, of New York City; and Hattie, an accomplished young lady in her teens.

~~~~~~✦~~~~~~

CHARLES C. LUTES, agent for the Wells, Fargo & Co. Express, and former agent for the New York & Lake Erie Railroad, came to Middletown in 1869 with the Erie Company, and about 1886 became their ticket agent at this place. He was also agent of the Erie Express until it was sold to Wells, Fargo & Co. In 1893 he resigned his position as agent for the Erie, and now devotes all of his time to his duties as agent for the former company. He was born in Sussex County, N. J., one mile from Unionville, N. Y., February 14, 1841, while his father, Samuel Lutes, was born in the town of Minisink, Orange County, as was his grandfather, Levi, and his great-grandfather, Godfrey. The latter, who at one time was the largest tax-payer in the town, was of German descent, and was a soldier in the Revolutionary War. Samuel Lutes was a farmer in Sussex County, N. J., and later removed to the town of Minisink, Orange County, where he followed the same occupation, and where he died in 1857. His wife, Lucinda Parker, was a daugh-

51

ter of Phineas Parker, who was born on Long Island, and settled in the town of Minisink at a very early day. Mrs. Lucinda Lutes died in 1882, at the age of seventy-two years, leaving three sons: Charles C., our subject; Phineas, in the employ of the New York, Ontario & Western Railway, and now residing in Middletown; and Levi, also residing in Middletown, and in the employ of the Erie Railroad.

Charles C. Lutes was reared on the farm in Minisink, and received his primary education in the public schools of that town, graduating at Unionville Academy at the age of seventeen. He then taught school in the vicinity of his home until the spring of 1862, when he went to Newburgh as a clerk. In the fall of that year he enlisted in Company A, One Hundred and Twenty-fourth New York Volunteer Infantry, from the town of Newburgh. During his three years of service he was in many important engagements, including Fredericksburg and Gettysburg; he was in the Wilderness campaign, and also stood on the hills of Appomattox and witnessed Lee's surrender to General Grant. At the close of the war he took part in the Grand Review at Washington, and was mustered out and honorably discharged at Newburgh in June, 1865.

On receiving his discharge Mr. Lutes went to Vermont, and for three years was telegraph operator for the Central Vermont Railway Company. In the spring of 1869 he returned to Orange County, and entered the employ of the Erie Railroad at Middletown, with which company he was engaged until 1893, when he resigned to devote his entire attention to his duties as agent for the Wells, Fargo & Co. Express. The office at Middletown is considered one of the best on the road. In the fall of 1893 he purchased Mr. Boyd's interest in the Boyd & Combs Real-estate and Insurance Agency, and continued as a partner of Mr. Combs, under the firm name of Combs & Lutes, until December, 1894, when he sold out to A. B. Wilbur. He is still a property-holder in Middletown, however.

In 1871, at Middletown, Mr. Lutes was married to Miss Alida Harding, who was born near Otisville. They have one son, Wilbur E., ticket agent for the Erie Railroad on Main Street, Middletown. Fraternally Mr. Lutes is a member of General Lyon Post, G. A. R.; of Hoffman Lodge, F. & A. M.; Midland Chapter, R. A. M.; of the Knights of Pythias; of Middletown Lodge, I. O. O. F.; and Ivanhoe Lodge No. 2103, K. of H. He is also a member of Excelsior Hook and Ladder Company, of which he has been a member for sixteen years, and is now the Vice-President. In politics he is a Republican, and has served his party as a member of the City Central Committee. Before the incorporation of the city he served one term as a member of the Board of Village Trustees, being elected on the Republican ticket.

JOHN W. GARDNER, proprietor of Oakland Place, Middletown, was born in 1866. His father, John W. Gardner, was born in the town of Warwick, while his grandfather, John Gardner, was born near Scranton, Pa., from which place he came to Warwick, where he died at the age of eighty-six years. His great-grandfather moved from Long Island to Pennsylvania, where his demise occurred. The Gardners trace their ancestry back to England, and some members of the family served in the Revolutionary War.

John W. Gardner, the father of our subject, was reared upon a farm until he was twenty-four years of age, when he went West, by way of Buffalo, to Chicago, and afterwards to Indiana, Iowa, Illinois and Wisconsin. He remained in the West ten years, the greater part of the time carrying on a successful grain business. Returning East, he purchased a farm of one hundred and fifty acres adjoining Middletown, which he improved and operated until his death, April 20, 1894, in his sixty-eighth year. In politics he was a Republican, and socially was a Master Mason. He was also an active member of the Presbyterian Church. His marriage with Anna E. Horton occurred in Middletown, of which place she is a native. She is a daughter of Parmenas H. Horton, who was born near Otisville, and who was descended from an old Orange County family. He was a farmer on the place which he sold to our subject's father. To John W. and Anna E. H. Gardner were born two children: Charles H., a commercial traveler, now residing in Chicago; and the subject of our sketch. The mother now makes her home with our subject.

John W. Gardner grew to manhood on his father's farm, and received his education in Wallkill Academy, and at Freehold Institute, the latter a military school in Freehold, N. J., where he spent two years. On leaving school, he returned to the home farm, but subsequently traveled extensively through the West, visiting nearly every state and territory, and also spent a short time in Canada. After having satisfied his appetite for travel, he returned to develop his present place, which he named Oakland Place, in honor of Oakland, Cal. He purchased the place in 1894, and had it surveyed and planted by C. J. Everson, C. E. The addition, which comprises ninety acres, was placed on the market in April, 1895, and many lots have already been sold. Nearly all his property lies within the city limits of Middletown, and the trolley cars pass through on East Main Street. He also has lots on the latter street, and on Horton, Gardner and Woodlawn Avenues.

≪+++++++++++◉+++++++++++≫

JOHN H. LITTLE. Although at the time of the breaking out of the Rebellion Mr. Little had reached an age when he was exempt from military duty, yet his patriotic impulses were aroused and his anger excited by the indignities heaped upon the Old Flag. Accordingly he enlisted as a member of the illustrious One Hundred and Twenty-fourth Regiment that won distinction on many a bloody battlefield. His service was of such a nature as to reflect credit upon his valor and add glory to the regiment. All the hardships incident to war he endured—the long and forced marches, the tedium of camp life, and the peril of an open conflict with the enemy. When he enlisted his hair was raven black, but

it was gray at the time he returned home. His eyesight, too, that had been unusually good prior to that, almost failed him. His patriotic spirit, however, knew no diminution, and he served loyally and well till the close of the war.

In the town of Wallkill, near Middletown, where he now resides, Mr. Little was born on the 1st of March, 1816. His father, Isaac, a native of this county, engaged in the carpenter's trade in early life, but later settled upon a farm in the town of Wallkill, where he remained until his death. Grandfather Eli Little was a farmer at Scotchtown, and was a descendant of Scotch-Irish ancestors. The mother of our subject, Abigail, was born on Long Island, and was a daughter of Eli Corwin, formerly a farmer at Scotchtown.

There were four daughters and six sons in the family of Isaac Little, but John H., and James, a retired citizen living on Mulberry Street, are the only survivors. John H. was reared on the home farm in Wallkill, and at the age of sixteen became an apprentice under Stephen Preston in Montgomery, where he remained nearly five years. About 1837 he began as a cabinet-maker on Main Street, Middletown, and for some years had the only furniture manufacturing and undertaking establishment in the city. Selling out after some years, he settled on a farm on the Bloomingburg Road, near Fair Oaks, but after a number of years on that place he came back to Middletown, where he fitted up the Congregational Church and superintended the building of the Methodist Episcopal Church. He then gave his whole attention to carpenter work, which he carried on until about 1893, when he retired. While at times he took contracts, he was sometimes employed as foreman on jobs.

In August, 1862, Mr. Little laid down his tools and entered the service of the Union, becoming a member of Company E, One Hundred and Twenty-fourth New York Infantry, and was mustered in at Goshen. Before leaving that city he was made Corporal. Accompanying his regiment South, he was with it at Fredericksburg and Chancellorsville, and at the latter place was obliged to remain in the hospital for a time, owing to sickness resulting from sunstroke. At

Gettysburg he was severely injured by the bursting of a shell near him, which threw him off his feet and rendered him insensible for a time. A few weeks were spent in the hospital, and on recovering he was placed in the invalid corps as Corporal, doing duty principally in Washington. He was there and helped guard the city at the time of Lincoln's assassination. At the close of the war he was mustered out of service and honorably discharged.

The home of Mr. Little is situated at No. 24 Grant Street, and is presided over by his wife, who was formerly Miss Josephine Jenkins and was born in this state. Prior to his marriage to her, Mr. Little had been married, in Scotchtown, to Miss Mary A. Young, who died in Middletown, leaving two children: Albert, who is engaged in the undertaking business in this city; and Frank Elizabeth, widow of Charles S. Burr, and at present residing with her father. Socially Mr. Little is connected with the Order of Royal Templars of Temperance and the Temple of Honor. He also belongs to General Lyon Post, G. A. R. In early days he was a Whig, and since the organization of the Republican party he has advocated its policy. For two years he was Overseer of the Poor of Middletown, and for one year he held the office of Collector of the town of Wallkill, including Middletown. As one of the oldest residents of this city, he takes a deep interest in its progress, and has been an eye-witness of much of its growth. His record is that of a brave, conscientious and honorable man, ready to do his duty in times of peace and war.

JOHN DONOVAN, an undertaker and liveryman at Nos. 122 and 124 North Street, Middletown, was born in Bullville, town of Crawford, in May, 1855. His father, James Donovan, who was born in County Kerry, Ireland, was a carpenter, and followed that occupation while in his native land. He there married Mary Dee, who was also born in County Kerry, and shortly after the birth of their first child the father came to America, reaching New York in

December, 1848. Not finding anything to do there, he walked with a comrade to Newburgh and thence to the town of Crawford, looking for work. They were offered work by a farmer, who would give them nothing but their board. His comrade accepted the offer, but Mr. Donovan found work on a farm elsewhere, receiving $4 per month during the winter. In the spring his wages were advanced, and after working two years he sent for his wife and child. As soon as possible he rented a farm in the town of Crawford, where he lived the remainder of his life, with the exception of two years spent in Bloomingburg. Later he bought a farm near Bullville, which he improved, and added to it until it comprised one hundred and seventy acres.

The father of our subject was one of the first three of the Irish race to settle in the town of Crawford, and was the first of them to locate permanently. During his life he was never sued, nor did he ever sue anyone. He was one of the founders of St. Paul's Catholic Church at Bullville in 1870, and one of its pillars until his death. Before this church was built he frequently walked to Goshen or Wurtsboro to attend church. He died April 7, 1892, and his remains were buried in St. Joseph's Cemetery at Middletown. He came of a long-lived race, his father, Timothy Donovan, who was a butcher by trade, dying in Ireland when over one hundred and eight, and his grandfather at the age of one hundred and twelve.

James and Mary Donovan were the parents of six children who grew to maturity. Michael resides in Middletown; John is the subject of this sketch; James, manufacturer and patentee of close-hitching road and speed carts, and also a carriage manufacturer and undertaker, resides at Goshen; Anna is Mrs. James Fitzgerald, of Goshen; Mary resides in Middletown; and Thomas is a successful coal merchant on Railroad Avenue, Middletown. The mother of these children resides with her son Thomas.

The childhood days of our subject were spent on the farm, and his education was received in the public schools. He remained at home, engaged in farm work, until 1880, when he located

at Circleville, and there engaged in farming for three years. He next moved to a farm near Bloomingburg, in the town of Wallkill, and there engaged in farming and in the livery business, and also operated a creamery for three years. In April, 1889, he located in Middletown, and engaged in the livery and undertaking business. He bought his present place, built a barn and driveway from North Street, and now has stable room for seventeen horses. Mr. Donovan is a graduate of Sullivan's School of Embalming of New York City, and thoroughly understands his business in every particular.

In Pittsfield, Mass., Mr. Donovan was united in marriage with Miss Annie Conway, born near New Lebanon, and a daughter of Patrick Conway. They have five children: James, Anna, Agnes, John and George. Our subject is a member of St. Joseph's Catholic Church at Middletown, and of the Ancient Order of Hibernians. He is a member of the Middletown Liverymen and Undertakers' Association, and is an honorary member of McQuaid Engine Company. In politics he is a Democrat.

※━━❈◀◈◐☺◐▶❈━━※

JOHN A. CROSS. Biographies of successful, upright men are great incentives, teaching noble thinking and energetic action. He who gives others an example of industry, sobriety and honesty of purpose in life has a present as well as a future influence upon the well-being of his community, for his life and character affect, unconsciously though it may be, the lives and characters of others, and thus the influence is unending.

The subject of this biographical review is one of the prominent residents of Orange County, and is the proprietor of the place known as Maple Lawn, in the town of Goshen. He was born February 9, 1830, in Brooklyn, N. Y., and was the eldest but one in the family of John A., Sr., and Isabella (Bates) Cross, also natives of this state, wherein they passed their entire lives. The father of our subject was a distiller during his lifetime, operating on an extensive scale. He was

prominent in local affairs in the city of Brooklyn, and for many years served as a member of the Board of Aldermen. From 1848 to 1850 he represented his district in the General Assembly, and for the next two years was State Senator. He was First Vice-President and Chairman of the convention held in Utica, N. Y., which nominated William Henry Harrison for President in August, 1840. For over thirty years he was an influential politician of Brooklyn, and became one of the organizers of the Republican party. His death occurred in the latter city November 21, 1867.

When ten years of age our subject went to sea, spending about nine months on board ship, and some three years later he again "shipped," working his way up until he became master. For seven years he was commander on a packet line between New York and Liverpool, being in the merchant service, and was on the water in all about thirty years. He is a finely educated gentleman, supplementing the knowledge gained in the public schools by a course in Delhi Institute, where he studied civil engineering. Later he entered Rensselaer College at Troy, graduating from the scientific course in 1847.

When the tocsin of war resounded over the land, Mr. Cross enlisted in the Thirteenth Regiment New York National Guard, serving for five months. He then entered the navy, and rendered efficient service as a member of the water forces until peace was established. Although escaping capture or bodily injuries, he contracted rheumatism as the result of exposures, and up to the present time has been a great sufferer from this disease.

In 1889 Mr. Cross retired, locating upon the beautiful place where he is now living, and which is known throughout this locality as Maple Lawn. It is a most beautiful and attractive place, and derives its name from the number of lovely maple trees which surround it. The marriage of our subject with Miss Elizabeth Howard, who was born in New York City, occurred in 1852, and to them was born a son, John Howard. Our subject's first wife departed this life in 1856, and his second marriage united him with Elizabeth

Joost, of Brooklyn. They had one daughter, Isabel. wife of Albert G. McDonald, present Corporation Counsel of the city of Brooklyn. In 1883 our subject chose for his third companion Jennie Guest. They had two children, James T. and John G., but both are deceased.

Mr. Cross is a devoted member of the Episcopal Church, while his wife belongs to the Baptist congregation. In social affairs he is a Mason of high standing, having attained to the Thirty-third degree, which is the highest degree known to Masonry. He is also a member of the Grand Army of the Republic. Of Republican candidates and measures he is an influential supporter, and never lets an opportunity pass by when he can be of use to his party.

CHARLES E. MANCE, Alderman from the Second Ward, Middletown, was born near Ellenville, Ulster County, November 28, 1852. At a very early day the Mances came from Holland and settled in the Shawangunk Mountains, the settlement long being known as the Mance Settlement. The great-grandfather of our subject, John Mance, was a prominent and active follower of Shank's Band. Shank was a half-breed Indian, who had formerly been friendly to the whites, but after he turned traitor John Mance took up arms against him and his band, and hunted them to the last, finally exterminating the entire band. After this he settled down to farm life at the settlement, where he died. Rhoadés Mance, the grandfather of our subject, and John S. Mance, the father, were both born at the Mance Settlement near Ellenville. Some years after his marriage the father located in Orange County, in the town of Wallkill, where he learned the trade of a mason, which he continued until the war. He then bought a sawmill on the Little Paughcaughnaughsinque, near Bullville, and ran a sawmill during the war, getting out ship-timber. Shortly after the close of the conflict he located in Middletown, where he engaged in contracting and

building until his death, in 1877, at the age of fifty-six years. He was a prominent and active worker in the Methodist Episcopal Church. His wife, Margaret M. Wilkinson, was born in the town of Wallkill, and was a daughter of Jonathan Wilkinson, also a native of that town, and of Scotch descent. She died in September, 1893, in her sixty-ninth year. They were the parents of the following children: Agnes, Mrs. Osborn, of Middletown; Alice, deceased; Charles E., our subject; Allie, who died at the age of twenty-nine; Jennie, deceased; and Lizzie, now Mrs. Millard, of Poughkeepsie.

The subject of this sketch was educated in a common school, and at the old Orchard Street School. In 1867 he went to Warwick and entered the employ of W. J. & J. J. Knapp, house and sign painters, with whom he remained two years as an apprentice, and then came to Middletown. After completing his trade with Col. M. I. McCornell, he formed a partnership with H. J. Randall, under the firm name of Randall & Mance, this connection continuing until March, 1878, at which time he entered the painting department of the New York, Ontario & Western Railroad. After continuing with the railroad company for three years he went to Bradford, Pa., and worked at his trade for a short time. Returning to this county, he located at Middletown, and again became identified with the New York, Ontario & Western. In 1883 he was appointed master painter by E. Minshull, and has since had charge of a painting department of the railroad shops, having about forty men under his supervision.

Mr. Mance was married, May 28, 1874, to Miss Augusta Taylor, born in Ulster County, and a daughter of Angus Taylor, a farmer in that county, who died in early manhood. Her grandfather, Daniel A. Taylor, was a farmer in Orange County, and died here many years ago. Her mother, Maria Bennett, who was born in Ulster County, after the death of her husband removed to Middletown, where she reared the family. She died here at the residence of our subject, October 19, 1894, at the age of sixty-six years, leaving four children: Louisa, Mrs. Timbrell, of Middletown; Cornelia, Mrs. A. D. Seamen, of this city; Mrs.

Mance, the wife of our subject; and Daniel, of Middletown. Mrs. Mance was reared and educated in this city, and here married our subject. They have two children: Frank A., attending Middletown Academy, a member of the Class of '96; and Mabel E.

In politics Mr. Mance is a Republican, and was elected on that ticket in 1892, as Alderman from the Second Ward. He was re-elected in 1894, and is Chairman of the Street and Railroad Committees, and is a member of the Lighting, Police, Auditing and Rules Committees. He is a member of Middletown Lodge No. 112, I. O. O. F., and of Lancelot Lodge, K. of P., and at present is an honorary member of Eagle Hose Company No. 2, of which he was foreman for four years. For two years he was first assistant chief of the Middletown Fire Department under F. M. Pronk. He belongs to the Master Car and Locomotive Painters of the United States and Canada, and for the past eight years has served on various committees in that organization. For many years he has been connected with the various band organizations of this city, and at present is a member of the Twenty-fourth Separate Company Military Band.

THE MIDDLETOWN STRAW WORKS is one of the principal industries in Middletown, and, under the able superintendency of H. C. Benson, has attained success equal to that of any other like institution in the country. The works were erected in 1885 by an incorporated company, known as the Middletown Straw Hat Works, for the manufacture of straw hats of every description. It then had a capacity of sixty dozen per day. Soon after the works were started, Edwin and H. C. Benson became stockholders of it, and in 1887 they leased it from the Middletown Straw Hat Works, remodeled it, put in new machinery, and engaged in the manufacture of men's hats exclusively. They have enlarged it so that it now has a capacity of two hundred and fifty dozen per day of ten hours.

The straw works are located on North Street and Low Avenue. The building is in the form of an "L," the main part being 45x235 feet, and the "L" 45x116. It is a solid brick structure, three stories in height. The first floor of the building is used for offices, packing, sizing, whittling-room, bandboxes and cases, bleaching, shipping and engine and boiler room. The engine is of thirty-five horse-power, and the boiler of sixty horse-power. The second floor is used for blocking, pressing and trimming. The third is used as a stockroom, sewing-room, machine and repairing room. The freight elevator connects the various stories.

Many of the machines used in the manufacture are the inventions of Mr. Benson, and improvements on others made by them. A few of them they have patented. They get the stock from which they manufacture from China, Japan, England, Switzerland, Belgium and Italy. It comes already plaited, or in the piece. The manufactured product is of men's straw hats of every description, shape and size. In 1894 they made three thousand different sample hats for their commission house alone. In the season of 1894–95 they manufactured over fifty thousand dozen hats. They originate their own styles and designs, and right here the work of H. C. Benson comes in play, for he is the principal designer, and all made by others have to be approved by him. The entire manufacture of the works is shipped to New York City, where all are sold through one commission house, that of Thom & Bayley, Nos. 14 and 16 Washington Place, New York, corner of Green Street, where the senior member of the firm, Edwin Benson, has his office.

The works give employment to from one hundred and fifty to one hundred and seventy-five hands. The season opens in September, and ends about the middle of July, making in all about ten and a-half months for the year. For bleaching they have an artesian well one hundred and thirty feet deep, which gives a sufficient supply of water for all purposes. They have two large pumps, with a capacity of seventy-five gallons per minute. The building is heated by steam, and in manufacturing they require a temperature of from eighty degrees to one hundred and twenty degrees in some of the rooms, while in the drying-room the temperature is still higher.

Edwin Benson, the senior member of the firm, is one of the veterans in the straw-hat manufacture in the United States. He has been in the business since about 1850, and is a practical man, both in the manufacture and in the business management of the business. H. C. Benson, the junior member, is a popular citizen of Middletown, and is a successful superintendent and manager of the works.

JAMES P. MULFORD is a very successful carriage manufacturer in Middletown. He was born in Hamptonburgh, December 25, 1845. His father, William B. Mulford, was born in the old town of Minisink, now Wawayanda. His grandfather, William Mulford, was born on Long Island, and located in the town of Minisink at an early day, where he improved a farm, and engaged in farming during the remainder of his life. He was a soldier in the Revolutionary War, and died at Minisink, and was buried in the old family cemetery at South Centreville. William B. Mulford, the father, was also a farmer, but later was interested in the running of canal-boats on the Delaware & Hudson Canal. He married Priscilla Van Auken, who was born in the town of Minisink, and who was of Holland-Dutch descent, being the only representative of the family then living. Her father was James Van Auken. In 1850 the family located in Middletown, where the father died one year later. The mother survived him many years, and died in 1892, when about sixty-five years of age. She was a devout member of the Presbyterian Church. Three children were born unto them, two of whom are yet living: Cornelia, now Mrs. Piatt, of Middletown; and our subject. It may here be mentioned that on the father's side, as well as the mother's, the family was of Holland-Dutch descent.

James P. Mulford, our subject, came to Middletown with his parents when but six years of age.

He was here reared, and educated in the Orchard Street public school, and finished his course in the academy. When fifteen years of age, he was apprenticed to learn the trade of carriage-making, and served three years at Middletown. He then went to Paterson, N. J., and was employed in Monroe & Van Idestine's Carriage Factory at No. 44 Broadway, the largest manufacturers in that city; from there he went to Bridgeport, Conn., in the employ of Hall Bros. Manufacturing Company, of which the great showman, P. T. Barnum, was the head, and where all the vehicles used in the great show were built. He was here foreman in the blacksmith department for two years. He then went to Tarrytown, in the employ of Daniel Shanahan, a carriage manufacturer, and had charge of his business twenty-one years. After having been away for twenty-five years, he returned to Middletown, and started in carriage manufacturing on the corner of North Street and Low Avenue. He continued there until the spring of 1894, when he removed to his present location, No. 243 North Street, a two-story building, 40x73 feet. In addition to manufacturing, he has a carriage repository, and carries in stock harness, blankets and horse supplies of all kinds. The second floor of his building is used for painting and storage. He does all kinds of job work, and sells wholesale and retail, having the largest business of the kind in the city.

While residing in Tarrytown, Mr. Mulford was united in marriage, June 5, 1871, to Mary Zell, a native of Philadelphia. Three children have been born unto them: Nettie, now Mrs. Piatt, of Middletown; Freddie and Alice. In politics Mr. Mulford is a stanch and straight Republican, and is a member of the First Presbyterian Church of Middletown, of which body his wife is also a member. Before leaving Middletown, Mr. Mulford was a member of Excelsior Hook and Ladder Company No. 1, and was assistant foreman at the time of his removal to Paterson. Since his return he has again become an active member of the company. While in Tarrytown, he was a member for fifteen years of Hope Hose Company No. 1, and was its foreman. He is at present a member of the Exempt Firemen's Association at

JAMES HALSEY HUNT, M. D.

Tarrytown. He attends its meetings, and is active in each year's tournament. In the twenty-five years in which he was absent from the city, many changes occurred, but on his return he has adapted himself to the new situation, and is now numbered among the leading and progressive business men of the city.

~~~~~⊛~~~~~

JAMES HALSEY HUNT, M. D., one of the most widely known surgeons in the southern part of New York State, was born in Sandyston, Sussex County, N. J., August 9, 1849. He was the son of Dr. Isaac S. and Sarah A. (Fleming) Hunt. His early education was obtained in the Travis Institute, at Newton, N. J. He began the study of medicine at Bellevue Medical College of New York City in 1869. Having mastered the prescribed course of study and graduated with honor at the above institute, he took a position on the staff of Bellevue Hospital, passing through the various grades of junior, senior and house surgeon, and acquiring much valuable information, especially in surgery, which proved of inestimable advantage to him when, in 1874, he located at Port Jervis in the practice of his profession. He was aided at the outset by his connection with his father, a physician of considerable repute.

The Doctor had a natural talent for surgery, and in this branch of the profession he had few superiors outside of the large cities. Possessed of an iron nerve, and with confidence in his own skill and judgment, gained by close study and experience, he did not hesitate to perform the most dangerous and difficult operations. That he was successful, was evidenced by his services being in demand for miles in every direction. In 1878 he purchased the old Savings Bank Building on the corner of Ball and Sussex Streets, and here established his offices. In 1888 he received the appointment of Surgeon for the Erie Railway Company at Port Jervis.

Recognizing the need of a hospital, Dr. Hunt was the first and only physician willing to risk his reputation on it proving a success. At his personal expense he enlarged and converted the building into a thoroughly equipped hospital, and in memory of his father, whom he greatly revered, he named the institution the "Hunt Memorial Hospital." He spared neither care nor expense to make it a model of its kind, and its marked success has been proven by the scores of Erie Railroad men who are living to bless the day when it was erected.

While pre-eminently a surgeon, Dr. Hunt yet felt a deep interest in the prosperity of his adopted village. He was a Director in the First National Bank, and one of the founders and a Director of the Deerpark Electric-light Company. One of his maxims was, "As a heath measure it is desirable, indeed almost essential, that those who are actively engaged in business should set aside a portion of each year for rest and recuperation." Reducing this theory to practice, he twice crossed the Atlantic and made several trips to the wilds of the Adirondacks and Canada. One of the last acts of his life was the publication of a souvenir volume entitled, "Three Runs in the Adirondacks."

In March, 1892, Dr. Hunt disposed of his hospital and extensive practice in the hope of restoring his health, which had become shattered by seventeen years of the most arduous and exacting labor. He planned an extensive trip through the Pacific Slope, Alaska, Southern California and New Mexico, returning by way of the Southern States. His hopes were never realized, for upon reaching Salt Lake City he was stricken with acute Bright's Disease, which resulted in his death, December 20, 1892.

Dr. Hunt's natural kindness and generosity of heart were demonstrated in his treatment of his poor patients. He never distressed one of them by enforcing the payment of a bill by legal process. In his practice he was governed and controlled by the spirit of the old Hippocratean oath, which required one receiving a license to practice medicine to pledge himself never to refuse professional aid and succor to the poor, to those who could not pay. His practice in this regard was true to the highest and noblest tradition of his profession. He enjoyed the respect and confidence of his fellow-citizens as a man, and dying at the comparatively early age of forty-three, he left behind him an example of success which most men would consider a rich reward for a lifetime of strenuous endeavor.

DR. ISAAC SHAFER HUNT, deceased, was one of the prominent and leading physicians of Port Jervis. He was born in Stillwater, N. J., November 1, 1819, and was a son of Thomas and Rebecca (Turner) Hunt. He was literally a self-made man, and whatever prominence he acquired in the profession to which he was so ardently devoted may be attributed mainly to his studious course in early life. In 1847 he was graduated from the medical department of Yale College, and was on his way to the Delaware Water Gap, where he intended to locate, when, passing through Sandyston, Sussex County, he found the "Finch" fever raging disastrously in that section. Immediately setting to work, he was eminently successful in the treatment of that dread disease, and was eventually taken down with the fever, barely recovering from the scourge.

Locating permanently at Sandyston, Dr. Hunt married Sarah A. Fleming, a well known lady of that place. He was the father of two sons and three daughters, namely: James Halsey, whose sketch precedes this; L. Victor, a resident of Port Jervis; Ella, widow of Walter L. Gallup, of Evanston, Ill.; Stella, wife of Herbert A. Shattuck, of Brooklyn, N. Y.; and Rebekah, wife of Charles E. Holmes, of Port Jervis. In 1865 the Doctor came to Port Jervis, where he gained the confidence and esteem of the people, as was shown by the extensive practice that he acquired. He was a member of the Masonic order, having taken the degree of Knight Templar. In politics he was a stanch Republican. He was a popular

man, and took an interest and active part in everything that would benefit the community. His death occurred November 26, 1875, when he was fifty-six years of age.

CHARLES B. BUCKHOUT, of Middletown, was born in Highland, Ulster County, N. Y., March 28, 1867. The family of which he is a member traces its lineage to England. His father, J. W. Buckhout, was the son of a cooper living at Highland and was born in that village, where the early years of his life were passed. For some time he engaged in the milling business there and later was similarly employed at Matteawan, where he built a mill and remained a number of years. From that place he accompanied O. D. Wickham to Middletown, where he has since resided.

The marriage of J. W. Buckhout united him with Lottie Weed, a native of Highland, and at present living in Middletown. She is the mother of two children, Charles B. and Nellie, of New York City. Her father, Barton Weed, was born in Highland, and there engaged in milling for some years. His invention for sharpening sickles brought him into prominence throughout this part of the country, and he manufactured large quantities of his patents, which he sold at retail in his own and other counties. His death occurred in Highland.

Gaining a good education in the public schools of his native village, Charles B. Buckhout was fitted for the successful prosecution of business affairs. Starting out for himself, he worked as bookkeeper in his father's employ until 1888, when he came to Middletown in the employ of O. D. Wickham, the lumber dealer and miller, with whom he remained as bookkeeper until 1892. He then accepted a position as traveling salesman in the employ of Stanton Brewster, a lumber merchant of Painted Post, Steuben County, N. Y., his territory lying between New York City and Albany. He was remarkably successful in his work, and in fact the trade assumed such proportions that it became advisable to establish a lumber-yard in Middletown, which he did in 1895. The yards are situated between Wawayanda and Benjamin Streets, near Fulton, and the sales, which are made principally direct to contractors, are very large.

In New York City Mr. Buckhout married Miss Phœbe Edwards, who was born in Sullivan County, N. Y., her father, Nathaniel Edwards, having been a farmer there. Our subject takes an intelligent interest in the questions of the age, and in both local and general elections gives his support to Republican candidates. He is a member of the First Presbyterian Church and a contributor to its good works.

※

FRANK ORCE, who is engineer on the Erie Railroad, with his headquarters at Port Jervis, resides on the bank of the Delaware River, just across the state line in the village of Matamoras, Pa. He was born in Borgo Taro, Italy, June 24, 1832, and in 1848 came to the United States in company with an uncle. The latter opened a boarding-house in New York City, and later conducted, one in Philadelphia. For some time the lad was an errand boy and purchased supplies for his uncle. They did not get along well together, however, and one night when the boy was sent to Jersey City on an errand he decided to go forth and seek his own fortune. Without a cent in the world, he tramped onward hoping to find work, but was disappointed. The people to whom he applied when he was hungry gave him something to eat, and huckleberries were plentiful at that season. After sixteen days he arrived, footsore and weary, at Hancock, a station on the Erie Railroad in New York. During this time he had slept each night in haystacks and barns, and had traveled one hundred and sixty-four miles. At the station just mentioned three or four men were standing by the side of a boarding-house. One spoke to him in German, asking him where he was going. He could not speak a word of English, but understood the German. He answered in his native tongue, and was surprised when one of the men

repeated the question in Italian and told him that it was thirteen miles to the nearest house in the direction he was going. This man, who proved to be very kind in his way, asked the boy to stay over night, which he did, and the next morning he was given work on the railroad, at eighty cents a day, though he had to board himself. His hands were soft, and at the end of a week he was discharged, as they were so swollen he could not handle the shovel. His employer did not pay him, but told him he could collect the money at Port Jervis, and so he tramped along for seventy-six miles in order to reach this city. He obtained the $2.40 which was due him, and this was his initial capital in business. He obtained board with a Mr. Warner, who also was proprietor of the boarding-house referred to at Hancock. The second day after Mr. Orce's arrival he assisted in raising the seminary, and though he worked for two days received nothing for his labor. For about a year he received seventy-five cents a day, but for four months, while working for the Delaware & Hudson Canal Company, he was paid but sixty cents a day. Returning to the Erie construction, he received eighty cents a day, and remained there until October, 1850.

After serving on a freight train with John Andrews, formerly conductor of the gravel train where he had previously worked, he was given a freight train in the Delaware Division, with headquarters at Port Jervis, his wages being $1 a day. He remained in the capacity of brakeman until 1857, a part of which time he obtained $1.25 per day. In November, 1857, he was made fireman on an engine, and September 10, 1861, became division engineer. For several years he ran a freight train, but gave up the place in 1874 in order to take charge of a freight train on the Honesdale Branch. This was his run for the next fourteen years, when, October 5, 1887, he was injured in a head and head collision at East Millville. The disaster occurred on a curve where the other train had no right to the track. Mr. Orce was buried beneath the wreckage, and was there probably forty minutes before he gained consciousness. When he was extricated it was found that his left arm was badly crushed, two ribs were broken, and severe scalds were about his head. His arm was useless for nine months. His hearing was permanently injured, and it was nine months before he could resume work. About 1870 he was in another collision near Rock Run. He obeyed his orders to enter a switch, and had left his engine when he had carried out the command; another freight train started off the main track, running into his own engine, with disastrous consequences. At another time a collision occurred one-half mile west of Baket Switch, in Delaware County, owing to conflicting orders. Both engines were totally demolished, cars were telescoped, and everything got on fire, but the company was saved thousands of dollars owing to the promptness with which the people of the vicinity turned out and with buckets of water assisted to put out the flames. Among his many other exciting experiences in railroading was when he was in charge of a passenger train. It was heavily loaded, and therefore he had two engines attached. The forward one broke down just as the train reached the three-span bridge across the Delaware at Deposit. The train was going at good speed and the momentum carried it across, the ties and tracks being broken away by the disabled engines. Thus the train went quite a distance on the stringers of the bridge, but no one was injured.

In May, 1852, Mr. Orce married Mary Kelley, of Port Jervis, who died in the spring of 1865. April 19, 1867, Mr. Orce wedded Catherine Madden, of New York City, but who was reared in Hancock, N. Y. By the first marriage there were born three sons now living, namely: Frank, a conductor on the Delaware Division; Stephen, a locomotive engineer; and Henry, who has charge of a stationary engine. By his second union Mr. Orce has one daughter, Mabel, who is a graduate of the academy and is a young lady of exceptional ability. A niece of our subject is also a member of the household. Mr. Orce has grown gray in the service of the Erie Railroad, and enjoys the good-will and friendship of every employe of the same. He is thoroughly acquainted with every curve of the one hundred and four miles of this division. Altogether he has

been for forty-six years in the railroad employ, and for thirty-four years has been an engineer, all of this work being on the Delaware Division. For over thirty years he did not speak to one of his own countrymen, but about 1874 his brother Louis, now of New York City, came to America, and after making inquiries succeeded in finding our subject and came to visit him.

JOHN P. SAYER, a musician in Middletown, and proprietor of a livery stable, was born in the town of Warwick, December 25, 1867. His father, Andrew Sayer, was also a native of that town, as was also his father, the grandfather of our subject, Decatur Sayer, who was a farmer. Andrew Sayer was engaged in farming in the town of Warwick for some years, and subsequently removed to Middletown and here engaged in the trucking business, which occupation he followed until his death. He married Sarah Corter, who was born in the town of Deerpark, and who now lives in Middletown. Of their nine children seven are yet living.

When the subject of this sketch was seven years old the family came to Middletown, where he grew to manhood and received his education in the academy. When but ten years of age, he began the study of music, taking lessons on the piano and cornet. At first he studied under Professor Doxey, later under Professor Stewart, and subsequently studied violin music under Professor Rosher. He became an expert musician on every instrument undertaken, and since 1886 has been a member of either Rosher's or Berg's Orchestra. In 1883 he began traveling for Wood & Ogden, selling pianos and other musical instruments, his territory lying in Orange, Sullivan and Delaware Counties. After continuing with that firm until its dissolution, he was employed by their successors, Morgan & Wilber, until 1893.

In January, 1894, Mr. Sayer purchased the livery business of L. B. Scott, which was the oldest and largest in Middletown. The building, which is two stories in height, and has a frontage of one hundred feet, extends back two hundred

HULET D. CLARK.

feet, and has thirty stalls. It accommodates a large number of carriages and buggies, and the stable is well equipped for supplying weddings and funerals.

In 1893 Mr. Sayer assisted in organizing the Twenty-fourth Separate Company Band, in which he plays solo alto. He is a member of the Baptist Church, and in politics is a Republican.

HULET D. CLARK. In the town of Minisink, where he has resided for many years, Mr. Clark is well known as a successful farmer and progressive business man. Since coming here he has been identified with the best interests of this locality, and has aided in all plans for the material advancement of the town. His has been a busy life, and as a result of his unwearied labors he has accumulated a competency, which will enable him, when he so desires, to retire from active business affairs and enjoy in his declining days the fruits of a life well spent.

Referring to the parental history of Mr. Clark, we find that his father, Benjamin G., was born in Connecticut, but in early manhood settled in New Jersey, and there married, his wife, Angeline Springsted, being a native of that state. Hulet D. was born in Sussex County, February 15, 1835, and was reared upon the home farm, gaining early in life a practical knowledge of agriculture, and receiving a fair education in the neighboring schools. He established domestic ties December 29, 1857, at which time he was united in marriage with Miss Margaret Swartwout, a daughter of James D. Swartwout, of Port Jervis, and a direct descendant in the seventh generation of Roeloff Swartwout, one of the pioneers of this country, who came from Holland in 1655, locating at Kingston, N. Y. They became the parents of five children, as follows: Deborah, who is the wife of Samuel Hornbeck; Naomi, who married John G. Beakes; Clarence G., who married Mary Horton; and Carrie M. and Niven H., who are still with their parents.

After his marriage Mr. Clark purchased a farm in the town of Mt. Hope, upon which he made

his home for six years, engaged in the cultivation of the place. In 1867 he bought one hundred and fifteen acres, comprising his present place, and here he has since resided, meantime bringing his place under a high state of cultivation. He followed general farming until 1884. Some two years later he started the flour and feed store in the village of Johnson, a station on the Susquehanna & Western Railroad, and he has since been connected with the firm of C. G. Clark & Co., of which his son, Clarence G., is the senior member.

In politics Mr. Clark is a Democrat, but is not radical in his political views, being willing that others should have the same independence that he asks for himself in voting for men and measures. He is an Elder in the Presbyterian Church at Westtown, and takes an active interest in all things that tend to the advancement of the Master's cause. He has been quite successful in the accumulation of this world's goods, which fact is largely due to his untiring industry and perseverance. All the improvements on his farm are the work of his hands and brains. As a citizen he is highly esteemed by all who know him, and is worthy of the regard in which he is held.

BEN D. DEWITT, junior member of the firm of Sliter & Dewitt, of Middletown, was born in Liberty, Sullivan County, N. Y., September 22, 1856. He traces his ancestry to the old Holland-Dutch family from which DeWitt Clinton was descended, and his forefathers were identified with the early history of this state, his grandfather serving in the War of 1812, and his great-grandfather taking part in the Revolution.

Elias Dewitt, father of our subject, was born in Orange County, and for many years gave his attention to general farming, but at present his home is used principally for the accommodation of summer boarders. In religious belief he is connected with the Methodist Episcopal Church. He is still hale and hearty, in spite of his seventy-six years. His wife, who bore the maiden name of Susan Tidd, was born in Downsville, Delaware County, N. Y., where her father, Elisha Tidd, was engaged in farming and the lumber business.

The parental family consisted of three daughters and five sons, of whom all the sons and one of the daughters survive. Of the brothers, two reside in Sullivan and three in Orange County. Eben, who was fifth in order of birth, was reared on the home farm, and attended the common schools and Jeffersonville Academy. For one year he was employed at the carpenter's trade in Laporte, Sullivan County, Pa., after which he worked near Hancock, Delaware County, N. Y., for two years. While there he was one of the first to open the blue-stone quarry at Hancock, which produced three-quarters of a million feet of stone. After closing that quarry he spent one year with the Inderlid Chemical and Stone Company at Rock Riff, being their salesman and general manager.

In 1892 Mr. Dewitt came to Middletown, where, in partnership with R. G. Sliter, he engaged in the blue-stone business at No. 5 Foundry Street, and they have since carried on a large wholesale and retail business. He has also a stone dock on the Ontario & Western at Montgomery Street. He has had important contracts for blue-stone sidewalks, curbings and trimmings for buildings, and furnishes any kind of stone wanted, his specialties being the Ohio sandstone, Warsaw blue stone and Connecticut brown stone. In addition to the sales made in this locality, shipments of stone are made to New Jersey and Pennsylvania.

In Delaware County, N. Y., Mr. Dewitt married Miss Leonora Porter, daughter of Levi Porter. Her father, who was a native of Oswego, N. Y., first followed his trade of a sawyer, later became a lumberman and jobber, and is now living retired from active labor at Hancock, Delaware County. Her mother, Mary J., was born in Oswego, where the maternal grandfather, Isaac Kipp, was a farmer and distiller. Her paternal grandfather, Selim Porter, was born in Cattaraugus County, N. Y., and engaged in farming and lumbering near Owego. Mrs. Dewitt

was the youngest of four children, all but one of whom are living, one of her sisters being a resident of Middletown. By her marriage she has had two children, viz.: Lottie, who is at home; and Fay, who died at the age of seven years. Politically Mr. Dewitt is a Republican, and is well informed regarding the questions of the age.

ANDREW BROWN, a dealer in meats and vegetables in Middletown, was born at Suspension Bridge, N. Y., and is a son of John W. and Margaret Brown, who were natives of Germany. His father was a stone mason by trade, which he learned in his native country. Shortly after his marriage he emigrated to the United States and located at Suspension Bridge, where he remained until 1865, when he came to Middletown, and has continued to work here at his trade ever since. While verging on old age, he is yet hale and hearty, and can do as much work as any man in the trade. During the war he was drafted, and responded to the call, but was rejected by the examining physician. His wife died at Suspension Bridge when our subject was a mere lad. They were the parents of two children, one of whom has passed to the better world.

Andrew Brown was born November 14, 1856, and remained with his father at Suspension Bridge until he was nearly nine years old, when they came to Middletown. While in Suspension Bridge he attended the public schools, and also those at Middletown for a short time. When but ten years of age he began in the meat-market of Louis Kammern, on East Main Street, with whom he learned the trade of a butcher. In 1872 he went to New York City with that gentleman, who had started in business in that city, and worked in his meat-market on Eighth Avenue for six months. As he did not like the business there, he returned to Middletown, and for three years was employed on the farm of George Wickham. On leaving the farm he commenced in business for himself, and November 14, 1876, started his present market at No. 82 North Street, where he occupies two floors. Here he has ample room for his stock of meat and vegetables, together with fish, oysters and clams in season. He has one refrigerator for fish and two for meat, and two delivery wagons are required in the delivery of goods. During the winter season he packs pork for summer use. In the manufacture of sausage he uses a three horse-power water motor.

Mr. Brown was married in Guilford, Chenango County, to Miss Cora E. Whiting, who was a native of that place, and daughter of E. M. Whiting. The latter was quite a politician, and for years was employed in the railway mail service. He died in 1890. One child was born to our subject and wife, Lena, who died at the age of eight years.

Mr. Brown is a member of the Legion of Honor, the Knights of Labor and the Eagle Hose Company. Of the latter organization he has been a member for thirteen years, being assistant foreman for one year and Treasurer three years. He is an attendant of the Congregational Church, and politically is a Republican. The family resides at No. 46 Wickham Avenue, in a neat and comfortable residence, which was built a few years ago.

F REDERICK W. LOWE. The business of which Mr. Lowe is the head was established by himself and sons in 1883, when he built a shop in Middletown, put in machinery at a cost of $2,700, and began in the manufacture of files and rasps. The plant is operated by an engine of fifteen horse-power, with a boiler of twenty horse-power, and there are two cutting-machines, together with a trip-hammer capable of making four hundred and fifty-four blows in a minute. The rasps are punched by hand, while the files are finished by machine work. Since 1890 he and his son Charles J. have been partners, under the firm name of F. W. Lowe & Son.

Mr. Lowe was born in Prussia, Germany, June 5, 1828, being a son of Henry and Dorothea (Sthan) Lowe, also natives of that place, where his father was a manufacturer of nails. The family consisted of fourteen children, of whom

our subject was seventh in respect to age, and he is one of the two survivors of the original number. He was a lad of fourteen when he began to learn the process of manufacturing nails, under the instruction of his father, and after gaining a thorough knowledge of the business he did journeyman work.

Taking passage on the sailing-vessel "Johan" at Bremen, Mr. Lowe came to America in 1853, reaching this country after a voyage of fifty-four days. From New York City he went to Connecticut, where he worked as blacksmith in a rolling-mill near Stamford. For a time he was employed in making chains. He learned the file business in that place, and was employed at it there until 1861, when he went to Sing Sing, N. Y., and secured a position with the Arcade File Works. So efficient did he become in the trade, that he was said to be the best workman in the factory. In 1862 he resigned and removed to Johnstown, N. Y., whence in the spring of the following year he came to Middletown, accepting a position in the Eagle File Works. Not feeling satisfied with the surroundings there, he went to Matteawan, but in a short time the superintendent of the works sent urgently requesting him to return to Middletown, which he did, taking a position as forger of files. For twenty-one years he remained with that concern, accompanying it in its three removals, and becoming thoroughly acquainted with every department of the work.

In 1883, resigning from the position he had so long held, Mr. Lowe started in business with his sons, and since then he has conducted a profitable and increasing trade. His main building is 200x 202 feet in dimensions, and is surrounded by a lot 106x153. He owns a neat residence, 79x200, at No. 180 East Main Street, near his shop. This property he purchased when it was in an unimproved condition, and planted shade and fruit trees, also small fruits and other produce, making the garden one of the finest in the city.

In New York City Mr. Lowe married Miss Eliza Spieker, who was born in Germany in 1826. Only three of their eight children attained years of maturity, and they were: William, who is a file-maker and resides in Philadelphia;

George, who died in Middletown in 1894; and Charles J. The last-named was born and reared in this city, receiving a good education in the academy here, and then began his trade under his father. He is a fine file-cutter and is said to be the best last rasp-maker in the country. Socially he is an active member of Eagle Hose Company No. 2.

For ten years Mr. Lowe was a Director of the first building and loan association organized in Middletown. He has served as Inspector of Elections and in other local positions. Politically his allegiance is given to the Republican party. In 1869 he joined Middletown Lodge No. 112, I. O. O. F., and belonged to it for seven years, when he became one of the principal organizers of Luther Lodge. In the latter organization he has served as First Noble Grand. He is a member of the Congregational Church and has held the office of Trustee of the congregation.

> ⸺ ❄✦❄✦❄ ⸺

WILLIAM J. NELSON, M. D., was born in Romney, Hampshire County, W. Va., April 30, 1860, and is a son of Rev. Joseph and grandson of Joseph Nelson, of County Antrim, Ireland. His father was educated in Belfast, Ireland, and graduated from Queen's College, with the degrees of A. B. and A. M. He then took a course in theology, and was ordained a minister in the Presbyterian Church, and preached in his native country until his removal to America, in 1857. On coming to the United States he located in Romney, W. Va., where he served as Principal and President of Romney Classical Institute until after the close of the war. He then removed to Cumberland, Md., where he was Principal of the Cumberland Classical Institute. Later he removed to Hartford County, Md., and was pastor of the Bethel Presbyterian Church. His next change was to Sussex County, N. J., where for four years he was pastor of the Clove Presbyterian Church. He later removed to South Centreville, where he was also pastor of the Presbyterian Church for four years. He then retired from the ministry, and

in the year 1892 his death occurred, at the age of seventy-four years. His wife, Janette McKibben, was born in County Antrim, Ireland, and was a daughter of Joseph McKibben, who was a salt manufacturer, and engaged in the shipping business at Belfast. He was the owner of several vessels, and did a thriving business there for many years. He died in Ireland. Mrs. Janette Nelson, who now resides in Middletown, is the mother of two daughters and one son.

The subject of this sketch spent his boyhood days in Maryland and New Jersey, and received his primary education in private schools, mostly in those presided over by his father. Later he entered Weston Military Institute, at Weston, Conn., where he remained three years. He then returned home, and went to school in Maryland for a time. From early childhood he had a desire to study medicine, and in the sessions of 1879-80 entered the medical department of the University of Maryland, from which he graduated in 1883, with the degree of M. D. By competitive examination he was appointed assistant in the University of Maryland Hospital and Infirmary, at Baltimore, where he remained two years, having the practical benefit of every department of that institution. He then located in Baltimore, where he engaged in the practice of his profession for one year, and then went to Clove, N. J., where he practiced for a time. In 1888 he removed to South Centreville, Orange County, where he remained in the practice of his profession until 1892, when he located in Middletown. His office is now at No. 66 East Main Street, where he is engaged in general practice and in surgery. He is at present the City Physician of Middletown, having received the appointment July 28, 1894, from the Mayor and Common Council. By virtue of his office he is a member of the Board of Health. In the four years in which he has resided in Middletown, he has built up an extensive and paying practice, of which he may well be proud.

Dr. Nelson was married, in Middletown, to Miss Cora J. Case, born in Turner, this county, and daughter of Ira L. Case, a sketch of whom appears elsewhere in this work. They have one

WILLIAM H. HALLOCK.
TOWN OF MONTGOMERY.

child, Olive L. Fraternally Dr. Nelson is a member of Hoffman Lodge, F. & A. M. He is also a member of Excelsior Hook and Ladder Company No. 1. Professionally he is connected with the Alumni Society of the University of Maryland, and of the Orange County Medical Society. Like his father, he is a member of the Presbyterian Church, and politically is a Republican.

WILLIAM H. HALLOCK. A pleasant and well improved farm in the town of Montgomery is the home of the gentleman above named, and under his able management the land produces crops which rank first both in quantity and quality. The estate comprises two hundred and eighty acres, upon which have been placed all the improvements of a model farm. The owner is an enterprising farmer, and a citizen whose worth is recognized by his fellow-men, by whom he is esteemed accordingly.

Mr. Hallock has spent his entire life in this town, and here he was born June 21, 1835, being the second in order of birth, and the only survivor, among three children comprising the family of Joshua G. and Mary (Brown) Hallock. His father was born and reared in Dutchess County, N. Y., and thence came to the town of Hamptonburgh, Orange County, where he married Miss Brown. Working on a farm by the month and operating rented land, he secured a start in life, and, carefully saving his earnings, he was enabled, in 1852, to purchase ninety-five acres of land in this town. From this small beginning he added to his property from time to time until his possessions aggregated two hundred and eighty acres. He continued to make his home upon this place until his death, which occurred at the age of eighty-five.

The life of Joshua G. Hallock was characterized by integrity and honesty, even in the smallest details of his business affairs, and no one could speak aught against his character. Possessing traits of perseverance and economy, he worked his way from poverty to affluence, and at his death left his son a valuable property. A Republican in political views, he was elected on that ticket to the position of County Supervisor, which he filled for several years. In connection with general farm work, he engaged in raising stock, a branch of agriculture in which he met with success. His parents were natives of Dutchess County, and the family dates back to 1640, when Peter Hallock, one of thirteen Pilgrim fathers, came from England and settled on Long Island. Our subject's mother was born in Dutchess County, and died in the town of Montgomery, at the age of eighty years, surviving her husband only four months.

Remaining with his parents until their death, our subject then inherited the old homestead, where he has since resided. His educational advantages were such as the public schools afforded, and being a man of close observation and a thoughtful reader of current literature, he is well posted concerning matters of general or local value. Like his father, he supports the principles of the Republican party, believing them best adapted to promote the welfare of our Government. March 4, 1874, he married Miss Harriet Barrett, of Sullivan County, N. Y., an estimable lady, whose efficient co-operation has been of the greatest assistance to him in his undertakings. Mr. Hallock and his wife are members of the Dutch Reformed Church.

DANIEL REEVE, deceased, was born in the town of Minisink, January 1, 1814, and was a son of Jeremiah and Hannah (Decker) Reeve, natives, respectively, of Long Island and Orange County. On the maternal side he traced his ancestry to Anthony and Hannah (Decker) Van Etten, members of pioneer families of this County. They resided in a stone house on a large farm, in what history calls the "lower" neighborhood, near the home of her brother, Maj. John Decker. In July, 1779, Captain Brandt, with a company of Tories and Indians, invaded this neighborhood, and Anthony, who

was Commissary for a company of American soldiers, was killed by a gunshot on going to duty.

Mary, a daughter of Anthony, married Isaiah
Decker in 1783, and at his death she was left with
three children, namely: Elizabeth, who became
the wife of Joseph Davis; Isaac, who died at the
age of eighty-four; and Hannah, who married
Jeremiah Reeve, son of Daniel and Martha (Rus-
sel) Reeve, of Suffolk County, L. I. Jeremiah
and Hannah Reeve had three children, those besides our subject being Isaiah, who grew to manhood and was accidentally killed by being thrown
from a horse in 1832; and Martha G., who remained at home.

The subject of this sketch grew to manhood on
the old farm and was educated in the public
schools, and in 1839 married Ruth Ann Carpenter. They became the parents of five children,
one of whom died in infancy. Daniel C., who
was graduated with honors from Union College,
Class of '63, and from Albany Law School,
practiced law in Middletown for a period of six
years, until a sudden cold developed into lung
trouble, resulting in his death, February 9, 1871,
at the age of thirty years. Valentine H., a successful farmer, resided on the old homestead until
his death, in 1886. Martha J. makes her home on
the farm where her grandparents settled in 1804.
Ruth A. is the wife of Edward Silk, of Middletown, and is the mother of one son, Reeve A.
Silk, an academic pupil.

The first representative of the Carpenter family
in the United States was William Carpenter, born
in 1576, who came from Wherwell, England, in
the good ship "Bevis" to New England, in May,
1638. His ancestry in England is traced back to
Richard, father of John Carpenter, who was Town
Clerk of London and a great promoter of education; he died in 1442. The descendants of William are (2d) William, (3d) John, (4th) John,
(5th) John, (6th) Isaac. The last-named was
born in Goshen, March 31, 1747. His father,
who was an early settler of Orange County, was
in July, 1721, one of the men who gave land
for the village of Goshen to be laid out, with its
church, parsonage, cemetery, etc. He had eight
children.

Isaac was married to Mrs. Susanna (McKinney) Thompson, of Scotch-Irish descent, a lady
several years younger than himself. Her parents
were Edward and Mary (Dekay) McKinney.
Isaac Carpenter and his wife lived on his large
estate, a part of which is now known as the Reeve
homestead, two and one-half miles south of Middletown. To them were given two daughters,
Susan and Ruth Ann, also a son, Isaac, who died
in childhood. Long before the abolishment of
slavery, Isaac, feeling it an unjust principle, gave
entire freedom to those he possessed, though he
retained them in his service for years afterward.
His daughter Susan married James Van Duzer
and reared a son, Isaac, who occupies a handsome residence upon part of the original tract
of his grandfather; also four daughters, all of
whom married farmers and settled near their old
home. The Carpenter family have a coat-of-
arms, and the present female representatives are
eligible to membership in the Society of Colonial
Daughters.

For many years our subject resided on the old
Carpenter homestead, where his death occurred
October 29, 1878; his remains were interred
in the Hillside Cemetery at Middletown. He
was a charter member of the Second Presbyterian
Church of Middletown and was active in religious
work. He was a patriotic man, interested in his
country's welfare, and in politics was a Republican. His death was mourned, not alone by his
family, but by a large circle of friends, who knew
and loved him. A quiet and retiring man, he
went forward in the discharge of such duties as
devolved upon him in such a manner as to win and
retain the friendship of every acquaintance.

CHARLES W. HILL, contractor and builder
of Middletown, was born in Newburgh, in
September, 1838. John Hill, his grandfather,
who was of English descent, was a cooper by trade,
and after residing in Newburgh for many years
removed to Haverstraw, dying there at the age of
eighty-eight years. He participated in the War
of 1812. Andrew Hill, the father of our subject,

was a native of Dutchess County, but in early life removed to Newburgh, and later to Haverstraw. In 1864 he located at Middletown, where he engaged in his trade as cooper He married Susan Wood, who was born in Haverstraw, and who was the daughter of John Wood, a farmer residing near that city. By their union eight children were born, six of whom grew to maturity, and three of whom are now living. In politics he was a Republican, and religiously was a member of the Methodist Episcopal Church, of which body his wife was also a member. She died in 1865, and he in 1882.

Charles W. Hill grew to manhood and was educated in the Haverstraw public schools. When a mere youth he commenced to learn the cooper's trade under his father, and continued in that occupation until twenty-one years of age, when he began to learn the carpenter's trade, spending two years in the Ramapo Car Shops. In 1864 he came to Middletown and commenced work, under instructions, at the carpenter's trade for Richard Van Horn, but received journeymen's wages from the start. He was with that gentleman three years, and then for one year was with Samuel Wilcox. At the end of that time he started in business for himself as a contractor and builder, and, with the exception of seven years spent on the police force, has since continued in that occupation. His first appointment on the police force was in 1875, when only two men were required to discharge the duties of that office. He served until 1882, during which time he had several exciting adventures, having had dirk knives drawn on him and revolvers fired at him. At the end of seven years he resigned his position, since which time he has been at work at his trade. Among the buildings erected by him are the Ropeno, Hornbeck, Stevens, Hinchcliff, Dicks and McGready & Finch, also two for Mrs. Annie Hill, and one for Mr. Tate, in Warwick, besides many others.

Mr. Hill was married at Sloatsburg to Miss Caroline Finch. Of their five children, only two grew to maturity, and only one is now living. Alice died at the age of two years; Charles E., who was engaged in the confectionery business,

and who was a very popular young man, being at one time a member of the Board of Aldermen, died in 1892, at the age of twenty-seven years; Gracie died at the age of four months; Mazie is yet at home.

Mr. Hill is a member of the Knights of Pythias and also of Middletown Lodge, I. O. O. F. Religiously he is a member of the Methodist Episcopal Church, in which he is a Class-leader and a member of the Official Board. In politics he is a Republican.

WALTER H. KNAPP comes of an old Orange County family of German extraction. He was born in the town of Canterbury, January 11, 1833, and is a son of James and Harriet (Knapp) Knapp, the former born in the town of Canterbury, and the latter born in the town of Little Britain. Though bearing the same name, she was not a relative of her husband. John Knapp, the grandfather of our subject, was a farmer by occupation, and died on the old homestead at the age of sixty-two years. Usal Knapp, a great-uncle of our subject, served for seven years in the Revolutionary War, and was the last of Washington's bodyguard to pass away, dying at the age of ninety-seven years at Little Britain. He was buried at Washington's Headquarters, where the state has erected a monument, on which is inscribed, "The last of the bodyguard." A company of Continentals from Albany had charge of the funeral services.

James Knapp, the father of our subject, was for many years engaged in farming in the town of New Windsor, and later in the town of Montgomery. He subsequently removed to a small farm in Coldenham, and died at the age of seventy-three years. In politics he was originally a Whig, and on the organization of the Republican party espoused its principles. He was a member of the Presbyterian Church, in which for many years he was chorister. He was buried in Goodwill Cemetery. His good wife, the mother of our subject, died at the age of seventy-seven years. Of the nine children in the parental family, all grew to maturity, and five are yet living. William, now deceased, was a member of the Sixty-ninth New York Volunteer Infantry, and was wounded by a shell, but served two years, and has since died. Helen, now Mrs. Higby, resides at Equinunk, Pa. Walter H. is our subject. James resides in Newburgh. Lavina, now deceased, was the wife of Benjamin Dawes, of the town of Montgomery, a soldier in the late war. Nelson enlisted in Company I, One Hundred and Twenty-fourth Infantry, under Captain Clark, and was all through the war; two years after his discharge he died suddenly. Edwin, a blacksmith, lives at Coldenham. Emily, who married William Corvey, of the town of Montgomery, is now deceased; and Hanford is a furniture dealer and undertaker at Equinunk, Pa.

The subject of this sketch was reared in the town of Montgomery, where he resided until eighteen years of age, assisting in the farm work and attending the public school. He then came to Middletown, which had but thirteen hundred inhabitants, and was apprenticed to learn the trade of the manufacture of sash, doors and blinds. He continued at this place until 1863, having been foreman of a factory for many years, and then removed to Warwick and engaged in the furniture and undertaking trade, together with carriage and sleigh painting. After following the business there for five years, he returned to Middletown, and engaged in undertaking on James Street. Later he bought property on the corner of James and West Main Streets. In 1881 he took in partnership his son W. Nelson, and the business was continued under the firm name of W. H. Knapp & Son. In 1891, after being in business thirty-two years, he retired.

Mr. Knapp was united in marriage in the city of Newburgh with Miss Martha J. Dickson, a native of Marlboro, N. J., and daughter of Selah Dickson, who was a carpenter at Newburgh. Two children have been born unto them: Mary A., now Mrs. Merritt, of Middletown; and W. Nelson, whose sketch appears on another page of this work. For many years Mr. Knapp has

been a member of St. Paul's Methodist Church, of which he is a Steward. In politics he is a Republican, and has ever been active in political affairs, having many times served as a delegate to county and state conventions. He served seven years in the old Protection Engine Company No. 2, which was one of the first fire companies started here, but which is now extinct. During the war he was a member of the Union League. In the spring of 1893 he was elected City Treasurer on the Republican ticket, was re-elected in 1894, serving two years, and was offered the nomination for a third term, but refused to accept. He is a member of Warwick Lodge No. 544, F. & A. M.; Midland Chapter No. 24, R. A. M.; Middletown Lodge No. 112, I. O. O. F.; Knights of Honor No. 2103, of which he is Past Dictator, and of which he was Treasurer for fourteen years; and is a member of Lancelot Lodge No. 169, K. of P. In each of these organizations he has taken an active part.

WILLIAM BURKE, proprietor of the Mud Mills Distillery, is a native of County Cork, Ireland, and was born in 1834. He remained at home until eighteen years of age, when he came to the United States and located in the town of Goshen, Orange County, where he first engaged in farming. Later he entered the employ of the Erie Railroad Company, remaining until 1864, when he came to Middletown and engaged in the liquor business. He has had distilleries at Centerville, Smith's Village and Mud Mills, and was connected with the old brewery where the Madison House now stands, and which was built by H. B. Ogden. Mr. Burke still owns the building, but leases it to other parties for hotel purposes. He was also connected with the old grain distillery on Canal Street, which was burned.

The Mud Mills Distillery is located two and a-half miles east of the city, and in connection with it is a forty-acre farm. Mr. Burke is now the oldest wholesale liquor dealer in the city, and, among his specialties is Burke's Cider Brandy

JAMES VANDEROEF.

or apple jack. In his business he has been very successful, and in addition to the fine brick block at No. 28 Union Street, which he occupies himself, he owns the adjoining building, besides considerable other real estate. His family consists of two children: Margaret, at home; and William, who is now engaged in the study of law with George H. Decker. Mrs. Burke is deceased.

Mr. Burke has been a resident of Middletown since 1864, and has witnessed its growth from a small village to a thriving city of over thirteen thousand inhabitants. He is one of the oldest business men in the place, and has been active in all the improvements of the city. When he located in Middletown it had but one railroad, the Erie. In religious belief he is a Catholic, and is at present Trustee of St. Joseph's Catholic Church.

JAMES VANDEROEF. The city of Montgomery, which lies on the east side of the Wallkill River, is one of the most desirable residence portions of Orange County, its citizens being foremost in educational, commercial and social projects. For twenty-eight years Mr. Vanderoef was one of its most prominent business men, as he is still one of its most progressive citizens. He came here in 1867 and embarked in the coal business, which he continued in conjunction with a large lumber and feed trade until 1895. Though still a member of the firm of James Vanderoef & Son, he has practically retired from business, having given to his son the management of his interests.

The first representatives of the Vanderoef family in America were three brothers, who came from Holland. The first of the name to settle in Orange County was the grandfather of our subject, Cornelius Vanderoef, who died before James was born. After his death his widow, whose maiden name was Dorothy Weisner, married William Shepard. She lived to the advanced age of ninety-six. One of her nieces, Temperance Weisner, died when ninety-seven years old.

John Weisner Vanderoef, our subject's father,

was born in Orange County, where he followed the trade of a carpenter, and later engaged in agricultural pursuits. His death occurred in the town of Warwick at the age of eighty-six. He first married Miss Dorothy Wheeler, who became the mother of two sons and a daughter, and died when James was three years of age. Later the father married Elizabeth (Rogers) Wheeler, the widow of Joel Wheeler, a brother of his first wife. Two children were born of that union. Both John W. Vanderoef and his brother-in-law, Joel Wheeler, were active in military circles.

The marriage of our subject, December 9, 1840, united him with Harriet, eldest daughter of James T. and Dorothy (Roe) Post, of the town of Warwick. She was born February 16, 1822, and is one of four children, the others being Jefferson, Moses and Louisa, of whom the only survivor besides Mrs. Vanderoef is Louisa, wife of John Ackerman, of Hartford, Conn. The grandparents of Mrs. Vanderoef were David and Nellie (Wisner) Post. Her father was born November 1, 1795, and died January 4, 1863; her mother was born May 16, 1802, and died April 3, 1879. Four generations, including the grandmother and mother of Mrs. Vanderoef, herself and her son, John James, were born on the 16th of the month.

After his marriage our subject remained for a time on his father's farm, then purchased one hundred acres, on which he resided until the outbreak of the Civil War. For a few years afterward he lived in the village of Florida, and later was for one year in the coal business at Goshen. In 1867 he came to Montgomery, where he has since resided. In connection with Chauncey Brooks, he has erected several houses in the town and has platted a large addition to the city. In addition to other enterprises he has purchased cattle by carload lots, disposing of them at a fair advance. Politically he is a Republican, but has never desired office nor mingled in public affairs, preferring to devote his attention to personal matters. With his wife he holds membership in the Presbyterian Church, in the prosperity of which he takes a deep interest.

For fifty-five years Mr. and Mrs. Vanderoef have traveled life's journey together, and by mutual sympathy have doubled their joys and divided their sorrows. Theirs has been a happy union, and in their declining years they have the affection of their children and grandchildren and the warm regard of a host of friends. Their family consisted of five sons and one daughter, viz.: John James, who is referred to elsewhere in this volume; Thomas Jefferson, who is in the mercantile business in Brooklyn; Charles Weisner, deceased, formerly a jeweler of Sing Sing, N. Y.; Hattie Louisa; William and Zebulon, who died in childhood. The two children of Charles, Harry Wilcox and Lizzie Charline, made their home with Mr. Vanderoef until their mother's marriage to Frederick Bodine, since which time they have resided in Montgomery. The only daughter of our subject is the wife of William I. Wallace, M. D., and she has two children, viz.: Bessie Louise, who was born February 10, 1892; and James, April 27, 1894. They reside on the old homestead with her parents.

JAMES C. SPIEGEL, M. D., comes of a noble German family, and traces his ancestry back to the year 1010. For hundreds of years his ancestors were court physicians to the ruler of Hesse-Cassel. His father, Christian Von Spiegel, was a baron, and was born in Hesse-Cassel. His grandfather, also named Christian Von Spiegel, was a court physician, as was also his great-grand-father, great-great-grandfather, and great-great-great-grandfather. Christian Von Spiegel, the father, was a graduate of Zurich University, both in the classical and medical departments. He took a prominent part in the Revolution of 1848, and for that reason was compelled to leave his native country. He came to America, and first located in New York City, then drifted South, and finally settled in Memphis, Tenn., where he engaged in the practice of his profession for many years. He was in Memphis the greater part of the war, but was a strong Union man, and a friend of General Grant. In 1870 he left Mem-

phis and located in Utica, N. Y., where he remained until 1887, and then removed to Saratoga, N. Y., where he now lives a retired life. He was in Memphis during the dreadful scourge of yellow fever, and also of cholera, and was active in the discharge of his duties as a physician. He is a member of the Presbyterian Church, and in politics is a Democrat. His wife, Martha E. Bosley, was born in Louisiana, and was a daughter of James Bosley, a cotton planter above Shreveport, on the Red River, where he had a large plantation, and was the owner of eight hundred slaves when the war broke out. He was a member of the Assembly in Louisiana, and was of English descent. Her mother was a Clark. By this marriage there was but one child, the subject of this sketch. Mrs. Von Spiegel died in 1862, and the Doctor subsequently married and became the father of two children by his second wife.

The subject of this sketch was born in Memphis, Tenn., December 23, 1856, and there remained with his father until 1870. His primary education was received in private schools in Memphis, and his course was completed at Whitestown Seminary, near Utica, from which he was graduated in 1873. He then commenced the study of medicine with his father, and in 1875 entered the medical department of the University of Buffalo, graduating therefrom in 1878, with the degree of M. D. During the summer of 1874 he went to Europe, and spent eight months in the hospitals of Berlin and Vienna. He then traveled over the continent, including England and Scotland, whence he returned and entered the medical college.

Soon after his graduation, in 1878, Dr. Spiegel located at Mt. Morris, Livingston County, where he engaged in practice for three years. He then traveled for a while through the North and West, and finally located in Schenectady, N. Y., where he remained for eleven years. During the following eighteen months he was traveling, principally in the South. He has traveled extensively in every state and territory in the Union. In October, 1893, he located in Middletown, principally for his health, but at once commenced the practice of his profession. He makes a specialty of chronic diseases and throat troubles, and has been very successful. In the treatment of chronic diseases he seldom uses a knife.

Dr. Spiegel was married in Utica, N. Y., to Miss Sarah E. Lord, a native of West Troy, N. Y., and daughter of A. N. Lord. They have one child, James Bosley. While in Schenectady he was County Coroner for six years. He is a member of the Odd Fellows, Red Men, Royal Arcanum and Chosen Friends, all of Schenectady, and has passed through nearly all the chairs of each of the orders. For a time he was a member of the Foresters. Religiously he is a Baptist, and politically a Republican. He was on the Republican Central Committee in Schenectady, and in 1889 was a member of the convention which nominated Donaldson for Senator. He is a member of the Alumni of Buffalo University.

As already stated, Dr. Spiegel has been an extensive traveler, and made his second visit to Europe in 1880, at which time he visited many points of interest. He is a good physician, well educated, and enjoys the respect and confidence of all who know him.

———⊙≷⊙———

WILLIAM L. DERR, Superintendent of the Delaware Division of the Erie Railroad at Port Jervis, is conceded to be one of the best practical railroad managers in the country, and is much esteemed by the employes as well as the officials of the company. While he was still a mere boy, his strong ambition and natural ability manifested themselves, and all his study and work has been toward practical ends. Mathematics of the most abstruse sort were easily mastered by him, and he is thoroughly informed on everything relating to railroad construction. He frequently contributes articles of scientific merit and bearing evidence of research to well known engineering journals, and his opinions meet with profound respect.

This noted railroad man was born at Charlestown, Cecil County, Md., in 1857. His ancestors were residents of Easton and Allentown, Pa., and his father, J. A. Derr, has been for a number of years Master Carpenter of the Delaware Division in this city. His mother, whose maiden name was Virginia Jones, is the daughter of a mill engineer and extensive land-owner in Maryland. Our subject received a good education, and by his own exertions made sufficient money to take a special course in engineering in the Polytechnic College of Philadelphia, graduating therefrom in the Class of '78.

Mr. Derr's first employment on public works was for the Phœnix Iron Bridge Company, and afterward he was with the Baltimore Bridge Company, thus obtaining practical knowledge of bridge-construction work. In March, 1875, he became an employe of the Philadelphia, Wilmington & Baltimore Railroad in the Susquehanna Bridge Division, and a year later was attached to the engineer corps as assistant civil engineer. In 1877 the bridge, over a mile long, at Havre de Grace was completed, Mr. Derr having been assistant engineer on construction for some time.

In April, 1877, our subject received an appointment from the Pittsburg, Cincinnati & St. Louis Railroad as assistant engineer in the Maintenance of War Department, and in August, 1879, was made Supervisor of Chartiers Division of the road. Then he obtained a better position with the New York & New England Railroad, with his headquarters at Boston, and in September, 1883, he was notified of his appointment as Roadmaster of the Woonsocket Division. Only a short time had elapsed ere he was promoted to be Assistant Superintendent of this division.

It was in February, 1886, that Mr. Derr became Roadmaster of the Buffalo Division of the Erie Railroad, and the following November he was made Roadmaster of the Delaware Division, with his headquarters at Port Jervis. In June, 1889, he was promoted to be Assistant Superintendent of the Susquehanna Division, and in June, 1890, Superintendent of the Jefferson Division. Finally, October 1, 1890, he was installed Superintendent of the Delaware Division, and is still serving as such. In his long years of service he has come into close contact with and served under many men who have been at the head of the engineering and railroad profession. While Roadmaster of the Delaware Division, he built the second track of the Jefferson Branch, and since becoming Superintendent of the Delaware Division has put in the block system the entire length of the branch, demonstrating that heavy traffic can be handled without delay or difficulty in this manner. He is a member of the American Society of Railroad Superintendents, and also belongs to the Buffalo Society of Railroad Superintendents.

March 24, 1893, Mr. Derr married Lillian A. Kies, of Putnam, Conn. They have had a family of four children, who are named in order of birth as follows: Orvill V., Pearl L., Alice F. and William T. Mr. Derr has a fine library of scientific volumes, the contents of which he has largely mastered. He is perfectly familiar with the geological formations in this portion of the state, and knows what rock is best for ballast, for building bridge abutments, etc. He is a man of broad mind and wide intelligence, these traits showing themselves plainly in his high, broad and full forehead. In manner he is very pleasant and cordial, and makes friends of all people with whom he is thrown in contact, whether in a business or social way.

CHARLES HIGHAM. During the early days in the history of this county, the Commercial Hotel, of Middletown, was a "half-way house" for the stage coaches running between Newburgh and Port Jervis. When the old stage line was superseded by the steam cars, and Middletown gained metropolitan activity, the hotel became the favorite stopping-place for tourists and commercial travelers. To-day, though one of the oldest hotels in the county, it loses nothing in competition with its more modern successors. It is situated on the corner of West Main and Canal Streets, and contains thirty-five or forty rooms, furnished with first-class improvements and all modern comforts.

The proprietor of the hotel, Mr. Higham, is also well known through his connection with the Middletown Wheelmen, of which he was one of the founders and has been President since its organization. In 1890 he joined the League of American Wheelmen, with which he has since been connected. For thirteen years he has been an active member of Monhagen Hose Company No. 1. In 1892 he served as second assistant engineer, and the following year he was promoted to be first assistant, which office he has since filled. In the Order of American Firemen he is a member of the Board of Directors of the Local Branch, Hamilton Council No. 14, and takes an active part in all its affairs. In 1894-95 he was delegate to the State Firemen's Convention, and has also been representative of the Monhagen Hose Company on the Board of Representatives of the Middletown Fire Department. In fact, he has been one of the most prominent firemen of the city.

A native of Manchester, England, the subject of this sketch was born in April, 1867. His father, a native of the same place, was engaged in business as a fancy-silk weaver, but in 1868 he came to America, and settled in Middletown in January of that year. He became proprietor of the Wallkill House, which he conducted until his death, in 1870. By his first marriage he had four children, of whom three are living. His second marriage was to Elizabeth Redfield, a native of Manchester, England, now living in Middletown. Two children were born of that union, Charles being the younger. He was reared in this city, receiving his education in Wallkill Academy. His mother continued to manage the Wallkill House until 1882, when she became proprietor of the Commercial House, and this later passed into the hands of our subject and his sister. In April, 1888, he purchased his sister's interest, and has since been proprietor of the hotel, into which he has put about $8,000 worth of improvements.

The first of the Higham family to come to America was John, an uncle of our subject, who settled in Jersey City and there carried on a hotel. From that place he came to Middletown, where he was prospered, acquiring the ownership of three hotels and a fine residence property. He

WILLIAM H. CARPENTER.

was a man of great liberality, and every enterprise that was calculated to benefit the city found
in him a warm friend. He continued to reside in
Middletown until his death, at which time his
property was distributed among his nephews and
nieces, he having no children of his own.

In Middletown, in 1890, Mr. Higham was
united in marriage with Miss Annie Colwell, a
native of this city and a daughter of J. M. Colwell, a retired tobacconist. Socially our subject
is connected with Hoffman Lodge, F. & A. M.
He is a genial, enterprising young man, and has
in this city a host of friends, who take a deep interest in his success. Already he has placed his
business affairs upon a substantial footing, and
financially ranks among the most prosperous men
of Middletown.

WILLIAM H. CARPENTER. This well
known resident of Orange County, whose
home is in the town of Hamptonburgh,
was born on the farm where he now resides December 24, 1824. He has been a life-long agriculturist, and is one of the best citizens of the
section. His father, Nathaniel Carpenter, was a
native of the town of Goshen, while his father,
the grandfather of our subject, was of English descent.

Nathaniel Carpenter married Miss Charlotte
Coleman, and to them was born a family of five
children. John C., a well-to-do farmer, departed
this life in 1882, when seventy-three years of age;
Oliver's death occurred in 1891; Julia A. is residing with her brother; Mary C. died in 1893; and
William H., of this sketch, was the youngest of
the household. The father of this family was a
mason, which trade he followed for a short time
after learning it, and then gave his attention to
farm pursuits.

The farm on which our subject now lives is a
very old one and was purchased by his father in
the year 1807. The house upon the place was
commenced in 1827 and was completed in 1829.

Though old, it is very substantial, having been
built of the very best materials. The barn and
outbuildings are large and commodious, and the
best arranged of any in the town for dairy purposes. The barn is one hundred and fifteen feet
long and thirty-two feet wide, and last season
(1894) it was filled to repletion with fine meadow hay, for the use of his large herd of Holstein
and graded cattle. Good spring water, cool and
refreshing, flows through the farm, making a
never failing stream. The location of this fine
estate is quite convenient to the Gerard station of
the Orange County Railroad. On this property
the father continued to live until his death, in
1846. He was very successful in all his undertakings, and although beginning in life a poor man,
left to his family a valuable estate, which was accumulated entirely by himself.

Our subject was reared on the home place, and
when a young man of thirty years purchased the
farm from the other heirs and has made it his
home ever since. It is one hundred and sixty-
eight acres in extent and comprises some of the
best farming land in the county. The greater
part of his attention, however, is given to dairy
farming, he selling his milk to the creamery near
his home. Besides the home farm he owns a
tract of one hundred and thirty-five acres, making in all three hundred and three acres.

In politics Mr. Carpenter always votes the
Democratic ticket. A man of generous disposition, he contributes liberally to the relief of others
and stands well with every class in the neighborhood, and is one of the town's most substantial and
progressive agriculturists.

NATHANIEL TAFT, whose home is at Matamoras, Pa., opposite Port Jervis, is the oldest engineer in continuous service on the Erie
Railroad. From October, 1856, to 1891, he ran
two express trains, and since then has been in
charge of the yard engine. He has calculated
that up to April 1, 1895, he has run one million,
five hundred and sixty thousand miles on an en-

gine, and this is the more notable in that he has never had a serious accident, and the loss of a single life cannot be laid to his charge.

Mr. Taft was born in Mendon, Mass., March 15, 1825, and is a son of Reuben and Sarah (Sterns) Taft. The former was born in 1788, and had a family of six sons and one daughter. His father, Nathaniel, born in 1747, had a family of five sons, and his grandfather, Thomas, had but two sons. Thomas, Sr., born in 1708, had a family of four sons, and he in turn was one of the six sons of Robert Taft, who was born in 1693.

The boyhood of Nathaniel Taft passed in a quiet manner in the town of his birth, and when he was but twelve years of age he commenced working on a farm, where he remained for two years. The succeeding year he drove a stage at Waterford, after which he became foreman of construction in a large mill, where sash and blinds were manufactured, and here he had about one hundred men under him. He put in the engine and machinery, and afterward ran the former for four years. It was in 1854 that he commenced his railroad career, for five months being fireman on the Worcester & Nashua Railroad. He was then given charge of an engine, which he operated until coming to Port Jervis, October 12, 1856.

Mr. Taft's connection with the Erie Road began at the time of the great strike of 1856. Colonel Philips, President of the road with which he had been employed, had placed on exhibition at the Crystal Palace Exposition in New York an engine barrel-cutting machine, and had our subject run the engine for the same. Homer Ramsdell, who was President of what is now the Erie Road, came in to see the exhibition, and asked Colonel Philips for one hundred engineers on account of the strike. This was agreed to, and Mr. Taft was among the first of the new engineers to take the place of the striking ones. He assumed charge of No. 1, the day express, running to Susquehanna, and brought back No. 8, an eastbound day express. The first time that he ran over the road he had charge of this train, which had been formerly intrusted only to old and experienced men on this line. In 1861, near Hales Eddy, the engine was overturned, falling down

an embankment, as it had struck a broken rail, but Mr. Taft, who went over with the engine, came out unhurt. At another time, near Carrskock, the engine ran into a large boulder that had fallen from the hillside, and had the train capsized on the other side it would have gone down ninety feet into the Delaware; but as it turned out no one was injured. Again, he ran over a drawhead on the track at Pond Eddy; the trucks were carried away, and the engine crashed into the bluff. The fireman, Virgil Bell, jumped, and was killed by having his neck broken.

August 17, 1847, Mr. Taft and Mahala Daymon, of Rutland, Mass., were united in marriage. She is the daughter of Galen P. and Ann B. (Beeman) Daymon, who came to live with their daughter a year or so ago. The father died in October, 1894, aged eighty-eight years, but the mother is still living, though she has now reached the extreme old age of ninety-four years. Mr. and Mrs. Taft have had the following children: Sarah, now the wife of John J. Reeder, of Middletown, N. Y.; Jane Elizabeth, who died at the age of ten years; Emma A., wife of John F. Tozer, of Waverly, N. Y.; Leonard N., a grocer and real-estate man of Ridgewood, N. J.; Frances I., widow of George Heidenthal, who was an engineer in the employ of the Delaware Division; and William A., Postmaster and station and express agent at Passaic Bridge, in New Jersey. In 1890 Mr. Taft built his present residence at Matamoras, and has since continued to reside therein. He has twenty-one living grandchildren.

In company with his son, Mr. Taft started the first skating rink in this city some years ago. He has been identified with almost every social movement here for thirty-five years, and at one time was a member of thirteen social and benevolent organizations. Among those to which he now belongs is the Deerpark Historical Society; the Protective Legion, of which he is a charter member and Past President; the Royal Templars; the Odd Fellows' Society, and the Masonic fraternity. He is a Master Mason, and belongs to the Order of the Eastern Star. For years he has been connected with the Brotherhood of Locomotive Engineers. He is a man of strict temperance, never having used tobacco or liquor in any form. Politically his franchise is used in favor of the Republican party. He has hosts of warm friends, many of whom have known him for more than half his lifetime. His favorite engine, No. 38, which was made in the Susquehanna shops, he ran for fourteen years. At a meeting of the Master Mechanics and Railroad Superintendents held in Chicago at the time the railways were made standard gauge, this engine was chosen as the type of the most economical and durable one. A record had been kept of all engines in the United States, and this one, with Mr. Taft as its master, received the honor. On the Fourth of July, 1876, this engine was gorgeously decorated with Washington's portrait at the head, and a sixteen-inch brass cannon, which had been cast and completely finished by Mr. Taft, crowned the pilot and added to the jubilation by being fired occasionally.

FRANK G. KAIN, of Middletown, was born near Pine Bush, Ulster County, in 1869, and comes of an old family of that county, who were of Scotch descent. His father, Andrew Kain, was born on the old homestead, and married Miss Alvina Niver, who was born in the same vicinity, and who came of an old family of Holland-Dutch descent. They were the parents of ten children, seven of whom are yet living.

The subject of this sketch, who is the second of the family, continued on the home farm until sixteen years of age, in the mean time attending the district school and assisting in the farm work. At that age he was apprenticed to learn the carpenter's trade at Fishkill, under B. F. Hall, with whom he remained three years. He then took up the machinist's trade at Cornwall, under Holland Emslie, with whom he continued about one year, at the expiration of which time he went to Newburgh, where he was superintendent of the sash, door and blind factory of Little & Hamilton, New York parties, for eighteen months. In the spring of 1891 he came to Middletown, and engaged as a carpenter and machinist with

Linsey & Co., with whom he is yet connected. In the mean time he purchased about five acres of land from B. F. Lowe, which, in 1893, he had platted into forty building lots, the greater number of which he has disposed of. On the tract he has built six residences, all of which have been sold but one. He also purchased seventeen lots on the main part of Watkins Avenue, on some of which he built, and all of which have been sold. He does his own architect work, and has built on North Beacon Street, Royce Avenue and Watkins Avenue.

In February, 1893, at Middletown, Mr. Kain was united in marriage with Miss Anna Bennett, born in Circleville, Orange County, and a daughter of Oliver Bennett, a carpenter and builder, now residing in this city. Her mother was Emily Williams, who is a native of Sullivan County, as is also her father. Mrs. Kain was reared and educated in Middletown, and by her marriage has one child, Mildred. Mrs. Kain is a member of the Second Presbyterian Church, and in religious and benevolent work takes a special interest. In politics Mr. Kain is a Prohibitionist.

JAMES H. CLARK occupies an important place in the farming community of the town of Hamptonburgh, but as a veteran of the late war he is perhaps known best. He served for three years during the conflict, and participated in eighteen of its most important battles. His birth occurred in the town of Warwick, December 19, 1840, he being a son of David Clark, a native of the same place, and a grandson of Timothy, likewise a native of Orange County. The last-named was in turn the son of Timothy, Sr., whose birth occurred in New Jersey. The first of this branch of the family to make their home in America was one William Clark, an Englishman by birth. He chose Orange County for his future home, coming here at an early day.

The father of our subject married Miss Hannah Gilson, and to them were granted ten children, namely: Jehial, Joseph, Elizabeth, John, Sarah, George, James, Albert, Annie and one who died unnamed. Our subject was a lad of eight years when the family removed to the tract on which he is now residing. Here he grew to manhood and was educated. When ready to establish a home of his own, in 1872, he was married to Miss Cornelia Vandervort, and two children were born to them: Henry, who is attending the normal school at New Paltz; and one who died in infancy.

The property of which Mr. Clark is the owner comprises a quarter-section of valuable land, on which he has made very many improvements since it came into his possession. In July, 1862, he offered his services in support of his country's flag, and was mustered into Company E, New York Artillery, whence he was ordered to Virginia. The first engagement in which Mr. Clark participated was the battle of Winchester. Later he was with General Hunter on his raid, after which he was transferred to the command of General Sheridan, fighting under him in nearly every battle which took place in West Virginia. He was present at Maryland Heights during that conflict; then fought at Harper's Ferry September 14 and 15, 1862; Lexington, Va., June 12, 1864; Buchanan, Va., two days later; was again at Harper's Ferry, July 4; Maryland Heights the following day; Winchester, July 24; Martinsburg, the same month; Cedar Creek, August 12; Charlestown, August 21; Halltown, August 25; Barrysville, September 3; Winchester, September 19; Fisher's Hill, September 22; Cedar Creek, October 13; and again at the same place, October 19, 1864. He was mustered out of service at Harper's Ferry, October 19, 1865, with the title of Sergeant, and soon thereafter was honorably discharged.

After the establishment of peace Mr. Clark returned home and took up the pursuits of farm life, which he has followed with success ever since. He is a straightforward Republican in politics and holds membership with the Grand Army post at Goshen. In religious affairs he is a devoted member of the Presbyterian Church, and takes an active part in the work of the same. He possesses intelligent views on all subjects of general interest, particularly on political questions, and is held in high regard by all who know him.

DAVID H. SPRAGUE, M. D., engaged in the practice of his profession at Middletown, was born in Princess Bay, Richmond County, N. Y., December 7, 1863. Both his father, Edward, and grandfather, John Sprague, were natives of the same place. The latter was a merchant, and was of an old family residing there. Edward Sprague, the father, was engaged in the shipping business on Staten Island for many years of his life. He is still living there, but has retired from active business. His wife, Susan Journeay, the mother of our subject, was also born at Princess Bay, and is a daughter of Henderson Journeay, also of that place. Her great-grandfather, Dr. Journeay, was born there, and for many years was a physician on Staten Island. The family were French-Huguenots, and were among the earliest settlers of Staten Island. They were members of the Methodist Episcopal Church. To Edward and Susan Sprague two children were born, a son and a daughter.

Our subject received his primary education in the schools on Staten Island, which he attended until fifteen years of age, and then entered the Normal School at Geneseo, N. Y. Later he began the study of medicine with Dr. George C. Hubbard, of Tottenville, N. Y., and subsequently entered the medical department of the University of New York, from which he graduated in 1886, with the degree of M. D. He was then appointed by competitive examination to Bellevue Hospital, but refused the appointment, and was examined for the city hospital, where he spent two years. In order to prepare himself for the cure of nervous diseases, he received an appointment at Ward's Island, and also spent some time in the Bloomingdale Asylum and the Butler Hospital. He then went abroad and made a tour of

JOHN JESSUP.

the Continent, including England, Scotland, Germany, Austria, Belgium, France and Switzerland, spending some five or six months in travel and visiting all the noted hospitals in those countries. In November, 1889, in partnership with Dr. James F. Ferguson, he started the Falkirk Sanitarium at Central Valley, N. Y., purchasing ground and erecting two buildings. He continued in charge, in connection with outside practice, until October, 1894, when he located in Middletown and opened his present office at No. 58 North Street, where he is engaged in general practice. He is a member of the City Hospital Alumni Medical Society of New York City; the Orange County Medical Society; and of the National Neurological Society. Fraternally he is a member of Standard Lodge, F. & A. M., of Monroe; Jerusalem Chapter, R. A. M., of New York City; of Delaware Commandery, K. T., of Port Jervis; of Mecca Temple, Nobles of the Mystic Shrine, of New York City, being a Thirty-second degree Mason; and of the Schunnemunk Lodge, K. of P., at Highland Mills. In politics he is a Republican. As a physician he has a fine reputation, and is a successful practitioner. While he has resided at Middletown but a short time, he has already succeeded in building up a practice.

JOHN JESSUP, one of the well-to-do and prosperous farmers of Orange County, has long been a resident of the town of Goshen. His homestead comprises one hundred and forty acres of valuable land, all of which has been acquired by his industry and frugality. From time to time he has made good improvements, and the appearance of the farm reflects credit upon his energy and thrift.

The subject of this sketch was born in the town of Warwick, April 18, 1824, and is the only child of Peter Clows and Anna (Gobel) Jessup. The father, who was likewise born in Orange County, where all of his life was passed, was very suc-

cessful in his farming ventures, and his last years were spent in retirement, free from the cares of managing his estate. He died in 1876, loved and respected by all who knew him. His wife, who was born in Sussex County, N. J., was a most estimable and intelligent lady, and aided him greatly in attaining his high position among the well-to-do residents of the county. She survived him four years, passing away in 1880. On his mother's side our subject is related to the Edsall family of Sussex County, N. J., who were among the first and most prominent residents of that portion of the state.

Mr. Jessup's advantages for obtaining an education were limited to the district school, where he gained a fair knowledge of the common branches taught. No pains, however, were spared in training him in farm work, and very early in life he performed his share of the labors on the homestead. Agriculture has been his life work, and he has made of it a success, so that now, in the closing years of his life, he can live in ease and comfort. The place is nicely improved with a neat set of farm buildings, and the residence, which is one of the finest in the town, is situated on an eminence some distance from the road. Mr. Jessup devotes the greater part of his time to dairy farming, not, however, to the neglect of grain-raising, as he has many acres from which he garners in an abundant harvest.

Miss Harriet Thorne Sayer, who became the wife of our subject October 5, 1848, was the daughter of William and Martha (Jackson) Sayer, and was born in the town of Goshen. Her education was gained in the district school, where she became well informed, and she trained her children to good and useful lives. Her family comprised three members, of whom the eldest, Henry H., died when three years old. William Sayer is at home; and Anna married Joel W. Houston, a prominent farmer of the town of Warwick.

The wife of our subject, who died in January, 1894, was a devoted member of the Presbyterian Church which meets at Goshen, and in the work of which she took an active part. Mr. Jessup has always affiliated with the Republican party.

All his life he has been a practical, industrious farmer, and a citizen who could be relied upon to advance any measure for the improvement and upbuilding of the community.

ANIEL B. SWEENEY, proprietor of Sweeney's Bottling Works, and manufacturer of soft drinks, is a native of Middletown, born October 27, 1864, and is a son of Miles and Margaret (Bradley) Sweeney, both of whom are natives of County Donegal, Ireland. When a youth of sixteen, Miles Sweeney came to the United States and located in New York City, where he was employed in Worley's Saw Works, and later, at the solicitation of the late Senator Madden, came to Middletown, where he was engaged in the first saw works started in this city. Until 1885 he had charge of the grinding and glazing department, and then, on account of ill-health, he was compelled to resign the position. One year later he died, at the age of forty years. His wife, Margaret Bradley, was a daughter of Daniel Bradley, a farmer in Goshen. She died in 1877, leaving five children: Margaret and Bridget, of Middletown; Miles, of Philadelphia, Pa.; Daniel B., our subject; and Joseph W., who makes his home with our subject.

Daniel B. Sweeney grew to manhood in his native city, and attended the First Ward School, completing his education at Wallkill Academy. On leaving school he entered the bottling works of W. F. C. Bastian, where he remained one year. At the age of sixteen he was an apprentice in the employ of the Eagle File Works, to learn the trade of file manufacturing. After completing his apprenticeship he resigned his position and was employed in the Cohalan Bottling Works. In 1887, in partnership with C. R. Smith, he purchased the works, and the business was continued under the firm name of Smith & Sweeney until May, 1895, when the partnership was dissolved, Mr. Sweeney retaining the works. He is now sole proprietor, and is located at Prince and Montgomery Streets, where he occupies a two-story and basement building, which has a frontage of one hundred feet and a depth of forty feet. Steam power is employed, and all kinds of sodas and soft drinks are manufactured. Mr. Sweeney also manufactures his own flavors. His icehouse has a capacity of two hundred tons, and two wagons are employed in conveying his manufactures to the railroad depots and local places of business. His trade extends over a radius of forty miles, and Mr. Sweeney himself travels over Orange, Sullivan and Ulster Counties. The Sweeney Bottling Works is the largest of its kind in the city and its capacity is unlimited.

April 26, 1892, Mr. Sweeney was united in marriage with Miss Mary McAloon, who is a native of Glenwood, Pa., and a daughter of Charles McAloon, now of Middletown. They have one child, Miles, and the family residence is at No. 54 Montgomery Street. Mr. Sweeney is a member of St. Joseph's Catholic Church, and of Division No. 1, A. O. H., of Middletown, of which he has been President for the last six years. He is also an honorary member of McQuoid Engine Company No. 3, of which he was Vice-President one term. In politics he is a Democrat. In 1894 he was Chairman of the Democratic City Committee and was re-elected in 1895, but resigned. He is a charter member of the Middletown branch of the New York Co-operative Banking and Building Association, and is also a member of the Columbus Club.

AVID P. WAGER, manager of C. W. Martin's blue-stone business at Middletown, was born near Cripple Bush, in Ulster County, December 25, 1849. The family is of German descent, his grandfather, Jonathan Wager, having emigrated from Germany to America in early manhood, and, after a short sojourn in Dutchess County, settled in Ulster County, where he engaged in farming until his death. He was a pioneer of the county, and made a farm out of the wilderness. His wife was also a native of Germany.

The father of our subject, David Wager, was born in Ulster County, and in early life learned the trades of mason and blacksmith, which he followed in addition to farming. He had a stone-shop, also a stone residence, which is still standing, though now over one hundred and thirty years old. His death occurred in 1862. when he was sixty-one years old. In religious belief he was identified with the Reformed Church. His wife, who was a Miss Pahlon, died in 1850, when David P. was eighteen months old. There were ten children in the family, of whom eight arrived at years of maturity, and four are living, all sons. One of them, Henry, was a member of the One Hundred and Twentieth New York Infantry, in which he served first as Sergeant and later for two years as Captain.

David P., who was the youngest of the children, was reared in Ulster County until thirteen years of age. His father dying about that time, he was forced to begin in life for himself. He started out for himself with a capital of $2.50, but with an abundance of determination and perseverance. Securing work with a carpenter, he remained with him about two years. In 1864 he went West, traveling through Canada, Michigan and Illinois, and spending two years in these various places. Returning to New York, he followed his trade for two years, then went to Pike County, Pa., where he worked for eighteen months. On again coming back to Ulster County, he began work as a stone-cutter, which trade he followed later in Chenango, Sullivan and Pike Counties. While in Sullivan County, he not only followed that occupation, but also carried on a grocery business at what is now Mountaindale. Afterward he clerked in a store at Ellenville.

In 1887 Mr. Wager came to Middletown and started in the retail blue and building stone business. In 1894 he sold out to C. W. Martin, with whom he continues as manager. While he was in business, he furnished the stone for the Todd, Central and Poppino Buildings, the Linden Avenue Schoolhouse, and did considerable work on the State Asylum, having the principal business of the kind in the city. Meantime he also carried on a hardware store on North Street, and

later had a grocery store on James Street. At present he is interested in the Mt. Adams Granite Company. During his active business career he has opened several quarries in Sullivan, Ulster and Pike Counties.

In Sullivan County, Mr. Wager married Miss Rozella Oliver, a native of Ulster County. They have five children, all at home, and named as follows: Leslie, Alva, Estella, Myra and Ethel. Socially Mr. Wager is connected with Ellenville Lodge No. 582, F. & A. M. Politically he supports Democratic principles, and is interested in everything pertaining to the success of his party.

<<+++++++++++++◉+++++++++++++>>

O. CARPENTER, a wholesale, retail and manufacturing confectioner of Middletown, was born in Monticello, Sullivan County, August 25, 1864. His grandfather, Nathaniel H. Carpenter, who was born near Thompsonville, Sullivan County, was a carpenter by trade, but has followed farming principally; now, however, he is living retired in Monticello. He is of Scotch and English descent. His son, Branson Carpenter, was born near Greenfield, Ulster County, and in his youth learned the carpenter's trade in Monticello, where he is now successfully engaged in contracting and building. He married Lucyette Culver, a native of Niagara County, N. Y., and daughter of Sylvester Culver, a farmer, who was also born in Niagara County. Three children were born unto them, two of whom are yet living: O. O., our subject; and George S., a traveling salesman for the latter.

The subject of this sketch was the second child in the parental family. He was reared in his native town, and received his primary education in the public schools of that place. He then attended the academy, and later took a business course at the Christie Business College at Lock Haven, Pa. On completing his course, he learned the carpenter's trade with his father, and also studied architecture. In 1887 he came to Middletown, and entered the employ of Linsey Brothers, with whom he continued two years, working at his trade. He then purchased the confectionery establishment of J. F. Colby, on James Street, and remained in that location for three years, in the mean time enlarging the business. The old location becoming too small for his trade, he removed to his present location in the Central Building, at No. 109 North Street. The main storeroom is 24x85 feet, with a basement the same size, in which he manufactures ice cream and confectionery, and part of which is used as a packing-room The power is furnished by a gas engine of eight horse-power. The business has constantly increased, until at present his trade extends throughout Orange and adjoining counties and into New Jersey. He has the largest ice-cream jobbing business, as well as retail business, in the city, and has a capacity of turning out five hundred gallons per day. His brother, George S., is constantly on the road, selling the manufactures of this establishment.

Mr. Carpenter was married, in Middletown, to Miss Carrie L. Kinnie, a native of this place, and they have three children: Harry C., Albert Branson and Percy. Religiously Mr. Carpenter is a member of the Methodist Episcopal Church, of which he has been Trustee. In politics he is a Republican. As a business man he is very popular, and has been very successful in the six years in which he has been engaged in business.

GEORGE STORCH is the oldest resident German citizen of Middletown, and has the finest and most complete fruit farm of any in this vicinity. He is a native of Germany, born at Hesse-Cassel, May 2, 1825. His father, Nicholaus, and his grandfather, Andreas, were also natives of the same place, and the latter was a cabinet-maker by trade, and served in the army with Napoleon. The father, Nicholaus Storch, was a mason and plasterer by trade, and died at the age of about fifty years. He married Anna Catherine Wetel, also a native of the same country, and who died at the age of sixty-five years,

leaving two children: Casper, and the subject of our sketch. The former resided in Middletown for some years, and here died in 1893.

George Storch, our subject, was reared in his native land, and when fourteen years of age was apprenticed as a buckle-maker, and continued with his employer there until twenty-six years of age. He married Miss Annie Christina Schmidt in 1849. She was a native of that country. In 1854 he brought his family to the United States, leaving Bremen on the sailing-vessel '' Martha,'' and after a voyage of seven weeks they landed at New York City, from which place they came direct to Middletown. Upon arriving here he found nothing.at his trade, and so sought employment in other lines. He secured employment with Wheeler, Madden & Clemson, in the tempering department of their machine-shop, where for twenty-nine years and six months he did all the tempering for the firm. He then resigned his position to live a more retired life. He first purchased two acres in the brush, which was in a wild state, and here built a residence and commenced the improvement of the place. At the present time every foot of ground is occupied, and on the place can be found almost every kind of fruit suitable for this latitude, including the largest vineyard in Middletown, together with more currants, gooseberries and pears than are raised by any other one person. During the war, Mr. Storch went to Rock Island, Ill., but remained there only seven weeks, and then returned to the sawshops at Middletown.

Mr. and Mrs. Storch became the parents of ten children, seven of whom grew to maturity, and six of whom are yet living: Mary, deceased; Carrie, residing at home; Lena, now Mrs. Klohs, of Middletown; Louisa Emma, Mrs. A. H. Loebs, of Rochester, N. Y.; and Amelia and Eliza, at home. Ann died at twenty-four years of age. Fraternally Mr. Storch is a member of Luther Lodge, I. O. O. F., of which he is a charter member, and also of the Knights of Honor. In national politics he is a Democrat, but in local matters votes as his conscience dictates. Religiously the family are Presbyterians.

W. H. Groo.

HON. WILLIAM JAY GROO. In perusing the record of the life of Judge Groo, one is impressed by the magnitude of his interests and the extent of his influence. As a citizen, as a professional man, and as an official, he has discharged every duty faithfully and well. He is now engaged, and for many years has been, in the active practice of law, having his office at No. 111 Broadway, New York, though his home is still in the city of Middletown, where he has resided since 1866.

The Groo family was represented among the earliest settlers of Sullivan County, N. Y., and from there the Judge's grandfather, Samuel, went forth to battle in his country's defence during the Revolution. His parents, Samuel, Jr., and Mercy (Tuttle) Groo, were natives of the town of Neversink, Sullivan County, the former born February 20, 1792, and the latter June 1, 1798. Of their marriage, which took place in 1814, the following-named children were born: David C., Sarah, Phebe, Nancy, John, Katharine, Isaac and William J. The only survivors besides the Judge are David C. and Katharine. The father, who followed agricultural pursuits, died in the town of Neversink at the age of forty-one.

The maternal grandfather of our subject was Selleck Tuttle, a member of a family that has become numerous in this country. Some years ago there was published a work giving a history of the different branches of the family, many of whom have become prominent in different professions. The paternal grandfather of our subject, who, as above stated, served in the Colonial army, died at the age af seventy-five. His wife, who bore the maiden name of Susanna Brooks, died at the age of sixty.

William Jay, who was the youngest of the family, was born in the town of Neversink, Sullivan County, September 9, 1831, and was only eighteen months old when his father died. At an early age he began to work upon the farm, while the winter seasons were devoted to study in the district schools. At the age of seventeen, with the means obtained by hard work, he entered a private school in Fallsburg, Sullivan County, where he was under the preceptorship of Henry

R. Low, afterward State Senator. The acquaintance thus formed ripened into a warm friendship, which terminated only with the Senator's death in 1888. After a year spent in that school he began to teach, in which way he gained the funds for continuing his education, and subsequently completed his studies at Monticello Academy. Having decided to enter the legal profession, in 1852 he entered the office of Gen. A. C. Niven, at Monticello, and was admitted to the Bar in 1855, receiving at the time from the examining committee a complimentary notice for having answered every question absolutely correctly. Before being admitted to the Bar he was appointed Deputy County Clerk, and continued to fill that office until 1854, when, upon the death of Philander Waring, the County Clerk, he succeeded to the position. At the close of the term he gave half of the net proceeds to Mrs. Waring, widow of the deceased clerk.

In the fall of 1856 Mr. Groo was elected to the office of District Attorney, and in that capacity he served for three years. He was formerly a Douglas Democrat, but immediately upon the outbreak of the Rebellion he espoused the Union cause, and subsequently became a Republican. When the statement is made that the county was strongly Democratic, it will be at once seen that he was influenced by no personal motives in making the change. In 1864 he was the delegate from his district to the Republican National Convention, and cast his ballot for the re-nomination of President Lincoln. His choice for Vice-President was Lyman Tremain, but Andrew Johnson finally received the nomination. While still a resident of Sullivan County, Governor Morgan appointed him one of the three Commissioners of Public Accounts, and he served in that position two years, when the pressure of other duties induced him to resign.

A few years after coming to Middletown, our subject was elected special Judge of Orange County, in the fall of 1868, running several hundred ahead of his ticket. While active in the Republican party, he used every effort to induce the leaders of that organization to legislate for the suppression of the manufacture and sale of intoxicating liquors. It was his opinion then, and to that principle he has since adhered, that the saloon is a greater evil than even human slavery ever was, and he had hoped that the party which had abolished the one would suppress the other; but when the local option bill was vetoed by Governor Dix, he saw clearly that all hopes in this direction were vain. The same conscientiousness which had led him to leave the Democratic party now caused him to become a Prohibitionist. In 1873 he united his influence with that party, and has ever since advocated its principles. In 1876 he was their candidate for Governor, and in 1886 was nominated for Judge of the Court of Appeals, at which time he received the largest number of votes ever polled for a Prohibition candidate up to that time, being thirty-six thousand four hundred and thirty-seven. Twice he served as Chairman of the Prohibition State Convention, three times was a delegate to the national convention, and in 1888 was Chairman of the New York delegation.

From the "Cotemporary Biography of New York," we quote the following: "Judge Groo has been an active worker in the temperance cause, devoting time and energy to its advancement, and assisting with other leaders in the movement to build up such a party as shall eventually triumph at the polls, and bring about that needed reform of which the grave necessity is admitted, even by those who do not uphold this means of its accomplishment. He is a platform orator of marked ability, and, gifted as he is with unusual rhetorical powers, a pleasing manner, together with a clear, argumentative faculty, his utterances have carried strong conviction to the minds of many of his hearers."

In one of the editorials of a local paper, we notice the following: "As a trial lawyer Judge Groo is eminently successful. In the management of a case he is cautious, yet at the same time bold and brilliant, always eager and watchful to protect his client's interests, and yet fair to his adversary. Always deeply impressed himself with the justice of any cause which he consents to espouse, he throws the weight of his personal convictions into the advocacy of his client's cause,

and wins his case as well by his manifest sincerity as by his professional skill and ability. Since he has been at the Orange County Bar he has tried many cases for other attorneys, and in his practice has been associated with, or pitted against, such men as Charles H. Winfield, Stephen W. Fullerton, David F. Gedney, Charles F. Brown and Lewis E. Carr."

In everything pertaining to the welfare of Middletown, Judge Groo is deeply interested, and the securing of the New York & Oswego Midland (now the New York, Ontario & Western) Railroad for the city was largely aided by his efforts. His connection with that enterprise may be judged from the following extracts from a letter written in 1891 by Hon. D. C. Littlejohn, former President of the Midland Road, in response to a request from a correspondent of the *Argus* as to the influences that were instrumental in locating the road at Middletown on its way to New York: "Of course it would be difficult at this late day to refer to all the circumstances that bore upon the question, but I remember distinctly that there was much opposition to going to Middletown, because of the cost of tunneling Shawangunk Mountain. * * * * I also remember well that at a meeting held by the Directors at Syracuse, among other things, the question of location of the road at Middletown was considered and virtually determined. A committee of prominent citizens from that village (H. H. Hunt, William Evans, M. Lewis Clark, John A. Wallace, William J. Groo and J. H. Norton) came before us, and Judge Groo addressed the board in behalf of the committee. The claims of Middletown, with its prospective growth and importance, as well as the great advantage to accrue to the company by locating its road there, were referred to and dwelt upon in a manner that had great weight with the Board of Directors. It is my candid opinion that, to that committee, more than to any other influence, is due the credit of having secured the location of the Midland Railroad at Middletown."

Fluent and gifted as a public speaker, Judge Groo's services are often called into requisition in that capacity. On the occasion of the centennial celebration of the battle of Minisink, July 22,

1879, on the scene of that conflict, he was the orator of the day, delivering an address that was afterward published. Space forbids any extensive quotations, but we take the following extracts from the oration: "One hundred years ago to-day, on the spot where we are assembled, now in the town of Highland, Sullivan County, N. Y., forty-five brave men gave up their lives at the call of duty and for the protection of their homes. If it be true, as some believe, that the spirits of the departed are conscious of the conduct of the living, we may well suppose that all who were present on that ever memorable day are now witnessing with the deepest interest our proceedings. May this thought inspire us to the utterance of such words as shall fitly commemorate their deeds. We are not here to simply express our admiration of the men who were killed in the battle of Minisink, but of all who fought in that engagement. Death has now overtaken them all, and we must remember and recognize the fact that he who survives the performance of a great duty ought to be awarded equal praise with him who loses his life before the contest is ended. * * * * The event we have been considering, although of local importance, was but a ripple on the bloody waters of revolution, then struggling on toward the broad bay of independence. Three years and eighteen days only had passed since from Independence Hall had been proclaimed that sublime declaration 'that all men are created equal.' This truth is the bed-rock upon which republican Government rests, and without its recognition no people can enjoy the full measure of human liberty regulated by law. The immortal fifty-six who signed the Declaration of Independence also expressed their 'firm reliance on the protection of Divine Providence.' Thus it will be seen that faith in God and the brotherhood of man are the two great principles that gave life to this nation—the lungs into which the infant Republic first breathed the vitalizing air of freedom."

On the occasion of the unveiling of the soldiers' and sailors' monument at Monticello, September 5, 1895, Judge Groo delivered the presentation speech, from which we quote as follows: "It seems eminently proper and praiseworthy that monuments like this should be erected to honor and perpetuate the memory of those who were in the military and naval service of their country. It stimulates and enhances patriotism and local pride; more than that, it manifests a just appreciation of the achievements of subordinate officers and private soldiers. The names of great commanders appear upon the pages of history, and are perpetuated in imposing mausoleums, so that their deeds will be remembered by a grateful people as long as the country they served so well shall endure. But it was the valor, the constancy, the strict obedience to orders of all subordinates, and especially the firm step and steady aim in battle of the private soldier that overcame the enemy and achieved the great victories which have added luster to American arms. From this platform and in this presence we proclaim honor to the private soldiers. They responded to their country's call, not moved by the paltry wages offered, but, prompted by the spirit of patriotism, they went forth to defend the Flag and preserve the Government to which, in its inception, their ancestors had solemnly pledged their lives, their fortune and their sacred honor."

Judge Groo is a member of St. Paul's Methodist Episcopal Church, and served as Chairman of the Board of Trustees and Building Committee. The elegant edifice, erected at a cost of $50,000, was materially aided by his efforts, and in addition to $2,800 personally contributed, he secured $2,200 from friends outside of the church. In 1872 he was one of the two lay delegates from the New York Conference to the General Conference of the church held in Brooklyn. By that conference he was chosen Vice-President of the Freedman's Aid Society. He has been connected with the church since September 9, 1866, and is recognized as one of its most valued members.

December 31, 1855, Judge Groo married Sarah G., only child of David and Margaret (Graham) Lines, of Monticello, N. Y. Her father was of New England stock, and her mother of Irish descent. Mrs. Groo was a lady of great beauty of face and character, and her death, May 12, 1870, was deeply mourned. Six children were born of this union, of whom Mary, Lines, Katharine and William Jay are still living. Mary and Lines were taught at home by their mother until the former was sent to Dr. Van Norman's school in New York City, and the latter to an academy in Delaware County, N. Y. Katharine was educated in the public schools and academy at Middletown. William J. was for some time a student in Hartwell's Seminary, and is now engaged in railroad work near Pittsburg, Pa. Mary married Rev. John T. Hargrave, now rector of Trinity Church, New Haven, Pa. Lines married Carrie E. Peters, of Lehighton, Pa., and they now reside at Bayonne, N. J. Katharine married John L. Wiggins, a lawyer of Middletown.

The present wife of Judge Groo, with whom he was united February 25, 1873, was Mary F., only daughter of David J. M. and Elmira (Lathrop) Sloat. Seven children were born unto this union, of whom Fannie, a remarkably sweet and bright child, died December 24, 1880. The others are as follows: Saidee B., Elmira Lathrop, Pearl, Lillian Lathrop, Frances Willard and Stanley, all at home. Mrs. Groo is a lady of unusual strength of character and intelligence, and has taken an active part in temperance work, having for many years served as President of the Woman's Christian Temperance Union of Middletown, which office she still fills. The Judge has been identified with almost all the temperance societies that have existed in New York for the last thirty years, among them the Sons of Temperance, Good Templars and Royal Templars of Temperance. His has been a busy and useful life, and he retains, though past life's prime, the energy, indomitable will and force of character that have ever been among his prominent personal attributes.

F. W. MATTHEWS, a contractor and builder of Middletown, was born in Andes, Delaware County, in 1848. His father, Thomas S. Matthews, was also a native of that county, and there died at the age of seventy-three years. By occupation he was a farmer, and followed that calling almost his entire life, but for a time was engaged as a buyer and speculator in lumber.

Politically he was a Democrat. He married Sarah J. Gregory, who was also born in the town of Andes, Delaware County, and was a daughter of Richard Gregory, likewise a native of Delaware County. Her father died in that county many years ago. During the War of 1812 he served his country faithfully as a soldier. To Thomas S. and Sarah J. Matthews were born eight children: Richard, who served in several different regiments during the late war, and is now a contractor and builder in Polo, Ill.; Charles, who served in the One Hundred and Forty-fourth New York Infantry during the Civil War, and now resides in Washington; Rensselaer, of Otsego County, N. Y.; Sylvester, a farmer and horse-trainer in Otsego County; Hannah, also residing in Otsego County; Phœbe, residing in Sullivan County; and James M., residing in Delaware County.

The subject of this sketch remained on the home farm until twenty years of age and received but a limited education in the schools of his native county. While generally employed at farm work, he also for a time worked at the carpenter's trade. On leaving home he began work at that trade as a journeyman, and two months later became the junior member of the firm of Shaeffer & Matthews, contractors and builders in Delaware County. He subsequently located at Walton, from which place he removed to Delhi, where he continued contracting and building for three years. He then returned to Walton and engaged in the flour and grain business, erecting there a small elevator with a capacity of ten thousand bushels. He purchased and shipped grain from the West all over Pennsylvania, New York and New Jersey, doing both a wholesale and retail business. For a time he ran a flour and feed mill, and in the three years in which he was engaged in business was quite successful. Later he sold out, and in 1887 removed to Binghamton, where he intended starting in the wholesale grain and produce business, but the competition was so great he abandoned the idea and resumed contracting and building. While residing in that place he built some large blocks, including that of Regan & McHale, and many fine residences.

JAMES H. SARVIS.

In 1892 he came to Middletown and entered the employ of Lindsey Bros., where he remained five or six months, when the firm failed. He then engaged in contracting and building for himself, and has continued in the business with good success. His shop and office are located on the corner of Prospect Street and Wickham Avenue, and his residence at No. 3 Linden Block.

While still residing in Delaware County Mr. Matthews was united in marriage with Miss Mary Neish, a native of that county. Two children have been born to them, Earl S. and Helen. While residing at Walton, Mr. Matthews was made a member of the Independent Order of Red Men, but does not at present hold membership with the order. Mrs. Matthews is a member of the Methodist Episcopal Church.

JAMES H. SARVIS. This well known citizen of Newburgh traces his ancestry to illustrious forefathers, who took an active part in the early wars of our country. His maternal grandfather, who was a valiant soldier in the War of 1812, was a son of Gen. Joseph Warren, of Revolutionary fame. The latter was born in Roxbury, Mass., June 11, 1741, and died at the battle of Bunker Hill, June 17, 1775. The family history in America can be traced back to the year 1659, when the name of Peter Warren appears on the town records of Boston as a mariner.

General Warren was graduated from Harvard College in 1759, and the following year was appointed master of the Roxbury School. He studied medicine with Dr. James Lloyd, and began to practice his profession in 1764. The passage of the stamp act the next year led him to publish several able articles in the Boston *Gazette*, and brought him into prominence as one of the supporters of the American cause. He was Chairman of the Committee of Safety, also served as President of the Provincial Congress that met at Watertown May 31, 1775, and thus became the chief executive officer of Massachusetts under the Provincial Government. June 14 he was chosen Major-General of the Massachusetts forces, and

three days later he was at Bunker Hill. It is said that both General Putnam and General Prescott successively signified their readiness to take orders from him, but he refused, and in the final struggle, when he was endeavoring to rally the militia, he was struck in the head by a musket-ball and instantly killed.

On the paternal side our subject traces his lineage to Holland. His paternal grandfather, John Jarvis (as the name was then spelled) came to America in early manhood and settled in Orange County, purchasing a large tract of land in Newburgh Town, where he remained until his death, at ninety-six years. He was a member of the Dutch Reformed Church. The house which he erected is still standing, being now occupied by his son Harvey.

The father of our subject, William Sarvis, was born in the town of Newburgh, and engaged in farming until 1842, when he removed to the city and embarked in the wholesale and retail fish business near the ferry. His trade was large, and he owned a number of boats and fishing outfits, having men constantly employed in fishing on the Hudson. His death occurred in 1884, when he was eighty-six years old. Politically he was a Democrat. His wife, whose maiden name was Mary Warren, was born in Marlborough, Ulster County, and died in the spring of 1894, aged ninety years.

Of the seven sons and two daughters of William Sarvis, we note the following: Lockwood, who died in Newburgh, was a member of the Fifty-sixth New York Infantry during the Civil War. John is a resident of Newburgh. William, deceased, served during the war as a member of the Nineteenth New York Infantry. Charles lives in Newburgh. James H., our subject, was born in the town of Newburgh, May 4, 1840. Daniel, who served throughout the entire period of the war, belonged to the Thirty-sixth New York Infantry, and now resides in Newburgh. George died in this city. Mary J. is the wife of George Mapes, of Newburgh. Josephine, deceased, was Mrs. George Mould.

From the age of three years our subject was reared in Newburgh, where he attended the Clinton Street and high schools. In 1855 he shipped on a sailing vessel that plied between Newburgh and Albany, and afterward was on various seagoing vessels in the coasting trade. Becoming an expert navigator, he was promoted to be first mate and then captain. While serving as captain of the "John R. Brick," a Hudson River sailing-vessel, he resigned, in July, 1862, to enter the Union army. He entered as a private in Company L, Nineteenth New York Infantry, and later was promoted to the Corporal's rank, his service being principally in Maryland.

Returning home at the expiration of his period of service, Mr. Sarvis entered the employ of Benjamin B. Odell in the ice business, and when the concern was merged into the Muchattoes Lake Ice Company, he remained with it as superintendent, filling that position for twenty-four years. When, in the spring of 1887, Mr. Odell was elected Mayor, he appointed Mr. Sarvis Chief of Police, and in that capacity he served until July, 1894. During his term of office he succeeded in breaking up the bridge bandits, and made a number of difficult arrests, among which were those of the infamous Thomas O'Brien and Red Orson. At present he has a forty-two-foot steam launch, a twenty-five-foot naphtha launch, and about forty small boats on Orange Lake, from the lease of which he derives a good income. He also owns a residence, a small summer hotel and boat houses at the lake.

The first wife of Mr. Sarvis was Susan M. Vredenburgh, who died in Newburgh, after having become the mother of four children, viz.: Jennie, Mrs. A. C. Smith; Mary, Mrs. Daniel Smith; James, who is connected with the West Shore Road at Kingston; and Frank, who is superintendent for a railroad contractor in Brooklyn. The second marriage of Mr. Sarvis united him with Miss Flora M. Bennett, who was born in Norfolk, Va., being a daughter of Richard Bennett, a farmer of the Old Dominion. They have three children: Flora M., who is married and resides in Newburgh; and Henry and Grace, who are with their parents.

In 1885-86 Mr. Sarvis was Almshouse Commissioner, but resigned upon being appointed

Chief of Police. When the Seventeenth Battalion of the National Guard was organized, he became a member of Company E, and was elected Corporal. He won the prize for the best marksman in the battalion, and was a member of the battalion team of marksmen that won the championship of the brigade. He is considered the best rifle-shot in the county, and his skill in that direction has brought him considerable local prominence. Socially he is a member of Ellis Post No. 52, G. A. R., the Veterans' Association or the Order of American Firemen, and the Veterans' Association of the fire department. A staunch Republican, he has been a member of city and county committees for thirty-five years, and is regarded as one of the most efficient workers of his party.

<hr/>

ANDREW J. BELL has been very active in the building up of the city of Middletown, and has erected many of the most substantial dwelling and business houses in the city. He was born near Syracuse, Onondaga County, in February, 1824, and is of Irish descent. His grandfather, John Bell, was a native of Ireland, and came over as a soldier in the English army under General Wolf, and was present when Quebec was taken by the Americans and when the General was killed. After the war he located in Schenectady, N. Y., where he was engaged in farming. Later he went to Onondaga County, and there died at an advanced age. His son, Joseph Bell, the father of our subject, was born in Schenectady, N. Y., and was by occupation a farmer. He there died at about the age of seventy-five years. Religiously he was a member of the Methodist Episcopal Church. He married Nancy Marcellus, who was born in Montgomery County, and who died at the age of seventy-five years. Of their family of two daughters and seven sons, only two are now living.

The subject of this sketch was the youngest in his family, and was reared on a farm, receiving only the advantages of a common-school education. When seventeen years old he was apprenticed to learn the trade of a carpenter at Preble, Cortland County, N. Y., where he remained two years, and then went to Syracuse and worked at his trade there for five years. From Syracuse he went to Washington, D. C., and during his residence there saw all the great men of that day, including Daniel Webster, Thomas H. Benton, Henry Clay and others. He next went to Boston, Mass., and then to Providence, R. I., and in 1847 went to Missouri, via the Ohio River, and up the Mississippi and the Missouri to Ft. Independence, where he located and worked at his trade. After remaining there a short time, he went through Arkansas, Texas and Louisiana, traveling principally by boat and on horseback. In all, he spent about five years in the West and South, and then returned and located in Monticello, Sullivan County, where he engaged in the wagon-making trade for ten years. He next removed to Thompsonville, where he engaged in the lumber trade and hotel business, in all about three years. While in Thompsonville he was also engaged in the manufacture of lumber of all kinds. Bloomingburg was his next place of operation. There he engaged in wagon-making, manufacturing the Bell Wagon, which at one time was well known throughout the entire state. He remained at Bloomingburg from 1865 until the spring of 1888, when he located in Middletown, purchased a lot, and built the residence at No. 295 North Street. Later he purchased lots and built over thirty residences, among them being fourteen on North Street, of which he now owns only one; three on Linden Terrace, of which all are sold; seven on Cottage Street, of which he yet owns three; two on Wisner Avenue, one yet remaining in his possession. He built and owns Nicholson's Hall on North Street, the first floor being used as a hall and the upper floor as flats.

Mr. Bell was united in marriage in 1853, at Bloomingburg, with Miss Mary Sinsabaugh, who was born there. They have one child grown to manhood, Marcellus S., who is engaged with his father in carpentering. In politics Mr. Bell is a Democrat, and is at present on the Democratic County Central Committee, and was on the old city and county committee until 1893. While

residing in Sullivan County he was nominated for the Assembly, but declined to make the race. In the councils of his party he has been very active and has served as a delegate of the county, congressional and state conventions. He is an out-and-out free-thinker, of the Bob Ingersoll stripe. In business he has been fairly successful, and in addition to his property interests is a stockholder in the Co-operative Store, also a stockholder in the Casino Theatre.

BUNO MUSBACH, slate, tin and metal roofer, and proprietor of the Midway Park Restaurant, was born in Langensalza, Thuringia, Saxony, April 1, 1865, and is the son of Christian Musbach, also a native of that country. He remained at home until eighteen years of age, attending school until fourteen, and then learning the trade of roofer under his father. In 1883 he came to Middletown and started in business alone. Two years later he entered into partnership with Alexander Bennett, under the firm name of Bennett & Musbach, but since the dissolution of the partnership Mr. Musbach has continued alone. Specimens of his work may be seen all over Middletown, including the Armory, State Hospital, Wickham Avenue Depot, and nearly all the business blocks that are covered with slate. Not only in Middletown, but throughout Orange County, including the schoolhouse at Goshen, may his work be seen. He has also done considerable work in Monticello, Sullivan County. During the busy seasons of the year he employs from twelve to fifteen men.

In July, 1895, Mr. Musbach became proprietor of the Midway Park Restaurant, which is beautifully located on Wallkill River. It has a frontage of over four hundred feet, and is sufficiently large to accommodate the immense crowds that assemble during the heated period of the year to enjoy the cooling breezes of the Wallkill. The resort has every convenience necessary to the comfort and well-being of its patrons, and the restaurant has a seating capacity of sixteen hundred people. The buildings are well planned and handsomely furnished, and are lighted by electricity.

Mr. Musbach was married in Middletown to Miss Mary L. Goldsmith, who was born in the town of Wallkill. Fraternally he is a member of Luther Lodge No. 380, having twice passed all the chairs, and has been a representative to the Grand Lodge of the state. He is also a member of Hoffman Lodge, F. & A. M.

CHARLES SCHWARTZ, dealer in fresh and salt meat at No. 21 West Main Street, Middletown, has been more than ordinarily successful. He was born in Halle, Wurtemberg, Germany, June 18, 1856. His father, Frederick Schwartz, was also a native of that place, and was engaged in the butcher and meat business there for many years. He married Lena Collins, born in Wurtemberg, where she died in 1878. The father died there in 1876, at the age of sixty-seven years. They were both devout members of the Lutheran Church. They were the parents of seven children, who grew to maturity, and four of that number are now living in America. One son, Christopher, now residing in Middletown, and engaged with our subject, was a member of a New York regiment during the late war. William, another son, also resides in Middletown, and was formerly in partnership with our subject; Sophia, now Mrs. Cochenderfer, resides in New York City.

The subject of this sketch was reared in his native country, and until the age of fourteen attended the common schools, and then entered the high school and took the Latin and French courses. Under his father he thoroughly learned the meat business, and continued in his father's shop until 1873, when he resolved to come to the United States; first, in order that he might better himself in life, and secondly, that he might escape military duty, which every able-bodied man was required to do in that country. He left Hamburg on the steamer "Harmony," and after a

voyage of fourteen days landed at New York, from which place he came directly to Middletown, and entered the employ of his brother Christopher, who was here engaged in the meat business. In 1882, having applied himself too closely to business, he found it necessary to recuperate, and therefore left the shop and entered Eastman's Business College, from which he subsequently graduated. In 1883, in company with his brother William, he engaged in the meat business, the firm being styled Schwartz Bros., and the location on East Main Street. For three years they continued in that location, and then removed to No. 21 West Main Street. The partnership of the brothers was continued until 1893, when our subject purchased the interest of his brother, and has since conducted the business alone. The market has a frontage of twenty feet, and a depth of one hundred and two feet. The location is an excellent one for business, and no market is kept in better order. Everything about it is neat and tidy, and with every convenience for the transaction of business. The refrigerator is a very large one, with a capacity of several tons. He has a large sausage-machine, which is capable of turning out an immense quantity of sausage, in which he has a very large trade. The market is the leading one in this city, and is supplied with every kind of fresh and salt meat, including pickled pork, ham and bacon. Two delivery wagons are constantly engaged in filling the orders of the market. In addition to what has already been mentioned, Mr. Schwartz carries fish of every kind, and manufactures a large amount of lard.

Mr. Schwartz is quite active in all matters pertaining to the material interest of his adopted city, and is at present the owner of the block in which his market is established, which has a frontage of thirty-eight feet and a depth of one hundred and two feet, three stories in height and built of brick. The neat residence in which the family resides, located at No. 127 South Street, he also owns. He has built two other houses, one of which he still owns. He is a member of the Orange County Telephone Company, and was one of the organizers of the Orange County Trust

EBER L. BROWN.

and Safe Deposit Company, of which he was a Director for a time. Fraternally he is a member of the Knights of Pythias, both of the subordinate and uniformed-rank degrees. He is also a member of Excelsior Hook and Ladder Company No. 1. In politics he is a thorough Republican, and in religious belief a Congregationalist. He is a Trustee of the Congregational Church of this place, and is very active in this work. Mr. Schwartz was here married to Miss Elizabeth Sears, born in the town of Montgomery, and daughter of Samuel Sears. They have one child, Winifred.

EBER LAIN BROWN. Working his way from poverty to wealth, from an humble position to a place of influence among his fellow-men, Mr. Brown has for years been a prosperous and successful business man, whose versatile ability and reliability in his dealings with others have brought to him the confidence of the public. At present he gives his time to the supervision of his farm, which consists of about seven hundred acres in the town of Minisink. Besides this property he owns seven tenement houses and a business block in Unionville, also several houses in Jersey City, the receipts from which form a very important addition to his income.

Our subject and his sister, Pamela, Mrs. Jonathan K. Burr (deceased), were the only children of Joseph and Phœbe (Lain) Brown. The father was born in the town of Minisink, on the farm now occupied by our subject, and was in early life a school-teacher, but later engaged in the mercantile business in Newburgh and New York. His father, who located in the town of Minisink in an early day, came to this locality from Long Island and was the first of the family to locate in this county. Eber L. was born in Sussex County, N. J., March 31, 1828, and in early boyhood attended the district schools of the home locality. When only eleven years

old he became a clerk in his uncle's store at Edenville, where he was employed a year. He then went to another uncle in Beemerville, Sussex County, N. J., where he stayed three years. For two years afterward he clerked in a store in Newburgh, and then went to New York City, where he was similarly occupied for a few years. Next we find him a member of the wholesale grocery firm of Stillwell, Brown & Co., of New York City, with which he was connected for about five years.

In the spring of 1848, shortly before the great gold discovery, Mr. Brown set sail for California, in company with the man who first discovered gold there. He was delayed for two months on the Isthmus of Panama, and the entire trip to San Francisco consumed four months. After having spent a short time in the last-named city, he began prospecting and mining at St. Mary's, which was back of Sacramento, and was fairly successful during the year he was at that place. His mining was altogether with the pan, in placer diggings. He often dug from $100 to $200 worth of gold per day, and a few times ran as high as $600. Expenses were correspondingly high, and he frequently paid $1 apiece for eggs, $1 a pound for bacon, and from twenty to forty cents per pound for flour. Besides this he did his own cooking and washing. He suffered many hardships, and in consequence contracted disease. Often he had to pay a doctor as high as $100 per visit. The climate, however, did not agree with him, and his failing health forced him to return East.

On his arrival at the old home, Mr. Brown at once resumed business. For about two years he was engaged in the wholesale dry-goods business in New York City, after which for three years he was a partner in a large wholesale grocery business. The pressure of business cares again caused the loss of his health, and, hoping to regain his strength, he came to Unionville and settled on the farm where his father was born. There he made his home, engaged in farming, for about twenty years. His next step was to open a wholesale and retail feed store in Unionville, which he sold six years later, having made a financial success of the enterprise. Turning his attention to a somewhat different line of work, he organized the Unionville Silk Manufacturing Company, of which he became President, and which invested about $25,000 in a silk plant, employing fifty hands. Unfortunately, the factory burned down in 1894, and the business has never since been resumed.

On Christmas Day of 1851 Mr. Brown married Miss Sarah E. Lewis, and one child blessed this union. His second marriage, June 1, 1863, united him with Caroline M. Lain, daughter of Richard A. Lain, and they became the parents of twelve children, but seven of the number have been taken by death. The survivors are Joseph M., Allison, Eber L., Phœbe and Millie M. The sons are all married. Mrs. Brown is a member of the Methodist Church. Mr. Brown has refused to be bound to any political organization in the matter of casting his ballot, but votes for the men whom he deems best qualified for office, irrespective of political ties. While serving as Supervisor, he rendered careful and satisfactory service in the interests of the people of the town. He is a man who is ever to be found on the side of progress, one who acts well his part in life and does all in his power to advance the material prosperity of the country. He was the first man who put up electric lights in Unionville, was also the first to use gas in the place, having his own private plant, and was the first to establish manufacturing plants there.

‿ ━━⊰❄⊱━ ⋇ ⊰❄⊱━━ ┿

WILLIAM S. CARPENTER has been from boyhood engaged in the railroad business in one capacity or another, and was promoted by degrees until he became engineer on the Erie Railroad. His residence is at No. 61 Orange Street, Port Jervis, where he has a pleasant home, and in addition to this he owns considerable property in other parts of the city. He is proprietor of the Deerpark Club House, one of the leading club houses (to which we will refer later on), owns one hundred and ten feet of land on Pike Street, and is interested in the Gorman & Abers-

dorf Livery Stable. He has erected two cottages, and is the owner of several tenement buildings on Franklin and Ball Streets.

Mr. Carpenter was born November 24, 1846, in Deposit, N. Y., his parents being Jesse and Sarah (Barlow) Carpenter. The latter is still living, her home being with her son William S. The father was an engineer on the Delaware Division, and for many years resided in this city. His death occurred February 20, 1876, as the result of an accident. The main connecting-rod broke and passed through the firebox of his engine, letting out steam and gases, which were inhaled by the unfortunate engineer, and his death took place ten days later, at the age of fifty-seven years. He had commenced railroading about 1854 as a fireman, and after the strike, two years later, returned to a brakeman's position, which he held for a year and a-half. About 1859 he was placed in charge of an engine, which he ran until his death. He was, like his son, a native of Broome County, his birth having occurred near Deposit.

Our subject was about ten or eleven years of age when the family removed to Port Jervis, and when in his thirteenth year he was made fireman on a switch engine. In September, 1863, though but seventeen years of age, he was made engineer on the main line, and soon afterward took charge of an engine on a freight train. In 1867 he assumed the responsibility of running a passenger engine, and now has the honor of running the No. 1 Westbound Chicago Express, and the No. 14 Eastbound Wells Fargo Express. Among the narrow escapes which befall all railroad men of long standing, he has had a few unpleasant experiences. At one time a freight train breaking left a drawhead on the track, which was struck by his engine, which capsized on the bank. The night express which his engine was drawing comprised twelve cars, which crashed into and completely demolished the engine. None of the passengers were killed, but the shooting steam so badly scalded Mr. Carpenter that he was laid up five months. Four miles west of this place a storm once washed out a space of thirty-five feet, leaving the rails and ties suspended without foundations. Mr. Carpenter's engine passed over before the rails gave way, but the twelve cars attached were plunged into the creek below. Marvelously, none of the passengers were injured. With the exception of three months, when he worked for the Morris & Essex Road, Mr. Carpenter has served continuously on the Erie lines since boyhood. He is a Master Mason, belonging to Port Jervis Lodge No. 328, F. & A. M.

The Deerpark Club House was originally built, in 1860, for a Baptist Church, and when the new house of worship was constructed Mr. Carpenter purchased the old building. He has made great changes, has partitioned it into elegant reception-rooms on the first floor, with ballroom and dressing-rooms on the second floor, and a well equipped kitchen in the basement. Here may be found china and silverware in sufficient quantities to set a table for one hundred and fifty guests, which number can be comfortably seated in the commodious dining-room. The club is arranged especially for social functions, and the enterprise displayed by the proprietor is fully appreciated by the citizens.

ECTOR OSTERHOUT, a photographer of Middletown, was born in Ulster County, near Kingston, in 1849, and traces his ancestry back to Tunis Osterhout, who came from Holland in 1640, and settled in the wilds of Ulster County. Abraham Osterhout, the grandfather of our subject, was born in Ulster County, and was a soldier in the War of 1812. He was honorably discharged from the service, and died at the age of eighty-six years. Kryneus Osterhout, the father of our subject, who was born in the town of Rochester, Ulster County, was by occupation a painter, but later engaged in farming, and though now over seventy-six years of age, yet follows that occupation near Stone Ridge, Ulster County. In politics he is a Republican, and is a member of the Reformed Church. He married Hannah J. Wood, born near Rosendale,

Ulster County, and a daughter of Frederick Wood, an old settler of that county, but of English descent. She is yet living, at the age of seventy-one. Of their eleven children, all grew to maturity, and ten survive.

The subject of this sketch remained at home on the farm until nineteen years of age, receiving his education in the public school and at Stone Ridge Academy. When nineteen he taught his first term of school, and then engaged as clerk in a store at Stone Ridge for one year, and later engaged in teaching for six months. In 1869 he commenced to learn the photograph business in Kingston, and for a time followed that occupation in Ulster, Greene and Columbia Counties, finally locating at Bennington, Vt., where he followed his profession for ten years. Desiring to make a change, he came to Middletown in December, 1884, and has since built up an extensive trade here. He has twice remodeled his place of business, which now covers an area of 24x130 feet, and his operating room is 15x40 feet. There are two reception-rooms and two showrooms, each of which is nicely furnished, and the gallery is well located on the first floor at No. 6 Main Street.

Mr. Osterhout was first married in Ulster County to Miss Katy Weeks, who died in Middletown in May, 1890. In Warwick he subsequently married Miss Martha Utter, by whom he has two children, Katy and Martha. The family reside in a pleasant home at No. 13 Wickham Avenue, of which he is the owner. Socially he is a member of the Knights of Honor, and in politics he is a Republican. Religiously he affiliates with the Congregational Church.

ARVEY LAMB is one of the prominent citizens of Port Jervis, Orange County, and is a conductor on the Erie Railroad. His life as a railroad man extends over forty-five years, during which time he has witnessed many changes and different systems. He ran on the road long before the telegraph was used, and recollects when Charles Minot, Superintendent of the Erie, wished to put up a telegraph system, but the

Board of Directors stood aloof. He also remembers when the old-style brakes at each end of the car, without ratchets and with a crank, were in common use.

Our subject was born in Jackson Township, Susquehanna County, Pa., November 7, 1830. When his father died he requested our subject to purchase the old homestead of his birth, saying that this farm was all that remained of the large estates which had formerly belonged to his father, and he desired that this one, at least, should remain in possession of the family. Accordingly Harvey Lamb carried out his father's wishes as soon as it was possible, and now owns the old farm in Jackson Township. His parents were Chauncy and Gratia (Wells) Lamb, both natives of Vermont, and the former born near Brattleboro. He was but nine years of age when he moved to Pennsylvania with his father, Maj. Joel Lamb, and settled in Susquehanna County when it was a wilderness. They were obliged to cut a road from their home to the Susquehanna depot, and for many years Chauncy Lamb was engaged in contracting for a turnpike. His death occurred at the age of seventy-five years, in 1888. His wife removed from the Green Mountain State with her sister when a young girl, and was married in Pennsylvania. Their father afterward came to live with these, his favorite daughters, and survived both of them. Mrs. Gratia Lamb was only thirty-seven years of age at the time of her death.

Until he was nineteen years of age Harvey Lamb was employed in farming, and for a few terms was engaged in teaching school. He was only fifteen when he was granted a certificate, and for his services received $11 per month and "boarded 'round.'' His higher education was obtained in Hartford Academy, in his home township, where for two terms he was under the instruction of "Uncle" Lyman Richardson. When in his twentieth year Harvey Lamb began railroading as a brakeman on the Delaware Division and as a flagman at Callicoon. At length he was promoted to be conductor of a freight train, and at the end of a year and a-half, or in 1852, came to Port Jervis. He was then a fireman, and about 1854 was given an engine. Then in 1856 occur-

red the great strike as the result of a rule which affected the engineers, but all the hands joined in expressing their disapprobation. Mr. Lamb left the company and went to the Chicago, Burlington & Quincy, where for three years he ran on the division between Galesburg and Aurora, one hundred and forty miles. In 1859 he went to Kansas as a pioneer, and settled on a farm near Le-Roy, in Coffey County. During his two years' residence there he became acquainted with many of the early settlers, among whom were John Brown and Jim Lane. In 1861 he was attached to Jennison's scouting brigade.

In 1861 Mr. Lamb again entered the employ of the Erie Railroad at Port Jervis and has since been one of their most trusted and capable men. For six years he ran a construction train, being his own engineer and conductor, and was then made conductor on a freight train, for a time doing extra duty. In 1874 he was given charge of a passenger train, and now, as for the past two and a-half years, has run the milk train, thus having every night for a rest. For seventeen years he ran No. 3 and No. 12 passenger trains, the former being the night express west and the latter the eastbound express. The lines traversed were from Jersey City to Port Jervis and from here to Susquehanna. The only accident of serious consequence which he has ever had was when No. 12 ran off the track at Tioga Station, six miles west of Owego, and collided with other cars. Six of the twelve cars were burned, two of these being express and mail cars, and four mail clerks, Murray, Fox, Reddinger and Sebolt, by name, lost their lives, and the express messenger, a Mr. Brewer, met a like fate. Mr. Lamb has had many hairbreadth escapes, but on the whole has been fortunate. A cinder which settled in his right eye caused him great suffering for months, as it could not be located, and finally he lost his sight in that eye. He is an honorary member of the Brotherhood of Locomotive Engineers, belonging to Division No. 54, and is a member of Division No. 9, Order of Railway Conductors.

October 28, 1863, Mr. Lamb and Marcella, daughter of Dr. Manley, were united in marriage in Susquehanna. Mrs. Lamb was born in Rut-

HENRY W. SMITH (85 YEARS).

land, Vt., of which state her father was also a native. For many years he was engaged in practice at Windsor, Broome County, N. Y. Mr. and Mrs. Lamb have no children of their own, but adopted a young girl, Bertha, who is now the wife of Don L. Sturgis, of Washington, D. C. Mr. and Mrs. Lamb attend the Baptist Church, of which the former is a Trustee. He is a liberal contributor to church enterprises and was one of the Building Committee. Politically Mr. Lamb is a Democrat.

HENRY W. SMITH. A history of the lives of the best residents of Orange County would in no wise be complete without an outline of the life of Mr. Smith, who has lived in the neighborhood of his present estate since 1849. He is now in the eighty-sixth year of his age, and is retired from labor on account of failing eyesight and old age. His farm is seventy-six acres in extent, and but few are superior in point of cultivation in the town of Goshen.

The subject of this sketch was born in Rockland County, this state, February 22, 1810, and is the youngest member of the family born to John and Mary Ann (Conkling) Smith, also natives of this state. The father, who was a farmer during his active years, was quiet and unassuming in manner, and although never seeking public office, was always willing to contribute his portion, either of money or time, toward the furthering of his community's interests. He died in 1813, when our subject was three years old.

Henry W., of this sketch, had very limited advantages for acquiring an education, as the schools of his day were few and far between, and as the class of teachers engaged was very inferior compared with what the youth of the present age enjoy. He was trained to farm work, and when ready to engage in business for himself went to New York City in order to learn the carpenter's trade under the best instructors. Meeting with an accident, however, he was compelled to return home, and since that time has given his attention to cultivating the soil. In this vocation he

has been successful and has built up for himself a name for honesty and fair dealing second to none in the county. In 1849 Mr. Smith located in this town, and has therefore made his home here for over forty-six years, and is now one of its oldest and most highly honored residents.

In 1832 occurred the marriage of Henry W. Smith with Miss Lucinda, daughter of Richard and Margaret Quackenbush, natives of this state. To them were born eight sons and daughters, five of whom have departed this life. Those now living are: Sarah, the wife of Ferdinand House, of this county; Joseph, engaged in the livery business in Warwick; and Caroline, who married John R. Van Nostrand, of this county. Mr. and Mrs. Van Nostrand reside at the old homestead and carry on the farm. The wife and mother passed from earth about 1885.

Mr. Smith is a Presbyterian in religious faith and during his early years took an active part in church work. In politics, he never fails to cast a vote in favor of Democratic candidates and principles. He is widely and favorably known, and his sterling worth and strict integrity have won for him the confidence and high regard of all with whom he has been brought in contact.

WILLIAM C. F. BASTIAN, Alderman from the Fourth Ward of Middletown, and one of the most enterprising men in the city, was born in Speier, Bavaria, January 27, 1839, and served his adopted country faithfully in the War for the Union. His father, William Bastian, was a native of Kreutznach, Prussia, and was a tanner and currier by trade. He had a tannery at Speier, which he operated for many years, and later took his son August into partnership, this connection continuing until the former's death, in 1894. In religious belief he was a Lutheran. His wife, Catherine Betsch, was born near Speier, and was a daughter of George Betsch, who was born in 1767, and died in 1851. Her father was an official of the Government, and served in the German army against Napoleon. He was also a member of the Lutheran Church. Mrs. Bas-

tian died in 1864, leaving six sons: William C.
F., our subject; Max, who died in Newburgh;
Louis C., who now resides in New York City,
and was formerly Lieutenant in the Fifteenth New
York Artillery under Colonel Dickey; George,
who resides in Speier, and is engaged in the
leather business; Philip, who also resides in
Speier, where he owns machine-shops; and August, who died in 1894, in Speier.

William C. F. Bastian was reared in his native
city, and until fourteen years of age attended the
public school. He then commenced to learn the
tanner's and currier's trade under his father,
where he remained until seventeen years of age,
when he came to the United States, being the
first of the family to locate in this country. He
sailed from Havre, and was thirty-five days on
the voyage to New York City. After remaining
there three weeks, he was engaged by Stephen
McKinstry, who owned a tannery on the Shawangunk, in Ulster County, and there remained
for some years, or until the tannery was closed
up. He then went to Newburgh with Mr. Mc-
Kinstry, who, under the firm name of Jennings
& McKinstry, conducted a tannery at that place.
In 1860 he went to Wawarsing, Ulster County,
where until 1861 he had charge of a department
in McKinstry & Child's tannery.

On the breaking out of the War for the Union,
our subject enlisted in Company A, Twentieth
New York Militia, under Colonel Pratt, and was
mustered into the service at Kingston for three
months. The regiment was sent to Baltimore,
where it remained until the expiration of its term
of service, when it was mustered out, and the
men honorably discharged. In August, 1862,
he assisted in recruiting Company E, One Hundred and Twentieth New York Infantry, and was
appointed First Sergeant of the company. On
examination, however, he was rejected by the
surgeon, and thus ended his military career.
Soon afterward he went to New York City, where
he engaged in business until 1869, and then went
to Wurtsboro, where he was married, the same
year, to Miss Louisa Belger, a native of that
place. In 1870 he opened a store in Wurtsboro
for the sale of fruits and confectionery, in which

he continued until 1872, when he located in Middletown, and built the Monopole House. He
continued in the hotel business until 1894, when
he sold out to Mr. Russell, who changed the
name of the house to the Oriental.

Mr. Bastian owns a nice residence at No. 97
East Main Street, where he resides with his wife.
One daughter, Millie, died in 1892, at the age of
nineteen years. In politics Mr. Bastian is a Republican, and in 1895 was elected on the Republican ticket as Alderman of the Fourth Ward.
He is Chairman of the Public Buildings and Park
Committees, and is a member of the Committees
on Light and Rules and Laws. Fraternally he
is a Master Mason, and first united with Monticello Lodge in 1871, from which he was demitted
to Hoffman Lodge. He is also a member of
Midland Chapter, R. A. M.; of Delaware Commandery at Port Jervis; and of Mecca Temple at
New York City. He is a charter member of
Luther Lodge No. 380, I. O. O. F., having twice
passed all its chairs, and has served as District
Deputy, and represented the local body in the
grand lodge. While at Port Jervis, he was a
member of the Encampment of Odd Fellows, but
is not active at the present time. He is also a
member of the Knights of Pythias, and is Vice-
Commander of W. A. Jackson Post No. 301, G.
A. R. Like most of his nationality, he is a natural musician, and for some years was Musical
Director of the Maennerchor. He has been connected with all the singing societies in the county, including the Port Jervis Maennerchor, of
which he was Musical Director, and also of a sim-
iliar society at Newburgh. While in New York
City, he was an active member of the Turn Verein.
Religiously he is a member of the Lutheran
Church.

GEORGE MAIER, manufacturer and wholesale dealer in cigars and tobacco, Middletown, was born in Constance, on Lake Constance, in Baden, Germany, near the head of the
Rhine, April 16, 1837. His father, Engelbert
Maier, was also a native of that place, and served
in the German army as a Corporal in the war

against Napoleon. He was the originator of the first bathing and swimming institution on Lake Constance. Since he first commenced in that business it has become very popular. He later formed a company, of which he was President until he died, the result of an accident, while yet in middle life. His wife, Rosa Frey, was born in Baden, and was a daughter of Michael Frey, a gardener of that city. She died in 1862. Of their family of five children, our subject is third in order of birth, and is the only representative in America. He was reared in his native village, and attended the public and high schools until the age of fourteen. He was but five years of age when his father died. His mother reared the family, and did her best by her children. At fourteen our subject commenced learning the trade of a shoemaker, and became a practical workman in his native place. He then traveled as a journeyman over Germany, Switzerland and France, after which he returned home and commenced the manufacture of shoes, and there remained until 1863.

With the desire of bettering himself in life, in August, 1863, Mr. Maier left his native land for the United States. The vessel on which he sailed was wrecked when in sight of the Jersey and Long Island shore. The passengers were rescued by a steamer sent from the city, and were landed in New York after a voyage of sixty-two days. While in New York he secured work at his trade, and for eighteen months resided in that city. He then went to New Paltz, Ulster County, and engaged in the manufacture of shoes, and there remained until 1868, when he removed to Kingston and continued to manufacture. In 1871 he started a large retail boot and shoe business in that place, which he continued until 1878, and then located in Middletown. Here he again engaged in the retail boot and shoe business, in which he remained one year; then sold out and engaged in the manufacture of boots and shoes, and in repairs, on West Main Street. His next location was on East Main Street, and in 1890 he removed to his present place of business. He built on the corner of Beadle and Railroad Avenue, now known as the Musbach Hotel, which

he subsequently sold. He also put up a double brick storeroom at Nos. 2 and 4 Beattie Avenue, and also erected his residence at No. 6 Beattie Avenue, where he is still engaged in the retail boot and shoe business, and in manufacturing, the business being in charge of his son Oscar.

In 1892 Mr. Maier began the manufacture of cigars, in partnership with another person, under the firm name of Eibing & Maier. The partnership lasted but one year, when our subject purchased the stock, and has since continued in business alone. His manufactory is located on the second floor of his building, and he employs about a half-dozen men. Among the brands of cigars manufactured by him are the "Rose of Sharon," a ten-cent Havana cigar; "Up to Make," a five-cent leader; and "G. M. S. Perfectos," another five-cent cigar. This is the largest cigar manufactory in the place. George Maier, his son, is continually on the road as a traveling salesman.

In addition to the lines already mentioned, Mr. Maier is engaged in the buying and selling of raw furs, and is the only buyer between New York City and Buffalo. He buys all kinds of furs, and expends thousands of dollars annually in the business. His sons assist him in the business. He is also interested in the Campbell Driving Park Association, and is a stockholder in the Co-operative Store. In politics he is a Democrat, and is a member of the County Central Committee from the First Ward. He has served his party as a delegate to County and Senatorial Conventions.

Mr. Maier was united in marriage in 1866, in New York City, with Anna Keck, a native of Germany, born near Stuttgart, in Wurtemberg. She died in Kingston, leaving five children: Oscar, in charge of the boot and shoe business; William, a plumber with Mr. Duryea; George, who is a traveling salesman for his father; Anna, now Mrs. Hess, living in Middletown; and Fred, who was accidentally killed on the New York Central Railway at Rome, at the age of twenty-one, while on his first trip out as a brakeman in the employ of that road. Mr. Maier's second marriage was with Miss Olivia Luckey, who was born in Bloomingburg, Sullivan County. Success has crowned the efforts of Mr. Maier in his adopted country, and his reputation as a citizen and a business man is one of which he may well be proud.

＊＊＊

JOHN F. WOOD belongs to a family that has long been noted for its patriotic zeal and devotion to the institutions of our Government. Two of his uncles served in the War of 1812, and three of his brothers were among the boys in blue who defended the Stars and Stripes. He himself did valiant service in the Union army, and the hardships he endured on the field and in the camp permanently affected his health. Since 1888 he has been obliged to use crutches, and for many years he has been unable to engage in active business, but he still maintains a general supervision of his interests and has at heart the welfare of his fellow-citizens.

The father of our subject, Jeremiah Wood, was born on Long Island, and was a carpenter by trade, which occupation he followed first in Warwick and later in Chester, his death occurring in the latter village. His wife, Frances Patton, was born in New York State, on the Hudson. They were the parents of five sons and five daughters, of whom eight attained years of maturity, and three sons and two daughters are now living. Of these, Charles B., William and Peter served in Company A, One Hundred and Twenty-fourth New York Infantry, while John F. was a member of Company E, Fifty-sixth New York Infantry. Personal mention of the first-named of these sons, Maj. Charles B., is made elsewhere in this volume.

In Warwick, this county, where he was born in July, 1824, the subject of this notice resided until sixteen years of age, and then accompanied his parents to Chester, where he learned the wagon-maker's trade. In 1850 he came to Middletown and secured employment in a foundry as a pattern-maker. After spending five years here, he went to Walled Lake, Oakland County, Mich., in 1855, and for two years worked at the carpen-

ter's trade, returning thence to Orange County. Near Port Jervis he was employed as assistant foreman in the building of the Erie Railroad, and remained there until 1859, after which he worked at the wagon-maker's trade for a year. He then turned his attention to the carpenter's trade, which he followed until the fall of 1862.

Coming to Middletown at that time, Mr. Wood worked at his trade, principally in the saw factory and hat works. In March, 1864, he enlisted in Company E, Fifty-sixth New York Infantry, and was sent to Albany as a recruit. From there he went to Hart's Island and then to Fortress Monroe. He was taken ill and for a time remained in the hospital, recovering from a severe attack of varioloid only to fall a victim to the typhoid fever. After rejoining his regiment in South Carolina in December, 1864, he continued to take part in its operations, and was with it in its engagements until October, 1865, when he was honorably discharged from the service.

As soon as his health permitted, Mr. Wood resumed work at the carpenter's trade in the hat shop and saw works, but he has continued to suffer from the effects of army life from that time to the present, and in 1880 he was obliged to retire altogether from work at his trade. He is an active member of General Lyon Post No. 266, G. A. R., and politically is a pronounced Republican. In this city, April 4, 1850, he married Miss Jane E. Compton, who was born in Deckertown, N. J., being the next to the youngest among six children. She was orphaned at the age of five years, and in 1845 came to Middletown, where she was a student in Denton Academy. By her marriage four children were born, namely: Frank W., who is flagman on the Erie Road at Port Jervis; Heman A., a carpenter at Middletown; Belle C., widow of Gerard Depeyster Saxon; and Fred, who is with his parents. Our subject's son-in-law was the son of Depeyster Saxon and a grandson of Abraham W. Depeyster, at one time Judge of the Supreme Court of New York. He was also a lineal descendant of Lord Saxon, of England, and a great-great-grandnephew of William Turner, the famous artist.

William C. Compton, father of Mrs. Wood,

SELDEN H. TALCOTT, M. D.

was born in Pompton, N. J., and was a millwright in that state until his death. Her grandfather, Jacob Compton, a native of England, was sent here as a soldier in the British army during the Revolutionary War, but deserted, and afterward fought in the American army as a commissioned officer. The mother of Mrs. Wood was in maidenhood Elizabeth Post. She was born in Sussex County, N. J., and died there when in middle life. Her parents were Gabriel and Anna (Wisner) Post, the former a soldier in the War of 1812. Her paternal great-grandfather was a resident of Warwick and a son of Anneke Jans, of Holland. The family was represented among the earliest settlers of this county, and has always been known for the honesty, uprightness and industry of its members.

SELDEN H. TALCOTT, M. D., Superintendent of the Middletown State Homeopathic Hospital, was born in Rome, N. Y., July 7, 1842. He traces his ancestry back to John Talcott, who came from England in the ship "Lyon," in 1632, in company with the Bradfords and other distinguished persons. He first located in Massachusetts and later in Connecticut. One son, James, born in Connecticut, was Governor of that state from 1723 to 1741. The great-grandfather of our subject, Jonathan Talcott, was born in Connecticut and was an ensign in the Revolutionary War. He was in the battle of Long Island, and at the close of the war settled in Rome, N. Y.

The grandfather of our subject, Siah Talcott, married Charlotte House, who was also a native of Connecticut. At an early day they removed to New York, where Jonathan Talcott, the father of our subject, was born. The grandfather was in the War of 1812, being engaged in the transportation of Government stores, and was a farmer near Rome. The father is also a farmer, a portion of his estate lying within the city limits of Rome, but he has retired from active life. In politics he is a Republican, and in religious belief a Presbyterian. He married Lucy Ann Shep-

54

hard, born at Brewerton, Onondaga County, at the foot of Oneida Lake. The Shephards are a New England family. The mother died in 1844, leaving a family of five children, and the father married a second time, by which union there are also five children.

Dr. Talcott, of this sketch, was reared in his native city, and there graduated from the Rome Academy, taking prizes in English composition and declamation. In 1862 he prepared for and attended Hamilton College one year. In 1864 he enlisted in Company K, Fifteenth New York Volunteer Engineers, and was mustered into the service at Elmira. The company was at once sent to the Army of the Potomac, which was then in front of Petersburg, and was among the first to enter the city after its capture. After serving faithfully until the close of the war, and being in the Grand Review at Washington, he was mustered out, in July, 1865, at Elmira, and received an honorable discharge. He then returned to Hamilton College, from which he graduated in 1869, with the degree of A. B. During his course he received the appointments of prize speaker and Clark prize orator. While in his junior and senior years he was one of the editors of *The Hamilton Campus*, a college weekly. Three years after graduating he received from his Alma Mater the degree of A. M., and twelve years later the degree of Ph. D. from the same college. In 1869 he commenced the study of medicine under Dr. E. A. Munger, of Waterville, and in 1870 entered the New York Homeopathic Medical College, from which he graduated in 1872. During his last course he was chosen Class President and was unanimously chosen valedictorian of the class, graduating with the highest standing of any in the class of thirty-six. Since his graduation he has had the degree of M. D. conferred on him by the Massachusetts Homeopathic Medical Society, and also by the Regents of the University of the State of New York.

In 1872 Dr. Talcott began the practice of his profession at Waterville, N. Y., where he remained until 1875, when he received the appointment of chief-of-staff of the Homeopathic Charity Hospital, located on Ward's Island, N. Y. The hospital had just been started, and Dr. Talcott was the first chief-of-staff. On taking charge of the hospital there was not a single patient, but when he left the institution there were some seven hundred. At the same time he was also in charge of the medical division of the Soldiers' Home in New York, with which institution he remained until it was disbanded and the inmates removed to the National Home. He was also in charge of the Inebriate Asylum of New York City, located in the southeast corner of Ward's Island, and had charge of one hundred and sixty insane patients.

In 1877 Dr. Talcott received the appointment from the Board of Trustees as Superintendent of the Middletown State Homeopathic Hospital, and after resigning his position on Ward's Island came at once to Middletown and took charge of this institution. At that time there were only about one hundred patients in the hospital, and only the main building was completed. At the present time there are between eleven and twelve hundred patients. Since taking the superintendency of the hospital, Dr. Talcott has managed the erection of over twenty buildings, large and small, and has had to approve every dollar expended during that time. The location of the hospital is a favorable one, and it has accommodations for about eleven hundred patients. The main building is one hundred and sixty-six feet long, while there are two pavilions, each two hundred feet in length. There are several cottages and halls on the grounds, which comprise about three hundred acres of land. Over two hundred and sixty men and women are employed in the hospital, together with six assistant surgeons.

Few physicians in the entire country have a larger practice or are more frequently called into consultation than the Doctor. He is consulting physician at Thrall Hospital; also occupies the same position in the new sanitarium at Easton, Pa., and is Professor of Nervous and Mental Diseases of the New York Homeopathic College. For four years he lectured on mental and nervous diseases at the Hahnemann Medical College at Philadelphia. Among the medical societies with

which he is now connected, or has been connected, may be mentioned the Orange County Homeopathic Medical Society, of which he has served as President; the Oneida County Homeopathic Medical Society, of which he was President in 1875; the New York County Homeopathic Medical Society; the New York State Homeopathic Medical Society, of which he has been President; the American National Institute of Homeopathy, of which he has been President; the Northern Homeopathic Medical Society of New York; the Inter-state Homeopathic Medical Society of New York and Pennsylvania, and an honorary member of the Massachusetts Homeopathic Medical Society. He is an associate member of the Royal Society of Medicine in Belgium. To the International Penal Association, held at Christiana, Norway, in 1891, he was sent as a delegate by the New York Medical-Legal Society of New York City, of which he is a member. In 1879 he was appointed a member of the State Board of Medical Examiners by the Regents of the University of New York.

Dr. Talcott has spent much time in travel in the interest of his profession. In 1883, 1888 and 1891 he traveled through the British Isles, France, Switzerland, Italy, Holland, Belgium, Prussia, Austria, Denmark, Sweden and Norway. On each visit he made a study of the asylum management in Scandinavia, Great Britain and the German States. He visited from forty to fifty asylums, and in 1891 made a report, giving the results of knowledge acquired. In his travels he met many distinguished physicians, among whom may be mentioned J. Al. Peeters, of Gheel; Jules Morel, of Ghent; Dr. Linboe, of Christiana; Joseph Lalor, of Dublin, and others.

Since he received his first appointment, Dr. Talcott has made twenty annual reports, eighteen of them covering his work in the Middletown State Homeopathic Hospital, and two for the hospitals on Ward's Island. He has written much on medical subjects which has been published in pamphlet form and in medical journals. Among the topics treated are "Prognosis in Insanity," "General Paresis," "Medical Notes on the Treatment of the Insane," "Mania, its

Causes, Course and Treatment," "Melancholia with Stupor," "Phimosis in its Relation to Insanity," "Delusions of the Insane," "The Insane Diathesis," "Sleep Without Narcotics, and The Hospital Idea." He was also editor of the "International Homeopathic Annual," published in Paris in 1894, to which he was a liberal contributor.

In 1873, at Waterville, N. Y., Dr. Talcott was united in marriage with Miss Sarah A., daughter of Dr. E. A. Munger, who was an old practitioner in that place, and for many years Coroner of Oneida County. Fraternally the Doctor is a member of Continental Lodge No. 287, F. & A. M., of New York City, and of Warren Chapter No. 22, R. A. M., of Waterville; and Rowell Post No. 23, G. A. R., of Waterville. In politics he is a Republican. Religiously he is a Presbyterian, and is a Trustee and Elder in that church. While his medical practice requires almost his entire attention, he is yet ready to do his part in all things pertaining to the welfare of his adopted city. Financially he has been quite successful, and is at present a Trustee of the Middletown Savings Bank, and a Director in the First National Bank of this place. As a physician his reputation is second to none in the country, and the success that has attended the Middletown State Homeopathic Hospital has been largely due to his persistent efforts. He perfected several of the plans of the buildings comprising the group, and assisted in devising the plans of each of them.

JOB B. GILES, junior member of the firm of Lindsey & Co., at Middletown, was born near Trowbridge, Wiltshire, England, March 21, 1865. The family of which he is a member, though for many years residents of England, originated in Wales. His father, Job, was born in Wiltshire, and was the son of James Giles, for a long time proprietor of an inn situated on the main road leading from Trowbridge to Frome. The father was also an innkeeper, succeeding the grandfather as landlord of the Royal Oak Hotel. For some time he also engaged in the mercantile

business. He spent his entire life in his native land, and died there in 1879, when forty-one years of age. In religious belief he was a Baptist, to which faith his progenitors had adhered for several generations.

The mother of our subject was Elizabeth Doel, a native of Wiltshire and a daughter of William Doel, a large and successful contractor. She still makes her home in her native shire, where she carries on the old Royal Oak Inn and the mercantile business established by her husband. Her ten children all attained years of maturity and are still living, but only two of the family ever came to America, these being our subject and his younger brother, W. H., superintendent for Lindsey & Co. J. B., who was sixth in order of birth, remained at home until eleven years of age, at which time he went to London and was apprenticed to the carpenter's trade under his uncle. Unable to carry on his studies in daytime, he attended the night schools of London until eighteen years of age.

In 1883 Mr. Giles came to America, the first of the family to establish his home in this country. Landing in New York, he came direct to Middletown, where he worked at the carpenter's trade with Lindsey Bros. About 1887 he became foreman of their factory, which position he held until the spring of 1892, and then entered the firm of Lindsey & Co. as a partner. The firm carries on a large trade as manufacturers of builders' materials, including sash, doors, blinds, hardwood trimmings and mantels. Their planing-mill is situated on Union Street, and the plant is operated by an engine of sixty horse-power and a boiler of eighty horse-power. For some of the finest residences of Middletown they have held the contracts, and they have also had contracts in Tuxedo Park, Orange (N. J.), Goshen, Warwick, Turner, Washingtonville, Liberty, and Morristown, N. J., as well as other places on the line of the Erie and the Ontario & Western. Mr. Giles is still manager of the mill and also furnishes the estimates on contracts.

In this city Mr. Giles married Miss Lillian Williamson, who was born here, being the daughter of John and Mary A. Williamson. In religious belief Mrs. Giles is identified with the Old-school Baptist Church. She is popular in social circles and unites with her husband in extending to their friends the hospitality of their cozy home at No. 21 Bonnell Street. As a Democrat, our subject has taken an active part in local affairs, and has been a member of the city and county committees, also has frequently attended county and state conventions of his party.

INCREASE CROSBY JORDAN. Noting the splendid success with which Mr. Jordan has met in his business enterprises, it may with justice be concluded that he is a man of large ability and shrewd discernment. He began as a dairy farmer, later became interested in the creamery and wholesale milk business, all of which he still continues. In fifteen or twenty creameries he holds a controlling interest, and the most of these were built by himself. Shipments are made to New York City over the Lackawanna, Lehigh Valley, Lehigh & Hudson River, Erie, Ontario, Susquehanna & Harlem, and other railroads.

In the town of Wallkill the subject of this notice was born August 18, 1849. He is a namesake of his father's maternal grandfather, Dr. Increase Crosby, a fine painting of whom adorns the walls of his city residence. Dr. Crosby was a pioneer of the town of Crawford, and for many years one of its most influential citizens. The Jordan family was founded in America by three brothers who emigrated from Ireland in an early day. Grandfather John Jordan, who was a civil engineer, was killed when a young man by the falling of a tree, and his body was buried with Masonic honors in Bloomingburg Cemetery.

The father of our subject, Increase C. Jordan, was a successful farmer and prominent Republican. His wife, who survives him, and who is now seventy-nine years of age, makes her home with her children. She bore the maiden name of Susan T. Norris, and was born near Hopewell, Sullivan Connty, being a member of an old Con-necticut family of Revolutionary connections. In religious belief she is identified with the Reformed Church. Of her seven children six are living, our subject being the fifth. He was reared on the home farm, of which, on arriving at man's estate, he became the owner. It consists of one hundred and ninety-five acres, and he has made of it a dairy farm, stocking it with about forty cows.

Forming a partnership with his brother, J. V., our subject in 1882 started in the creamery business, building the creamery at Hurleyville, Sullivan County. In the fall of the same year he built at Liberty a creamery which he still runs. His next venture was the erection of a creamery at Stevensville, and afterward he was similarly engaged in the counties of Madison, Chenango, Broome and Otsego, N. Y., Hunterdon and Warren, N. J., Susquehanna and Wayne, Pa., from all of which places he makes shipments to New York City. The shipments aggregate twelve hundred cans daily, and each can holds ten gallons. Recently he opened a creamery at Mt. Rose, Pa., which bids fair to be as successful as his previous ventures in a similar line. Each of his creameries is managed by an efficient Superintendent. His partner, John P. Werk, has charge of the Brooklyn office, located at Nos. 488-90 Broadway, that city, where a large wholesale and retail business is carried on.

In addition to the enterprise with which his name is most closely associated, Mr. Jordan is interested in the glass factory, has served as Treasurer of the Unadilla Valley Milk and Cream Company, and is a charter member and Director of the Orange County Trust and Safe Deposit Company. He is also connected with the City Club. In 1894 he bought his present residence in Middletown, and has here established his permanent home. His marriage, in 1881, united him with Miss Sarah E., daughter of P. L. Seybolt, and a native of the town of Mt. Hope, having been born near Otisville. Five children complete the family circle, namely: Lena, Cora, Antoinette, Louise and Gertrude.

In 1892 Mr. Jordan was elected a member of the Board of Education, but resigned the position after holding it for two years. Socially he is

THERON CRAWFORD.

12

connected with Hoffman Lodge, F. & A. M., and Midland Chapter, R. A. M. Though not active in political affairs, he is a firm defender of Republican principles, which he upholds by his ballot in local and national elections. He was a member of the committee that organized the Milk Exchange of New York City, and in other ways he has been associated with many of the important enterprises and organizations of Middletown, of which he is an honored citizen.

THERON CRAWFORD, one of the progressive and influential farmers of Orange County, is living in the town of Crawford, where he was born June 26, 1823, on the same farm and in the same house where he now resides. His parents, Robert I. and Deborah (Dickerson) Crawford, had eleven children, of whom Theron was the youngest but one.

We make the following mention of the brothers and sisters of our subject: Emeline, who never married, lived to be eighty-five years of age; Leander was seventy-three at the time of his decease; Millicent, died July 23, 1864; John A. was eighty-one years of age at the time of his death; Albert was thirty-nine years old; George is living retired in Middletown; Sarah E. is deceased, as is also Esther; Robert is a well-to-do farmer of this town; and Angeline still makes her home in this locality.

The father of the above family was born at Bloomingburg, Sullivan County, N. Y., and while young he was brought to the town of Crawford by his parents, John and Sarah (Barkley) Crawford, the former of whom was a native of this state. He was among the first to settle in the town of Crawford, which was named in his honor. His parents were both born in Ireland. The paternal grandmother of our subject was a native of this county, while her parents were born in Scotland. The father of our subject was reared to a useful life and became successful as an agriculturist in this town. He was a stanch Republican in politics and took a very active part in local affairs, giving of his time and means to-

ward the furtherance of all worthy measures. He possessed the entire confidence of the people, and was often called upon to settle estates, which he was always able to do in a satisfactory manner. In the Hopewell Presbyterian Church he was an Elder for a great many years, and was also an active worker. His death occurred here on the old homestead, September 15, 1860, and it was with deep regret that his many friends heard of the sad event, for in him the community lost one of its best citizens.

Our subject's mother was a native of the town of Crawford, and for many years prior to her decease, which occurred April 28, 1851, was a devoted member of the Hopewell Presbyterian Church. She was the daughter of Benjamin and Esther (Ogden) Dickerson, both born in Connecticut.

On the death of his parents, Theron Crawford found himself in possession of the old homestead, on which he still resides. It comprises ninety-nine acres of excellent land, and has been handed down in the family from father to son for one hundred years. Our subject was married, November 24, 1870, to Miss Anna F. Cooper, of New Windsor.

In politics Mr. Crawford is a stanch Republican, but has never aspired to official honors, as he finds his time fully employed in the management of his farm. Following in the footsteps of his honored parents, he, too, is a member of the Hopewell Church, which he has served as Trustee for many years. He is both enterprising and energetic, and has won the good-will of all with whom he has come in contact.

AUGUST PFAFF, proprietor of the Wallkill House, and one of the well known citizens of Middletown, was born in Hanover, Germany, in 1861. He is the eldest of the four children of George and Louisa (Wilkening) Pfaff, natives of Hanover, where they still reside, the father being City Morgue-keeper and also proprietor of a transfer line. August, who is the only member of the family that emigrated to the United States, was educated in the public schools of his native place, and at an early age developed a fondness for a seafaring life. At the age of fourteen he shipped with an uncle, who was captain in charge of the trans-Atlantic vessels of Knoppe & Co., and, beginning in an humble position, worked his way upward, continuing before the mast for three years. His first trip was to Brazil, where he spent six months. Afterward he went on a voyage to Siam, Bangcock, Singapore, the East Indies and Portugal, spending one year in that part of the world. He also made several trips between Bremen and New York City, and in the latter place his uncle died.

In 1877 Mr. Pfaff came to the United States, intending to return to Germany after a short visit in New York, but he afterward decided to establish his permanent home in this country. For a time he was employed in a cousin's grocery store, then was employed by others in the same city, and later started in business for himself, but retired after his wife's death. In 1888 he came to Middletown, where for five years he was in the employ of Mr. Gunther in the restaurant business. In 1893 he leased the Wallkill House, which he remodeled and improved, and of which he has since been the proprietor. The hotel is one of the finest north of New York, and is conducted upon the European plan. The barroom is the most elegant in the city, and everything about the place is first-class. In the rear is a summer-garden, the only one in the city.

One of the attractions of the hotel is the splendid collection of curios. The natural-history cabinet, which is displayed with four electric lights, surpasses anything of the kind in Orange County, and contains more than two hundred and fifty specimens of the birds, reptiles, rodents and wild animals of the county. Mr. Pfaff's collection of coins and postage stamps is also very complete and interesting. In addition to these he has specimens of animals from the West and from the Old Country, including among the latter the only genuine German wild boar's head in America. This was secured from the imperial forest by a brother-in-law of Mr. Pfaff.

The first marriage of Mr. Pfaff took place in New York City, his wife being Miss Emma Buehler, who was born there, and died eighteen months after their marriage. His second wife, whom he married in Middletown, bore the maiden name of Emma Wendt, and was born in Germany. They are the parents of two children, Lucy Irene and Elsie. Socially our subject ranks high in the Masonic order, belonging to Hoffman Lodge No. 412, F. & A. M.; Midland Chapter No. 240, R. A. M.; Delaware Commandery No. 44, K. T.; Union Consistory No. 59; and Mecca Temple, Nobles of the Mystic Shrine. He also belongs to Luther Lodge, I. O. O. F.; Knights and Ladies of the Golden Star; Morning Star Lodge No. 40, in New York City; and Jefferson Lodge No. 268, of the German Order of Haugai, in that city. In the Maennerchor of Middletown he has held the offices of Treasurer and Vice-President, and has served as fireman in Wallkill Engine Company No. 6. In religious belief he is a Lutheran, but as there is no church of that denomination in Middletown he attends Grace Episcopal Church.

<hr/>

ROBERT LAWRENCE, of Middletown, was born in Birmingham, England, in 1849, and is the son of Samuel, a native of Gloucestershire, and a grandson of John Lawrence, a farmer of that country. His father was reared to manhood upon a farm, and in youth became a gun-barrel grinder, which occupation he followed until coming to this country. In his native land he married Ann, daughter of Robert Smith, a shoemaker of Gloucestershire. Accompanied by all the members of his family excepting our subject, who joined him three years later, he came to America in 1863, and for a short time was employed in the Colt Pistol Works at Hartford, Conn., from which place he came to Middletown, and secured a position as a grinder in the Monhagen saw factory, now the National Saw Works. There he remained until his death, in 1886, at the age of sixty years. His wife, who was a lady of amiable disposition and noble life, and a member of the Episcopal Church, died in this city in 1889. Of their four children, two are living, Robert and Francis Samuel, both of Middletown.

The subject of this sketch was reared in Birmingham, where, prior to the age of eleven years, he attended the common schools. He then commenced to learn the butcher's trade, and after completing his apprenticeship he continued to work at that occupation in Birmingham until 1866, the year of his emigration to America. In June of that year he took passage at Liverpool on the steamer "City of Dublin," which arrived in New York City on the 3d of July. At once coming to Middletown, he has since made his home in this city. Here he apprenticed himself to the saw-maker's trade under Wheeler, Madden & Clemson, with whom he remained, in various capacities, for twenty-two years altogether. In 1888 he resigned from their employ, and accepted a position with the Columbia Dye and Print Works, and has since been with that concern, at present being in charge of the steaming-room.

With various social, business and religious enterprises originated for the benefit of this city Mr. Lawrence has been intimately associated. He is interested in the Homestead Building and Loan Association, now one of the well known institutions of the city. A Republican in politics, he is a stalwart adherent of the principles of that party, and for one term served as a member of the Board of Health. Fraternally he is connected with Middletown Lodge No. 112, I. O. O. F., in which he has passed all the chairs, and has filled the position of Past District Deputy Grand Master. He is also a member of the American Legion of Honor, and Ivanhoe Lodge No. 2103, K. of H., in which he has served as Financial Reporter for the past eleven years. In the Methodist Episcopal Church, of which he is an active member, he has served as Steward, and for eight years was Superintendent of the Sunday-school. His residence, at No. 24 Myrtle Avenue, is presided over by his wife, formerly Miss Amelia Thornton, with whom he was united in marriage at Homowack (now Spring Glen), Ulster County, N. Y. She was formerly a resident of that village, where her father, Charles Thornton, was a speculator and

prominent citizen. They are the parents of three children now living, namely: Cora B., who is employed as bookkeeper in Predmore's grocery store; Howard R., clerk in a clothing store in this city; and Ethel A.

CHARLES E. MILLER, a representative of the young business men of Middletown, was born in the town of Wallkill in 1861, being a son of Silas J. Miller, a native of the adjoining county of Sullivan. His grandfather, Abraham, was born in Dutchess County, whence he removed to Sullivan County and engaged in farming there. Tracing the ancestral history back one generation further, we find that the great-grandfather was a native of England, and founded the family in America, coming here in early years and making settlement in Dutchess County.

In youth Silas J. Miller learned the carpenter's trade in Middletown, and followed that occupation here and in other parts of Orange County, being quite successful as a contractor and builder. When past middle age he removed to a farm situated near Walker Valley, on the line between Sullivan and Ulster Counties, and there he still resides, being now about fifty-two years of age. The Brookside Farm, as the place is known, is advantageously situated on the Plattekill, and the scenery and climate being all that could be desired, a large summer boarding-house has been erected for the accommodation of city guests, to whose entertainment Mr. Miller gives much of his time.

The mother of our subject was Nettie Dailey, whose father was a farmer of the town of Wallkill, though she was born in Middletown. She had three children, of whom Charles E. is the eldest and the only son. He was reared in Orange and Sullivan Counties and attended the district schools in boyhood. Under his father's instructions he commenced to learn the carpenter's trade, which he later carried on with his uncle, T. W. Dailey, of Middletown. After gaining a thorough knowledge of the trade, he became his uncle's foreman, working in that capacity until the spring of 1895, when he started out independently as a contractor and builder. During the five months that have since elapsed he has completed two houses and has seven partially finished. Among them are two fine residences on Beattie Avenue for C. B. Warner, the Morris home on Royce Avenue, three houses on Cottage Avenue, and one on Woodlawn Avenue.

The residence occupied by Mr. Miller is situated at No. 304 North Street, and is presided over by his accomplished wife, formerly Miss Carrie E. Mulford. Mrs. Miller was born in Ulster County, a daughter of Ford Mulford, and by her marriage she has one child, a daughter, Hazel Undine. They attend the Methodist Episcopal Church and are well liked in social circles. While Mr. Miller has not taken an active part in politics, he is unswerving in his allegiance to the Democratic party, and always votes that ticket at elections. In addition to his work as a contractor, he manifests considerable ability as an architect, and his plans commend themselves to the critic by reason of their adaptability to the wants and needs of the people. If the future may be judged by the past, he will certainly attain success in his vocation.

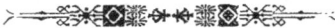

>═══✦✹◆❀✦◆❀✧◆✦✹═══<

SYLVANUS GREER, one of the brave men who did service in the illustrious One Hundred and Twenty-fourth Regiment, was born in March, 1827, near Mt. Hope, in the town of Wallkill, three and one-half miles from the present place of his residence in the city of Middletown. His father, James, was born in the town of Blooming Grove, this county, where the paternal grandfather had made settlement on coming hither from New England. During the War of 1812 James Greer rendered brave service for his country. Afterward he moved to the town of Wallkill and followed the blacksmith's trade throughout the remaining years of his active life. His death occurred at the age of seventy-six. His wife, Mary, was born near Bloomingburg, Sullivan County, and died at the age of seventy-five. Her father, Jonathan Martine, was a farmer, and made his home in Sullivan County.

The parental family consisted of nine children, all of whom attained years of maturity, and two sons and three daughters are now living, Sylvanus and Alpheus (twins) being the youngest. Our subject was reared in the town of Wallkill. On coming to Middletown he entered the employ of Henry Little in the Monhagen Mill, where he worked for eight years. In the spring of 1862 he settled on a farm in the town of Goshen, but did not long remain there, as a call was made for soldiers and he responded promptly to the appeal.

At Goshen Mr. Greer was mustered into service as a member of Company K, One Hundred and Twenty-fourth New York Infantry. In December, 1862, he was at Fredericksburg. May 3, 1863, he took part in the engagement at Chancellorsville, and during that battle a ball entered his head below the left temple and came out in the right eye, which it turned out on his face. The ball was extracted and is still in his possession. Taken prisoner by the enemy, he was held two weeks on the field, deprived of necessary medical and surgical attention. At the end of that time he was exchanged and taken to the Aqua Creek field hospital, where he remained two weeks. June 9 he returned to Middletown, but after a furlough of thirty days reported at headquarters. This he continued to do until he was honorably discharged in October, 1864, on account of physical disability. Since the unfortunate catastrophe in battle he has been almost blind, able only to distinguish daylight and the outline of large objects, and as a partial compensation for this affliction and for his valor in war, he receives from the Government a pension of $72 per month.

Until 1868 Mr. Greer remained with his parents, but he then came to Middletown, where he has since resided, his home being on the corner of Mill and Fulton Streets. For five years he engaged in the grocery business with J. P. Updegrove, but in 1885 he bought a farm, to which he moved, making it his home for four years. Since his return to Middletown he has lived in retire-

WILLIAM D. STRATTON.

ment from business. He was first married, in Middletown, to Miss Catherine Carpenter, who was born in the town of Wallkill and died in this city in April, 1862; she was a daughter of Edward, and a sister of William W., Carpenter, of whom mention is elsewhere made.

In New York City, in 1867, Mr. Greer married Miss Sarah A., daughter of John and Hannah (Moore) Wait, and a native of New York City. Her father and grandfather, both of whom were named John, were natives of Boston, whence the former removed to New York prior to his marriage. He was engaged as a truckman for many years, and died in Brooklyn at an advanced age. Grandfather William Moore was born in Scotland. On emigrating to America he settled in Boston, but later removed to the town of Wallkill, this county. His wife bore the maiden name of Letitia Sutherland, and was of Quaker faith. Mrs. Hannah Wait died in New York City, after having become the mother of seven daughters and one son, of whom six attained mature years and four survive. Those living are Sarah A.; Mrs. Mary Corby, of Brooklyn; Mrs. Hannah Higgins, of Jersey City; and Mrs. Sophia Hunt, of Mt. Vernon, N. Y.

Politically Mr. Greer has been a believer in Republican principles since the organization of the party. Socially he is connected with General Lyon Post No. 266, G. A. R., of which he is a charter member. His wife is connected with the Woman's Relief Corps, in which she is a leading worker. Both are connected with the Second Presbyterian Church of this city, and are highly respected by the best people of the place.

WILLIAM D. STRATTON. There is perhaps no railroad contractor in our country whose career has been more successful than that of W. D. Stratton, of Middletown. In 1891 he was an active factor in securing the incorporation of the Drake-Stratton Company, which began in business with a capital stock of $100,000,

but which has since been increased to $1,000,000. He was chosen Treasurer and General Manager, but the oversight of affairs entailed so much labor on his part that he resigned as Treasurer, and has since devoted his entire attention to the management of the business.

The Stratton family was founded in America by a native of England, who on coming to this country settled in Massachusetts. The next in line of descent was our subject's great-grandfather, who was born in Massachusetts, removed thence to Connecticut, and later became a pioneer of the town of Thompson, Sullivan County, N. Y. His son Eliphalet was born in Connecticut and served in the War of 1812; he passed away suddenly, being found dead, at the age of eighty-one years.

William Benjamin, son of Eliphalet, was born in Thompsonville, Sullivan County, and there learned the trade of a millwright, which he followed for some years, building a large number of saw and grist mills. Later he settled on a farm between Thompsonville and Fallsburg, in what is now the town of Fallsburg, and there engaged in general farming until his death, in 1887, at the age of seventy-seven. Politically he was a Democrat, and in religious belief an Episcopalian. His wife, Sarah Elizabeth, was born in Connecticut, as was also her father, Nelson Canfield, who was a mason and builder, and became an early settler of Thompsonville. Mrs. Stratton resides on the old homestead, and is now seventy-one years of age.

Of the six children of William B. and Sarah E. Stratton, three are now living, namely: William D.; James, who is a general contractor in New Jersey; and Benjamin, who resides on the home farm. The first-named son was born in Thompsonville, Sullivan County, in November, 1844, and was reared in the place of his birth, receiving a district-school education. In boyhood he learned the millwright's trade, at which he worked until his enlistment, in 1864, as a member of Company K, Fifty-sixth New York Infantry. He joined his regiment at Charleston, S. C., and did picket duty on the island off that city. In the spring his regiment was attached to

Sherman's army and moved up toward Richmond, but later was sent back to Charleston, where he was mustered out and honorably discharged in July, 1865.

For two years after his return from the South, Mr. Stratton worked at his trade in Sullivan County, after which he became a journeyman carpenter on the Wallkill Valley Railroad, and later was promoted to the position of foreman. He spent five years as foreman of the erection and construction of bridges, his business taking him throughout the entire country. At the expiration of that period he resolved to embark in business for himself, which he did, and after considerable effort and having overcome the numerous obstacles in the way, he gained a substantial foothold.

In 1878 Mr. Stratton formed a partnership with his brother-in-law, Mr. Drake, and the first contract taken by the firm of Drake & Stratton was that of rebuilding the bridge over the canal at Huguenot. Later they had the contract for building the New York & New England Road between Waterbury and Brewster, after which they received orders from various parts of the country. They had one hundred and nine consecutive monthly estimates from the Pennsylvania Road, for which they worked nine years or more; built thirty-eight miles between Monroe and Madison, Wis., and then double-tracked the Mahoning Valley Railroad between Youngstown and Cleveland. The McKeesport & Belle Vernon Road, of thirty miles in Pennsylvania, was built and equipped by them, and afterward sold. For a number of years they were employed on the Lake Shore & Michigan Southern, working from Dunkirk east and west. They are now building a railroad of fifty miles on the island of San Domingo, upon which eighteen hundred men are employed, and which will require two years to complete. This contract, which was made with the San Domingo Improvement Company of New York, calls for Government protection.

The firm also built fifty miles of the Pittsburg, McKeesport & Allegheny Road, and five miles of the Schuylkill Valley Railroad for the Pennsylvania. They are now building one hundred miles

of railroad between Charleston, Kanawha and Sutton, the charter of which they have purchased. Twenty-eight miles are now in operation, and fifty miles have been graded. The only work they have done west of the Mississippi was a contract for masonry for the Chicago, Burlington & Quincy at Rulo, Neb. They bridged the Tombigbee River at Jackson, Ala., on the Mobile & Birmingham Railway, and have a contract for repairing and straightening out the Delaware & Hudson Railroad between Albany and Schenectady; also for a bridge over the Delaware River at Philadelphia for the Pennsylvania Railroad, and for the stone arches for the Conestoga Bridge on a branch line of the Pennsylvania. In Maryland, West Virginia and other states they have similar contracts. One of their contracts is for the erection of a bridge over the Monongahela River at Pittsburg. They have a five-years contract with the Oliver Mining Company and the Ohio Mining Company of Minnesota, and a contract for the A. W. Byers Ore Company of Minneapolis. In addition to their other enterprises they are operating a large quarry at Sandy Hill, Washington County, N. Y. They furnished the stone for the Poughkeepsie Bridge, and have done considerable work for the Baltimore & Ohio, also for the Erie. While it is difficult to approximate the gross amount of their contracts per annum, yet it is safe to say that $4,000,000 would be a conservative estimate of their operations. They own and operate the Akron & Chenango Falls Railroad, which runs from Barberton, Ohio, via Akron, to Cuyahoga Falls.

The history of the firm since 1883 is one of unvarying and remarkable success. They have never failed on a contract, nor refused to meet an obligation, and as a business concern their reputation is an enviable one. Their remarkable prosperity is largely due to the judicious efforts of Mr. Stratton. Prior to 1888 he resided in Sullivan County and New York City, but in that year he came to Middletown, where he owns and occupies an elegant residence on Wisner Avenue, opposite Grand. Aside from this property, he owns a number of acres within the city limits and also has four farms in Sullivan County. The

Hogan Boiler Company, one of the growing concerns of this city, owes much to his wise counsel and interest, and he is now serving as its President. He is also a Director of the First National Bank, the Orange County Trust and Safety Deposit Company, and the New York Construction Company of Philadelphia, and is a stockholder in the West End Trust and Safe Deposit Company of Philadelphia. In politics a Democrat, he was elected a member of the Board of Water Commissioners in 1893, being the nominee of both political organizations, a fact which attests his popularity with the citizens. In Fallsburg, N.Y., he married Miss Mary C., daughter of James O'Niell, a farmer of that place. They have three children, namely: Frank M., whose sketch appears on another page; Ralph and Grace, who reside with their parents.

EORGE W. O'NEAL, traveling engineer for the New York, Ontario & Western Railroad, was born in Laurel, Sussex County, Del., November 10, 1851, and is the son of George and Margaret (Boyce) O'Neal, also natives of Delaware. The former remained on his father's farm until nineteen years of age, when he began to learn the cabinet-maker's trade, and on completing his apprenticeship he followed that occupation for a time, but later was employed as a carpenter and ship-builder on the Chester River. Afterward he was proprietor of a large mill on that river, then turned his attention to agriculture, and for some years he has made his home upon a valuable farm which he cultivates. His father died in early life. His father-in-law, Hosea Boyce, was born in Delaware, and was a sea-captain, owning a vessel and engaging in the coasting trade. After retiring from the sea he devoted his time to the management of his three large plantations until his death, which occurred at the age of sixty-two.

In the family of George and Margaret O'Neal there were ten children, all of whom reached mature years, and nine are now living. One of the sons, Andrew, is an engineer on the Ontario &

Western, and resides at Norwich. George W., who is the fourth among the children in respect to age, was reared on the home farm, receiving his education in the public school and Laurel Academy. In the spring of 1869 he began his railroad career, going at that time to Norwich, where for nine months he was employed on construction by the New York & Oswego Midland, now the New York, Ontario & Western Railway Company. In October, 1869, he went back home, but in April, 1870, returned to Norwich, where he was employed in the roundhouse a short time, and then became fireman between Norwich, Sidney and Oswego.

Going West in 1873, Mr. O'Neal was employed for three months as fireman on the St. Louis & Iron Mountain Road, after which he was promoted to engineer, his run being between St. Louis and Poplar Bluffs. In the spring of 1875 he returned to New York and resumed work for the New York, Ontario & Western, having the promise of a new engine, but as the road was embarrassed he continued as fireman until 1877, when he was made engineer of a milk train between Middletown and Liberty. At that time only seven cans of milk daily were secured from the district north of Summitville, but the dairy industry has developed to such an extent that now there are over five thousand cans per day.

In 1878 Mr. O'Neal went to New Berlin, and for eight years was engineer on the New Berlin Branch of the Ontario & Western. On his return to the main line he ran the night express between Middletown and Norwich, later had the train between Liberty and New York for eighteen months, and then took the day express west and the night express east between Middletown and Norwich. In March, 1892, he was promoted to the position of road foreman of engines, and in the discharge of his duties he spends a large portion of his time traveling, inspecting engines at different points.

The residence of Mr. O'Neal is situated at No. 33 Linden Avenue, Middletown. He married in this city, in 1877, Miss Ruth Etta Seaman, who was born in Spring Glen, Sullivan County, N. Y. Her father, Rev. Isaac Seaman, was born in Newburgh, this state, and was educated for the min--

istry of the Wesleyan Methodist Church, which profession he followed until failing health obliged him to retire. He died in Mountain Dale, Sullivan County, in the autumn of 1860. In politics he was a Republican. His wife, who bore the maiden name of Christina Frantz, was born in Mamakating, and died in New Berlin, at our subject's home. Her father, Joseph Frantz, was for many years a grocer at Spring Glen. She was the mother of nine children, of whom seven are living, Mrs. O'Neal being the youngest. Two of the sons served in the Civil War, namely: Harrison, who was a member of the One Hundred and Twenty-fourth Regiment, and is now a resident of Maryland; and Alfred, who was in the Fifty-sixth New York Infantry, and now lives in Mountain Dale. Mr. and Mrs. O'Neal are the parents of four children: Howard H., Daisy D., Clarence G. and Irma.

Socially Mr. O'Neal is a member of Phœbus Lodge No. 82, F. & A. M., at New Berlin, and Hillington Chapter No. 224, R. A. M. For three terms he was Chief of the United Division No. 292, Brotherhood of Locomotive Engineers, at Middletown, and was their delegate to the convention at Denver in 1891. He is identified with the Traveling Engineers' Association, and attends the annual meetings of that organization. In politics he affiliates with the Democratic party.

<figure><<++++++++++++++❋++++++++++++>></figure>

HENRY MOREY, JR., engineer on the New York, Ontario & Western Railroad, between Middletown and Weehawken, was born in the town of Mt. Hope, February 25, 1853. His grandfather, Eben Morey, was born in Rhode Island, whence in the early days he came to Orange County and settled in the town of Mt. Hope, about two and one-half miles from Howells. There he established his home in a primitive log cabin and set about the task of developing a farm from the wilderness. Here he spent the remainder of his life, dying when advanced in years. His wife, Prudence, attained the great age of ninety-seven years and six months. His ances-

tors were of Scotch-Irish lineage and were early settlers of Rhode Island.

Henry Morey, Sr., father of our subject, was born in Rhode Island, whence he accompanied the other members of the family to Orange County and settled in the town of Mt. Hope. His entire active life was spent there, but on reaching advanced years he retired from business and went to East St. Louis, Ill., where he makes his home with his older son John, a manufacturer of that place. His wife, who died at the home of our subject in 1888, bore the maiden name of Mary Hunter and was born in Ireland. Her father, John Hunter, also a native of the Emerald Isle, brought the family to America and settled in Paterson, N. J., where he engaged in the mercantile business until he fell a victim to cholera. Mrs. Morey by her first marriage had two sons, one of whom spent seven years at sea, and died in New York. The other, James A., was Major of the One Hundred and Fifty-sixth New York Infantry throughout the entire period of the Civil War; he also served in the Mexican War, and is now a resident of Tioga, Pa.

Our subject is the younger of two sons born of his mother's second marriage. He remained on the home farm in the town of Mt. Hope until 1869, when he began to work in the construction department of the New York, Oswego & Midland, now the New York, Ontario & Western, his work being between Winterton, N. Y., and Franklin, N. J. After being engaged in that capacity for twenty-two months, he came to Middletown and became an employe in Babcock & Fuller's hat shop, later working in Fuller Bros.' hat shop. March 9, 1880, he resigned from his position there and entered the employ of the Ontario & Western as watchman in the roundhouse, remaining in that capacity about one year. In June, 1881, he was promoted to be fireman between Middletown and Norwich. In September, 1883, he was made engineer on a freight train, and now runs both freight and passenger trains, at present having charge of the "Liberty" from Liberty to Weehawken. He is known as a reliable and efficient engineer, and has been fortunate, in that he has had very few accidents. At

WILLIAM VANAMEE.

one time his train collided with another at Hancock, Delaware County, but no one was injured. In Middletown Mr. Morey owns a residence at No. 135 Wickham Avenue, where he and his wife, with their two children, Harry and Lillian, make their home. Mrs. Morey bore the maiden name of Mary Murphy, and was born in England, but was reared, educated and married in this city. The family attends the Second Presbyterian Church. Politically our subject is a Republican, and socially he is identified with Hoffman Lodge No. 412, F. & A. M. He is connected with the Brotherhood of Locomotive Engineers, his membership being with the United Division No. 292, at Middletown.

WILLIAM VANAMEE. The subject of this sketch was born in Albany, N. Y., January 9, 1847, of mingled Dutch and Scotch descent, his father, Dr. Simon Vanamee, being a descendant of one of the early settlers from Holland, and his mother, Anna (Graham) Vanamee, being of Scotch extraction. While he was yet a child his parents removed to Kingston, Ulster County, N. Y., where he received an education at the Kingston Academy. When he was nineteen years old he went to Middletown, Orange County, to study law with Judge Groo. Two years afterwards he was admitted to practice at the General Term of the Supreme Court held at Poughkeepsie in May, 1868. He began the practice of law in Middletown, where he has ever since continued it, and he has been connected with many important cases. He was the sole counsel for the Receiver of the Middletown National Bank for eight years after its failure in 1884. The complicated litigations following that failure, some of which required his presence and arguments in the United States Circuit Court in the state of Nebraska, resulted invariably in favor of the Receiver, and saved to the depositors a large portion of the assets of the bank.

After the death of Judge Wilkin in 1889, Mr. Vanamee was appointed attorney for the Middletown Savings Bank, which position he still retains. In the same year he was appointed the attorney for the New York, Ontario & Western Railway Company for the county of Orange, and he has conducted many important cases for it. At the same time he has not allowed himself to be exclusively a corporation lawyer, and he has frequently brought actions against railroad companies. The verdict of $18,500 obtained by him in favor of Gabriel Tuthill against the Long Island Railroad Company is a well known case. He was the specially retained attorney for the city of Middletown in the action brought by Jehiel Vaughn against the city for $40,000. He secured a favorable ruling, which defeated a large portion of the claim, and the remaining portion was then compromised.

Mr. Vanamee has always enjoyed the confidence of the courts. He was appointed by the General Term upon the committee to examine applicants for admission to the Bar. In 1894 he was appointed one of the Commissioners of Appraisal to determine and award the damages sustained by property-owners in Putnam County in the proceeding taken by the city of New York to acquire land for a pure-water supply.

Mr. Vanamee has always been a Democrat, casting his first vote in 1868 for Horatio Seymour for President. He does not take an active interest in politics, though he has occasionally responded to the demand for a speech in important campaigns. He was never a candidate for public office, except once, when, in 1888, he was the unsuccessful nominee of his party for County Judge. This was the year in which Harrison was elected President, and when Orange County was overwhelmingly Republican. For almost twenty years he has been a Trustee of the Middletown State Homeopathic Hospital.

For four years Mr. Vanamee was a member of the Middletown Board of Education. In 1880 he was chiefly instrumental in securing the election of the very first women who were elected in the state of New York to positions upon school boards. Five women were elected, Mrs. Persis A. Marvin, Mrs. Sophronia B. Corwin, Mrs. Harriet B. Morgan, Mrs. Lydia Sayer Hasbrouck and Mrs. Mary A. Moore. Mrs. Corwin declined to serve, and Mr. Vanamee was invited by the board to accept the position thus left vacant. He did so, chiefly because he was anxious to observe closely the working of the new system. He came to the conclusion, which he has always cherished, that women are peculiarly fitted for the successful discharge of such duties, and that they are more faithful and conscientious than men in the performance of them. Afterwards he was elected by the people to a three-years term of office on the board.

Mr. Vanamee did not have the benefit of a collegiate course, but in 1886 Hamilton College conferred upon him the degree of A. M., which was considered to be a well deserved mark of high distinction. Mr. Vanamee's tastes are literary When he was twenty years old he founded a department in the *Orange County Press*, entitled "Society and Literature," to which he contributed social and literary discussions. He is frequently in demand for memorial and public occasions. He was one of the speakers at the New Windsor Centennial, held at Temple Hill in 1883, and at the celebration of the Middletown City Charter in 1888. His tributes to the memory of Judge Wilkin, Judge Gedney and David A. Scott are especially remembered.

In October, 1889, Mr. Vanamee presented the name of Hon. J. O. Dykman to the Judicial Convention held in Brooklyn; and in October, 1893, Mr. Vanamee, at the request of the friends of Judge Isaac H. Maynard, presented his name to the Democratic State Convention at Saratoga Springs. Without reference to the political issues involved, his address upon this occasion was complimented by members of both parties.

Mr. Vanamee has made three trips to Europe, in 1878, 1887 and 1892. He has accumulated an extensive law and miscellaneous library. He is a member of the Bar Association of the City of New York and of the Reform Club. He is also a member of Winnisook Club, founded by Judge Alton B. Parker, Hon. Thomas E. Benedict and others, owning a portion of Slide Mountain in the Catskills; and of Camp Sabael, an association founded by Hon. Roswell C. Coleman upon the shores of Indian Lake, in the Adirondacks.

In the year 1871 Mr. Vanamee was married to Lida Ostrom, daughter of Dr. J. W. Ostrom, of Goshen. He has three children, Talcott, Theodora and Parker. By his untiring industry in the preparation of his cases and by his able, eloquent and convincing presentation of them in court and before juries, Mr. Vanamee has obtained a front rank in his profession.

OSCAR MILTON TERWILLIGER, freight agent for the New York, Lake Erie & Western Railroad at Middletown, was born in the town of Crawford July 2, 1852. His father, Milton, and grandfather, Samuel, were of Holland-Dutch descent, and were farmers in the town of Crawford, occupying a farm three miles east of Pine Bush. The former, upon reaching advanced years, retired from active labor and removed to Pine Bush, where he is now living, at the age of seventy-four. Politically he is a Republican. He is one of the oldest living members of the Prospect Reformed Church, in which he has been an officer, and contributed liberally to the erection of the edifice.

The mother of our subject, Mary (Moffatt) Terwilliger, was born in the town of Shawangunk, Ulster County, and was a daughter of Thomas Moffatt, a native of New England, and for many years a farmer of Ulster County, where he died. The family of Milton and Mary Terwilliger consisted of four children, but the only survivor besides our subject is Charles H., who is baggagemaster on the Crawford Branch of the Erie at Pine Bush. Oscar M. was reared on his father's farm and attended the public school at Pine Bush. In the spring of 1873 he began for himself, and for three years following he was employed in the works of the New York Knife Company, becoming thoroughly initiated into the process of manufacturing knives.

In 1878 Mr. Terwilliger came to Middletown and here for nearly four years he was employed in S. S. Wickham's mill. In 1882 he accepted a position in the freight department of the Ontario & Western, remaining with that company for two years. In 1884 he became yardmaster .for the Erie Railroad Company, but after two years he was transferred to the freight office, where he held the position of way-bill clerk until July 1, 1893. Since then he has been freight agent at Middletown, which is the largest station between Jersey City and Binghamton. In the freight department he has nine men under him, and a very large business is carried on.

The marriage of Mr. Terwilliger, at Walden, united him with Miss Amelia Samuel, daughter of Charles Samuel, and a native of that village. Mrs. Terwilliger is a member of the Presbyterian Church and is popular in society, receiving with grace and hospitality the many friends who visit her in her pleasant home at No. 69 Academy Avenue. Socially our subject is actively connected with Middletown Lodge No. 112, I.O.O.F., in which he has held official position, and he is also a member of Lancelot Lodge No. 169, K. of P., in this city. In politics he votes the Republican ticket.

WILLIAM H. KIRBY, passenger conductor on the New York, Ontario & Western Railroad, was born in South Centreville, N. Y., January 17, 1866, and is of direct English descent. His father, Oscar, was born near Honesdale, Wayne County, Pa., August 11, 1843, being a son of David, a native of Orange County, and a grandson of John Kirby, whose birthplace was in England. The latter, who was the son of an English merchant, was pressed into the English army for the War of 1812. One day, when injuries received prevented him from keeping up with the other soldiers in the line of march, he was struck by an English officer with a sword, which so aroused him that he deserted. After secreting himself for about a year, he managed to reach American lines, and finally came to Orange County, where he settled permanently.

From Wayne County, Pa., where he had engaged in farming, David Kirby came to Orange County, and in 1852 settled in the town of Wallkill, where he was similarly occupied until his death, at the age of sixty-three. Politically he was a Democrat, and for some time he served as Justice of the Peace. In religious belief he identified himself with the Old-school Baptists. His wife, Esther, was born in the town of Wawayanda as was also her father, Abraham Bennett; he was a farmer, and was massacred with the other people of that locality in the battle of Minisink.

The father of our subject was seventh among ten children, all of whom attained mature years, and seven are still living. In 1852 he came to Orange County, where he attended the district schools and Wallkill Academy. In 1862 he went to Pennsylvania in the employ of the Pennsylvania Coal Company as brakeman on their road between Holly and Dunmore. Two years later, in 1864, he became conductor on the same road, continuing there until 1871, when he resigned to enter the employ of the Erie Company. In 1880 he accepted a position as conductor on the Ontario & Western, with which road he has since remained, his home being in Middletown.

Though born in Orange County, the first six years in our subject's life were spent principally in Pennsylvania, but since then he has resided in Orange County. He began life for himself as clerk in a grocery store, and later was express messenger on the Ontario & Western Railroad between Ellenville and Middletown, with the American Express Company. In 1883 he became brakeman on a milk train between Middletown and Sidney, on the Ontario & Western, which position he filled for two years. Then, going to the western part of the state, he became conductor on a construction train with the Syracuse & Phœnix Railway Company, but had been there only three weeks when he was dragged under the wheels of a car, the flange of the right wheel entering his left limb. He was brought home, and for a year was unable to resume work, but fortunately, and as it seemed almost miraculously, he saved both limbs.

For seven months after his recovery Mr. Kirby was employed in the Homeopathic Hospital. In

1888 he was made baggagemaster at the Ontario & Western Depot, Middletown, where he remained for a year. Next he became flagman between Middletown and Weehawken. In August, 1890, he was promoted to be conductor, and during the winters since that time has made the run with engines Nos. 29, 30, 31 and 32, while in the summer he has charge of the through freight and extra passenger trains. In 1890, while coupling the cars in the dark, his thumb was smashed, inflicting a painful and serious wound; but, with his usual fortitude, he rode back eighty-two miles before he had it dressed, and was on duty again eight weeks afterward.

In Ellenville Mr. Kirby married Miss Carrie A. Kuhfeldt, who was born in that village. They are the parents of one son, Ralph. Politically our subject is a Republican. He is a Director in the Ontario & Western Branch at Middletown of the Western Building and Savings Association of Rochester. In religious belief he is connected with Grace Episcopal Church. Socially he belongs to Owosling Lodge, K. of P., at Ellenville, and Millard Division No. 52, Order of Railway Conductors, at Middletown, in which he has been active on various committees and has passed most of the chairs.

━━━━━━━━❁❄❁━━━━━━━━

ELTING DuBOIS FRANCE, of the firm of C. E. Crawford & Co., Middletown, was born near Ulsterville, in the town of Shawangunk, Ulster County, N. Y., September 17, 1854. The family which he represents originated in France, and was numbered among the pioneers of Ulster County. The grandfather, Elting France, was born near New Paltz in 1800, and married Catherine DuBois. Settling near Ulsterville, he was engaged as a tanner and scythe manufacturer there until his death in 1872. The France, Elting, DuBois and Schoonmaker families of Ulster County were all related to one another.

The father of our subject, Oliver D. France, was born in Ulster County, and in early life engaged with his father in the tanning business and manufacture of scythes, gradually giving the latter industry a larger share of his attention, until he followed it exclusively. The burning of his shops caused him subsequently to turn his attention to agriculture. He purchased a tract of one hundred and five acres, and built up a valuable farm, upon which he died in 1890, at the age of fifty-eight. He was well informed regarding public questions, and advocated the Democratic policy. His wife, whose maiden name was Mary Crist, was born near Pine Bush, Orange County, and died in 1875, at the age of forty-two. She was a daughter of Milton Crist, who in early life carried on a hotel, but later turned his attention to farming.

There were seven children born to the union of Oliver and Mary France, as follows: Elting DuBois; Bernice, of Middletown; Clarence, a farmer residing at Syracuse, Otoe County, Neb.; Abbie, who lives at Pine Bush; Mona J., wife of John Beckwith, of Frankfort, N. Y.; Theresa, Mrs. George Andrews, of Syracuse, Neb.; and Oliver, who resides in California. Our subject, who is the eldest of the family, remained with his parents until he attained his majority, when he started out for himself. About 1880 he came to Middletown, and for six months was employed in the delivery department of C. E. Crawford's store, after which he was in the packing department two years. He then became a salesman, and continued as such until February, 1891, when he became a member of the firm of C. E. Crawford & Co. The following year the firm opened a branch store in Port Jervis, and in 1894 commenced business in Goshen, and they now carry on a large trade in the three cities. They carry in stock the finest grades of furniture and buy in large quantities, in order to compete with the New York City trade.

The family residence at No. 15 Grove Street is presided over by our subject's wife and brightened by the presence of their two daughters, Ethel M. and Alice. Mrs. France, who bore the maiden name of Alida Boyd, was born in Mt. Hope, this county, being a daughter of Tooker Boyd, who died in Middletown. In Binghamton, this state, she received an excellent education, which fitted her for life's duties. Though

SAMUEL C. DURYEA.

not neglectful of the duties she owes to society, she finds her greatest happiness in contributing to the pleasure and promoting the welfare of her husband and children. The family attends the Second Presbyterian Church, in which Mr. and Mrs. France hold membership.

—⊶⊷⊷⋯◊⊰⊰◉⊱◌⊱⋯⊶⊷⊶—

SAMUEL CRAWFORD DURYEA. The family of which this gentleman is a member originated in France, and was of the Huguenot faith. After the revocation of the Edict of Nantes, in 1582, the ancestors were compelled to flee to other lands, leaving their possessions to be confiscated by the enemy. Joost Duryea, the founder of the family in this country, came to Long Island from Holland in 1675; and from Jamaica, Queens County, Yost, or George, our subject's great-grandfather, came to Orange County and settled in the town of Blooming Grove, of which he was a pioneer. He died in 1760 and was buried at Greycourt. His three children were George, Garret and Hannah.

George, our subject's grandfather, was a farmer, and a valuable factor in the pioneer development of his section. During the Revolution he was in active service in the cavalry department of the Colonial army. At his death, in 1832, at the age of eighty-six, he was buried on the homestead where his life was passed. His wife was Hannah Hudson, of Goshen, whose father came from New London, Conn., and was the first Sheriff of Orange County. Their family consisted of five sons and four daughters, viz.: George, John, Henry, Garret and Hudson; Hannah, who married Cornelius Decker, of the town of Montgomery; Dolly, Mrs. John Rosa, of Sullivan County; Betsey, who became the wife of Pierson Geming, of Blooming Grove; and Mitte, who never married.

At the old homestead in Blooming Grove, John Duryea, father of our subject, was born December 29, 1778. In early life he learned the blacksmith's trade. February 18, 1800, he married Mary, daughter of Samuel and Jeannette (Mc-

Curdy) Crawford, of the town of Montgomery. This lady was born May 27, 1778, and died November 27, 1857. After their marriage they removed to the town of Wallkill and settled two miles east of Bloomingburg, where he engaged in farming until his death, January 21, 1859. Of his children we note the following: Nancy married Daniel Brush, then of Bloomingburg, subsequently a farmer of the town of Crawford; Jeannette became the wife of Horace Mills, of Bloomingburg; Hannah married James G. Thompson, of Craigsville; Mary A. formerly resided in Middletown; John H. was for fifty years pastor of the Second Reformed Church of Paterson, N. J.; Samuel C., our subject, is the only surviving child of the parental family; Jonathan for many years occupied his father's homestead, but afterward lived in Middletown until his death; and two other children died in youth.

The mother of our subject was born in the town of Crawford and was the daughter of Samuel I. and Jeannette (McCurdy) Crawford. The former, who was born in the same town, December 18, 1750, and died October 17, 1828, was a son of James Crawford, a native of Ireland, who settled in this country in the early part of the last century. Jeannette McCurdy was born February 14, 1757, in Pennsylvania, and died January 12, 1839.

In the town of Wallkill, where he was born July 16, 1815, the subject of this notice was reared to manhood. April 6, 1838, he removed to the town of Crawford and purchased the farm where he now resides. His first marriage occurred January 24, 1838, and united him with Miss Emily Tuthill, who was born in the town of Blooming Grove, December 1, 1814, being a daughter of James and Sarah (Wells) Tuthill. She died July 2, 1850, leaving one son, John E. January 7, 1852, our subject married Mary E. Bull, daughter of Henry Bull and a native of the town of Crawford. She died April 20, 1892. Our subject commenced life with but limited capital and now owns one hundred and forty acres of valuable land. Politically he is a Republican, and since 1870 he has been Railroad Bonding Commissioner. Though now eighty years old, he is an active, hale and well preserved man. The accompanying portrait was taken after his eightieth birthday.

John E., our subject's son, was born in the town of Crawford, September 6, 1840, and has always remained on the home farm, which he now superintends. December 2, 1863, he married Miss Jane Frances Hunter, who was born in the town of Montgomery March 20, 1842, and died March 19, 1883, leaving four daughters: Emily C., wife of Murray M. Hunter, of Milwaukee, Wis.; Mary F., Edna H. and Anna Z., accomplished young ladies who are with their father. As a Republican John E. Duryea takes an active interest in political affairs. For twelve years he has been Justice of the Peace, and for four years Justice of the Session of Orange County. He is a member of Wallkill Lodge No. 627, F. & A. M., at Walden, and Hiawatha Lodge, K. of P., at Pine Bush.

~~~~~~

GEORGE L. KNOX. Though for about thirty years connected with the Caldwell Lead Works of New York City, and a resident of Jersey City, Mr. Knox has never lost interest in old Orange, the county of his birth, nor his love for Middletown, where his childhood days were spent. No one takes a deeper interest in its welfare or greater delight in its progress than does he, and by his frequent visits here he is enabled to keep in touch with the material advancement made in every line.

Mr. Knox is a member of an old and honored family of this county, and full mention of his parental and ancestral history will be found in the sketch of his brother-in-law, Isaac L. Cassell, presented on another page. He was born in Middletown May 2, 1828, and was reared there and in New Vernon, receiving his education in the common schools and in Liberty Institute, at Liberty, Sullivan County, where he was under the preceptorship of Prof. John S. Stoddard. After completing his studies he engaged in teaching for three years at Matamoras, Pa., and Wurtsboro and White Lake, N. Y. He then took up civil-engineering, which he followed for a few

years, becoming very proficient in that occupation. While thus employed he ran the line from Suffern to Jersey City, double-tracking the old narrow gauge to a six-foot gauge.

Going West in 1858, Mr. Knox became paymaster for a contract on what is now the Lake Shore & Michigan Southern Railroad, and was employed in that capacity about three years, having his headquarters near Erie, Pa. On his return to New York, he had charge of a contract for the building of the Warwick Railroad, now the Lehigh & Hudson River Railroad, between Greycourt and Warwick, and on closing that contract he became timekeeper and paymaster in the yards at Jersey City.

In January, 1866, when his uncles started the Caldwell Lead Works, Mr. Knox became bookkeeper for the concern, and upon the incorporation of the company, in 1869, he became a stockholder. For some time he has been a Trustee and the Treasurer of the company. The works are situated at No. 63 Center Street, New York City, and a specialty is made of the manufacture of shot and of plumbers and steam-fitters' supplies. There is a shot tower one hundred and seventy-four feet high, together with two large lead presses and a rolling-mill. The founders of the enterprise, his uncles, are dead, and he is the only one of the original members left. As a business man he is keen, shrewd and discriminating, and the success of the business is due not a little to his zeal and energy. The firm carries a capital stock of $250,000, and is conducting business upon a sound financial basis.

The home of Mr. Knox is at No. 218 Eighth Street, Jersey City, and he belongs to the Second Presbyterian Church of that place; also to Mechanics Lodge No. 66, I. O. O. F., of that city, in which he has been an officer and its representative to the grand lodge. At one time he was a member of the encampment. Since the nomination of Abraham Lincoln for the Presidency, he has advocated the principles of the Republican party and has cast his ballot for its candidates. He was united in marriage, in Monroe, Orange County, with Miss Fannie Mapes, who was born there, being the daughter of Julius and Samantha Mapes, prominent farmers of that locality. Mrs. Knox passed from earth February 8, 1894, and was laid to rest in Hillside Cemetery, Middletown, where a monument has been erected to her memory, bearing the simple inscription, "She has gone home."

AMZY A. TURNER, a veteran of the Tenth Legion, residing in Middletown, was born in Fishkill, Dutchess County, N Y., May 15, 1843, and is a son of Stephen M. and Delia A. (Moshier) Turner, the former a native of Dutchess County, and the latter of Newburgh, Orange County. The father was a farmer in his native county, and also engaged in raising thoroughbred fast horses. Late in life he retired from the business and located at Canterbury, where he died. His wife, the mother of our subject, comes of an old Revolutionary family of German descent, her grandfather, Captain Moshier, being an aide-de-camp on the staff of General Washington. He was wounded in the arm, although he recovered and died at Newburgh. The mother died when eighty-nine years of age. She had a brother who lived in Newburgh and who died in 1894, at the age of one hundred and three years. Of the children born to Stephen M. and Delia A. Turner, we mention the following: Harvey, who was a soldier in Company D, Fifty-sixth New York Infantry, now resides in the Black Hills; Isaac, who was in Company K, of the same regiment, resides in Newburgh; John, who was in Company C, of the Fifty-sixth, also makes his home in Newburgh; Amzy is the subject of this sketch; Joseph N., who also served in the Fifty-sixth, resides at No. 84 Grand Avenue, Middletown; Phœbe now resides in Montana; Mary, who became Mrs. Knoff, died in Middletown; and one daughter died in infancy.

The subject of this sketch was reared in his native village, and received a limited education in its public schools. As his father met with misfortune when he was but seven years of age, he was compelled to start out in life for himself, and began work on a farm in the town of Goshen,

where he remained until he was thirteen years old. In 1856 he began work in the brickyard of Solomon Wood, of Goshen, with whom he learned the trade of brick-making, and then went to Ridgebury, and in Cummings' brickyard was employed until in July, 1861, when he enlisted in Company D, Fifty-sixth New York Infantry, or the Tenth Legion, under Colonel Van Wyck. He was mustered into the service at New Windsor. While the regiment was being enlisted, he spent $400 in enlisting and taking men to the regiment, and took down about one-third of the regiment. Soon after being mustered in, the regiment was ordered South, and was in active service until it was mustered out. Among the battles and skirmishes in which our subject participated, may be mentioned Lee's Mill, Baltimore Cross-roads, Chickihominy Swamp, Yorktown, Williamsburg, Seven Pines, Fair Oaks, Malvern Hill, Newport News (N. C.), Charleston, Honey Hill, Ladies' Island, John's Island and Secessionville.

In front of Charleston he volunteered to go out for the boys and get water which was in the magazine. He was the only one that had courage enough to go, and for the service he was offered $20. He refused it, however, both before and after his return with the water. Gathering up the canteens, about thirty in number, and stringing them over his neck, he passed out to the magazine, filled the canteens and returned in full range of the rebels. He walked stooping, and had just reached the riflepit, into which he was ready to jump, when a rebel sharpshooter shot at him, the ball striking the edge of one eye and lodging in the skull. He jumped up, however, and the boys dragged him into the riflepits. This was on Sunday morning, and he had to lie there until about ten o'clock in the evening, when he was taken to the field hospital. For a time he was blind in both eyes. The ball was extracted, however, and in seven weeks he returned to the field again. The eye was damaged, and at times even now is painful, and his sight is defective. Rejoining his regiment, he was with it on the Peninsula, where he received a sunstroke, and later he was mustered out and honorably discharged, in 1864, just before the expiration of his term of service. While in the service, in Maryland, the regiment was ordered to make a raid. As a result they obtained about two thousand head of swine, fifteen hundred head of sheep, fifteen hundred head of horses, about the same number of cows, four hundred and fifty head of steers and numerous fowls.

At Fair Oaks, while on picket duty, a rebel crawled up to our subject, with the intention of shooting him. Hearing him, Mr. Turner reached out his hat, which was fired upon by the rebel. Mr. Turner fired back and killed the latter. Mr. Turner was one of the color guards of his regiment, and was often a mark for rebel bullets. Several balls were shot through his clothes, and his canteen was shot several times.

On receiving his discharge Mr. Turner came to Middletown, and for a long time he was unable to do any work, and has never been in good health. In 1866 he was united in marriage with Miss Catherine Knoff, who was born here, and who died March 28, 1892. They were the parents of six children, five of whom are yet living. Georgiana is deceased; Arthur W. is in the employ of the Tompkins Hat Works; and Mary, Bell, Louis S. and Stella are at home. Mr. Turner is a member of General Lyon Post, G. A. R., and in religious belief he is a Methodist, being a member of the Methodist Episcopal Church at Middletown. Politically he is a true-blue Republican, and cast his first Presidential vote for Abraham Lincoln in 1860. While in North Carolina he voted for him the second time.

JOHN ALFONSUS GANNON has been in the employ of the New York, Susquehanna & Western Railway Company since 1870, and in point of years of service is the oldest engineer on the present railroad system in Middletown. He is of Irish parentage, but American birth, and with the versatility of one race combines the energy characteristic of the other. His father, John Gannon, was born in Ireland,

being the son of a large land-owner there. After his marriage he came to America, and for a time sojourned in Spring Valley, Rockland County, from which place he removed to Piermont, and became an employe of the Erie Railroad there. Thence he went to Port Jervis in 1864, still, however, continuing with the Erie, and he has remained an employe of that company up to the present time, having been with them forty-seven years. He is now railroad baggagemaster between New York and Dunkirk, and though past the prime of life is still active and robust. His wife, who bore the maiden name of Mary Galancy, was born in Ireland, and died in Port Jervis.

The family of John and Mary Gannon comprised nine children, all of whom attained years of maturity. The first death among them was that of Edward, the third eldest, who held the position of engineer on the New York & Northern Railroad. During a severe blizzard in 1888 he was opening the track with a snow plow, and through an accident was killed instantly. Frank, the eldest son, and a twin of our subject, is a very successful and prominent railroad man. He is Superintendent of the Baltimore & Ohio between Staten Island and Pennsylvania, and President and Superintendent of the Staten Island Railroad, also manager of the boats. Mrs. Kate McGovern, the eldest daughter, is a widow and lives in Port Jervis. James is an engine-dispatcher at High Bridge, on the New York Central Railroad. Thomas is an operator on the Erie at Port Jervis. Bernard, the youngest son, is ticket agent on the Staten Island Road at Perth Amboy. The youngest children, Mary and Lizzie, reside with their father in Port Jervis.

At Spring Valley, Rockland County, N. Y., the subject of this sketch was born September 24, 1852. He was reared in Piermont until twelve years of age, when he accompanied the other members of the family to Port Jervis, and there he attended school. Commencing for himself, he was for eighteen months employed in the Erie shops in Port Jervis, after which he was clerk in Turner's Hotel for eighteen months. In 1870 he became brakeman on the Jersey & Midland, now

ABNER S. WELLS.

the New York, Susquehanna & Western, and after six months in that capacity he took a position as fireman between Middletown and Ellenville. In June, 1874, he was promoted to engineer, in which position he has since been employed, being with a freight train the first six months, and afterward on a passenger train. For the past sixteen years his run has been on a milk train between Middletown and Jersey City. Since 1879 he has made his home in Middletown, where he owns residence property at No. 158 Railroad Avenue.

At Port Jervis Mr. Gannon was united in marriage with Miss Mary A. Cuff, who was born there, and died in January, 1894, leaving four children, Frank, Andrew, Regina and Winnifred. In national politics our subject is a Democrat, though in local elections he is inclined to be independent, giving his ballot to the man whom he considers best qualified for office. He is identified with the Brotherhood of Locomotive Engineers, belonging to Silk Division No. 521, at Paterson, N. J.

ABNER S. WELLS. There are no names more worthy to be perpetuated than those of our brave soldier boys, some of whom have passed away to join the great army of the dead, but many remain, boys no longer, though still as devoted to our country as in the days of their youth. In the list of brave men whom Orange County sent to the front in defense of the institutions of our Government, we find the name of Abner S. Wells, of Middletown. During his long service in the army he was ever gallant, brave and loyal, and as in war, so in peace he has displayed the noblest principles and highest honor in his life work.

The birth of Mr. Wells occurred June 3, 1838, in the town of Wawayanda, on the Wallkill line, four and a-half miles southwest of Middletown. His father, Abner S., Sr., was also born in that town, being a son of William Wells, who with five or six brothers came from Long Island, some of them settling in this locality. During the

Revolutionary War Grandfather Wells rendered loyal service in the army. He gained considerable prominence in this county, and the farm owned by him in the town of Wawayanda became the center of a settlement known as Wells' Corner. There one of his sons, Abijah, ran a hotel. The place is now known as South Centreville, and in it the grandfather's death occurred at the age of about seventy.

In the town of Wawayanda, near the Wallkill line, Abner S. Wells, Sr., cultivated his finely improved farm, following agricultural pursuits until he became blind, when he was obliged to retire from active labor. He died when seventy-one years old. He had served valiantly in the War of 1812, and politically was first a Whig and later a Republican. In religious belief he was connected with the Methodist Episcopal Church. His wife, whose maiden name was Mary Hunter, was born in Slate Hill, and was a daughter of Robert Hunter, a descendant of Dutch ancestors. She passed from earth in 1893, aged ninety-four years. Of her thirteen children, ten attained years of maturity and five are still living. George, one of the sons, was for a short time a member of a New York battery.

From an early age our subject displayed a remarkable aptitude for music, his favorite instrument being the violin, on which he soon acquired such proficiency as to attract attention. While he learned the trade of a carpenter under a cousin in Pennsylvania and later followed that occupation, yet he still devoted a large share of his attention to music, and for ten or twelve years after the war his time was largely spent in travel, visiting different cities, where he gave concerts. The Wells Orchestra, of which he was the leader, consisted of five pieces, and possessed a high order of merit. Finally, however, owing to the ill effects of the night work upon his health, he retired from the profession.

In September, 1861, at the opening of the Civil War, Mr. Wells enlisted in the Second Cavalry Company of the Tenth Legion, or Fifty-sixth Regiment New York State Volunteers, Col. C. H. Van Wyck commanding, and was mustered into the United States service the following November. The regiment was ordered to Washington, and went into camp on Calorama Heights. Thence they removed to Rock Creek, and afterwards proceeded to Meridian Hill. From this place the two cavalry companies were detached for Fortress Monroe, where they formed the First New York Mounted Rifles, commanded by C. C. Dodge. Mr. Wells was here taken ill with the black measles, followed by typhoid fever, and for a long time he was so ill that many considered his recovery impossible. However, his good constitution enabled him to conquer the disease, and in time he regained his strength. At Williamsburg, Va., in 1863, he was assigned to the veteran corps, and in July, 1865, the First New York and the Third New York Cavalry were consolidated and mustered out as the Fourth Provisional Cavalry at City Point, Va.

Locating in Middletown at the close of the war, Mr. Wells became leader of the orchestra that bore his name, and with it traveled throughout the country. In 1876 he began the occupation of contracting and building, in which he continued for a number of years, but later retired from active business. Among the residences erected by him is his elegant home at No. 86 Monhagen Avenue, where the commodious house is surrounded by four and a-half acres of ground. He has built three residences for himself, and still owns two, and he has also erected a number of houses owned by the most prominent men of the city.

In Middletown occurred the marriage of Mr. Wells and Miss Libbie Van Inwegen, who was born in Huguenot, in the town of Deerpark. Her father, David, who was born in the same place, was a farmer by occupation, and died near Monticello. Her paternal grandfather, Harmonis Van Inwegen, was of Holland-Dutch descent. Her mother, Sallie Van Inwegen in maidenhood, though bearing the same name as her husband, was in no way related to him. The maternal grandfather, John Van Inwegen, was a farmer of Huguenot, and served in the War of 1812. His wife, who was a Miss Van Fleet, was of Dutch extraction, and died in Port Jervis. Mrs. Wells was the eldest of four children, all of whom are

living. By her marriage she is the mother of a daughter, Lottie Mae, a talented violinist and a member of the Class of '96, Wallkill Academy.

Every old soldier is interested in Grand Army affairs, and Mr. Wells is a member of Capt. W. A. Jackson Post No. 301. He and his wife and daughter belong to the Methodist Episcopal Church and are regular attendants at the services. In national affairs he favors protection of home interests, and therefore upholds the principles of the Republican party, but in local matters he works for prohibition, believing that the country will be benefited and the people elevated when the liquor traffic is exterminated.

REV. FRANK ARTHUR HEATH, pastor of the First Baptist Church at Middletown, is one of the most popular ministers in the city. He was born March 20, 1860, at Boston, Mass., and is a son of Thomas and Caroline (Pierce) Heath, the former a native of Rhode Island, and the latter of Fall River, Mass. On his father's side he is of English, and on his mother's side of Scotch, ancestry. His grandfather, Capt. William Vose Heath, was a native of Newport, R. I., and for many years was a sea-captain, engaged in the coasting trade. On one of his trips he fell from his vessel and received injuries which resulted in his death. Thomas Heath, the father of our subject, is a carriage manufacturer, and has been engaged in the business in Boston, in one location, since 1858. While somewhat advanced in years, he is hale and hearty. He is very prominent in social and benevolent societies, and has been District Deputy Grand Master of the Independent Order of Odd Fellows for years. He is also a prominent member of the Knights of Pythias, having filled all the offices in the local lodge, and of the uniformed rank. He is a very sociable man, and a very successful after-dinner speaker. His wife, the mother of our subject, is an active worker in the Woman's Christian Temperance Union, and in the Pythian Sisterhood. They have three sons and one daughter, all living. William H. is a chief engineer in Brooklyn. Frederick, blind from infancy, is a natural musician, and a graduate of Perkins' Institute for the Blind in South Boston. He is an instructor on the organ and piano, and is also an eminent soloist. Mary is now Mrs. Warren M. Blood, of East Pepperell, Mass.; and Frank Arthur is the subject of this sketch.

Rev. Frank Arthur Heath graduated from the Boston Latin School, an institution formerly attended by Charles Sumner, Wendell Phillips, and other prominent men, and then entered Colgate University, at Hamilton, N. Y., from which he graduated in 1885 with the degree of A. B. Three years later, on the completion of his course in theology, he received from that institution the degree of A. M. While in college he was a member of the Delta Upsilon fraternity. On completing his regular course, he entered the theological seminary at Hamilton, from which he graduated in 1888. After he entered the sophomore year, he preached continually, and in that way mainly secured the means to pay his way through college. While at Hamilton he preached four years steadily at Unadilla, N. Y., and after his ordination, July 7, 1888, at Acton, Mass., an old Revolutionary town, whence Capt. Isaac Davis and his minutemen went and met the British on the old North Bridge at Concord. He remained at Acton, Mass., as pastor of the Baptist Church until 1891, when he received an urgent call to Binghamton, N. Y., to take charge of a new mission church at that place.

While at Binghamton, our subject bought new ground, on which he moved the chapel, and during his two-years pastorate received one hundred and fifty new members, leaving the church in excellent condition. In August, 1893, he was called to the pastorate of the First Baptist Church at Middletown, as successor to Rev. Christian J. Page. The church here is an old society, and for some years had been burdened with debt, but Mr. Page aided greatly in clearing it, and the balance was paid within four months after Mr. Heath took charge of the church. In October, 1893, on payment of the debt, the church had a jubilee, which was participated in by Rev. Mr.

Page. With a present membership of over three hundred and fifty, which is constantly growing, the church has a bright future before it. Soon after coming here, Mr. Heath began the agitation for having Sunday services at Midway Park, which was opposed by some of the clergy, but Mr. Heath was determined, and began the work, in which he has been eminently successful, being able to reach a class of people there that never go to church. In his work he now has the co-operation of the majority of the people of Middletown, who bid him God-speed.

Mr. Heath was married, in Boston, to Miss May Walker, born in Kingston, Nova Scotia, and daughter of John Walker, who died there, after which the family removed to Cambridge, where Mrs. Heath was educated. Three children have been born unto them: Genevieve, Sherburne and Marjorie.

Mr. Heath is a member of the Masonic fraternity, holding membership with the lodge at Unadilla. He is also a member of Middletown Lodge No. 112, I. O. O. F., and of the Independent Order of Good Templars. In politics he is independent, with strong Republican and Prohibition leanings. For years he has been a valued contributor to various religious journals. His pulpit ability is of the highest order, and it is a delight to sit under his ministration. In his pastoral work he is very successful, and is popular with those inside and outside of his church.

JAMES G. MARTIN, a practical moulder in Middletown, was born in Dublin, Ireland, in 1852, and is a son of John and Ann Martin. His father, and also his grandfather, Peter Martin, were architects and builders in Dublin, of which city they were both natives. They were the architects and builders of Conciliation Hall, built at the time of the repeal of the Union. His father did quite a large business, and died in Australia, about 1880. To John and Ann Martin were born two children, our subject being the only living one.

James G. Martin was educated in Dublin, at

Clongeswood College, and then took up the study of law with John D. Rosenthal, remaining with him three years. In 1869 he left Dublin for Liverpool, and from there took the steamer "Queen" for New York City. After remaining there a couple of months, he came to Middletown, and entered the employ of Howell, Hinchman & Co., tanners, with whom he remained until October of that year, and then began to learn the moulder's trade with E. P. Wheeler, one of the pioneers of Middletown. After continuing with that gentleman four years, he worked for him as a journeyman until his death, with the exception of a short time spent at Goshen, New York City and Franklin. While in Mr. Wheeler's employ, he made several trips to the Old Country, and in 1886 took his family with him, with some idea of remaining there. His presence in Dublin was rendered necessary in the settlement of his father's estate. Disposing of his interest in that city, he returned to Middletown, and engaged in whittling blocks for straw hats, remaining in the business, more or less, for sixteen years. In 1891 he formed a partnership with Thomas H. Butler, a practical moulder, and, under the firm name of Butler & Martin, built the present shop, which has a capacity of five tons per day. After continuing the business one year, our subject purchased Mr. Butler's interest, and has since continued alone. The main building is 50x100 feet, fronting on Wisner Avenue, and is on the line of the New York, Ontario & Western Railway. The engine is of twenty-four horsepower, and the boiler of forty horse-power. Mr. Martin makes a specialty of green sand work, and has quite a trade with New York parties, besides a local trade. He also does considerable work for the New York, Ontario & Western Railway.

In 1871 Mr. Martin was married, in Middletown, to Mary A. Cunningham, whose birth occurred here. She died in October, 1886, on the voyage from Greenock to New York, when five days out, and was buried in midocean. At her death she left five children, four of whom are living: Annie, now Mrs. Andrew Riley, of New York; James, who, at this writing, is in China; and Michael and Gregory, at home. Mr. Martin's

second marriage was with Mrs. Annie (Houston) Killbride, who was born in Middletown, but who resided in Newark. They have two children, Kevin and Kathleen. Mr. Martin is a member of St. Joseph's Catholic Church, and in politics is independent.

GEORGE HEATER, a contractor and builder residing at Middletown, was born in the town of Wantage, Sussex County, N. J., October 12, 1832. His father, Martin, who was born in Warren County, that state, was of German ancestry, and was a son of a hero of the War of 1812, who engaged in farm pursuits in New Jersey. In early life he learned the trade of a moulder at Oxford, and later removed to Deckertown, where he died at the age of seventy-seven. His wife, Eliza Ketcham, was born in Warren County, and there died. Of their eight children, all of whom arrived at mature years, only four are now living, George being the eldest.

The subject of this notice spent his boyhood years principally in the vicinity of Hamburg and Newton, Sussex County. In every respect he is entitled to be called a self-made man, for he never attended school, nor did he have any opportunities for advancing himself in the world save those which he made for himself. When only eight years old he began for himself, and from that time forward he was self-supporting. For a while he was employed on a farm, later worked in a blast furnace in Hamburg, and afterward learned the cooper's trade in Sussex County, N. J., near Unionville, N. Y., where he followed his chosen occupation.

Going South, Mr. Heater was for six years foreman of a shop in Murfreesboro, Tenn. While there the war broke out, and owing to his location he was harassed considerably. When Buell's army fell back to Tennessee, he joined them and returned with them to Louisville, Ky., from which city he came to his former home. He soon afterward engaged in the grocery business in Jersey City, where he remained until May, 1863, the date of his arrival in Middletown. For

MILTON C. CONNER, M. D.

a time he worked at the cooper's trade in this place, and had a shop on John Street, near Linden Avenue, which was burned down once, but afterward rebuilt. In 1880 he worked at his trade with P. F. Miller, and later was with other parties until 1894, when he began as a contractor and builder. Among the residences erected under his supervision are those of W. Adams, Emery Van Keuren and George Jacobs.

In Shelbyville, Tenn., in 1862, Mr. Heater married Miss Annie Ruth, daughter of David Ruth, a carriage-painter of that place. Four children survive of the eight born unto them, Elsie, William, Lizzie and Mamie being deceased. Mrs. Mattie Hoyt, the eldest daughter, lives in Middletown. George is engaged in the milk business in New York City. Annie and Edgar are with their parents, the family occupying a neat residence on Sprague Avenue. Socially Mr. Heater is connected with the Knights of Honor and also with Hoffman Lodge No. 412, F. & A. M. In politics he votes for the men and principles advocated by the Republican party.

✦❧━━━▲✦◆✖◆✖◆✦◆━━❧✦

MILTON C. CONNER, M. D. Since the completion of his medical course and his graduation from college, Dr. Conner has practiced his profession in Middletown, and the flattering success with which he has met is indicated by his constantly increasing practice. While he is skilled in the treatment of all diseases, his specialty has been diseases of the eye and ear, concerning which he is accurately informed, and in the treatment of which he has few superiors. He has an office in the Everett Building, on the corner of Main and North Streets; also at his residence. In addition to his general practice, he was for four years Health Officer of Middletown, and for one year served as City Physician.

The Conner family originated in Ireland, and was first represented in America by the Doctor's grandfather, William Conner, who emigrated to this country and settled in the town of Wallkill, Orange County, where he was variously employed as a mason, distiller and farmer. His death oc-

curred when he was about seventy years of age. The father of our subject, Hezekiah, was born in the town of Wallkill, where he spent his entire life, following the occupations of mason and farmer. In religious views he was a Presbyterian, while politically he supported the Republican party. In 1889, at the age of eighty-one, while on his way to the city one day, he was thrown from the wagon and run over by the team, sustaining fatal injuries.

Three times married, Hezekiah Conner had two children by his first marriage and five by his second, four of them surviving; his third union was childless. His second wife, our subject's mother, was Caroline, daughter of Phineas Corwin, a farmer of the town of Wallkill. She died at the age of forty-six years. Milton C. is the youngest of the family, and was born on the home farm near Scotchtown, town of Wallkill, September 6, 1853. In boyhood he attended the Wallkill Academy for a time, but was obliged to temporarily discontinue his studies on account of his father having broken his leg, which rendered it necessary for him to manage the home place. He then entered the Ft. Edward Institute, and later was a student in the Cazenovia Seminary, spending two years in each institution. Meantime he taught school at Ft. Ann, N. Y., for one year.

Having resolved to become a physician, our subject entered the Detroit Medical College, in which his brother was a professor. Two years were spent there, after which he became a student in the College of Physicians and Surgeons of New York, from which, after two years, he was graduated, in 1883, with the degree of M. D. Upon completing his studies he opened an office in Middletown, where he has since had charge of a general practice. He is examining surgeon for numerous insurance companies, and is one of the most popular physicians of the city. Interested in everything that pertains to the science, he holds membership in the New York State Medical Association, and is serving on the Executive Committee of the Fifth District Branch of that organization. He is also identified with the American Medical Association, and was a delegate to the conventions of that body held at Detroit, Milwaukee, San Francisco and Baltimore.

The marriage of Dr. Conner took place in this city and united him with Frances Adelaide Cox, who was born in Bloomingburg, N. Y., being the daughter of the late George Cox, formerly an attorney of Middletown. Socially the Doctor is connected with Hoffman Lodge No. 412, F. & A. M., and Midland Chapter No. 240, R. A. M. He is intelligently posted upon public questions, and believes that the policy of the Republican party is best calculated to advance the welfare of the people; hence he gives it his unqualified support.

L EWIS STEWART STIVERS. One of the influential Republican papers of Orange County is the Middletown *Daily Times*, a nine-column folio, devoted especially to the interests of Middletown. It has the largest circulation of any daily between Paterson and Binghamton, and is surpassed by only one paper in this county, the Newburgh *News*. Through the Associated Press reports, it is enabled to furnish its readers the latest and most authentic news from every part of the world. Not a little of its success is due to the zeal and ability of the subject of this notice, who is one of its editors and proprietors. Aside from this paper, he is also one of the publishers of the *Semi-weekly Times*, a nine-column folio, and read by a large number of subscribers in this and adjoining counties. In addition to the newspaper work, there is a large and well equipped job office, from which work of the highest grade is turned out, and which is liberally patronized by the people of the city.

In the town of Wawayanda the subject of this sketch was born April 20, 1859. After attending the public schools and Wallkill Academy, he entered Peekskill Military Academy, from which he was graduated in 1876. On concluding his studies, he entered the office of the Middletown *Press*, of which his father was editor and part owner. In 1891, with his brother,

John D. Stivers, he began publishing the Middletown *Daily Times* and the *Orange County Times*, a semi-weekly paper.

Mr. Stivers was one of the original members and organizers of the Twenty-fourth Separate Company National Guard of New York, which was organized in 1887. For three years he was Second Lieutenant of the company, and in 1890 was promoted to the rank of First Lieutenant, which he still holds.

Besides his other interests Mr. Stivers is a charter member and Director of the Orange County Telephone Company. Now an honorary member of the Excelsior Hook and Ladder Company, he was for several years an officer of the organization, and for two years he was Secretary of the Middletown Fire Department. For a number of years he was a member and officer of the Bachelors' Social Club. He was united in marriage, in this city, with Miss Cora D. Mackay, daughter of John Mackay, who for many years was connected with the Orange County Foundry Company. They are the parents of two children, Christina and Gladys.

C HARLES TIERNEY, who is an engineer on the New York, Ontario & Western Railroad, was born at Howells Depot, this county, March 14, 1852. His father, James, was born in County Tyrone, Ireland, and when a young man emigrated to America, and bought a farm at Howells Depot, where for a short time he carried on agricultural pursuits. Later he was employed as section man on the Erie Railroad, and afterward became section foreman, in which capacity he was employed until his retirement from business. He died at Howells Depot, at the age of fifty-two years. His wife, whose maiden name was Ellen Gibbon, was born in County Donegal, Ireland, and died in Middletown, at the home of our subject, July 4, 1889.

The family of James and Ellen Tierney consisted of nine children, of whom five are living, Charles being next to the eldest. He was reared in the place of his birth, and at the age of ten began to work on a farm adjoining his home. In 1869 he was employed on the construction of the New York & Oswego Midland, now known as the New York, Ontario & Western, working at Summitville until the fall of 1870, when he came to Middletown. He was brakeman on the first train that was put on at Middletown, being under Engineer McNiff. In the spring of 1871 he began as fireman on a switch engine, afterward was fireman between Middletown and Liberty, and in 1872 was promoted to engineer, running a switch engine in the Middletown yards. Next he was employed as fireman on the New York Division of the New York & Oswego Midland, between Middletown and Jersey City. In 1874 he was again made engineer, and from that time until 1883 his run was on the New Jersey Midland, and the New York, Susquehanna & Western. During the last-named year, he resigned to accept a position as engineer on the New York, Ontario & Western, between Middletown and Norwich. Until 1886 his run was on a freight train, but from that time until 1891 he had charge of a passenger train, and since the latter year he has been extra passenger and yard engineer.

Only one serious accident has happened to Mr. Tierney during his long railroad experience. This was near Stockholm, N. J., in October, 1873, when he was in the employ of the New Jersey Midland. A bank had washed away from under a bridge, and the train, running on the bridge, precipitated the structure into the water. The engine turned over, throwing him into the water, but he made his way to the shore, where he was soon found. Though severely bruised, his injuries were not serious, and he was able to resume work in six weeks from the time of the accident.

At No. 27 Broad, corner of Prince, Street, Mr. Tierney has a neat and comfortable home, where he and his family reside. He was married in this city, his wife being Ellen Murphy, daughter of Thomas Murphy, formerly a railroad man residing in this city. Their family consists of four children: George, Charles, Frank and Ellen. Active in the ranks of the Democratic party, Mr. Tierney has served as a member of the City Com-

mittee, and in other local positions. In religious connections he is a member of St. Joseph's Catholic Church. He is a member of the Brotherhood of Locomotive Engineers, and is first engineer of United Division No. 292.

DANIEL BAILEY HARDENBERGH, M. D. The son of a physician and the grandson of a physician, the subject of this sketch may claim his profession through heritage as well as by the unusual zeal and advantages devoted to its acquirement. The genealogy of the Hardenbergh family has already been reviewed in the sketches of the subject's father, Dr. Henry Hardenbergh, and grandfather, Dr. Charles Hardenbergh. His mother, Delia, was born in Wallkill, the daughter of Nathaniel Bailey, and a descendant of Capt. Daniel Bailey, an officer in the Revolutionary War.

Daniel Bailey Hardenbergh was born in Port Jervis, March 13, 1866, and graduated from the Port Jervis Academy as valedictorian of his class in 1883. After a year spent under private tuition to complete preparation, he entered Yale College, from which he was graduated in 1888, with the degree of A. B. In his sophomore year he secured a position in his class crew, and after two winters' training with the university crew, through the spring of the junior year he acted as stroke-oar of the class crew, and was also a member of the university tug-of-war team. In his junior year he was elected a member of the Delta Kappa Epsilon Society, a social fraternity; and in his senior year, through rank in scholarship, was made a member of the Phi Beta Kappa fraternity. At graduation he was a Commencement-day speaker, and a member of the Ivy Committee. In the fall of the same year he entered the College of Physicians and Surgeons of New York City, which is the medical department of Columbia College. During these three years of study he obtained practical experience in minor surgery at the Chambers Street Hospital, and in obstetrics at the Sloane Maternity Hospital and Broome Street Lying-in Dispensary.

Our subject received the degree of M. D. in 1891, and through a competitive examination, participated in by the graduates of the three regular medical schools of New York City, obtained an appointment in Bellevue Hospital, securing the first place as results of the examination. The Doctor remained as *interne* two years in the hospital, acting for nine months of the time as house physician, In addition to a wide medical service the two years were spent in constant operative gynecological work under the visiting surgeon, Dr. W. Gill Wylie. The experience here gained and associations formed in turn opened opportunities for greater advantages, and in the summer of 1893, following the hospital service, Dr. Hardenbergh became connected with the Post-Graduate Medical School and Hospital, conducting the clinics and delivering the lectures during the summer months, in place of Prof. F. Ferguson, upon the subject of "Physical Diagnosis and Clinical Medicine" to the older practitioners, who return to become more familiar with the recent views in medical science. The material for these clinics was drawn from the out-patient department of the New York Hospital, with which Dr. Hardenbergh was connected for one and a-half years. Later he was appointed provisional assistant, assistant and full attending physician to the out-patient department. The following winter he severed his connection with the Post-Graduate Medical School in order to become associated once more with Prof. W. Gill Wylie, at the New York Polyclinic Medical School, acting as instructor in gynecology and delivering the lectures during the summer months and during the absence of Professor Wylie. About the same time he was appointed Assistant-Surgeon to the New York Cancer Hospital, and delivered frequent lectures to the training schools for nurses of the Post-Graduate and Cancer Hospitals.

For private practice Dr. Hardenbergh located with Dr. William B. Coley at No. 52 West Thirty-fifth Street, New York City. His first contribution to medical literature was an article upon "Salophen in Acute Rheumatism," to the New York *Medical Record*. He became assistant editor of the *Epitome of Medicine*, having charge of

the department in gynecology, and later assistant editor of the *American Medico-Surgical Bulletin*, with which he is still connected in the same capacity. In the fall of 1893 there was held in Washington, D. C., a medical congress from the different countries of the Western Hemisphere, the first "Pan-American Medical Congress." Dr. Hardenbergh was chosen by the editor of the New York *Medical Record* to report for that journal the transactions of the section in "Abdominal Surgery and Gynecology," which he did in an article running through successive numbers of that journal. October 1, 1894, after having enjoyed six years in New York City as student, practitioner and instructor, Dr. Hardenbergh chose Middletown as the field of his endeavor. A most favorable introduction had been obtained through Dr. Theo D. Mills, whose practice for several years he had conducted during his absence on vacations.

ROBERT D. MAPES, who is engaged in the wholesale and retail milk business, and also has a growing trade as a dealer in agricultural implements in Middletown, was born at Howells Depot, in the town of Wallkill, September 14, 1862. His grandfather, John V. Mapes, was born in this county, and for many years was a farmer near Howells Depot. The father, Albert, was born in the town of Wallkill, one mile from Howells Depot, and still makes his home in the house where he was born. As a general farmer he has met with considerable success, and he now also runs a large dairy. His wife, Frances, was born in Mt. Hope, where her father, Seth Mapes, was a farmer. The two families, though bearing the same name, were not related to each other. The parents are members of the Congregational Church at Howells Depot, and have reared their nine children in the doctrines of that denomination.

Robert D., who is the eldest of the family, was reared on the home farm and received a district-school education. He remained at home until

about 1877. In May of that year he and his father started a milk route in Middletown, and continued in partnership until 1886, when our subject purchased his father's interest in the business, and established a retail trade in Middletown. Since that time he has carried on business at No. 4 Knapp Avenue, where he has increased the capacity of the building by adding a milk and cooling room. He has one delivery wagon, with which he supplies the retail trade. In 1890 he started in the agricultural-implement business, and now keeps on hand, in the warehouse on Knapp Avenue, a stock of Deering mowing-machines and hay rakes and New York Champion horse rakes.

At Howells Depot, in 1886, Mr. Mapes married Miss Margaret Isabelle Axford, who was born in Port Jervis. Her father, the late Calvin Axford, was for many years a farmer in the town of Wallkill. For eight years Mr. Mapes has served as Inspector of Elections, and at different times he has served in other local positions, the duties of which he has always discharged in a manner satisfactory to the people and reflecting credit upon himself. Politically he is firm in his advocacy of Republican principles, and invariably votes for the candidates of that party.

❮❮✦✦✦✦✦✦✦✦✦✦✦✦✦✦❀✦✦✦✦✦✦✦✦✦✦✦✦✦✦❯❯

WILLIAM E. DOUGLASS, M. D., has been in practice in Middletown since 1881. He was born in Franklin, Delaware County, July 14, 1853, and is of good old Revolutionary stock, his great-grandfather, Asa Douglass, serving as Captain during that struggle. For his services he was granted a tract of land, supposed to have been in Massachusetts, but on surveying it was found between the two states, now in Rensselaer County, N. Y. He was born in Franklin, Delaware County. Judge Amos Douglass, the grandfather, was born in Stephentown, in Rensselaer County, and in early life moved to Franklin, Delaware County, where he was one of the first attorneys. He was subsequently County Judge there, which office he held for many years. The father of our subject, who was also named Amos,

was a native of Franklin, and for twenty-five years was engaged in the mercantile business, and later in the banking business. He was one of the organizers of the First National Bank of Franklin, and was President of the same for more than twenty-five years. He married Miss Marriette Hine, who was also a native of Franklin, and was a daughter of William Hine, a native of Woodbridge, now New Milford, Conn. He was, however, an early settler in Franklin, and was by occupation a farmer. His grandfather, the great-grandfather of Mrs. Douglass, who was named Stephen Hine, served in the Revolutionary War, and died in Connecticut. Her father was a Deacon in the Congregational Church for many years. Amos Douglass, the father of our subject, was a strong Republican, but one who never aspired to official position. He was Clerk in the Congregational Church for many years, or until he gave it up on account of ill-health. He died in Franklin in 1888, and his wife died in 1886. They were the parents of four children, three of whom grew to maturity, and two are yet living: Amos Stanley, who resides in Middletown, and who is a special insurance adjustor; and Dr. William E., the subject of this sketch. Charles A. grew to manhood and was Cashier of the First National Bank of Middletown, but resigned, and has since died.

The subject of this notice was reared in Franklin, and received his education in the literary institute at that place, from which he graduated. At the age of sixteen he began reading medicine in the office of Dr. Ira Wilcox, and subsequently entered Bellevue Hospital Medical College, New York City, where he remained four and a-half years, taking his degree of M. D. in 1876. On graduating, he removed to Lisle, Broome County, where he opened an office and commenced the practice of his profession. He remained there until 1881, when, as already stated, he located in Middletown, where he has since resided, and where he has built up an extensive practice, being recognized as one of the leading physicians of the county. Since the institution was started he has been on the medical staff of Thrall Hospital. He is a member of the State Medical Society, is ex-President of the Orange County Medical Society, and is examiner for several life-insurance companies, besides being a Director of the First National Bank at Middletown, and a member of the Board of Water Commissioners.

Dr. Douglass was married, in Broome County, to Miss Katharine Whitney, a native of that county, and they have one child, Amos Stanley, Jr. Fraternally the Doctor holds membership with the Odd Fellows and the Knights of Pythias, and politically is a Republican. He is a member of the Congregational Church of Middletown and is Chairman of its Board of Trustees. Personally he is very popular and is held in high esteem by those who know him.

LEVI VANDERLYN SINSABAUGH. On the corner of Linden Avenue and John Street is located one of the prominent industries of Middletown. Here, in 1888, Mr. Sinsabaugh embarked in the lumber business, which he has since enlarged and is now conducting with flattering success. His planing-mill is 130x130 feet in dimensions, two stories in height, with a basement containing a thirty-five horse-power engine. The first floor is devoted to the planing of the lumber and to the manufacture of sash, doors and blinds, while the upper floor contains the turning and carpenter's department. Adjoining this place is a large ware and store room. The principal lumber-yard is situated on Union Street.

Careful management on the part of Mr. Sinsabaugh has secured success for the enterprise. Since purchasing the factory he has introduced a full equipment of modern machinery for turning and planing, and now has all the essential appurtenances to secure the patronage of the builders of the city and surrounding country. Being a man of great energy, he has not limited himself to the management of the factory, but has gained other important interests. He has devoted some attention to contracting and building, and has

built a number of cottages at Tuxedo and Arverne-by-the-sea. In Middletown he has erected about twenty houses, which he has sold on easy terms to working men, in that way promoting the growth of the place. He owns four acres on Monhagen Avenue, near the state hospital, which he is improving and will plat for residences. His own residence he has built there, it being a commodious and elegant structure, an ornament to that part of the city.

A native of this county, Mr. Sinsabaugh was born in the town of Montgomery, July 28, 1857. His father, R. P. L. Sinsabaugh, was born in the town of Crawford, of which the grandfather was a pioneer farmer. The former, who is still living in the town of Montgomery, is a man of upright character, the possessor of a host of friends in his community, and a prominent leader in local Republican ranks. Fruit-growing and the dairy business have received his attention throughout life.

The mother of our subject, Elizabeth, was born in the town of Montgomery and was a daughter of Levi Vanderlyn, a native of New Jersey, who early settled in Montgomery and became a large and successful farmer there. The first representative of the family in America was Peter Vanderlyn, who came hither from Holland. One of his descendants was the famous artist Vanderlyn, whose painting, "Landing of Columbus," adorns the walls of the capitol in Washington. Levi Vanderlyn was a prominent Republican in his locality and a well informed, intelligent man. One of his sons, Abraham, a soldier in the Civil War, fell in the battle of the Wilderness. Another son, John N., was for two terms District Attorney of Ulster County, and now has a large practice at New Paltz. The great-grandfather, Abraham, was a farmer of New Jersey, and his father, Jacobus, was the son of Peter Vanderlyn, the original settler in this country. Grandfather Vanderlyn married Elizabeth, daughter of Charles Newkirk, a farmer of the town of Montgomery One of her brothers was Judge John Newkirk, who resided at Hudson, Columbia County, N. Y., and died there in 1894.

In the parental family, which consisted of five

children, our subject is the eldest. He was reared on the home farm and learned the carpenter's trade in Walden. In 1886 he came to Middletown, and two years later bought the Piatt sash and blind factory, on Linden Avenue. This, as above stated, he improved and enlarged and is still conducting with success. He is a Director in the Orange County Telephone Company, also Vice-President and a Director of the Industrial Building and Loan Association. On the 29th of September, 1886, at the time of coming to Middletown, he married here Mrs. Eldora Simpson *nee* Brown, of Goshen, an accomplished lady and a graduate of Seward Seminary at Florida. She is a daughter of Martin Washburn and Elizabeth (Ward) Brown, both of whom are now deceased. Mr. Brown was formerly a wholesale jeweler in New York City, but resided in Goshen, that being a more healthful location. Mrs. Sinsabaugh has one daughter, Bessie, by her former husband.

A Republican in politics, Mr. Sinsabaugh has been intimately connected with public affairs in this city since becoming a resident of this place. In 1893 he was elected Alderman from the Second Ward, and so satisfactory was his service that he was re-elected two years afterward. Since becoming a member of the council he has been Chairman of the Fire Department Committee and the Committee on Law, and has also served on the Committees on Sewers, on Ways and Means and on Public Buildings and Grounds. He is a member of the Excelsior Fire Company and Vice-President of the Royal Arcanum. He is a member of the Board of Trade and is connected with other enterprises and organizations that have promoted the progress of this city. In Grace Episcopal Church, of which he and his wife are members, he officiates as Vestryman.

March 1, 1895, Mr. Sinsabaugh took into partnership his former superintendent, John H. Burch, who has been employed in the factory since the spring of 1890, and who now gives his attention to the factory business and lumber-yards on Union Street. The business has enjoyed a constant growth, and during the past year (1894) it was estimated that the sale of lumber was two million feet, the value of the sales aggregating

over $100,000. The firm of L. V. Sinsabaugh & Co. is one of the most progressive in the city, and is carrying on business in such a manner as to prove remunerative. The finances are on a substantial basis, and every indication points to years of uninterrupted business prosperity and growth.

IRA DORRANCE, ex-Postmaster, and President of the Board of Aldermen of Middletown, was born in Mamakating, in Sullivan County, N. Y., in 1832. His father, George Dorrance, was also a native of Sullivan County, while his grandfather, David Dorrance, was a native of Rhode Island, and settled in Sullivan County at a very early day. By occupation David Dorrance was a farmer, and during the Revolutionary War served as a Captain under General LaFayette. He died in Sullivan County many years ago. George Dorrance, who for many years was a hotel-keeper and forwarding merchant on the canal, also died in Sullivan County some years ago, at the age of seventy-six years. He married Martha Beyea, whose family were from Westchester County, N. Y., and who came of old Revolutionary stock, of French extraction. They were the parents of three children, all of whom are yet living, our subject being second in order of birth.

Ira Dorrance grew to manhood in his native county and received his education in the common school. In early life he was engaged with his father in forwarding and merchandising between Wurtsboro, Albany and New York City. They had a very large business, and our subject continued to serve in this line until 1862, when he enlisted in the service of his country. He raised a company of men, principally from the neighborhood where he resided, which became Company E of the One Hundred and Forty-third New York Infantry, and was commissioned Captain. Soon after his enlistment, his regiment was ordered to the front in the defense of Washington

Unfortunately, the Captain was taken sick and

subsequently resigned, and our subject returned to his old home, taking up his former business again. He continued to follow this until 1866, when he received the appointment of postal clerk in the Railway Mail Service, being assigned to the Erie Railroad, between New York and Buffalo. After holding this position until 1884, he was appointed Postmaster at Middletown by President Arthur, filling the office until 1889, when he was removed by President Cleveland. However, he was only out of the office three months, the man appointed by President Cleveland failing of confirmation. In March, 1889, he was re-appointed Postmaster by President Harrison, being one of the first appointed by the new administration. Captain Dorrance continued in the office until August, 1893, when he stepped out on account of his politics. During his time the postoffice was enlarged, free delivery established, and other improvements made, and it goes without saying that he made a most popular and efficient official.

In 1894 Captain Dorrance was elected Alderman-at-large for the city, and was made President of the Board, which position he still retains. His progressive spirit is such that he is ever ready to undertake any work that tends toward the upbuilding of his adopted city. Socially he is a member of General Lyon Post No. 146, G. A. R. In politics he is a Republican, and cast his first Presidential vote for the first nominee of that party, Gen. John C. Fremont.

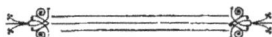

WILLIAM H. PERLEE, an engineer on the New York, Ontario & Western Railroad, and also a member of the firm of George H. Hill & Co., druggists of Middletown, was born in Schenectady, N. Y., in July, 1848. He is the son of Henry Perlee, a native of Canada, whose father, Henry, Sr., had emigrated to that country from France. In early days Henry, Jr., engaged in merchandising in Grand Trunk, but later settled in Schenectady, N. Y., where he

was employed in the locomotive works until his death. Prior to leaving Canada he married Eliza Perlee, a native of that country, who died in New York State in 1856. Of their three children, William H. is the sole survivor. He was orphaned at the age of thirteen years, but continued for a time afterward to make his home in Schenectady, being employed in the office of the locomotive works.

At the age of sixteen Mr. Perlee went to Syracuse, where he was employed in a drug store and studied pharmacy for eighteen months. When about nineteen years old he began as fireman on the New York Central Railroad, being employed in the yards at Syracuse and on the Western Division of the road, between Syracuse and Buffalo. Sickness, however, soon forced him to discontinue work for two seasons. In 1873 he went to Oswego, in the employ of the New York & Oswego Midland, now the Ontario & Western Railroad, and first had charge of the engines at Sidney, but later was made fireman of a passenger train on the main line between Norwich and Middletown. When the road went into the hands of a receiver, he was thrown out of a position, but soon secured work as a machinist on the Delaware & Hudson Railroad. After a short time he resumed work on the New York, Ontario & Western road, on the main line, later on the Delhi Branch, and was fireman on the passenger train between Middletown and Norwich. In 1881 he was promoted to the position of engineer, and ran the pusher engine at Sidney for six months; then had the Delhi Branch engine for five months, and afterwards ran an engine on the construction of the West Shore Railroad in New Jersey for eighteen months.

In June, 1883, Mr. Perlee became an engineer on the milk train between Middletown and Weehawken, a distance of seventy-eight miles, making the round trip, one hundred and fifty-six miles. He has since served in that capacity, and is known as one of the most reliable engineers on the road. In addition to this work he is owner of the principal drug store in Middletown, situated on the corner of North and Courtland Streets, and carried on under the firm style of George H.

J. FRANCIS MATTHEWS.

Hill & Co. In former years he had extensive agricultural interests, but he is not interested in agriculture at present. His residence at No. 12 Albert Street, Middletown, is the finest on the street and one of the best in the city.

The first wife of Mr. Perlee bore the maiden name of Emma Alcott, and she died in this city. His second marriage, which took place here, united him with Mrs. Edith (Decker) Younglove, a native of Middletown, and daughter of Jesse F. and Sarah E. (Crans) Decker, old and prominent residents of this county. Her father, in 1894 and 1895, entertained the members of the Decker and Crans families on the occasion of their reunion. Our subject and his wife are the parents of one son, Ross H. Socially Mr. Perlee is identified with Lancelot Lodge, K. of P., and the United Division No. 292, Brotherhood of Locomotive Engineers, of which he was First Assistant Engineer for four years. Politically he is a Republican.

JARED FRANCIS MATTHEWS was born in Southington, Conn., in 1815, and was one of a family of twelve children. After coming of age, he with two brothers, Miles and Elbert, joined a colony of men who moved with their families to Greene County, and engaged in a manufacturing business, which they afterward removed to Middletown, N. Y., where they conducted a most successful business in leather goods, manufacturing bags, belts, etc., in connection with their large carpet store of that place, widely known throughout the county as the Matthews Brothers' Carpet Bag Factory. Their good standing and sterling integrity in conducting their business insured their success. Their salesrooms were in Dey Street, New York, but they afterward built and removed to their fine store at No. 92 (now known as No. 168) Church Street.

Among other things, Mr. Matthews became interested in farming. He was a good judge of and was fond of fine horses; he also owned a choice dairy of cows. He was identified with many other enterprises and progressive movements in Orange County. He retired from active business four years before his death. For many years he was a devoted member and faithful officer in the Episcopal Church. After an exemplary, useful life, he passed away, August 29, 1884.

The lady who became the wife of Mr. Matthews February 10, 1859, and who from that time until his death was his devoted helpmate, bore the maiden name of Sarah Thurman Thorne, a relative of the late Judge John Thurman, of New York. She was born in the house where she still resides, where her father lived for seventy years. Notwithstanding the fact that the house is about one hundred and fifty years old, it presents as substantial an appearance as the homes of the present decade. The beautiful farm adjoining the house has been in the possession of the family over a century, and consists of seventy acres of highly cultivated land, well equipped as a grazing farm, with a number of outbuildings, etc., all within the corporate limits of the village of Goshen.

The grandfather of Mrs. Matthews was Richard Thorne, a native of England, who settled at Great Neck, L. I., and was living there at the time of the Revolutionary War. He was wealthy, and when his property was invaded by the Hessian soldiers his family buried their valuables in the garden to save them. He and his son John took part in the defense of the Colonists and were taken by the British and imprisoned in the old Sugar House in New York. Among his eleven children was Thomas Thorne, father of Mrs. Matthews, and a native of Great Neck, L. I. He married Elizabeth, daughter of Thomas Waters, a wealthy man residing on the Florida Road and the owner of extensive tracts of land. He was proprietor of a racecourse, and at one time held the office of Sheriff of Orange County. In early life he owned a number of slaves, but, being opposed to the system of slavery, he gave them all their liberty. During the war with England he succeeded in taking a fine span of horses from the British camp near his home. His sister married Gabriel Wisner, who was one of the slain in the massacre at the battle of Minisink.

When only sixteen years of age Thomas Thorne

came to Goshen in order to enjoy the school privileges here. Later he bought the farm where his remaining years were spent, becoming the owner of one hundred acres of valuable land. In addition to farming he conducted a tannery for years, and was also prominent in public affairs, serving as Commissioner of the county and as Supervisor for one term. For years he was Senior Warden in the Episcopal Church and died firm in the faith in 1859, aged eighty-six. His first wife was the widow of Robert Seeley, her maiden name being Hatfield. His second wife, Elizabeth Waters, was related to the Wisner family of Goshen; she died about 1864, at the age of seventy-five. Of her three children, Mary died at the age of seven years, and John passed away soon after reaching his majority.

The union of Mr. and Mrs. Matthews was blessed by the birth of five children, three of whom are living, namely: Thomas A., William Thorne and Elizabeth Montague. Mrs. Matthews is connected with the Episcopal Church, and is generous in her benefactions to the poor and unfortunate. She still superintends the management of her valuable property, which she does in such a manner as to prove her executive ability and secure the largest possible returns.

UGUST KROEGER. Though he had been in the United States only about one year when the Rebellion broke out, Mr. Kroeger displayed a patriotism equal to that of any native-born son of the country. He enlisted in the Union army, and did valiant service in the defense of the Stars and Stripes, taking part in a number of memorable engagements, as well as in many skirmishes, where the peril to life was equally great, though the results to the nation were less important. Since 1872 he has made his home in Middletown, and is the proprietor of a merchant-tailoring establishment situated at No. 43 James Street.

February 21, 1838, the subject of this sketch was born in Oldesloe, Holstein, Germany, where also were born his father, Henry Kroeger, and

his mother, known in maidenhood as Gretchen Grapp. The former engaged in the manufacture of paper in his native land until his death. Of his four children, two are now living, August being the only one who ever came to the United States. He was reared in Holstein and attended the common schools until fourteen years of age, at which time he was apprenticed to the tailor's trade. In 1860, hoping to better his fortunes in America, and at the same time to escape military oppression, he emigrated to this country, leaving Hamburg on the sailing-vessel "C. Robert Peal," and arriving in New York City after an uneventful voyage of seven weeks. He remained in New York, working at his trade, until April, 1861.

At the first tap of the drum, in the opening of the mighty conflict between the North and the South, Mr. Kroeger enlisted in the Union army, becoming a member of Company E, Twentieth New York Infantry. He was mustered into service at New York City, and went at once to the front, taking part in the engagement at Ft. Hatteras, the seven-days battle at Richmond, the second battle of Bull Run, and the two engagements at Fredericksburg. In the latter engagement a bullet grazed his neck, inflicting a slight wound, but with that exception he escaped uninjured. In all the battles this regiment was conspicuous for bravery, and at Antietam their loss was heavier than that of any regiment. After two years of service, he was honorably discharged, June 14, 1863, immediately after the battle of Fredericksburg.

Returning to New York City, Mr. Kroeger continued at his trade there until 1872, when he came to Middletown and started a merchant-tailoring business at the corner of Main and North Streets. For one year he was a member of the firm of Wolf & Kroeger, after which he was alone until 1894, and then formed a partnership with G. Gunther, the firm name being now Kroeger & Gunther. His residence, which was erected by himself, is situated at No. 16 Liberty Street. In religious belief he is a Lutheran. Politically he is a Republican in the national issues, but somewhat independent in local affairs. He is one of the officers of Capt. W. A. Jackson Post, G. A. R., and is a member of the Twentieth New York Infantry Veterans' Association, the annual reunions of which in New York City he always attends.

In New York City, in 1864, Mr. Kroeger married Miss Fredricka Badd, who was born in Westphalia, Germany, and died in New York in 1871. The following year he married Miss Mary Roed, a native of Frieburg, Baden, and they are the parents of six children, four of whom survive. Dora died of diphtheria at the age of four years. Andrew, who was a youth of unusual promise, and very popular among his associates, was drowned while swimming in Dewsnap Pond at Mechanicstown, June 10, 1891, at the age of fifteen years. He was a member of the Episcopal Church choir and belonged to the Young Men's Christian Association. The four surviving children are Henry, who is engaged in business in this city, and is an active member of DeWitt Camp, Sons of Veterans; Augusta; Charles, who is associated in business with his elder brother; and Hilda, who is at home.

—————————◦✧◦⊛◦✧◦—————————

ROBERT HIGHAM. For twenty-six years Mr. Higham was proprietor of the oldest hotel in Middletown, the Wallkill House, situated at the corner of James and Depot Streets, but in 1893 he retired from the business and leased the hotel to other parties. Since that time he has given his attention to the supervision of his general real-estate and other interests, and though he is not actively engaged in business his life is nevertheless a busy one.

Born in Manchester, England, in 1844, the subject of this notice is a son of Robert, Sr., a native of the same place and for many years a cotton warper there. After the death of the wife and mother, the father came to America, in 1866, and soon afterward with his son opened the Wallkill House, continuing its management until the death of the senior Mr. Higham a few years later. At a very early age our subject began to support himself, and when only eight years old he com-

menced to work in the cotton-mills of Manchester. There he remained until 1861, meantime working in every department of the mills.

Believing that America offered him better opportunities for advance than England, our subject determined to come hither. Accordingly, in 1861, he took passage on a ship bound for this country, and after landing proceeded at once to Middletown, reaching this city May 4 of the same year. To this place his uncle, John Higham, had preceded him, becoming proprietor of the Holden (now the Jefferson) House. He was the second male representative of the Higham family to seek a home in this country. Three years after coming here, in 1864, he enlisted in the United States navy as landsman in the South Atlantic Squadron. Later he became an ordinary seaman. He proceeded on the gunboat "Florida" to Port Royal and Ft. Sumter, and at the latter place took part in a severe conflict with the Confederates. Later he was on the "New Hampshire," the "Tallapoosa" and the "Inoe."

At the expiration of a year, his term of enlistment, Mr. Higham was honorably discharged from the service at the Brooklyn Navy-yards. On his return to Middletown, he remained for a time with his uncle, then with his father assumed the management of the Wallkill House, which has the best location of any hotel in the city. He still owns it, though since 1893 he has not been engaged in the hotel business. He expects soon to build a residence in Oakland Place, on East Main Street, where he will establish his permanent home. His wife, with whom he was united in Middletown, bore the maiden name of Lydia E. Walker, and was born in London, England. They are the parents of two daughters, Edith E. and Alice M.

Prior to the war Mr. Higham served in the old Middletown Militia Company until its disbandment. He served for a time in the Eagle Hose Company, of which he is now an honorary member. In his fraternal relations he is connected with Middletown Lodge No. 112, I. O. O. F., and with General Lyon Post No. 266, G. A. R. While not a member of any religious body, he is a regular attendant at the services of the

Grace Episcopal Church and a contributor to its maintenance. Politically he has always advocated Republican principles, which he believes best adapted to promote our country's welfare.

HARVEY MOORE, engineer on the New York, Ontario & Western Railroad, between Middletown and Norwich, was born in Monticello, N. Y., August 21, 1846. His father, William J., was born in Canada, of Irish descent, and when a young man came to Montgomery, Orange County, where he learned the blacksmith's trade. Later settling in Monticello, he resided there for a short time, then removed to a farm in Thompsonville, Sullivan County, where he carried on agricultural pursuits for ten years. When advanced in years he retired from active labor and returned to Monticello, where he is now living with a daughter, being hale and robust, notwithstanding his ninety years. Politically he is a Republican.

Twice married, William J. Moore has two daughters and one son surviving of his first union. Of his second marriage, six children were born, of whom two are deceased. The mother of our subject, Eleanor L., was born in Connecticut, and died in Ulster County at the age of seventy-three years. Her father, John Crumley, came from Connecticut to New York, and settled in Bethel, Sullivan County, where the closing years of his life were spent. Harvey Moore was reared principally in Monticello, and attended the public schools of that village. In April, 1861, when less than fifteen years of age, he began driving a stage and carrying mail between Monticello and Grahamsville. After fifteen months spent in that way, he drove a mail-coach between Monticello and Liberty for three years. He next drove the four-horse stage between Monticello and Middletown, via Wurtsboro, a distance of twenty-five miles, the round trip consuming three days. This coach was sufficiently large to accommodate seventeen passengers and their baggage, as well as the express and mail.

In 1870 Mr. Moore discontinued work as a stage-driver, and began the manufacture of nitroglycerine for the tunnel at Bloomingburg. After six months in that capacity, he went to Monticello, where he resumed his former occupation, and drove the stage between Monticello and Neversink, connecting with the terminus of the Oswego Midland Road. August 7, 1871, he became an employe on the Jersey Midland, now the Ontario & Western Railroad, and for thirteen months he was fireman between Unionville and Franklin. In September, 1872, he was made engineer, and has since been retained in that capacity. His first position was on the work train at Ellenville, but in 1875 he was transferred to the freight running between Middletown and Walton, and two years later he began to run the milk train between Middletown and Livingston Manor and Sidney. In 1882 he was transferred to the night passenger train from Middletown to Norwich, afterward was placed on the day run, and since then he has held one of these positions, at present being engineer on Nos. 1 and 2 day trains, between Middletown and Norwich. During his long experience in railroading he has had only one serious accident, and that was caused by the opposite crew mistaking a train. His car collided with the other, his fireman being killed, and he escaped only by jumping from the train.

In addition to his other interests, Mr. Moore is a Director in the Granite State Providence Building and Loan Association. Politically he is a Republican, and socially holds membership in Unity Division No. 292, Brotherhood of Locomotive Engineers, and the Royal Templars of Temperance. His religious connections are with the Methodist Episcopal Church. He was united in marriage, in Liberty, N. Y., with Miss Anna A. Crispell, a native of that city, and daughter of David P. and Grace E. (Adgate) Crispell, natives, respectively, of Orange and Sullivan Counties. Her grandfather, Richard D. Crispell, was a carpenter, which trade her father also followed, being a contractor in Liberty. Hoping to regain his health, which was poor, he went to Leadville, Colo., but the change did not prove beneficial, and in a short time he died, leaving an only child, Mrs. Moore.

DAVID R. MILLER.

AVID R. MILLER, of Middletown, one of the largest real-estate dealers in Orange County, is also one of the most liberal and enterprising men in the business, and to the growth of this city he has probably contributed more than any other man. His addition to Middletown, known as Central Park Addition, contains about two hundred and fifty acres, and is beautifully located, running north from Wisner Avenue. Already nearly two hundred acres have been platted, from which more lots have been sold than from any other addition in the city.

Mr. Miller was born in South Centreville, Orange County, March 13, 1848, and is a son of Charles S. and Jane (Robertson) Miller, the former born near Dover, N. J., but of Scotch descent, and the latter born in South Centreville. When a youth the father was bound out to learn the trade of a carpenter, his apprenticeship continuing until he was twenty-one years of age, when he received $100 in cash. On completing his apprenticeship, he located at South Centreville, where he followed his trade for over thirty years, and among the buildings which he assisted in erecting was the Orange County Almshouse. He was quite successful as a contractor, and became the owner of two good farms near Centreville. His death occurred when he was seventy-two years of age. Religiously he was a devout member of the Methodist Episcopal Church, and in politics was first a Whig and then a Republican. He married Jane Robertson, who, as already stated, was born in South Centreville. Her father, David Robertson, was born in Scotland, and, in company with two brothers, William and Robert, came from that country and settled on adjoining farms in Orange County, and reared large families. To Charles S. and Jane Miller were born three children, two of whom grew to maturity, David R. and George R., the latter residing in Middletown.

When our subject was but fourteen years of age, his mother died. He grew to manhood in his native town and received his early education in the public schools, later attending Unionville Academy one term. From boyhood he was handy with tools, and at an early age commenced work

as a carpenter and mason. He remained at home and worked with his father until past eighteen, when he rented one of his father's farms, which he operated for three years. He then became the possessor of the George W. Robertson Farm, consisting of one hundred acres, to which he removed in 1860. In 1870 he located in Middletown, bought the old Webb Farm of seventy-five acres, and later purchased the old Everett Farm of eighty-one acres, on which he yet resides. Another farm which he purchased later is known as the Dan Wood Farm. Besides engaging in farming, he also deals in real estate, making several additions to the city, and has given away several acres for manufacturing and other purposes. He laid out Washington Square of several acres, and gave the right of way to the Street Railway Company. In addition to what has already been mentioned, Mr. Miller owns one hundred and seventy-four acres at Midway Park, on the Wallkill, which he improved, and which he operates. He also owns one hundred and sixty acres at Livingston Manor, Sullivan County, which is principally timber-land.

March 19, 1867, Mr. Miller was married, in Centreville, to Miss Eliza J. Mulford, who was a native of that place and the daughter of Linden Mulford, who is there engaged in farming. Five children were born to them, as follows: Annie B., who died at the age of five years; Emily B., now Mrs. Josiah Miller, of Wallkill; Nellie K., the wife of Rev. Gilbert A. Shaw, of Clayton, N. Y.; Hermon C., of the firm of Ritter & Miller, grocers of Middletown; and Viola S., at home.

Mr. Miller has been quite successful in life and is actively engaged in his business, sparing no pains to make Middletown one of the best cities in Orange County. He is a stockholder and Director in the Middletown & Goshen Traction Company, of which he was one of the organizers, and was also the largest stockholder in the old Horse Street Railway Company. He is a strong temperance man, and is a member and Lodge Deputy of the Independent Order of Good Templars. Religiously he is a member of the Methodist Episcopal Church, of which he has been Class-leader and Trustee for many years. He assisted in starting the North Street Methodist Episcopal Mission, and gave the lot for the church site. The Sunday-school finds in him a warm supporter, and he has served as Superintendent for many years. In politics he is a Republican.

Among other enterprises which Mr. Miller has assisted in starting are the Middletown City Iron Works and the North End Machine-shops, in both of which a large number of men are employed. He has ever been ready to assist, with his counsel and his means, any enterprise calculated to advance the interests of Middletown.

HENRY L. ADAMS, agent for the Adams Express Company at Middletown, was born in Minisink, this county, in 1843. He is a representative of a family that has long been connected with the history of America, being the fifth in line of descent from the first of the name to come hither. Little is known of this ancestor save that he purchased from King George a tract of land lying near Deckertown, N. J., and there established his permanent home.

The grandfather of our subject, Crowell Adams, was born in New Jersey, and followed agricultural pursuits until his death, in the city of Newark. Next in line of descent was Samuel C., a native of Deckertown, N. J., who selected agriculture for his occupation, and was thus engaged in the town of Wallkill, Orange County, two miles from Middletown. When advanced in years he retired from active work, and his closing days were spent in this city, where he died at the age of sixty-nine. In religious belief he was a member of the Presbyterian Church, and politically he affiliated with the Republicans. His wife, whose maiden name was Sarah Van Cleft, was born in Minisink, and died in Middletown when more than sixty-six years of age. She was a sister of Lewis, father of Joseph Van Cleft, of Newburgh, whose sketch is presented on another page.

The family of Samuel C. and Sarah Adams consisted of five children, three of whom attained years of maturity. Henry L. was reared in the town of Wallkill and attended the public schools

and Wallkill Academy, completing his education in the latter institution. He was engaged in farming until 1868, when he came to Middletown, and here for six years he carried on a boot and shoe business. In 1874 he entered the employ of the American Express Company, as messenger on the Susquehanna & Western Railroad from New York to Middletown. In 1883 he was made agent for the company, remaining with them for the succeeding ten years, and was also agent for the National Express. In 1893 he resigned in order to accept a similar position with the Adams Express Company. He commenced his duties in 1893, and started the business for the company, being their first agent at this point. His office is located at No. 5 North Street.

The pleasant home of Mr. Adams at No. 45 South Street is presided over by his wife, a native of this city and known in maidenhood as Charity Weed. They are members of the First Presbyterian Church and sing in the choir, besides which he is chorister of the Sunday-school. Since 1869 he has been connected with the Excelsior Hook and Ladder Company No. 1, of which he was assistant foreman and is a member of the Board of Trustees. Aside from other interests, he is a member of the Board of Trade. In politics he favors Republican principles. His experience in the express business, covering a period of twenty-one years, has made him familiar with every detail connected with it, and his good management has brought the well deserved commendation of superior officials of the company.

GEORGE W. REED, the present Alderman of the Fourth Ward, Middletown, was born in July, 1844, at South Centreville, in what was then the town of Minisink, but is now the town of Wawayanda. His father, Alonzo, and grandfather, James Reed, were born in the same place, and were of Scotch descent. The latter, who was a farmer by occupation, served in the War of 1812. The former, also an agriculturist, spent his active life at South Centreville, but now, at the age of eighty-one, he is living retired at Denton. His wife, who bore the maiden name of Mary Carr, was born in the town of Wawayanda, where her father, Peter Carr, followed the shoemaker's trade. Her ancestors were of Scotch-Irish origin. She is still living and is now in her eighty-second year. In religious belief she is connected with the Methodist Episcopal Church, to which her husband also belongs.

The family of Alonzo and Mary Reed consisted of ten children, nine of whom attained years of maturity, and seven are now living, George W. being the eldest. Three of the sons served in the Union army during the Civil War. Benjamin F. was a member of the Thirteenth New York Battery, and died soon after the close of the Rebellion; and Charles H., a member of the Eighteenth New York Infantry, died during the Peninsula campaign. Our subject was reared on the home farm and received a common-school education. At the opening of the war, though he was then only in his teens, he enlisted in the Union army, and in October, 1861, his name was enrolled as a member of Company C, First New York Mounted Rifles. He was mustered into service at Newburgh, sent South from there, and engaged in duty in Virginia, participating in the battle of Petersburg and other engagements of the war. He veteranized in 1863 and continued with his regiment until the close of the Rebellion, when he was mustered out as Corporal at Albany, in December, 1865, having served for more than four years.

After retiring from the army Mr. Reed spent a year in South Centerville, and in 1866 came to Middletown, where he was for five years an apprentice to the carpenter's trade under Theodore W. Dailey. At the expiration of that time he became foreman for Edwin McWilliams, and has since followed his trade in this city and the surrounding country. He erected a number of buildings, which he afterward sold at a profit, and has done some contract work. Aside from his other interests he is a Director in the Middletown Co-operation Company. He is a charter member of Capt. William A. Jackson Post No. 301, G. A. R.,

and is its Commander. With his family he belongs to the First Congregational Church of Middletown. Politically he is active in the ranks of the Republican party, and is a member of the Republican City Committee. In the spring of 1894 he was nominated and elected Alderman from the Fourth Ward, and is now serving his second year in that office, having acted as President of the Board during the summer of 1895. He has served as Chairman of the Committee on Ways and Means, also as a member of the Street, Sewer and Fire Committees.

The first marriage of Mr. Reed took place at Middletown in 1867, uniting him with Phœbe Decker, daughter of Densmore Decker, of this city. She died in 1879, leaving three children: Ida U., wife of John Moshier, of Middletown; Jennie A., Mrs. W. H. Mapes, also of this city; and Henry W., who is connected with a New York store, and is Quartermaster of DeWitt Camp No. 37, Sons of Veterans. At New Vernon, in 1881, Mr. Reed was united in marriage with Miss Susan F. Corwin, a native of that place, her father, J. P. Corwin, having been a farmer there.

HORACE W. COREY, real-estate dealer and manager of the Casino Theatre, Middletown, was born at Port Jervis, August 16, 1859, and is a son of Alexander and Cordelia (House) Corey, the former a native of Goshen, N. Y., and the latter of Newton, N. J. He traces his ancestry back to David Corey, who came from Wales during Cromwell's time, and located first in Connecticut, and later settled on Long Island. Alexander Corey, the great-grandfather of our subject, was born on Long Island, and commanded a company from that island and Connecticut during the Revolution. While on the heights of Quebec he was shot through one of his lungs. Afterwards he settled in the town of Goshen, where the grandfather of our subject, Benjamin Corey, was born. The latter was a soldier in a New York regiment, and served in the War of 1812. For many years he was a farmer in the old town of Minisink, but late in life retired, and resided in Middletown until his death, at the age of eighty-six. He was a member of the Old-school Baptist Church.

Alexander Corey, the father of our subject, learned the carpenter's trade in Port Jervis, and followed the occupation of a contractor and builder for many years in Newburgh, as the senior member of the firm of Corey & Crumbley. He continued to work at his trade until age rendered it necessary for him to retire from active business, when he removed to Middletown, and here died at the age of seventy-two years. His wife, Cordelia House, was a daughter of Thomas House, who was born at Ft. Orange, now Albany, N. Y. Her great-grandfather, Ephraim House, was born in Alsace-Lorraine, France, coming to New York at the age of eighteen, and during the Revolutionary War served in the defense of his adopted country. He settled at Ft. Orange, and later removed to New Jersey, where he died. Her grandfather settled in Sussex County, N. J., where he engaged in farming, and later in hotel-keeping. He died in 1876, at the age of eighty-eight. The mother of Cordelia House was of French extraction and bore the maiden name of Annie Rousselle, which has been Anglicized as Russell. She was born in Lorraine, and her father, Col. Derrick Rousselle, was also in the Revolutionary War, as a Colonel with La Fayette. Many of his letters during this period are still in the possession of our subject. Mrs. Cordelia Corey is yet living and resides at Middletown. She became the mother of four children, all of whom are yet living.

Horace W. was reared in Newburgh and Port Jervis, and in both places received his education in the public and high schools. After leaving school he entered the office of W. E. McCormick, real-estate dealer and civil engineer of Port Jervis, and on the Erie Railroad took his first lessons in surveying. He was afterward with the Marvin Safe Company for four years, traveling as their salesman through the Middle and Southern States. He continued traveling until 1884, when he located in Middletown and engaged in the real-estate business for several years, having charge of Senator Low's real-estate interests in Middletown. He acted as agent for Mr. Low until the latter's death, since which time he has been in the real-estate business for himself. In 1887, in company with I. F. Van Duzer and R. O. Lewis, he purchased the old Casino Rink, which was altered and converted into the Casino Theatre. One year later it was burned down, when a stock company was organized, known as the Casino Theatre Company, which built the present fine theatre building. The company was organized with a capital stock of $40,000, but the building and the land cost about $67,000. Mr. Corey has been manager of the business from the start. The plans of the building were drawn by Leon H. Lempert, of Rochester. It has a frontage of sixty-two feet and a depth of one hundred and fifty feet. The first floor is devoted to stores and the electric plant, and the remainder to the theatre and offices. Including the balcony and gallery, it has a seating capacity of twelve hundred. The stage is 40x57 feet and is provided with a fine drop-curtain and scenery sufficient for the production of almost any ordinary play. The house is seated with upholstered red plush chairs. During the regular seasons it is engaged about four nights during each week.

Richmond Hill, the largest and most popular addition ever laid out in Middletown, and probably the most successful financially, comprised the Rockafellow Farm of about seventy-five acres. It is in the southern portion of the city, and through it run Conkling Avenue, Mountain Avenue and a number of the city's best streets. It was laid out in February, 1895, and one hundred and twenty-five lots were sold in four months. In less than six months $10,000 worth of building lots were sold, and $75,000 worth of buildings were erected. This addition is the property of Stratton & Corey, and is handled exclusively by Mr. Corey. While engaged with the firm of Ferguson & Corey, they platted the North End Addition, and Highland Avenue, the property of the late Judge Low.

In 1885 Mr. Corey was married, in Middletown, to Miss Sadie Mapes, who was born in Goshen, N. Y., a daughter of John W. Mapes. In

DANIEL T. WEED.

politics Mr. Corey is a Democrat. He is a member of the Managerial National Association of Theatres, and takes a great interest in all theatrical matters. Mr. Corey's residence is at "Locksley Hall," in the southern end of the city, and comprises about fifteen acres, on which he has made an artificial lake, well stocked with bass, pickerel, etc. It is one of the neatest suburban residences about the city, and here may probably be found the finest apple orchard in Orange County, comprising about eight acres of land. He has taken from this orchard seven hundred barrels of apples in a season, the famous Conkling Seedling being the only apple of the kind on the market.

ANIEL T. WEED is Superintendent of Downing Park, which is located in the suburbs of Newburgh, and which was named in honor of his personal friend, Charles Downing, now deceased. Horticulture has always been an interesting subject to Mr. Weed, and it would indeed be difficult to find a man better qualified to hold the position which he so ably fills. He is a member of the Agricultural Society of Orange County, and is a member of its Advisory Committee. For many years he and Mr. Downing were judges of fruits and vegetables at the state and county fairs, they being considered authorities on these subjects.

The grandfather of our subject came to the United States from Ireland at an early day, settling in Newburgh, where his son David, the father of Daniel T., was born. The father was a farmer by occupation, and died in early life as the result of an accident. His wife, whose maiden name was Deborah Noyes, and who was also born in Newburgh, was thus left a widow with seven children, only three of whom are now living. She died at the ripe old age of seventy-three years. Her brother, Aaron Noyes, who was well known in the early history of Newburgh, owned a brickyard where the West Shore freight depot now stands.

Daniel T. Weed was born in Bethlehem, this county, March 13, 1820, and until he was in his fourteenth year lived on a farm, his educational privileges being very limited. His first employment in the business world was in the Roseville brickyards, of which in time he became the proprietor, and for twenty years was engaged successfully in the manufacture of brick, at the same time taking contracts. About 1852 he settled upon a farm of one hundred acres at Middle Hope, where he made a specialty of raising fruits and vegetables and also conducted a large dairy. He still engaged in general contracting, building or superintending many of the roads in the town. For twelve years he was one of the Commissioners of the town of Newburgh, and in 1877 located here permanently, engaging in the hardware business with Joseph Van Cleft, and having charge of one of the stores for five years. Then he became agent for the Newburgh & Albany Transportation Company in the Albany freight office, acting in that capacity for seven years. The following four years he was Assistant Superintendent of the Newburgh Street Committee, and in 1894, when extensive improvements were inaugurated in the beautiful thirty-acre Downing Park, he was placed in charge of the work as Superintendent by the Park Commissioners. He brings to bear upon this wide experience and a great love of the business.

January 16, 1840, Mr. Weed was married, in the town of Newburgh, to Elizabeth A. Westlake, who was born in Middle Hope, N. Y., and whose father, Daniel Westlake, was a farmer in that vicinity. Six children, of whom four are now living, were born to our subject and wife, and are as follows: Juliet, wife of Leander Clark, Jr., of this city; J. Irving, a gold miner in Denver, Colo.; Adolphus, baggagemaster for the West Shore Railroad in Newburgh; and Emma, wife of Joseph Simpson, of Passaic, N. J.

In company with his brother, Jonathan N. Weed, our subject has been greatly interested in the upbuilding of Trinity Methodist Episcopal Church. He has been one of the most liberal donors to its various departments of activity, and also aided in the erection of the beautiful house of worship. For twenty years he was a member of the Official Board, serving as Steward, Trustee, etc. For two years he was one of Newburgh's Assessors, and politically he is a stanch Republican. Formerly he was a member of the Union League, and for years he has been one of the most active promoters of general works of benevolence and progress.

JOHN CUMMINGS is senior member of the firm of J. & P. Cummings, wholesale grocers and liquor dealers, and also of the firm of Cummings Brothers, wholesale liquor dealers. He was born in County Meath, Ireland, in 1839, and landed in New York December 25, 1854, making the voyage in twenty-three days. (For an account of the ancestry of our subject, see sketch of Peter Cummings, on another page of this work.) On arriving in New York, he proceeded at once to Otisville, where he entered the employ of the Erie Railroad, but later removed to Naglesville, near Scranton, Pa. Soon afterwards, however, he left the railroad and purchased a boat, which he ran on the Delaware & Hudson Canal, in which business he was later joined by his brother Peter. After selling his interest in the canal-boat, he purchased the boat "National," and ran on the Erie Canal from Buffalo to New York City and to Baltimore for three years. Subsequently he sold out his boating interests and with his brother devoted his attention to mercantile pursuits. Under the firm name of J. & P. Cummings our subject erected a building on the corner of what is now Fulton Street and East Avenue, then Water Street and East Avenue, where they engaged in the wholesale and retail grocery and liquor business. Soon afterwards they rented the place to Frank Murphy, and started a canal store in Honesdale, Pa., which was in charge of our subject for three years. Peter went to Acadia, but subsequently returned and continued the grocery and liquor business. In 1880 the brothers bought the dis-

tillery of Jefferson Roberts, at South Centreville, which they enlarged, putting in new machinery. This distillery they yet operate, manufacturing apple brandy, and they carry a full line of liquors from Kentucky, having a large trade in Orange, Sullivan and Ulster Counties, and New York City. Some shipments are made as far west as Ohio. In 1893 they started a wholesale and liquor business at No. 100 North Street, the fine building in which it is located being owned by Peter Cummings. Their manager at this place is Peter T. Kirk.

In addition to his mercantile interests, in company with his brother Peter, our subject is interested in fine horses, and owns a number of thorough-breds. He is individually interested in the real-estate business, and is the owner of lots in various parts of the city. The large brick block on the corner of East Main Street and Railroad Avenue was erected by him some years ago.

Mr. Cummings was married, in Middletown, to Miss Margaret F. Sheridan, a native of Howells Depot, and daughter of Dennis Sheridan, a farmer of that place. She died in December, 1881, leaving three children: Myrtie J., attending school at the Ursuline Academy; John, at Middletown Academy; and Christopher.

Mr. Cummings is a member of St. Joseph's Catholic Church, and in politics is a Democrat. He is now an honorary member of McQuaid Hose Company, and for some time was an active member, being one of the original number forming the company.

EDWARD FITZGERALD. The scenery of the Hudson has been immortalized in song and story by some of the greatest writers America has produced. The serene flow of the river, the beauty of the adjacent valley, with its low-drooping trees, and the grand old forests through which the sunlight steals, all these and many other attractions of the vicinity have been made familiar to the people of the United States. Of late years a portion of the valley, more beautiful even than that which enjoys a wider fame, has been gaining an increased amount of attention from the lovers of the beautiful in nature.

Orange Lake is situated in the town of Newburgh, about three miles from the city of that name. It is a mile and a-half long and one mile in width, and furnishes excellent facilities for boating, bathing and fishing. It is not strange, therefore, that it is popular among the people by whom its beauties and attractions are known. The subject of this sketch had the shrewdness to see that in coming years visitors would be drawn hither in ever-increasing numbers, and he invested largely in property on the lake. He was born in Cornwall, N. Y., December 5, 1865, and has spent his entire life in this county, so that he is well known among the citizens.

In 1890 Mr. Fitzgerald purchased the Orange Lake Hotel, with the surrounding grounds, covering about thirty-three acres. Two years later he took charge of the hotel, of which he has since been proprietor. The house is roomy, conveniently arranged and admirably adapted for the purpose for which it is used. The farm has for years been a noted one, and has a good half-mile race-track. It is known as the place where "George Wilkes" was born and bred, and other horses have been trained here that have made excellent records on the turf. Two steamers ply the waters of the lake, enabling the guests of the hotel to enjoy a pleasant outing on the water. No pains are spared to secure the comfort of visitors, who welcome with delight every opportunity to enjoy a few days' recreation at Orange Lake.

CHARLES ZACHARY TAYLOR, contractor and builder of Middletown, was born in New York City in 1846, and is a son of Abraham L. and Eliza G. (Reed) Taylor, the former a native of Yonkers, and the latter of New York City. Grandfather Taylor, an uncle of the ex-President of that name, was a soldier in the War of 1812, and carried on a farm near Yonkers. Abraham L. Taylor, the father of our subject,

was a builder, having learned the carpenter's trade when a boy, and for many years was engaged in contracting and building in New York City. From 1849 to 1854 he was at Dunkirk, N. Y., engaged at his trade and in farming. He was a Captain in the New York City Militia, and had charge of the fort at Central Park. In politics he was a Democrat. He died in 1871, at the age of about fifty-four years. His wife, Eliza G. Reed, was a daughter of James Reed, a gardener, who was born in Edinburgh, Scotland, and who died of cholera in New York. Mrs. Taylor died in 1890. Three of the five children in the parental family are now living. Jacob, who was a Captain of a pioneer corps in a New York regiment during the Civil War, now resides in Harlem, N. Y., where he is engaged in the real-estate business; and George is an electrician in Mt. Vernon.

The subject of this sketch was reared in New York City and at Dunkirk, and was educated in the high schools, graduating from a New York academy when seventeen years old. While in Dunkirk he saw the Erie Railroad opened, and regards it as one of the grandest sights that he ever saw. He learned the carpenter trade under his father, and completed it under an architect and builder in New York City. He then engaged in business with his father and brother, under the firm name of Taylor & Sons, until 1871, when his father died. The firm did quite an extensive business in the erection of residences and school buildings. After the death of the father the business was continued by our subject and brother until 1875, when the partnership was dissolved. Mr. Taylor then removed to Middletown, where he continued contracting and building until 1882, when the Anglo-Swiss Condensing Company was organized, and he was made superintendent of the building department, having charge of the erection of all the buildings of the company. He continued as superintendent until 1892, when he resigned and again engaged in contracting and building. In the spring of 1895 he built the shop and moved to his present location, No. 1 Railroad Avenue.

Mr. Taylor was married in Middletown to Miss

Adelia Parson, who was born in the town of
Wallkill, and is a daughter of Gilbert L. Parson,
who was a farmer, and who died in January,
1894, at the age of ninety years. Mrs. Taylor
is a graduate of Wallkill Academy, and is a
highly educated and acomplished woman. Five
children were born unto them, four of whom are
living, viz.: Mary, Emma, Grace and Cora, all
of whom are at home, and the two oldest are attending Middletown Academy. Bertha, the fourth
child, died at the age of eight.

Fraternally Mr. Taylor is a member of the
Knights of Honor and of the Knights of Pythias.
He is an active member of Eagle Hose Company
No. 2. Religiously he is a Baptist, and is a Trustee of the church in Middletown. Politically he
is an active and straightforward Republican. He
was Chairman of the Ward Republican Committee for many years, and has been a member of
the City Central Committee and also of the County Central Committee.

CHARLES PIATT, a retired business man of
Middletown, was born in the town of Mt.
Hope, near Otisville, November 1, 1825.
His grandfather Piatt was born in New Jersey,
where he lived and died. He was of French
descent. His father, Daniel Piatt, was also a native of New Jersey, but located in the town of
Mt. Hope at an early day, and later removed to
Mamakating, Sullivan County, where he was engaged in farming until his death, at the age of
eighty-three years. He married Rhoda Campbell, who was born in Mt. Hope, and who died
in early womanhood. Her father, David Campbell, the grandfather of our subject, was a native
of Virginia, who came to Orange County during
the last century, and located adjoining the village of Otisville, where he farmed and worked
at his trades of gunsmith and blacksmith. The
family was driven from Virginia by the Indians,
and he escaped to Orange County, crossing the
Delaware River with his little sister on his back.
None of the family were injuried. His death
occurred when past eighty years. He was of

Scotch descent, and a member of the old-school
Baptist Church. To Daniel and Rhoda Piatt
were born three children, our subject being the
only one now living. After the death of his first
wife, Daniel Piatt again married, and by his second wife had five children, three of whom are
now living. One son, John, enlisted in the late
war from Sullivan County, under Colonel De-
Witt, was wounded, taken prisoner and sent to
Andersonville, where he died. Another son, William Lewis, was also in the service, and now resides in Sullivan County, engaged in farming.

After the death of his mother our subject resided with his grandfather Campbell until ten
years of age, and then went to work on a farm
in Mt. Hope with an uncle, John M. Piatt. All
the educational advantages enjoyed were in the
district subscription schools. In 1841, when but
sixteen years of age, he came to Middletown,
and was apprenticed under Robert Cavanaugh
as a cabinet-maker, with whom he remained four
years. He continued to work at his trade both
in Middletown and Goshen as a journeyman for
a few years, and about 1850 purchased an interest
in a door, sash and blind factory, in partnership
with Mr. Clawson, H. Williams, William Wilkinson and T. P. Ogden, and continued that
business for several years. About 1861 he purchased the interest of all his partners, and continued the business alone, at the old location on
James Street, and then, about 1876, located on
the corner of John Street and Linden Avenue,
erected a building, put in machinery and engaged
in the manufacture of doors, sashes, blinds and
mouldings, and also did a planing-mill business.
During that time he erected his present residence
at No. 18 Highland Avenue, and rebuilt the old
factory on James Street, converting it into brick
stores, which he still owns. He continued the
planing-mill business until 1887, when he sold out
and retired from active business.

Mr. Piatt was married, in Middletown, to Miss
Juliet Swayze, a native of New Jersey, and a
daughter of Gabriel Swayze, also a native of
that state, but who was then engaged in farming
in the town of Wallkill. She died here, leaving
three children: Emmett, in the United States

PROF. JOHN H. BURROWS.

Custom House in New York City; Eva, who died at the age of five years; and Burt S., of Middletown.

Mr. Piatt's second marriage occurred in March, 1887, when he married Mrs. Cornelia A. Hill, *nee* Mulford, a native of the town of Minisink, and daughter of William Mulford, also of Minisink, and a sister of J. P. Mulford, of Middletown, whose sketch appears elsewhere in this work. She grew to womanhood at Centreville and Hamptonburgh, and at Middletown first married William F. Hill, who was a carpenter by trade, and who died here. By her first husband she had one child, James M., residing in Middletown.

Mr. Piatt is a member of the First Presbyterian Church, and since its organization has been a member of the Republican party. For some years he was a member of the Odd Fellows, but does not at the present time hold membership in the order. In early days he was an active member of the fire department.

PROF. JOHN H. BURROWS. There is no resident of Orange County whose life affords a better illustration of what may be accomplished by determination and indefatigable industry than Professor Burrows, the efficient Principal of the schools of Washingtonville. During his experience of seventeen years as an instructor of youth, he has gained the confidence of the people and considerable prominence as a successful educator. In the fall of 1891 he came to this village, and has since filled the position of Principal of the schools, which under his energetic management have been raised in standard until they now rank with the best of any village in the county.

The Burrows family is of English origin, and its members have been honest, industrious and persevering people. The Professor's parents, Richard and Mary Ann (Holman) Burrows, spent their entire lives in England, and there the father, who was a miner by occupation, died at sixty years of age. The mother also died in that country, in 1860. By their union they had twelve children, three of whom are now living, namely: Eliza, whose home is in Pennsylvania; John H.; and Elizabeth, a resident of Iron Mountain, Mich. By another wife Richard Burrows had two daughters: Thirza, who makes her home in Crystal Falls, Mich.; and Agnes N., the only member of the family remaining in England.

In St. Pinnock, England, Professor Burrows was born October 21, 1849, and he spent the first twenty-one years of his life in the vicinity of Liskeard. At the age of ten he commenced to work in the mines, being obliged to earn his own livelihood. His educational advantages were exceedingly meager, and the prospects for the future seemed almost hopeless. But he was not easily discouraged, and in the face of apparently insurmountable obstacles he persevered until he had achieved the goal of his ambition and obtained an education. At the age of twenty-one he emigrated to America, and for the four years following he worked in the mines of Essex County, N. Y. Saving his money, he was at last enabled to carry out his plan of attending school. He entered the Ft. Edward Institute, where he remained for two terms. Subsequently he taught school, and in the intervals between terms he attended that well known educational institution as his funds enabled him, finally graduating in 1879. In the spring of 1881 he became a tutor in the Ft. Edward Institute, where he remained as instructor for four years, also teaching the union school of that place. Later he attended the State Normal School for one and one-half years, perfecting himself in his chosen profession, and is now recognized as one of the best teachers in the state. Since coming to Washingtonville he has built up the school at this place, and now has four teachers under him and one hundred and fifty pupils. Not only is he an excellent instructor, but he is a good disciplinarian as well, being kind, yet firm and efficient, and by his effective methods of imparting knowledge he has materially promoted the welfare of his pupils.

In 1880 Professor Burrows was united in marriage with Camilla Kessler, of Altoona, Pa., who died the following year, leaving an infant son, who died six months later. In 1891 he married Miss Nellie McDonald, of Ft. Edward, N. Y., and they have one child, Helen May. Believing that the greatest question before the people to-day is not the protection of home industries or the adoption of free-trade principles, but the prohibition of the liquor traffic, and the destruction of the saloons which have brought dishonor and death to so many of our countrymen, Professor Burrows gives his support to the party whose platform is pledged against the saloon element and the licensing of the sale of intoxicating liquors. Socially he is identified with the Masonic fraternity. In his religious views he is liberal, and while a believer in the Christian religion, he does not uphold the creeds and doctrines of denominationalism. He attends the Methodist Episcopal Church, because it most nearly carries out his idea of what a church should be, though, were it in his power to do so, some of the features of that denomination would be eliminated.

JOHN DUNNING STIVERS, one of the editors of the Middletown *Times*, was born in Middletown, August 30, 1861. In boyhood he attended the public schools of this city and Wallkill Academy, where the rudiments of his education were obtained. Later he became a student in Peekskill Military Academy, from which institution he was graduated in 1878, at the age of seventeen. He then began his journalistic career, entering the office of the *Press* as bookkeeper, and later filling the position of city editor.

Resigning from the *Press*, Mr. Stivers became private secretary to his father, Hon. M. D. Stivers, during his term as Member of Congress from this district. Upon the latter's retirement from office, he returned to Middletown, and with his brother, Lewis S., established the Middletown *Times*, which has now gained a place among the most influential organs of the Republican party in this section. He was elected to

take his father's place as Trustee of the Orange County Trust and Safety Deposit Company.

Mr. Stivers is one of the oldest members of the Bachelors' Social Club, and for five years officiated as its President. He is also identified with Lancelot Lodge No. 169, K. of P., and Hoffman Lodge No. 412, F. & A. M., at Middletown. He is an honorary member of Excelsior Hook and Ladder Company No. 1, and was Secretary of the organization for several years. Upon the organization of the Twenty-fourth Separate Company, New York National Guard, in 1887, in which he aided, he was elected Sergeant, and served in that capacity until 1891, since which time he has been Second Lieutenant.

EDWARD AYERS, senior member of the firm of Ayers & Rodgers and a rising young business man of Middletown, was born in Wantage, Sussex County, N. J., January 5, 1866, being the son of David B. and Hulda (Beemer) Ayers, natives of the same county as himself. His paternal grandfather, who was of English descent, was a farmer there; his maternal grandfather, who became a member of a New Jersey regiment during the Civil War, served with valor until he fell in an engagement with the Confederates.

In 1880 David B. Ayers came to Middletown, where he remained until his death. Here he was for some time extensively engaged in the stock business, buying cattle and horses and shipping them by carload lots. His yards and stables were situated on the Dolsontown Road, where his son Edward now has a farm. At the age of fifty-six years he passed away, in 1889, in the faith of the Presbyterian Church, to which he belonged. In politics he affiliated with the Republican party. His widow still makes her home in this city, and their three children also reside here, namely: Edward, of this sketch; Gabriel B., who is engaged in the livery business on Canal Street; and David B., who is with his eldest brother.

Until fourteen years of age our subject resided in Sussex County, where he attended the common schools. After coming to Orange County he was a student in Wallkill Academy. At an early age he helped to drive stock from Western New York to New Jersey, his first work in that line being when only about nine years old. After his father's death in 1889, he took charge of the business, which he ran for his mother one year and then became sole proprietor. In 1895 he bought the place on Academy Avenue, including residence, barns and substantial outbuildings adapted for the successful prosecution of a stock business. In April, 1894, he formed a partnership with William H. Rodgers, under the firm title of Ayers & Rodgers, and started in the livery business on Sprague Avenue. They have large and well equipped stables, with vehicles of every kind, and all the conveniences for carrying on the enterprise successfully.

Aside from his interest in the livery, Mr. Ayers has been prospered in his work as a stock-dealer. Many of his purchases are made in western Pennsylvania and the cattle are shipped here and sold from his stock-yards. He has for sale both milch and beef cattle, carrying on a large trade in that line, and also deals extensively in horses. Politically he is a Republican, and socially holds membership in the Excelsior Hook and Ladder Company No. 1, at Middletown. In Middletown he married Miss Carrie May, daughter of William H. Rodgers, his partner and the manager of the livery business. Mrs. Ayers was born in Port Jervis, and by her marriage is the mother of one child, named Rema.

<<++++++++++++◉++++++++++++>>

JOSEPH B. PENNY, of Middletown, was born in Ellenville, Ulster County, May 11, 1859, and is a son of Jonathan and Angeline (Williams) Penny, both of whom were born near Ellenville. The grandfather, Daniel Penny, was a native of Holland, and came to this country in early life, locating in Ulster County, where he followed the occupation of a farmer until his death. Jonathan Penny remained upon the old homestead until seventeen years of age, assisting his father in the cultivation of the farm, and then went to Sullivan County, where for one year he worked for his board, at the same time attending school. At the expiration of this time he secured a school in Sullivan County and began teaching. The following year he went to Pennsylvania, and there taught one or more terms, when he removed to Ulster County and engaged in the same occupation. Later Mr. Penny engaged in the mercantile business at Ellenville for a few years, and then again engaged in teaching, which profession he continued until 1885, when he located in Sparrow Bush. He is now living a retired life, at the age of seventy-five years. In politics he is a strong Republican. In Ulster County he was married to Angeline Williams, a daughter of Joseph Banks Williams. The latter was a native of Connecticut, but removed at an early day to Ulster County, where he engaged in farming and school teaching. All of their six children are yet living. Charles A. resides in Port Jervis; Joseph B. is the subject of this sketch; David L. is a tanner in Newark, N. J.; Carrie is Mrs. Vannoy, of Sparrow Bush; Ira B. is a tanner in Chicago; and William is a tanner of Sparrow Bush.

The subject of this sketch was reared in Ellenville, and until ten years of age attended the public schools of that place. For three years he followed the baker's trade, and later was employed as a clerk in a general store at Ellenville, where he remained as general salesman until 1887. After severing his connection with the store, he started in the grocery business, under the firm name of J. B. Penny & Co., but in 1890 sold out and removed to Middletown, engaging as a traveling salesman for the Prior Medicine Company, his route being from Philadelphia to Binghamton. After traveling for this firm two years he entered the employ of the New York, Ontario & Western Railway, where he remained until January, 1895, when he was elected Truant Officer by the Board of Education. During the ten months of the school year his entire time is taken up in the discharge of his duties. His office is in the rooms of the Board of Education.

Mr. Penny was married, in Ellenville, to Miss Elizabeth Sherwood, who was born in Ulster County, and who is a daughter of John E. and Sarah J. (Terwilliger) Sherwood, the former a native of Ulster County, and the latter of Sullivan County. Both parents are yet living, Mr. Sherwood being a general carpenter for the Delaware & Hudson Canal. Three children have been born unto them, Cora E., Addie M. and Joseph S. In politics Mr. Penny is a Republican, and fraternally is a member of the Knights of Pythias.

CHARLES H. BABCOCK, who resides on Beattie Avenue, Middletown, and is employed as a conductor on the New York, Ontario & Western Railroad, was born in the town of Warwick, December 5, 1860. His father, J. M. Babcock, a native of the same place as himself, was a son of Erastus Babcock, who was born in this county, was of English descent, and followed the occupation of a farmer in the town of Warwick. J. M. Babcock, whose life occupation has been that of an agriculturist, still resides on the old homestead five miles from Warwick, and there his wife, formerly Keziah Rainer, resided until her death.

Of nine children, all still living, the subject of this notice is fifth in order of birth. He remained on the home farm until nineteen years of age, meantime attending the district schools. In 1879 he went to Illinois and embarked in farming near Rochelle, Ogle County, where he remained until 1886. The attractions of old Orange, however, were greater than those of the West, and in 1886 we find him back at his boyhood's home. Soon afterward he entered the employ of the Erie Railway Company as a brakeman between Port Jervis and Jersey City, his run being on a through freight. In the fall of 1889 he became brakeman for the Ontario & Western on a local freight train between Cornwall and Livingston Manor. One year later, in November, 1890, he was promoted to the position of conductor, remaining on the same train for two years. Since then he has had the freight train between

Middletown and Mayfield, Pa., a run of one hundred and twenty-two miles, which is made in eleven hours. In his railroad experiences he has been exceedingly fortunate, having never had a serious accident on his train.

Since coming to Middletown, Mr. Babcock has built his residence on Beattie Avenue, near Albert Street. While not active in politics, he is known as a stanch and pronounced Republican, always upholding party principles. Socially he is connected with Middletown Lodge No. 112, I. O. O. F., and United Division No. 104, Order of Railway Conductors. In this city, in 1886, he married Miss Elizabeth Brown, a native of this place and daughter of William Brown, one of the well known business men and old residents of Middletown.

GABRIEL B. AYERS, one of the rising young business men of Middletown, is proprietor and owner of the livery, boarding and sale stables at No. 28 Canal Street. In his barns are twenty stalls, and the sheds in the rear have an equal capacity. He carries a full line of buggies, carriages, hacks and phaetons—in fact, everything necessary for the proper management of the business. Though he has been in the business for a short time only, he has already gained a large trade and the confidence of the people as a man of honorable dealings with all.

By referring to the sketch of Edward Ayers, which is presented upon another page of this volume, mention will be found of David B. Ayers, our subject's father. Gabriel B. is the second among three children, and was born in Beemerville, town of Wantage, Sussex County, N. J., in 1869. From the age of eleven years he was reared in Middletown, and his education was principally received in the schools of this place. He remained at home, assisting his father in the stock business, until the death of that parent, when he began in the world for himself. For a

GEORGE W. PETERS.

time he was employed in New York City, after which he spent ten months in Scranton as a conductor in the employ of the Street-railway Company. Returning from there to New York City, he secured a position on the Eighth Avenue line of the city street railroad.

April 15, 1894, Mr. Ayers embarked in the business which he has since conducted. From the start he has met with encouraging success, and without doubt will in time build up a very large and profitable business. He gives his attention principally to its management, though he is also prominent in social circles and popular among the best people of the place. In his fraternal relations he is identified with Paughcaughnaughsinque Tribe of Red Men. He is an enterprising and capable young man, and will without doubt gain an influential position among the business men of Middletown.

GEORGE W. PETERS, one of the well-to-do and retired business men of Newburgh, resides at No. 148 Montgomery Street. Under Mayor Doyle he was Superintendent of Streets for two terms, and has always been very active in Democratic campaign work, serving on executive and ordinary committees. He is a stockholder in the Palatine Hotel, is a stockholder and member of the City Club, and belongs to the Board of Trade. For years he has been President of the Society for the Prevention of Cruelty to Animals, helped to obtain a separate charter, and was the first President of the new organization. For the past twenty-five years he has been a member of the Newburgh and New Windsor Horse-thief Protective Society, of which he is also President.

Mr. Peters was born in Poughkeepsie, N. Y., September 27, 1826, his parents being Charles and Phœbe (Dean) Peters. The father was a native of Pleasant Valley, Dutchess County, and the grandfather came from a Long Island family. Charles Peters was proprietor of a butcher-shop in Poughkeepsie, and afterward in Washington Market, in New York City. He was a soldier in the War of 1812, and at the time

of his death, which occurred in New York, he was in his sixty-third year. His wife was also a native of Pleasant Valley, Dutchess County, in which locality her father, Gilbert Dean, a native of Long Island, had settled at an early day. He was a boot and shoe maker by trade and followed that occupation until shortly before his death. Mrs. Peters died in New York City, at the age of fifty-two years. Both parents were members of the Methodist Episcopal Church.

Our subject is one of sixteen children, all but two of whom grew to maturity, though only seven survive. He was reared in Poughkeepsie, attending the public schools of that place, and in his sixteenth year he moved to New York City and learned his father's business. At that time his stand was located in the old Washington Market, formerly known as Bear Market, but afterward the father and son opened a shop on Eighth Avenue, near the corner of Twenty-third Street, under the old Knickerbocker Hall, where the present Grand Opera House stands. On reaching his majority, young Peters became a member of the firm, which for ten years was known as Charles Peters & Son, and from that time up to 1863 he was sole proprietor. In the year last mentioned he sold out his interest and moved to Newburgh, buying a farm on the northern plank road, four and a-half miles from the city, and for two years was engaged in agricultural pursuits. Then for a like period of time he operated a farm near Monticello, N. Y. In 1869 he opened a meat-market at No. 113 Water Street, and continued at that location for four or five years, when he took his two sons, Charles and William T., into partnership. Five years later the former died, and at the end of three years more the senior Mr. Peters retired from the firm. The other son, William T., continued to engage in trade until his death, which occurred in January, 1892. Besides his home our subject owns three other residences, one at No. 146 Montgomery Street, another at No. 3 Catlin Street, and the third at No. 263 Grand Street.

In 1852 Mr. Peters was initiated into the Masonic order, becoming a member of Hope Lodge, of New York City, and in later years was Master of Hiram Lodge, of the same city. He is now a member of Hudson River Lodge No. 607; of Highland Chapter No. 52, R. A. M.; and of Hudson River Commandery No. 35, K. T. He is a member of the Veteran Association and is with one exception the oldest Mason in Newburgh. While in New York he was a member of Hose Company No. 30 for several years, and belonged to the Eighth Regiment of the National Guard, known as the Washington Grays. His son, William T., was Quartermaster of the Tenth Separate Regiment of the New York National Guard, was identified with Lawson Hose Company, and was also a Mason.

The first marriage of our subject occurred in New York City in 1845, when his union with Miss Marinda Wallace was celebrated. Of the five children born to them Charles and William T. were the only ones that grew to maturity. The former died at the age of twenty-six years, and the latter, who died in his forty-sixth year, left two daughters, who reside with their grandfather. The second marriage of Mr. Peters was with Miss Mary Whitney, who was a native of Germany, and who died in Newburgh. His present wife was formerly Miss Georgiana Wier, whose birth occurred in Newburgh. Mr Peters is a member of the Unitarian Church, being a member of the Board of Trustees, while his wife is a member of Calvary Presbyterian Church.

⋆ ⸺ ⸻ ❊ ⸻ ⸺ ⊷

ISAAC L. CASSELL, one of the oldest engineers on the New York, Lake Erie & Western Railroad, was born in New York City in 1833. His parents, William and Hannah (Lilly) Cassell, were natives, respectively, of France and Wales, and the former, who emigrated to America in early manhood, was employed in New York City as a teacher of languages. After his death, which occurred in middle life, his widow took charge of the children, whom she reared to fill positions of trust and usefulness in the world. She attained an advanced age, dying at the age of seventy-six.

Of the eight children comprising the family,

two grew to years of maturity, the other besides our subject being Mrs. Mary Hill, who died when visiting in Chicago. Isaac L. was reared in New York City until ten years old, when he went to West Point as messenger boy for the civilian treasurer at the post. Three years were spent there, after which he returned to New York City and served an eighteen-months apprenticeship to the gold-beating trade. In 1850 he secured a position on the Harlem Railroad, working first in an humble capacity, but was soon promoted to be fireman. In 1853 he went into the employ of the Erie, with headquarters at Port Jervis, being fireman between that city and Piermont. In 1855 he became engineer, his run being into Jersey City.

Going west to St. Louis in 1856, Mr. Cassell secured a position as engineer on the Missouri Pacific Road between St. Louis and Jefferson City. Three years were spent there, after which he made a short visit to Orange County. On again going West, he stopped in Indiana, where he was engineer on a passenger train between Richmond and Logansport for five years. On his second return to Orange County he secured employment as engineer on the Erie between Port Jervis and Jersey City. In 1867 he went to Ohio, where for two years he ran a passenger train on the Cincinnati, Hamilton & Dayton between Cincinnati and Dayton. On his return to Orange County in 1869, he became freight engineer, and continued in that capacity until 1884, since which time he has run the passenger train, and since 1888 he has had the Middletown way-train local between this place and Jersey City.

At Middletown, in 1858, Mr. Cassell married Miss Frances Knox, who was born in this county. Her father, James, was born in the town of Crawford, to which place her grandfather, John Knox, had emigrated from the North of Ireland. Though of direct Irish descent, the family is of remote Scotch lineage, their ancestors having been prominent Protestants during the days of religious agitations. In the town of Crawford, where he was reared, James Knox learned the carpenter's trade, and afterward he settled near New Vernon, where he was engaged as a contractor and builder.

In 1855 he purchased a farm of eighty-seven acres within the limits of the city of Middletown, and lying between the Asylum and Hillside Cemetery, on the Erie Railroad. Here he died in 1863, at the age of sixty-three. In politics he was a Jacksonian Democrat, and in religious belief an Old-school Baptist. His wife, who bore the maiden name of Vashti Caldwell, was born in Dutchess County, and died in 1869. Her father, Joseph Caldwell, was a native of that county, and a farmer there, and her grandfather, who also resided there, was a soldier in the Revolutionary War.

Mrs. Cassell is the youngest of six children, the others being as follows: Nelson, who died in Brooklyn; George L., Treasurer of the Caldwell Lead Company of New York City, and of whom mention is elsewhere made; Henry, who is living near Topeka, Kan.; Harrison, who was a member of the First California Infantry in the Civil War, and served principally in the West, running the Apache blockade; and Eliza, wife of Charles Robbins, of New York City. The old Knox homestead is now either built up or laid off in lots, its principal streets being Monhagen, Knox and California Avenues, and West Main and Erie Streets. Mrs. Robbins was the first to build here, after which Mr. Cassell erected his elegant residence at No. 173 West Main Street.

Socially Mr. Cassell is identified with Hoffman Lodge No. 412, F. & A. M., and Midland Chapter, R. A. M. He and his wife also belong to the Order of United Friends, in Jersey City. They are members of the Second Presbyterian Church, and politically he is a Republican.

GEORGE W. HESS, senior member of the firm of Hess & Van Ness, proprietors of the North End Machine-shops, at No. 325 North Street, is a fine machinist and electrical engineer. He was born in Scranton, Pa., July 4, 1862, and is a son of Hieronymus and Margaret (Wolfinger) Hess, the former a native of Germany, and the latter of Oxford, N. J., but of German descent. The father came to the United States when but eighteen years of age, and was employed as a stationary engineer at Scranton, and later was with the Lackawanna Iron and Coal Company as engineer, remaining there until his death, at the age of sixty-four years. His wife, who was a member of the German Methodist Church, died in Scranton, leaving five children, four of whom are yet living.

George W. Hess was second in the parental family of five children. He grew to manhood in his native city, and there had the advantage of the public and high schools. When sixteen he was apprenticed as a machinist in the shops of the Lackawanna Iron and Coal Company, and after serving five years became an engineer under his father. Subsequently he was with A. B. Sturgis, as electrical engineer, and later was chief engineer of the suburban electric station. Then for a time he was with Mr. Whiting, of Scranton, as superintendent of the electric plant at that place. In April, 1894, he came to Middletown as chief engineer of the Middletown & Goshen Traction Company, and has had charge of the construction of the power-house and electric-plant in this city. After the completion of the building, he was chief engineer until April 1, 1895, when he resigned to go into business, forming the present partnership with Richard Van Ness, and under the firm name of Hess & Van Ness they leased the building, put in new machinery, including planers, drills and lathes, and in fact everything needed in modern machine works. The engine is six horse-power and the boiler ten horse-power. They do machine work of all kinds, but make a specialty of electrical work, and manufacture the safety brake and the feeder combined for electric-street cars. In the short time they have been engaged in business, they have had remarkable success, and are securing orders from many points. They do general job work, and have a blacksmith-shop in connection.

Mr. Hess was married, in Scranton, to Miss Sarah Parsons, a native of that city, and they have three children: Arlington, Margaret and Ella May. The family resides at No. 19 Prince Street. While in Scranton Mr. Hess was a member of the Patriotic Order Sons of America, and

of the Scranton Branch of the United Order of
Machinists of America. He is a member of the
Methodist Episcopal Church, and is an active
worker in that body. In politics he has always
been a Republican.

EWIS G. WILSON, general manager of the
Middletown Ice Company, was born at Plaistow, Rockingham County, N. H., February 15, 1853, being a member of an old Scotch
family that was early represented in Vermont.
His father, George M., who was born in Top-
sham, Vt., was a carpenter by trade, and early in
life settled in Plaistow, N. H., on the Massachusetts line, where he was engaged as a contractor
and builder. After many years in that place, he
removed to Haverhill, Mass., and there he died
at eighty-three years of age.

Though beyond the limit of age for military
service, George M. Wilson enlisted in the Union
army during the Civil War, and was Corporal of
Company K, Fifth New Hampshire Infantry, in
which he served until he was discharged on account of physical disability. In religious belief
he was a Baptist, devoted to the doctrines of that
denomination. For his wife he chose Harriet M.
George, who was born in Plaistow, N. H., and
died at the age of sixty-six. Her father, Jesse
George, was an extensive farmer and successful
hotelman, and at one time held the office of High
Sheriff of Rockingham County.

The subject of this sketch is next to the youngest of eight children, and is the only son among
the five children who attained years of maturity,
and of whom three are now living. At the age
of thirteen he accompanied his father from Plaistow to Haverhill, five miles distant. About the
same time he was graduated from Phillips Academy, at Andover, Mass. He then secured a position as clerk in a dry-goods store at Haverhill,
where he remained until January, 1873, and
thence moved to Port Jervis, N. Y., where he became fireman on the Erie Road between Jersey

City and Port Jervis. For seven years he was
employed in that capacity, and for the two following years was engineer between the same
points, after which he retired from railroading and
bought a meat-market in Chester. For eighteen
months he was a member of the firm of Rundell
& Wilson, after which he bought out his partner's interest, and soon took in a Mr. Osborn,
under the firm title of Wilson & Osborn, continuing as such until December, 1888, when he sold
out to his partner. Shortly afterward he came to
Middletown, where he has since resided.

Forming a partnership with John D. Wood,
under the firm name of Wilson & Wood, our
subject bought the Consumers' Ice Company's
plant, and carried on the business until 1892,
when the concern was merged into the Middletown Ice Company, with himself as general manager. Later he bought out Josiah Miller's ice
business, which he consolidated with the Middletown Ice Company, and the firm now has an icehouse at the Summit, and also at Miller's Lake.
During the summer months eight wagons are
used for delivery, and the business is a very large
one. The icehouses have a capacity of twelve
thousand tons.

Meantime our subject commenced in the coal
business as a member of the firm of Bodine &
Co., and after the death of Mr. Bodine in 1895,
the concern was carried on by the firm of Wilson
& Wood. As a business man Mr. Wilson is
sagacious and progressive, and his large trade
has been secured through his earnest efforts and
untiring energy. While residing in Chester, he
married Miss Mary E. Fredricks, who was born
in that village. Her father, Henry P. Fredricks, was a business man of that place for many
years, and also engaged in business at Washington Market in New York City.

Politically a Republican, Mr. Wilson represents the Second Ward on the Republican County Committee, and is also a member of the City
Committee. In 1892 he was elected, without
opposition, a member of the Board of Excise
Commissioners, of which he was Treasurer for
two terms, and is now President. While a resident of Chester, he was elected Collector by the

JOSEPH GAVIN.

largest majority ever given any candidate. Socially he is connected with Hoffman Lodge No. 412, F. & A. M.; Mt. William Lodge, K. of P., at Port Jervis; and the Esther Anthony Lodge, I. O. O. F., at Port Jervis. Since September, 1889, he has been a member of the Excelsior Hose and Ladder Company No. 1.

---⚙☸⚙---

JOSEPH GAVIN, a prominent citizen of Orange County, was born in County Galway, Ireland, June 18, 1833, a son of John and Bridget (Moore) Gavin, both natives of Ireland, where they spent the greater part of their lives. In 1853 they emigrated to this country, and in October, 1854, they came to Chester, N. Y., where they passed their last days. John Gavin met with an accident April 24, 1856, which resulted in his death a few days subsequently. Strange to relate, Mrs. Gavin, the mother of our subject, also met an accidental death. With her daughter, she was sitting near an Erie Railroad track when a train came along unexpectedly and caught a cow on the cow-catcher. The animal was thrown with great force against Mrs. Gavin, and her death occurred a few days later. This was also in 1856.

Joseph Gavin, our subject, received a limited education in Ireland during his youth. His father being a blacksmith, Joseph learned that trade with him, and was engaged in that work in his native land until the age of twenty, when he came to America and soon after located at Chester, this state. He established a blacksmith business at this place, and successfully conducted the same from April 1, 1858, until 1865, when he disposed of his property and business. He then moved to Middletown, where for six months he was engaged in blacksmithing, when, in 1866, he purchased a farm of one hundred and forty-one acres near Goshen, for which he paid $11,000. Six years later, or in 1872, he sold that farm for $20,-000, and bought one hundred and ten acres near Stony Ford, Orange County. In 1878 he purchased a lovely home where he now lives, which comprises fifty-five acres of finely improved land

near the village of Chester, and which is part of the farm formerly owned by the famous Ristick, owner of "Hambletonian."

Mr. Gavin is comparatively a self-made man, and has made some very profitable deals in horses. He was married, in 1859, to Miss Ann Burke, a daughter of Martin Burke, of Ireland. Five children were born of this union, three of whom are yet living: Mary B., of New York City; Anna, wife of F. W. Downey, of Dobb's Ferry; and Katie E., also of New York City. Mrs. Gavin died in February, 1870, and in 1872 Mr. Gavin married Ann Sullivan, daughter of David Sullivan, of Ireland. By this marriage there are six children: Elizabeth May, Joseph, Emily G., David, Mary Lucy and Helen, all of whom are yet at home with their parents.

Mr. and Mrs. Gavin and their children are members of the Catholic Church, and Mr. Gavin was largely instrumental in erecting the church at Chester. He is a Democrat at all times and under all circumstances; however, in local politics he is conservative. He has never aspired to official position, preferring to attend to his own affairs, and is a kind husband, an indulgent parent and an accommodating neighbor.

---◈━━━◈---

WILLIAM M. O'NEAL, a veteran of the late war, and at present a contractor and builder at Middletown, was born in Scottstown, town of Wallkill, January 16, 1842. The family of which he is a member originated in Ireland on the paternal side, and in Holland on the maternal side. Our subject's great-grandfather was born in the North of Ireland, and, emigrating to America, settled in Orange County. Edward, who was next in line of descent, was born in the town of Monroe, but spent his life principally at Scotchtown, where he engaged in farm pursuits. His wife was a native of Scotland. During the War of 1812 he enlisted in the defense of our country and served until the close of the conflict. The father of our subject, Samuel O'Neal, was born in the town of Wallkill, and in youth learned the stone-mason's trade, but made farming his principal occupation. In 1852 he settled near Ellenville, where he improved his land and made of it a fine dairy farm. He died May 5, 1895, when over seventy-four years old. His wife, who was known in maidenhood as Margaret Bennett, was born in the town of Mamakating, Sullivan County, and was of Holland-Dutch descent. She died in 1888. They were the parents of ten children, eight of whom arrived at years of maturity, and seven are now living, William M. being the eldest. The others are Sarah, Samuel, Helen, Martha, Lottie and James.

The first ten years of our subject's life were passed in Scotchtown, whence in 1853 he accompanied his parents to Ellenville, Ulster County, where he was reared to manhood on a farm. At Lackawack, the same county, he was employed on a farm and in the lumber business. In June, 1862, he enlisted in Company D, One Hundred and Fifty-sixth New York Infantry, being mustered into the state service at Kingston, Ulster County, and into the United States service at New York City. He was assigned to the Army of the Gulf, under General Banks, and started South, but the transports were wrecked off the coast of Florida. The soldiers were taken on the "Blackstone," a mail steamer, and "Gemsbock," a blockading steamer, which landed them at Ft. Taylor December 12, 1862, and shortly afterward they reached New Orleans. From there they were sent up to Camp Carlton, where they drilled; next went to Baton Rouge, then to Port Hudson, falling back to New Orleans, and then going to Burwick's Bay, and up the bayous until they reached Alexandria. In the battle of Ft. Bisslin the First Lieutenant of the company was killed. The troops also took part in the battles of Alexandria and Port Hudson, and in a large number of skirmishes.

After the surrender at Port Hudson, July 8, 1863, the company was sent back to New Orleans on a steamer, and in the spring of 1864 they went to the bayous and Opelousas. After the battle of Mansoria they went to Alexandria, and from there accompanied Banks to Shreveport and Sa-

bine Cross Roads, fighting during the entire journey. After that expedition was concluded our subject was sent farther east and assigned to duty in the Shenandoah Valley, under Gen. Phil Sheridan, taking part in the battles of Winchester (September 19, 1864), Fisher's Hill, Mt. Crawford and Cedar Creek. In the last-named engagement he was wounded three times within ten minutes, but refused to leave the field, and in spite of three troublesome flesh wounds he stayed on picket duty all night. In the morning, however, he had become so weak that it was necessary to convey him to the hospital, and an ambulance was sent for him by Harry Lockwood, the Lieutenant in charge of Company D, who also dressed his wounds. The regiment went to Winchester, thence to Baltimore, from there to Ft. Pulaski, Savannah, Goldsboro, Morehead City and Newbern, N. C. After the surrender at Raleigh, they were sent to Athens, Ga., thence to Savannah, and in September, 1865, were mustered out of the service.

Upon being honorably discharged from the army, Mr. O'Neal returned to New York State, and for a year was unable to engage in active business. As soon as he partially regained his strength, he became employed in a lumber manufacturing business, and later was variously occupied at different places. Having learned the mason's trade with his father, in 1869 he began work at that occupation. The following year he went to Bradford County, Pa., where he spent a year. For two years he was a clerk in a grocery business, after which, in 1877, he came to Middletown and started to work at his trade, and with the exception of three years spent in Sullivan County he has ever since remained in Middletown. Since January, 1893, he has done contract work, and has erected residences in various parts of the city.

In Phillipsport, Sullivan County, Mr. O'Neal married Miss Suestia Richerson, who was born there. They have five children living, namely: Charlotte A., Mrs. O. Simpson, of Hurleyville; Mary M., Mrs. S. Chambers, of Middletown; Franklin N., a mason, living in Middletown; Cora E. and Edna D., who are at home. Ida M.

died at the age of fifteen years. The family attends the Methodist Episcopal Church. Politically Mr. O'Neal is a Republican, and socially he is connected with Lancelot Lodge, K. of P.; Monticello Lodge No. 532, F. & A. M.; and Capt. W. A. Jackson Post, G. A. R., of which he is a charter member.

B YRON S. DAYTON, senior member of the firm of B. S. Dayton & Co., merchants at Middletown and Liberty. was born near Napanoch, Ulster County, N. Y., July 12, 1847. The family of which he is a representative originated in England, and was founded in America by three brothers, who came from that country and made settlement in Connecticut. Thence Joseph Dayton, the great-grandfather of Byron S., emigrated to Ulster County, and became the founder of the family in this locality. He was one of the brave soldiers of the Revolution, in which memorable contest he fought for liberty and independence. His son, William I., was born in Ulster County, at a place known as Dayton's Corner, and he spent his entire life in that vicinity, engaged in agricultural pursuits.

Marinus Dayton, father of our subject, was born near Modena, in Ulster County, and while yet a boy began boating on the Hudson. In partnership with his cousin, Morgan A. Dayton, he owned and ran the sloop "Othello" for years between Albany and New York City, but his wife's failing health induced him to abandon that occupation, and he purchased a farm north of Napanoch, Ulster County. Later he spent a few years in Sullivan County, whence he went back to Ulster County. After the death of his wife, he came to make his home with his son Byron S. in Middletown, and here he now resides, being in the eighty-sixth year of his age.

The mother of our subject, Jane Barnes, was born on a sailing-vessel on the Atlantic Ocean when her parents were en route from Ireland to America. They settled in Philadelphia, and then

went to Poughkeepsie, N. Y., where she was reared, educated and married. Her death occurred in Ulster County in 1878, when she was about sixty-three years of age. She became the mother of five children, all of whom are still living, Byron S. being the eldest of the number. His boyhood years were spent in Napanoch, Ulster County, and Grahamville, Sullivan County, where he gained a common-school education. In the latter place he assisted his father, who was proprietor of a hotel there.

At the age of seventeen years, in the summer of 1864, Mr. Dayton volunteered in the Union army, and became a member of the First New York Mounted Rifles. He was mustered into the service at Kingston, and joined his regiment before Richmond, where within six days he was under fire in the skirmish line. In the various cavalry charges and dashes made by the regiment he took a valiant part. In a cavalry charge into Murfreesboro in 1865 his horse fell, throwing him on the ground, where his own and another horse fell over him, injuring him severely in the back. In June, 1865, he was mustered out of the service and honorably discharged at Richmond, Va.

On returning to New York, Mr. Dayton joined his parents in their home at Phillipsport, Sullivan County. Soon afterward he purchased a boating outfit for the Delaware & Hudson Canal, and this he ran between Honesdale and New York for two seasons, later trading it for a grocery store at Napanoch, on the canal. In 1870 he removed from that village westward, and settled in Madison County, Neb., becoming a pioneer of that now thickly populated state. He pre-empted one hundred and sixty acres, a portion of which occupied the present site of the county seat. After six months he proved possession to the property, and then took advantage of his homestead right, locating at Traceyville, Platte County, near the present site of Humphrey. While proving that claim, he also took up a tree claim, but disposed of it before it had been proved up. He remained on his homestead claim for the required period of five years, less the time of his army service, and then located at Columbus, where he was proprietor of a boarding-house, the hotels in the West at that time being boarding-houses and quite distinct from a bar. At one time he owned a portion of the site of Humphrey, but this he sold.

In 1876 Mr. Dayton disposed of all his Nebraska property excepting his homestead, which he sold many years later. Immediately after disposing of his interest there, he returned to New York and engaged in merchandising at Hunk Hill, north of Napanoch. Later he went to Ellenville and opened a general store there. In 1886 he came to Middletown and started a novelty store on North Street. Some time afterward he opened branch stores in Goshen and Otisville, and for two years made his home in the former village. On returning to Middletown he started a store on James Street, but after a short time sold the concern and took a position as traveling salesman. Later he carried on a grocery business on East Main Street, and was thus engaged until he opened his present store on North and King Streets. In addition to this, he has a branch store at Liberty. His son Warren F. has been in partnership with him since he was eighteen years of age, and is now in charge of the Liberty store. Besides his mercantile interests, Mr. Dayton does some real-estate business, and erected his residence at No. 36 Broad Street.

At Omaha, Neb., in 1870, Mr. Dayton married Miss Lydia Potter, who was born in Potterville, Ulster County, being a daughter of Francis Potter, formerly a lumberman of that county. They have two children, namely: Thornton Byron, proprietor of a novelty store at Walden, N. Y.; and Warren Francis, junior member of the firm of B. S. Dayton & Son. While in Nebraska Mr. Dayton was a Supervisor in Platte County. He is now a member of the Board of Education of Middletown, and is an active factor in the promotion of the educational interests of the city. Politically he is a Republican. Socially he is identified with Paughcaughnaughsinque Tribe, Improved Order of Red Men, and is keeper of the Wampum. For a time he held official position in General Lyon Post No. 266, G. A. R., from which he was demitted; he is now

connected with Capt. W. A. Jackson Post, and on Decoration Day of 1894 and 1895 served as Marshal of the day for that post. As a business man he is unusually keen, vigorous and efficient, and his financial success has been achieved through his indomitable perseverance and persistence.

J MILTON BARNES, a merchant of Central Valley, Orange County, New York, was born in Cornwall, Orange County, October 9, 1844, and is the youngest of a family of twelve children born to Matthew and Mary (Van Duser) Barnes, the former a native of Otsego County, N. Y., and the latter of the town of Cornwall, Orange County, N. Y. Our subject was reared in his native town, and attended what is now known as a "mountain school" until the death of his father, which occurred when he was about seventeen years of age. Being thrown on his own resources, he first engaged as a clerk in a store in the village of Canterbury, now Cornwall. He continued as clerk for a few months, and then learned the carpenter's trade, which he followed until the spring of 1876, working in all parts of Orange County. During the year 1875 he worked at his trade in Central Valley, and, liking the place, he formed a partnership in a mercantile business with Alfred Cooper, succeeding the firm of Cooper & Ackerman. This partnership continued eight years, when Henry C. Thorn purchased the interest of Mr. Cooper, and the firm name became Barnes & Thorn. At the end of two years, Ambrose Duran succeeded Mr. Thorn, and the business was continued under the name of Barnes & Duran for one year, and then changed to J. M. Barnes & Co. Mr. Duran continued with the firm three years, since which time Mr. Barnes has been alone, but until January 1, 1894, the firm name was not changed. At that time the "Co." was dropped. Mr. Barnes was appointed Postmaster in 1885, and again in 1892, and is the present incumbent.

On the 6th of November, 1884, Mr. Barnes was united in marriage with Miss Hannah Shuit, a native of Highland Mills, and a daughter

CHARLES L. MEAD.

of Morgan and Mary Ann (Titus) Shuit. (See sketch of Morgan Shuit in another part of this work.) In politics Mr. Barnes is a Democrat, and has supported that party during his entire life. He never sought or desired public office, and only served a short time as Highway Commissioner by earnest request. He was elected Justice of the Peace, but refused to qualify.

The mercantile business of Mr. Barnes has been developed, until it is more than double what it was when he first became a member of the firm of Cooper & Barnes. After being in business three years, he purchased the building in which the store is located, which is a two-story building, with basement and attic. He carries a full line of general merchandise, having added hardware, wall-paper and other lines to the stock. As a citizen, he enjoys the confidence and respect of the community, and is ever ready to do his part in building up his adopted village.

CHARLES L. MEAD, LL. B. This prominent attorney of Middletown comes of an old and honored family of New York State. He is a popular gentleman, and is at present serving as Treasurer of Orange County. His birth occurred in the town of Wawayanda, August 27, 1851, and he is a son of William H. Mead, also a native of that town. His grandfather, Roswell Mead, was a native of Connecticut, but became one of the pioneers of the town of Minisink, where his death occurred. He was one of the prominent residents of this section, and for many years served as Justice of the Peace, also filled the office of Supervisor. On one occasion he was elected a Member of the Assembly on the Democratic ticket. During the War of 1812 he served as a soldier in the ranks and rendered his country efficient service at that time. He married Hannah Cash, whose parents were also well known residents of this portion of the state.

The great-grandfather of our subject was Lieut.-Col. Matthew Mead, who was born in 1736, and died in 1816. He served as Captain of the Fifth Regiment Connecticut Line, under Col. David

Waterbury, and was wounded at St. John's, Canada, September 6, 1775. The following year he became Captain of the Ninth Regiment Connecticut Militia, and shortly afterward was made Major of the First Battalion Connecticut State Troops, under Col. G. S. Sulliman. December 25, 1776, he was made Lieutenant-Colonel of the Fifth Regiment Connecticut Line, Col. P. B. Bradley, serving in that capacity from January 1, 1777, until May 25, 1778. Col. Matthew Mead served as Lieutenant-Colonel during the Revolutionary War on the staff of General Washington. His brother John was a soldier in the Revolution and died during the service. (For further information relative to the Mead and Cash families, see sketch of Judge Roswell Coleman on another page.)

The father of our subject was an extensive land-owner of Orange County, where he died in 1876, at the age of fifty years. He had held many of the town offices and enjoyed the high regard of all who knew him. His wife, Cornelia, was a daughter of Hon. Joseph Davis, a Member of the Assembly and Supervisor of the town of Minisink for many years. From the time of its organization until his death, at the age of threescore years and ten, he was President of the Middletown National Bank. He was born in the town of Minisink and was there buried. The great-grandfather of Mrs. Mead was John Davis, a Scotchman. Her father married Elizabeth Decker.

The parental family included four children, namely: Hannah Davis Mead, deceased; Roswell, now a resident of St. Joseph, Mo.; Lizzie Decker Mead, who resides in Middletown; and our subject. The last-named, who was the eldest of the family, remained on the home farm until fourteen years of age, when he became a student in the Wallkill Academy. He then took a course in Claverack College, Columbia County, N. Y., from which he was graduated in 1873. He next entered Princeton with the Class of '77, where he was a student for two years.

Being desirous of following the profession of law, Mr. Mead, in 1875, entered Columbia Law School at New York City, from which he was graduated in 1877, with the degree of LL. B. He at once settled at Goshen for practice. In the fall of 1892 he was elected Treasurer of Orange County, by a majority of over nine hundred, carrying the town of Wawayanda, which was strongly Democratic. In January, 1893, he assumed the duties of his office, which he is still filling.

In Middletown, June 5, 1878, Mr. Mead married Miss Fannie, daughter of William Tuthill, a large farmer, owning extensive tracts near Middletown, in which place he resides. From 1891 to 1893 Mr. Mead was a member of the City Council, representing the Third Ward, and during that time aided greatly in securing the building of the electric street railway of the city. He is a member of the Sons of the Revolution. Politically a stanch Republican, he has represented his party in various conventions for many years, and at this writing is a member of the County Committee.

ILAND H. BLANCHARD, general superintendent of the National Saw Company, Middletown, was born in Acra, Greene County, near Catskill, N. Y., February 18, 1850. He is a descendant of French ancestors, the first of whom to cross the Atlantic was his paternal great-grandfather, one of the pioneers of the Hudson Valley and a jeweler by occupation. From their French-Huguenot ancestors the family has inherited that rectitude of character and uprightness of action which were dominant traits of their forefathers.

Our subject's father, Justus, and grandfather, Dr. Joseph Blanchard, were natives of Greene County, where the latter practiced medicine for many years. The former, who for a time engaged in the hotel business, afterward settled on a farm, and there he died at the age of thirty-five years. His wife, Emeline, was born in Greene County, where her father, Miles Darby, was a blacksmith. She survived her husband's death many years,

passing away at the age of seventy. She reared her two children in Greene County, and her younger child, Elizabeth, married Myron F. Gage, and went to New York City, where she died, leaving one son.

The only surviving member of the family is the subject of this sketch. He was reared at Acra, Greene County, where he attended the public school. In 1865 he entered Wallkill Academy at Middletown, where he remained until completing the course. In the fall of 1868 he became an employe of Wheeler, Madden & Clemson, saw manufacturers, being in their packing department for several years, though from 1870 he was in charge as shipping clerk. In 1888 he was made superintendent of the works, which position he continued to occupy after the concern was merged into the National Saw Company. He is one of the oldest of the three hundred or more employes of the company. That he has been energetic, capable and efficient, is proved by his long service with this concern, and also by the fact that he has worked his way upward to a position of great trust and responsibility.

Until 1883 Mr. Blanchard resided in Middletown, but he then removed to his eighty-acre farm adjoining Fair Oaks. This place is situated on a branch of the Erie and on the main line of the New York, Ontario & Western Railroad, about three and one-half miles from the city of Middletown. Politically a Democrat, Mr. Blanchard has been active in political clubs, and has served as a member of city and county committees. Socially he is connected with Hoffman Lodge No. 412, F. & A. M., of which he was Treasurer for a number of years. He is also associated with the Knights of Pythias at Middletown, and with the Legion of Honor. For one year he was Secretary of Excelsior Hose and Ladder Company No. 1, Fire Department. In religious matters he is connected with Grace Episcopal Church.

In Middletown Mr. Blanchard married Miss Sarah Biggin, who was born in Sheffield, England. Her father, Samuel Biggin, was a large saw manufacturer in that place until 1857, when he came to America and settled in Middletown. Here he had charge of the saw-manufacturing

department of Wheeler, Madden & Clemson for a
number of years. Wishing to revisit the scenes
of his youth and renew old associations, he started across the Atlantic, but died on the voyage.
Four children comprise the family of Mr. and
Mrs. Blanchard, namely: Hiland H., who is employed as a mechanic in the saw works; George
R., Maude and Edith. Mr. Blanchard possesses
to an unusual extent that happy combination of
traits which marks him at once as a man who is
prompt in action, yet prudent and cautious in
carrying out his undertakings, and he looks zeal-
ously after the interests of the company.

DAVID E. LAIN, who is a member of the
Orange County Roofing Company at Middletown, was born July 31, 1861, on a farm
adjoining the old Lain homestead near Westtown,
in the town of Minisink. His father, L. L., and
grandfather, David Lain, were born on the homestead. The great-grandfather, William, was born
on Long Island in 1743, and was orphaned by his
mother's death when an infant. He was then
taken by his father to Moorestown, N. J., where
his boyhood years were passed in the home of
maternal relatives. On attaining manhood he
settled in the town of Minisink, in 1765, and purchased a tract of unimproved land, upon which
he built a log house. In 1785 the log cabin was
replaced by a substantial stone dwelling, which
still stands, being occupied by our subject's brother, Milton A., whose children represent the fifth
generation of Lains residing there. William Lain
married Keziah Mather, a lineal descendant of a
brother of Cotton Mather, and they had ten children. Of these the youngest, David, became the
owner of the farm.

David Lain was born January 28, 1791, and was
twice married, his first wife being Millicent Aber,
and his second Rhoda Lee. Lebeus L., who was
born of the first marriage, grew to manhood on
the old homestead, and combined farming pursuits with the mercantile business, having a store
in Westtown. On retiring from business he purchased the old home farm from the widow of his

youngest brother, Mortimer, and there he still
makes his home. He is interested with our subject in the Orange County Roofing Company. In
politics he is a Republican, and religiously holds
membership with the Baptist Church at Unionville.

The mother of our subject, Arminda Terry,
was born near Liberty Corners, Orange County,
and spent her girlhood there, being a member of
an old and honored family of this locality. Her
father, Uriah Terry, who was born in this county,
owned a farm at Liberty Corners, comprising the
present site of the Drake & Stratton stock farm.
On retiring from agricultural pursuits, he retired
to Westtown, where he died at the age of about
sixty-five years. In religious belief he was a
Presbyterian, and his daughter is a Baptist.

The parental family consisted of three children,
namely: Milton A., who occupies the home farm;
David E.; and Millicent J., Principal of the Middletown School of Stenography and Typewriting.
Our subject was reared in Westtown and on the
homestead. He attended the public schools until 1870, after which he prepared for college under
private instruction, and also attended Wallkill
Academy. In 1881 he entered Cornell University and four years later was graduated, receiving
the degree of B. S. in electrical engineering. He
was a member of the first class that graduated in
electrical engineering from that institution. While
there he served for one year as editor of the Cornell *Daily Sun.*

In 1885 Mr. Lain became associated with the
electrician, Stephen D. Field, as his assistant, and
while engaged in that capacity they built a large
electric motor for use on elevated roads. This
was successfully completed and was run in 1887
for Cyrus Field. In 1888, when Mr. Field associated himself with Rudolph Eickemeyer, of
Yonkers, in electrical-railway work, Mr. Lain
entered their employ and assisted in developing
an electrical-railway system, which they sold in
1893. He also invented several valuable patents,
including a trolley and magnetic ore separator.
In 1893 he located in Middletown, where he and
his father have since been proprietors of the Orange County Roofing Company, with an office on

Franklin Square. They manufacture a roof paint from our subject's own formula, and have had a number of important contracts. Through their agents the company do business in this and adjoining counties.

Recently Mr. Lain has introduced and commenced to use Sackett's Wall-board, a new invention, for which he has the agency in this section. The board is built of composite layers of plaster of paris and paper, and is proving a splendid success. The outside can be finished in any style, which adds greatly to its desirability. A residence has been built of it in the North End, and it will undoubtedly soon become popular, as its desirable features become more generally known. While living in Yonkers Mr. Lain married Miss Maude Bonham, who was born in Cincinnati, Ohio, and who is the daughter of the late N. A. Bonham, of that city. Her mother, Lydia J., was a sister of George W. Barnum, of Monticello, N. Y., in whose home, after her mother's death, she was reared to womanhood. Two children bless the union, Marion A. and David L. Mr. Lain is a member of the American Institute of Electrical Engineers, and while engaged in electrical work contributed largely to the electrical literature of that time. Politically he is a Republican, and has been elected to offices of trust in his own church and allied societies.

─────⊙✳⊙─────

PETER CUMMINGS, of the firm of J. & P. Cummings, distillers, and wholesale and retail grocery and liquor dealers in Middletown, was born in County Meath, Ireland, in 1846, and is the son of Christopher and Frances (O'Keefe) Cummings, the former a native of County Meath, and the latter of County Kildare, Ireland. For several generations the Cummingses were interested in fine horses, the grandfather of our subject being a thorough sportsman, and a breeder of some of the finest horses in his native country. In his native land Christopher Cummings, the father of our subject, was an inn-keeper.

James, an elder brother of our subject, came to America in 1851, and in 1854 John also crossed

the Atlantic. Two years later the father and mother, together with our subject, came to this country. They settled at Otisville, in the town of Mt. Hope, where they remained until 1872, when they removed to Middletown, where the father died at the age of seventy-four years. The mother, who was a daughter of James O'Keefe, a gardener in his native land, lived until 1888, and died in Middletown at the age of eighty-four. Both parents were devout members of the Catholic Church. Their three children are yet living. James, now residing at Kingston, was Alderman of the Ninth Ward for many years; John's sketch appears on another page of this work; and Peter is the subject of this sketch.

Soon after arriving here, Peter Cummings was employed on the farm of William Wilkins, in the town of Wallkill, and remained with him for three years, working steadily in the summer and attending school in the winter. At the expiration of three years he secured a position as driver on the Delaware & Hudson Canal, with his brother John. As soon as his age would permit he was made captain of the boat, which ran between Honesdale and Rondout, carrying coal and merchandise. In connection with this duty, our subject was the agent for the brewery in Kingston now owned by his brother James. Feeling the necessity of a better education, our subject attended Wallkill Academy one year, and then studied in Otisville for two years. He left before graduating in order to enter into business with his brother John at Middletown.

Since coming here in 1868, Mr. Cummings' mercantile interests have increased year by year, and his surplus earnings have been judiciously invested in real estate, both in Middletown and New York City, he having built many private residences and business houses. His love for fine horses, which he doubtless inherited, is such that he has made many investments in this direction, and has bred some of the best horses in this region. He now owns "Lady C.," by "Clay," a Hambletonian, dam by "Messenger Durrock." She has raised three fine colts, two by "Alberton," sired by "Kentucky Prince," and one by "Old Sweepstakes," all promising horses.

WILLIAM C. TRIMBLE.

Mr. Cummings was married, in Port Jervis, to Mary F. Sheridan, born in New York City, and daughter of John and Mary Sheridan, both of whom are now deceased. Her father was a merchant of that city. Three children have been born unto them: John H., a graduate of Manhattan College; Mary, now attending Mt. St. Vincent Academy, on the Hudson; and Annie, attending the Ursuline Academy of Middletown.

Mr. Cummings is a member of St. Joseph's Catholic Church, and was a member of the Building Committee at the time of the construction of the church edifice. In politics he is a Democrat. He resides in a beautiful residence on Monhagen Avenue, adjoining the city limits, his grounds comprising four acres of land.

> ══════════════ ⁄

WILLIAM C. TRIMBLE is the senior member of the firm of W. C. Trimble & Son, proprietors of a livery, boarding, training and sales stable at Newburgh. With one exception, he is the oldest driver on the turf to-day. By those who are competent to judge, he is considered the best trainer of horses in the Hudson Valley, and the animals that have been trained by him have made the best record of any in Orange County. The junior member of the firm is his son, George E., who attends to the business part of the concern and has personal supervision of the stable.

The Trimbles are of Irish extraction. The father and grandfather of our subject, both of whom were named John, were natives of Crown Point, N. Y., but the latter, who engaged in teaching school there, finally removed to Pike County, Pa., where he died. John, Jr., when a boy, came to Orange County, and made his home with an aunt, Mrs. Hill, in the town of Montgomery. On arriving at man's estate he began to farm, afterward acquiring the ownership of one hundred acres. In 1850 he removed to Fox Lake, Dodge County, Wis., where he engaged in farming for a number of years. His death occurred in 1856, when he was fifty-six years of age.

The mother of our subject, Margaret, was a daughter of Cadwallader Colden, a farmer of Orange County. By her marriage she had seven children, of whom only three are living. Our subject was born in the town of Montgomery, this county, December 29, 1826, and was reared upon a farm there, receiving a common-school education. In 1849 he went, via the Lakes and rail, to Chicago, thence by canal to St. Louis, from there down the Mississippi to New Orleans, and on the coast in Louisiana he engaged in the race-horse business with D. F. Kenner, remaining there for seven years. In 1857 he located near Newburgh, and engaged in general farming, also devoting considerable attention to raising horses. In 1862 he came to Newburgh, where he commenced to deal in horses. Five years later he opened a livery stable on Third Street, where he carried on business until 1872.

In 1876 Mr. Trimble built a livery stable on the corner of Chambers and First Streets, and here he has engaged in the livery business since 1878. The building which he occupies is 50x135 feet in dimensions and three stories in height. It contains fifty stalls, an elevator, and everything necessary for the successful prosecution of the business. Among the noted horses which Mr. Trimble has trained, we mention the following: "Mountain Boy," a fine racing horse, that was sold to Commodore Vanderbilt, in 1865, for $12,000; "Judge Fullerton," which was bought for $3,000 and sold three months later for $20,000; "Commodore," purchased for $700, and sold for $8,000 four years later; "Music," a sorrel filly, that was bought at the age of three years for $325 and sold five years afterwards to Robert Bonner for $8,500; "Cornelia," a black mare, bought for $2,000 and sold for $13,000; "Inez," a black mare that was bought for $2,000 and sold for $8,000, after having been on the turf as a trotting-horse for two years; "Garnet," a well known trotter, purchased for $1,000, by J. G. Coster, who two years later refused ten times that sum for him; "Zenobia Moore," purchased for $1,000, eight times that sum being refused for her three months later, but she afterward died; "Patience," purchase price $1,000, trotted for one year, then sold as a brood mare; "Instant," bought in 1890

Mr. Trimble owning a half-interest in her, trotted for two years, and sold for $4,200, after having made a record of 2:14 1/4; "S. J.," a chestnut horse belonging to Gen. Austin Lathrop, trained here, trotted for one year, gained a mark of 2:16 1/4, and is now on the road in New York; and "Cobweb," a young horse condemned in California when five years old, but bought in New York for $550 by John Turl's sons, and given to our subject May 9, 1894, for the purpose of training for the turf. This horse is the finest perhaps of any trained by Mr. Trimble, as he has made a record of 2:12 and won $6,600. At present our subject has in training the filly "Morwent," five years old, foaled by "Instant," and sired by "Kentucky Prince." This filly had been condemned by three or four trainers, but Mr. Trimble is proving that she has good qualities, and is getting work out of her for her owners, Colonel Page and Dean Sage.

In 1857 Mr. Trimble married Miss Abbie Woodruff, who was born in this county. Their only child, George E., was born in Newburgh, June 6, 1862, and received a good education, graduating from Siglar's Academy, at the age of eighteen. He then entered into business with his father, and has since had charge of the stable and livery trade. November 10, 1892, he married Miss Lizzie Town Stocker, a native of Boston, and a graduate of the Conservatory of Music in that city, also at one time a teacher in the Newburgh Academy. George E. is a member of the Orange Lake Ice Yacht Club and the Newburgh Gun and Rifle Club.

GEORGE CRAWFORD, for many years one of the influential and enterprising business men of Middletown, is now living retired at his beautiful home in this city. He has shown marked ability as a business man, and has been very successful in all that he has undertaken.

Our subject was born September 10, 1816, in the town of Crawford, which was named in honor of his grandfather, who located here many years ago. The parental family included eleven children, of whom we make the following mention: Emeline, who never married, died when eighty years of age; Leander at the time of his death was in his seventy-third year; Millicent was sixty-five years at the time of her death; John A. lived to be eighty-one; Albert was sixty-three years old when he died; George, of this sketch, was the next-born; Sarah E. is deceased, as is also Esther; Theron is one of the most prominent agriculturists of this section, and occupies the old home farm; Robert is a substantial farmer of the town of Crawford; and Angeline is also living in the town of Crawford.

The father of our subject, Robert I. Crawford, was born in Sullivan County, N. Y., to which locality he was brought by his parents when young. He was here reared to mature years, and led an honorable and useful life. He was a very prominent man in the affairs of his locality, and in settling up estates there was none better. Honorable and upright in all his dealings, he won many friends, who held him in high esteem.

The mother of our subject, Deborah (Dickerson) Crawford, was a native of the town of Crawford, and was the daughter of Benjamin and Esther (Ogden) Dickerson, who were born in Dutchess County. She belonged to the Hopewell Presbyterian Church, with which denomination her husband was also connected, and of which he was an Elder for many years.

Our subject passed the first thirty years of his life on the old homestead, in the meantime acquiring a good education. On starting out for himself, he purchased a farm in the town of Montgomery, which he operated with success for ten years. At the end of that time he rented his estate, and, moving into Middletown, engaged in the crockery and woodenware business. Several years later he opened up a grocery store, and for four years conducted a thriving trade among the best people of the locality. He is now living retired, giving his attention to looking after his real-estate interests.

November 5, 1846, Mr. Crawford married Miss Mary E. Crawford, a native of Orange County, and to them have been born two children: Emma, at home; and Frank, a merchant of Middletown. Mr. Crawford owns three residences in this place, which he rents, and in this way derives a good income. He is a stanch Republican in politics, and is actively interested in the success of his party. Like the other members of his family, he belongs to the Presbyterian Church.

ABRAM VAN NEST POWELSON is engaged in general law practice at Middletown, and in addition to protecting the interests of a large clientage, he is filling the positions of Assistant District Attorney and Justice of the Peace. The latter office he has held since 1869, being elected to succeed himself every four years. His political views are in accordance with the declarations of the Republican party, and in its progress he takes a great interest, for he believes its teaching and policy are best fitted to insure the welfare of the country and the prosperity of the citizens.

The Powelson family is of Dutch descent. The subject of this notice was born in Somerville, N. J., April 15, 1842, and both his father, Abraham, and his grandfather, John, were born near the same place, and were farmers by occupation. The former, who is still living, is now seventy-nine years of age. He still takes an interest in public affairs, and in politics is a Republican. His religious connections are with the Presbyterian Church. The lady whom he married was, like himself, of Dutch descent. She bore the maiden name of Sarah A. Van Nest, and was born near Somerville, N. J., where her father, John, was engaged in farming pursuits.

The parental family consisted of three children, those besides our subject being John A., President of the Somerville Woolen Manufacturing Company; and Mrs. Adeline Hagaman, who lives near Somerville. Our subject was prepared under a special tutor for Union College, which he attended for some terms, graduating in 1864 with the degree of Bachelor of Arts. Three years later the degree of Master of Arts was conferred

upon him. In 1864 he came to Middletown as instructor in the classics and higher mathematics at Wallkill Academy, remaining in that position for two years. Believing, however, that the law offered greater opportunities for advancement than the teacher's profession, he began its study under Judge John G. Wilkin, and carried it on for two years during his leisure hours, while engaged as Superintendent of the public schools. Since his admission to the Bar in 1869, he has carried on an extensive practice, giving his attention, to some extent, to his official duties, but finding sufficient time outside of them to manage the interests of his clients. Interested in educational matters, he is a member of the Board of Education and is Chairman of the Academy Committee, the duties of which are very important and responsible.

At Neversink, Sullivan County, Mr. Powelson married Miss Adeline Palen, a native of that place, and a daughter of Arthur Palen, who is head of the firm of Palen, Fleager & Co., the largest tanners there. Six children blessed the union of Mr. and Mrs. Powelson. The older ones have attained years of maturity and have proved themselves not only the joy and comfort of their parents, but of value in the world. Unusually brilliant in intellect, they have gained distinction by their culture and mental acumen. Arthur P., the eldest son, is a graduate of the Middletown High School and the New York Homeopathic Medical College, Class of '94, in which he was Class Prophet. He took a post-graduate course in Europe at the University of Gottingen, and on returning to the United States opened an office in Middletown, N. Y., where he has since practiced his profession.

Wilfred Van Nest, the second son, entered the United States Naval Academy at the age of sixteen, where, in the first year's examination, he was placed seventh among seventy-two. In the second year he rose to the second place, and in the third year stood at the head of the class. In his last year he fell back to second place, but his average for the four years was so much better than that of anyone else that he was the undisputed "honor man" of the class. Before the age of twenty-one, he joined the "Bennington," as a midshipman, and later went on the "Chicago" to Europe. He was sent by the Government to the University of Glasgow, where he took a special course, receiving the first prize. On his return to the United States, he was assigned to duty on the "New York," and is now an ensign on the personal staff of Admiral Bunce, of the North Atlantic Squadron. The third son, Howard J., is a graduate of the academy and the Hahnemann Medical College of Philadelphia, completing the studies of the latter institution in 1895, at the age of twenty-one, and standing third in his class, with a percentage of ninety-eight and one-fifth. The three youngest children, Nellie, Louise and John, are students in the academy.

A. V. BOAK, President of the Board of Trade of Middletown, was born in the town of Wallkill, Orange County, and is of Irish and English descent. James Boak, his grandfather, was born in the North of Ireland, and came to this country in early life, locating in the town of Wallkill, where he died many years since, having passed his fourscore years. James F. Boak, the father, was born in the town of Wallkill, and was reared to the life of a farmer, which occupation he ever afterward followed. In that town he married Martha Vail, a native of the same town, and a daughter of Abraham Vail, who was also born there, and who was of English descent. He was a farmer by occupation, and served as Supervisor for some years. The Vail family was a prominent one, General Vail being one of its members. The father was a member of the Presbyterian Church, and for years held the office of Trustee. He died on the farm near Scotchtown in 1890, at the age of seventy-one. The mother also died there some years ago. Four children were born to James F. Boak and his wife, two of whom are now living: James E., living on the old homestead; and A. V., the subject of this sketch.

The latter was reared in his native town, and

received his primary education in the common schools. Later he entered Wallkill Academy, from which he graduated with honors, and then entered Eastman's Business College at Poughkeepsie, from which he graduated in 1869. Three years later he came to Middletown, and, in partnership with M. Lewis Clark, he engaged in the real-estate and insurance business, the partnership continuing two years, when Mr. Clark withdrew from the firm, since which time Mr. Boak has been alone. On the retirement of Mr. Clark, he abandoned the insurance business, and confined himself exclusively to dealing in real-estate. His office is now the oldest established real-estate office in Middletown.

In 1878 Mr. Boak was united in marriage, in Baltimore, Md., with Miss Frances M. Brewster, a native of that city, and a daughter of James Brewster, now deceased. At that time he was engaged in the machinery business in Baltimore, having retired from the practice of homeopathy, which was unpopular there. In Maryland he was a prominent Mason, and had taken the highest degrees in the order. Mrs. Boak was educated in Baltimore, and is a lady of great refinement and intelligence. By her union with our subject, three children were born: Frankie, Eleanora and Ada Lynda.

Since coming to Middletown Mr. Boak has been an active business man. He owns seventeen acres inside the city limits, has laid out several additions to the city, and handles the property of others who have made additions to the city plat. Experience in the real-estate business for over twenty-three years has made Mr. Boak an authority on Orange County real estate, and his appreciation of present and prospective values of property is reliability itself. He makes a specialty of handling Middletown residences, city lots, business and investment properties, hotels, and Orange County farms, and has sold more of the latter than any other firm in the county,

Mr. Boak was one of the originators of the Board of Trade, and was one of its first Trustees. In the re-organization of the Board about five years ago, he was elected President, and has since held the office. Twice he was elected Alderman

REV. PHILIP E. AHERN.

from the Second Ward, and is a member and Presiding Officer of the Board of Water Commissioners of the city, being made a Commissioner at the time of the completion of the last reservoir. Socially Mr. Boak is a charter member of the Knights of Honor of Middletown, and religiously is a member of the Second Presbyterian Church, taking an active interest in the affairs of that body. For seven years he was a member of the Excelsior Hook and Ladder Company, and is now an honorary member. In politics he is a Democrat, and has been Chairman of the City Central Committee. Few men in Orange County are better known and none more highly esteemed, and the success which has attended him he richly deserves.

REV. PHILIP E. AHERN, pastor of St. Thomas' Roman Catholic Church at Cornwall on the Hudson, has had charge of this congregation for the past two years. In it there are about eighty families represented, over whom he is a faithful shepherd, and, being a close and earnest student, he is a general favorite in the community. Rev. Mr. Ahern is the successor of Rev. Henry G. Gordon, who was pastor here for five years. The church was incorporated November 17, 1870, and the Trustees who executed the certificate were Most Rev. John McCloskey, Archbishop; Rev. William Starr, Vicar-General; and Rev. John Keogh, pastor; the laymen being James Sheridan and Patrick Piggott. This was the legal organization of a society founded by the indefatigable labors of Father Keogh, who was appointed to the Cornwall mission by the Archbishop of New York.

For some years prior to this time Catholic services had been held in a small brick church which had been erected in 1860, under the direction of Rev. Edward J. O'Reilly, subsequently pastor of St. Mary's of New York City. Father Keogh resolved on having a better edifice in which to meet, and after the ground was secured excavation was made by voluntary labor in the winter of 1870–71. The corner-stone was laid in the spring following by the Bishop of Rochester, Rt.-

Rev. D. McQuade (assisted by several prominent priests from New York and elsewhere), in the presence of a large concourse of citizens. The work was pushed with great energy, so that both the church and pastoral residence were enclosed before the fall. In the spring of 1872 the old church property was disposed of, and in the month of June the altar was moved to the basement of the new edifice, which had been fitted up as a chapel.

Father Keogh retired from this charge April 1, 1876, and was succeeded by Father Stephen Mackin. The latter was followed by Father William Ward, who found here a debt of about $25,000. Through his indefatigable efforts, however, $20,000 of the amount was paid off during his stay. His work was carried on later by Rev. Henry G. Gordon. Although a comparatively new priest here, our subject has shown himself to be a conscientious worker and a valued acquisition to the moral force of the community.

The subject of this sketch was born in New York City, June 9, 1854, and was the son of Philip and Margaret (Smith) Ahern, natives of Ireland. Father Ahern was given the best advantages for gaining an education, attending first the public schools of the metropolis, and in 1867 became a student of St. John's College, Brooklyn. After pursuing the higher studies, he was regularly graduated in 1872, and then attended St. Joseph's Seminary, completing the course in that institution in 1877. May 26 of that year he was ordained and stationed in New York City, but remained there only three months, however, when he was sent to take charge of the congregation of St. Peter's at Poughkeepsie, holding the same for three years. At the end of that time he returned to New York, and for the same length of time was pastor of a congregation. We next find him in Ulster County, where he remained for nine years, having charge of two missions besides the regular charge. It may thus be seen that his preparation has been thorough, and his popularity here attests the high standing in which he is regarded by the people. The church is finely located, and is a large structure, built of brick. It is not entirely completed,

58

but will be ere long. It has a large seating capacity, and was planned to accommodate the members of the surrounding villages and towns of the county.

VIRGIL COX, Vice-President of the New York & New Jersey Roller Coaster Company, of Middletown, was born near Deckertown, Sussex County, N. J., in January, 1863. The first of the family to come to America was his grandfather, George Cox, a native of England, who emigrated to this country and, settling in Orange County, became proprietor of the Salisbury Mills. There our subject's father, George W., was born and reared. In youth he learned the carpenter's trade, and became a contractor and builder in the vicinity of Deckertown and Port Jervis. He finally came to Middletown, where his closing years were spent and where his death occurred. His wife, Mary A., was born in Sussex County, as was also her father, Amos Mead, but the latter removed from there to Montrose, Pa., where he died.

The subject of this sketch is the second among four children, his brothers and sister being William H., General Manager and Secretary of the Roller Coaster Company; Frank, who is in the employ of the *Times* at Middletown; and Carrie, Mrs. John Dreher, of Hornellsville, N. Y. Virgil was reared in the vicinity of Deckertown, N. J., where he received a public-school education. In 1880 he came to Middletown as an apprentice to the carpenter's trade under Lemon & Madden, with whom he remained about two years. Afterward for a year he was with Mead & Taft at Cornwall. Next he went to Orange, N. J., where he worked at his trade, gradually turning his attention to contracting and building. He was employed in that way both in Orange and East Orange, N. J. In the fall of 1893 he came back to Middletown, where he has since engaged in building. He has erected two residences on Prince Street and sold to other parties,

and also erected the residence he now occupies on Spring Street, being also the owner of the three adjoining lots.

In the summer of 1894 Mr. Cox and his brother secured the necessary lease from the traction company and erected the Roller Coaster building at Midway Park. When the enterprise was almost completed, they formed a company, which was incorporated as the New York & New Jersey Roller Coaster Company, our subject being Vice-President, and his brother Secretary and General Manager. The scheme has proved a successful one, and will undoubtedly be remunerative to the proprietors. The building is arranged so that there is an elevation of one hundred and twenty-five feet and an incline of four hundred feet, the coaster being three-fourths of a mile in length. It has proved one of the greatest attractions of the park, and as a business venture is a success. In his political belief Mr. Cox is a Republican, but has never taken an active part in public affairs, preferring to give his business matters his entire attention.

AB. WHEELER, a veteran of the late war, was born in Craigsville, town of Blooming Grove, Orange County, August 31, 1846. His grandfather, Seth Wheeler, was the youngest of ten brothers, born in Danbury, Conn., all of whom went to sea excepting him, and he remained on the home farm, giving his attention principally to the carpenter's trade. From Connecticut, after a time, he went to New York City, where he was employed as a contractor. Later he went to Bloomingburg, Sullivan County; thence, a few years later, to Fishkill, N. Y., where he worked as a contractor. In 1830 he settled in Craigsville, and there he died in 1863, at the age of eighty-four. During the War of 1812 he served in defense of this country. In religious belief he was connected with the Methodist Episcopal Church.

The marriage of Seth Wheeler united him with

Mary Hulse, who was born in the town of Blooming Grove, her father, Benjamin Hulse, having been an early settler there. They became the parents of two sons and one daughter. Their son Henry, who was a carpenter and wheelwright, spent his early life principally in Blooming Grove, thence removed to Newburgh, and fifteen years later settled in Jersey City, where he now resides. The other son, William, our subject's father, was born in New York City, and in youth served a seven-years apprenticeship to the trades of carpenter and wheelwright at Fishkill; later worked for a similar period at Brooklyn, becoming a thorough master of these trades. He was a Drum Major in the Twenty-second New York State Militia, the brigade that was commanded by Gen. William C. Little, of Goshen. Settling at Craigsville, he was engaged there as a contractor and builder until his death, which occurred July 1, 1859, at the age of forty-three.

The mother of our subject bore the maiden name of Sarah E. Braffett, and was born in Monroe, this county, as was also her father, Hezekiah, while her mother, Elizabeth (Newbury) Braffett, was from Kingston. At the time of her husband's death, she was left with six children, the eldest of whom was thirteen years, and the youngest six months old. She afterward married again, and now makes her home in Philadelphia. Of the children of her first marriage, only three are living, our subject being the eldest of the number. He was reared at Craigsville, and from the age of nine years was self-supporting, as he then began to work at the cotton-spinner's trade in Craigsville.

At the outbreak of the Civil War, Mr. Wheeler's sympathies were aroused in behalf of the Union, and five times he endeavored to enlist in the army, but was refused on account of youth. The sixth attempt, however, proved successful, and August 22, 1864, he was accepted as a soldier, though at the time he weighed only ninety pounds. At Goshen he was assigned to Company C, Fifty-sixth New York Infantry, and joined his regiment at Charleston Harbor, September 16, 1864, entering active service immediately. He was

in the engagements at Graham's Station, Honey Hill, Boyd's Landing, Devore's Neck and Gregory's Farm, and participated in three different engagements, on the 6th, 7th and 9th of December. At the battle of Coosacatcha, December 29, he was wounded with a musket-ball, when firing from the skirmish line, the ball entering the bridge of the nose from the left flank, and passing across the right eye. After being wounded, he walked three miles to the field hospital, being obliged to ford the river with the water rising as high as his neck. On reaching the hospital, the wound was dressed, and he was removed from the active list. January 31, 1865, he was sent to the general hospital at Port Royal, from there went to David's Island, New York Harbor, and was honorably discharged May 30, 1865, on account of disability resulting from injuries received in action.

As soon as the condition of his health permitted, Mr. Wheeler resumed work at spinning in Craigsville. Soon, however, he abandoned that occupation and engaged in farming in the town of Blooming Grove. In 1868 he removed to Hamptonburgh, where he spent one year, and afterward for ten years cultivated a farm in the town of Goshen. In 1878 he came to Middletown, but continued farm work for a couple of years, after which for five years he was superintendent of what is now the Middletown Ice Company, and then for one year was with C. L. Webster & Co. In August, 1877, he was appointed a letter-carrier for the city, and continued in Government employ until September 10, 1894, when political reasons led to his removal, after he had served for seven years and one month. Since then he has been traveling salesman for the Household Supply Company at Danbury, Conn., with branch office in the Central Building at Middletown.

In the town of Blooming Grove, May 30, 1867, Mr. Wheeler married Miss Hannah W. Oldfield, who was born in the town of Warwick, as was also her father, Joel Oldfield. Her grandfather, Nathaniel Oldfield, was an old settler and pioneer farmer of Warwick. Her father, who was born in 1812, resided in Tompkins County from 1843 until 1865, returning thence to Blooming Grove,

where he died in May, 1891. He married Melissa
Moon, who was born in Monroe, this county, and
was orphaned in infancy. Five children were
born to the union of Mr. and Mrs. Wheeler,
namely: Melissa A., who is married, and lives in
Middletown; Harrison W., who is in the engineer
corps, United States regular army, stationed at
West Point, and was formerly Lieutenant of
General Custer Camp No. 96; Joel B., who is in
the employ of the National Saw Company, and is
Captain of General Custer Camp No. 96; Emma
E. and Sarah L.

Politically Mr. Wheeler is a stanch Republican.
Socially he belongs to Hoffman Lodge No. 412,
F. & A. M.; Paughcaughnaughsinque Tribe No.
77, I. O. R. M., in which he has held official
position; Knights of Labor, in which he was for
five years Master Workman of his lodge, the
strongest of the district; the Tenth Legion Veterans' Association, in which he was Vice-President
for four years; and General Lyon Post No. 266,
G. A. R., in which he was Commander for seven
years in succession. Since becoming a member
of the latter organization, he has personally recruited one hundred and sixty-five members. In
1894 he was Aide-de-camp, under Gen. J. G. B.
Adams, of General Lauder Post No. 5, G. A. R.,
at Lynn, Mass. In religious belief he is a Methodist. He is prominent among the veterans of the
war, with whom he loves to meet and recount
the thrilling events connected with those stirring
times.

JOHN I. BRADLEY. Since the age of fourteen years the subject of this sketch has
made his home upon his present farm in the
town of Wawayanda. The land which he owns
and operates is finely improved, and here may be
found all the accessories of a model estate, including a large and commodious residence.
Through his persevering efforts he has become
one of the most prosperous farmers of his locality,
and is known as a man of upright character and
accommodating disposition.

The subject of this notice and his brother, Benjamin W., were the only children born to the

union of Simeon and Eleanor (Williams) Bradley. The father was a native of Fairfield, Conn.,
as was also the grandfather, John Bradley. The
great-grandfather, also John Bradley, emigrated
with his family from England and settled in
Fairfield County, Conn., about the year 1730.
He was still living at the time the British soldiers burned Danbury, Conn., during the Revolution, and he hauled powder for the Continental
troops.

Simeon Bradley was born in Fairfield County,
Conn., in 1795, and when eighteen years old
came to Orange County, and taught school for
six or seven years north of Newburgh. At Middle-
Hope he was married to the daughter of Benjamin
Williams, the latter one of the descendants of the
Williams family who came from England at an
early day and settled Williams Bridge, in Westchester County, N. Y. The father purchased
a tract of land near Middle Hope, but in 1847 he
disposed of that place and removed to Brock-
port, Monroe County. Seven years later, in 1854,
he came to the town of Wawayanda and purchased two hundred and forty acres known as the
old Dalton Homestead, and which is now the
place owned by his son John I. Here he died in
1889, at the age of ninety-four years, and his
remains were interred in Cedar Hill Cemetery.
A devout Christian man, he held membership in
the Presbyterian Church, of which he was a loyal
supporter. His wife, who died in 1885, was likewise a member of the Presbyterian Church, and
possessed many noble qualities.

In the town of Newburgh our subject was
born August 20, 1840. When the family removed to his present home, he was a lad of fourteen years, and here he has since remained, eu-
gaged in agricultural pursuits. His primary education was obtained in a private school, and afterward he was a student in the Middletown
Academy. In 1868 he was united in marriage
with Sarah Little, the daughter of William and
Emma (Andrews) Little, both of whom were
from well known families of the town of Wawayanda. Mr. Little died in 1870. His widow still
lives on the old homestead, which adjoins Mr.
Bradley's farm. Our subject and his wife became

H. H. ROBINSON, M. D.

the parents of four children. Eleanor was the eldest. William L. graduated from Princeton College in 1892, and from the College of Physicians and Surgeons of New York City in June, 1895; he is now on the staff of the New York Hospital. Mary B. and John I. are pupils in the district schools. It is a fact worthy of note that there has been a John I. Bradley for four generations.

At the time of his marriage Mr. Bradley took charge of the home place, where he has since been extensively engaged in general farming. The farm is under a high state of cultivation and produces bounteous harvests. In politics he is a Democrat. For three terms he has served as Supervisor of the town of Wawayanda, has also been Commissioner of Highways, and is a Director in the First National Bank of Middletown, and President of the Pine Hill Cemetery Association. He is a member of the Presbyterian Church, with which his wife, who died May 19, 1889, was also identified. She was buried in Pine Hill Cemetery. A good man and an honest citizen, Mr. Bradley is worthy of the respect and confidence of his neighbors and friends.

> ❧───✦◆✦──✦──✦✦◆✦───✦───<

HEMAN HUMPHREY ROBINSON, M. D., stands at the head of the medical profession in Goshen, where he is located for practice. He was born in Bellport, L. I., August 20, 1838, and is a son of Rev. Phineas Robinson, whose birth also occurred at the above place. The latter was graduated at Hamilton College, and prepared for the ministry at Princeton. He first preached on Long Island, and in 1841 and 1842 taught in Middletown Academy. He afterward was pastor of a congregation at Washingtonville for five years, and for four years held a charge in Jefferson, Schoharie County. For a period of nine years he taught the languages and mathematics in Chester Academy. After being retired from the ministry for some years, he again began preaching the Gospel on Long Island, being at that time seventy-five years of age. He was recognized as one of the able Presbyterian clergymen of the state, and was also a noted educator. As a poet he had gained considerable fame, and one edition of his writings has been published.

Our subject's mother was known in maidenhood as Eliza Day, and was born in Connecticut. She departed this life at Middletown, when sixty-five years of age. In the parental family were twelve children, ten of whom grew to mature years. Of these seven were sons, two of whom became physicians and one an attorney. Heman H. attended the Middletown Academy for five years, and was a student in Chester Academy, where his father taught for nine years. When in his seventeenth year he went to Seamen's Retreat Hospital, on Staten Island, in order to study medicine, remaining there two years. In 1859 he entered the medical department of the University of New York, from which he was graduated with the Class of '60. He was therefore ready to commence the practice of medicine when just past the age of twenty-one. Finding a good opening in Jeffersonville, Sullivan County, he opened an office there, and soon became noted as a skillful and successful practitioner. He remained there until 1870, when he came to Goshen, where he has for years had a very extensive practice. He now occupies with his family a fine residence on Murray Avenue, which is a model in its arrangement and furnished in a manner indicating the occupants to be people of taste and means.

In 1861 Dr. Robinson was married, in Sullivan County, to Miss Maria Pendell, a native of Schoharie County, and the daughter of Lemuel Pendell, a manufacturer in Gilboa, Schoharie County. Her paternal grandfather was a Methodist minister, and met with great success in preaching the Gospel. The Doctor and his wife have seven living children: Josephine, Kittie, Mary, Robert Thomas, Harry H., Lee and Florence, who are at home. Dr. Robinson has been physician on the Board of Health for many years, for two years was President of the Orange County Medical Society, and for three years served as its Treasurer. He is now filling the position of local surgeon of the New York, Lake Erie & Western Railroad, and is also Medical Examiner for the New York Mutual Life Insurance Company, the New York Life Insurance Company, Equitable Insurance Company, besides others. He is an Elder in the Presbyterian Church, and one of its valued and most active workers. In politics he is a strong supporter of Republican principles, and rejoices greatly in the success of that party.

MICHAEL F. FRITZ, of Port Jervis, has been an engineer on the Delaware Division of the Erie Railroad for seventeen years and is one of their most efficient employes. Perhaps his most notable experience during this time was in the well remembered accident of August 13, 1888. He was in charge of engine No. 672, which was drawing a stock-train. It struck the rocks that had fallen on the track near Schohola and the engine upset at a point eighty-five feet perpendicularly above the Delaware River and only one hundred and fifteen feet from the edge of the bank. The engine, or at least the boiler thereof, remained on the bank, but the cars carried away the cab, in which were Mr. Fritz and a fireman. The former's clothes caught fire and he was pinned down by a timber, but the river water put out the fire and he, lying in such a position, was wonderfully saved from drowning. Though suffering terribly and with death staring him in the face, the thought crossed his mind that the night express No. 3 westbound was due. He shouted to the conductor, who was standing on the bank, to flag the train. The whistles of the fated train were already heard in the distance. The fireman had fainted, and the lights of the approaching engine had no witness but our subject. He was well acquainted with John Kinsella, the engineer, and Alexander Newman, the fireman. They were running on fast time, as they were a little late, and as it was on a curve they could see but a little way in advance. The express engine struck the fore part of Mr. Fritz's engine, which was still lying on the track, bounded into the river, and some of the forward cars followed, though

the Pullman stopped on the brink. Language is inadequate to describe the sight which our subject witnessed as the immense engine, its wheels revolving like lightning, struck fire from the stones which it hit in its descent, and, with fire and steam bursting from every side, finally plunged, hissing and snorting, a few feet beyond him into the river. The fireman was killed and engineer Kinsella was badly injured, but though the ladies' car was full of passengers when it went over the bank only one was killed, though nearly thirty were more or less wounded. At length some order was evolved from the chaos, and when all the passengers were extricated, Mr. Fritz was released from his unhappy position, and was taken to the opposite shore in a boat. His hip was seriously hurt and he was completely covered with bruises, so that his life was despaired of, but after careful nursing his strong constitution brought him through. Mr. Abbey, Mrs. Langtry's manager, was on the train, en route to California.

M. F. Fritz was born in Corning, N. Y., September 14, 1853, his parents being John and Mary Grace (Webber) Fritz. The former was an old railroad man, being in the service for many years. At one time he was a conductor on the Rochester Division, and for a time ran on the Coshocton Railroad from Corning to Rochester. He was a native of Germany, and died in 1875, when sixty-two years old. He was accidentally drowned during a spring freshet at Corning while standing on the bank of the river, the earth caving in and precipitating him into the water, and as he was unable to swim he was drowned before assistance could reach him. He was one of the best known men on the Susquehanna Division of the Erie.

The boyhood of Michael Fritz, until reaching his fifteenth year, was passed quietly in his native city. Soon afterwards he took a position as brakeman on the Delaware Division, this being in September, 1869. For two years he was a brakeman, after which he was made baggage-master on the Jefferson Division, and thus acted until 1871. The following year he was promoted to a conductorship on the Delaware Division, and a few months later commenced running on an engine as fireman. During the succeeding four years he was much of the time in the roundhouse as a hostler, and finally, in February, 1878, was given an engine. While serving as an extra conductor, February 13, 1872, the engine exploded and a man who was sitting next him in the caboose was killed instantly. For nearly twenty years Mr. Fritz has been a member of Mt. William Lodge No. 105, K. of P. He is also connected with the Brotherhood of Locomotive Engineers, and is Secretary of the General Grievance Committee of the Erie System, all complaints along the lines from New York to Chicago coming under his notice. He is a Republican in his political views. At the time of the serious accident in which he was so badly injured and to which we have referred at length in the beginning of this sketch, he received the kindest possible attention from Superintendent W. A. Starr of the Erie Road, and all expenses, such as doctor's bills, etc., were met by the company. It was a matter of wonder to his physicians that he ever recovered and that blood poisoning did not set in, as, with the exception of the palm of his right hand and the sole of his right foot, he was literally black and blue.

September 7, 1875, Mr. Fritz and Alice Spencer, of Port Jervis, were united in marriage. The father of Mrs. Fritz is William Spencer, who is now a blacksmith in the railroad shops. Our subject and wife have three children, Albert, Grace and Walter, who are all at home.

HENRY L. BEAKES is a representative of one of the oldest families in Orange County, and no family is more highly honored or respected. Wherever found, the Beakes are honest, industrious and upright, and are very successful in their various avocations. November 7, 1824, our subject was born on the present homestead, which adjoins Middletown, and where the father, Joseph, was also born. Stacey Beakes, the grandfather, was a native of New Jersey, where he married Miss Yard. The young couple came from Trenton and located on the farm now owned by our subject, who has the original deed, signed January 3, 1781. Orange County at that time was a part of Ulster County. On locating here, Stacey Beakes built a house and improved the farm, and there three sons and four daughters were born. Stacey, who was a merchant and a Member of the Assembly, served in the War of 1812, and died in Middletown; Joseph was the father of our subject: Mahlon died near Ann Arbor, Mich.; Mary A., Mrs. William Murray, now deceased, had one son, Ambrose Spencer Murray, who became a Member of Congress; Ruth died in this county; Martha passed away in Michigan; and Agnes died in Pennsylvania.

Joseph Beakes, the father of our subject, bought the one-third interest of his brother Mahlon in the home farm, and inherited one-third, which gave him a farm of one hundred and thirty-eight acres. He continued to cultivate the farm until his death, in 1857, at the age of seventy-seven years. He was an attendant at the Old-school Baptist Church, and in politics was originally a Whig, and afterwards a Republican. He married Anna Witter, who was born in Wallkill, half a mile from the Beakes place. Her grandfather, Isaac Witter, was born in the town of Wallkill, where he engaged in farming. Later, however, he sold out and located at Canadaigua, Ontario County, N. Y., where he continued farming until his death. Mrs. Anna Beakes died in 1879, after having become the mother of eleven children, ten of whom grew to maturity. Maria, who married Isaac Decker, died at Monticello; William O. died in Wallkill in 1893; Lucinda, who married Daniel Harding, died in Mt. Hope in 1844; Sally Jane, who married S. C. Howell, resides at Howells Depot; Alanson died in Wallkill; Mahlon Stacey died in Wallkill in 1891; Mariam is the widow of Thomas P. Pitts and resides in Middletown; Fannie married Cyrus Tuttle, and died in Dowagiac, Cass County, Mich.; Henry L. is our subject; Hiram, an attorney, and a great friend of Judge Cooley, died in Ann Arbor, Mich.; and George M., a prominent physician at Bloomingburg, was educated at the University of New York, and graduated from the medical department. He was Surgeon in the Fifty-sixth

New York Volunteer Infantry, and is an ex-Representative in the General Assembly.

The subject of this sketch was reared on the old homestead, and was educated in the district schools. He remained on the home farm and gradually took charge of its management, and when the father died, in 1857, he willed it to our subject. The latter paid off the legacies required in the will to the brothers and sisters. Our subject has shown himself an enterprising farmer, and has made many improvements on the place. The farm is well watered by springs and is well improved in every respect. In connection with general farming, Mr. Beakes is engaged in the dairy business, and has from thirty-five to forty head of cows.

Mr. Beakes' first marriage occurred in Florida, Orange County, and united him with Miss Amelia Gardner, who was born near Florida, and who died on the home farm, leaving one child, John G. The latter is a graduate of Eastman's Business College, and is now engaged in the flour, feed and coal business at Unionville. The second marriage of Mr. Beakes occurred at Middletown in 1865, with Miss Jennie Norris. She was born near Bloomingburg, Sullivan County, and was a daughter of Alfred Norris, also a native of Sullivan County, but whose family were originally from Connecticut, and whose father served in the Revolutionary War. Alfred Norris, who was a farmer of Sullivan County, was also a merchant for many years, but now resides on the old homestead, at the age of eighty-five years. His wife, Catherine Bull, was born in Bullville, and was a daughter of Thomas Bull, who was there engaged in farming. She died in Sullivan County, at the age of about eighty years. They were the parents of six children, three of whom are now living, Mrs. Beakes being fourth in order of birth.

To Henry L. and Jennie Beakes were born three children: Jennie, who married E. Sanford Crowell, of New York City, manager of the Marlboro Hotel; S. Murray and Ada May, at home. Mr. and Mrs. Beakes are members of the First Presbyterian Church at Middletown, of which he was formerly Trustee, and when the

present handsome church edifice was erected was a member of the Building Committee. In politics he is a Republican, and was a member of the Union League during the war. As already stated, he is an enterprising man. His farm is fenced into convenient fields, and is well improved in every respect. It has a splendid location, and part of the farm lies within the city limits of Middletown.

———————++++++●●●++++———————

WILMOT DURYEA, a plumber, steam and gas fitter at Middletown, is a native of the town of Wallkill, born May 26, 1856, and is a descendant of a French-Huguenot family, who were early settlers of Orange County. His grandfather, John, and his father, Jonathan C., were both born upon the same farm as was the subject of this sketch. The father was engaged in general farming and dairying until his retirement in 1870, when he removed to Middletown, and there died in 1891, at the age of seventy-six years. While not a politician in the ordinary sense of the term, he was a strong believer in the principles of the Republican party, and an earnest advocate of the same. He married Ruth L. Seeley, a native of Blooming Grove, who died in 1861, leaving five children, who grew to maturity. Three are now living: Arietta T., now Mrs. Hutting, of Jamaica, L. I.; Wilmot, our subject; and Jennie S., Mrs. Bradner, of Middletown.

The subject of this sketch remained at home with his parents until 1870, when he came to Middletown, where he received his education in the academy. In 1873 he was apprenticed to learn the plumbing trade with I. F. Van Duzer & Co., and after serving his time continued with the firm until 1888, when he started in business for himself, first locating on the corner of Depot and North Streets. In 1889 he removed to his present location, No. 50 North Street, occupying the basement of the Gothic building. The room he occupies is 30x70 feet in size, and here he carries a full line of everything required in his business. He usually employs from six to eight

SAMUEL C. VAN VLIET, JR.

hands. Among the residences and places of business that he has furnished may be named those of Mrs. Merritt, Frank Madden, P. F. Miller, George E. Adams and W. E. McWilliams, and he has also done work in Goshen, Tuxedo, and many towns in Sullivan County, and across the line in New Jersey. He is the oldest practical plumber in the city, and his work is always satisfactory.

Mr. Duryea was married, in Middletown, to Jennette E. Mills, who was born in Bloomingburg, and who is a daughter of William H. Mills, a farmer of that town. Two children have been born unto them, Ethel R. and Alafair. Mr. Duryea is interested in the Middletown Driving Park Association, and is an honorary member of Phœnix Hose Company No. 4, having served for five years as an active member. In politics he is a Republican, but has never aspired to local office. Fraternally he is a member of the Independent Order of Odd Fellows, Middletown Lodge No. 112, and of Lancelot Lodge.

SAMUEL C. VAN VLIET, JR. The principal resident of Oxford, the one to whom the management of its interests is largely due, and whose devotion to its welfare has been the source of its advancement, is the subject of this notice, who is engaged in a general mercantile business at this place, and is also Postmaster, express agent and railroad agent for the Erie. He is a man who, from an humble beginning, has risen to a position of prominence in the community, and who, while gaining a competency, has not done so at the expense of others, but throughout life has maintained a reputation for probity and honor.

The Van Vliet family, as the name indicates, is of Holland extraction, and the ancestors were among the original settlers of New Amsterdam. The father of our subject, Samuel, and grandfather, Alva, were born in Dutchess County, N. Y., and were farmers by occupation, the

former dying at the age of eighty-four years. The mother of our subject, Keturah Owen, died in 1858, at the age of fifty-nine years. Her eleven children were as follows: Lavinia, deceased; Ann Eliza, Mrs. Franklin Bull; Martha R., who married J. R. Hoffman, of West Virginia, and is now deceased; James H.; Samuel C.; Lavinia B., Mrs. Henry Shaw, deceased; William D., of Goshen; Esther and Charles E., who died in infancy; Chauncey O.; and Sarah Frances, who is deceased.

The subject of this sketch was born in the town of Blooming Grove, December 29, 1833, and was reared on a farm until seventeen years of age. His education has been gained rather by practical observation and reading than by attendance at schools. At an early age he was apprenticed to the blacksmith's trade, at which he worked five years, but discontinued it on account of illness. Subsequently for two years he was clerk in a railroad office, for three years was employed in a dry-goods store at Monroe, and for three years was in a general merchandise business for himself there. In March, 1861, he came to Oxford, where he has since engaged in general merchandising, being the principal business man of the vicinity.

In 1858 Mr. Van Vliet married Miss Euphemia L. Jenkins, a native of Monroe and a daughter of Ira and Millie (Smith) Jenkins, both deceased. Two daughters bless their union. The elder, Elsie J., is the wife of S. G. Lent, and has one child, Helen Grace. The younger, Effie L., lives at Chester, and is the wife of Fred L. Conklin.

Politically Mr. Van Vliet is a Republican, and for thirty-four years has been Postmaster through different political administrations. For four years, from 1868 to 1872, he was a member of the Board of Supervisors, and one of its valued and active workers. He does not advocate a gold standard exclusively, but insists that it is neither wise nor just to insist on gold as the only unit of value. His membership is in the Presbyterian Church, in which he has long been an active worker. Since 1875 he has been an Elder, and has taken part in most of the councils of the church for many years. His religion, however, does not make him narrow-minded nor bigoted, but he is liberal in his views and charitable in his judgment of others. His character is a noble one, thoughtful, considerate, just and energetic, and the large measure of success which he has gained belongs to him deservedly.

ROBERT A. SAYER, proprietor and manager of the Crescent Steam Laundry at Middletown, was born July 1, 1867, in Warwick, where also his father, Andrew Sayer, was born. The latter was the youngest son of James H. Sayer, who was also a native of that town, and who married Sarah E. Courter, likewise a native of Warwick. They resided there until 1868, when they located in Middletown, where the father engaged in trucking, and had the contract for lighting the street lamps. He died in May, 1885. For many years he was an earnest and devoted member of the Baptist Church. Of their family of nine children, seven are yet living, all sons.

The subject of this sketch grew to manhood in Middletown, being only six months old when his parents removed to this city. He was here educated in the public schools and the academy, and when thirteen years of age was thrown on his own resources. He then accepted a position in the store of Stephen Wolfe, merchant tailor and dealer in men's furnishing goods, as a clerk, remaining there five years. He then entered the office of the Middletown *Press*, and learned the printer's trade, being in the job department. During the last six months he was foreman of the office, succeeding L. S. Stivers, when they started the *Times*. He remained there until September 2, 1890, when his right hand was accidentally caught in the bed of the big press, resulting in the loss of his thumb and three fingers. He was laid up for three months, and on his recovery, after having passed the civil-service examination, he was appointed clerk in the postoffice, but on account of the loss of his fingers he resigned six weeks later.

On leaving the postoffice, he purchased the cigar business of J. J. Kirkpatrick at No. 12 North Street, which had been established forty-nine years, but the trade of which had been allowed to run down. He improved the business until he had the best cigar trade in the city, and continued in the business until June 11, 1895, when he sold out. The following day he purchased the laundry which he now operates. He does the finest work in the country and has offices in all the adjoining villages. The laundry, which is located at No. 101 Fulton Street, has a frontage of thirty feet and a depth of one hundred and twenty-seven feet. About twenty hands are constantly employed, and two wagons are run for city trade. A part of the shirts manufactured by Millen & Co., of New York City, are laundried at this establishment.

Mr. Sayer was married, July 24, 1889, in Middletown, to Miss Effie Colville, who is a native of this place and a daughter of Robert Colville. They have one child, Harold. In politics Mr. Sayer is an active Republican, and fraternally is a member of the Knights of Pythias.

BENJAMIN BROWN WILLIAMS, of Middletown, is a wholesale liquor dealer, and a jobber of foreign and domestic cigars. His grandparents were Leonard and Eleanora (Bullard) Williams, the former a farmer in the town of Newburgh. They were of Welsh descent, and reared a family of sixteen children, one of whom was James, the father of our subject. When a mere lad he left home and engaged as clerk for an uncle in Auburn, N. Y., where he remained some two or three years. Afterward he went to Monticello, where for a time he clerked for James H. Foster, and then purchased a store in partnership with J. C. Holly, the partnership continuing for fifteen years. During a portion of this time Mr. Williams served as Postmaster of the city. His mercantile career in that place covered a period of thirty years. As Treasurer of Sullivan County, he served for a term of three years, and was re-elected four times in succession, serving in all fifteen years.

Disposing of his interest in Sullivan County, Mr. Williams came to Middletown in 1875, and with the exception of a short time when he was in partnership with the subject of this sketch in the clothing and men's furnishing-goods trade, lived a retired life. For two terms, or six years, he served as Treasurer of Orange County. His term of office expired January 1, 1891, and on the 27th of that month he passed to the better world. He was a life-long Democrat, and in Sullivan County was a Master Mason. He married Abigail Brown, who was born near Monticello, and who was a daughter of Benjamin Brown, whose birth occurred near Elmira, N. Y. Mrs. Williams died in Middletown in 1886, at the age of fifty-three years. In the parents' family were four children: Nellie, Mrs. T. S. Tenny, of Jersey City; Adelaide S., Mrs. Kernochan, of Middletown; Benjamin B., our subject; and James H., also of Middletown.

The subject of this sketch was born in Monticello in 1857, grew to manhood in his native city, and was educated in the Monticello Academy, from which he graduated. Soon after coming to this city with the family, he started in business with his father, the partnership continuing until the election of the latter as County Treasurer. They then sold the establishment, and for two years and a-half our subject assisted his father in the Treasurer's office. In 1886 he engaged in the liquor business with his brother-in-law, T. S. Tenny, under the firm name of Tenny & Williams, but in 1891 he purchased the interest of Mr. Tenny, and has since continued the business alone. His present location is on James and King Streets, where he has a fine brick building 22x100 feet in dimensions, the first floor and basement being occupied by himself. He conducts a wholesale business exclusively. In April, 1895, he was burned out, but he refitted his storeroom in an elegant manner, and has the largest and finest establishment in the city.

Mr. Williams was married, in Newburgh, to Miss Minnie P. Goodale, born in Coldenham,

Orange County, and daughter of J. H. Goodale, ex-Deputy Sheriff, and ex-Superintendent of the Poor Farm of Orange County. They have one child, Highland Goodale. In politics Mr. Williams is a Democrat. He served for a time in Excelsior Hook and Ladder Company No. 1, and is interested in the Casino Theatre, and the Middletown Ice Company. Mr. Williams is a lover of fine horses, owning several fine specimens of standard-bred trotters, and from its inception he has been interested in the Middletown Driving Park Association. The family resides on West Main Street.

❮❮✛✛✛✛✛✛✛✛✛✛✛✛✛✛✛✛✛✛✛✛✛✛✛✛✛❯❯

BENJAMIN F. LOW, of Middletown, one of the leading attorneys of Orange County, was born in the town of Fallsburg, Sullivan County, April 1, 1828. His grandfather, John Low, was one of the French-Huguenots who came from Holland and settled in Ulster County, becoming one of its pioneers, and there lived and died. His son, John A. Low, the father of our subject, located at Fallsburg, Sullivan County, where he was extensively engaged in farming until his death, in 1862, when sixty-two years old. His farm comprised four hundred acres of land, which he had under a high state of cultivation. In politics he was a Democrat. His wife, Charlotte Drake, was born in the town of Neversink, Sullivan County, and was a daughter of Jeremiah Drake, a native of Connecticut. He married Miss Phœbe Reynolds, a daughter of Henry Reynolds, who was a prominent factor in the Revolutionary War. On one occasion the Tories made an attack on Mr. Reynolds, and with swords inflicted twenty-three wounds on his person, and then hung him up in a chimney, leaving him for dead. On leaving they stated they would shoot the first one who came outside, but his daughter Phœbe ran out, cut him down and resuscitated him, and together they started for Washington's camp, which they reached before morning. Soldiers from the camp at once started in pursuit of the Tories, whom they captured and shot. Mr. Reynolds was in charge of all the munition of war of the American army, and served until the close of the conflict, then settling in Neversink, Sullivan County, where he died, his remains being interred in Pound Hill Cemetery. Jeremiah Drake was in the cavalry service in the Revolutionary War, and at its close settled in Sullivan County, where he engaged in farming until his death. Mrs. Charlotte Low died in 1850, leaving two children, Henry R. and Benjamin F. The former was County Judge of Sullivan County for several years, and was a member of the Assembly and Senate of New York for twelve years. At the time of his death, December 1, 1888, he was President of the Senate. Politically he was a thorough Republican.

Benjamin F. Low grew to manhood in his native county, received his primary education in the public schools, and at the age of eighteen commenced teaching, in which occupation he continued for some years. Until twenty-one he taught school during the winter months, and assisted on the farm the remainder of the year. With his brother, he opened a select school at Monticello, which was the foundation of the Monticello Academy. This school was continued until 1850, when he engaged in farming and lumbering in the town of Liberty, on the home farm, which comprised about four hundred acres. On the farm was a sawmill, which he operated in the manufacture of lumber, drawing it to Ellenville, and thence shipping it by canal to various markets. He carried on this industry quite extensively until 1859, when he began the study of law under O. Porter, at Homer, N. Y. Three years later he was admitted to the Bar at Binghamton, Broome County, and at once located at Monticello, as a partner of his brother, under the firm name of Low & Low. This partnership continued during the war and up to 1870, when his brother's private business had become so extensive that his removal was rendered necessary, and he therefore opened an office in New York City. Our subject continued alone until 1873, when he located in Middletown and continued the practice of his profession. Shortly afterwards he was admitted to practice before the courts of New Jersey at Trenton. He then located in

New York City, and again formed a partnership with his brother, at No. 120 Broadway, which continued until the removal of his brother to Pittsburg. While in New York his practice was very extensive, but failing health necessitated his removal, and in 1877 he returned to Middletown, opened an office there, and in 1886 erected the Low Building, where he has been located since 1887. The building has a frontage of fifty feet and a depth of ninety feet, and comprises three stories and basement, the first floor of which is used for stores, the second for law offices, and the third for lodge rooms. His residence is at No. 100 Highland Avenue, where he has the finest well of water in Orange County.

Mr. Low has tried a great many important cases to a successful issue, and has been one of the leading attorneys, not alone of Orange County, but of the entire state. He has had as many as fifty cases on the calendar at one time. He makes a specialty of no particular line of practice, but transacts a general law business in both civil and criminal courts. His practice extends throughout Orange, Sullivan, Delaware and Westchester Counties, New York City and into New Jersey. He has quite an extensive practice in the United States Courts. At the present time, however, he tries to confine himself as much as possible to office work as a counselor.

In 1850 Mr. Low was united in marriage, in the town of Liberty, Sullivan County, to Miss Harriet A. Porter, a native of that town, and daughter of Granville Porter, a native of Connecticut, and a large farmer and lumberman of the town of Liberty. Five children were born unto them, four of whom grew to maturity, and two are now living. Henry R., an attorney-at-law, practiced his profession for some time at Atchison, Kan., and at the corner of Reed Street and Broadway, New York City. He died in 1890, in the latter city, at the age of thirty-nine years. Walter, who was a literary man and good composer, died in 1883, at the age of thirty years. Mary C. is at home. Carrie is deceased. John A., who was educated at Wallkill Academy, is now assisting in his father's office.

Mr. Low has been quite prominent in the af-

HARRY M. WARING.

fairs of Middletown, and has contributed extensively in its upbuilding, especially in the northern part of Highland Avenue and along Watkins, Royce and Wisner Avenues and Beacon Street. He has always been a liberal contributor towards everything calculated to improve his adopted city, and helps every good cause financially. In politics he is a Republican, having advocated the principles of that party since 1860, prior to which date he was a Democrat.

HARRY M. WARING has the reputation of being a strictly first-class business man, reliable and energetic, and is now proprietor of the Newburgh Ice Company. He was born in the town of Newburgh, October 13, 1865, and is a son of Daniel S. and Phebe A. (Moffat) Waring, the former born in the town of Newburgh, and the latter in the town of Blooming Grove. The mother departed this life in 1889, leaving a son and daughter.

Daniel S. Waring remained upon the home farm until 1853, when he embarked in the coffee and spice business in Brooklyn, and in the year that Newburgh became a city he located here, erecting a coffee and spice mill, which he operated for one year. He then entered the firm of D. S. & C. S. Lockwood, in the coal business, and in 1873 succeeded those gentlemen in the proprietorship of the yard on Mailler's Dock. In 1885 he opened a coal-yard on the corner of Lake Street and Broadway, and in 1890 George S. Weller was admitted to partnership. The following year Mr. Waring sold out his interest in the other yard to W. O. Mailler, and became a large stockholder and Trustee in the Kilmer Manufacturing Company. In 1885, in connection with our subject, he organized the Newburgh Ice Company, and five years later purchased the Walsh Paper Mill property, where he commenced the manufacture of ice by the Pictet process.

Daniel S. Waring was a stockholder and Secretary of the Newburgh Highland Hotel Company, which erected the large building afterward known as the Baldwin House, and The Leslie,

and is a Trustee of the Newburgh Savings Bank, and a Director of the Highland National Bank. He has given his aid and influence to many public movements, and does all he can to encourage the growth and prosperity of the city. From the organization of the Board of Trade he was its President until a few years ago, when he declined the position in favor of Robert Whitehill. He has been foremost in all the good work the Board has accomplished, and rendered invaluable service in securing the removal of the Kilmer Manufacturing Company to Newburgh. He is a member of the Newburgh Real-estate Company, which purchased the Roe property, between Grand and Montgomery Streets, now occupied by a number of handsome dwellings and the Misses Mackie's large boarding-school. He built a number of fine dwellings on Grand Street, and has otherwise dealt considerably in real estate. In 1872 Mr. Waring represented the Third Ward on the Board of Supervisors, and afterwards served for twelve terms on the Board.

On the death of Dr. Forsyth he was chosen President of the Woodlawn Cemetery Association, which office he still holds, and he is also Elder in the First Presbyterian Church of Newburgh. In 1891 he was appointed by Mayor Doyle as Alderman from the Third Ward to fill a vacancy.

Almost the entire life of Harry M. Waring has been passed in the city of Newburgh, from whose academy he graduated in 1882, and is now a member of the Alumni Association. On leaving school he engaged in the coal business at the corner of Third and Front Streets in connection with his father, being quite successful, but in 1889 disposed of the same in order to give more attention to the manufacture of ice. As before stated, the Newburgh Ice Company was formed in 1885, and it has since grown to extensive proportions. The plant is located at No. 442 Broadway, occupies five acres from Broadway to First Street, and is supplied with a ninety-horse-power engine and boiler. The ice is made by the Pictet process, and they can turn out fifteen tons per day. During the busy season twenty hands are employed, and the ice is delivered all through the city and suburbs. In 1892 our subject became sole proprietor, now having complete charge of the extensive business, with a main office at the place of manufacture and another on Front Street.

Mr. Waring was married, in Newburgh, to Miss Jessie Chambers, of which place she is a native, and they now reside at No. 6 Dubois Street. He is a prominent member of the Masonic order, belonging to Hudson River Lodge No. 607, F. & A. M.; Highland Chapter No. 52, R. A. M.; Hudson River Commandery No. 35, K. T.; and Mecca Temple, M. O. M. S., of New York City. For seven years he has been a member of the Ringgold Hose Company, and is a charter member of the City Club, of which he has served as Secretary since January, 1894, being one of its leading and most popular members. Mr. Waring is President of the Newburgh branch of the New York Mutual Savings and Loan Association, which office he held at the time of its organization here, and is also connected with the Newburgh Building and Loan Association. From 1885 to 1888 he was Assistant Secretary and Treasurer of the Orange County Agricultural Society. In 1894 he held the same position, and in the fall of that year was elected Treasurer. Politically he is a loyal adherent of the principles of the Republican party, while in religious faith he is a Presbyterian, belonging to the First Presbyterian Church of Newburgh.

JAMES SHAFER, a farmer in the town of Crawford, was born December 2, 1826, on the farm that he now owns. He was second in a family of three children born to John and Hannah (Confort) Shafer, both of whom were natives of the town of Crawford, and who spent their entire lives here. The parents of John Shafer were natives of Orange County and were among the early settlers of this region. To John Shafer and his first wife, Hannah Confort, were born three children. Frederick, a farmer in the town of Crawford, married Harriet Linderman, a daughter of Absalom Linderman. After a few months of married life she died, and Mr. Shafer chose for his second wife Mary Smith, of Che-

nango County, N. Y., by whom he has three children living. James, our subject, was next in order of birth. Ruth Elizabeth is now the wife of William Weller, a farmer in the town of Crawford. They have two sons and two daughters. John Shafer had no children by his second wife, Phœbe Maria Confort, a sister of his former wife. The father was quite successful in life, and a member of the Presbyterian Church. The mother of our subject belonged to the Reformed Church. The parents were earnest Christian people, whose memory is cherished by all who knew them. The father died at the age of eighty, and the mother when sixty-one years old.

The subject of this sketch remained with his parents until their death, when he inherited the old homestead. On the 4th of March, 1880, he married Miss Elizabeth Weller, daughter of Peter and Margaret (Elder) Weller. The former was born in the town of Montgomery, and came to Crawford with his parents when he was two years old. He remained on the farm until his death, when seventy years of age. He was greatly respected by all acquaintances and beloved by his friends, and at his death he was deeply mourned, all feeling that a kind friend had left them. He was known as "Uncle Peter" the county round. His parents were born in the town of Montgomery, but were of Holland-Dutch extraction. The mother of Mrs. Shafer was born in the town of Crawford, and her death occurred at the age of seventy-six. Her parents, the grandparents of Mrs. Shafer, were also born in the town of Crawford, but were of Irish and German extraction. Mrs. Shafer's mother was a descendant of Rev. Joseph Houston, first minister of the Goodwill Church of Montgomery, Orange County. To Peter and Margaret Weller were born ten children, as follows: George, deceased, formerly a farmer of this town; William, a resident of Crawford; Elizbeth, Mrs. Shafer, Catherine Sinclair, who died in infancy; Charles, a resident of Bullville; Peter, a resident of Colorado; Susan Jenneatte, who married H. H. Brown, and is living in Brooklyn; John Seibert, of Norfolk, Va.; Joseph Wilkin and Sidney, both deceased.

To James Shafer and wife has been born one

son, John Weller Shafer, who was born April 12, 1881, and who yet resides at home. Politically our subject is a Democrat, and at present occupies the position of Excise Commissioner of the town. Both he and his wife are members of the Presbyterian Church. The home farm, which consists of one hundred and seven acres, has been in the family a great many years. Among the old families of Orange County none are held in higher esteem than that of the subject of this sketch.

<hr/>

REV. ROBERT BRUCE CLARK is one of the most popular clergymen of Orange County, and is highly esteemed in the community where it has been his good fortune to be located since the beginning of 1886. He has varied abilities and many accomplishments, which have been devoted to the benefit of his church, the village in which he resides, and to the entire western section of the county, where his influence is felt. As preacher and pastor he is warmly commended by those who know him and his work most intimately. Executive ability of a rare nature is manifested and marked by the smooth and successful work of his large church and in the operation of many enterprises in which Mr. Clark has been interested. Many of the substantial interests of the village of Goshen have been planned and promoted by his untiring industry, among which might be mentioned the Music Hall, the Goshen Library, the Electric-light Company and the Goshen Vocal Society, whose reputation has gone out into the musical circles of the country. Mr. Clark has exhibited skill and prudence, and has shown himself such a man of affairs that he commands the respect and confidence of the business interests, with whose co-operation he has made himself seemingly indispensable to the beautiful and aristocratic county seat.

Mr. Clark comes of a patriotic and distinguished family. His great-grandsire was a hero of the Revolutionary War, and his grandfather, Israel Clark, for many years a well known and re-spected resident of New York City, inherited a strong and upright character. Mr. Clark was the second son and last child of William H. Clark and Elizabeth S. Munn, and was born in Newark, N. J., September 22, 1852. The only other offspring of this union was a brother, now a well known and successful physician, Dr. W. B. Clark, of New York City. On his mother's side the ancestry was also distinguished. She was the eldest child of Albert Munn, for many years identified with the public affairs of Newark and a man of ample means. Her grandfather was Judge Munn, a jurist of wide reputation both in his own state and throughout the Middle States. Mr. Clark, therefore, was fortunate in his ancestry. His mother was a woman of great accomplishment as a lady, a scholar and a musician. His father, who was an officer in the Civil War for three years, was seriously wounded, being confined to the hospital for several weeks, and was mustered out of the service with distinction. Afterward he became a leading factor in the Grand Army of the Republic. It was thus that the subject of this sketch was early impressed with the influences that have asserted their effects in his own public life. Those who have heard Mr. Clark's voice upon a patriotic occasion (for he is frequently in demand for addresses upon Lincoln's anniversary, Washington's birthday and Memorial Day) will understand the vigor of his patriotism and sturdy Americanism.

Mr. Clark felt the bent of commercial pursuits, and at the age of fourteen entered a large wholesale commission house in the hosiery and woolen trade in New York. At seventeen he occupied a responsible position, taking charge of the receiving and shipping department of the firm, the volume of whose business was $2,000,000 annually. Not long after uniting with the Presbyterian Church the desire to enter college and prepare for the ministry asserted itself. For this purpose Mr. Clark left business, sacrificing thus unmistakable prospects of commercial success and wealth, and fitted himself in the preparatory studies under private tutors, covering all the requirements in twelve months' time, and entered the Class of '76 at Amherst College. While there he was a member of the Alexandria Society and of the Alpha Delta Phi fraternity. He was college organist during his course; leader of the choir and of the glee club the last two years, and graduated in the honorary division of his class. Then he entered Union Theological Seminary, and completed his studies in divinity in the spring of 1879. The Presbytery of Newark licensed him to preach, and he at once went West and was ordained by the Presbytery of Waterloo and installed pastor of the Presbyterian Church at State Centre, Iowa, in October, 1879. After a pastorate of four years, which was singularly successful, he became pastor of the Forty-first Street Presbyterian Church of Chicago. From this field of labor Mr. Clark was invited to become the successor of Dr. Snodgrass, a man of great eminence, in the pastorate of the large and influential Presbyterian Church of Goshen. His ministry in this charming village began in January, 1886. Mr. Clark is the tenth pastor in succession (now in his tenth year of incumbency) of this church, which has just celebrated its one hundred and seventy-fifth anniversary with a fitting jubilee.

After graduating from the seminary, Mr. Clark married Miss Adelaide Roome, the eldest daughter of Lewis E. Clark, of Plainfield, N. J. Four children, three sons and one daughter, have blessed their union. In addition to his accumulated duties as a busy pastor of a large congregation, and the many demands upon him from his own community and from repeated calls to ministerial service outside his own town, Mr. Clark has been able to devote considerable of his time to music. This is noticeable in the services of his own church, where upon special occasions it has been of a very high order. The name of Goshen has become famous as the center of the best musical influence. This is due to the prestige and concerts of the Goshen Vocal Society, which was organized in 1887 by Mr. Clark, and has been directed by him with signal social and artistic success ever since. The standard and classical works of the great composers are rendered by this society under the able conductorship of Mr. Clark every season, with the use of the most affluent accessories. In the line of this recreation Mr. Clark has extended his acquaintance and usefulness over a large territory, yet without detriment to his reputation as a warmhearted friend and pastor and an eloquent and forcible preacher. His apparently inexhaustible energy and fertility of resource are richly esteemed by the people of his village, who delight to do him honor.

CHARLES H. BRINK. A representative of the young business men of Middletown, to whose energy the city is largely indebted for its recent progress, and through whose wise policy it will undoubtedly broaden its commercial activity in the coming years, Charles H. Brink is justly entitled to rank among the successful and prominent citizens of the place. The plumbing, steam and gas fitting establishment of which he is the owner and proprietor is situated at No. 14 King Street, where the building, 20x85 feet, is stocked with a full line of everything pertaining to the business. Employment is furnishd to eight or ten plumbers, whose work is guaranteed to be first-class. In this way the most satisfactory results are secured for every customer.

The history of the Brink family is given in the sketch of Leander Brink, father of Charles H., presented on another page. Our subject, who is the only child of his parents, was born in the town of Wallkill, September 14, 1860, and was reared in Middletown, receiving his education in Wallkill Academy, from which he was graduated at the age of eighteen. He then took a position in his father's hardware store, where he learned the tinsmith's trade and became a practical workman. In December, 1889, he left the employ of Brink & Clark and embarked in his present enterprise, buying out Vanduzer Brothers. He has since carried on an increasing business, and has become known as a judicious and energetic business man. He has had the contract for plumbing in many of the most substantial and elegant residences of Middletown, among them

JOHN J. POPPINO.

those of I. C. Jordan, B. F. Low, Albert Bull, Frank Harding, Nathan Hallock, R. M. Smiley, Alton J. Vail, C. E. Gardner, James A. Clark, W. N. Knapp, W. H. Knapp, H. H. Crane, E. T. Hanford, Clarence Sweezy, Mrs. E. K. Reed and F. McWilliams. In addition to his work in this city, he has also had contracts for work in the cities of Goshen, Montgomery and Monroe.

In Rochester, this state, Mr. Brink married Miss Sarah Douglass, who was born in Mt. Hope, this county, and is a daughter of James Douglass. Mr. and Mrs. Brink, with their children, William D., Harry and Bessie, occupy a pleasant residence at No. 24 Wickham Avenue. The various enterprises inaugurated for the promotion of the welfare of the people receive the cordial and substantial support of our subject, and he may at all times be relied upon to aid in worthy projects. He is a member of the Orange County Telephone Company, and of the Middletown & Bloomingburg Traction Company. He is intelligently informed regarding the great public questions of the age, and in politics favors the platform adopted by the Republican party.

⁕⋯═❦◖◧◉◖▷❧═⋯

JOHN J. POPPINO. The gentleman whose honored name appears at the head of this sketch is a representative of the men of energy, ability and enterprise who have made Orange County so prominent in the state. His name is associated with agriculture as one who has made a success of tilling the soil, and as one who has helped to improve the stock of the county by careful breeding. He is greatly interested in dairy farming, which branch of husbandry he finds to be very profitable.

A native of this county, our subject was born December 12, 1853, and is the eldest son of James G. and Frances (Hulse) Poppino, also natives of this county. The father's birth occurred on the estate where his son, our subject, now makes his home. He was also an agriculturist of prominence and high standing in the community, and although quiet and unassuming in manner, his death, which occurred in August, 1894, was

59

greatly felt in the community where his entire life had been passed. He attended strictly to his own affairs, and was contented with the results of his labors. The family is of French-Huguenot descent, and an old one in the county, and its various members, who have taken a prominent part in local affairs, are deserving of the respect which has been accorded them. The first of the name who is known to have located in the county was one Major Poppino, a Revolutionary officer, who took up his abode in this portion of the state prior to the outbreak of that war.

The mother of our subject is still living, at the age of sixty-six years. John J. received his primary education in the district schools, and subsequently took a course of study in the academy at Goshen. He was reared on the home farm, and when ready to begin in life for himself very naturally chose this as his vocation. When twenty-three years of age he left the parental roof and located on the tract of one hundred and sixteen acres where he is at present residing. This farm has been in the family for nearly one hundred years, the grandfather having purchased the place in 1823. It is very productive, being cultivated after the most approved methods, and is adorned with a neat set of buildings, including a substantial residence, pleasantly located and conveniently arranged. In addition to the dairy business Mr. Poppino is interested in the growing of onions.

October 4, 1876, our subject and Miss Catherine B. Elston were united in marriage. The lady was the daughter of Charles and Elizabeth (Space) Elston, natives of this county. Of their union four children were born: Carrie A., James G., Elizabeth E. and Agnes, all at home. The wife and mother departed this life September 10, 1885, and December 19, 1889, our subject married Mary C., daughter of Nathaniel and Sarah (Poppino) Roe, of Florida, N. Y. To them has been born a daughter, Sarah Helen. Both Mr. and Mrs. Poppino are members of the Presbyterian Church of Florida, in which the former is Elder. In politics he casts his vote with the Democratic party. He takes a great interest in political matters, and for several years past has been Election Inspector. With intelligent conception of his duties as a citizen, with a feeling of good-will toward mankind, and a deep regard for his family, he endeavors to honorably fulfill all the duties which devolve upon him, and in so doing has gained the respect of all with whom he comes in contact.

ON. JOSEPH D. FRIEND, M. D. Not only has Middletown gained prominence as a commercial centre, but in the professions, in literature, science and art, it has given many noble thinkers and workers to the world. In these latter departments its reputation has been heightened by the labors of Dr. Friend, for many years one of its most honored residents. It may be said, and with justice, of Dr. Friend, that as a legislator he was incorruptible and liberal-spirited; as a physician, skilled; as a medical lecturer, profound; as an editor, discriminating and full of resources; and as a writer, terse, clear, fluent and entertaining. His death, which occurred February 19, 1889, was a loss to the profession he had honored and to the city whose welfare he had promoted.

The Friend family originated in England and is in the direct line of descent from Sir John Friend, whose life in the service of the British Government is a matter of history and dates back to 1687. In the fierce struggles of opposing factions, contests between Catholics and Protestants, rendered the lives of legislators exceedingly difficult and dangerous. From him descended the coat-of-arms in the Friend family in Gloucester, Mass., now in a good state of preservation, although yellow with age. The next in descent was Dr. John Friend, a few of whose many writings are as follows: "Nine Commentaries upon Fevers and Two Epistles Concerning the Small-pox;" "Emmenologea," written in Latin, and translated into English by Thomas Dale, M. D., who said: "I am not ignorant of how difficult a task I assumed in attempting to translate so masterly a writer, who by his polite discourses has done honor to our country and profession."

Some of these writings are in the possession of the Friend family in Middletown. He was appointed Physician to the Queen in 1828, and the papers giving this appointment were in the Friend family at a late date.

The Doctor's father, Solomon, was a son of Richard Friend, and was born in Massachusetts, where his entire life was passed and where, at an advanced age, he died in Gloucester. He married Belinda Richmond Dunham, whose father at one time owned Martha's Vineyard, and they became the parents of seven children. Joseph D., who was the youngest of the family, was born in Salem, Mass., November 12, 1819, and passed his youthful years in his native place, receiving his primary education in the common schools. Afterward he went to Hartford, Conn., where he prepared for college, and when quite young he matriculated as a student in Madison University. His devotion to his studies, while it brought him a high grade in scholarship, injured his health to such an extent as to force him to leave college.

Restored to health through the skill of Dr. Isaac Sperry, then a prominent physician of New England, our subject afterward began the study of medicine under that gentleman, and a few years later he was graduated with honors from the Metropolitan Medical College of New York. In 1842 he came to Middletown, and here he spent the most of the intervening years until his death. Soon after settling in this city he became the editor of the Middletown *Mercury*, with which he was connected about five years, and afterward he published and edited the Middletown *Mail* for many years. His editorials attracted widespread attention, and his views upon political questions, while decidedly Democratic in their tenor, won not only the enthusiastic endorsement of his party, but the admiration of the opposing political organization.

From 1852 until 1854 Dr. Friend was editor-in-chief of the *Medical Journal of Reform*, published in New York. During this period he was also Professor of Obstetrics in the college from which he was graduated. While the positions of editor and professor would seem to demand radically differing characteristics, yet in both he achieved remarkable success. His lectures, although prepared for undergraduates, attracted even physicians in practice, and young men from other institutions often came there to hear him. It is said of him that he won the friendship, as well as the admiration, of every student. Multiplicity of duties never caused him to lose that geniality of manner which was one of his distinguishing characteristics. When he retired from the professorship it was with sincere regret on the part of the students and other members of the faculty.

In fields of public activity, too, the name of Dr. Friend was well known. In 1877 he served as a Member of the New York State Assembly, and in that responsible position was able to render lasting service in behalf of his constituents. He was a pioneer in the cause of popular free education, and a prime mover in the founding and maintenance of public libraries. Socially he identified himself with the Independent Order of Odd Fellows. He was a man of sincere Christian faith, upright and consistent character, and though gifted far above most men, he delighted in the society of others, and his companionable nature won the regard of his associates.

November 12, 1843, at Middletown, Dr. Friend was united in marriage with Miss Susan A. Coleman, who was born in this city, as was also her father, Charles Coleman. The Coleman family was founded in this country by five brothers who came hither from Wales at the time of the Revolutionary War, and made settlement in Orange County. Her grandfather, Samuel Coleman, was born in the town of Warwick, but made his home in the town of Wallkill, where he became a wealthy farmer. He was a man of the greatest integrity of character, an enemy to vice and intemperance even in those early days. "He loved his fellow-men." Many incidents are remembered of his kindliness of heart and great benevolence. He had only two faults, great pride and a hasty temper. He married Elizabeth Burt, who was of French descent and belonged to one of the prominent families of the county. They had three children, Annie, Harry and Charles. Annie married Thomas Welling, who came of a wealthy and

leading family of Warwick. Harry and Charles, both very young men at their father's death, opened a store in Mt. Hope, but Harry later settled in Newburgh and Charles in Middletown. Harry had two beautiful daughters, Anna M. and Harriet E., and two sons. Mrs. Dr. Barclay and W. W. H. Armstrong, of Newburgh, are his great-grandchildren.

The wife of Charles Coleman, Catherine, was born in Sullivan County, N. Y., and was a daughter of Thomas and Susanna (DeCamp) Norris, natives, respectively, of Morristown and Newark, N. J. The latter's father, Dr. John DeCamp, accompanied General La Fayette from France during the Revolutionary War, in which he served as Surgeon. At the batttle of Trenton he was shot from his horse and killed, and a few hours afterward a riderless horse returned to his old home. His wife died three years after his death. She was a granddaughter of Samuel Sanford, of Newark, N. J., where many of both the DeCamp and Sanford families now reside.

The Norris family is of Scotch origin, but was early established in New Jersey. Subsequently grandfather Thomas Norris settled in Sullivan County, N. Y., but the large tracts of land he owned there were so wholly destitute of improvement that he removed to the town of Mt. Hope, in Orange County. There Mrs. Coleman was reared and educated. After her husband's death she continued to reside in Middletown, where she reared her children, fitting them for honorable positions in the world. Hers was a beautiful character, and her memory is sacred to her descendants. She passed away at the age of eighty-three.

Mrs. Friend is one of seven children, of whom six attained years of maturity, namely: Mrs. Julia Stubbs, who died in Wellsboro, Pa.; Adeline, who married George W. Bailey, and resides in Great Bend, N. Y.; Augustus Ludlow, formerly a farmer near Milwaukee, Wis., where he died; Oliver Perry, for many years Postmaster of Middletown, where his death occurred; Thomas N., who served in a Wisconsin regiment for three years during the Civil War, and afterward returned to Orange County where he died; and

Susan, Mrs. Friend. The last-named was reared in Middletown, receiving her education in Wallkill Academy. She has been a member of the First Presbyterian Church of this place since childhood, and is warmly interested in every enterprise that will elevate mankind. Her tastes are refined, and in literary ability she was the peer of her gifted husband. Their children, too, are unusually gifted intellectually and have attained positions of prominence in the literary world. The two daughters, Catherine Dunham and Anna, are connected editorially with *L'Art de la Mode* office at No. 3 East Nineteenth Street, New York City, and the former is also editor of the fashion columns of the New York *Evening Post*, while the latter has attained signal success as a writer of original stories. The eldest son, Dr. Frederick N. Friend, who was a soldier in the Union army during the Civil War, is now a practicing dentist of Middletown. The second son, Herbert S., was lost at sea, and the youngest sons, William and James W., are reporters in New York City.

J AMES H. CONKLING, who is proprietor of a tin and hardware store at No. 9 Depot Street, Middletown, is a member of the family to which the illustrious statesman, Roscoe Conkling, belonged. He was born in Newburgh, in March, 1844, being a son of James R. and Frances W. (Parshall) Conkling, natives of this county, who died and were buried in Goshen. His father was born near Conklingtown, named in honor of the family, and grew to manhood there, afterward going to Newburgh and engaging in the hotel business. Later he came to Middletown, where the closing years of his life were spent.

The family of James R. and Frances W. Conkling consisted of four sons and three daughters, and three of the number are living. John Augustus and William H. served in the Union army during the Civil War, the former belonging to a Wisconsin regiment, and the latter being a member of a Pennsylvania regiment; both are deceased. James H., who was next to the youngest of the family, came to Middletown with his parents when he was seven years of age, and here he attended the old Orchard Street School for some time. At the age of thirteen he was apprenticed to the tinsmith's trade under Joseph Crawford, with whom he remained for one year, after which he was with A. C. King for five years. He then was hired by Scott Brothers, and later was foreman in a shop at Westtown for two years. On his return to Middletown, he took a position with Armstrong & Lyon, being their foreman for five years. In 1878 he embarked in business for himself, occupying for the first eight months a shop adjacent to his present store at No. 9 Depot Street. He carries a full line of tinware and hardware, stoves, pumps and house-furnishing goods. He has made a specialty of tin and sheet-iron roofing, and does more than one-half of the work in that line in the city, as well as some in neighboring villages. His manufacturing department is situated on the second floor of his store.

Among the buildings for which Mr. Conkling has held the contracts for roofing, may be mentioned the Howell & Hinchman tannery, Ontario & Western shops, Eagle Hose Company's building, the Armory, Casino Theatre, Russell House, Academy Building, Wallkill House and Ontario Hose building. As a business man he is sturdy, progressive, honest and capable, and bears a reputation for probity which has never been assailed. At one time a Republican, he now affiliates with the Democratic party, and is a member of the City Democratic Committee, and has served as a delegate to county and congressional conventions. In 1887 he was Collector of the town of Wallkill and village of Middletown. In 1892 he was elected, on the Democratic ticket, to represent the Fourth Ward on the Board of Aldermen, and served for one term of two years, retiring in 1894. Since the organization of the Homestead Building and Loan Association he has been one of its Trustees. Socially he is connected with the Knights of Honor, and in religious matters, while not identified with any denomination, attends the First

THOMAS H. ORAM.

Baptist Church. He is a member of the Board of Trade, and formerly belonged to Excelsior Hook and Ladder Company No. 1.

In Gardnerville, this county, Mr. Conkling married Miss Phœbe C. Tuthill, a native of the town of Minisink, and six children bless their union, namely: George M.; John W., who married a daughter of Dr. James D. Johnston, and is employed as a mail-carrier in the Middletown Postoffice; Arthur, who is a tinsmith by trade, and is assisting his father in the store; Eugene; Alice A., who is married and lives in this city; and Addie. Mrs. Conkling is a daughter of Abraham P. Tuthill, a farmer of this county. She had three brothers, George M., Eugene and William, who served in the Union army as members of a western regiment, and all died soon after the close of that memorable conflict.

THOMAS H. ORAM. Since the close of the war Mr. Oram has been a resident of Ft. Montgomery, town of Highland, where he is now officiating as Postmaster, and is also carrying on a general mercantile business. For twenty-three years he was closely associated with the Forest of Dean Iron Ore Company's works, of which he was general superintendent. During the long period of his residence here he has been distinguished for the uprightness and honesty of his business transactions, as well as for his firmness of convictions and unflinching integrity.

The ancestors of Mr. Oram were of English birth and were natives of Cornwall. His father, Thomas, was born in that county, and there learned the trade of a mining engineer, which he made his life work. After his marriage he came to America and resided in Pennsylvania for one year, then returned to England for his family, bringing them back with him to Pennsylvania. He continued to reside there until 1849, when he removed to New Jersey and began work in the Boonton Iron Works of Fuller, Lord & Co., remaining with them for six years. Going from there to St. Lawrence County, he was connected with the Rossie Lead Works. Later he

went to Tennessee and assisted in opening the copper mines in Ducktown, Polk County, but subsequently returned to New Jersey and continued to make his home on his farm until he died, at the age of eighty-two. His wife, who bore the maiden name of Ann Gundry, is now eighty years old, and makes her home on a large farm in New Jersey, which was bequeathed her by her husband.

Thirteen children comprised the family of Thomas and Ann Oram, and it is a notable fact that all of them attained mature years, none dying under twenty-three years of age. Thomas H., our subject, is the eldest; Elizabeth lives in New Jersey; Benjamin is deceased; Lovdie and Alice make their home in New Jersey; Joseph is dead; Frank is a farmer of Central Valley; Robert, who was an agriculturist by occupation, went West and died in Colorado; Serena is the wife of George Connell, an insurance agent of Central Valley; and Louisa married Dr. Dalrymple, a well known physician of New York City.

The subject of this sketch was born in Cornwall, England, February 22, 1837, and was brought to this country when a child. Passing his early years in Pennsylvania, New Jersey and New York, he received excellent educational advantages in the schools of those states. His tastes led him to adopt his father's occupation, and he soon became an expert mining engineer, having gained a thorough knowledge of every detail of the business when only seventeen years old. Before he was twenty he had charge of public works, filling with efficiency a position of great responsibility. For some time he was employed in the copper mines of Tennessee, forty miles east of Cleveland, Tenn.

Upon attaining his majority, Mr. Oram started out for himself, going to Chattanooga, Tenn., where he opened the coal mines on the Nashville & Chattanooga Railroad. Thence he went to Tuscarawas County, Ohio, and for one year was engaged in the iron mines near Massillon, after which for three years he was in the coal business in Pennsylvania. In 1864 he connected himself with Colonel Almy of the Union army, and served until the close of the war, his services being of great practical help by reason of his knowledge and experience as a mining engineer. Soon after peace was declared he came to Ft. Montgomery and took charge of the Forest of Dean Iron Ore Works, near this place, being connected with that enterprise for the ensuing twenty-three years. Meantime he took a trip to Mexico and investigated the gold and silver mines there.

On retiring from his connection with the iron ore company, Mr. Oram embarked in the mercantile business, which he has since conducted. He also has charge of the postoffice, which he has in his store. Aside from his other interests, he is connected with the Ramapo Water Works, and his advice in matters of a public nature is of much value. Just before he went to Ohio he was united in marriage with Miss Mary E. Green, of Maine, and they are the parents of a son and daughter, Thomas and Alice, both at home. Socially he is identified with the Masonic fraternity, while in political matters, he is inclined to be independent and liberal, supporting the men best qualified for office, irrespective of political ties.

B V. WOLF, Vice-President of the Homestead Building and Loan Association, is one of the oldest business men of Middletown, having commenced business here in 1853. He was born near Frankfort-on-the-Main, Germany, in July, 1817, and is a son of Victor and Esther (Rothschild) Wolf, both of whom were natives of that country. The former was reared in his native country, and was engaged in business near Frankfort. His primary education was received in the common schools, and he finished his course at Fulda College, where he mastered three ancient languages, Hebrew, Greek and Latin, and two modern languages, German and French. On leaving college, he went to Frankfort as bookkeeper in a large mercantile establishment, remaining there until 1847, when he came to the

United States via Havre, and arrived in New York City after a voyage of thirty-five days.

After mastering the English language, Mr. Wolf filled a position as bookkeeper in a mercantile establishment in New York City until 1853, when he came to Middletown and engaged in business, being among the first Germans to locate here. In 1860 he put up the first four-story building on North Street, and there began the manufacture of clothing. During the war he manufactured extensively, having in his employ over one hundred men and women, and he continued in this business until 1875, when he closed out. His son Morris B. afterward engaged in the same line, and is still in business opposite the old place.

In 1875 Mr. Wolf engaged in a real-estate and general office business, including conveyancing, collection and the settlement of estates. He is also a Notary Public, and represents the North German Lloyd Steamship Company. During his long residence here he has satisfactorily discharged all business entrusted to his care, and he has the entire confidence of the people. His office is also the headquarters of the Homestead Building and Loan Association, an institution which has been eminently successful.

Mr. Wolf was married, in New York City, to Miss Caroline Ehrenreich, a native of that city, and daughter of Jacob Ehrenreich, who was there engaged in merchandising. She died in Middletown, in September, 1890, leaving seven children: Victor B., of Brooklyn, a large wall-paper dealer at No. 829 Broadway, who married a Miss Hart, a sister of Maj. G. E. B. Hart, of New York; Bertrand B., who is interested in business with his brother Victor B.; Morris B., a manufacturer and retail clothier of Middletown; Moses, engaged with his brother Morris in Middletown; Joseph B., an employe of his brothers at Brooklyn; and Esther and Celia, at home.

Mr. Wolf is a member of the Legion of Honor, and was one of the charter members of Empire Council. Subsequently he became a charter member of Harmonia Council, and is a past officer and an ex-representative to the grand lodge. Formerly he was a member of Hoffman Lodge,

F. & A. M., but is now demitted. He is the oldest fireman in Middletown, having been a member since 1859, and helped to organize Eagle Hose Company No. 2, of which he was Trustee for years, and of which he was Vice-President for several years. In politics he was formerly a Democrat, but at present takes little interest in political matters. He was City and Town Collector in 1878, and in 1879 was Town Clerk. Mr. Wolf has always been active in forwarding the business and material interests of Middletown.

R. ANDREW J. THOMPSON. one of the oldest veterinary surgeons in the state, was born in the town of Goshen, January 26, 1834, and is a son of Robert and Susan (Johnson) Thompson. His father was born in the town of Goshen, as was also his grandfather, William Thompson. Dr. J. H. Thompson, of Goshen, is an own cousin of our subject. Robert Thompson, the father, was a carpenter by trade, but the greater part of his life was spent in farming. He owned one hundred and thirty acres near Goshen, which he operated until his death in 1875, at the age of eighty-five years. In the Presbyterian Church, of which he was a member, he was quite an active worker. Susan Johnson, his wife, was also a native of Goshen, and was a daughter of John Johnson, a tanner in the town of Wallkill. She died in Middletown, at the age of ninety-four years, having been the mother of six children: Olivia, Mrs. Berthol, of Middletown; Mary, wife of William Thompson; Ann, who resides in Middletown; Mittie, Mrs. Weller, who formerly resided near Bullville, but who died in September, 1895, aged eighty-three; Dr. Benjamin and Dr. Andrew J. Benjamin was a graduate of the New York Medical College, and practiced at Goshen. There he married Miss St. John, of Port Jervis, and later removed to Muscatine, Iowa, where he has since died.

The subject of this sketch was reared on the farm, and attended Blooming Grove and Chester Academies. For three years he then studied medicine with his brother Benjamin, part of the time being engaged in practice. Subsequently he studied veterinary surgery under English George, of New York City, for seven years. On the death of Dr. George, our subject took charge of his practice, which he continued until the death of his father, when he returned to Goshen and operated the old farm for a few years, at the same time practicing his profession. In 1870 he located at Middletown, where he has since continued to reside. For over fifty years he has been in the general practice of veterinary surgery, and has had calls in every adjoining county, Long Island, Philadelphia, Albany, and along the line of the Erie Road for many miles. At present he has about all the practice from the various livery barns in Middletown.

Dr. Thompson has been twice married, his first marriage being with Miss Harriet Merritt, of Blooming Grove, where she was born. She died in Goshen, leaving three children: Robert, who was foreman in the machine-shops of Middletown, but is now deceased; Anna, Mrs. Darby, of Middletown; and Susie, who married David Mulloch, but is now deceased. For his second wife the Doctor married Mrs. Hattie L. (Parson) Joyce, a native of the town of Wallkill, and daughter of Hudson L. Parson, a blacksmith by trade, who served thirty-three years as Police Constable in Middletown. Her mother was Julia Jamp. In politics Dr. Thompson is a Democrat, but has never accepted political office. For some years he was a member of the Old Thirty-fourth Fire Engine Company of New York City. His wife is a member of St. Paul's Episcopal Church in Middletown.

HARLES GARDNER, a contractor and builder residing in Middletown, was born in Monticello, N. Y., November 19, 1845. His father, George H., and grandfather, Henry Gardner, were natives of Orange County, where their English ancestors had settled in an early day. The former, who is a carpenter by trade, removed to the vicinity of Monticello, where he occupied and operated a farm, though also giving a large share of his attention to his trade. In those days it was the custom for the carpenter to go to the woods with his men and there hew out the timber for a house. From Sullivan County he removed to Broome County, where he became superintendent of a stock farm. He is still living, and is hale and hearty, notwithstanding his eighty-six years. His wife, who was known in maidenhood as Sarah Tharp, was born in Washingtonville, in the town of Blooming Grove, and died in Sullivan County in 1865. She was a sister of James Tharp, the old and well known merchant of Washingtonville.

Of four children comprising the parental family, three are now living, Charles being the next to the youngest. He was reared on a farm near Monticello and in boyhood attended the district schools. At the age of eighteen he was apprenticed to the carpenter's trade in Monticello, and worked at that occupation for the twelve years ensuing, after which he learned the trade of a mason, which he carried on for a time in that vicinity. In 1870, in New York City, he married Miss Harriet N. Taylor, who was born in Washingtonville, as was also her father, Robert Taylor. The latter, who was a life-long farmer, married Fannie Jacques, a member of an old family of the town of Blooming Grove. They were faithful members of the Methodist Episcopal Church until death. Of their ten children, five are now living, Mrs. Gardner being the youngest of the family.

For three years after his marriage Mr. Gardner resided in Monticello, whence, in 1873, he went to Washingtonville and for some years was superintendent of Mr. Howell's farm. Later, for four years, he superintended a farm owned by Mrs. Hulse. He next leased the Barber Farm in that locality, which he operated for four years as a dairy farm, having thirty cows. At the expiration of that time he transferred his attention to the mason's trade, and began contract work. In November, 1889, he came to Middletown, and here for two years he followed his trade, after which, in 1891, he began as a contractor and builder. In this line of work he has been very successful, and this season (1895) he has fifteen contracts for residences, of which he has completed six. He gives constant employment to eight or ten men, and is regarded as one of the reliable, progressive business men of the city. Among the houses he has erected are those for Messrs. Osterhout, Waterbury, Cheney, Davis, D. R. Miller, William Logan, Isaac Miller and Wilbur Hill. Politically he is a Republican.

WILLIAM G. TAGGART. This very prominent and energetic gentleman is the popular Clerk of Orange County. He was born in Newburgh in 1856, and is the son of Archibald Taggart, a native of Ireland, in which country his father, George Taggart, was also born. The father emigrated to America when nineteen years of age, at once making his home in Newburgh. Later he engaged in the meat business, in which he has built up a large trade. Mr. Taggart and his family are devoted members of the Presbyterian Church, in which body he is an active and valued worker.

William G., of this sketch, is the eldest in the parental family of four children. He was graduated from Newburgh Academy in 1873, after which he was associated in business with his father, aiding him greatly in establishing the business on a sound basis. April 2, 1891, however, he was obliged to abandon his operations in this line, as he was then appointed by President Harrison Postmaster of Newburgh, succeeding William R. Brown. This office he held acceptably and efficiently until February, 1892, when he resigned to assume new duties.

In the fall of 1892 Mr. Taggart was elected on the Republican ticket to the office of County Clerk, and January following took the oath of office. He has under his supervision seven employes and they occupy large rooms in Goshen. Mr. Taggart is interested in the Muchattoes Lake Ice Company, of which he is one of the Directors. They do a large wholesale and retail business and supply their customers with the purest of ice.

WILLIAM H. SOARE.

In social matters our subject is a Mason, having attained the degree of Knight Templar, and is a member of the Order of Foresters. He is one of the Directors of the Masonic Hall Association, and has been a member of the County Republican Committee for years, representing his party in both county and state conventions. He enjoys the esteem and confidence of the entire community, and as an official his record is above reproach.

<hr/>

WILLIAM HUNT SOARE was a native of Warwickshire, England, born near Coventry, November 30, 1805, and was a son of Thomas Soare, whose birth occurred in the same country. He grew to manhood in England, learning the trade of a silk weaver, and when twenty-one years of age he emigrated to the United States, sailing on the "Little Briton." He came at once to Orange County, N. Y., where he became acquainted with Sarah Ann Fulton, their marriage being solemnized February 14, 1839. She was a native of New York State, born October 13, 1816, and a daughter of Robert and Margaret (Cooper) Fulton, both of whom were born in New York State.

After his marriage Mr. Soare with his young bride removed to West Newburgh, where they lived for a time, and where he was engaged in teaching. Later he settled on a farm near his wife's father, in the town of New Windsor, and followed farming for twenty-two years. Selling his place, he purchased another near Canterbury, in the town of Cornwall, where he lived a few years, after which he removed to Blooming Grove, where he resided for a short time. He then purchased a farm near Bethlehem Church, one and a-half miles from his old home, and resided there until 1866, his wife dying July 17 of that year. Three children were born to Mr. and Mrs. Soare, Robert Fulton, William Hunt and Mary Elizabeth.

On the death of his wife, Mr. Soare, accompanied by his daughter, returned to his old home near Coventry, England, and visited among old friends and relatives for some months. Returning to America, he came to Cornwall, Orange County, where he again taught school for a time, and then removed with his daughter to Virginia, locating on a farm thirty-five miles west of Richmond. In the management of this place he was assisted by his son, William Hunt. On leaving Virginia he returned to New York, locating in Ulster County, where he purchased what is now known as the Borden Mill, which he operated until his death, which occurred in 1886.

Mr. Soare was a whole-souled man, a gentleman by birth, education and practice, thoroughly honest and successful in all his business ventures. He was not a politician, nor did he ever aspire to hold public office. He was a true Christian in his life, a member of the Church of England, and was a warm friend and neighbor. All who knew him greatly admired his sterling worth and placed the greatest reliance in him as an honorable man.

Since the death of her father, Mary Elizabeth Soare has purchased the mansion known as the Embler House, standing on a commanding eminence near the Wallkill River, with a view unsurpassed. The house is a large, roomy structure, and the grounds on which it is located comprise sixteen acres. Its mistress, a lady of refinement, was always a companion to her father and was most ardently loved by him. In her elegant home she delights to entertain her many friends, and is loved and respected by all who know her.

<hr/>

PATRICK LARKIN, engineer on the through fast passenger train of the New York, Ontario & Western Railroad, has been connected with the road since 1870. He was born in Rome, N. Y., in 1848, and is eleventh in a family of twelve children born to Paul and Mary (Kennedy) Larkin, both of whom were natives of Ireland, where they remained some years after their marriage. Desiring to give their growing family the advantages of a free country, they came to the United States, and located in Rome, N. Y., where the father died some years ago. The mother still resides in Rome. One son, Michael, who was a soldier in the War for the Union, was wounded in battle, and died from the effects of his wound and exposure after the war.

Patrick Larkin was educated in the public and high schools of Rome, and there grew to manhood. When sixteen years of age he accepted a position on the Rome, Watertown & Ogdensburg Railroad as a wiper, then as watchman, and later fireman between Rome and Watertown. In May, 1870, he entered the employ of the New York, Oswego & Midland Railroad, now the New York, Ontario & Western, in the Northern Division, as fireman for Edward McNiff. He remained with that gentleman for eighteen months, and in September, 1872, was made engineer on the road, with a run between Middletown and Jersey City, on what was called the New Jersey Midland. When the Midland Division was opened in 1873, he was given a run between Middletown and Norwich. For about twenty years he ran the local passenger, and is now running a fast passenger express between Middletown and Norwich, a distance of one hundred and fifty miles.

In Middletown, Mr. Larkin was married to Miss Mary Murphy, who was born in this city. Three children have been born unto them: James, who resides at home; and Thomas and Mary, residing in Rome. Mr. Larkin is a member of Middletown Division No. 292 of the Board of Locomotive Engineers. He has been a life-long member of St. Joseph's Catholic Church, and in politics is a Democrat.

> ⸙ ════✦✧✦✧✦ ════ ⸙

CHARLES J. BOYD, the junior editor and proprietor of the Middletown *Press*, was born a newspaper man, so to speak. Early he took a deep interest in the "art preservative," and had, at the age of ten years, an outfit with which he published a miniature paper. While attending school he spent his Saturdays in the *Whig Press* office.

Mr. Boyd was born of Orange County parents, in New York City, February 19, 1847, on Greenwich Street, near Warren, then a residence section, now a busy mercantile thoroughfare. His ancestors on his father's side were Scotch, descending from a younger son of the illustrious lord, the first High Steward of Scotland, who was murdered by Macbeth, the usurper, in 1043. The name came from Simon, the third son of Alan, the second Lord High Steward, whose eldest son, Robert, being of fair complexion, was named "Boyt" or "Boyd," from the Gaelic, meaning "fair." His great-grandfather Boyd went to Philadelphia before the Revolutionary War. His maternal ancestry was the numerous French family of Fosters, who settled in Newark. The father of Charles J. was David Robertson Boyd, who became a druggist and chemist in New York, which business he gave up to join a colony seeking gold in California, and spent seven years, from 1852 to 1859, in the mines within sight of Mt. Shasta. He died in Middletown in 1881. His mother was Miss Frances Amelia Jackson, with whom his father became acquainted at Montgomery, to which place Mr. Boyd's family removed when he was a lad.

Charles J. was an only child. He received his education in the Middletown schools, and in 1862, at the age of fifteen, entered the *Whig Press* office as apprentice under the administration of John W. Hasbrouck. Abraham Lincoln's call for troops almost depleted the *Press* office of its force the first year of his apprenticeship, and he gained rapid promotion. The last two years that he served Mr. Hasbrouck was foreman and assistant editor. In 1866 Mr. Boyd entered Wallkill Academy, and graduated December 6, 1866, delivering the valedictory of his class before an audience that packed "Gothic Hall" to the very doors. It is somewhat remarkable that in his later years as a journalist he should labor in the same building—for the former Gothic Hall is the home of the *Press*, which has grown from a small weekly until now it holds an influential place in the newspapers of the county, having daily and semi-weekly issues.

The next day after graduating from Wallkill Academy (December 7, 1866), Mr. Boyd entered Eastman's Business College at Poughkeepsie. Before graduating at Eastman's, a fine opening presented itself in the city of Newburgh as confidential clerk to John R. Wiltsie, Assistant Assessor of Internal Revenue for that district, who also controlled a large and increasing insurance and real-estate agency. In 1868 a business opportunity brought him back to Middletown, where his school days were passed, and he entered the insurance agency of Selah R. Corwin, who was also Assistant Assessor of Internal Revenue.

In a short time he became a partner with Mr. Corwin, and as a member of the firm of Selah R. Corwin & Co. he was actively engaged in that line of work until 1880, when Mr. Corwin retired by reason of age. Soon thereafter he accepted a proposition to return to his favored profession, and became a partner with Mr. Slauson in publishing the *Press*, and sold his insurance interests to Douglas & Dolson.

Mr. Boyd early manifested an interest in the Republican party. His first nomination for official position was as Inspector of Elections in the village of Middletown, and while the Democratic ticket was successful at that election, he was chosen by three majority. He always looks back to that with pride as the greatest triumph of his life. In 1875 he was appointed Village Clerk, which included at that time the clerical work of the Water Board, and held that position for seven years. His next office was that of Supervisor of the Second Ward, for which he was nominated by acclamation when Middletown became a city. He has had six successive nominations by acclamation, and is still holding this office. He was the only Republican elected in the city in 1890, his ward showing a Democratic Alderman and other Democratic ward officers. His largest majority was the last time he ran, in 1894, when he received one hundred and ninety-seven votes more than his opponent, who had both the Democratic and Prohibition nominations.

In 1892 Mr. Boyd was honored with the position of Chairman of the Orange County Board of Supervisors, and again, without soliciting the office, he was unanimously chosen to the position of Chairman in 1894. In the month of June last, while absent from home, he was selected by Governor Morton as the Representative of this, the Second Judicial, district on the new Commis-

sion of Prisons for the state, which commission was provided for by the new Constitution, and had the first intimation of his selection by reading the announcement in the telegraphic dispatches from Albany.

Mr. Boyd has twice represented his district in the Republican State Convention, of 1891 and 1895. In 1892 he was selected to make the canvass for Member of Assembly in what had for thirty years been a strong Democratic district, and, while defeated, he polled a vote fully equal to that given General Harrison for President.

For many years Mr. Boyd was a Director in the First National Bank of Middletown, and has, since its organization, been the Treasurer of the Homestead Building and Loan Association, the assets of which now reach $300,000. He is identified with the Masonic, Odd Fellows and Knights of Pythias orders, with Excelsior Hook and Ladder Company, and the First Presbyterian Church, in all of which he has held office.

Mr. Boyd is clear, positive and convincing in his editorial writing, and of late years has contributed his share of the political articles which have made the *Press* an influential party journal. He is firm in his party convictions, and, while dealing hard blows, has the respect and confidence of his political opponents. His family consists of a wife, Mary E., daughter of Stephen S. Conkling (who was a lumber dealer in Middletown during his business life), and two daughters: Ada Stewart Boyd, sixteen years of age; and Helen Ames Boyd, in her fourth year.

IRA L. CASE, real-estate dealer and insurance agent at Middletown, was born in Sullivan County, near Monticello, in 1844. His father, E. Inman, was born near Unionville, Orange County, and his grandfather, John Case, also resided near that place, dying there many years ago. E. Inman Case, the father of our subject, was a well educated man, and in early life read medicine. He took a course of lectures, but, be-

coming dissatisfied with the profession, never engaged in practice. Later he engaged in teaching
near Monticello, where he also purchased a farm,
and divided his time between teaching and farm-.
ing. In 1856 he returned to Orange County,
locating near Unionville on a farm, and there
continued until the death of his wife, when he
removed to Middletown, and died at the home of
our subject, when past seventy-six years of age.
In the Baptist Church he served in the capacity
of Deacon. He married Lydia A. Mather, who
was born near Westtown, and who was a daughter of Jonathan Mather, also a native of Orange
County, and who was by occupation a farmer and
wagon-maker. Six children were born of this
union, five of whom grew to maturity, but only
one of them is living, the subject of this sketch.
One son, Joseph M., enlisted in an independent
regiment and served through the late war, and at
its close entered the regular army. He died in
Virginia, of yellow fever, some years ago.

Ira L. Case, our subject, received his primary
education in the public schools, and finished his
school life in the academy at Unionville, where
he graduated at the age of eighteen. He then
commenced teaching school in the vicinity of his
home, and also in New Jersey for two years. He
later taught in his home district for two years,
when he went to Washington, N. J., where he
spent two years associated with his eldest brother
in the mercantile business, under the firm name
of John M. Case & Bro. He then went to Pine
Bush, where he remained one year as Principal
of the public school, and then was at Turner in
the same capacity four years. In the fall of 1874
he was made Vice-Principal of Wallkill Academy,
and had charge of the school until his election, in
1884, as School Commissioner on the Democratic
ticket from the Second Assembly District of
Orange County. He was re-elected, and served
until January 1, 1891. During his term the uniform examination was adopted in his district,
under State Superintendant Draper, and also the
revision of the school code. He made many important changes in school work which have been
satisfactory to the people.

In January, 1885, Mr. Case became a partner

of J. M. H. Little in the real-estate and insurance
business, buying out Wood T. Ogden. During
his terms as School Commissioner he gave only so
much of his time to the real-estate business as he
could spare from official duties. Since his retirement from office, however, he has devoted his
entire attention to it. Some years ago the business was consolidated with that of T. K. Walker,
and the firm became Little, Walker & Case. Six
months later Archibald Taylor bought out Mr.
Walker, and the firm became Little, Case & Taylor for one year, at which time the agency was
divided, Mr. Little taking the former agency of
Little & Case, and Mr. Case and Mr. Taylor taking that of T. K. Walker, and continuing the
business under the firm name of Case & Taylor.
This change was made in 1889.

In connection with the real-estate business, the
firm of Case & Taylor has the agency for many
of the best insurance companies in the country,
including the Liverpool, London & Globe, Home,
Hanover, Phoenix of Hartford, Orient of Hartford, Glens Falls, Fire Association of Philadelphia,
Manchester of England, London & Lancashire,
North British & Mercantile, Caledonian, Travelers'
Life and Accident, New York Life, Metropolitan
Plate-glass and Hartford Steam Boiler. Their
business covers a large extent of territory, and is
constantly increasing. The company now own
valuable property in Middletown, which they
handle exclusively, beside having charge of a
number of properties belonging to other parties.

November 24, 1869, Mr. Case was married, in
Pine Bush, to Miss Bella G. Taylor, a native of
that place, and daughter of James and Ann M.
Taylor. Four children have been born unto them:
Cora J., now Mrs. Dr. W. J. Nelson, of Middletown; Florence and Wilhemetta, at home; and
Anabelle, who died in infancy. In politics Mr.
Case is a Democrat, and has been quite active in
the councils of his party. In addition to the office
of County Commissioner, he held the office of
member of the Board of Education of the city
of Middletown for three years, commencing in
1891, during which time he was Chairman of the
Committee on the Academy. He is a Master
Mason of Hoffman Lodge, in which he is at pres-

HON. MOSES DUNNING STIVERS.

ent Junior Warden, and is also a member of Midland Chapter, R. A. M., having passed all the chairs. For nine years he was High Priest of the chapter, and for three years was Assistant Grand Lecturer of the chapter for this district. He is an honorary member of the Excelsior Hook and Ladder Company, and has been Vice-President of the organization. He is a successful insurance and real-estate man, and is popular in the community where he resides.

HON. MOSES DUNNING STIVERS, for many years one of the most influential citizens of Middletown, was born December 30, 1828, and died February 2, 1895. He was the son of John Stivers, and grandson of Randal Stivers, both natives of Middlesex County, N. J., residing near New Brunswick. From there, in the early part of the present century, the latter moved to Sussex County and settled in the town of Frankford, where his remaining years were spent.

Born October 3, 1802, John Stivers was reared to manhood in Sussex County, having but meager educational advantages. March 22, 1828, he married Margaret Dunning, who was born near Scotchtown, Orange County, July 1, 1803, and at the age of about three years was taken by her parents, Jonathan and Rachel (Crans) Dunning, to the town of Wantage, Sussex County, N. J. Her father was a private soldier in the American army during the War of 1812. After their marriage, John and Margaret Stivers settled on a farm near Beemerville, N. J., where their three children, Moses D., Randal and Jesse L., were born. In 1845 they removed to Ridgebury, Orange County, where Mr. Stivers purchased the old Deacon Hallock Farm. There he died February 21, 1865, and upon that place his son Randal still resides. The wife and mother died in Middletown March 19, 1883.

The youngest son, Jesse L., enlisted in Company B, Fifty-sixth New York Infantry, known

as the Tenth Legion, and commanded by Col. Charles H. Van Wyck. With his regiment he participated in the campaign in front of Richmond and the battle of Fair Oaks, where he was wounded. Afterward he was stationed at Yorktown, Va., and subsequently on Morris Island, S. C. After having served for three years, he re-enlisted for a similar period, and for some time served as Second Lieutenant. The hardships incident to camp life and enforced marches, however, undermined his health, which had never been robust, and he was obliged to resign his commission in 1865, when he received an honorable discharge. Afterward he was associated with his brother as part-owner of the *Orange County Press*. He died of heart disease in New York City, April 30, 1871, aged thirty years.

The subject of this memorial attended the common schools in youth, and at the age of fourteen was sent to the private school kept by Edward A. Stiles, in the town of Wantage, Sussex County, N. J., afterward known as Mt. Retirement Seminary. In that school he remained for two and one-half years, after which he studied for a term in a select school at Beemerville, and also for a time attended the academy at Ridgebury, Orange County. His studies concluded, he worked upon his father's farm in the summer seasons, while during the winters, for ten years, he engaged in teaching in Sussex and Orange Counties.

September 26, 1855, Mr. Stivers married Mary Elizabeth, second daughter of the late Lewis and Christina Stewart, of the town of Wawayanda. Five children were born unto them, namely: Mary Ellen, wife of Edwin T. Hanford, of the firm of Hanford & Horton; Lewis Stewart and John Dunning, concerning whom mention is made upon another page of this volume; Christina S., wife of Dr. Theodore D. Mills, of Middletown; and Dr. Moses Ashby, Assistant Superintendent of the New York Cancer Hospital in New York City. There are four living grandchildren, as follows: Christina Mills and Gladys Mackay, daughters of Lewis S. Stivers; and Samuel Wickham and Elizabeth Stivers, children of Dr. Mills.

For two years after his marriage Mr. Stivers was proprietor of a country store at Ridgebury.

In the spring of 1859 he came to Middletown, where his widow still resides, and where he remained, with the exception of three years in Goshen, until his death. Forming a partnership with William Evans, the firm of Evans & Stivers for five years carried on a mercantile establishment on West Main Street, when Mr. Evans sold his interest to Harvey Wallace, of Goshen, and John A. Wallace, of Middletown. The business was continued under the title of Stivers & Wallace until the election of Mr. Stivers to the office of County Clerk in the fall of 1864.

At the expiration of his term of office, in March, 1868, Mr. Stivers purchased from John W. Hasbrouck the printing-press and weekly paper, the *Orange County Press*. Though he had no practical experience in the field of journalism, he at once met with flattering success. The paper was improved and enlarged, and from a circulation of between six and seven hundred, it ran up in a few months to three times that amount, and subsequently equalled or surpassed the circulation of any paper in the county. For a time his brother, Jesse L., was associated with him, and in December, 1869, Albert Kessinger, of Rome, N. Y., was taken into partnership, the latter remaining until his death, August 5, 1872.

Meantime the firm also established the Middletown *Tri-weekly Press*. After the death of Mr. Kessinger, in order to make a settlement with his heirs, Mr. Stivers sold the plant to F. Stanhope Hill, of Chester, Pa., who associated with himself John W. Slauson, and continued the business under the firm name of Hill & Slauson. In the summer of 1873 Mr. Stivers made a tour of Europe, visiting Great Britain and the Continent, and attending the International Exposition at Vienna. Just prior to his departure he again became part-owner of the *Press*, by repurchase from Mr. Hill of his two-third interest therein, and he admitted Mr. Slauson to an equal partnership in the business. On his return from abroad in September, 1873, he resumed the editorship of the paper (the *Daily Press* having meantime been established), and remained connected with it until December, 1880, when he sold his interest to C. J. Boyd. In August, 1882, he again became

connected with the *Press* by purchasing a third-interest in the plant, the firm becoming Stivers, Slauson & Boyd, and he was a member of the firm until his return from Congress in 1891, when he sold to Slauson & Boyd.

In 1873 Mr. Stivers erected the building now occupied by the Middletown Savings Bank. The following year, with Linus B. Babcock, he built the Masonic Block, on North Street. He also made the first Casino into a public hall. For some time he was connected with the Orange County Agricultural Society, and served for some years as its President. In 1859 he aided in the organization of the Eagle Engine Company, of which he was foreman, and later President until his death. For a number of years before his death he was a member of the Middletown Club. He was a regular attendant at the services of the First Presbyterian Church, and was a member of its Board of Trustees for several years. Socially he was identified with Hoffman Lodge No. 412, F. & A. M., and in 1871-72 served as Master of the lodge. He was also connected with Midland Chapter No. 240, R. A. M., and was associated with Middletown Lodge No. 112, I. O. O. F., and Ivanhoe Lodge No. 2103, K. of H. In 1890 he was elected President of the Mt. Retirement Alumni Association, was later re-elected, and was the incumbent of the office at the time of his death. There were few who took a deeper interest in the establishment of the State Homeopathic Hospital in this city than did he, and to that enterprise he contributed liberally of his time and means, and after it was located in Middletown he was chosen a member of its Board of Trustees, being Secretary of that body until his death.

At its annual gathering at Washington, D. C., Mr. Stivers was elected President of the New York Press Association. During his incumbency of the office, the association made a trip to Boston and points in the New England States, where it was entertained by like organizations and city officials. For a time he was a Director of the Middletown, Unionville & Water Gap Railroad, and also of the Port Jervis, Monticello & New York Railroad. Until he resigned, he was a Trustee of the Hillside Cemetery Association; for many years was a Trustee of the Middletown Savings Bank; one of the organizers, and until his resignation in July, 1892, a Director, of the Merchants' and Manufacturers' National Bank of Middletown, and one of the originators, and during its period of organization Treasurer, of the Orange County Trust and Safe Deposit Company, of which successful financial institution he took the presidency July 1, 1892, holding the position at the time of his death.

A sketch of the life of Mr. Stivers would be incomplete were no mention made of his political and public career. From the time of coming to Middletown, he was a leader in the ranks of the Republican party, and his fellow-citizens, appreciating his large talents and keen judgment, frequently chose him to represent them in positions of honor and trust. As has been already mentioned, he served as County Clerk of Orange County for three years. In October, 1869, he was appointed by President Grant Collector of United States Internal Revenue for the Eleventh District of New York, which then comprised the counties of Orange and Sullivan. In 1873 Ulster and Greene Counties were consolidated with the Eleventh, and Mr. Stivers was retained as Collector for the new district. He continued to serve in that capacity until the district was consolidated with the Albany district in 1882, a period of about fourteen years. During that time millions of dollars of the public money passed through his hands, and every cent was properly accounted for. At the close of his administration he received from the Internal Revenue Department at Washington a very complimentary letter, referring to the fidelity with which he had executed his trust.

In February, 1880, Mr. Stivers was selected to represent his party at the Republican National Convention in Chicago the following June. From the outset he insisted that he would obey the wishes of his constituents rather than the instructions of the state convention, and joined with a number of other delegates in opposition to the unit rule, which position was sustained by the subsequent action of the National Convention. He voted in the convention for James G. Blaine

until the name of General Garfield was presented, when he assisted in securing his nomination.

The death of Hon. Lewis Beach, M. C., in 1886, left his position vacant, and at a convention of the Fifteenth Congressional District, held in Middletown, Mr. Stivers was nominated for the office. He accepted only on condition that he should not be expected to use any money in the purchasing of votes, which practice he condemned in pointed terms. The sentiment which he expressed regarding this matter proved popular, and he was sustained by his party in his action. He succeeded in cutting the usual Democratic majority down from fifteen hundred to four hundred, and received the largest vote ever given a Republican in this district for Member of Congress.

In 1888 Mr. Stivers was again nominated for Member of Congress, his competitor being Hon. Henry Bacon, his former successful opponent. He was elected by a plurality of seventy-four votes, and had the honor of being the second Republican elected from this district since Rockland County, with its large Democratic majority, had become a part of it. The responsibilities of the position were many, but all of them he discharged in a manner reflecting the greatest credit upon his own ability and the judgment of his constituents. Aside from his duties in the House, he gave personal attention to the wants of his constituents, and rendered valuable service, especially in the matter of pensions. He took great interest in securing a Government building for Newburgh, and it was largely through his efforts that a bill was passed appropriating $100,000 for that purpose. He was a member of the Committee on Militia, of which Gen. D. B. Henderson, of Iowa, was Chairman. He also served on the Committee on Printing, of which Hon. Charles A. Russell, of Connecticut, was Chairman, and Hon. J. D. Richardson, of Tennessee, the other member. This is one of the few joint committees of the House and Senate, and is a Privilege Committee, having permission to report at any time. Many large and important contracts, involving the expenditure of immense sums of money, came before it for consideration, and were awarded by it. Just before the nominating convention met in 1890, Mr. Stivers published a letter positively declining renomination for Congress.

From this resume of the life of Mr. Stivers it will be seen that he was for many years intimately associated with the progress of this city and the development of its material, commercial and financial interests. In the varied duties of his active and busy life he made many warm friends, and won the highest regard even of those whose political opinions differed from his own. His death was mourned by a host of acquaintances, and it was felt that one of the best friends the city had ever had was called from the scene of his former activities. The good that he accomplished, the enterprises that he fostered, the projects that he planned for the welfare of the people, remain to testify as to the value of his life and the stability of his character.

——•—•——•▷❉◁•◦❊◦•▷❉◁•——•—•——

GEORGE BARTLE, Superintendent of Bridge-building on the New York, Susquehanna & Western Railroad, and the Wilkes Barre & Western Railroad, is one of the oldest bridge-builders in the country. When he began building bridges, they were constructed of wood, but these have since been removed, and he has constructed iron bridges in their places. He was born in Cuba, N. Y., June 1, 1831, while his father, Stephen, and his grandfather, Andrew, were born in Chenango County. By trade the father was a millwright and mason, and located in Cuba as superintendent of the locks on the Genesee Canal. He died there at the age of sixty-four. In early life he was a Jackson Democrat, then an Abolitionist, and later a Republican. For many years he was a Deacon in the Presbyterian Church, in which he was a faithful and active worker. His wife, Sarah Keller, who was born in Mechlenberg, Pa., was a daughter of Andrew Keller, a farmer in Allegheny County, who was of German descent. She died at the age of eighty-

four years. In the parental family were nine children, seven of whom are yet living. One son, Stephen, was a private in the Twenty-third New York Infantry, in which he served two years, and was then Sergeant in the Second New York Mounted Rifles. While leading a charge in the absence of all the commissioned officers of his company at the battle of Cold Harbor, he was killed and his body was brought home by his brother Birney G., who was in the commissary department of the regiment. The Grand Army regiment post at Cuba, N. Y., is named in his honor.

The subject of this sketch is second in order of birth in the family of Stephen and Sarah Bartle, and grew to manhood in his native town, where he was educated in a public school. Under his father he learned the carpenter's trade, and in 1857, when the Buffalo, Bradford & Pittsburg Railroad was being built, he was erecting a mill near Bradford, Pa. He later entered the employ of R. Cummings, a contractor and bridge-builder, and continued with him seven years. Among others he has built bridges for the Erie, the Dutchess & Columbia, the New York, Ontario & Western, the Grand Trunk and the Evansville & Crawfordville Railroads. At Meredosia he built a draw-bridge across the Illinois River. It was all built of wood and was the largest ever constructed up to that time.

During the war Mr. Bartle was engaged in farming in Allegheny County, where he still owns one hundred and twenty acres of fine land. In 1870 he first came to Middletown on the construction of the New York & Oswego Midland and the New Jersey Railroads. The same year he was also engaged with the Wallkill Valley Railroad, and March 1, 1872, was made Superintendent of Buildings and Bridges on what was then the New Jersey Midland, afterward known as the Oswego Midland, then as the New Jersey Midland, but which is now the New York, Susquehanna & Western Railroad. His position has been the same during all this time, with the exception of one year, when he also performed the duties of Roadmaster of the whole of the New Jersey Midland. In his position as Superintendent

JAMES A. CLARK.

of Bridges he has charge of over two hundred miles of road, with headquarters at Middletown. He has also taken some outside contracts, and has built all the bridges on the Stroudsburg Branch, and on the Lake Erie & Hudson Railroad. He built a bridge across the Wallkill for the Middletown & Goshen Traction Company at Midway Park.

Mr. Bartle was first married at Friendship, N. Y., to Miss Flora Utter, who was born there, and who was a daughter of Judge Josiah Utter. The latter was Judge of the Allegheny County Court for twenty years, and served in the War of 1812. Mrs. Bartle died in Middletown, leaving one child, Vina, now Mrs. Amsden, of Cuba. Mr. Bartle subsequently married Miss Ella Stout, a native of Sussex County, N. J., and they have two children, Charles and Evelyn. In politics Mr. Bartle is a Republican, on which ticket he was elected Trustee from the First Ward in Middletown, serving two years. Fraternally he is a member of the Legion of Honor. Mrs. Bartle is a member of the Congregational Church.

JAMES ALONZO CLARK. In point of years of experience in the business, the junior member of the firm of Brink & Clark is one of the oldest hardware men in Middletown. Beginning in 1862 as a clerk in the hardware store of Scott Brothers, he continued with them and with their successors, gaining a thorough knowledge of every department of the business, and finally he was taken into partnership. The success of the enterprise is due to his energy in no small degree. Aside from business interests, he is prominent socially, and is identified with various fraternal organizations, prominent among these being the New York Sons of the Revolution, of which he has been a member for some years.

Like many of the influential families of this county, the Clarks came here from Long Island. James, our subject's grandfather, was a son of John Clark, and engaged in farm pursuits in this county, his death occurring in the town of Wall-

60

kill. The father of our subject, Mortimer S., was born in this county in 1803, and followed the trade of wagon-maker until his death, which took place in Middletown in 1860. His marriage united him with Mary Jane Bailey, who was born in 1813, in the old Millspaugh homestead, on the banks of the Wallkill River, below Hopkins' Bridge.

The maternal grandfather of our subject, Oliver Bailey, was born in the town of Wallkill, near Phillipsburg, December 18, 1788, and he and his wife, whose maiden name was Susan Millspaugh, resided on a farm near Scotchtown, but afterward settled in the town of Goshen. He died in 1867, when about seventy-nine years of age. Oliver was a son of Capt. Daniel Bailey, who was born in Jamaica, L. I., in 1757, and at the age of nineteen enlisted in Captain Wright's company, Col. John Lasher's battalion, a regiment made up of men from Long Island and New York. After his first enlistment he came to Orange County, where he again enlisted, becoming a member of Colonel Allison's regiment. His entire service was for three years.

On coming to this county, Captain Bailey settled west of the city limits of Middletown, where he built a log cabin and began the improvement of a farm. In 1783 he bought the farm at Phillipsburg now owned by Edwin Mills. His death occurred in Middletown May 16, 1841. He was a man of splendid physique, tall and robust, and retained his mental and physical vigor to the last. In religious belief he was a Presbyterian, and served as an Elder in the church at Goshen. His wife, Mary Tuthill, was a daughter of Nathaniel Tuthill, and traced her ancestry back to John Tuthill, who came to this country in the good ship "Swallow," some time between 1633 and 1638, and settled in New Haven, but later removed to Southold, L. I. Nathaniel Tuthill was one of the minutemen of Orange County and participated in the battle of Ft. Montgomery.

The Baileys originally spelled their name Baylis, from which form it was changed to Bayley, and finally became Bailey. Daniel, father of Captain Bailey, was born in England, and emigrated to Long Island, where he made his home in Jamaica. During the Revolutionary War he served in the Colonial army, and was a stanch patriot. Taken prisoner by the British, he was confined in the old Presbyterian Church in Jamaica, of which he was an Elder, but which had been seized by the British and converted by them into a prison. He was a member of Capt. John Skidmore's company of minutemen of Jamaica. On one occasion, it is said that a British officer remarked to him, "You'll see England yet." He promptly replied, " 'Twill be a sight, won't it?"

The mother of our subject was a member of the Presbyterian Church, and was a woman of sincere Christian faith, which found expression in many kindly deeds and encouraging words to those in need. She died October 3, 1893, in her eightieth year. Of her three sons and two daughters, we note the following: Oliver B. died in 1866 on the old homestead; Theron B., who was a member of the Tenth Legion band during the late war, is now a coal merchant of Elizabeth, N. J.; Margaret died in infancy; Mary E. died in 1877; James A., our subject, who was the youngest of the family, was born on William Street, Middletown, March 26, 1845. He was reared in this city, and in boyhood attended the old school on Orchard Street. In 1860, when a lad of fifteen, he began to clerk in Alexander Wilson's book store on North Street, remaining in that place for two years. In June, 1862, he secured a clerkship in Scott Brothers' hardware store, and, as above stated, remained with the concern through various changes until he became a member of the firm in 1879. The title was then Vail, Brink & Clark, but in 1884 the senior member sold out, and the firm became Brink & Clark, which name it has since retained.

In his pleasant home at No. 89 Highland Avenue, Mr. Clark enjoys, in the society of his wife and child and of those friends whom his genial nature draws to himself, a needed relaxation from business cares. His marriage, which took place in this city in 1887, united him with Mrs. Emma (Cole) Dunning, daughter of David B. Cole, formerly a confectioner of this city. Mrs. Clark was born in New York City. One daugh-

ter, Mildred Murray, was born to them October 23, 1888. Mr. Clark is a Trustee in the Middletown Savings Bank, and has other responsible interests in this place. Since 1865 he has been connected with the Excelsior Hook and Ladder Company, one of the oldest and finest organizations of the kind in the county, and in it he has filled all the offices. His interest in the New York Society of Sons of the Revolution is deep, and he is justly proud of the fact that he is the descendant of one of the heroes of that desperate struggle which ended in securing liberty for the colonies. Socially he is connected with Hoffman Lodge, F. & A. M., Midland Chapter, R. A. M., and is also identified with the Knights of Pythias.

JOHN A WALLACE, coal dealer, No. 14 Railroad Avenue, Middletown, was born in Bullville, this county, April 23, 1838. He is of Scotch descent, his grandfather, William, and his great-grandfather being natives of Scotland. With his wife and five children the latter came to the United States, settling first in Virginia, and subsequently in New York. At an early date the grandfather located near Scotchtown, where he engaged in farming, and here died when past eighty years of age. William W. Wallace, the father of our subject, who was born in Orange County, was a wagon-maker by trade. After locating in Bullville, he engaged in the mercantile business, but later sold out and removed to Middletown, where he died at the age of fifty-six years. He was a Presbyterian in religious belief. For many years he was Justice of the Peace, and was also Postmaster at Bullville for more than twenty years. He married Mary Thompson, whose birth occurred at Thompson Ridge, and who was a daughter of Robert A. Thompson, a farmer. She died in Middletown in 1892, at the age of seventy-seven years. In the parental family were four children, three of whom grew to maturity: John A., our subject; Mary, who married John Rotherham, but who is now deceased; and Frances, Mrs. James W. Philips, of Middletown.

John A. Wallace remained with his parents until fifteen years of age, during which time he attended the district schools whenever possible. He then went to Goshen and engaged as a clerk for H. & F. B. Wallace, general merchants of that place. After remaining in their employ for about fifteen months, he came to Middletown, in the fall of 1854, and clerked for Little & Evans, who were engaged in a general merchandise business on East Main Street. After continuing with that firm for several years, he went to Newburgh, where he remained one year, later spent one year at Goshen, and then was in New York City for two years. In 1864 he returned to Middletown, and bought out his old employers, and, forming a partnership with M. D. Stivers, under the firm name of Stivers & Wallace, they continued a dry-goods business for one year. As Mr. Stivers was elected County Clerk, he sold his interest to J. D. Horton, and the business was continued by Wallace & Horton for about five years, when the former retired from the firm, disposing of his interest to G. A. Owen. Mr. Wallace then purchased the building on North Street now occupied by the Merchants' Bank, and opened a dry-goods store, under the name of J. A. Wallace & Co., his partner being his uncle, Harvey Wallace. Three years later his uncle died, and his widow continued as the partner for two years, when Eli Rightmeyer purchased her interest, and Wallace & Rightmeyer continued in partnership for two years more. Our subject then purchased the interest of his partner, but immediately admitted into the firm R. H. Dolson, and for one year business was continued under the name of Wallace & Dolson, when the firm moved into Bull's Opera House. Later Chancy Horton was admitted to the firm. The business was now enlarged and continued by Wallace, Dolson & Horton for three years, when Mr. Horton disposed of his interest to the company and retired from the firm.

In the fall of 1876 Mr. Wallace was elected County Clerk on the Democratic ticket, and January 1, 1877, took the oath of office. This position he held for three years, his deputy during this time being C. G. Elliott. In 1878 Mr. Wallace sold his interest in the dry-goods store, in order to give his undivided attention to his official duties. After the close of his term he returned to Middletown, and in January, 1880, bought out Mr. Dolson, who was engaged in the dry-goods business, and for two years continued alone. He then took into partnership C. H. Winfield, and business was continued by Wallace & Winfield. Later Mr. Winfield retired, and Mr. Wallace continued alone until 1889, having in the mean time removed the stock to a new location on West Main Street. In 1889 he sold out to Benjamin Smith, and retired from the dry-goods business. Soon afterward he was appointed the Main Street station agent for the New York, Ontario & Western Railway, which position he held for four years, when he resigned, and formed a partnership with S. H. Bodine in the coal business. The firm of Bodine & Wallace was located on Depot Street, and continued in partnership three and a-half years, when Mr. Wallace withdrew and commenced business alone at No. 14 Railroad Avenue, the old McKee stand. He handles all kinds of coal, and has a storage capacity of three hundred tons.

Mr. Wallace was married in Goshen, in 1861, to Miss Abbie M. Wood, who was a native of that place. Four children were born unto them: Lena, now Mrs. B. A. Bordwell, of Chicago; Harvey Clifford, in the dry-goods business at Scranton, Pa.; William W., a graduate of Wallkill Academy and Hamilton College, now in his senior year at Yale College; and George E., bookkeeper for the Merchants and Manufacturers' Bank of Middletown. Mrs. Wallace died here in 1873, and in February, 1875, Mr. Wallace married Miss Adeline Hill, born at Liberty, and daughter of George Hill, a farmer. Two children have been born to this union, Blake L. and Mary.

Mr. Wallace has filled other official positions besides County Clerk. Before his election to that office he was Trustee of the village of Middletown three years, and after his return home, having filled out his term as County Clerk, he was elected President of the Village Board of Trustees for two years. Since the incorporation of the village as a city, he has served two terms as

Treasurer, and was School Trustee of the town of Wallkill when there was but one school in the present city of Middletown, known as the Orchard Street School. In politics he is a Democrat, and each time has been elected on the Democratic ticket. Socially he is a member of the Masonic fraternity, and is Past Master of the Blue Lodge, Past High Priest of Midland Chapter, R. A. M., and has been Secretary of the latter for ten years. He is a member of the Second Presbyterian Church, and has held the position of Trustee of that body. He was interested in the building of the Middletown, Unionville & Water Gap Railroad, now the Susquehanna. In the councils of the Democratic party his advice is often sought, and he has been sent as a delegate to state conventions. A successful man and energetic citizen, he enjoys the respect and esteem of all who know him.

CORNELIUS E. CUDDEBACK, one of the leading attorneys of Orange County, located at Port Jervis, is an able counselor and a man of wide information. In many of the leading enterprises of this vicinity he has been interested. Recently he has taken an active part in the re-adjustment of the affairs of the Port Jervis, Monticello & New York Railroad Company, and was Chairman of the Re-organization Committee, through whose efforts an indebtedness of $650,000 was reduced to $225,000, and the corporation restored to solvency.

C. E. Cuddeback is the eldest in a family of four children, who reached mature years and whose parents were Elting and Ann B. (Elting) Cuddeback. He was born March 10, 1849, and after obtaining a good common-school education entered Prof. A. B. Wilbur's Academy. In 1867 he was enrolled as a student at Yale College, and graduated from the classical course in the Class of '71. with the degree of Bachelor of Arts.

On considering the question of his life vocation, Mr. Cuddeback determined to read law, and took the regular course in the Columbia Law School

of New York City, from which he graduated in 1873. In order to pay his way through the school, he taught private classes of students who were preparing for college. In August, 1873, he opened an office in Port Jervis, where he has since been engaged in general practice. He is particularly versed in corporation law, and has been interested in many important legal contests. For ten consecutive years he served as Village Attorney, and for a long time held a like position for the town of Deerpark. He has often acted for the village and town as their legal advisor, and was attorney for the receiver of the Port Jervis & Monticello Railroad. His attention is chiefly given to counsel and corporation law, and as a rule he prefers to defend cases.

October 6, 1875, Mr. Cuddeback married Esther, daughter of Rev. S. W. Mill, D. D. She was born in Bloomingburg, and was educated in what was then known as the Neversink Female Seminary of Port Jervis. Our subject and wife have had born to them five children, but two of the number. are deceased, Harry having died when four and a-half years of age, and Nellie in infancy. Those living are: Samuel M., Anna M. and Cornelius E., Jr. The parents are members of the Reformed Church. Mr. Cuddeback is very domestic in his tastes and has a very pleasant home. He is classed among the prominent and representative citizens of the county. Politically he is a Democrat.

WILLIAM H. McGOWAN, who is a prominent citizen of the town of Wallkill, was born in Circleville, N. Y., in 1827, and is a son of John and Melissa (Fowler) McGowan, both of whom were natives of Orange County, and spent their entire lives within its limits. His father, when a young man, learned the trade of a blacksmith, and this occupation he followed for several years. Later he became interested in farming pursuits, and he was successfully employed at that vocation until advancing years caused his

FRED HERMAN.

retirement from active work. He passed from earth in 1878, having long survived his wife, whose death occurred in 1864.

The rudiments of his education Mr. McGowan gained in the district schools, and the knowledge there acquired was supplemented by systematic reading and self-culture in later years. His entire life has been spent upon a farm, with the exception of some six years, during which time he was collecting agent and Treasurer of the Farmers' Milk Association of Circleville, N. Y. His property consists of thirty-two acres in the home farm, which is embellished with a neat residence, and contains all the equipments necessary for the successful prosecution of the work. The principal industry in which Mr. McGowan engages is the milk business, and of this he has made a decided success.

In 1858 our subject and Miss Sophia Horton were united in marriage, and their union has been one of mutual helpfulness and happiness. Mrs. McGowan was born in this county, of which her father, Hiram Horton, was a worthy citizen. In religious belief she affiliates with the Baptist Church, and her Christian character has won the esteem of the people of this locality. Being opposed to monopolies, Mr. McGowan naturally finds a home in the Democratic party, of which he is a stanch adherent. However, while he uniformly votes that ticket in national affairs, he is conservative in local matters, voting for the man whom he deems best qualified for official position, no matter what his politics may be.

RED HERMAN, a prosperous business man in the western part of Newburgh, is an active Republican, and at one time served as Alderman from the First Ward. Besides serving on local and county committees, he has also been Chairman of the Fire Department Committee. In 1891 he was elected to serve as one of the Almshouse Commissioners, and at the end of three years was re-elected, being made Chairman of the Outdoor Relief Committee and a member of the Children's Home Committee. He is engaged in

the hide and leather business, and is Secretary and Treasurer of the Newburgh Rendering Company.

Mr. Herman was born in Canterbury, town of Cornwall, Orange County, February 9, 1848. His father, Jacob Herman, was a native of Zweibrucken, Germany, on the River Rhine, and there learned the tanner's trade. In his early manhood he emigrated to the United States, and, settling in the vicinity of Newburgh, conducted a tannery on his own account. Later he moved to West Newburgh and built the tannery now operated by his son. He was actively engaged in business up to the time of his death, which occurred in February, 1862, when he was nearly sixty-one years of age. Religiously he was a Lutheran, and in his political faith was a Republican. His wife, who was a Miss Riedinger before their marriage, was born in Germany, and died when her son Fred was only a year old. The father afterward married Catherine Van Aiken, who was born in Newburgh, and who is still living here. Her two sons are Jacob, who is in the grocery business; and Robert, who is in the postoffice, both being residents of Newburgh. The only sister of our subject is Mary, who is now living in New York City.

Until he was thirteen years of age, Mr. Herman attended the Newburgh schools, and was then apprenticed to the tanner's trade under his father, continuing with him until the latter's death. For the following five years he and his brother Jacob managed the business, but at the end of that time the partnership was dissolved. Since then our subject has carried on a hide, leather and findings trade, his business location being at No. 531 Broadway. In May, 1894, he helped to incorporate the Newburgh Rendering Company, he being made Secretary and Treasurer. The company has a capital stock of $3,000, and the plant is located adjacent to the city.

In Port Jervis, in 1873, Mr. Herman was married to Florence E. Sawyer, who was born in Pike County, Pa. Mr. and Mrs. Herman became the parents of five children, the eldest of whom, Celim, was drowned when the steamer "Elbe" sank; Homer is attending the academy; and Fulton is engaged in the tinsmith and plumbing business. The two daughters, Katie and Belle, are still living at the parents' home, which is situated on Broadway. Mr. Herman is a member of the Knights of Honor, and belongs to Newburgh Lodge No. 309, F. & A. M. He is a charter member of Highland Steamer Company No. 3, of the fire department, with which he has served for thirty years. Among his business associates he bears a well deserved name as a man of strict integrity and honor.

WILLETT J. MARSHALL is one of the largest wholesale provision merchants in Newburgh. His well equipped establishment is also devoted to the sale of all kinds of cured and smoked meats, and in the prosecution of this business he is meeting with success.

Mr. Marshall is a native of this state, having been born in Hyde Park, Dutchess County, August 6, 1837. This was also the birthplace of his father, Hiram, and grandfather, Willett. The latter was a farmer by occupation, and during the War of 1812 served as a soldier in its ranks. His son Hiram was likewise a tiller of the soil, and owned a splendid property four miles east of Hyde Park, where he died when fifty-five years of age. The mother of our subject, Hannah (Haight) Marshall, was born in Clinton, Dutchess County, and was a daughter of Isaac Haight, a Quaker and farmer of Clinton.

The parental family included six children, all of whom are living, and of whom Willett J. was the eldest. He was reared to farm life and educated in the Quaker schools of Washington, remaining at home until his father died, in 1855. That year he went west to Illinois, locating on a farm in Knox County, within one mile of Galesburg, where he engaged in farming for two years, when he returned to his native state and began working on the old homestead. In May, 1867, he located on Gidney Avenue, Newburgh, and engaged in his present business, which was the

first of the kind carried on in the city, and for the first three years he operated alone. Mr. Coles then became his partner, and the firm known as Coles, Marshall & Co. has existed up to the present time. After six years spent at the old stand, they moved to Nos. 21 and 23 South Water Street, where they have a large and well equipped eestablishment, conducted on strictly business principles. The senior member of the firm and Mr. Gidney reside in New York City, looking after their interests there. They also do a wholesale provision business in that city, their house being located at No. 100 Forsyth Street. They purchase their own stock and cure their meats, the establishment for that purpose being located in Jersey City. Their house in Newburgh, which our subject conducts, occupies five floors. The firm of Coles, Marshall & Co. is well known throughout the East, the business extending to almost every city on the Atlantic Coast. Two traveling salesmen are kept on the road during the entire year, looking after the firm's interests in Newburgh and New York City.

Mr. Marshall was married in Hyde Park, in 1859, to Miss Emeline Avery, who was born at Lima, Livingston County, this state, in 1841. To them has been born a son, Hiram, who is at present residing in Middle Hope. Mr. Marshall occupies one of the pleasantest homes in the city, and surrounds his family with all of the comforts and many of the luxuries of life. In politics he is a supporter of Republican principles, and religiously belongs to the Society of Friends.

JOHN J. HOGAN. The name of this gentleman deserves to be perpetuated as a public benefactor, for through the exercise of his mechanical genius he has been enabled to wholly revolutionize the science of boiler-making. He is mechanical engineer of the Hogan Boiler Company, of Middletown, the other officers being W. D. Stratton, President; G. N. Clemson, Vice-President; C. Macardell, Treasurer; and C. L. Merritt, Secretary and Manager. Mr. Hogan himself is the founder of the works, the success and rapid growth of which are due almost entirely to his skill and inventive ability. The Hogan Water Tube Boiler, which he has perfected, and through which his name has become widely known, possesses a three-fold advantage over the ordinary boiler, in that it saves first cost, space and fuel.

Among the advantages of this boiler we note the following: instant and continuous precipitation of all sediment in the water and its certain deposit in the mud drum; steady water line at all pressures, irrespective of capacity or forcing; introduction of the feed-water in a way to promote and assist circulation instead of retarding it; the impossibility of water of low temperature coming in contact with the surfaces which are exposed to the heated gases; positive vertical circulation and continuous circulation, insuring clean surfaces and freedom from accumulation of sediment in tubes and cylinders, irrespective of the kind of water used; vertical water tubes, insuring natural circulation; free expansion of all parts without any strain on the joints; dry steam at all times, no matter what the conditions of firing and use may be; and the heating surfaces located directly above the fire surfaces in one chamber of large volume.

That the boiler is economical, may be inferred from the fact that a plant of one thousand horse-power will save $5,000 in fuel above what any other boiler has been able to accomplish. Its operative economy is also very large, as it generates more steam per pound of coal used than any other boiler ever made. It is admirably adapted for marine purposes, and is now being introduced into shipping. The boilers have been tried at sea and it has been found that four of the Hogan Boilers can replace twelve of the largest size of others, and twenty-eight of the smaller size. There is, therefore, in view of their great economy of fuel and space, a probability that these boilers will entirely replace the others in use at the present time, for the cost of operation is materially smaller and the space occupied is two-thirds less than that taken by other boilers.

Of this line of work Mr. Hogan has made a specialty since boyhood. He studied mechanical

engineering in England, and was a pupil in the Reading Iron Works, near London, paying a tuition fee of $1,500 and receiving in wages for the five years from sixty cents to $1.25 per week. Believing that America offered a wider field for work in his occupation, he came hither, and for some time was with Alexander L. Holley, designing and erecting the Bessemer Process. Not infrequently, in the erection of plants, it was necessary to put in from ninety to a hundred of the largest boilers of that day. He spent some time in this business both at Scranton, Pa., and St. Louis, Mo. In 1893 he came to Middletown and erected the necessary buildings for the manufacture of boilers, completing them so as to begin in business early in 1894. Since that time he has conducted a large contract business, manufacturing boilers of from seventy-five to eight hundred horse-power. The Hogan Boiler Company has a capital stock of $300,000 and owns five acres of land within the city limits, on which they intend in the near future to build large shops, sufficient to furnish employment to four or five hundred mechanics.

Since 1871 Mr. Hogan has been perfecting the boiler which now bears his name, and he now has about one hundred different patents upon it. The Novelty Hot Water Circulator and Novelty Steam Boiler are manufactured by the Model Heating Company of Philadelphia, under their patents. The Hogan Metallic Joint, used on the boiler, is a valuable patent. The whole structure is supported on a wrought-iron frame, neatly enclosed and covered with brick. The front is of wrought and steel plates, secured with long bolts in a way to prevent all movement of the brickwork. In addition to these steel plates and bolts, the brickwork of the furnace has air spaces between it and the external walls. The man-holes are provided with copper seats in their joints, which are under compression at all times. The man-holes are especially designed for high pressure, and the covers may be replaced without renewal of copper seat. The opening of two or three man-holes, the number varying according to the type of boiler, gives access to the inside of the boiler.

One of the most important contracts taken by

the Hogan Boiler Company was for the erection of a boiler in the State Hospital for the Insane at Middletown. The grate area of this boiler is a little more than eighty square feet, being $11\frac{1}{2}$ x7. The heating surface is equal to four thousand and one hundred square feet, and the floor space occupied by the boiler is 20×11^2 $_3$. The height of the chimney from ground to top is fifty feet. These figures will serve to give an idea of the magnitude of this enterprise, which was one of the most important ever undertaken by the company.

In everything pertaining to the business Mr. Hogan is deeply interested, and probably few men are better informed concerning every detail of boiler-making than is he. A considerable portion of his time is devoted to the publication of the "Boiler Review," a magazine for the trade, in which are technically reviewed theory and practice relating to the design, construction and operation of stationary, marine and locomotive boilers.

LOUIS DOUGLAS FOUQUET, Assistant Engineer on the New York, Ontario & Western Railway, with headquarters at Middletown, was born in the village of Fishkill, N. Y., October 12, 1867. The family of which he is a member has been represented in this country since the Revolution, when his paternal great-grandfather accompanied General LaFayette from France to America. The grandfather, D. L. Fouquet, was proprietor of the Fouquet House at Plattsburg, Clinton County, N. Y., and owned a number of stage lines running to the Adirondack Mountains.

Our subject's father, John D., was born in Plattsburg, and took a course in civil-engineering at the Troy Polytechnic Institute, from which he was graduated. He was a civil engineer on the Atlantic & Great Western, the Erie and in the United States navy under Admiral Bailey, on the frigate "St. Lawrence." Later he settled at Fishkill, where he was a division engineer on the Dutchess & Columbia Railroad, then became

architect for the large print works of Garner & Co., and afterward was architect for the West Shore Railroad, with headquarters at Weehawken, N. J.; he also served as superintendent of buildings and construction for the same road. His next position was that of architect for the New York Central at Grand Central Station, New York. About 1894 he resigned this position and established an office at No. 35 Broadway, New York, where he has since been engaged as a civil engineer and architect, making a specialty of railroad work. In religious belief he is an Episcopalian.

The mother of our subject, whose maiden name was Emma J. Leffingwell, was born at Athens, Greene County, N. Y., and is of English descent. Her father, Capt. John Leffingwell, was for a long time a captain on the Hudson, and owned a number of sloops and barges that plied the waters of that river. Our subject is the elder of the two children, and has a brother, M. L., who is Assistant Engineer on the New York Central Railroad. Louis D. was reared in Fishkill, where he attended the public schools. At the age of seventeen he went to Pittsfield, Mass., where he was clerk in a pharmacy for one year, but not liking the business, he took up civil-engineering. His first position was as clerk and draughtsman in the West Shore Railway office, after which he was chainman for the New Jersey Railroad between Weehawken and Jersey City, and later was draughtsman for the same company. For one year he was draughtsman on the New York Central Railroad at Grand Central Depot, New York, and then was transferred to One Hundred and Thirty-eighth Street, the same city, as rodman on the Harlem Depression. He was also employed on the construction of the Mott Haven yards.

Resigning that position in 1889, Mr. Fouquet became leveler on the construction of the zig-zag tunnel in Delaware County, on the New York, Ontario & Western. From that position he was promoted to transitman, and in 1891, while working on the tunnel, he became assistant engineer. The construction of the tunnel required two years and eleven months, and he was the first to pass

HARVEY ALEXANDER.

through it upon its completion. The work of building it was done very rapidly, the world's record on that score being broken by their speed. Not only was the work rapidly done, but it was done well, and when the two lines met there was not the least variation in them.

In 1891 Mr. Fouquet came to Middletown as Assistant Engineer of the entire system, but in 1893, when the railroad was divided, he became Assistant Engineer of the Southern Division. His entire time is given to the duties of his position, which he fills most efficiently and satisfactorily. He has superintended the building of a number of bridges and viaducts of steel, and aided in the construction of the Ellenville Bridge. He is a Junior in the American Society of Civil Engineers, and takes a warm interest in everything pertaining to the science. Like his parents, he is an Episcopalian, his membership being in Grace Church. Fraternally he is identified with Hoffman Lodge No. 412, F. & A. M.; Midland Chapter No. 240, at Middletown; Delaware Commandery No. 44, at Port Jervis; and Mecca Temple Shrine in New York City.

HARVEY ALEXANDER. This worthy old settler of the town of New Windsor has dwelt on his present farm uninterruptedly since 1846, with the exception of one year, which was passed in Cornwall. Though now in his seventy-ninth year, he still enjoys good health and carries on the work of his farm in a manner befitting a man of half his years. He is mainly self-educated, for in his boyhood he had little chance for attending school, and was obliged to rely upon private study and general observation. His first Presidential ballot was cast for William Henry Harrison, and he also had the privilege of voting for his grandson in 1888. He has always been a stalwart Republican, and has held a number of local offices of trust and honor, having served as Town Trustee for fourteen years.

The parents of our subject were James and Catherine F. (Bullard) Alexander, the former of whom was born in Belfast, Ireland, November 2, 1770, and the latter in Connecticut, December 29, 1780. Their family numbered thirteen children, of whom John died in 1858, aged fifty-eight years; Thomas died January 1, 1895, when in his ninety-fourth year; Joseph, born in 1804, is still living; James died in 1888, when in his eighty-third year; Franklin, born March 9, 1808, is a resident of Cleveland, Ohio; Annie E., born January 16, 1810, and now living in Mt. Pleasant, Pa., is the widow of Thomas McClellan; Jane, born February 14, 1812, married Daniel Sayer, and died March 12, 1895; Catherine, born December 27, 1813, is the widow of A. T. Rumsey, and resides in Newburgh; Rebecca, who was born April 13, 1818, and was the wife of Samuel McCoon, died May 28, 1857; Mary, born January 17, 1821, the widow of Mathew Crist, lives in Newburgh; Daniel M., born January 9, 1824, is a resident of Morristown, N. J.; Rhoda, born October 24, 1827, is the wife of George W. Shaw; and our subject completes the family. The father of this large family was a weaver by trade. In 1798 he came to America on a sailing-vessel, and from that time onward lived in Newburgh.

Harvey Alexander is a native of this town, having been born within its limits February 15, 1816, and was reared on the farm now owned by James Corwin. When he was about sixteen years of age he commenced working at the carpenter's trade, serving for three years as an apprentice, and receiving therefor his board and about $40 per year. Later he worked at his trade for a short time, but since 1846, when he moved to the farm which he still owns, he has given his principal attention to agriculture.

April 7, 1841, Mr. Alexander married Amanda Kernaghan, who was born in this town, April 27, 1817, being a daughter of William and Sarah Kernaghan. Three children came to bless the home of our subject and wife. Sophia C. lives at home and is keeping house for her father; George B. is ex-Under Sheriff of Orange County; and Joseph K. is ex-Sheriff. The mother died March 6, 1884, and was buried in Bethlehem Cemetery. She was a faithful member of the Presbyterian

Church, to which Mr. Alexander and daughter also belong. The former has served as Trustee in the Methodist Church at Little Britain, and has always taken great interest in religious affairs.

> ━━━━ ⚜❖⚜ ❖✦❖ ⚜❖⚜ ━━━━ ⟨

CHARLES G. BALDWIN is the junior member of the firm of Wood & Baldwin, proprietors of a livery, boarding and sales stable at Middletown, and who are also operating a sandbank with great success. In public affairs he is a man of influence. In 1890 he was elected to represent the Third Ward on the Board of Aldermen, and two years later he was re-elected, serving four years, but refusing further nomination for the position. While a member of the Council he served as a member of almost all of the committees and was Chairman of the Street and Police Committees.

Mr. Baldwin was born in East Fishkill, Dutchess County, February 27, 1861, and his father, Peter A., and grandfather, Elisha, were born at the same place. His great-grandfather, Daniel, removed from Connecticut to New York and settled on a farm near Fishkill, remaining there until his death. Peter A. Baldwin has for years been successfully engaged in farming and stock-raising, and still makes his home in Dutchess County, near Hopewell, being quite robust though sixty-four years of age. He has been active in local matters and has served as Supervisor, his popularity being shown by the fact that he ran considerably ahead of his ticket at election. Socially he is a Mason. His wife, whose maiden name was Mary Green, was born in the town of Hyde Park, Dutchess County, and was a daughter of Charles Green, a shoe merchant of New York City. She is identified with the Dutch Reformed Church in religious belief.

There are three children in the family of Peter A. and Mary Baldwin, of whom our subject is the eldest. The others are Frank, a farmer living near Poughkeepsie; and Aletta, who is with her parents. Charles G. remained on the home farm until twenty-one years of age, meantime attending Monticello Academy, from which he was graduated in 1879. In boyhood he frequently rode on horseback to and from Ohio, driving from two to three hundred head of cattle, and from twenty-five to fifty head of horses, from the Buckeye State to New York City.

Going to New York City in 1882, Mr. Baldwin became bookkeeper for the Syndicate Mining Company, at No. 2 Wall Street. After three months there, he secured a position as claim clerk of the live-stock department of the Erie Railroad in New York, being with his uncle, A. S. Baldwin. In 1885 he went to Camden, N. J., and formed a partnership with his father-in-law in the lumber business, under the firm name of L. M. Stanton & Co., but one month after starting in business Mr. Stanton died. The business was then sold out and Mr. Baldwin went to Fishkill, where he engaged in dealing in horses. In December, 1888, he came to Middletown, where he began as a horse dealer, and later bought and opened a sandbank of thirty acres, one mile from the city, on South Street, lying on the line of the Susquehanna & Western Railroad, with which it is connected by a switch. There is also a large supply of clay here, and it is the intention of the firm to start a brickyard at some future time. From two to six men are employed at the bank, and a very extensive business is done, large sales being made of moulding, building, gravel and paving sand.

In 1893 Mr. Baldwin started in the livery business on James Street, and here he has since carried on a large trade. He sells large numbers of horses, both for himself and other parties, and raises a few standard horses for sale. He is a stockholder and Director of the Driving Park Association and has twelve or more horses at the park, where they are being trained. Politically he is a Republican, but does not care for prominence in public affairs, preferring to give his attention to business matters.

In Monticello Mr. Baldwin married Miss May Stanton, daughter of Lewis Stanton, at one time County Clerk of Sullivan County, but now deceased. Mrs. May Baldwin died in Middletown, after having become the mother of two children, Elizabeth and Adriance. The present wife of Mr. Baldwin was Miss Anna B. Harman, who was born in Middletown, being a daughter of Frank Harman, a resident of this city and connected with the Erie grain elevator at Jersey City. One child blesses this union. Mrs. Baldwin is a member of Grace Episcopal Church, and moves in the best society in this city. As a representative and successful business man, Mr. Baldwin has won a place among the prominent men of the city, and is rapidly gaining a solid and substantial prosperity, of which he is well deserving.

ILLIAM M. CORNELL, one of the well-to-do farmers of the town of Cornwall, was born in the town of Monroe, August 19, 1826. He attended school for some time in his native place, but since 1842 has made his home in this locality, where his father, Josiah Cornell, was the proprietor of a large tract of land, comprising over seven hundred acres. This property was inherited by his two sons, James and William, the latter receiving two hundred and fifty acres.

The paternal grandparents of our subject were Josiah and Catherine (Maillor) Cornell, natives, respectively, of Westchester and Orange Counties, this state. Josiah was but a small boy when his father, Daniel, came to this county, soon after the close of the Revolutionary War. The latter lost much property in the way of cattle, etc., during that period, and on one occasion two soldiers were compelled to run the gauntlet for stealing some carpet which belonged to him.

Daniel Cornell married Miss Mary Quimby, to whom were born three daughters and three sons, and of these Josiah was the third. He married Catherine Maillor, and lived on the farm adjoining that occupied by our subject. Their family included eight children. Of these, Charity is living in this section; James and Esther are deceased; William, our subject, was the next-born; Mary Ann is the wife of Charles Ryder, of Brooklyn; Rebecca makes her home at Mineola, L. I.;

Elizabeth married Reuben Birdsell, a native of Chappaqua, but now living in Mineola; and the youngest member of the household died in infancy.

Our subject was married in Highland Mills, November 24, 1859, to Miss Sarah Cornell, the daughter of Harrison and Charity (Earl) Cornell. Her father was the son of Samuel Cornell, a native of Westchester County, and by his union with Miss Earl there were born the following eleven children: Samuel, Hannah, John, Mary, David, Elizabeth, James, Charles, Charlotte (the wife of Charles S. Ostrander, now living in Portland, Ore.), Sarah, and one who died unnamed.

To our subject and his estimable wife there have been born six sons and daughters. Charlotte married John S. Drake, of Green Point, L. I.; Harrison is a farmer living on a farm adjoining his father's; Josiah is a farmer in the town of Woodbury; Charity is at home; Sidney is also a farmer of Woodbury; and Charles is also at home. The parents are members of the Society of Friends. In politics Mr. Cornell is a Democrat of the old-fashioned type. He has been active in public affairs and for some time served as Road Overseer. He is an influential worker in his church and has been overseer of his congregation. The land which he cultivates is a very productive tract and yields him a good income.

HE MIDDLETOWN PRESS, which is one of the oldest and most widely circulated newspapers in southern New York, was established in Middletown as a weekly in 1851, by John W. Hasbrouck, who is still living, an honored resident of this city. It was from the first strongly Republican in politics, and then, as now, made the local news a leading feature. Mr. Hasbrouck conducted the paper, with unvarying success, for seventeen years, and then sold out to Moses D. Stivers, who had then just completed a term as Clerk of Orange County. He was an ardent Republican, and proved to be a "born newspaper man."

The first paper under the editorship of Mr.

Stivers was issued April 3, 1868. December 3, 1869, he formed a partnership with Albert Kessinger, and the paper was issued by the firm of Stivers & Kessinger until the sad death of the junior of the firm in 1872. During this interval, May 24, 1870, a tri-weekly edition of the paper, known as the Middletown *Evening Press*, was started and was a great success. The paper was sold in 1872 in order to settle Mr. Kessinger's estate, and was bought by F. Stanhope Hill, an experienced newspaper man of Chester, Pa., who at once sold an interest to John W. Slauson, one of the present proprietors.

Feeling that the time for a daily paper in Middletown (which then had a population of over six thousand) had arrived, the new firm of Hill & Slauson changed the tri-weekly to a daily, and sent out the first issue of the Middletown *Daily Press* October 26, 1872. Mr. Hill remained in the firm only nine months, when he resold to Mr. Stivers, and the paper had a very prosperous period, under the firm of Stivers & Slauson, from July 2, 1873, to December 14, 1880. At the latter date Mr. Stivers sold his interest to his partner, who at once sold the same to Charles J. Boyd, one of the present proprietors, and the firm of Slauson & Boyd was formed. This firm existed three years, during which the weekly edition of the paper—the *Orange County Press*—was changed to a semi-weekly, the first issue bearing date July 24, 1883. This was the first semi-weekly paper in this part of the state, and its success was remarkable from the start.

In August, 1883, Mr. Stivers repurchased an interest in the paper, and the firm became Stivers, Slauson & Boyd. He remained in active connection with the firm until elected to the Fifty-first Congress, in the fall of 1888. During his term of office he was necessarily absent from his newspaper work. At the close of his official term he decided to dispose of his interest in the paper, a decision to which his partners gave reluctant consent. They finally purchased Mr. Stivers' share in the establishment, and for the second time the firm became Slauson & Boyd, and has so continued ever since. While there have been several changes of firm

titles, as mentioned above, the real changes in proprietorship were few, one of the present owners having been connected with the paper for twenty-three years and the other for about fifteen.

The paper owns its own real estate, is equipped with modern and rapid-printing machinery, has a large job-printing department, and has always been in a flourishing and healthful condition The building in which the paper has large and commodious quarters was once the only public hall of the town, and its walls have echoed the voices of the leading orators and statesmen of the country. The following mention of the character and influence of the paper was prepared for this volume by W. T. Doty, editor of the *Orange County Farmer:*

"The career of the Middletown *Press* has been onward and upward. With no faltering step, it has worked its way from a mere 'diminutive chronicler' of events to an eminence of ability and far-reaching influence,—a credit to the great 'art preservative' and an example of thorough, high-toned, even-tempered management.

"The *Press* has made a record of great usefulness. It has nearly reached its half-century mark, being now in its forty-fourth year. During that time it has seen its birthplace grow from a hamlet to a prosperous, beautiful, busy city; its own state from greatness to grandeur; and its own Republic from a border-land of struggling civilization to an empire of enlightenment.

"Its own columns have grown from few to many. In size and usefulness it has kept pace with the march of events, never slighting a duty or evading an issue. Steadfastness to principle has ever found it in the columns of the Republican party's army of occupation. Boys have become men and men have grown gray in its service.

"The *Press* has always been one of the cleanest of journals,—the steadfast aim of its successive proprietors having been a continuity of noble purpose and a marvel of attainment. The writer of these lines has been more or less familiar with the work,—he may say the domestic work,—

PROF. LOUIS J. DIEMER.

of the office for more than thirty years, and during that time he has found so much to commend and so little to condemn in the conduct of the *Press*, that he takes pride in pointing to it as a model newspaper establishment in every respect. This term, 'model newspaper,' is so often misused that it generally fails to convey its true meaning; but in this case the highest application of encomium expresses only the truth.''

LOUIS J. DIEMER. Newburgh is known among the other cities of the Hudson Valley as having among her citizens a number of gentlemen whose superior musical ability and skill have won for them an enviable reputation, and whose public-spirited service has raised their city to a high position in artistic circles. Such is Professor Diemer, who is recognized as one of the most skilled pianists and organists, not only of Newburgh, but also of this part of the state. As an instructor in music he has earned a widespread reputation for thoroughness and accuracy. In addition to instruction in the art, he is officiating as organist of St. Paul's Protestant Episcopal Church and of the Jewish Temple, Congregation Beth Jacob.

Though of German parentage and ancestry, Professor Diemer is a native of New York, and was born in Newburgh, October 18, 1858. His educational advantages, both literary and musical, were of the very best, and being naturally of a bright and assimilative nature, he acquired a broad knowledge of the sciences, literature and art while still quite young. From early childhood he displayed a predilection for music, and the talent which it was seen that he possessed he was given the best opportunities to cultivate. When only eight years of age he began the study of music under the instruction of Prof. Louis Hammerstein, with whom he continued for six years.

The first public work done by Professor Diemer was in May, 1878, when he secured the position

of organist at St. George's Episcopal Church of Newburgh. The following year he studied organ and harmony with Prof. C. B. Rutenber, of New York, remaining under his instruction for one term. In 1880 he studied piano, organ and harmony with Dr. E. Eberhard, President of the Grand Conservatory of Music of New York City. Later he studied the piano with Otto Hackh, A. M.

The ability of Professor Diemer was recognized by his appointment as a member of the faculty of the Grand Conservatory in 1883, and during the following year he accepted the position of organist of St. Mary's Catholic Church. Later he was organist for the American Reformed and the Trinity Methodist Episcopal Churches, and at present, as before stated, he is organist for Congregation Beth Jacob and St. Paul's Protestant Episcopal Church. At the early age of twelve years he began to compose music, and this he has since continued, but has modestly declined to publish any of his compositions, not deeming them of sufficient merit. If the opinions of others may be relied upon, however, in preference to his own estimate of his ability, he is without doubt one of the most efficient musicians and skilled composers of the state. In the profession he stands very high, while his genial manners and unvarying courtesy of demeanor have brought him equal prominence in social circles.

The marriage of the Professor occurred October 15, 1884, uniting him with Miss Josephine M. Waring, of Newburgh, and daughter of James K. and Sarah K. (VanWyck) Waring. To our subject and wife have been born four children.

CARL KEEHNER, or Charles Keener, as he is best known (the change in name being rendered necessary on account of the persistency of the people in calling him so), is a manufacturer of fine hand-cut files, and is a successor to the Homebreaker-Keener Company. He was born in Germany, at Rheinpfalz, about thirty miles from the Rhine, November 5, 1852. His parents, Mathias and Susanna (Flockerzie) Keehner, were also natives of the same country. His paternal grandfather was an officer in the French army in the Napoleonic Wars. During the Revolutionary War he came to America to assist the Colonists, after which he returned to Germany, where he held the position of Forester to the king. He was a prominent man, a valiant fighter, and had many medals bestowed upon him for his bravery in action. He passed away at the age of eighty-five years.

Mathias Keehner, the father of our subject, was by trade a stone-cutter and general contractor in street paving. He died in his native land at the age of fifty-two years, firm in the faith of the Evangelical Church. The mother of our subject, as already stated, was a native of Germany. Her father was also a Government officer, and held high rank in the German army. When he retired from the army he was employed as Head Forester to the king. Of their family of four sons and one daughter, all are yet living, two of the number residing in America: David, who resides in Middletown, and who is a contracting mason; and the subject of this sketch.

Charles Keener attended the public schools of his native country until fourteen years of age, when he was apprenticed to learn the trade of a dyer in a large woolen-manufacturing establishment. For nearly two years he worked at this trade, when, his health failing him, he decided to come to America. In the spring of 1869 he left home, sailing from Hamburg in the steamer "Zumbria," and after spending eleven days on the water landed in New York, from which place he went to Saugerties and engaged in cutting bluestone for two years. He then removed to Grahamsville, Sullivan County, and for two years and eight months was employed in a tanning establishment. The firm with which he was employed having failed, our subject then came to Middletown and entered Howell & Hinchman's tannery, where he worked for eighteen months. In 1878 he entered the sawshops of Wheeler, Madden & Clemson, now the National Saw Works, where he remained three years. He then formed a partnership with his brother-in-law, Herman Homebreaker, a practical file-maker, to manufacture files and rasps, and erected a build-

ing for their works. Business was conducted under the name of the Homebreaker-Keener Company until July, 1894, when the partnership was dissolved. Mr. Keener then purchased the interest of his partner, and has since continued alone in business. The location of the house is at No. 37 Broad Street, where, in addition to the manufacture of files and rasps, he cuts, tempers, hardens and finishes up steel for various manufacturing purposes. He manufactures rasps from bar steel, and files from the rough. The house has a capacity for turning out from one hundred and seventy-five to two hundred files every twenty-four hours. The business amounts to several thousand dollars each year, and the products are shipped from the Atlantic to the Pacific, and North and South. Mr. Keener himself does much of the traveling for the house.

In 1878 Mr. Keener was united in marriage in Middletown with Miss Matilda Homebreaker, a native of Germany, and daughter of Peter and Wilhelmina (Schilling) Homebreaker. Her father was a file manufacturer by trade, and followed that work both in his native land and after he came to America. On coming to this country, he located in Pompton, N. J., where he was employed at his trade for a short time. After living in various places, he came to Middletown, about 1858, and entered the employ of Wheeler, Madden & Clemson, file manufacturers. He yet resides in this city, and works at his trade. Mrs. Keener was reared in this country, and she has become the mother of six children: Mabel, Emma M., Clara J., Florence, Grover Cleveland and Alfred Robert, all of whom reside at home.

Since coming to Middletown Mr. Keener has been quite successful, and in addition to his business interests owns property at Nos. 37 and 47 Broad Street. Fraternally he is a member of Luther Lodge No. 380, I. O. O. F., in which he has passed all the chairs, and has twice represented the lodge in the grand lodge of the state. He is Trustee of the Odd Fellows' Home in Westchester County, this state. He is also a member of the Maennerchor, and was Second President of the association. As a business man he is conservative, and is a member of the Middletown Co-operative Store Company. The files which he manufactures are considered the best in the country. Both parents are members of the Congregational Church.

≈⇒◄|◙✸◙►|⊱≈

CHARLES H. SMITH, of Middletown, is a successful architect and civil engineer, and at present is serving in the latter capacity, the duties of which office he has discharged in a manner eminently satisfactory to the people. His office is located in the Trust Building, at No. 75 North Street, and his time is busily occupied in the management of his extensive business and professional interests.

The first representative of this branch of the Smith family in Orange County was our subject's grandfather, Melancton, a native of New York, and a farmer in Chenango County, whence he removed to the town of Wallkill. When advanced in years he came to Middletown and settled at No. 12 William Street, where he lived retired until his death, at the age of seventy-five. Our subject's father, George, was born in Oxford, Chenango County, but was reared in Orange County. Early in life he entered the employ of the Erie Road, and after a time became Roadmaster of the Eastern Division of the Erie. In 1887 he accepted a position as Roadmaster for the New York, Susquehanna & Western Railroad, which position he still holds, with headquarters at Middletown. His wife, Abbie J. Horton, was born in the town of Wallkill, and was the daughter of A. J. Horton, who for many years served as station agent and Postmaster at Howells.

The family of George and Abbie J. Smith consisted of seven children, of whom all but one are living. Charles H., who is next to the eldest, was born in Howells, this county, in 1861, and was reared principally in Paterson, N. J., where he resided from the age of six to sixteen. From that place he came to Middletown, where he has since resided. After graduating from Wallkill Academy, at the age of nineteen, he took up civil-engineering, and spent two years in practical work under Chief Engineer O. Chanute, of the Erie Road. He then entered Lehigh University, and for two years was a student in the department of civil-engineering. Later he was Assistant Engineer between Ridgewood and Rutherford, N. J., after which he was promoted to the position of Division Engineer on the Erie, his headquarters being at Elmira for two years. He was then transferred to a similar position on the Western Division, with headquarters at Hornellsville, his territory being between that city and Dunkirk, also the Bradford (Pa.) Branch. In that capacity he was employed for two and one-half years.

At Hornellsville, N. Y., in 1890, Mr. Smith married Miss Minnie A. Hollands, whose father, George Hollands, was a prominent business man of that place and at one time Sheriff of Steuben County. In 1890 Mr. Smith was appointed Assistant Chief Engineer of the New York, Ontario & Western Railway, with headquarters at Middletown. For three years he held that position, being under E. Canfield, Chief Engineer, and having charge of the division extending from Oswego to New York City, with all the branches. In 1893 he resigned in order to give his attention wholly to civil-engineering, and in the spring of the following year he opened an office in Middletown. About the same time he was appointed City Engineer by the Council, in which capacity he has since served.

A number of new streets in this city have been opened by Mr. Smith. He is Chief Engineer of the Middletown & Goshen Traction Company, of which he was one of the organizers, and in which he is a stockholder and Director. He laid out the Central Park Addition to the city, comprising six hundred acres, also the R. N. Boak tract of forty acres, Columbia Park, Richmond Hill and other portions of the city that are fast growing in popularity. He had the contract for the engineering of water works at various towns in the county, and is now making surveys, and is Chief Engineer, for the Middletown & Bloomingburg Electric Street Railroad, being one of the organizers and Directors of that company. Recently he completed an elegant residence for his family at No.

129 South Street, and in addition to this property he owns nine acres of land in the southern part of the city.

It has been Mr. Smith's custom to attend the annual meetings of the American Society of Civil Engineers, of which he is a member. He is connected with the Middletown Club, the Board of Trade, and is an honorary member of the Excelsior Hook and Ladder Company. In religious belief he is associated with the Second Presbyterian Church of Middletown. He is an enterprising business man, and employs four assistants in his office.

COL. CHARLES WILLIAM LARNED, Professor of Drawing in the United States Military Academy at West Point, was born in the city of New York, March 9, 1850, and is the son of William Larned, Additional Paymaster in the United States army, who died of disease contracted in the field in the performance of his duties during the War of the Rebellion. His great-grandfather, William Larned, was an officer of the Revolutionary War, and his progenitor, William Larned, came over to Charlestown, Mass., among the early Puritans, in 1632, and was one of the Selectmen of that town.

Colonel Larned entered the United States military as cadet July 1, 1866, and was graduated from that institution June 15, 1870. His graduating leave was spent in Europe during the Franco-Prussian War. His first assignment was to the Third United States Cavalry, but before reporting for duty he was transferred to the Seventh Cavalry, which regiment he joined at Ft. Hays, Kan., in October, 1870. He was temporarily assigned to "D" Troop, and commanded it during the march to Ft. Leavenworth, where he wintered. In March of the following year the regiment was selected for service in the South during the reconstruction period, and Lieutenant Larned moved with the headquarters to Louisville, Ky., where he remained with his troop until sent in command of a detachment of men to Livingston, Ky., for the purpose of assisting the United States

Marshal in his raids upon illicit distilleries during the winter and spring of 1873. In April of that year the regiment was ordered to Dakota to protect the survey of the Northern Pacific Road, and rendezvoused at Yankton, where, after being buried under the snow in a blizzard, it marched to Ft. Lincoln, and thence, under command of Gens. D. S. Stanley and G. A. Custer, it penetrated the then unknown region of the Yellowstone and Musselshell Rivers.

As topographical officer, Lieutenant Larned mapped the route of the expedition, and was present at the fight with Sitting Bull, at the mouth of the Big Horn River. During the winter of 1873-74, he was ordered to Washington on special duty in the office of the Secretary of War, and the following August was ordered to report to the Military Academy for duty as instructor in the department of drawing, under Prof. Robert Weir. In July, 1876, after receiving his promotion to a First Lieutenancy in the cavalry, he was, upon the retirement of Professor Weir, appointed to succeed him, and has continuously held the chair of Drawing up to the present, with the assimilated rank of Colonel since 1886.

Colonel Larned is a member of the Century, the Union League and Church Clubs of New York; he is also a member of the Federation of Fine Arts and the Architectural League of that city, and a member of the American Philological Association. He has been a frequent contributor to art and other periodicals.

DANIEL H. MERRITT, one of the prominent general farmers of this county, was born January 1, 1835, on the farm which he now occupies. Here he has passed his entire life, and has aided, by his perseverance and honesty, in making the community one of the best of the county. His father, Daniel, was also born on this farm, the year of his birth being 1799. The grandfather, Underhill Merritt, was a descendant of French ancestry, and was born in Westchester County, this state. Prior to the Revolutionary War, Humphrey, the grandfather of Underhill

JOSEPH BOARD.

Merritt, settled on the land now owned by our subject. He became the owner of a very large tract of land, and a portion of the property has been handed down from generation to generation, being retained in the family all these years.

On this place the father of Daniel H. died May 7, 1867. His wife, who bore the maiden name of Eliza Hait, was born in Ulster County in 1805, being a daughter of John and Jennie Hait, who were old residents of that county. Mrs. Merritt died on the old homestead in August, 1891, and her body was buried beside that of her husband in Cedar Hill Cemetery. Her children, four in number, were as follows: Daniel H., of this sketch; Hiram, who is engaged in the real-estate business in New York City; Mary J., who is the wife of Daniel T. McFarlan, of Yonkers, N. Y.; and Theodore, a druggist of Newburgh.

The educational advantages which the schools of the district afforded were given to our subject, and he also early acquired a thorough knowledge of farm work. As a result of the manner in which he was trained to agricultural pursuits, he is now enabled to superintend the operations of his farm in a most efficient manner. In addition to raising the usual amount of grain, he devotes some attention to breeding live stock, and has on his place a number of fine horses, cattle and swine. He has never desired office, but is content to use his influence in a quiet way, upholding the principles of the Republican party in a loyal manner. If the citizens of New York were all of this type, our state, which we love so dearly, would increase in prosperity tenfold.

JOSEPH BOARD, a prominent business man of Chester, was born in the town of Chester, November 9, 1842. He is the eldest child of Peter S. and Madeline (Conklin) Board, the former a native of Boardville, N. J., where he remained until twenty years of age, when he came to Chester and took up his abode with his uncle. Peter Board, who was a quiet, unassuming man, was engaged in agricultural pursuits until his death, in September, 1853, and was respected by all who knew him. He was a son of Gen. Charles Board, also born in Boardville, N. J., where he spent his entire life. The latter was prominent in New Jersey politics and represented his county several times in the Legislature. He was a son of Joseph Board, who was born at Bloomfield, N. J., and who spent his entire life there and at Boardville. With his brother he pre-empted the land on which our subject's father and grandfather were born. Joseph Board was a Captain in the Revolutionary War, and was a son of Cornelius Board, who emigrated from England to America in 1730. It is the impression that he was sent here by Lord Sterling to establish an iron manufactory. We quote the following testimony of James, son of Cornelius Board, in a controversy as to the boundary line between the Wawayanda and Cheesecock Patents:

"James Board, born in England. Came with my parents to America in 1730. My father was sent by Lord Sterling to discover copper mines, and purchased one hundred acres at what is now known as Sterling Pond, under the New Jersey grant of 1736. He afterwards made further location of one hundred and fifty acres. Later, in 1738, he built a forge. In 1740 he removed to Ringwood, and soon after the forge was started sold it to Colden & Ward."

Our subject, who has spent considerable time in tracing the genealogy of the Board family, thinks that Cornelius Board came from Bristol, England. Mrs. Board, the mother of our subject, was a native of the town of Warwick, and died in 1884.

Joseph Board, the subject of this sketch, received his primary education in Chester, under Prof. Edward Orton. At the age of twenty he entered Amherst College in Massachusetts, finishing the course in 1867. He then returned to Chester, and January 1, 1868, engaged in the feed and lumber business. In 1883 he added coal, and has since been successfully engaged in this trade. He is among the oldest established business men in the village.

Joseph Board was united in marriage, January 3, 1868, with Miss Josephine Bradbury Curry, a daughter of Benjamin and Hannah (Tebbetts)

Curry, natives of Sanbornton, N. H., where Mrs. Board was born. She died April 6, 1869. She was a prominent teacher in the Chester schools prior to her marriage, and her health was seriously impaired while engaged in this profession. November 2, 1870, Mr. Board was married to Hannah A. Curry, a sister of his former wife, who was also born in New Hampshire. This union was blessed by the birth of five children, one of whom, Helen, died at the age of two and a-half years. Those living are: Joseph Orton, who was so named by his father to perpetuate the name in the family; Anna Tebbetts, Ben Curry and Josephine Clough, all of whom yet reside at home. Mr. Board is a member of the Presbyterian Church and Mrs. Board of the Episcopal Church. Socially he is a member of the D. K. E., a college society, and of the Phi Beta Kappa Society.

The Board family was of Democratic extraction, but our subject associated himself with the Republican party when a young man, and cast his first presidential vote for Abraham Lincoln, in 1864. He has ever since affiliated with that party and has been active in its councils. In 1877 he was elected Excise Commissioner, and in 1878 he was elected Supervisor of this town, creditably filling the position for three years. In 1883 he was again chosen for this position and served for two years. He has served on the Board of Education for the past twenty years, and is at present the President of that body. In 1892 he served as managing superintendent of the laying of the pipes for the Chester Water Works. At present he is the efficient clerk of the Village Board of Chester.

Joseph Board is well and favorably known throughout the county and has several times been chosen as administrator of estates. In 1869 he was commissioned to deliver two new passenger cars on the Union Pacific Road, and he extended his tour to California, spending some two months in the Golden State. In 1883 he made an extensive trip through the Southwest, visiting Texas, Arizona and several of the Southern and Western States. In 1887 he made a trip to England, Ireland, Scotland, Belgium, France, Italy, Germany, Austria and Switzerland, spending some four months in his foreign travels, and in the near future he contemplates another trip to the Old Country. In 1884 he was nominated by his party for the Assembly, and although the county is largely Democratic, he came within sixty-seven votes of election.

CHARLES W. DOELL, of Middletown, entered the employ of the New York, Ontario & Western Railway Company April 30, 1886, as a brakeman, later became a flagman, and October 12, 1889, was promoted to the position of conductor, which he has since held. He was born in the Tenth Ward, New York City, April 7, 1860. The family of which he was a member originated in Germany, and his paternal grandfather, Charles A. Doell, was born in Minden, from which place he emigrated to America and settled in New York City. He was a brewer of Weiss beer, and was the first to introduce it into New York. His death occurred when he was eighty-two.

The father of our subject, whose name was also Charles, was born in New York City, and was a civil engineer by occupation, being employed principally by the Government, and making surveys throughout almost the entire country. His last work was in Duluth, Minn., where he surveyed a township for three hundred families. Later he took passage on the steamship "Henry Ames," bound for New Orleans for a coast survey, but while on board ship he died at Cairo, Ill. This was in 1873, and he was forty-three years of age. During the War of the Rebellion he had served for three years and six months as Corporal in Company A, Seventy-third New York Infantry, Excelsior Brigade, under Gen. D. E. Sickles. His wife, Mary, was born in Germany, and died in Port Jervis in 1876. She was a daughter of Jacob Hauber, who for a time was employed as horseman in the king's stables in his native land, and who died on board ship as the family were en route to America.

There were five children in the family of Charles

and Mary (Hauber) Doell, of whom three are living, viz.: Charles; George, a railroad man, residing in Paterson, N. J.; and James, who is employed in the saw works at Middletown. At the age of nine years our subject accompanied the family from New York City to Providence, R. I., and one year later he removed with them to Port Jervis. There he learned the trade of glove-cutting and kid-leather dressing. In 1886 he came to Middletown and entered the employ of the Ontario & Western as brakeman between Norwich and Weehawken, later worked as flagman between Middletown and Weehawken, and in 1889 was made conductor, his run being between Middletown and Weehawken on the express freight.

In Port Jervis Mr. Doell married Miss Mary Green, who was born in Mongaup, Sullivan County, N. Y., her father, Gabriel Green, having been a farmer there. One child, Mary, blesses their union. Since January, 1885, Mr. Doell has been a member of Middletown Lodge No. 40, Order of Railway Trainmen, and has been a delegate to the biennial conventions of the order at St. Paul, Minn., in 1889; Galesburg, Ill., in 1891; Boston, in 1893; and Galesburg, Ill., in 1895. For five years he was Secretary of his lodge, served as Master one year, and is now serving his second year as Financier. The lodge has increased in numbers since he united with it, and now has ninety-three members. In national politics he is a Democrat.

FRANK M. STRATTON. To those who, appreciating the vast possibilities offered by the real-estate business, embark therein, guiding their transactions with caution, discrimination and sagacity, success almost invariably comes. Such has been the fortunate experience of Mr. Stratton, who is not only one of the youngest real-estate men of Middletown, but one of the shrewdest and most enterprising as well.

For the history of the Stratton family, the reader is referred to the sketch of our subject's father, William D. Stratton, which appears else-

where in this volume. Frank M. was born in Thompsonville, Sullivan County, March 1, 1872, and was reared in his native place, receiving his rudimentary education there. He prepared for college at Wallkill Academy, and in 1891 entered Columbia College, where he remained one year, leaving to engage in business for himself. His first venture was the West View tract of land, situated in New Jersey, eight miles from New York City, and which his father had purchased and commenced to improve. In 1892 he took charge of the property, of which he took possession the following year. It consists of eighty-two acres, subdivided into one thousand lots, and situated on the Hackensack River, and on the West Shore and the Susquehanna & Western Railroads. The entire property is platted into residence lots, with the exception of twelve acres of river frontage, to be utilized for manufacturing purposes. The tract adjoins Ridgefield Park, and is within the limits of the same.

In 1893 Mr. Stratton purchased the River Edge tract of forty acres, of which one-half has been platted and is rapidly building up. This property is situated sixteen miles out of New York City, on the New Jersey & New York Railroad, a branch of the Erie, and also on the Hackensack River. In 1894 Mr. Stratton bought the Cherry Hill property of forty acres, which he intends to develop soon. He has an office in New York City, at No. 1 Park Row, and at Middletown in the Casino Theatre Building. He is interested in the foundry property on Kings Street, Middletown, which has been platted into lots, and also in the Eagle Hose Company's building, a brick business block in the center of the city.

The firm of Stratton & Corey, in December, 1894, bought fifty-eight acres, comprising the old Rockafellow Farm, which they have laid out into a beautiful addition at an expense of $3,000. This is proving one of the most successful of their ventures. Aside from his other interests, Mr. Stratton is a stockholder in the Casino Theatre Building and Secretary of the company that owns it. He is also interested in the Orange County Telephone Company, of which he is a Director. Since August, 1888, he has made his home in

Middletown, where he owns a beautiful residence on the corner of Wisner and Grand Avenues. He was married in this city, his wife being Miss Delle Wilkes, daughter of Mrs. Theodore Wilkes, of Middletown. Politically he affiliates with the Democratic party. He is a member of the Board of Trade, and socially is connected with the Middletown Club.

ANIEL FINN, a leading and successful attorney of Middletown, traces his ancestry back to his great-great-grandfather, Dr. Finn, who came from Finland, leaving home when a mere lad. After landing in New York City, he went to Goshen, where he was educated, and where he began the study of medicine. He commenced to practice his profession near Little Britain, at a time when this section of the country was known as Ulster County. In 1750 one of his descendants was Surrogate of Orange County, and Assemblyman of this district. The great-grandfather was a Baptist minister, and preached in New Jersey and Pennsylvania. For some time before the massacre he was an inmate of the old fort of Wyoming, and while there his vigilance kept the Indians out and none of their stratagems succeeded, but after he left the fort the fearful massacre occurred.

Daniel Finn, the grandfather of our subject, was a native of Beaver County, Pa., and served in the War of 1812. Shortly after the war he settled in Warwick, where he worked at his trade of blacksmith, and subsequently engaged in farming until old age compelled him to retire, when he moved to Middletown, and died at the residence of his son-in-law, Rev. Dr. Seward. His wife, Alice Armstrong, was born near Florida, Orange County, and her ancestors came from England in the same vessel with the Clintons.

William Finn, the father of our subject, was a native of Orange County, and was born near Warwick. By occupation he was a farmer, and followed that vocation almost his entire life, but

shortly before his death removed to Vineland, N. J., where he died at the age of sixty-six years. He was an Elder in the Presbyterian Church at Florida, as was also his father before him. His wife, Frances Halsey, was born in Morris County, N. J., and was a daughter of Alexander Halsey, who was also a native of that state. The Halseys were originally from Long Island. Her mother, formerly a Miss Hedge, was a lineal descendant of Henry Hudson. She died in 1867. In the parental family were four children, three of whom are now living.

Daniel Finn, the subject of this sketch, was the eldest in the family, his birth occurring in Westfield, Chautauqua County, N. Y., November 9, 1843, and he is the only one of the family in Orange County bearing the name of Finn. He was reared on a farm near Florida, and attended Seward Institute, where he prepared for college. After teaching school for a time, he entered Union College, where he spent part of one year, and then entered Hamilton College, in the third term of the freshman class. In 1868 he graduated with the degree of A. B., and during his last year, in addition to the regular course, took a course in the Hamilton Law School. On graduating, he studied in the law office of McQuoid, at Middletown, and in the office of Osborn & Swayne, of Toledo, Ohio. He was admitted to the New York Bar in the fall of 1870, and in the spring of 1871 opened an office in Middletown, where the Merchants' Bank is now located, and there remained until 1873, at which time the firm of Hulse, Little & Finn was formed. This lasted two years, and was then succeeded by the firm of Hulse & Finn, which one year later was dissolved, since which time Mr. Finn has conducted his practice alone. Since 1873 he has been in his present location, in what is now known as the Lipfeld Building, but which was formerly known as the Postoffice Building.

Since commencing practice, Mr. Finn has been a very active man. While he conducts a general practice, his business is mostly of a chancery nature. In the settlement of estates, and in litigation that frequently follows, he has had wide experience. Since its organization he has been at-

LEANDER BRINK.

torney for the Merchants' Bank, and is also attorney for the Cosmopolitan Theatre Company, in both of which he is a stockholder. Socially he is a member of Clinton Lodge, F. & A. M.; Midland Chapter, R. A. M.; and Delaware Commandery at Port Jervis. While in college he became a member of the Delta Kappa Epsilon Society. He is a member of the First Presbyterian Church of Middletown, in which he is Trustee. In politics he is a Republican, but has never held a civic office.

Mr. Finn married Miss Clara S. Slauson, of Wawayanda, and a sister of N. W. Slauson. They have one child, Frank Halsey, a graduate of the Class of '94, of Middletown Academy, and who is now attending Hamilton College, a member of the Class of '98.

In the quarter of a century Mr. Finn has practiced his profession in Middletown, success has crowned his efforts in almost every direction. As an attorney he ranks high, and as a counselor he is reliable. By consanguinity he is related to the Sewards, and is well posted in their family history.

LEANDER BRINK. The history of the hardware business of which Mr. Brink is proprietor extends back to the year 1842, when I. O. Beattie opened a store in Middletown. He was succeeded by the firm of King & DeWitt, after which the establishment was owned successively by King, DeWitt & King, A. C. King & Scott, and Sayer & Scott. When Mr. Sayer entered the Union army during the Civil War, the title was changed to Scott Brothers, but soon one of the latter became a soldier and went to the front, where he was killed during the engagement in the Wilderness.

Afterward the business was carried on by Scott & Vail and Vail & Brink until 1879, when the firm name was changed to Vail, Brink & Clark, and in 1885 the present title of Brink & Clark was adopted. In spite of these frequent changes of name, the business has been conducted on practically the same site since it was founded,

April 1, 1845. The present building was erected in 1865, and the extension to King Street added in 1877. The structure has a frontage on North Street, with dimensions of 24x120, and on King Street 18x60. Each of the four floors is occupied, the first floor containing the heavy goods, the second or main floor being utilized for the retail trade, while on the third floor tinware and stoves are manufactured. On the fourth floor are stored goods not in present demand. The stock is unusually large, and comprises every variety of heavy and shelf hardware, furnaces and heating apparatus of all kinds. Employment is furnished to five clerks and four workmen in the factory.

The subject of this notice, to whom the success of the enterprise is largely due, is one of Middletown's most public-spirited citizens. He was born in the town of Shawangunk, Ulster County, January 30, 1833, and is a son of James Brink, whose birth occurred in the town of Wallkill, Orange County, in 1804. The grandfather, Cornelius, was born on Long Island, and settled in Wallkill, becoming a prominent farmer there. He served in the American army during the War of 1812. Until his death, which occurred at eighty-four years, he had been for some years an Elder in the Dutch Reformed Church in Bloomingburg. The great-grandfather, Cornelius, Sr., was a life-long resident of Long Island. The family is of Dutch lineage and of sturdy old Knickerbocker stock.

After his marriage to Jane Horton, in 1827, the father of our subject settled in Shawangunk, Ulster County, where for a time he engaged in farming. In 1835 he removed to Schuyler County, and settled near the head of Seneca Lake, at the present city of Watkins. The journey thither was made with teams and wagons, his family accompanying him. That part of the state was then considered the far West, and he was entitled to the title of pioneer. In 1852 he moved to Genoa, Cayuga County, where he successfully conducted farm pursuits. There his death occurred June 1, 1895, at the age of ninety years, seven months and one day. He was a stockholder in the Tompkins National Bank, and in politics ad-

hered to Jacksonian principles. A man of remarkable character, tireless energy, unflinching
integrity and blameless life, he was loved, not
alone by his family, but by all with whom he had
business or social relations.

The mother of our subject was born in the
town of Wallkill, where her father, Silas D. Horton, engaged in farming until his death at the
age of more than fourscore years; she died in
1840, aged twenty-nine. Afterward the father
married Miss Delilah Martin, a native of Tompkins County, and unto them were born six children, all still living. Of the first marriage, four
children were born, all living, as follows: Maria,
Mrs. Williams, of Burdett, N. Y.; Leander; Mrs.
Eliza Hollister, of Cayuga County; and Harriet,
who is at home. At the funeral of the father,
three sons and three sons-in-law were the pall-
bearers.

When two years old our subject was taken by
his parents to Schuyler County, and his boyhood
days were passed on a farm near Watkins. When
five years of age he was brought to Orange County on a visit. In 1854 he came to Middletown
and began as clerk for his uncle, Hiram Brink, a
furniture dealer, with whom he remained as clerk
until October, 1857. He was then admitted as
partner, the firm name becoming H. & L. Brink.
In 1864 he went to Saginaw, Mich., and engaged
in the manufacture of salt, making it by the Syracuse process. The capacity of the works was
one hundred and fifty thousand barrels a year.
A joint-stock company was formed, known as
the Orange County Salt Company, and of it he
was made Superintendent. He continued the
operation of the works until 1867, when he returned to Middletown. However, he retained
his interest in the salt works for seven years, selling out in 1876.

When business affairs are in a condition to permit a vacation, Mr. Brink is accustomed to take
a relaxation from work. He has visited the
Rocky Mountains, and enjoyed the sport of hunt-
ing the animals of that region. In 1884 he took
a trip to Europe, accompanied by his wife. Leaving June 11 of that year, they spent three months
visiting England, Ireland, Scotland, France,

Switzerland and Germany, and thoroughly enjoyed this glimpse of European customs and
towns. Interested in mines, he owns a number
of these in Colorado, and is interested in manufacturing enterprises in Nebraska. While a Republican in politics, he inclines toward Prohibition principles and is a man of strong temperance
sentiment. He has made a remarkable success
both of the wholesale and retail departments of
his business, and at the fairs his exhibitions invariably receive first premium.

At Middletown, in 1857, Mr. Brink married
Miss Mary Horton, daughter of Hiram Horton, a
farmer of the town of Wallkill. They reside at
No. 39 South Street, and their younger child,
Jennie, a graduate of Ursuline Convent, is now
with them. Their son, Charles H., is engaged
in the plumbing business in this city. Mrs. Brink
is a member of the Second Presbyterian Church,
and interested in all its good works. The family
rank high socially and are highly esteemed wherever known.

WILLIAM E. McWILLIAMS, Assessor of
Middletown, is a representative of the
young and enterprising business men of
the place, and was born in the town of Wallkill,
near Scotchtown, in 1861. His great-grandfather,
John McWilliams, was a native of Scotland, and
was one of three brothers who came from that
country to America. He settled in the town of
Wallkill, and the village of Scotchtown was so
named on account of a Scotch settlement at that
place. Here Stewart McWilliams, the grandfather, and J. Spencer McWilliams, the father, of
our subject, were born. The latter is one of the
most extensive drovers and stock-dealers in the
vicinity, and now resides on Wickham Avenue,
Middletown. He married Susan Bailey Coleman,
who was born near Scotchtown, and whose father,
William N. Coleman, was born at Amity, Orange
County. Her great-great-grandfather, Nathaniel
Finch, was an Adjutant in the Minisink Massacre under Colonel Tusten, and perished with the
rest of his comrades. His name is inscribed on

the monument at Goshen. Her mother, Margaret Bailey, was a daughter of Oliver Bailey, who was a son of Capt. Daniel Bailey, of Revolutionary fame. The latter was born in Jamaica, L. I., in 1757, and at the age of nineteen enlisted in Captain Wright's company and Col. John Lasher's battalion, a regiment made up of men from Long Island and New York. After his first enlistment he came to Orange County, where he again enlisted, becoming a member of Colonel Allison's regiment. His entire service was for three years. On coming to this county, Captain Bailey settled west of the city limits of Middletown, where he built a log cabin and began the improvement of a farm. In 1783 he bought the farm at Phillipsburg now owned by Edwin Mills. His death occurred in Middletown, May 16, 1841. He was a man of splendid physique, tall and robust, and retained his mental and physical vigor to the last. In religious belief he was a Presbyterian, and served as an Elder in the church at Goshen. His wife, Mary Tuthill, was a daughter of Nathaniel Tuthill, and traced her ancestry back to John Tuthill, who came to this country in the good ship "Swallow" some time between 1633 and 1638, and settled in New Haven, but later removed to Southold, L. I. Nathaniel Tuthill was one of the minutemen of Orange County, and participated in the battle of Ft. Montgomery.

When our subject was but nine years of age his parents removed to Middletown, and he here completed his education in the Middletown Academy. In 1879, at the age of seventeen, he engaged in the mercantile business at No. 7 West Main Street, and continued the same for about eleven years. He then engaged in the insurance and real-estate business, in company with John McWilliams, under the firm name of J. & W. E. McWilliams. They were located at No. 25 North Street, where the business was successfully continued until 1893, when our subject sold his interest, since which time he has been engaged individually in buying and selling real estate. He is Secretary of the Central Building Association, of which he was one of the incorporators.

Mr. McWilliams was married in Bloomingburg

to Miss Carrie T. Shearer, who is a native of that village, and a daughter of the late William T. Shearer, who was there engaged in farming. She is a great-great-great-granddaughter of William Bull and Sarah Wells, so largely connected in Orange County. Mr. McWilliams and his wife have two children, Edgar Coleman and Lester Shearer. In politics Mr. McWilliams is a Republican, and in 1895 was elected City Assessor on that party ticket. He is a member of the Second Presbyterian Church, and has served that body as a member of its Board of Trustees. In business affairs he is active, with an eye single to the best interests of his adopted city, and is a member of the Board of Trade of Middletown.

⁂

ARCHIBALD C. REYNOLDS, chief clerk in the transportation department of the New York, Ontario & Western Railway, was born in Ellenville, Ulster County, N. Y., March 26, 1867, and is a son of S. H. and Mary (Childs) Reynolds, both natives of Neversink, Sullivan County, N. Y. He traces his ancestry back to his geat-grandfather, Henry Reynolds, who lived near Vail's Gate, and as a minuteman served under Gen. Anthony Wayne at the storming of Stony Point, July 16, 1779. At one time he was attacked by Tories and Indians, under the leadership of Benjamin Kelly, who murderously assaulted him and left him hanging in his fireplace, as they supposed dead, but he was rescued after their departure by his daughter. A few years after the war he located in Sullivan County, where he reared his family, and where his son Hophni, the grandfather of our subject, was born. The latter was a mechanic and miller by occupation, and lived and died in Sullivan County.

S. H. Reynolds, the father of our subject, was a millwright and machinist by trade. For some years he was engaged in building mills and tanneries in Sullivan and Ulster Counties, N. Y., and in Pennsylvania. From 1870 to 1884 he resided at Tunkhannock, Pa., and from there removed to Middletown, where he now resides, and where he is a general inspector of motive power for the New York, Ontario & Western Railway. His wife, Mary Childs, is a daughter of John G. Childs, an attorney and ex-Sheriff of Sullivan County.

The subject of this sketch is the only surviving child of the parental family. He attended the common and high schools at Tunkhannock, Pa., until 1883, when he went to Walton, N. Y., and spent one year in the academy at that place. In July, 1884, he came to Middletown, and at once secured a clerkship in the office of the purchasing agent and paymaster of the New York, Ontario & Western Railway, where he remained until May, 1887, when he was transferred to New York, and later became secretary to the General Manager. He remained in that office until December 1, 1893, when he was again transferred and made chief clerk in the transportation department of the same road.

Fraternally Mr. Reynolds is a member of Hoffman Lodge, F. & A. M.; Midland Chapter, R. A. M.; Union Consistory at Middletown; and Mecca Temple, N. M. S., at New York. In politics he is a Democrat. While yet a young man, he has had nearly twelve years' experience in the railroad business, and in every position occupied he has served with fidelity, and has received the approval of his superior officers. No man on the line of the New York, Ontario & Western Railway is more popular than the subject of this sketch.

R O. LEWIS, mason and contractor at Middletown, was one of the youngest soldiers in the late Civil War. He was born in Westchester County, N. Y., in December, 1848, and is eighth in the family of thirteen children born to William I. and Eliza (Mangum) Lewis. His father was also a native of Westchester County, and there resided until 1866, when he located at Port Jervis, where he followed his trade of contractor and builder until his death, at the age of sixty-eight. His wife, Eliza Mangum, was also a native of Westchester County, and was a daughter of William Mangum, who for many years was engaged in the real-estate and

hotel business in that county. Of their thirteen children, eight are yet living. One son, Gilbert M., was a member of the Seventieth New York Infantry, which was a part of Gen. Dan Sickle's brigade. He was transferred to the First New York Mounted Rifles, and served until the close of the war, a period of four and a-half years. In one of the engagements in the Wilderness campaign he was shot in the arm. He was mustered out as Quartermaster-Sergeant, and now lives in Scranton, Pa., where he is engaged in farming.

The subject of this sketch remained in Westchester County until twelve years of age, and then attended school at Monticello. In June, 1864, he enlisted as a private in Company G, First New York Light Artillery, and was mustered in at New York City. He was at once sent to his battery at City Point, opposite Petersburg, Va., and participated in the siege of Petersburg, and also took part in all the movements around Richmond, resulting in its capture. He served until October, 1865, and was then mustered out at Elmira, N. Y.

On receiving his discharge, Mr. Lewis went to Sullivan County, where he remained until 1866, and then came to Port Jervis, but remained there only a short time, going thence to New York City, where he worked under instruction as a mason for three years. He then engaged in contracting and building in New York City, where he remained until 1875, and then returned to Port Jervis, where he contracted as a mason and builder until 1885. Since that time he has made his home in Middletown, where he has erected scores of buildings, among which is the Opera House. In addition to contracting and building, he has engaged to some extent in buying and selling real estate. He is one of the originators of the Cosmopolitan Theatre Company, of which he was a Director, but has since sold out.

While a resident of Port Jervis, Mr. Lewis married Miss Kate Stearns, a native of that place, and a daughter of Josiah Stearns, a farmer, who has resided at Port Jervis fifty-two years. Four children have been born unto them: Lena, Eva, Stella and Roberta.

DWIGHT W. BERRY.

Fraternally Mr. Lewis is a member of the Independent Order of Odd Fellows, of the Knights of Pythias, and is a charter member of Capt. William A. Jackson Post, G. A. R. He also served five years in the Excelsior Hook and Ladder Company of Middletown. All work entrusted to him is completed with the utmost care. As a citizen he is enterprising and progressive, and is willing to do all in his power in building up and maintaining the reputation of his adopted city.

DWIGHT W. BERRY. The first creamery established in Middletown was started in April, 1892, by Mr. Berry, whose thorough familiarity with every detail of the business enabled him to manage this enterprise successfully. The building is situated on Cottage Street, near Wickham Avenue, and the plant has a capacity of four thousand quarts per day, transportation being rendered easy through a switch of the New York, Ontario, & Western Railroad. In addition to this concern, he owns a creamery at Circleville, with the same capacity as this. He makes large shipments of milk and cream, the latter, however, being his specialty. In the creamery there are fine coolers, and an icehouse with a capacity of six hundred tons, every effort being made to secure purity and sweetness on the part of the products. For more than twenty-five years he has shipped cream to the well known J. M. Horton Ice-cream Company, of New York City, and still continues to furnish their regular supply.

In Pharsalia, Chenango County, N. Y., Mr. Berry was born, June 5, 1839. His father, Richard Wayne, was born in Stonington, Conn., and was a son of Richard W. Berry, Sr., a native of Connecticut, but a pioneer of Chenango County, N. Y. The father, who was a farmer of Chenango County, was a man of remarkable industry and perseverance, and possessed considerable influence in his community. For two terms he was Superintendent of the Poor, and was the sole Building Committee for the Chenango County

Poor House. He also served as Supervisor. In politics he was a Democrat until the candidacy of General Fremont for President, after which he voted with the Republicans. In religion he was a Universalist. While hauling timber one day, he was accidentally killed. His wife, Lucy, was a daughter of Luther Osgood, a farmer of Chenango, where she was born, and where she remained until death.

Of four children now living, our subject is the eldest. His sisters are: Mary D., of Norwich, and Lucy O., wife of George D. Brown, of Scranton, Pa. His brother, Hon. Silas W. Berry, now of Norwich, N. Y., has held many important public positions, having been Supervisor, Superintendent of the Poor of Chenango County two terms, Member of the Legislature two terms, and Deputy Internal Revenue Collector of his district. He is a man of considerable influence, and a local leader in the Republican party. Our subject was reared on the home farm, and in youth received a good education in Oxford Academy, where he completed the course of instruction. He taught school for five successive winters, the first three terms being in Chenango County. After coming to Orange County, he taught one term in Wallkill and another in Minisink.

The year 1862 witnessed the arrival of Mr. Berry in this county, where for a short time he was employed in Alanson Slaughter's co-operative creamery. Later, for three years, he was in charge of Brown & Bailey's creamery at Glenwood, N. J., after which he purchased a creamery three miles north of Middletown, known as the Rockville Creamery, carrying it on for twenty-five years. His next purchase was the Circleville Creamery, which he still operates. He was also a partner with Pound & Tayntor at New Berlin, Chenango County, establishing a creamery there, and conducting it for three years, after which the connection was dissolved. For three years he owned and operated the Holmesville Creamery, and for about the same length of time he carried on a creamery at Morrisville, Madison County, N. Y. In April, 1892, he established the creamery at Middletown, which he has since conducted in a most efficient manner.

In this city Mr. Berry married Miss Mary S. Boyd, who was born in Rockland County, being a daughter of Rev. John N. Boyd, a Presbyterian clergyman of this part of the state. Mr. Berry has taken a commendable interest in questions affecting the public welfare. For one term he represented the First Ward on the Board of Aldermen. He was the first member of the first Board of Water Commissioners elected under the new city charter, and served the full term of five years, during which time the Highland Lake reservoir was built. His popularity was attested by his election, on the Republican ticket, by a majority of fifty-seven in a ward that usually gave one hundred Democratic majority, to represent the First Ward on the Board of Supervisors. In the Milk Exchange Limited he held the office of Director for ten years. No one takes a deeper interest in the progress of the city than does he, and certainly no one labors more to secure its advancement. His prominence has led to his election as a member of the County Republican Committee, and he has also served as delegate to county, senatorial and congressional conventions.

<<++++++++++++++✵++++++++++++++>>

CORNELIUS CASKEY was born in the town of Deerpark, on the banks of the Delaware River, August 11, 1819. His father, Martin Caskey, was born in the old Buckley House of Port Jervis, February 11, 1783, and was a son of Samuel and Sarah (Decker) Caskey, who located there before the Revolution. Martin Caskey was married, December 30, 1808, to Jane Meaddagh, daughter of Henry C. Meaddagh, who cleared the flats on the Pennsylvania side below where Matamoras now stands, and ran the ferry. He lived there before the War for Independence. Martin Caskey died February 2, 1839. He owned all the property along the Delaware River now included in Germantown, and was a lumberman and raftsman, piloting the rafts down the river to the Philadelphia market.

Cornelius Caskey began this work as a boy, and at the age of fourteen became a steersman, steering a raft the third time he went down the river. During his first years' work at that business he made five trips and has made as high as thirteen trips in a season, receiving from $40 to $55 per trip, and each trip took from two and a-half to seven days. During all the time he was on the river he never had but one mishap; his third raft, however, ran into the rocks at Trenton Falls, where he did not know the stream very well, and was broken into pieces. The Delaware contains a number of dangerous rapids, but he was careful and painstaking, and therefore had but one accident. On one occasion he took a company of tourists from Port Jervis to Philadelphia on a flatboat. When the Erie Railroad bridge, two miles above Port Jervis, was carried off by the ice, he was called upon to take a rope across the river, and just a few days before this he and his son were engaged in ferrying passengers across the river at Matamoras. When the bridge was destroyed the Supervisor, E. J. Thomas, sent for Mr. Caskey, told him to get what supplies he needed and begin the work of repairing the bridge, which he did on the 19th of March, and on the 27th the cars were able to cross. The railroad company had ordered out two thousand men, and they spent two days in doing nothing, but Mr. Caskey dispatched the work quickly and faithfully. He and his son moved the stone of the old abutments of the old bridge on flatboats to the position for the new bridge. He has been connected with nearly every piece of work on the river and knows every turn and bend in the stream.

In 1868, when an engine exploded at bridge No. 1, and the engineer was thrown into the canal, the company had several men out searching for the body for hours, but they were not successful, and called upon Mr. Caskey, who found the body in a few minutes. On another occasion when a car loaded with cheese ran off of bridge No. 2 into the river, he succeeded in recovering within a short time seven of the cheeses, and the next day a number of additional ones. No one is more familiar with the Delaware, and several times he has crossed the stream when no one else would attempt it. He has almost made the fastest time with rafts that has ever been made on the river, and in his work was usually assisted by his son, who was also an expert in such work. He had many narrow escapes, but his thorough knowledge of every rock and bend in the river enabled him to always reach home in safety.

Mr. Caskey was married, June 5, 1841, to Catherine J. Stearns, who died December 8, 1886. Their children were as follows: Margaret, wife of Sanford Clawson, of Port Jervis; Joel, who died in infancy; Elizabeth, wife of John Osterhout; Naomi, who was the wife of John McAllister, and died May 1, 1882; Asenath, wife of Joseph Westbrook, of New Jersey; Martha Alice, wife of Ford Ackerson, of New Jersey; Ada Hortense, widow of Hon. Charles St. John; Urilla E., wife of Benjamin Carpenter, of Jersey City; and Samuel F., who married Annie Westbrook, of Port Jervis. Mr. Caskey is a Democrat in politics. Some fifteen years ago he retired from the river and has since lived upon his farm in the neighborhood where his entire life has been passed, and where he is an honored and respected citizen.

JOHN WIGGINS, Justice of the Peace at Middletown, was born in Mt. Hope, N. J., September 22, 1826. His father, William H. Wiggins, was born in the town of Mt. Hope, Orange County, and for some years was engaged as a clerk in Newburgh, and subsequently as a clerk for Mr. Phillips, at Phillipsburg. He then had charge of the Mount Hope Iron Mines, and later removed to Ramapo, N. Y., and was appointed superintendent of the large manufacturing establishment of William Parsons, where he remained until his death in 1833, at the age of thirty-eight years. His father, William Wiggins, the grandfather of our subject, was a farmer in the town of Mt. Hope.

William H. Wiggins married Catherine E. Lewis, a native of Wales, and a daughter of Richard Lewis, who first located in Goshen on a farm, whence he removed to Sullivan County, and later to Chenango County, where he was quite successful in his business affairs. Two

years after the death of her first husband, Mrs. Catherine E. Wiggins married George F. Seybolt, who was a soldier in the War of 1812. Three children were born of her first marriage, our subject being the only one that grew to maturity.

After the death of his father, our subject moved with his mother to the town of Mt. Hope, where he grew to manhood, receiving his education in the common schools in the winter months, and assisting in the farm work the remainder of the year. On attaining his majority he became possessor of the home farm, to which he added from time to time, until he was the owner of three hundred and forty acres. While carrying on the farm, he was also for a time engaged in lead mining in the Shawangunk Mountains, on a portion of his own farm, one mine being known as the "Empire" and the other as the "Washington." In his mining operations he was quite successful, and continued farming and mining until 1887, when he removed to Middletown. The farm was between Otisville and Port Jervis, and while residing there he was Justice of the Peace of his town for a period of sixteen years. Shortly after locating in Middletown he was elected Justice of the Peace, was re-elected in 1892, and is still serving in that capacity, his office being at No. 11 North Street.

On the 7th of February, 1850, Mr. Wiggins was united in marriage with Miss Antoinette Mullock, a daughter of Joshua Mullock, who was for many years a Justice of the Peace and Supervisor of the town of Mt. Hope, where he was engaged in farming. He also served in the War of 1812. Mrs. Wiggins died February 7, 1875, leaving seven children: Willis H., a railroad attorney and ex-Representative in the Ohio Legislature, now residing at Chillicothe, Ohio; Erwin A., Assistant Traveling Auditor of the Erie Railroad; John L., an attorney, and now Corporation Counsel for the city of Middletown; Catherine, Mrs. F. W. Pyatt, of Charles City, Iowa; George M., in the cigar business at Binghamton, N. Y.; Lillian A., a teacher in the Highland Avenue School, residing at home; and Ella A., also at home.

Fraternally Mr. Wiggins is a member of Hoff-man Lodge, F. & A. M., and religiously is a member of the First Presbyterian Church in Middletown. In politics he was originally a Whig, and since the organization of the Republican party has been an earnest and enthusiastic advocate of its principles. As a Justice of the Peace, he brings to bear a strong judicial mind and the exercise of good common-sense. His decisions are seldom, if ever, set aside by the higher courts. As a citizen he is enterprising, and has ever at heart the best interests of his adopted city. His popularity is attested by his repeated election to office.

STEPHEN ST. JOHN, an old and honored resident of this village, departed this life at his home August 30, 1870, at the age of eighty-two years. He was born at Norwalk, Conn., November 16, 1788, and when a lad of fourteen years left home and made his way to New York City, where he apprenticed himself to learn the shoemaker's trade. He afterward came to the town of Deerpark, before Port Jervis was ever dreamed of, and here he opened a small store.

Mr. St. John remained at the above location until 1808, when he formed a partnership with a Mr. Holly and built a tannery at a point between Middletown and Mt. Hope, where they were soon in command of a good business. He was drafted into the War of 1812 about this time, and in order to enter the service postponed his marriage, which was to have taken place very soon, until October 16, 1816. The lady on this occasion was Miss Abigail Horton, of Mt. Hope, who departed this life just four months prior to his death.

At the close of the war the country lying about Port Jervis contained but few Dutch settlers, but as it was a good business point, it soon grew to large numbers. Our subject came hither about that time with Benjamin Dodge and, pur-chasing land, erected thereon a store, which he operated. He also bought what was known as the Stone House Farm, the residence standing on which was originally built as a fort during the War of the Revolution.

Meantime our subject removed his store to Mt. Hope, a distance of twelve miles, although his family still continued to reside on the Stone House Farm, he walking home every Saturday evening in order to spend Sunday there. In 1828 the building of the Delaware & Hudson Canal was begun, a project which had long been talked of. It was destined to pass through Mr. St. John's farm, and it was not long before the engineers, Mauruce Wurts, Philip Hone and John B. Jervis, had obtained his consent. This now flourishing village was named in honor of the latter, who was the engineer, and as soon as the canal was completed the settlers began to flock in, as it was an important point on the route and was destined to become an enterprising city.

In the year 1828 Mr. St. John was appointed Collector of Port Jervis, holding the responsible office for a period of forty-two years, or until his decease. In 1825 the firm of St. John & Dodge, in addition to their general merchandise business, began dealing extensively in pine lands. They erected large mills, and until 1840 turned out annually large quantities of pine and hemlock timber, which was rafted to points down the Delaware River. Soon after the canal was completed they erected a storehouse on its western bank, and "Dodge, St. John & Co." may still be read upon its sides.

Our subject continued in active business until 1839, when he was succeeded by his son Charles, an enterprising and energetic young man. In 1846 the Erie Railroad survey showed it to pass through a portion of his farm, and later he sold sixty acres to the company at $100 per acre, which at that time was considered a remarkable price. After retiring from the store Mr. St. John devoted himself to looking after the financial part of the business until his death, in 1870. October 16, 1866, occurred his golden wedding, which was the first ever held in Port Jervis. His ancestors were Quakers, and although he did not

A. W. CUDDEBACK.

1420

belong to that sect, his religious views strongly inclined that way. He was a member of the Reformed Church. He was a Mason of fifty years' standing and took an active part in the workings of that order. His home was always open to the deserving, and more than one young man owes his success in life to the assistance received from Mr. St. John. He was plain, temperate, frugal and faithful in his friendships, kind as a parent and kind and social to all. He had been in feeble health for many years before his demise, so that his death was not unlooked for.

ABRAHAM WESTBROOK CUDDEBACK is a representative of one of the old and honored families of the Empire State. Jacob Caudebec came from France in 1685, and died when about one hundred years of age. He married Margaret Provost, and their children were: Benjamin, who died at the age of eighty; William, who married Jemima Elting, and died at the age of seventy-four; James, who married Antje Decker, and died at the age of thirty; Abraham, who married Eleanor Swartwout, and died at the age of eighty-eight; Jacob, who married Jeannette Westbrook; Elsie, who became the wife of Harmonas Van Gordon, and died at the age of eighty; Morice or Maria, who married George Westfall, and afterward a Mr. Cole, and died at the age of one hundred; Dinah, who married Abraham Low, and died at the age of seventy-four; Eleanor, who married Evert Hoornbeek, and died at the age of seventy; and Naomi, who married Lodiowyke Hoornbeek.

In the line of direct descent is William Cuddeback, who married Jemima Elting. Their children were James, who died at the age of eighty; Capt. Abraham, who married Esther Gumaer, and died at the age of eighty-two; Benjamin, who married Catherine Van Fleet, and died at the age of forty-five; Roulif, who died at the age of fifty; and Sarah, who became the wife of Daniel Van Fleet.

The great-grandparents of our subject, Abraham and Esther Cuddeback, had six children:

Col. William A.; Peter G.; Jacob; Cornelius; Esther, wife of Ernest Hornbeck; and Jemima, wife of David Westfall. The grandparents, Col. William A. and Charlotte (Van Inwegen) Cuddeback, had nine children, namely: Samuel, Abraham, Margaret, Ezekiel, Harmonas, William, Col. Peter, James and Lewis.

The father of our subject, William Cuddeback, wedded Mary, daughter of Abraham T. and Mary (Van Keuren) Westbrook. Mr. Cuddeback died in October, 1866, at the age of seventy-four, and his wife passed away January 1, 1864, at the age of sixty-three. The record of their children is as follows: Abraham W. is the subject of this review; Margaret is the wife of Elting Cuddeback; Mary is the wife of John Van Etten; Sarah is the widow of Martin Wheeler; Elsie is the widow of William Mapes, of Otisville, N. Y.; Charlotte resides in Grand Rapids, Mich.; Minerva is the wife of Rev. Egbert Winter, of Grand Rapids; Harriet is also living in that place; and Catherine died in childhood.

William Cuddeback spent his entire life on the farm which is now the home of our subject, the place comprising two hundred acres of land, on which he erected in 1822 a good residence. He carried on lumbering for a time, but devoted the greater part of his life to agricultural pursuits. At the time when the canal was built, he and his father and brother Abraham built one mile of the same. In politics he was a stanch Democrat and served for some years as Justice of the Peace and Supervisor. He was a man of fine physique and was said to have been one of the strongest men in the county. His remains were interred in the cemetery at Cuddebackville, and in his death the community lost one of its best citizens.

Abraham Westbrook Cuddeback was born in an old log house on his present farm, April 27, 1816, and was reared in the usual manner of farmer lads, spending a part of the time with his maternal grandfather at Westbrookville. Having arrived at years of maturity, he was married, March 25, 1843, to Miss Emeline, daughter of William and Mary (Van Inwegen) Penny. She was born March 10, 1825, and is also a representative of an honored old family. The children born of this union are Horace and George, at home; Edgar, Herbert and John, who are engaged in the milk business in New York City; Yancey and Mary, at home; and Maggie, who died in her twenty-sixth year.

Mr. Cuddeback is a supporter of the Democracy, and his wife belongs to the Reformed Church. He is one of the oldest living descendants of an illustrious family, and is a well preserved man, on whom the long years rest lightly, although his hair has been whitened by the snows of many winters. He is a genial, whole-souled gentleman, who has hosts of warm friends and no enemies, and his well spent life is worthy of emulation.

PETER G. LEWIS, a progressive agriculturist, whose farm is situated near Mt. Basha Lake, in the town of Monroe, was born at Turner August 16, 1833. In boyhood he attended school at Turner and Forshee Hill, and upon discontinuing his studies he gave his attention to farm work. He remained with his parents until his marriage, after which he rented a farm adjoining the old homestead for three years. In 1859 he purchased a portion of his present farm, and to this he has added until he now owns two hundred and forty acres, extending down to the shores of the pond. A portion of the farm has been in cultivation for many years, while the remainder is utilized for the pasturage of stock, and one meadow has not been turned with a plow for over one hundred years. When he took the place twelve acres would produce only seven loads of hay, but he has, by his practical methods of work, increased the amount to thirty-five. Possessing an unusual knowledge of agriculture as a science, he has been enabled to secure the very best results from his property, and justly ranks among the most capable farmers of his locality. He makes a specialty of the dairy business, which he conducts on a large scale, shipping as high as one hundred and eighty gallons of milk per day.

The father of our subject, Thomas Lewis, was a son of Isaac and Hannah (Galloway) Lewis, who died when ninety years and six months and seventy-five years, respectively. He was born in 1803, and spent his entire life on the farm where he was born, and which his father had bought one hundred years ago. His death, which was the result of an accident, occurred in June, 1876. His maternal grandfather, Jacobus Galloway, lived to the age of almost one hundred years, and died on a farm adjoining that now owned by our subject. The mother of our subject, Mary Ann Bush, was born May 2, 1809, and died May 20, 1894. She was a daughter of Peter and Mary (Smith) Bush, both of whom were born near Turner, the latter being a daughter of James Smith.

In New York City, March 10, 1853, Mr. Lewis was united in marriage with Miss Adelia Ann Davis, a native of that city and a daughter of John, Sr., and Catherine (Seward) Davis. Her father was at one time a farmer, but later dealt in real estate. Eleven children were born to the union of Mr. and Mrs. Lewis, of whom the fourth died in infancy unnamed. Of the others we note the following: George and Mary Catherine died at the ages of eleven and three months, respectively. Sarah Frances passed away when two and one-half years old. Emma married Sylvanus Roberts, a farmer of the town of Chester, and they have two children. Tillie, Mrs. Harley Smith, resides in the town of Monroe and has two children. Lemuel, a carpenter of the village of Monroe, married Maria Webb, and they have two children. Isaac, who married Ella Smith and has two children, is a farmer of the town of Monroe. Henry assists our subject on the farm. Abbie is the wife of Fred Smith, of the town of Monroe, and they have one child. Adelia, the youngest, resides with her parents.

The political belief of Mr. Lewis brings him into active co-operation with the Republican party, and he may always be relied upon to support its county, state and national tickets. For six years he filled the office of Road Commissioner, and he also served as School Collector and in other positions of trust and responsibility. His ancestors were men of patriotic spirit, and his grandfather was a soldier in the War of 1812. Their love of country and devotion to its welfare has descended to him, and he is always ready to champion any cause that will benefit the people and promote the general welfare.

JOHN L. WIGGINS, City Attorney of Middletown, was born in the town of Mt. Hope, March 21, 1855, and is a son of John and Antoinette (Mullock) Wiggins, a sketch of whom appears on another page of this work. Our subject traces his ancestry back many generations to the barony of Wigen in England. Jacob Wiggins, who was the great-grandfather of our subject, first located on Long Island, from which place he came to Orange County and settled in the town of Mt. Hope. During the French and Indian War, which followed shortly after his arrival in this country, he was a member of the Home Guards, and providentially escaped death at the battle of Minisink.

John L. Wiggins spent his boyhood days in the town of Mt. Hope, and until fifteen years of age attended the common schools of that town, and also assisted in the farm work. He then took the course of study under private tutors at home, and later at New Haven, Conn., where he received instructions in both the sciences and classics. While pursuing his studies in New Haven he taught several terms of school, and also engaged in the study of law. From the latter city he came to Middletown, continuing the study of law, and was admitted to the Bar in 1878. He then went to Chillicothe, Ohio, and entered the office of McClintock & Smith, who were then the General Counsel for the Marietta & Cincinnati Railroad, now the Baltimore & Ohio Southwestern, where he remained two years. In 1881 he came to Middletown and entered into partnership with Judge Groo, which partnership continued until 1886. He has a large clientage, and is a very successful practitioner of his chosen profession. In 1894 he was appointed City Attorney, and was re-appointed in 1895. He has been exceedingly successful in taking care of the city's interests, and has won several important cases since he has been such Corporation Counsel.

In 1886 Mr. Wiggins was united in marriage with Miss Katharine Groo, a daughter of Judge W. J. Groo. They have one child, Ada, who is the pet of the household. Fraternally Mr. Wiggins is a member of Middletown Lodge, I. O. O. F. His wife is a member of Grace Episcopal Church, and is very popular in church and social circles. In politics Mr. Wiggins is a Republican. A number of years ago he purchased the old King place on Highland Avenue, which he has occupied since coming to Middletown. His offices at No. 11 North Street are the same ones he has occupied since 1881.

As an attorney Mr. Wiggins takes high rank in the profession, and enjoys the confidence and esteem of those associated with him in practice, and also of the general public. He is counsel for several corporations, and is regarded as a sound and safe legal adviser. In the trial of cases he is quick to see and take advantage of any points of law or practice that might result to his client's interests, but is always fair and courteous to his opponents. As a speaker Mr. Wiggins is forcible and possesses marked ability, and seems always ready with an address for almost any occasion. He is a hard worker, and believes that in order to accomplish any great achievement one must work hard, early and all the time.

DAVID DILL HOUSTON, a native of Orange County, born in Middletown in 1833, is of Irish descent, and traces his ancestry back to his great-great-grandfather, Rev. Joseph Houston, who, with his two brothers, John and James, emigrated from the North of Ireland in the beginning of the eighteenth century and landed in Jamestown, Va. James remained near there, and John settled in Pennsylvania. After preaching a few years at Jamestown Rev. Joseph came North, and was the first settled pastor of the Goodwill Presbyterian Church in the town of Montgomery, Orange County. There he purchased some six hundred acres of land, upon which he resided until his death, and upon which his sons, Joseph and James, resided.

James, the great-grandfather of our subject, married Anna, daughter of Rev. George Carr, a Presbyterian minister of Goshen, who bore him the following children: Joseph, George, Thomas, James, John, Samuel, Andrew, Polly (wife of Robert Wilkin) and Jane (wife of Adam Dickerson). Of these children George was the grandfather of our subject. For a few months during the Revolutionary War he was on guard in the Mamakating Valley, to protect the whites from the incursion of the Indians. He was born in 1763, and died in December, 1825. His wife, Jane, the daughter of Robert Hunter, of the town of Montgomery, died in 1801, aged about thirty-two, leaving the following children: Ann, Mrs. Samuel W. Brown, of Scotchtown; John G., James G., Robert H. and George. The latter cultivated land on which part of Middletown is now located, and afterward was a merchant and Justice of the Peace. For his second wife he married Julia, widow of Chester Gale, and daughter of William Thompson, of Goshen, who bore him the following children: Anthony and Jane, twins, the latter becoming the wife of Charles Heard, of Hamptonburgh; Henry; Sally, wife of Hector VanCleft; Samuel and Theodore, who died young; Almira, wife of Orange Horton, of White Plains; Elizabeth, the wife of William Church, of Orange; and Thomas. George Houston, the grandfather, settled on a farm at Scotchtown in 1787, where he remained until 1805, when he located in the town of Wallkill, there residing the remainder of his life. He was one of the founders of the Presbyterian Church at Scotchtown; for many years was one of its Elders, and gave the site for the church edifice at that place.

Robert H. Houston, the father of our subject, was born in the town of Wallkill, August 20, 1798. At sixteen he began learning the tanner's and currier's trade, completing it when twenty years old, and then for six years had charge of his father's farm. In 1826 he came to Middletown, and, in company with Charles Dill, rented, and afterwards purchased, the Anderson Tannery,

which is located across the street from the Commercial Hotel. For a time business was conducted under the firm name of Dill & Houston, but later they sold out and built another tannery on the site of the present Anglo-Swiss Condensing Building, continuing there until 1846. In 1831 they purchased a farm of sixty acres adjoining the village, which they also operated. In 1846 the partnership was dissolved, Samuel S. Wickham purchasing an interest in the factory, and business was continued under the firm name of Houston & Wickham until 1851, when the former sold out to Mr. Wickham. Mr. Houston retained the original farm, however, laying it out as an addition to Middletown, and it has since been well built up. He laid out East Avenue, east of the railroad; Prospect Avenue, and Sprague, Spring, Houston, Washington, Fulton and Grant Streets, all of which were formerly comprised in his old farm. He bought part of the Bennet Farm, to which he added later, and bought land adjoining the Reeve Farm, subdividing all these tracts. For many years he was also engaged in the lumber business in Sullivan County. He assisted in the extension of the Erie Railroad after its completion to Goshen, and also in the erection of two churches, besides other institutions. He was an active Presbyterian, and died in that faith in 1889, at the age of ninety-three years. His wife, the mother of our subject, was Mary Dill, daughter of David and Elizabeth (Houston) Dill. She died in 1883, at the age of about eighty.

The subject of this sketch is the only living child of Robert and Mary Houston. He was educated in the public schools and in the academy, and spent his early life on the home farm. In 1875 he bought the old Monhagen Mill of Mr. Little and started in the feed business. Later he sold the same to his father, since which time he has devoted all his time to farming and the dairy business, having about thirty head of cows. He still has the old farm of eighty acres in the southern part of the city, and from time to time he has platted a portion of the same. For over forty years he has resided in the neighborhood of his present residence.

Mr. Houston was married, in Middletown, to

HON. GILBERT O. HULSE.

Catherine Moore, who was born in Slate Hill, and who is a daughter of John K. Moore, a carpenter by trade, now residing in San Francisco. Four children have been born unto them: Frances, Mrs. Oscar J. Worley, of Middletown; Robert H., engaged in the feed business, and at the head of the firm of Houston, Webster & Co.; Mary, Mrs. Madden, of Middletown; and John, of the firm of Houston, Webster & Co. In politics Mr. Houston is a Republican, and during the war was a member of the Union League. For a great many years he has been a member of the Presbyterian Church. For one term he was Trustee of Middletown, and throughout this section of the country he is well and favorably known.

ON. GILBERT O. HULSE. Without doubt no attorney in the Hudson Valley is more favorably known for ability and keenness of intellect than the influential and able lawyer whose name introduces this sketch. Having offices in both New York City and Middletown, he spends three days of the week in each. In the former city he occupied an office at No. 167 Broadway until 1886, when his son Levi S. was admitted into partnership. They then removed to No. 120 Broadway, and now have their office at No. 52 Exchange Place, where, under the firm title of G. O. & L. S. Hulse, they have charge of an extensive legal business.

The Middletown firm, which bears the name of Hulse & Melick, has a suite of rooms in the Duzenberry Building at No. 16 North Street. The junior member, J. Elmer Melick, was admitted into partnership June 1, 1895, prior to which time Mr. Hulse had for some years been alone. While he has met with flattering success in every branch of the profession, perhaps his greatest triumphs have been gained in cases of civil law. Some of the suits in which he has been attorney have become famous, and the decisions rendered have established important precedents. Among these we mention the Everett case, the

62

main facts of which were as follows: Walter Everett, who lived on North Street in Middletown, had a son, Collins, the owner of large tracts of land. The latter died unmarried in 1842, and left a will, which his father secured possession of and destroyed. In 1848 Walter Everett died and willed his son's property to other parties. A sister, in 1862, after having consulted a number of lawers, all of whom told her there was no hope, asked the advice of Mr. Hulse regarding the matter. He said the lost will could be proved, and at once commenced action in the Supreme Court for that purpose. Though the opposing counsel was able, he succeeded in establishing the will as lost, under Judge John W. Brown, at a special term of court. This decision was afterward sustained by the general term of the same court. After the property, valued at $30,000, was sold, he was the attorney to recover it, which after seven years he succeeded in doing. This was the first record of proof of a lost will in any of the courts of the state, and was a very intricate and complicated case, the last settlement not being made until twenty-seven years after the death of Collins Everett.

Another noted case was that of Howell vs Hurtin. General Hurtin had a farm at Scotchtown that had been given him by his father for life, after which it was to go to his sons. He borrowed $2,000 from Howell, an attorney at Goshen. Not long afterward he failed, and Howell brought a partition suit. The place was sold to the eldest son for $3,000 in that action and the latter re-mortgaged it to Howell for $9,000. One of the sons was a minor at the time of the sale, and through his father, in an action in the Supreme Court, consulted Mr. Hulse when the family was about to be dispossessed under the foreclosure of the $9,000 mortgage. Mr. Hulse began proceedings in the partition action by motion to set aside the partition sale, which was denied at a special term, and on appeal from the order to the general term the same was affirmed. He then took it to the Court of Appeals, which reversed the decision, set aside the sale, and gave the son his half of the property.

In the well known case of Brown vs Knapp,

Brown sued an executor of his grandfather's estate in an action in the Supreme Court. The grandfather in his will bequeathed him a legacy of $3,000, to be paid to him at the age of twenty-one. If he died before that age the legacy was to be given to a son of the testator, who was executor of the will, but the executor refused to pay the interest on the same to the grandson. Seven or eight years after the grandfather's death the mother of the grandson began suit to recover interest on the legacy. The case was tried before Judge Pratt and was defended by Close & Robertson, a well known legal firm of Westchester County. Mr. Hulse won the case for his client, whereupon the defendant appealed, first in the general term of said court, and later in the Court of Appeals, but in both instances the first decision was sustained.

Mr. Hulse is a native of the town of Wallkill, and was born three miles from Middletown, on the 22d of September, 1824. His grandfather, Thomas Hulse, engaged in farming upon the old family homestead three miles from the city, and there Oliver, our subject's father, was born January 1, 1794, being the third among a large number of children. He was a soldier in the War of 1812, serving first as Corporal and later as Sergeant. The family was founded in this country by three brothers who came from England and settled on Long Island. Later one of the brothers removed to Orange County and settled in the town of Wallkill, becoming the founder of the family of which our subject is a descendant. About 1725 our subject's great-grandfather settled on the ground now adjoining the State Hospital, in the suburbs of the city, and there he reared a large family and continued to reside until his death. Upon the old homestead, which consisted of two hundred and thirty acres, our subject's father engaged in general farming, and there his death occurred July 27, 1871. Politically he was a Democrat.

The mother of our subject, whose maiden name was Eleanor Oakley, was born in Fairfield, Conn., and died in Orange County, in April, 1875. She was a daughter of Gilbert and Eleanor (Wakeman) Oakley, natives of Connecticut,

where the former was engaged in tilling the soil. During the Revolutionary War, in which he was a brave soldier, he was wounded in the leg, and from the effects of that wound he died in 1805. Our subject was one of ten children, of whom eight attained years of maturity, and three daughters and one son are now living.

The subject of this sketch was reared on the old homestead, and after spending a short time in a district school in Middletown, he entered the Jessup private school, and later was a student in Wallkill Academy for eighteen months. On leaving school he went back to the farm, where he remained until 1845. At that time his father purchased the Franklin House, now known as the Holden House. In December, 1847, he began the study of law under Asa D. Jansen, of Goshen, and was admitted to the Bar in Brooklyn November 9, 1849.

Locating in Middletown, Mr. Hulse at once began the practice of his profession. In 1850 he moved his office to the building that stood on the site of his present office. In August, 1851, he located at Elmira, and there, in December of the same year, he married Miss Sarah E. Schoonmaker, who was born in Searsville, Orange County, and was the daughter of Levi Schoonmaker, a native of Ulster County. Mr. Hulse remained in Elmira until the fall of 1854, when he went to New York City and opened an office with ex-Gov. Lucius Robinson, and in the spring of 1855 opened an office at No. 61 Wall Street. In 1865 he returned to Middletown and opened an office. Two years later he was elected Surrogate on the Democratic ticket, which carried the county for the first time since 1856. Entering upon his duties in January, 1868, he filled the office with conspicuous ability until his retirement in January, 1872. During that time he never had but one case appealed, and that was sustained upon appeal. In 1872 he became a member of the firm of Hulse, Little & Finn, which firm three years later was changed to Hulse & Finn, continuing in that way for one year. In 1878 he established an office in New York City, where, as before stated, he spends three days of each week.

By his marriage Mr. Hulse had four children. M. Louisa is the wife of John Wilkin, of Middletown. Oliver Gilbert, a graduate of Wallkill Academy, is one of the leading stenographers of New York City, where he has an office at No. 10 Wall Street. Levi Schoonmaker, the younger son, is also a graduate of Wallkill Academy, and studied law under his father; he is now the junior member of the New York firm. Sarah Frances died at the age of four years and three months. Politically Mr. Hulse is firm in his allegiance to the Democratic party, the principles of which he supports by his ballot. In 1850 he served as Town Clerk, and he has held other local positions, but it has been his preference to give his attention wholly to his practice, to the exclusion of public offices. He assisted in the organization of the Savings Bank and served as one of its Trustees until other duties induced him to resign. As a lawyer he has great energy and tenacity of purpose. He is a strong and tireless combatant, devoted to his clients' interests; an able advocate, logical and convincing in argument, attractive in address and fluent in speech. He is a man of ardent temperament and strong convictions, an interesting companion and popular with all who know him.

H. FARNUM, deceased, was one of the most prominent citizens of Port Jervis. He was a wealthy man, and was very generous and liberal in his charities. It will never be known how many he has assisted, for he was modest and retiring and made no ostentatious display, but certain it is that numerous local industries owe to him their prosperity, and his memory is cherished and honored in thousands of homes. Just before his death, which occurred suddenly, October 11, 1879, the result of heart disease, he had contributed $15,000 to the new chapel of the Reformed Church.

Mr. Farnum was born May 10, 1808, in Litchfield, Conn., being a son of Peter Farnum, who removed to Butternut, Otsego County, N. Y., in 1815 with his family. Our subject received a fair education, and in 1827 attended the Albany Academy for six months. It was in the fall of that year that he came to Port Jervis, joining the corps of engineers then surveying the Delaware & Hudson Canal, and at the same time the late R. F. Lord became a member of the corps. John B. Jervis was the chief engineer, and Mr. Farnum was made resident engineer of this section. He continued to do efficient service on the canal construction until it was completed, in 1828, and was then made superintendent of the section which had been built under his jurisdiction. He held this office until 1832, being succeeded by his brother, S. B. Farnum, and was promoted to be assistant engineer under R. F. Lord. During the last years of his service, which terminated in 1838, he had entire charge of the canal from Rondout to Lackawaxen. In 1838 he became resident engineer of the Black River Canal, having his headquarters at Boonville, N. Y., until 1842, his former co-laborer, Mr. Root, being his immediate superior. Many important works which added greatly to his reputation were instituted in this period. When the state put a stop to work on the canal Mr. Farnum returned to Port Jervis and soon afterward entered into partnership with Charles St. John, son of Stephen St. John, in a general dry-goods trade. Mr. St. John retired from the firm about a year later, Mr. Farnum continuing the business until 1854, when he took in as partners his nephews, H. C. Cunningham and A. H. Peck, the style being H. H. Farnum & Co. Five years later Mr. Cunningham retired and Messrs. Farnum & Peck continued their connection until 1861. From that time onward our subject was not actively engaged in commercial pursuits. He was a Director in the Bank of Port Jervis, which he organized in 1863, with Thomas King President, and after the latter's death, in 1867, Mr. Farnum was elected President, holding that position until his death. He was the first President of the local gas-light company, which was organized in 1860. In 1871 he became interested in the organization of the Barrett Bridge Company, and a year later was made Vice-President of the concern. He was a clear-headed, far-seeing business man, and owned a large share of the town, his investments rarely turning out to be anything but remunerative.

The first marriage of Mr. Farnum was celebrated January 11, 1837, with Abigail Ann, daughter of the late Stephen St. John. Her death occurred May 4, 1874, in Washington, D. C., at the age of fifty-six years, nine months and fifteen days. She had gone South the previous October, hoping to regain her health, but was not materially benefited. She was a warm-hearted, loving Christian woman, ever ready to lend her aid to the poor and needy, and was very active in church work. October 8, 1879, Mr. Farnum married Diana Zearfoss, widow of George W. Farnum, his eldest brother. She died March 24, 1885. Of the eleven brothers and one sister of our subject, but four survive, namely: Harriet, wife of. Rev. Levi Peck, of this city; Caroline, Mrs. Henry Tervell; Samuel B., of Port Jervis; and the widow of Rodman M. Fuller, of Pond Eddy.

In May, 1868, Mr. Farnum became a member of the Reformed Church, and contributed about $13,000 to the present house of worship, which was erected at a cost of $40,000, and contains a fine organ, valued at $3,000. Mr. Farnum was very much interested in the construction of this edifice, and was an active member of the Building Committee. On several occasions he was elected to church offices, but peremptorily declined to serve. He contributed $2,500 for enlarging the theological library of the seminary at New Brunswick, N. J. His portrait and name are to be found in an alcove of the library, thus perpetuating his memory. A local coal dealer states that on various occasions during severe winters Mr. Farnum instructed him to supply poor families, saying nothing as to the donor, and present the bill to him. We will mention but one other incident of his undoubted liberality of heart: In 1859 Rev. Samuel R. Brown, then on the point of sailing as a missionary to Japan, was much troubled about the education of his son. It seemed best to leave the youth in America, and he was without means for his support. Mr. Far-

num learned of the case and at once contributed $650, the amount necessary for the education of the youth. He was a believer in the great value of learning, and contributed $500 to the college at New Brunswick for founding a perpetual scholarship.

ANDREW JACKSON DOWNING. More than forty years have passed since the tragic death of this gentleman terminated the existence of one of Newburgh's most illustrious citizens. As an author he won for himself a national reputation, and his works are still considered authorities upon the subjects of which they treat. His literary career began in 1841, with the publication of the "Treatise and Practice of Landscape-gardening, Adapted to North America, with a View to the Improvement of Country Residences; with Remarks on Rural Architecture." The book leaped into instant popularity, and the orders to his publishers for copies of the work were followed by orders for the construction of houses and decoration of grounds.

In 1842 "Cottage Residences" was published, and was received with equal favor. "The Fruits and Fruit Trees of America" was printed simultaneously in London and New York in 1845, and five years later a second edition, with colored plates, appeared. In 1846 he became connected with the "Horticulturist," for which he wrote an article every month until his death. In 1849 he wrote "Additional Notes and Hints about Building in the Country," for an American reprint of Wightwick's "Hints to Young Architects." The summer of 1850 he spent in England, visiting the great country-seats, of which he wrote descriptions, and in that year he published his "Architecture of Country Houses." His remaining work is an edition of Mrs. Loudon's "Landscape-gardening for Ladies."

The entire life of Mr. Downing was spent at the homestead in Newburgh, where he was born October 30, 1815. From boyhood his tastes were directed to the natural sciences, his inclination be-

DR. G. J. APPLETON.

ing fostered by his father, a practical nurseryman. His education was gained principally in
the academy of the village of Montgomery. At the
age of sixteen, with his brother Charles, he began the management of the nursery, and by visiting the estates of gentlemen in his neighborhood, he studied the forms of plant life and cultivated a taste for landscape-gardening. In June,
1838, he married the daughter of John Peter De
Wint, of Fishkill, and during that year he built on
his estate a beautiful mansion in the Elizabethan
style, which was the first practical illustration of
what an American home might be. In 1851 he
was commissioned to lay out and plant the public grounds of the Capitol, the White House and
the Smithsonian Building at Washington. These
and other professional labors occupied his remaining years.

On the 28th of July, 1852, Mr. Downing left
Newburgh on the steamer "Henry Clay," but
he never reached his destination, the city of Newport. On the Hudson the boat entered a contest
with the "Armenia," and when near Yonkers
was discovered to be on fire. In his heroic efforts to save other passengers, he perished in the
flames. His "Rural Essays" were collected and
published in 1853, with a memoir by Frederika
Bremer, who was Mr. Downing's guest during a
portion of her visit to the United States, and was
an enthusiastic admirer of him and his works.

ETHEN J. APPLETON, D. V. S., one of
the best known men of Orange County,
makes his home at New Windsor. Besides
devoting his attention to the practice of veterinary
surgery, he takes an active interest in the work
of the Humane Society for the prevention of
cruelty to animals, and has accomplished great
results by insisting on the rules of the society being observed. Like many of the best residents of
this portion of the state, Dr. Appleton was born
in England, his birth occurring near the city of
London, October 28, 1831.

John Appleton, the father of our subject, was
a real-estate man in his native land, and in 1849

came with his family to America, locating in the
town of Hamptonburg, near Goshen. There he
purchased a small farm, and for seven years was
employed in its cultivation. He then moved to
the town of Newburgh, and gave his attention
to stock-farming, importing many fine horses.
Among them was "Tom Cribb," a thoroughbred
race-horse, who was well known to the stockmen
of the county. When advanced in years he retired from active business, and lived in New
Windsor until his decease, which occurred when
he was in his eighty-sixth year. In religious
matters he was an Episcopalian. The grandfather of our subject, Joseph, was also born in England, and lived a retired life.

The mother of our subject, who bore the maiden
name of Eliza Bailey, was likewise a native of
England, and died in this county when in her
seventy-fourth year. She was the mother of three
children, all of whom are living, Gethen being
the eldest. His sisters are Eliza Julia and Elizabeth, both single, and residents of New Windsor.
Our subject is finely educated, and upon completing the course of study at the Blue Coat School,
or what is now called Christ Hospital, took a
course in the Royal Veterinary College of London.

In 1849 our subject accompanied the rest of
the family on their journey to America, coming
hither on the sailing-vessel "Henry Hudson,"
which was five weeks in making the trip. He
continued to make his home with his parents for
a number of years, then became assistant to Dr.
Grice, of New York City. After remaining with
him for three years, he returned to Orange County and began practicing at Newburgh. In 1870,
however, he located in New Windsor, which is
the seat of his operations. His practice is very
large, extending throughout Orange County, and
he is often called upon to make visits in adjoining counties. He is thoroughly qualified for the
work in which he is engaged, and his services are
in great demand by the horsemen of this locality.

December 22, 1865, the Doctor married Mrs.
Mary Amelia Havemeyer, widow of Charles H.
Havemeyer, of New Windsor. She died July 30,
1868, since which time he has made his home
with his sisters. The Doctor is a Democrat in

politics, although not radical in his views. So-cially he is a Mason, belonging to Newburgh Lodge No. 309. In him the Episcopal Church has a valued member, he being actively interest-ed in the work of that denomination, and to its support is a regular contributor.

─── ※✦◈✦◆✦◆✦◆❀◆◈✦◈✦✦ ───

EDWARD McNIFF is the oldest engineer in point of service on the New York, Ontario & Western Railway, having run the first construction train on the road and set up the first engine. He was born in the province of Quebec, Canada, in 1842, and his father, John McNiff, was born in County Sligo, Ireland, where he grew to manhood on a farm. He married Nancy McLaughlin, a native of Scotland, whose parents emigrated from the Highlands of Scotland to Ireland. Soon after their marriage they moved to Canada, where they remained a few years, and finally located in St. Lawrence County, N. Y., where the father followed contracting and build-ing, and where he died some years ago. They had a family of eight children, five of whom grew to maturity, two sons and three daughters. Of their two sons, Patrick is an engineer on the Rome, Watertown & Ogdensburg Railroad.

Edward McNiff removed with his parents from Canada to Norwood, St. Lawrence County, in early childhood, and in the common schools of that place he received a very limited education. At the tender age of nine years he commenced work on a farm in that county, and from that time he has made his own way in the world. At the age of fifteen he secured employment as brakeman on the old Potsdam & Watertown Rail-road, now a part of the Rome, Watertown & Ogdensburg System. He soon began firing, and January 1, 1862, before he was twenty years of age, became an engineer on that road, having charge of a freight train. Later he ran the pass-enger train between Watertown and Ogdens-burg. In 1869 he went to Oneida, N. Y., as en-gineer for the New York, Oswego & Midland Railroad, now the New York, Ontario & Western Railway. He set up engine No. 5 on the side

track of the New York Central Railroad at that place, ran a construction train, and built one hundred miles of the road from Oswego to Nor-wich. He opened up the first section of the road from Oneida to Central Square, and then pulled the first regular passenger train from Oswego to Norwich. He thus opened the first one hundred miles of the road, and continued that run until the spring of 1871, when the section below was opened up.

Taking engine No. 5 to Syracuse and over the Central to Binghamton, and then to Middle-town, Mr. McNiff unloaded it and set it upon temporary tracks. He then took a construction train and ballasted ten miles of road between Middletown and Bloomingburg, and the same summer had charge of the motive power in con-structing the Crawford Road. That fall he built this road as far as Liberty Falls, and then re-turned to Oswego, remaining there until Septem-ber, 1872, when he returned to Middletown and ran a passenger train from Ellenville to Jersey City, over the new Jersey Midland Road. He re-mained there until the road was given up by the Ontario & Western, and then returned to Middle-town and ran mail trains No. 1 and No. 2 from Middletown to Norwich, on the Midland Division. In 1874 he took leave of absence and accepted a position on the Canada Southern Railroad, run-ning from Buffalo to St. Thomas, but remained there only four months, when he returned and took the same train on the Ontario & Western that he had given up. Soon afterwards, how-ever, he took charge of a train between Ellenville and Middletown, and later had charge of a milk train between Delhi and Middletown. In 1888, he took charge of the yard engine at Middletown, which position he yet holds, his engine being known as No. 49. He has never been injured, al-though he has had some narrow escapes.

Mr. McNiff was married, in Mountain Dale, N. Y., to Miss Henrietta Cox, who was born in that place, and who is a daughter of Mitchell Cox, a tanner by trade. They have one child, Elizabeth. The family residence is on East Main Street. Mr. McNiff and wife are members of Grace Episcopal Church, of which he is a Vestryman. In politics he is a Democrat, but in local affairs is quite liberal. He is a charter member of Oswego Lodge No. 152, B. of L. E., and is a member and Chief Engineer of Division No. 292, in Middletown. He is Chairman of the Board of Adjustment of the Ontario & Western System for the Board of Locomotive Engineers.

WILLIAM REID THOMAS, D. D., was appointed Archdeacon of Orange County, diocese of New York, in 1887, which office he still holds. He was also elected Bishop of Northern Michigan at the general convention of 1892. Our subject was born at Schenectady, N. Y., and when a child removed with his parents, Rev. William B. and Jane P. (Livingston) Thomas, to Poughkeepsie.

The subject of this sketch was educated in Dutchess County Academy at Poughkeepsie, St. Stephen's College at Annandale, and the General Theological Seminary of New York City. He was graduated from college with the Class of '69, and from the seminary in 1872. He was ordained Deacon by Rt.-Rev. Horatio Potter, Bishop of New York, June 30, 1872, and Priest November 14 of that year.

Rev. William R. Thomas received the degree of Bachelor of Arts in 1869, Master of Arts in 1872, Bachelor of Divinity in 1884, and Doctor of Divinity in 1889, and has been Rector of the Church of the Holy Innocents at Highland Falls since his ordination. Dr. Thomas is President of the Morgan Library and Reading Room, and takes a warm interest in all local movements tending toward good government and the improvement of the village.

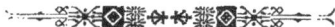

REV. AME VENNEMA, pastor of the Reformed Church of Deerpark at Port Jervis, is a native of Holland, Ottawa County, Mich., his birth occurring May 25, 1857. His parents were Ame and Elizabeth M. (Vanderthaar) Vennema, the former of whom is a native

of Holland. He crossed the Atlantic in 1847, making his way westward to Holland, Mich. When a lad of fifteen years our subject began working in a furniture factory in Grand Rapids, but was employed there only a few months however. He afterward spent two years as a student in Hope College, and after completing his education returned to Grand Rapids, where he lived for a time, and then was engaged in teaching school for two years in Ottawa County. When eighteen years of age he again entered college, graduating with the Class of '79, with the degree of Bachelor of Arts. Three years later the college conferred upon him the degree of Master of Arts.

Desirous of following the ministry, Mr. Vennema went to New Brunswick, N. J., where he entered the theological seminary of the Reformed Church, completing the course in 1882. He was then licensed to preach, and received a call from a church in Ulster County. In July of that year he was ordained, remaining at that place for over three years. Later our subject went to Kalamazoo, Mich., where for three years he was pastor of the new Reformed Church of that city, preaching in the English language. Previous to this time he had used the Dutch dialect. While there he was instrumental in securing the erection of a new building, which was paid for before he left. From Michigan Mr. Vennema returned to New York and accepted a call to Rochester, which was the center of his pastoral work for the following two years. From there he came to Port Jervis, entering upon his duties here in January, 1892. The church numbers about four hundred and fifty members, about one hundred and fifty of whom have joined during the past three years. There was an indebtedness of $6,000 on the building when he came here, but this has since been paid off, and the congregation is now free to spend its means in making additions and improvements on the premises.

Rev. Mr. Vennema is interested in the work of the Riverside Mission, and is correspondent from this section for the *Christian Intelligencer*, the church organ, and also edits the *Church Life*, a local paper. He is connected with W. G. Baas in translating and publishing the writings of Rev. Dr. Theodore Cuyler, a noted divine of Brooklyn, distributing them among the Dutch-speaking people of the state. Our subject is a member of the Board of Education of his church, which has a general oversight of the educational work in the United States, and which numbers about eighteen members. While at New Paltz he received a call to the Reformed Church at New Durham, N. J., and while at Kalamazoo was solicited to take charge of the work of the First Reformed Church at New Brownsville, N. J.

Rev Mr. Vennema was married, June 7, 1882, to Miss Henriette LeFebre, of Holland, Mich., a lady whom he had known for many years. To them have been born three children: Edith May, born August 29, 1883; Augustus Whiton, May 13, 1887; and Florence Elizabeth, December 3, 1891.

―――――⟨○⟩⁂⟨○⟩―――――

WILLIAM H. SHAW. The life record of this gentleman has been one reflecting credit upon himself. In the town of Wallkill he owns and operates a finely improved farm of sixty-seven acres, upon which he has erected modern and substantial buildings, and from the cultivation of which he derives a fair income. For three years, or since Mr. Shaw has resided upon his present farm, he has devoted much of his time and attention to raising veal for the New York market, which has proved remunerative. His success is especially commendable when the fact is taken into consideration that from youthful years he has been obliged to earn his own livelihood, his father's death forcing him to begin life's struggles at an early age.

In the town of Wallkill, in 1836, the subject of this notice was born to the union of Alexander W. and Adeline (Welch) Shaw. His father, who was a native of Connecticut, learned the tanner's trade in the place where he was born. Coming to Orange County in early manhood, he began in that occupation, forming a partnership with his brother William. Subsequently he purchased a farm near Middletown, and there he spent the re-

mainder of his life, passing away in 1852. He served his fellow-citizens creditably in the capacity of Assessor of the town, and held other local offices. He was also a Trustee of Wallkill Academy, and assisted in drawing to the grounds the material for the construction of the building. His wife, who was a native of this county, passed away ten years after his demise.

In the academy of which his father was a Trustee, the subject of this sketch received excellent educational advantages, attending that institution for some terms. For twelve years he was express agent at Middletown, but with that exception he has followed agricultural pursuits through all his active life. His father died when he was sixteen, and since that time he has struggled for himself, with what success his valuable farm attests. June 17, 1857, he married Miss Arminda H., daughter of Dr. Cyrenus Crosby, a physician of the town of Crawford. His father, Dr. Increase Crosby, was a very prominent physician in his day. He was an early settler in the town of Crawford, and the second practicing physician in Orange County. The only child born of the union of our subject and wife was Charles A., who was called from earth at the age of sixteen, his death being a deep bereavement to his devoted parents, who had cherished the brightest hopes for his future. In religious connections Mr. Shaw is identified with the First Presbyterian Church of Middletown, to which his wife also belongs. Socially he is identified with the Masonic order.

When the tocsin of war was sounded, Mr. Shaw donned the blue and went in answer to his country's call for volunteers. He served for three months in the Seventy-first New York State Militia, returning home at the end of his period of service. Like all old soldiers, he is interested in the Grand Army, his membership being in Capt. William A. Jackson Post. In politics he may always be depended upon to give his vote and influence to the Democratic party, and upon that ticket he has been chosen to serve in important capacities. For three years he was a member of the Board of Supervisors of Tioga County. He has also served as Constable, Justice of the Peace and Trustee of the Fourth Ward of Middletown.

MARTIN C. EVERITT.

He at one time made the race for Assemblyman in Tioga County, which stood one thousand majority for the Republican party, but he succeeded in reducing this majority to four hundred and twenty-nine, a fact which shows the confidence reposed in him by those of the opposite party. He has served efficiently as President of the Agricultural Society of this county, and in whatever position to which he has been called he has displayed sound common-sense and excellent judgment.

MARTIN COLE EVERITT, President of the First National Bank of Port Jervis, has the reputation of being a strictly first-class business man, reliable and energetic, and is a citizen of whom Orange County may be justly proud. He was born in Montague, Sussex County, N. J., on the 4th of February, 1828, and is a son of John D. and Roanna (Decker) Everitt. His grandfather, Isaac Everitt, who was a farmer, was a son of Dr. Everitt, the founder of the family in America. The latter was a native of Germany, and located in Hunterdon County, N. J., prior to the Revolutionary War. He was the author of a medical work used by the professors in his native land. On his grandmother's side Mr. Everitt is descended from Holland-Dutch ancestors. The father of our subject was a teacher by profession, but in later life followed merchandising and farming. He served as Justice of the Peace for many years, and also as Associate Judge. In politics he was an old-line Whig. His death occurred at the age of seventy-nine, while his wife, who was a daughter of Daniel Decker, died at the age of sixty years. In their family of six children our subject is the fourth in order of birth; his youngest brother died in 1851, at the age of twenty-one years; Daniel D. is a resident of Montague, N. J.; and Robert lives in Centreville, N. J.

M. C. Everitt remained on the home farm until reaching the age of sixteen years, when he began clerking in a country store. In connec-

tion with a brother-in-law, he later embarked in merchandising in Centreville, N. J., near the old home, starting with a capital of only $300, and they continued to conduct that store for two years and a-half, when, in 1851, Mr. Everitt sold out to his partner and came to Port Jervis. For a year he was employed by St. John & Birdsall, and then for a year by Charles St. John, when he purchased a half-interest in the business, the firm name becoming St. John & Everitt. For ten years they engaged in general merchandising near where Farnum's store now stands. Although Mr. Everitt had to borrow money to start, a successful and lucrative business was carried on. In 1861 the firm sold out, and in connection with Henry Nooney our subject started a general store, which was carried on for two years and a-half with first-class results.

On his retirement from that firm in 1864, Mr. Everitt took the contract for supplying the Erie Railroad with wood, and furnished from eight to ten thousand cords of wood annually. He bought lands covered with timber and hired men to cut the same, which business he followed for five years, and during that time made his home at Port Jervis. At the same time he converted the land into farms, and still owns one in Broome County of four hundred and fifty acres, and another one of two hundred and forty-four acres. In 1868 he formed a partnership with John T. Van Etten in general merchandising, but later John Rightmeyer took the latter's place, and they continued business for two or three years, when our subject retired from the firm.

In 1870 a stock company was formed to purchase the First National Bank of Delhi, and by a special permit from Congress it was removed to this place and the name changed. It became the First National Bank of Port Jervis, with a capital of $100,000, and Mr. Everitt became its first Vice-President, while Jacob Hornbeck was President, and George A. Guernsey Cashier. In January, 1871, our subject was elected Cashier, and took charge of its affairs, but in 1874 he was elected President, which office he has since filled; and at the same time C. F. Van Inwegen was made Cashier, which position he still continues to fill. Eli Van Inwegen is Vice-President. Mr. Everitt devotes his time and energy to the interests of the bank, which does a strictly legitimate banking business. The capital stock has remained the same, and their present location is at the corner of Ball and Sussex Streets.

On the 9th of October, 1860, Mr. Everitt was married to Miss Louisa Armstrong, of Montague, N. J. At her death, in 1865, she left a family of three children: John E., a conductor on the Erie Railroad; Charles B., of Waterbury, Conn., superintendent of the blanking room in the Plume & Atwood Manufactory; and George, who was a railroad employe, but who died in April, 1892, at the age of twenty-seven years. Mr. Everitt has always been true to his first love and has never married again. He is a man of pleasing address, slender build, clear-cut features and open expression. He is a stalwart supporter of the Republican party, and takes an active interest in its welfare. He attends the Presbyterian Church, though not a member of the same, but gives liberally to its support. Socially he belongs to Port Jervis Lodge No. 328, F. & A. M., serving as Secretary of the Blue Lodge many years, and is a member of Neversink Chapter, R. A. M. He is held in the highest respect throughout Orange County, and has the confidence and esteem of all with whom he comes in contact.

≪+++++++++++++◉+++++++++++++≫

GEORGE W. WEST, Superintendent of Motive Power of the New York, Ontario & Western Railway, was born in Troy, N. Y., April 3, 1847. His father, Capt. James D. West, was born in Exeter, N. H., but came of a Massachusetts family. As a boy he ran on sloops, and later was owner and captain of sloops before steamers were placed on the river. After the discovery of steam power and the manufacture of steamboats, he became the owner and captain of several boats. He had two steamers, "A. A. Watkins No. 1" and "A. A. Watkins No. 2," both of which he sold to the Government. The first was a very fast boat, and was used by the Government between Washington and Alexandria during the war. Soon after the disposal of these boats he was taken sick, and died at the age of sixty-eight years. In the forty years that he ran upon the Hudson River, he never lost but one trip. He ran between Troy and New York City, and also to Boston in early days, and for many years he acted as pilot on the river. At Troy he married Electa Wager, who was born in Keene, N. H., and who died at the age of about sixty-eight years. Of their eight children, six grew to maturity, but only two are now living. One son, Chester, was on the Hudson River as pilot and captain, and fell from the mast of a barge. After that event he quit the business, and is now located in West Newburgh, in the employ of the Erie Railway.

The subject of this sketch was the seventh in the parental family, and grew to manhood in his native city, receiving his education in the public schools. From early childhood he was on his father's boat, and went with his father and brothers to Washington on the steamer "A. A. Watkins" at the beginning of the war. He did not remain there, however, but returned to the Hudson and ran on the river between Troy and New York until 1862, when he accepted a position as wiper on the Troy & Greenbush, now the New York Central, Railroad. Soon after he was made fireman, and ran between Troy and Greenbush. Two years later he went to Baldwinsville, N. Y., and entered a machine-shop as an apprentice, in which an elder brother, Mason West, was general foreman. After being there about two and a-half years the works were shut down and he went to Schenectady, and in the New York Central Car-shops completed his trade. He continued work there until that shop was abandoned, when he was transferred to Syracuse, remaining there until 1872, when he was made Master Mechanic of the Chenango Valley Railroad, with headquarters at Syracuse. In 1883 this road was absorbed by the West Shore Railroad, and the shops were abandoned.

Mr. West was general foreman of the West Shore Railroad Shops at East Buffalo for one year, when he was appointed Master Mechanic of the Buffalo Division of the West Shore, with which he remained until 1886. He then became Master Mechanic of the Mahoning Division of the Erie Railroad, with headquarters at Cleveland, but after holding that position about nine months he was transferred to their main shops at Meadville, Pa., as Master Mechanic. In February, 1888, he was transferred to the Eastern Division at Jersey City as Master Mechanic. Up to this time there had been two departments, the car department and the locomotive department, but these were now consolidated and Mr. West was made Master Mechanic of the consolidation, holding the position until February, 1890, when he resigned to accept the Superintendency of Motive Power of the New York, Ontario & Western, with headquarters at Middletown. In 1893, on the completion of the new depot, he was among the first to occupy offices in the building. He has now entire charge of the motive power on the main line from Oswego to New York, and also on the Scranton, Utica, New Berlin, Delhi and Rome Divisions, in all four hundred and twenty-four miles. Since beginning railroad service he has never been a day out of employment, his positions being changed by transferring from one department or place to another. He has been a very successful man in every position occupied, and his success is due to the fact that he thoroughly understands his business and has acquired his knowledge by actual work in every department.

Mr. West was united in marriage in Schenectady, N. Y., with Miss Jennie Van Slyck, a native of that place and daughter of Jacob and Ann Van Slyck, the former being engaged in merchandising in that place. They have one child, Arthur Conklin. Fraternally Mr. West is a member of Central City Lodge, F. & A. M., at Syracuse, and of Union Consistory at Middletown. He is also a member of the American Railway Master Mechanics' Association; of the Master Car Builders' Association, with which he meets every year; and is President of the New York Railway Club, with headquarters at New York City. Politically he is a true Republican. Religiously he is a member of the Methodist Epis-

copal Church, and of the Railroad Young Men's Christian Association at Middletown. He is also President of the Ontario & Western branch of the Western Savings and Loan Association.

GEORGE KETCHAM, a miller at Middletown, is a native of the town of Mt. Hope, born in 1837, and there both his father and grandfather were also born. Amos Ketcham, the father, was a miller by trade, and for many years ran a mill which was erected by Isaac Ketcham, the grandfather. In 1848 the father repaired the old mill, operating the same until he retired, and it is now carried on by his son Isaac Edward. The father was an old-line Whig, and died in 1888, at the age of seventy-five. He was twice married, first to Sallie Eliza Seybolt, who was born near Otisville, and who was a daughter of George Seybolt, a farmer at that place. She died in 1870, leaving four children: Lamira, now Mrs. Sweezy, of Unionville; George, the subject of this sketch; C. C. B., formerly a grain dealer in Middletown, who died here some years ago; and Isaac E., who has charge of the old mill. The second marriage of Amos Ketcham was with Miss Margaret Seybolt.

The subject of this sketch was reared near the old mill, and had the advantages of a common-school education. He learned the trade of a miller with his father, and remained with him until twenty-two years of age, when he located on a farm near Otisville. After operating that eighteen months, he opened a butcher-shop in Otisville, which he continued some three or four years. His next business enterprise was in New York City, where he purchased a milk route, and engaged in the milk business for several years.

Closing out that industry, he came to Orange County, and for eleven years conducted the Salisbury Mills, doing custom work. In 1881 he took charge of the Wickham Mill, which is connected with the Erie Road by a side track. This mill he superintended for sixteen months, when it was sold to Drake & Dewitt, and for the succeeding eighteen months he superintended it for that firm. He then leased it, and has continued to operate it since that time, making a specialty of the manufacture of buckwheat flour, and doing custom work exclusively. The mill is an old structure, with four floors and an elevator, and is run by a fifty horse-power engine. In addition to milling, he does a wholesale and retail business in feed and grain.

Mr. Ketcham was married in the town of Mt. Hope to Miss Minnie A. Harding, who was born there, and who is a daughter of J. Columbus Harding, a farmer in that locality. Four children have been born unto them: Georgianna, a dressmaker of Middletown; Ida M., a trained nurse, and graduate of Mt. Sinai Hospital; Melvin H., a printer, residing in Brooklyn; and Ira B., at home. In politics Mr. Ketcham is a Democrat. The family resides at No. 147 Academy Avenue.

JOHN L. HART, Justice of the Peace of Walden, Ulster County, was born in Shawangunk, Ulster County, on the 26th of August, 1815, and is a son of Thomas and Susan (Colden) Hart, the latter being a widow at the time of her marriage with Mr. Hart. The father was also a native of the Empire State, and resided in one neighborhood all his life. He died at the age of fifty-nine. There were six children in the family, of whom our subject is the only one now living. A brother of Thomas, Cadwallader C. Hart, was for many years captain of a Hudson River steamboat of the Caledonia & Susquehanna Line, and resided at Newburgh. He died at Orange, N. J., at the age of seventy-four.

The subject of this sketch remained on his father's farm until 1840, when he removed to Wallkill, Ulster County, where for five years he was engaged in the hotel business. In 1850 he came to Walden, and first engaged in running an oyster saloon, and was also in the meat business for fourteen years in connection with Mr. Hepper.

In 1861 he was elected Justice of the Peace, and with the exception of about one year has served in that office ever since, his terms being each of four years. Politically he is a Republican, but has ever been popular with both parties.

On the 21st of October, 1840, Mr. Hart was united in marriage with Miss Cornelia Ostrander, who resided in the same neighborhood near the old home farm. Three children were born unto them, but they all died in childhood. Mrs. Hart is a member of the Reformed Church.

FRED R. WILLIAMS, of Newburgh, was born in Glens Falls, N. Y., in 1858, and is the son of Stephen I. and Jane A. (Ray) Williams, natives, respectively, of Glens Falls and Virgil, N. Y. His father, who was for some years a merchant tailor in Glens Falls, and also served as Postmaster of the place, removed from there at the time of the burning of the town, in 1865, and settled in Chestertown, this state. In 1880 he came to Newburgh, where he remained until his death. His widow at present makes her home in Jersey City.

The subject of this sketch passed the first twelve years of his life in the city were he was born, and there and in Chestertown his education was conducted in the public schools. In 1876 he came to Newburgh, where he served an apprenticeship to the printer's trade in the composing-room of the *Daily Mail*, of which his brother was one of the owners. On the consolidation of that paper with the *Telegraph*, and the subsequent change of the name to the *Register*, he remained with the different proprietors, being a compositor there for twelve years.

Afterward, for one year, Mr. Williams was employed as bookkeeper and advertising agent, and later for two years he was local editor for the Newburgh *Daily News*. His next position was that of solicitor for the Calcium-light Advertising Company of Newburgh, in which capacity he remained for three years. In Septem-

THEODORE D. MILLS, M. D.

ber, 1893, he aided in the organization of the Lime-light Advertising Company, of which he is manager and part-owner. This enterprise has been successful, and has been introduced into eight states.

The marriage of Mr. Williams united him with Miss Lettie Johnson, daughter of John D. Johnson, who was formerly proprietor of the City Hotel of Newburgh. They are the parents of three children, Clifford, Ray and Grace.

THEODORE D. MILLS, M. D., one of the leading physicians in Middletown, is a native of Bloomingburg, N. Y., born June 9, 1852, a son of Rev. S. W. Mills, D. D., a sketch of whom appears elsewhere in this work. The family remained in Bloomingburg until our subject was six years of age, when they removed to Port Jervis, where Theodore received his primary education in the public school, preparing for college in the select school of Professor Wilbur. In 1870 he entered Rutgers College at New Brunswick, N. J., where he pursued the classical course, and was graduated in 1874 with the degree of A. B. At the expiration of three years he received the degree of A. M. from the same college. He was elected a member of the Phi Beta Kappa and D. K. E. fraternities. Soon after his graduation he began to read medicine in the office of Dr. H. R. Baldwin, of New Brunswick, and in 1874 entered the College of Physicians and Surgeons of New York City, from which he was graduated in 1876. He then passed a competitive examination at Bellevue Hospital in New York, and was made house surgeon in that institution.

After completing his hospital service Dr. Mills returned to Port Jervis and opened an office in connection with Dr. Henry Hardenbergh, and there he continued in practice from October, 1877, to January 28, 1881, when he removed to Middletown, his office now being located at No. 60 West Main Street. Since locating here the Doctor has built up a very extensive practice, and as a skilled physician and surgeon has a reputation

second to none in Orange County. He has been called into consultation by leading physicians in his section of the country, and his merits have been recognized by various bodies. For about twelve years he has been surgeon for the New York, Ontario & Western Railway, and is also attending surgeon at Thrall Hospital.

While Dr. Mills is engaged in general practice he pays special attention to general surgery and the treatment of the eye and ear. He is Secretary of the Orange County Medical Society, of which he was formerly President, and has always taken an active interest in its proceedings, at times contributing papers that have received marked attention. In the State Association of Railway Surgeons, of which he is a member, he takes an active interest. He is also a member of the National Association of Railway Surgeons, and attended its sessions in Omaha in 1893, and in Galveston, Tex., in 1894. The Tri-State Medical Society and the New York State Medical Society, in both of which he is a member, also require a share of his attention. The Doctor is a very close student and is ever abreast of the times in all medical research. In 1887 he took a post-graduate course in the New York Post-Graduate College, thus preparing himself for greater usefulness. He is examiner for the Royal Arcanum and the Legion of Honor, in both of which he holds membership, as well as numerous old-line companies.

October 20, 1887, Dr. Mills was united in marriage in Middletown with Miss Christina S. Stivers, who is a native of Middletown and daughter of Hon. M. D. Stivers. Three children were born unto them, two of whom are living: Samuel Wickham, Jr., and Elizabeth Stivers. Theodore D., Jr., died at the age of nine weeks.

While Dr. Mills is an active man in his profession, he yet finds time to devote to social and business intercourse, and ever takes an active interest in all things tending to advance his adopted city. He is one of the Trustees of the Orange County Trust and Safe Deposit Company, and is a Director of the Orange County Telephone Company, of which he was one of the incorporators. He is a member of the Middletown Club and also of the Board of Trade. Religiously he holds membership with the Presbyterian Church, in which body he is active and influential. Politically he is independent.

Dr. Mills is yet in the prime of life, and with his studious habits and careful attention to all details of his business and profession, has a bright future before him. Not only in the practice of his profession has success attended him, but in a business way as well. As a citizen he stands high in the estimation of his fellow-men.

EVANDER M. HAMILTON, City Clerk and Collector of Middletown, was one of the Union defenders during the late war. He was born near Auburn, N. Y., December 10, 1842, and is a son of James W. and Elizabeth Catherine (Taylor) Hamilton, the former a native of Scotland, and the latter of Orange County. William Hamilton, the grandfather of our subject, was a machinist by trade. He came to this country at an early date, first locating in Philadelphia, and subsequently lived for a time in Brandywine, Md.; Walden, N. Y., and New York City, at which latter place he died many years ago.

James W. Hamilton, the father, was a millwright by trade, learning the same in Orange and Dutchess Counties, N. Y. Later he settled at Auburn, from which place he went to St. Paul, Minn., there building the first flourmill ever erected in Minnesota, on the falls of St. Anthony. His family followed him to St. Paul, and he there resided for some years, engaged in the erection of mills, and subsequently located at Toledo, Ohio, where he still followed his trade. From Toledo he went South, spending some years in the erection of cotton-mills, and was in Alabama when the war broke out. Returning to Toledo, Ohio, he ran the Toledo Novelty Works for a time, and then engaged in the oil-refining business. In 1864 he located at Middletown, where for ten years he carried on the latter business, but was then forced out of business by the Standard Oil Company. From that time he lived a retired life until his death, in February, 1892. In politics

he was a Republican, and religiously a Presbyterian. His wife, Elizabeth C. Taylor, was a daughter of William Taylor, who was a native of Ireland, but who came to this country prior to the Revolutionary War, and served his adopted country in the struggle for independence until the close of the war. He located near Montgomery, where he engaged in farming, and where his last days were spent. He was a member of the Presbyterian Church. Mrs. Elizabeth C. Hamilton died May 30, 1893.

The subject of this sketch was the eldest of four children, and remained on the farm near Auburn, N. Y., until fourteen years of age. He then removed with the family to St. Paul, and subsequently to Toledo, Ohio. His education was received in a common school near Auburn, and in the high schools of St. Paul and Toledo. In May, 1862, he enlisted in Company B, One Hundred and Thirtieth Ohio Infantry, and was mustered in as Second Sergeant at Johnson's Island, where for a time the regiment was stationed guarding prisoners, and from there was sent to Petersburg, Va. Mr. Hamilton continued with the regiment in active duty until he was mustered out and honorably discharged, in September, 1864. In November following he came to Middletown and engaged with his father in the oil-refining business, under the firm name of J. W. Hamilton & Son. Their business was the first one established on Genung Street, and was continued until 1874, when, as already stated, the firm was forced out of business by the Standard Oil Company.

Soon after retiring from the oil business, Mr. Hamilton went to New York City, and for four years w .s engaged in the manufacture and sale of tobacco and cigars. He next removed to Sheffield, Pa., where he remained one year, and the succeeding eighteen months he was in the employ of Wells, Fargo & Co. Returning to Middletown, he was made inspector for the city in the construction of the Highland Lake Reservoir, and also the principal sewers of the city. He continued in this occupation until 1892, when he was made Superintendent of Streets. In March, 1893, he was appointed City Clerk and Collector by the Common Council, and has been twice re-appointed. From June, 1886, until June, 1893, he was Chief Engineer of the fire department in Middletown. Before leaving the place for New York City, he had had experience in the fire department, being a member of Excelsior Hook and Ladder Company No. 1, of which he was foreman three and a-half years, resigning the position on his removal from the city. He still retains his interest in the fire department, and has been President of Hamilton Council No. 14, Order of American Firemen. He assisted in the organization of the council and has been its President ever since. In politics he is a Republican, and has served his party in various conventions.

ELLSWORTH A. WHEELER, a horse-shoer in Middletown, was born in Shoemakersville, in Berks County, Pa., September 16, 1864. His grandfather, Henry Wheeler, was also a native of that county, and was by occupation a farmer. Isaac and Lovina (Adams) Wheeler, the parents of our subject, were likewise natives of Berks County. There the former grew to manhood and learned the trade of a mason, which occupation he followed for many years, and finally located on the farm on which he still resides. He is an old Jacksonian Democrat, and is a member of the Methodist Episcopal Church. He is of English ancestry, although for many generations the family have lived in Pennsylvania. Of the seven children in the parental family, six grew to maturity, and five are yet living.

The subject of this sketch is second in order of birth of the children born to Isaac and Lovina Wheeler. Until the age of seventeen he was reared on the home farm, receiving the advantages of the common school only. In 1881 he left the parental roof and went to Gardiner, Ulster County, being employed by his uncle, Peter Adams, who was then engaged in farming. Two years later he left his uncle and commenced to learn the trade of a blacksmith at New Paltz, where he remained one year, and then went to

Gardiner and finished his trade under Mike Dugan. After remaining in the latter village for three years, he went to Florida, Orange County, as a journeyman blacksmith, remaining there two years and seven months. In November, 1890, he came to Middletown and entered into partnership with John Boland, under the firm name of Boland & Wheeler. This partnership continued two years and ten months, when Irving Barr purchased the interest of Mr. Boland, and the business was continued by Wheeler & Barr, who are at present engaged in general blacksmithing, although they make a specialty of horse-shoeing. They have a good reputation in this section of the country, and shoe the fastest horses in Middletown, including "Nora L.," Robert Lemon's mare. They also shoe the horses of Messrs. Tyndale, Donovan, Wilkinson, Hansford, Clemson and Sweager.

Mr. Wheeler was married, in Florida, Orange County, to Miss Jennie Chambers, a native of that place, and they have one child, Jennie. The family resides at No. 14 Watkins Avenue, in a neat residence which Mr. Wheeler has erected since coming to Middletown. His business location is at No. 96 North Street. In politics he is a Democrat.

ROBERT I. CRAWFORD, a farmer residing in the town of Crawford, was born August 23, 1822, in this town. (See sketch of Theron Crawford for family record.) His early life was spent on the home farm, and his education was received in the district schools of his native town and in the academy of Montgomery. When he attained his majority, his father gave him part of the old homestead, where he now lives, and where he has since made his home. He married Miss Nancy J. Thompson, who was a daughter of James R. Thompson, and who died in March, 1887, leaving seven children: Elmer, a prosperous farmer of the town of Crawford; Emily J., who married C. B. Martin, a farmer in Ulster County; Robert, Jr., now residing in this town on his great-grandfather's old place; Leander, a farmer just across the line in Sullivan County; Deborah, who married William Decker, a farmer of the town of Crawford; Agnes, the wife of Watson Ellivy, of Ulster County; and James, who runs the old home farm in connection with his father.

The subject of this sketch is a stanch Republican in his political views, and is an active worker in local political affairs. He has been a member of the Hopewell Presbyterian Church for forty years, and has been an Elder in the same for thirty years. His wife was also a member of that body, as are all the children. Mr. Crawford has been quite successful in life, has given his children all the advantages possible, and has lived to see each well settled in life.

GEORGE A. ELSTON, the genial and popular Postmaster of Port Jervis, assumed the duties of that position January 1, 1894, and is proving that the best interests of the public are very near to his heart by giving them prompt and faithful attention. His appointment to this position was secured by the earnest efforts of his many friends in Democratic circles, and previously, in 1890 and 1891, he filled the position of Secretary of the County Democratic Committee. At various times he has been a delegate to county and district conventions, and for years he has been very active and influential in political affairs.

The Elston family was represented among the early settlers of Orange County. Capt. David Elston, our subject's grandfather, was born here, and by occupation was a farmer. For many years he was active in the Greenville Baptist Church, and assisted in the organization of the first Baptist Church in Port Jervis. Though his home was about seven miles east of this place, he often walked the distance when well along in years. His mental vigor and physical strength, which he retained to an advanced age, were due largely to his regular and temperate habits. A man of patriotic spirit and loyal devotion to his

native country, he ever upheld those interests which tended to the advancement of his community and fellow-citizens. He won his title in the militia service, and his old Queen Anne musket is now in possession of his only male descendant, our subject. His last years were spent in Unionville, N. Y., where he died at the age of seventy-seven. His wife, who bore the maiden name of Lydia Schoonover, died at the age of eighty-nine. Their son Abraham departed this life leaving no children.

The parents of our subject, George and Deborah Jane (Hawkins) Elston, were natives of the towns of Greenville and Mt. Hope, Orange County, respectively, the latter being a daughter of Eliab Hawkins, a farmer. When a young man, George Elston started in the dry-goods business in Port Jervis, being one of the first merchants of the village. After a time he became a member of the firm of Elston & Green, but in 1876 retired from that concern and embarked in business in Middletown. In early years he was a Democrat, but after 1872 he affiliated with the Republican party. His death occurred March 5, 1887, and his wife passed away December 17, 1888. Their eldest son, David, died when eighteen years of age, and their daughter, Ida J., is the wife of Floyd W. Cole, junior member of the firm of Farnum & Cole, of Port Jervis.

In Port Jervis, where he was born September 24, 1859, the subject of this notice has spent his entire life. At the age of sixteen he entered the general store of Nearpass & Bro., with whom he remained for six years, learning all branches of the business. For some nine years afterward, or until 1890, he was employed as bookkeeper and manager of the Port Jervis Flint Glass Works, having charge of the greater part of the business. Upon leaving that firm, he took a place as bookkeeper in the office of Swift's branch of the Chicago Beef Company in Port Jervis.

As assistant to Charles M. Preston, Superintendent of the Banking Department of the State of New York, Mr. Elston held a very responsible position, and during his two years of labor as an examiner he acquitted himself creditably in every way, the books of banks and building and

ISAAC BANKER.

MRS. ISAAC BANKER.

loan associations coming constantly under his notice. That position he resigned that he might enter upon his present work, to which he devotes his earnest attention. Though often urged to accept nomination for local offices, he has invariably declined, the only exception to this being when he served one year as Clerk to the Board of Education. Socially he is identified with the Order of United Friends and the American Legion of Honor, and for several years was District Deputy of the former organization.

September 29. 1881, Mr. Elston was united in marriage with Miss Jennie Caskey, adopted daughter of John Caskey. They are members of the Presbyterian Church and have the friendship of a large circle of acquaintances. There is no citizen of Port Jervis more interested in its progress than Mr. Elston, nor one who has displayed a more commendable degree of public spirit. By fostering progressive enterprises, he has done not a little to promote the interests of the place, and justly ranks among its most influential citizens and prominent men.

ISAAC BANKER, one of the most prominent and highly respected agriculturists of Orange County, is the owner of one hundred and forty-one acres in the town of Goshen. His career has been upright, and his neighbors and friends may hold him up as an example of what may be accomplished by zeal and energy.

Our subject was born in Washingtonville, in 1829, and was the youngest son born to Isaac and Sallie (Denton) Banker, natives of Orange County. Here the father was identified with farm pursuits, in which he was more than ordinarily successful. He owned the farm upon which his son Isaac is now living, and which has descended from father to son for three generations. The father was a man who attended strictly to his own affairs, and was well and favorably known throughout the county. In politics he was a Whig until the formation of the Repub-

63

lican party, when he joined its ranks. He closed his eyes to the scenes of this life in 1870. His wife had died five years previously, in 1865.

Isaac, of this life sketch, gained his first knowledge of the common branches in the schools taught in his district. He was later sent to the Chester Academy, and after finishing his education returned to the old home farm, where he has since made his home, and to which he has devoted his attention up to the present time, each year garnering abundant harvests. Dairying, however, forms his principal industry, and on his place he has a large herd of fine cattle of the best breeds. His residence, which is of a modern style of architecture, is one of the most attractive in the county, and is presided over by his estimable wife, to whom he was married in 1870. She was formerly Miss Martha L. Howell, and is the daughter of Joseph B. and Elizabeth Jane (Weeden) Howell, both of whom are deceased, as are all of their family, with the exception of Mrs. Banker. The parents were natives of this state, and the former was a prominent man in what is now the town of Chester, having served as Justice of the Peace for many years.

Mrs. Banker is a member in excellent standing of the Methodist Episcopal Church, and is one of its most influential workers. Her husband always takes a great interest in the same church, and is one of its liberal supporters. Both Mr. and Mrs. Banker are always foremost in every good work, and give liberally of their means toward the spread of the Gospel. In politics he is a Republican, and therefore gives his support to the success of its chosen leaders.

SAMUEL S. TOOKER, one of the oldest and most highly respected citizens of Orange County, was born in what was formerly the old town of Minisink, but what is now the town of Wawayanda, near Slate Hill. September 8, 1824. His grandfather, Samuel Tooker, was born on Long Island, and located near Slate Hill at a very early day. There Charles P. Tooker, the father of our subject, was born. By profession the grandfather was a surveyor, and also engaged in teaching and farming. On locating here, he purchased one hundred and sixty acres of land, which he improved, and which is now owned by a grandson, Prof. James H. Tooker.

Charles P. Tooker, the father of our subject, was a farmer on the old Tooker place. By his marriage with Hannah Neeley, who was also a native of the old town of Minisink, five children were born: Prof. James H., now residing on the old homestead; Samuel S., our subject; Charles L., who died on the old place in 1845; Catherine J., who married Albert Wickham, and died in 1850; and Julia A., the widow of Fletcher Vail, of Middletown. The father died March 15, 1865, at the age of sixty-six years. He was a successful farmer, and a very popular man in the community. Originally he was a Democrat, with which party he affiliated until the organization of the Republican party, with which he united because of his hatred of slavery. The mother died August 10, 1873, at the age of seventy-six years.

The subject of this sketch grew to manhood on the old homestead, and in his youth attended the subscription schools of his neighborhood. There he learned geography, grammar, spelling, reading and arithmetic, going in the last-named study as far as the "double rule of three." From a boy he turned his attention to farming, which occupation he followed until his retirement in 1867. He was married, February 21, 1850, in the town of Wawayanda, to Miss Emeline R. Stanton, who was born in the town of Deerpark, and who was the daughter of Samuel Stanton, the latter of whom engaged in farming in that town. At the time of her marriage her father had moved to Wawayanda, which was subsequently divided into three towns, Minisink, Greenville and Wawayanda. After the division our subject's house was in Wawayanda. He continued to farm there for two years after his marriage, and in 1853 removed to the town of Wallkill, two and a-half miles west of Middletown, where he also carried on farming. His first purchase there was of eighty-nine acres, to which by subsequent purchase he added twenty-two acres from the Everett Farm and engaged in general farming and the dairy business for about four-

teen years, when he removed to Middletown, and has since virtually lived a retired life. However, he is a stockholder in the Merchants and Manufacturers' Bank, and is interested in other financial operations. He has a fine place at No. 10 Highland Avenue, where he keeps open house, and where he has entertained many friends in past years. His wife died December 15, 1890. In politics he is an old Jacksonian Democrat, and has voted the ticket for fifty years. He is a liberal and public-spirited man, whom it is a pleasure to meet.

EDWARD E. CONKLING is the oldest real-estate and insurance agent in Middletown. The agency was started in 1851 by Selah R. Corwin, and in the mean time has undergone many changes. Our subject is a native of Middletown, born August 20, 1860. His grandfather, William Conkling, was for many years a resident of Pennsylvania, where he was engaged in merchandising, and later removed to Westtown, N. Y., where he engaged in farming. He died in Middletown many years ago. The noted Roscoe Conkling came from the same family as did he.

Stephen S. Conkling, the father of our subject, was born in Westtown, and in early manhood removed to Middletown, where for many years he was engaged in the lumber trade. He was also engaged in building and in the real-estate business, and laid out many lots and additions to the city. Among the streets and avenues that he laid out were Everett Street, Genung Street, Liberty Street, Lake Avenue and Academy Avenue. His lumber-yard was located near the Erie depot. He is now living a retired life in his beautiful residence located on Wickham Avenue. In politics he is a strong Democrat. Religiously he is a member of the Congregational Church, in which body he has always taken an active interest, is a member of the Official Board, and served on the Building Committee when the present church building was erected. His wife, Phœbe J. Lathrop, was born in the town of Wawayanda, and is a daughter of David Lathrop, a farmer of that town. Nine children were born unto them, seven of whom are now living. The subject of this sketch grew to manhood in his native city, and received his education in the academy here. When seventeen he entered the employ of his brother-in-law, C. J. Boyd, with whom he remained until January 12, 1880, when he commenced clerking for Boyd & Corwin, who were in the insurance and real-estate business. Here he remained through all the changes of the firm, including Boyd & Douglas, who soon succeeded Boyd & Corwin. In April, 1881, Mr. Boyd sold out to Mr. Dolson, and the firm became Douglas & Dolson. In 1885 Mr. Conkling bought a one-fourth interest and the firm became Douglas, Dolson & Co. This lasted until 1891, when Mr. Douglas sold his interest to Mr. Conkling, and the firm became Dolson & Conkling, continuing thus until December 28, 1893, when Mr. Conkling purchased the entire business, and has since conducted it alone. The following old reliable companies are represented in the insurance department: Continental; German-American; Niagara and Williamsburg City, of New York; Franklin, of Philadelphia; Sun and Phœnix, of London; Hartford and Ætna, of Hartford; Queen, of New York; Springfield, of Springfield, Mass.; Dutchess County Mutual, of Poughkeepsie; and the Imperial, of London; also the Inter-state Casualty Company, an accident-insurance company; and the Mutual Life, of New York.

In the real-estate business, Mr. Conkling handles the new addition of Vail & Foote, besides much other west-end property. He has on his list farms all over the country, including New York and the Southern States. He has made many improvements in the city, including two neat residences erected for himself, one on East Avenue, which he sold, and the other at No. 103 Highland Avenue, in which he resides. In all matters pertaining to the business interest of Middletown, he takes a lively interest. He is a member of the Orange County Telephone Company, and is interested in the Driving Park and Building Bank.

Mr. Conkling was married, in Scotchtown, to

Miss Florence Sutherland, who was born in Orange County, and who is a daughter of Abraham Sutherland, a wholesale merchant of New York City. They have two children, Lawrence S. and Anna L. Mr. and Mrs. Conkling are members of the Congregational Church of Middletown, in the work of which they take an active interest. Our subject is a member of the Orange County Underwriters' Association, and of the Middletown Board of Underwriters. In the latter he serves as Treasurer, and in both organizations is a member of the rating committee. He is an active member of Excelsior Hook and Ladder Company No. 1. As a citizen he enjoys the respect and confidence of his fellow-men, and is ever ready to give of his means and time to the advancement of the material interests of his native city.

THOMAS S. HUTCHISON. Superintendent of the Columbia Dye and Print Works, is at the head of the silk-printing in America. He is a native of Lanarkshire, Scotland, and was born August 24, 1854, a son of George and Christine (Stodhard) Hutchison, both of whom were also natives of Scotland. George Hutchison was a fancy weaver, a trade which he learned in youth, and which he followed until his retirement on account of age. He worked at his trade in his native country until 1873, when he located at South Manchester, Conn., and there continued in the same line. Now, however, he is living a retired life, at the age of sixty-eight. In religious belief he is a Presbyterian, and comes of an old Scotch family of the Highlands. His wife, Christine Stodhard, is a daughter of Thomas Stodhard, who served in the English army as a private in the Ninety-second Highlanders. He was in the war against Napoleon, and also in Egypt. The Stodhards came from the Lowlands, where they had long been established. To George and Christine Hutchison were born twelve children, ten of whom grew to maturity, and nine of whom are yet living, and all residing in America. Three brothers are with our subject; two reside in South Manchester; one, James, is superintendent of Cheney Brothers' weaving establishment; and three daughters are in South Manchester.

Thomas S. Hutchison was the third-born in the family. His educational advantages were very limited, but, by reading and observation, he is now a well informed man. When nine years of age, he commenced to learn the weaver's trade under his father, with whom he continued until he was past sixteen, when, in company with his brother James, he came to America. He left Glasgow in May, 1871, on the steamer "Australia," bound for New York City. After his arrival he at once proceeded to South Manchester, where he worked at weaving about one year, when, on account of failing health, he was compelled to seek outdoor employment. For six months he was fireman of an engine on the railroad, and later apprenticed himself to learn the trade of silk printing with Cheney Brothers, that industry then being in its infancy in this country. Commencing at the bottom, he worked his way up through every department until he had mastered the business in all its parts, and to-day is credited with being the most experienced silk-printer in America. When he began, the printing was all done by hand, but at the present time it is principally done by machinery.

Our subject learned the business under Robert Melville, who was from an old family of printers in Scotland, and who has since returned to his native land. On the return of Mr. Melville to Scotland, Mr. Hutchison was made foreman of the printing department. He subsequently resigned his position, however, and went to Paterson, N. J., with the Hawthorne Works, or Ames Dyeing, Finishing and Printing Company, as superintendent. He remained there but six months, when he was offered his present position. For some time he had been flooded with letters offering him positions, but on account of his wife's ill-health he decided to come to Middletown, and in April, 1891, took charge of the Columbia Dye and Print Works as superintendent and manager. The works have since been enlarged by the addi-

tion of two printing-machines, and now have a capacity of thirteen thousand yards of silk per day. They are located on the corner of Railroad and Grove Streets, the main building being 100 x 150 feet, five stories in height. All of the building is occupied and used in the business, and five engines are required. The success of the mills has been unprecedented, and the proprietors are branching out into other lines, now printing flannels and woolens. Employment is given to about one hundred and ten hands, and the payroll amounts to over $1,000 per week.

Mr. Hutchison was married in South Manchester, Conn., to Miss Hattie Stebbins, a native of Hadley, Mass., and of old Puritan stock. She died in Manchester, leaving one child, George E., who is a practical color-maker. Mr. Hutchison subsequently married Matilda Christine Nelson, a native of Sweden, but who came to this country in early childhood, and was here reared and educated. They have four children living: Joseph Nelson, Thomas C., Carrie Agnes and Marjorie A.

Mrs. Hutchison is a lady of superior ability, and is well educated. Her father was a professor in the schools of Sweden, having been educated at Guttenberg. Her mother, Caisa Peterson, is also a native of Sweden. The parents still reside in their native country, but their four children reside in America.

Fraternally Mr. Hutchison is a member of Middletown Lodge No. 112, I. O. O. F., and religiously is identified with the First Presbyterian Church of Middletown, of which body his wife is also a member, although she was reared a Lutheran. While in South Manchester, Mr. Hutchison was a member of the Congregational Church. Since coming to Middletown he has been active in religious work, and for one year was superintendent of the Sunday-school. He is an active worker and director of the Young Men's Christian Association of this place. In politics he is a Republican.

Mr. and Mrs. Hutchison reside in a beautiful home on Ridge Street, which has a frontage of two hundred and forty feet, and a depth of two hundred and fifty feet. Coming to this country

HON. D. H. BAILEY.

a poor boy, by industry and faithful discharge of all duties devolving upon him he has worked his way up to his present enviable position. In handling men he has been very successful, and has never had a strike among those in his employ. As a testimonial of their regard, the employes of the print works presented him with a handsome cane, and his wife a handsome chair. In this country there are at present but three silk-printing works, the Hawthorne, Cheney Brothers' and the Columbia Dye and Print Works, of which our subject is the manager. The latter leads them all, and its success is largely due to the enterprise of the subject of this sketch.

―――――――◈❀◈―――――――

HON. DANIEL H. BAILEY, Secretary and Treasurer of the Middletown Savings Bank, was born near the village of Mechanicstown, Orange County, in June, 1834, and is a son of Deacon Nathaniel and Mahala (Dunning) Bailey. The former was born in the town of Wallkill, and the latter near Middletown, this county. They were of Revolutionary stock, the grandfather of our subject having served in the War for Independence as a Captain. By occupation Deacon Bailey was a farmer, spending the greater part of his life in agricultural pursuits, but his later years were spent in Middletown. He purchased a tract of land on High Street, on which he erected a comfortable home, and there spent his declining days. His death occurred some years ago, and his wife has since passed away. They were both members of the Presbyterian Church, in which body he was first a Deacon, and subsequently an Elder for many years. In politics he was originally a Whig, but on the organization of the Republican party allied himself with it, and was a strong advocate of its principles. Deacon Bailey was twice married, and by his first wife had one child. His second wife was a daughter of Jacob Dunning, who was a farmer living north of Middletown, on the plank road. By this marriage there were four children, three of whom were daughters, our subject being the only son. Almeda J. was the first wife of Dr. S. W. Mills;

Harriet E. became the first wife of Theodore J. Denton; and Delia married Dr. Henry W. Hardenbergh.

Daniel H. Bailey received his primary education in the public schools, later attended Wallkill Academy, and subsequently studied under the direction of Mr. Freeman. His first business experience was in the capacity of clerk in the employ of T. J. Denton, with whom he remained only a few months, however, when, in 1856, he engaged with Bull & Van Fleet, then doing business in Middletown. In 1858 he accepted a situation with the dry-goods firm of Lord & Taylor in New York City, remaining with them two years, and at the expiration of that time he entered into partnership with T. J. Denton. His father dying about a year afterward, he sold out to his partner and came to Middletown. Home affairs occupied his attention for several years, after which for one year he was in the employ of the American Express Company as agent and messenger. On the 1st of December, 1873, he entered the Middletown Savings Bank, and in July, 1885, he was elected Secretary and Treasurer of the same, which position he has since continued to hold. The bank is recognized as one of the solid institutions of Orange County, and under the management of Mr. Bailey it has gradually increased its business from a very small beginning, until now it has deposits aggregating $1,500,000. It has occupied its present location since 1874.

The life of Mr. Bailey has been a most active one. Notwithstanding the arduous duties devolving upon him as Secretary and Treasurer of the Savings Bank, he has yet found time to devote to public interests and social intercourse. In politics he has always been a Republican, and cast his first Presidential vote for John C. Fremont, the first candidate of the party for President. In 1868 he was elected President of the Village Board, was re-elected to that position in 1869, the term of office being for one year, and in 1880 he was elected for a term of two years. During his term of office there was much to make the position a busy one. The first sewer was built during his administration; it is called the Trunk Sewer, and extends from John Street to

Monhagen Brook, being a very expensive piece of work. Main and High Streets were widened, a drinking fountain erected, North Street was paved with Belgian block, and other improvements were made. In 1892 Mr. Bailey was elected Mayor of the city, and during his term the trolley was built and completed. He served from March, 1892, until March, 1894, and refused a re-nomination. In his election to office he was always a candidate on the Republican ticket.

Personally Mr. Bailey is a man of very quiet tastes and habits. He is possessed of excellent judgment and is one not likely to be led astray by a boom in stocks or any investment not particularly substantial. He ever has the interests of his city at heart, being willing to make many sacrifices in building it up, and at the time of the location of the asylum here he took an active part. He has been a member of the First Presbyterian Church for over forty years, and has been Trustee and Chairman of its board several times. Since 1863 he has been a member of Phœnix Engine Company No. 4, and travels with the company every fall. He served as first President of the company, and continued to hold this position until elected Mayor, when he resigned. During the war he was a member of the Union League and served as Trustee. Mr. Bailey was married, in January, 1862, to Sarah E., daughter of John H. Robertson.

—+·+· —·|>×°◦•◉◦•×◦|·—·+·+·—

CHARLES DOWNING. While it is impossible, within the limits of this volume, to review in detail the life of the illustrious gentleman above named, it is fitting that some mention be made of his honorable and useful career. A life-long resident of Newburgh, he was here born July 9, 1802, and died January 18, 1885. His parents, Samuel and Eunice Downing, were natives of Lexington, Mass., and upon their marriage removed from Cambridge to Newburgh, but later went to Montgomery, where the father intended to follow his trade of carriage-maker.

Ill-health, however, caused him to return to Newburgh, where, about the beginning of the present century, he established a shop for the manufacture of wagons, on the northeast corner of Broad and Liberty Streets. Within a few years he abandoned his trade to become a nurseryman, in which he was the first in the county to successfully engage. He died November 1, 1822, and his wife passed away October 29, 1838.

The four children of Samuel and Eunice Downing were: Emily, born in 1801, married Sylvester Ferry, and died in 1864; Charles, of this sketch; George W., born in 1804, and died in 1846; and Andrew J., whose biography is presented on another page of this volume. The early years of our subject were passed under the careful training of his father in the nursery business and in attendance upon the common schools of his day. Before he had attained his majority his father died, and the responsibility of conducting the business, and the support of the family, to a large degree devolved upon him.

Forming a partnership with his brother, under the firm name of C. & A. J. Downing, our subject embarked in the nursery business, but a few years later the connection was dissolved, and in 1837 he removed to the outskirts of the city. He continued in the nursery business for thirty years and became the most prominent pomologist of the United States. His was a penetrating and inquiring mind, that led him to study carefully the forms, varieties and qualities of the different fruits that came under his observation, and by experimenting and proving he was enabled to improve many varieties of fruits and originate others, some of which bear his name to this day. His last years were passed at his home on the corner of Chambers and South Streets, where, free from business cares, he was at liberty to pursue his pomological investigations and literary work with greater assiduity than in former years.

In his earlier years Mr. Downing devoted his attention principally to the cultivation of fruits, but in later life he became a regular contributor to periodicals, and twice revised "The Fruits and Fruit Trees of America," written by his brother, and after the last revision he added two appendices, containing new fruits, corrections, etc., making the work twice its original size. It has become a classic, and is regarded as the highest authority on the subjects of which it treats. Increasing honors came to Mr. Downing with his advancing years. In his chosen field he gained high renown. People from all parts of the country sought his advice and deferred to his judgment, and he was conceded to be the authority on pomology. Largely through his influence Newburgh became the center of a great fruit-growing district, and thus he was instrumental in promoting the prosperity of the locality.

September 20, 1830, Mr. Downing married Miss Mary, daughter of Samuel Wait, of Montgomery, N. Y. For fifty years they lived happily together, sharing their joys and sorrows, until they were separated by her death, October 18, 1880.

A. KETCHUM, a lumber and coal dealer at Middletown, was born in the town of Mamakating, near Wurtsboro, in Sullivan County, January 24, 1831. His father, James Ketchum, was born in Putnam County about 1800. His grandfather, Daniel Ketchum, who was of Welsh descent, was long a resident of that county, but removed with his family to Sullivan County, where he died. In early life the father learned the trade of a millwright, and erected and equipped many mills throughout Putnam and Sullivan Counties. Later he engaged in the manufacture of cart felloes and wheelbarrows at Oakland, N. Y. About 1845 he purchased a farm near Oakland, which he improved, and on which he passed the remainder of his life, dying at the age of seventy-six years. His wife, the mother of our subject, was Miss Harriet C. Fields. She was born in Putnam County, near where the Ketchums lived. Her grandfather, Joseph Coles Fields, was also a resident of Putnam County, in the town of Southeast, where his death occurred. Mrs. Harriet C. Ketchum died in 1878, at the age of seventy-seven years.

In the parental family were ten children who grew to maturity, and eight of the number are now living. Hiram was a member of the One Hundred and Twenty-fourth New York Infantry, and was wounded in the thigh at the battle of Chancellorsville. He now resides in Middletown. The subject of this sketch was fifth in the family, and was reared on the farm, receiving his education in the district school. Later he took charge of the home farm, and operated it until 1857, when he engaged in business in Oakland, manufacturing lumber and wheelbarrows. For a time the business was run under the firm name of Ketchum Brothers and later by our subject alone. He operated two sawmills in Oakland, and largely engaged in the manufacture of wheelbarrows, tray, coal and garden barrows. Thousands of them were carted to Otisville, then sent to New York City, and from there were shipped all over the country. After operating the two branches of business for a number of years, Mr. Ketchum gave up manufacturing and engaged in the lumber business exclusively. Much of the lumber was supplied to the Erie Railroad, being used in car-manufacturing, and he ran the mill until he came to Middletown in 1886. In carrying on the business, he found it necessary to purchase a great deal of timber-land, and he is to-day the owner of over seventeen hundred acres on the Neversink.

Since locating in Middletown Mr. Ketchum has been engaged in the lumber and coal business at No. 245 North Street. He has a frontage of one hundred and fifty feet running back to the Ontario & Western Railroad, where he has a coal-pocket and siding, the pocket being 144x18 feet. He carries from three hundred to six hundred tons of coal, and is the largest dealer in coal in the city. He has a fine arrangement with drop-screen in the wagon. His main shed is 100x20 feet, with an addition adjoining of 50x18 feet. Everything is well and conveniently arranged, and Mr. Ketchum does a large wholesale and retail business both in lumber and coal. He was one of the first to locate on North Street.

In 1858 Mr. Ketchum was united in marriage with Miss Susan J. Williams, who was born in Forestburg, Sullivan County. To them five children have been born: A. F., residing in Middletown; John A., with his father in the office; Charles H., in the insurance business at Cleveland, Ohio; and Clara C. and D. Albert, at home. The family resides in a neat and comfortable house at No. 202 North Street, which was erected by Mr. Ketchum on coming to this city. Politically he is a Republican.

MARCUS S. HAYNE, M. D. During the long period of his residence in Unionville, no one accomplished more in behalf of its progress, or became more thoroughly identified with its best interests, than did the late Dr. Hayne. He was known throughout this locality as one of the most honorable and straightforward of men, upright in every respect. For some time prior to his demise, failing health prevented him from actively participating in public affairs, and he lived retired, rejoicing in the good-will of his acquaintances, and filling up the measure of his days with good works. Laying down the burdens of life at length, he entered into rest April 8, 1891, and his body was buried in the cemetery which his efforts had secured for the village nearly twenty-five years before.

The Hayne family is of German origin. The first representative in this country was our subject's great-grandfather, who emigrated from Germany, and settled in Wantage, N. J., in 1775. The Doctor was born near Deckertown, that state, January 23, 1816, and was the son of Benjamin and Millie (Whittaker) Hayne, of the town of Minisink. After carrying on the studies of the district school at Unionville, he attended the well known school of William Rankin at Deckertown, N. J., where he was later a teacher. In 1838 he commenced to study medicine with Dr. Lynn, of Deckertown, and afterward entered the office of Dr. Sylvester Austin, in Ontario County, N. Y. Later he became a student in the Geneva Medical College, from which he was graduated in 1841.

Opening an office in Westtown, the Doctor began the practice of his profession, remaining there until 1844, when he moved to Mt. Salem,

Sussex County, N. J. In 1846 he came to Unionville, where he resided until his death. Until 1870 he gave his attention assiduously to his profession, and had a large practice among the people of the town and of the country round about. In 1870 he relinquished general practice, though still retaining professional work in consultations, and he then turned his attention to business matters. In 1865 he had become interested, with his father-in-law, in the Unionville Creamery, and later in the creamery at Wantage. Both of these enterprises he managed until shortly before his death, when he transferred them to his son, S. Christie, who runs them successfully, and in addition to the regular work manufactures sugar of milk in the Unionville Creamery.

In 1843 Dr. Hayne married Amelia VanFleet, who died January 30, 1848. Their two children died in infancy. In 1849 he was united with Jane Decker, who died July 16, 1856. The children by that marriage were Albert B., who died October 12, 1876, aged twenty-six; Annie M., deceased; and Marcus P., an attorney of Minneapolis. The third marriage of the Doctor took place in January, 1858, when Eliza A., daughter of Samuel and Jane Christie, of Wantage, became his wife. Mrs. Hayne, with one son, S. Christie, an enterprising and capable business man, survives.

The brothers and sisters of Dr. Hayne were as follows: Peter, who lives in Goshen; Millie, wife of Henry B. Lee, of Waverly, N. Y.; Frances, Mrs. A. W. Van Fleet, of Unionville; Caroline, Mrs. O. W. Cooke, of New York City; Jacob, who lives in Goshen; Martha, wife of J. B. Hendershot, of Newton, N. J.; and Lewis and Henry, deceased. Interested in everything pertaining to his profession, Dr. Hayne identified himself with the Orange County Medical Society in 1841 and remained a member of it until his death. In 1868 he was instrumental in laying out the Unionville Cemetery, and this he managed as a private enterprise for some years, but afterward transferred it to a Board of Trustees, by whom it was incorporated.

In early life a Whig, Dr. Hayne joined the

ELTING CUDDEBACK.

Republican party at its organization, and was always true to its principles. In April, 1879, he was appointed Postmaster at Unionville, and served efficiently in that capacity until removed by the Cleveland administration. Upon settling in Unionville, he joined the Presbyterian Church, and of it he remained a consistent member until his death. In addition to his residence in the village, he owned another dwelling here and a valuable farm over the Jersey line.

In all his enterprises he was assisted by his devoted wife, who survives him, and who occupies a high place in the regard of the people of this community. Her husband's energy and excellent judgment secured a comfortable property, and she is surrounded by every comfort which enhances the pleasure of living. The estate is in charge of her son, S. C., a young man of superior ability, who looks after affairs in a most praiseworthy manner.

———※———

ELTING CUDDEBACK, one of the reliable and representative agriculturists of the town of Deerpark, was born October 10, 1816, on the farm where he now resides, although at the present time it is within the corporation limits of Port Jervis. His parents, Benjamin and Blandina (Van Etten) Cuddeback, were well known people of this community, and the former was a son of Benjamin and Catherine (Van Fleet) Cuddeback. The grandfather of our subject lived about two miles from Huguenot, in an old stone house, which is still used as a residence. There his death occurred when his son Benjamin was only eight years old. He had three sons, Benjamin, Henry and William, and two daughters, Synche and Jemima. William, of the town of Deerpark, who wedded Miss Van Inwegen, had a large family, none of whom now live in this county, and his death occurred on the old homestead when he had reached the age of ninety years. Henry, also of this town, married Esther Gumaer, and bought a farm on the east side of the Neversink, where his grandson, Henry G., now lives; he also reached the age of ninety years. Synche married Simon Westfall, of Port Jervis;

and Jemima became the wife of Anthony Van Etten, of the town of Owasco, Cayuga County.

Benjamin Cuddeback, the father of our subject, was united in marriage with Blandina Van Etten, a daughter of Levi and Jane (Westbrook) Van Etten, who lived where Levi Van Etten, his grandson, now resides, on the east bank of the Neversink. The farm purchased by his father is the one on which Elting now makes his home, and there he carried on agricultural pursuits until his death. Politically he gave his support to the Democracy, and was a public-spirited, enterprising man. In early days he had engaged in teaching, but later learned the weaver's trade, which he followed for many years. Each house then had a loom of its own, but employed some skilled workman to do the weaving. He served as Town Supervisor, and was Justice of the Peace for a number of years, holding that office at the time of the building of the canal. The Irish workmen would often get into a pitched battle, and on Monday morning they would be brought before him, and he would send them to jail at Goshen by the wagon-load. He had more power as a Justice of the Peace than those in that office to-day. He was quite an active politician, being one of the leaders of his party in Orange County. His death occurred on the 25th of July, 1870, at the age of ninety-one years, and his wife, who was two years his junior, passed away in 1868. He was a stout, strong, robust man, an able successor and a noble ancestor. For forty years he was Elder in the Reformed Church, of which he was a staunch supporter.

Of the present family we make the following mention: Catherine married James Cuddeback, who, though of the same name, was not a relative, and she died at the age of seventy-eight years. Jane, who wedded Alex Johnson, a teacher and farmer, lives in Port Jervis. Asenath became the wife of Samuel B. Farnum, of Port Jervis. (See sketch elsewhere.) Elting is the next in order of birth. Hannah, who married Peter P. Swartwout, father of Dr. Henry Swartwout, makes her home in Huguenot, Orange County. Thomas, a doctor, practiced here for a time, but later removed to Big Flats, Chemung County, where he died at the age of seventy-four years. Jemima became the wife of Lemuel S. Chapin, now of Crete, Neb. Lydia married Wallace Titsworth, a farmer residing near Deckertown, N. J. All but two of the family are still living.

Elting Cuddeback was named in honor of Rev. Cornelius C. Elting, who had recently arrived in Port Jervis at the time of his birth, but preached in this place for twenty-five years. His boyhood was passed upon the home farm, and when he was ten years of age the canal was cut through his father's land, and he became familiar with every detail of canal-building. All his life has been devoted to the labors of an agriculturist, and he now keeps on hand about fifty cows for dairy purposes. Besides the Delaware & Hudson Canal, the Monticello Railroad also crossed his property, about ten acres of which he has platted and built upon, and it now forms an addition to Port Jervis. He uses his right of franchise in support of the Democratic party, but takes no active part in political matters. He is a man of remarkably good judgment, sound common-sense and ability, which traits have made him prosperous and influential; and the respect in which he is held is due to his high moral character and his disinterested benevolence.

On the 18th of September, 1844, Mr. Cuddeback was united in marriage with Miss Ann B. Elting, who was born April 29, 1820, in New Jersey, and was a daughter of Rev. C. C. and Anna Maria (Bevier) Elting, the latter a native of Rochester, Ulster County, N. Y. Mrs. Cuddeback was called to her final rest January 20, 1862, and she left four children. Cornelius Elting is an attorney of Port Jervis, of whom see sketch elsewhere in this volume; Benjamin, who died June 17, 1892, at the age of forty-two years, was engaged in farming on the old home place, and he left a widow and four children, who are now living in Port Jervis; William L. is a physician and surgeon of the same place; and Blandina Maria is the wife of Rev. John L. Stilwell, pastor of the Reformed Church of Bloomingburg, Sullivan County, N. Y. Mr. Cuddeback was again married, on the 10th of August, 1871, this union being with Margaret Cuddeback, who was born

April 10, 1818, and was a daughter of William and Mary (Westbrook) Cuddeback, of Cuddebackville. Her death occurred on the 21st of October, 1884. Her sister Sarah, the widow of Martin Wheeler, who was a carpenter of Cuddebackville and died in Newburgh in 1862, has for ten years been housekeeper for our subject. She has two sons, Frank W. and William H. Wheeler, printers of Waterbury, Conn., where she made her home for some years.

JAMES A. BEAKES was one of the brave boys in blue in the One Hundred and Twenty-fourth New York Infantry, which was principally made up of men from Orange and Sullivan Counties. He was born at Middletown, on the North Plank Road, February 5, 1841, and is a son of Mahlon Stacey and Emeline (Carpenter) Beakes, both of whom were natives of the town of Wallkill. They were the parents of eleven children, ten of whom are yet living: James A., our subject; George E.; Charles H. C., of Cornwall; and Mary F., William B., Joseph E., Albert S., Abbie J., Annie M. and Sarah E. Spencer M. died at the age of two years.

James A. Beakes was reared on the home farm, where he remained until his enlistment in the United States service during the War of the Rebellion. He received his primary education in the district school, and completed it in Wallkill Academy. On the 5th of August, 1862, he enlisted in Company E, One Hundred and Twenty-fourth New York Infantry, and as a private was mustered into service at Goshen. Among the engagements in which he participated were Fredericksburg, Chancellorsville and Gettysburg. In the last-mentioned engagement, in which they were engaged three days, all the officers of his company were either killed or wounded, and he was left in command of the company. After the battle, with nine others of his regiment, he was on detached service, and was sent to Hart's Island to forward troops, where he remained until the close of the war.

HON. CHARLES ST. JOHN.

He was mustered out and honorably discharged at the latter place, June 15, 1865, at which time he was a sergeant in the company.

Returning home, he engaged in farm labor on his father's place until his marriage, in 1867, near Mt. Hope, with Miss Mary Augusta Mapes. Her birth occurred near that place, and she was a daughter of Stephen S. Mapes, who was also born in the same locality. Her grandfather, Seth Mapes, was a farmer by occupation, and served in the War of 1812. Her great-grandfather, Erastus Mapes, lived to be nearly one hundred years of age. Mrs. Beakes grew to womanhood in her native town, where she received her primary education, completing her course in the Wallkill Academy. Six children were born unto them: Fred M., employed by C. H. C. Beakes, of New York City; Janet, at home; Laura, who died in 1893, at the age of seventeen years, in the year of her graduation from Wallkill Academy; Albert L. and Mary Augusta, at home; and Harry, who died in infancy.

In 1867 Mr. Beakes purchased his father's farm of one hundred acres, continuing in farm work and in the dairy business at that place for four years, when he removed to New York City, and engaged in the retail milk business. Three years later he sold out and returned to his farm, where he remained two years, and then leased a creamery at Dwaar Kill, Ulster County, which he operated for nine years. After closing out the same he went to Merrickville, Delaware County, and purchased a creamery, which he has since continued to operate. In 1894 he purchased a creamery at Franklin, that county, which he also operates. He is engaged in shipping milk and cream to New York City, and also engages in the manufacture of butter and cheese. His creameries have a capacity of about three hundred and fifty cans per day. Mr. Beakes is interested in the raising of blooded cattle, especially Jerseys, and has upon his place a herd of twenty-five head.

In the spring of 1890 Mr. Beakes removed his family to Middletown, and purchased his present residence at No. 27 Washington Street. In politics he is a Republican, and while residing in Ulster County was Commissioner of the town of Shawangunk. Religiously he is a member of the First Presbyterian Church, as is also his wife. He is a member of the Board of Trade at Middletown, taking an active interest in its proceedings, and fraternally is a member of Hoffman Lodge No. 412, F. & A. M., and of Capt. W. A. Jackson Post No. 203, G. A. R.

HON. CHARLES ST. JOHN. Treasured in the hearts of the men and women of Orange County is the memory of the honored dead, those who once lived and labored among us, but who now have gone away. By the remembrance of their progressive spirit and noble deeds, the young are stimulated to action and the old are cheered and soothed. From the life of Hon. Charles St. John there may be gleaned may lessons of honor, truth and lofty principle. For many years a resident of Port Jervis, he was known and honored by all the citizens of this place, and by them he will be remembered with affection through the years to come.

A volume of this character would be incomplete were no mention made of Mr. St. John, for at one time he was more widely known than any other citizen of the county. His public service was of a useful and important nature, and he contributed effectively to the development of the resources of this section. It is fitting, therefore, that we should perpetuate, through these pages, the record of his honorable career. A life-long resident of this county, his birth occurred in the town of Mt. Hope, October 8, 1818. He was the son of Stephen and Abigail (Horton) St. John, whose family consisted of eight children. His sister, Mrs. Amelia Marvin, who died in 1894, was for many years one of the most cultured ladies and prominent social leaders of Port Jervis.

The boyhood years of Mr. St. John were passed in the village of Port Jervis, whither his parents removed when he was about two years of age, and he early identified himself with public affairs, ever maintaining an interest in matters relating to the public welfare. Politically he espoused

PORTRAIT AND BIOGRAPHICAL RECORD.

the principles of the Republican party, and to its tenets he was ever loyal and true. He became one of the leaders of his party, and his superior ability led to his selection to serve in important official positions. It is unnecessary to state that in every office to which he was called he served with credit to himself and to the satisfaction of his fellow-citizens. In 1870 he was elected Representative to Congress, and was re-elected in 1872. As a member of that honorable body, he was enabled to present and support many measures helpful to his constituents, and having in view the advancement of the general welfare of the people. He was a stockholder in the National Bank of Port Jervis, being Vice-President at the time that Henry H. Farnum was President. After that gentleman's death, Mr. St. John became President, and held the office until his death. He was engaged in many business enterprises, and in the early days was greatly interested in the lumber business, floating large rafts of lumber down both the Susquehanna and Delaware Rivers to the markets of Baltimore and Philadelphia. For many years he was a prominent merchant in Port Jervis, and was also interested in a foundry.

Mr. St. John owned a farm in every state in the Union at one time and several in some states. These he rented on shares, refusing to rent for money, but aiding every man who needed assistance. In some places he owned a number of farms, and in South Dakota he owned a half-interest in a farm of twenty-five hundred acres. He also owned an orange grove and valuable real estate at Palatka, Fla., and much of his time was spent in that place, superintending his important interests there, as well as gaining needed recuperation. For a time he was engaged in business in New York City, but, preferring a country life, he sold out his interest there and returned to Port Jervis.

Mr. St. John's first wife was Ellen S. Thompson, who at the time of her death left three sons and three daughters: Ellen; Elizabeth, wife of Alonzo Stryker; Stephen, a druggist in Port Jervis; Charles, proprietor of the Port Jervis *Union* and the *Orange County Farmer*; George; and Amelia, wife of Lewis Goldsmith. Two children died in infancy. For his second wife Mr. St. John married Frances Reed, who died leaving no children. His third wife, Ada Hortense, was a daughter of Cornelius Caskey, a life-long friend of Mr. St. John, and of whom mention is made on another page. They were united in marriage October 10, 1888, three years prior to his decease. He was taken ill June 6, 1891, and on the 6th of the next month he died at his home in Port Jervis. He was mourned by hundreds of men and women, who numbered him among their friends, and his death was regarded as a public loss.

Mr. St. John never held membership with any fraternal organizations, nor was he a church member, though in early life he attended the Dutch Reformed Church and sang in the choir, but later, becoming dissatisfied, he withdrew. His family was reared in the faith of the Presbyterian Church, and he was one of the most liberal supporters of and contributors to that organization. He was a man of the greatest generosity; in fact, his constant benevolences prevented him from ever gaining wealth, though he was in comfortable circumstances. His friends, when in need, he assisted to the extent of his ability, and no needy person ever appealed in vain to him for help. His benevolence was well known, and he was often imposed upon. Generosity may be said to be his leading characteristic, and there are scores of poor persons who remember him with the greatest reverence as their friend in time of trouble.

EDWARD R. RUSSELL, proprietor of the Oriental Hotel at Middletown, was born in Honesdale, Pa., November 25, 1850, and is of Scotch descent, his great-grandfather coming from Scotland and locating in New York at a very early day. His father, Albert H. Russell, was born in Fredonia, N. Y., grew to manhood in his native state, and subsequently removed to Honesdale, Pa., where he engaged in the mercantile trade with his brother, Zenos H. Russell. The latter was also President of the Honesdale

WICKHAM C. McNISH.

National Bank. From Honesdale Albert H. Russell removed to New York City, and at No. 99 Barclay Street was engaged in the wholesale provision trade. He later removed to Narrowsburg, and became proprietor of Murray's Hotel. In 1863 Mr. Russell came to Middletown and purchased the Ogden House, which he continued three years, and then engaged in the retail lumber business, the firm being Eaton & Russell. They remained on the corner of Main and Canal Streets until 1879, when Mr. Russell sold out and again engaged in the hotel business, taking charge of the old Taylor House. In 1881 he rebuilt the old Grand Central, and changed the name to the Russell House, which he continued to operate until his death, in 1885. He was quite prominent in local affairs, and was Supervisor of the town of Wallkill, when the town and village of Middletown comprised one district. He was a member of the Board of Education for nine years, and was for some years Trustee of the Middletown Savings Bank. In politics he was a Republican, and religiously he was a Baptist. His wife, Harriet Babcock, who was born near Westerly, R. I., and died in 1868, came of an old Eastern family. The parental family comprised the following children: Edward R., our subject; Albert H., of the McQuaid Iron Company, of Brooklyn, N. Y.; and Sarah B., Mrs. Lucky, of Middletown.

For the most part the childhood days of our subject were spent in Middletown, and his education was received in Wallkill and Monticello Academies. He began his business life as a clerk in the lumber-yard of Eaton & Russell, remaining with them as bookkeeper for eight or nine years, then accepting a clerkship in the Middletown Water Works Company, and later with Denton & Barker, clothiers. He was next private secretary to C. W. Douglass, General Superintendent of the New York & Oswego Midland Railroad, and in 1878 he became conductor on the New York, Ontario & Western Railroad, running between Middletown and Norwich. He remained with that company until 1893, and then bought the Monopole Hotel, remodeled it and changed its name to the Oriental Hotel. It is now

a first-class house, located on East Main Street, near the Main Street Depot, and has a frontage of one hundred and two feet.

Mr. Russell was married, in Bloomingburg, to Miss Ella N. Hennion, a native of New York City, and a daughter of David Hennion, one of the first to engage in the creamery business, and the first to take Orange County milk to New York City. One child has been born unto them, Henry Z. Mr. Russell is an active member of Millard Division of the Order of Railway Conductors, and takes great interest in its proceedings, although he is not at present on the road. He is a member of Grace Episcopal Church of Middletown, and in politics is a Republican.

───────────✦───────────

WICKHAM C. McNISH, one of the oldest and best known residents of Middletown, is a descendant in the fifth generation from Rev. George McNish, a native of Scotland, who came to America in 1705, upon the solicitation of Rev. Francis Mackenzie, who was afterward styled "the father of the Presbyterian Church in America." Rev. George McNish was licensed to preach here by Rev. Mr. Seymore, of Maryland, in 1706. He was one of the members of the first Presbytery formed in America, and upon the first vacancy in the pulpit after the formation of the Philadelphia Presbytery, he was called to the Presbyterian Church at Jamaica, L. I., in 1710. He began to preach there in 1711, and is called "the father of the Presbyterian Church on Long Island," being among the first Presbyterians in the province of New York. He was a man of much Christian zeal, and was well prepared to meet with determined resistance the aggression of the English Church on the island. When the latter finally succeeded in taking from the Presbyterians their church property, Mr. McNish preached to his congregation in private places. He owned one thousand acres of land in the town of Wallkill, which after his death became the property of his only child, Rev. George McNish. He died March 10, 1722.

Rev. George McNish, the son of the above,

married a daughter of Joseph Smith, of Jamaica, and settled in New Jersey, preaching at Newtown, now Newton, between 1744 and 1746. He subsequently preached in Goshen, and spent his life in the ministry. He died in Wallkill in 1779, aged sixty-five. His children were: Andrew Clark, who served in the Revolutionary War, and fortunately escaped from Ft. Montgomery when taken by the British; Peggy; and Polly, wife of George Conkling, of Goshen.

Andrew Clark McNish, the grandfather of our subject, was born August 17, 1752, and died February 12, 1805. He owned one hundred acres of land within what is now the corporation limits of Middletown, where he built a log house and barn and where he resided until his death. His wife was Elizabeth Davis, of Long Island. Their eldest child, Joshua, the father of our subject, was born September 1, 1779, and served in the War of 1812. For fifteen months he was stationed on Long Island. As he was the eldest child, upon the death of his parents he succeeded to the homestead, and gave, as requested in his father's will, each of his brothers and sister $75 each, and a trade if they chose to learn one. He resided upon the homestead during his entire life. His marriage united him with Mary M. Reeve, a daughter of Deacon James Reeve, one of the founders and the first Deacon of the Congregational Church in Middletown. He came from Long Island and settled in the town of Wawayanda, where he reared a family of thirteen children. The parental family comprised six children, three of whom are now living. George C. died at the age of twenty-one; Andrew C. died at the age of thirty-seven; Elizabeth resides in Middletown; Wickham C. is our subject; Sarah married James B. Crawford, of Middletown, and died at the age of sixty-two; Phebe J. is now Mrs. Oliver B. Carpenter, of Wawayanda. After the death of her husband, Mrs. McNish managed the homestead farm with superior ability and judgment, and reared her children with all the care and devotion of a Christian mother until her death, in December, 1863.

Wickham C. McNish was born on the old homestead, August 25, 1823, and grew to man-

hood on the farm. His education was received in the Wallkill Academy, from which he was graduated, and he then taught school for six years during the winter months and assisted on the farm in the summer. In 1850 he took a steamer for California, via Panama, where he waited six weeks, and then took passage on the propellor "Columbus" for San Francisco, but before arriving there was taken sick with Panama fever, from which he did not recover for six months. He finally arrived in San Francisco, and in the fall began clerking in a boot and shoe store. Later, in company with J. B. Roberts, he engaged in the same line of business under the firm name of Roberts & McNish. He returned home after he had been gone from New York City just three years to a day. Subsequently he located in Boston as buyer for the business in California, forwarding the merchandise by vessel to California around Cape Horn, afterwards across the Isthmus, and thence by steamer to San Francisco. This partnership continued until 1869, when it was dissolved by mutual consent, Mr. McNish returning to California by rail to make the final settlement. Mr. Roberts still resides there. Mr. McNish and his partner began a small retail business but soon entered a jobbing trade, their sales being over half a million a year.

About 1866 our subject became interested in the oil regions of Pennsylvania, and took stock in a company formed the previous year at Boston, known as the Phœnix Oil and Land Company. He held the controlling interest and became manager, removing to Titusville, Pa., where he remained until 1873, when the company sold out. He has, however, been interested in the oil business almost ever since. Many wells were sunk by his company, and a great deal of land was bought and sold. Of late years his interest has been chiefly in the Bradford fields.

Mr. McNish was married in Middletown, January 14, 1857, to Miss Mary Etta Reeve, who was born near Middletown. Her parents were William Wickham and Jane (Ayers) Reeve, the former of whom was born here in April, 1802. Her father was an engineer and surveyor, being one of the oldest surveyors in the country, and laid out the Erie Plank Road, the grounds on which the water works of this city are located, and the asylum grounds. His farm comprised the land now occupied by the asylum He sold this, however, and removed to the city, building a neat and comfortable residence at No. 150 East Main Street. For many years he was Supervisor of Wallkill, and for several years was a Member of the Legislature. He was a well known and popular Democrat, and a Trustee and member of the Congregational Church. He died here in 1876. His wife, Jane Ayers, was born in the town of Wallkill, and was a daughter of David and Martha (Crawford) Ayers. She died in 1892, in her eighty-seventh year. Mrs. McNish received her education in Middletown and New York City. Mr. and Mrs. McNish were the parents of two children, one of whom died in infancy. Mary J., the surviving one, resides with her parents.

Mr. McNish and family are members of the Congregational Church, and he has ever been active in the Master's work. For several years he has filled the office of Deacon, and has also been President of the Board of Trustees. He was Chairman of the Building Committee during the erection of the present church edifice in 1873, and was the largest contributor to the building fund. Politically he is a Republican. With his family he resides in a fine residence at No. 146 East Main Street, which was erected in 1892.

GEORGE SMITH, Roadmaster of the New York, Susquehanna & Western Railroad, is one of the oldest railroad men in Middletown, having commenced work with the Erie Railroad in 1849. He was born in Sullivan County, near Bloomingburg, December 16, 1834, and his father, Melancthon, and his grandfather, George, were also natives of that county. His paternal great-grandfather came from the North of Ireland and settled in Sullivan County, where he was one of the pioneer farmers. Melancthon Smith, the father, was a farmer in Mamakating,

Sullivan County, and later removed to Oxford, Chenango County, where he remained for a time. and then located at Middletown, where he died at the age of seventy-five years. His wife was Amanda Harding, a native of Sullivan County, and a daughter of Charles Harding, who was an old settler of that county, and a farmer by occupation. For many years she was a member of the Old-school Baptist Church, and died in Goshen at the age of seventy-five years. The parental family comprised the following children: Charles H., a graduate of the Albany Medical School, who died soon after his graduation; Augustus B., a saw maker by trade, who now resides in the far West; George, our subject; Mary A., Mrs. Mapes, of Goshen; and Helen M., Mrs. Oakley, of Newark.

The subject of this sketch was but two years old when his parents moved to Chenango County, where they remained some years and then removed back to Sullivan County. He had only the advantages of a common-school education, and in 1849 entered the employ of the Erie Railroad at Middletown. At that time the road had but a single track, the rails being laid on hardwood stringers, and the longest rail was sixteen feet. After three months' service he was made foreman of a section of four miles, one mile from Middletown, and was thus engaged for twelve years; afterward he was made Supervisor over thirty-one miles of road through New Jersey, from Suffern to Jersey City. This position he held for six years, and was then made track foreman of the Eastern Division and branches of the Erie Railroad, covering about six hundred miles, including Newburgh, Newark, Pine Island and Montgomery Branches. During this time he had charge of laying the third rail from Port Jervis to Jersey City, and of narrowing the track from a six-foot to a four-foot eight and a-half inch gauge. March 20, 1883, he resigned in order to accept the position of Roadmaster of the New York, Susquehanna & Western Railroad, which position he still holds. His territory includes one hundred and fifty-six miles on the main line, and fifteen miles known as the Winton Branch, and covers twenty-eight sections.

Mr. Smith was married, at Howells Depot, to Miss Abbie J. Horton, born in the town of Wallkill, and a daughter of A. J. Horton, a merchant at Howells Depot. Seven children were born unto them: Emma, Mrs. Mills, of Middletown; Charles H., City Engineer; M. Ada, a successful artist in oils; Jennie, deceased; Alfred K., a graduate of the medical department of Columbia College and the College of Pharmacy; Cora G., a successful school teacher; and George A., at home. Fraternally Mr. Smith is a member of the Royal Arcanum, and in politics is a Republican. Religiously he is a member of the Second Presbyterian Church.

JOHN F. JOHNSON, Assistant Roadmaster of the Hudson River Division of the West Shore Railroad, was born in Sweden, July 4, 1858. His father, Olaf, also a native of Sweden, brought the family to America during the progress of the Civil War, settling at Mont Clair, N. J., and removing thence to Hancock, Delaware County, N. Y., where he still resides. His life occupation has been that of an agriculturist, and he is the owner of a well improved farm of two hundred and sixty acres. He is still in the prime of life, being fifty-six years of age. In religious belief he is actively identified with the Lutheran Church.

By his marriage with Johanna Oleson, also a native of Sweden, Olaf Johnson had five children, namely: John F., Charles, Frank, August and Lottie, all of whom are with their parents excepting the eldest. Upon the home farm in Delaware County the childhood years of our subject were passed, his education being such as the neighboring schools afforded. From boyhood he evinced a preference for railroading, and at the age of sixteen he entered the employ of the Oswego & Midland Railroad as section hand. When twenty he became foreman of the same section, remaining at Hancock for one year, after which he had charge of a "floating" gang on the road for over three years. His next position was

that of superintendent in the laying of the new track on the Oswego & Midland between Midland and Cornwall.

Upon completing that job, Mr. Johnson went to Haverstraw, and in the fall of 1882 became an employe of what is now the West Shore Road, his duty being to ballast the track between Haverstraw and Ft. Montgomery. While thus engaged, he had more than a hundred men under him. From Haverstraw he went to Weehawken, N. J., to ballast the yards there and put in the tracks. On the completion of that work, the majority of the employes were discharged, but he was retained as foreman of the Weehawken yards for three years, being general foreman the last year. May 1, 1886, he was made Assistant Roadmaster between Weehawken and Kingston, his headquarters the first year being at Weehawken and the second year at Cornwall. In 1888 he was transferred to Newburgh, where he has since held the position of Assistant Roadmaster between Newburgh and Weehawken, also of the Thirty-fifth Street yards in New York City, and the New Jersey Branch of the West Shore, his route extending over fifty-eight miles of the main line, five miles of the branch road, and all the yards. He travels over the road every day, sometimes twice a day. Under his supervision are thirteen sections on the main line, one on the branch, and a floating and two tunnel gangs.

September 21, 1892, at Newburgh, occurred the marriage of John F. Johnson and Miss Emma Bennett, a native of this city. Her father, George Bennett, was born near London, England, whence he accompanied his grandfather, William Bennett, to America. The latter engaged in farm work in Orange County for some time, but later went to Colorado, where he died. Her father was in the United States navy during the Civil War. For some years he was a machinist in the western part of Colorado, but after his return to Newburgh he entered the Whitehall Engine Works, where he is now the oldest employe. His wife, Mary, was born in Poughkeepsie, being a daughter of Aaron Van Vlack, a farmer, who died in Dutchess County. They were the parents of six children,

of whom four survive, Mrs. Johnson being next to the youngest. Socially our subject is connected with the Good Templars and the Young Men's Christian Association of Railroad Men. While taking no active part in politics, he has decided opinions regarding national questions, and advocates Republican principles. His wife is a member of St. John's Methodist Episcopal Church, to the support of which he is a liberal contributor.

SAMUEL RITCHIE, senior member of the firm of Ritchie & Hull, editors of the *Journal* at Newburgh, was born in Larne, Ireland, July 3, 1836, being the second son of Robert L. and Sarah E. Ritchie. At the age of three years he was brought by his parents to this country, and has made his home in Newburgh since then, with the exception of the year 1867. His connection with the *Journal* began March 1, 1865, and he has been its editor and one of its proprietors since March 1, 1877. He was united in marriage, in May, 1869, with Kate L., daughter of the late James F. Kelly.

FRANK S. HULL, who is associated with Samuel Ritchie in the publication of the *Journal* at Newburgh, was born in this city June 6, 1853. His education was received in the public schools of this place, and he also attended a number of private schools. He is the eldest son of Dr. Duane and Sarah S. Hull, the former at one time a well known dentist of Newburgh, but known principally through several important inventions. The most valuable of these was the facing of the iron guards on the mowing-machines with cast steel to afford a keen and durable cutting-edge for the knives to operate across. This invention proved to be so great an improvement over the cutting apparatus previously used, that

64

it was universally adopted, though, through some defect in his formal application, Dr. Hull did not secure a patent for his invention.

From boyhood Mr. Hull displayed a predilection for journalism, and when only thirteen years of age he began to publish the *American Eagle*. This he published with little interruption until 1868, the paper being enlarged several times during that period. The place of publication was changed from Newburgh to Millerton and West New Brighton, N. Y., respectively, as his residence was removed thereto. In 1870 he returned to Newburgh and accepted a position in the *Journal* office. In 1876 he was foreman of the office of the Middletown *Press*, but resigned that position, and March 1, 1877, formed a partnership with Samuel Ritchie and Lawrence C. Bodine, purchasing the *Journal* establishment from Cyrus B. Martin. In December following he and Mr. Ritchie purchased Mr. Bodine's interest, and have since carried on the publishing, printing and book-binding business.

Mr. Hull has served as President of the Young Men's Christian Association, and in religious connections is identified with the Trinity Methodist Episcopal Church, of which he is a Steward. He is one of the five Newburgh representatives in the Advisory Board of the Orange County Agricultural Society. In 1882 he married Miss Ida, daughter of the late James Weygant, and they have two children, Marjorie W. and Stanley W.

GEORGE W. DECKER, of Newburgh, Superintendent and Cashier of the Pennsylvania Coal Company, is a native of Orange County, born in Minisink, June 16, 1846, and is a son of DeWitt and Jane (Duryea) Decker, both of whom are also natives of Orange County. The Deckers were early settlers of this county, the first of the name being Jacob, the grandfather of our subject. Mrs. Decker was a daughter of Henry Duryea, who was well known as an extensive farmer of this county. She was born near Craigsville, Blooming Grove Township, and died in 1872, at the age of sixty-four years. The father died in his eighty-sixth year. They were the parents of six children, five of whom are now living, George W. being the eldest. One brother resides on the old farm, two in New York City, and a sister on a farm near the old homestead.

The subject of this sketch was reared on the farm and remained at home until March, 1864, when he came to Newburgh and engaged as a clerk in the store of Isaac Wood, Jr. He continued in the employ of Mr. Wood until May, 1867, when he entered the employ of the Pennsylvania Coal Company, with which he has ever since been connected. He was elected Cashier of the company on entering its employ, and has continued to hold that office until the present time. In February, 1894, he was also elected Superintendent of the company at this place.

The Pennsylvania Coal Company is an incorporated institution and one of the oldest and strongest in this state, with shipping points at Buffalo, Cleveland, Duluth, Milwaukee and Newburgh. Its mines are located at Dunmore, Pa., and the Wyoming region, near Scranton. It has a great many collieries and employs about three thousand men. At Newburgh the company's docks are very large, and about one-half of the product of the mines, or nine hundred and seventy-five thousand tons, is handled each year at this point. The business was first begun here in 1864, when the docks were built. The storage capacity at Newburgh is about seventy-five thousand tons, and about three hundred men are employed in different capacities in the yards. The river and canal boats owned and used by the company are about two hundred in number. About twenty acres of ground are required at this point. The office is located on South Water Street, and is a large, roomy structure, well adapted for its use. The main office of the company is located at No. 1 Broadway, New York, and is connected by telephone with the one at Newburgh.

Mr. Decker was married, in Newburgh, to Miss Sarah Allard, born in New York City, and a daughter of Noham Allard, a native of Massachusetts, but who lived and did business in New York City, afterward coming to Newburgh, where

he died. Two children have been born to Mr. and Mrs. Decker, Henry P. and Elizabeth.

George W. Decker is recognized as one of the best business men in Newburgh; beginning life here, as already stated, as a clerk, he has worked his way up until he is now the manager of one of the largest institutions in this section. In business he is very methodical and punctual in all his appointments. His office is always neatly kept, and the surroundings are also in the best of order. His residence is at No. 154 Grand Street, and his home life is a most pleasant one.

MOSES M. CLARK, of the town of Woodbury, was born at Croton-on-Hudson, Westchester County, N. Y., August 4, 1815. He remained in the place of his birth until he was sixteen, when he went to New York and served an apprenticeship of four years to the trade of a carriage-maker. After having worked in the employ of others for a number of years, he embarked in business for himself, and was successfully engaged in that way for some time. About 1853 he brought his family to his present home, in order that his wife might take care of her parents, whose farm it was. For ten years afterward he continued his business, going home about once a week, as his trade permitted. In 1863, however, he retired from business, and since then has made this his permanent home.

The father of our subject, John Clark, Jr., was born at Dikeman's Place, N. Y., August 12, 1775, and died in February, 1852, at the age of seventy-seven. He was twice married, his first wife being Sarah Clark, who was born at Dikeman's Place shortly after the Revolution. Their union resulted in the birth of ten children, one of whom died unnamed in infancy. The others were William, Elizabeth, Thomas, States, Samuel, Moses, Rebecca, Maria and Sarah Matilda. By his second marriage, one son and one daughter were born.

The Clark family originated in Scotland, from

which country our subject's grandfather, John Clark, Sr., emigrated to America. At the age of eleven years he secured work as a cabin-boy on an ocean steamer, and at various times received promotions, until finally he was a captain. During his voyages he visited almost every port in the world. He married Maria Dikeman, a member of one of the oldest families of New York, whose ancestors in 1663 purchased five hundred acres near Kingsbridge, the patent for which was signed by the Duke of York, and afterward again signed by George IV. and the Governor of New York.

Soon after his marriage, John Clark, Sr., purchased a tract of five hundred acres near Croton-on-Hudson, and upon that place he built a large stone house. During the Revolutionary War, in which he took part, the Hessians took possession of the house, and some of them slept in his garret. Some years after the close of the war, Mr. Clark sold his farm and bought another tract of five hundred acres farther up in the lumber districts. The deed for this property was registered at White Plains, on the 4th of July, over a hundred years ago. His wife, Maria, was a daughter of Hans Dikeman, a native of Holland, who emigrated to this country and settled on the Harlem River.

The mother of our subject was born in 1785, and died in 1825. Her father, Thomas Clark, was a farmer by occupation, and a son of Capt. William Clark, a native of Virginia, and a Captain in a company in Washington's army. Thomas, then a lad of sixteen, was mail-carrier during the war. The Clark family first settled near Jamestown, Va., but finding the country there thickly settled, moved to the vicinity of Mt. Vernon, General Washington's home, where the Captain engaged in agricultural pursuits. He was of English birth, but a loyal patriot, and devoted to the welfare of the Colonies.

In the city of New York, July 4, 1837, the subject of this notice married Miss Mahitable, daughter of Elam and Eunice (Clark) Earl. She was born July 16, 1817, in a house that stood on the site of her present home. Her father was a son of Peter and Elizabeth (Bull) Earl, the form-

er of whom was one of three brothers, who came from England and settled in this country. One brother located in New England, John went to New Jersey, while Peter came to Orange County, and settled near Highland Mills, taking under patent over fifteen hundred acres, all the land lying between the present homestead and Highland Mills. He and his wife were the parents of nine daughters and three sons.

Elam Earl was born on a farm adjoining the present homestead, and spent his entire life in this vicinity, following agriculture for his occupation. In his youth he attended the district schools at Bakertown and Highland Mills, but his educational advantages were very meager, and his knowledge was mainly acquired by self-culture. Unto his marriage seven children were born, namely: Elizabeth, Mrs. Jacob Blaheney, deceased, formerly of New York City, and who had four sons in the war; Mahitable; Mary, deceased, wife of Simeon Howell, of Blooming Grove; Rachel, who married Charles Mapes, of Monroe; Nathaniel, who resides on a farm lying between Highland Mills and Central Valley; Matilda, whose first husband was Charles Peters, and her second Henry Mapes; and Peter, who married Hannah Conklin, and is now deceased.

The union of our subject and his wife resulted in the birth of eight children. Moses E., the eldest, was born May 29, 1838, makes his home in Jersey City, N. J., and is engaged in business in New York; he married Emma Tanner, and their children are: Albert; Francis Herman, of Jersey City; Emily Jessica, who married Oscar Whitney; Moses Ernest, Jr.; and Henry Holmes, deceased. Albert, the eldest son of Moses E., Sr., married Louise Fronk, May 21, 1885, and they have three children, Louise, Emma Maude and Gladys Earl.

The second son of our subject, Isaac A., resides at Suffern, Rockland County, and is conductor on the elevated railroad in New York City; he is married and has one child. Mary E., the eldest daughter, is the deceased wife of George W. Green, of Highland Mills. Charles A. and Sarah E. are deceased. Matilda Julia married James Hall, of Roslyn, L. I., and they have two children. Simeon H. is a car-painter of New York. Ida A. married William S. Andrews, a confectioner of New York.

It is a remarkable fact that in the house where our subject now resides four generations are living under the same roof, and the land has been in possession of the family for two generations previous, making six generations that have resided here. In their younger years, Mr. and Mrs. Clark were active workers in the Methodist Episcopal Church, but they are prevented now, by the infirmities of age, from taking the active part in religious affairs they formerly maintained. Mrs. Clark has had a number of remarkable visions during her life, one of which was four nights before the assassination of President Lincoln, when she saw him fall, and also saw the assassin trip, fall and injure himself.

During the existence of the Whig party, Mr. Clark gave it his allegiance, and he also advocated the principles of the "Know-Nothings." Since the organization of the Republican party he has upheld its principles. Notwithstanding their advanced years, he and his good wife are hale and hearty, retaining to a large extent the possession of their mental and physical faculties. They are an honored and worthy couple, and their memory will be held in love and affectionate esteem by their descendants long after they shall have been called to their rest.

＞ ＝ ❊✦◈✦◈❊ ＝ ＜

EDGAR SMITH. The attention of the traveler passing through Orange County is invariably attracted to the many pleasant country homes which have been built up through the perseverance and industry of a more than ordinarily intelligent class of men. A number of these farms have been in the possession of the same family, descending from father to son, for several generations. This is true of the farm where Mr. Smith resides. Bequeathed to him by his father, it consists of ninety acres of fertile land, which he devotes to general farming and dairying, and upon which he has placed a number of valuable improvements.

The elder of the two children of Alonzo and Rachel (Baker) Smith, the subject of this biography was born in the village of Montgomery, this county, August 28, 1856. His father was born in a log house situated on the farm now owned by our subject. On this place he was reared to manhood, but then removed to Montgomery, and for a number of years successfully engaged in the manufacture of cigars and the tobacco business. Accumulating a comfortable competence, his last years were spent in retirement from business, and he remained a resident of the village until his death, at the age of sixty-seven. His parents were born in this county, whither his grandparents had emigrated from Holland. Our subject's mother was born in Ulster County, N. Y., and her parents were also natives of this state, though of English extraction.

In the public schools of Montgomery our subject was the recipient of excellent educational advantages. Upon attaining his majority he began the management of the old homestead, which he has since conducted. January 17, 1878, he married Miss Mary L. Kidd, a native of the town of Montgomery, and the eldest daughter of Herman Edgar and Susan (Leeds) Kidd. She has two sisters, namely: Emma W., wife of Edward L. Anderson, of Montgomery; and Frances, who married Frank V. Leeds, a commission merchant of New York City.

Born near the village of Walden, Herman E. Kidd spent his entire life upon a farm, his ventures as an agriculturist being quite successful. He was prominent in local affairs, and filled the majority of the town offices. His death occurred when he was about sixty years old. It is worthy of note that his father and grandfather were born in the same house, on the old homestead near Walden. The family history in America dates back to Alexander Kidd, who came to this country from the North of Ireland in 1732, and settled near Walden, being one of the first settlers of that part of Orange County. The mother of Mrs. Smith was also born near Walden, being a daughter of Silas and Susan Weed Leeds, who settled in this town about 1815. She spent her

AMOS F. HOLDEN.

entire life in this locality, and died at the age of fifty-eight. Grandfather Kidd was one of the heroes of the War of 1812, and his father, Alexander, rendered valiant service in the Revolution. Two daughters comprise the family of Mr. and Mrs. Smith, namely, Alta L. and Mary L., who are receiving excellent advantages and are being prepared for positions of honor in social circles. Socially Mr. Smith is connected with Freeman Lodge No. 120, I. O. O. F., at Walden. With his wife he holds membership in the German Reformed Church, and his contributions to religious and benevolent enterprises are as generous as his means permit. Politically he upholds the policy of the Democratic party, and maintains the intelligent interest in public affairs which every citizen should feel.

A MOS F. HOLDEN is one of the proprietors and is sole manager of The Little Falls Paper-mills, situated on the Quassaick Creek, Newburgh. This is one of the leading industries of Orange County. The mill has a capacity of five tons per day, the product of which is used almost exclusively by the Albany Paper Company, of Albany.

In Little Falls, N. Y., Mr. Holden and his partner also operate a paper-mill, which has a capacity of about half the extent of the former, and this mill is also managed by our subject. Another mill, situated a few miles from Syracuse, has recently been leased by The Little Falls Paper Company, as the demands for their product were beyond what could be supplied by the two former mills. The capacity of these three mills is about ten tons per day. All the mills are furnished with the finest machinery and equipment for the manufacture of the various grades of tissue and manilla paper for toilet use.

Abel Holden, father of our subject, was born in the Bay State, and in mature life operated a farm in Rutland County, Vt. He is now in his eighty-fourth year, and is living retired, his home being in Charleston, N. H. His wife, who was before their marriage a Miss Mary Sterns,

was also a native of Massachusetts, and at the time of her demise was eighty years old. They were the parents of eight children. The birth of A. F. Holden occurred in Mt. Holly, Vt., in April, 1848, he being the youngest in his father's family. He was educated in the district schools, and remained on the old homestead until shortly before reaching his majority, when his father sold the farm. For a few years after this, Mr. Holden clerked in a boot, shoe and clothing store at Springfield, Vt. Subsequently he purchased one-half interest in the business, but sold out within a year. Then, locating at Bellows Falls, he operated a retail boot and shoe and men's furnishing-goods store for ten years.

About this time Mr. Holden became desirous of engaging in business as a manufacturer, and in February, 1885, in association with H. W. Church and O. M. George, a company was formed. An old mill was purchased at Livingston, Columbia County, N. Y., fitted with new machinery, and they engaged in the manufacture of paper. After running between three and four years, they purchased the Little Falls Mills, on the Mohawk River, the latter having greater advantages in water-power. This is an extensive mill, built substantially of stone, and completely fitted up with the most approved machinery.

In 1891 Mr. Holden and his partners purchased the Orange County Mills of Newburgh, to which were built new additions; new machinery was put in, besides the best of the machinery from the Livingston Mills, and other extensive alterations made. A switch from the Erie Railroad has recently been placed, thereby greatly facilitating the shipping, and the mills are kept running night and day. In November, 1891, Mr. Church died, and Mr. Holden and his surviving partner, Mr. George, bought out the interests of their deceased partner's heirs. The whole interest in the mills now belongs to Mr. Holden and Mr. George.

In 1872 Mr. Holden was married in Springfield, Vt., to Miss Sarah Spencer, who was born in that locality, and whose father was a well-to-do farmer. In 1892 Mr. Holden built a comfortable residence at No. 80 First Street, Newburgh. He is a member of the Bellows Falls Lodge No. 41,

F. & A. M., and politically is an ardent Republican. Both Mr. and Mrs. Holden are members of the Methodist Episcopal Church.

CORNELIUS MACARDELL, President of the First National Bank of Middletown, Treasurer of the Middletown State Homeopathic Hospital, and proprietor of the *Daily Argus* and the *Semi-Weekly Mercury*, was born in Darien, Ga., October 24, 1836. He is the son of Cornelius Macardell, a native of Dublin, Ireland, who, after having graduated from Trinity College, came to America, and after a brief sojourn in New York City went to Georgia, settling in Darien, where he published the Darien *Telegraph*, and afterwards the Savannah *Daily Telegraph*. In 1841 he returned North, making his home in Brooklyn, N. Y., and following journalistic work. He was a writer of marked ability, but his career was cut short by death in early manhood.

The marriage of Cornelius Macardell, Sr., united him with Rebecca Campbell, who was born in Ireland, and who died in Orange County. Their only son, the subject of this sketch, was a child of five years when in 1841 the family came North. Educated in the public schools of Brooklyn, before attaining his majority Mr. Macardell engaged in journalism. In 1859 he became interested in a business newspaper venture in New Orleans, an enterprise which proved most profitable, but which came to a sudden termination through the outbreak of the Civil War. Returning North in 1861, he became interested in Wall Street activities and in 1866 was elected to membership in the New York Stock Exchange, and his name is still upon its roll-book.

Retiring from business in New York in 1871, Mr. Macardell came to Middletown. In 1876 he founded the *Daily Argus*; two years later the *Argus* and the *Middletown Mercury*, a weekly publication, joined fortunes and were for several years published by Thompson & Macardell. By purchase of Mr. Thompson's interest Mr. Macardell some years since became sole owner of both papers. The *Argus* first appeared as a folio,

but it has been enlarged several times and is now a six-column quarto. The *Mercury* was founded in 1858. Both papers are strongly Democratic.

In 1877 Mr. Macardell resumed active work in the New York Stock Exchange, but after eleven years in the business retired. In 1891 he became interested in the First National Bank as a Director, and the following year he was made President.

The marriage of Mr. Macardell, in Orange County, united him with Esther, daughter of Oliver and Penelope Crawford. Of their numerous offspring seven are living. Their eldest son, Cornelius, Jr., is business manager of his father's newspaper properties.

Mr. Macardell has had his share of adversities; several times he has had to begin the fight anew, but always with good name untarnished and with debts paid in full.

JAMES P. CHAMBERS, a contractor and builder residing in Middletown, was born in the town of Blooming Grove, near Washingtonville, January 5, 1845. His parents, James H. and Ann (Redner) Chambers, were natives, respectively, of Succasunna Plains, N. J., and the town of Monroe, Orange County, N. Y., the former being of English descent. For some years the father followed the blacksmith's trade, after which he engaged in farming in the towns of Blooming Grove and Monroe. He now resides in the town of Goshen, and is about eighty years of age. During the late war he enlisted in the One Hundred and Seventy-sixth New York Infantry, and after serving one year was honorably discharged, having contracted rheumatism, that rendered him unfit for service.

The mother of our subject was a daughter of Peter Redner, and was descended from English progenitors. She died when thirty-eight years of age, having been the mother of seven children, five of whom are living. Cornelius, one of her sons, served first in the Nineteenth New York Infantry, and on the expiration of his term of service enlisted in the One Hundred and Seventy-sixth New York Infantry, in which he served one year.

The subject of this sketch was reared in the towns of Monroe and Cornwall, and was educated in the public schools. In 1864 he commenced to learn the carpenter's trade at Ramapo, Rockland County, where he remained one year: he then went to Hohokus, N. J., where he likewise remained one year, and then to Sloatsburg, N. Y., where he remained one year. In 1867 he located in Middletown and began working at his trade for Theodore Wilkes, and continued with him and others until 1872, when he began contracting and building for himself. He was at first in partnership with John H. Little, and then with Martin B. Van Fleet. Since the dissolution of the partnership with the latter, he has been alone. While a journeyman he assisted in the erection of the Methodist Episcopal and Congregational Churches. Among the buildings erected by himself was one for George Bartle. He also built a two-story dwelling for John E. Iseman, on Liberty Street: Mrs. Smith, Knapp Avenue; Frank Tanney, Lake Avenue; Thomas A. Mapes, Bennett Street; Jonathan C. Duryea, Grand Avenue; Carl A. Iseman, corner of Prince Street and Grand Avenue; F. M. Barnes (two), Beattie Avenue; Allan Ridgeway (three); John J. Silk (three): Miss Bennett, Albert Street: Dr. E. R. Varcoe, of Goshen; James H. Wallace, of Pine Bush; and Eli Mapes. He has erected scores of other buildings, including his own residence at No. 36 Knapp Avenue, and one at Nos. 37 and 37½ Knapp Avenue, which he owns and leases. In the prosecution of his work he frequently employs ten or twelve men.

Mr. Chambers was married in 1866, at Paterson, N. J., to Miss Margaret J. Barbarow, a native of Bergen County, N. J., and daughter of John J. Barbarow, a retired shoe manufacturer of Sloatsburg. She died in 1892, at the age of forty-six years, leaving five children who grew to maturity: John J., in the drug business at No. 57 North Street; William H., in carpentering with his father; Samuel B., a carpenter of Middletown: Frank T., a drug clerk

of Monroe; and Ida M., at home. Freddie died at the age of seven years. Mr. Chambers' second marriage was with Charlotte Talmadge, a native of the town of Monroe, and daughter of Nathaniel Talmadge, who died in Monroe.

Socially Mr. Chambers is a member of Hoffman Lodge No. 412, F. & A. M., of which he has been a member over twenty years. He is also a member of the Knights of Pythias, and of St. Paul's Methodist Episcopal Church, of which he has been a member since 1866. In politics he is a Prohibitionist, but was originally a Republican.

EDWIN S. MERRILL, A. B., B. L., is one of the rising young attorneys of Middletown. He is a native of Maine, born in Pownal in 1863, and is a son of Horace P. and Adelia A. P. (Wait) Merrill, both of whom are natives of Freeport, Me. His father was a sea-captain, in charge of a merchant vessel engaged in the coasting trade, and during the late war enlisted in Company B, Twenty-fifth Maine Volunteer Infantry, continuing in the service until the expiration of his time. He still resides at his Maine home, and is a member of the Grand Army of the Republic, of which he is Past Commander. In politics he is a Republican. Adelia A. P. Wait, the mother of our subject, was a daughter of Capt. Charles Wait, who was engaged in the coasting trade and resided at Freeport, Me. She was of English descent, and died in 1876. Moses Merrill, the grandfather of our subject, was of English descent, and lived and died in Maine. To Horace P. and Adelia A. P. Merrill were born six children, four sons and two daughters.

The subject of this sketch was fourth in the family and grew to manhood in his native state. Before attaining his majority he taught school at Milan, N. H. Subsequently he entered Maine Wesleyan Seminary at Kent's Hill, from which he went to Williams College, at Williamstown, Mass. He entered college in 1885, and graduated in 1889, with the degree of A. B., making a special study of history and political science, in which he won first prize. After his graduation he entered the law department of Columbia University, at Washington, D. C., from which he graduated in 1892, with the degree of B. L. The law lectures being conducted in evening session gave opportunity for employment during the day, and during his course he was employed in the United States Census Bureau, and was later stock clerk in the equipment division of the Postoffice Department, under the Second Assistant Postmaster-General.

In October, 1892, Mr. Merrill located in Middletown and entered the office of Judge T. N. Little, where he remained one year, and in February, 1894, was admitted at the Brooklyn General Term to practice in the courts of New York. He now has a law office in the Winter's Building, No. 16 East Main Street, Middletown, where he has built up a good practice.

Mr. Merrill is a member of Metropolis Lodge No. 16, I. O. O. F., of Washington, D. C., and is Secretary of Monhagen Hose Company No. 1. In 1892 he organized Gen. D. P. DeWitt Camp No. 37, Sons of Veterans, and was its first Captain, holding the position for two years. In politics he is a Democrat, and is taking an active interest in political affairs. Religiously he is a member of the Congregational Church. In September, 1895, Mr. Merrill was married to Estella May, daughter of Merritt H. Parsons, of Middletown.

JOHN M. GARDNER, an attorney of Newburgh, was born in the town of Warwick, Orange County, N. Y., in 1858. His father, W. H. Gardner, as was also his grandfather, W. H. Gardner, Sr., was a native of Columbia County, N. Y. The latter was a prominent and successful woolen manufacturer, and also a lay minister in the Methodist Episcopal Church. Originally the Gardners were from Scotland, and first settled at Nantucket, whence they removed to Columbia County.

The father was a teacher in that county, and while still a young man came to Orange County and engaged as Principal of the Warwick public schools, where he remained until he retired from the profession of teaching. He married Caroline Flagler, who was born in Bellvale, Orange County. Her father was Hiram Flagler, and her mother was originally Miss Wiley. The Wiley family are the oldest, and were the original, settlers of the town of Cornwall, and until a few years ago they continued to occupy the old homestead, where the military academy now stands. The grandfather of Mrs. Gardner was a well known and prominent Judge in his day. The parents of our subject are yet living and reside in Ironton, N. J.

John M. Gardner is the second in a family of four children. His primary education was obtained in the public schools of Warwick, and his law studies were commenced in Goshen, but concluded at Fulton County, N. Y. He was admitted to the Bar in Ithaca, N. Y., in 1881, and at once commenced the practice of his profession in Fulton County, where he remained until 1887, when he removed to Newburgh, opened an office, and began practice. While still a resident of Fulton County he married Miss Eugenia Northrup, a daughter of Leonard Northrup, at one time one of the best known and successful manufacturers of that county.

On his arrival in Newburgh, Mr. Gardner at once secured a fine practice, which has constantly increased up to the present time. His office is now located in the Townsend Building. In 1891 he established an office in the Bennett Building, at the corner of Nassau and Fulton Streets in New York City, in partnership with Mr. Linehan, under the firm name of Gardner & Linehan. His business has increased so rapidly in New York, that he now spends about three-fourths of his time in that city. During the past few years his practice has consisted, to a great extent, of damage cases against railroads and other corporations, and in the prosecution of claims he has been very successful. From others the biographer has learned many facts in connection with the business of Mr. Gardner. It is said of him that he has prosecuted to a successful termination more damage and personal-injury cases than any other attorney in

DR. EDWIN R. VARCOE.

Orange County. Among the many cases was that of Mowett *vs.* Mowett, which was very closely contested, but he succeeded in recovering over $6,000. In the Cookedale *vs.* Brown case, one in which the former had been defrauded out of about $40,000 real estate, Mr. Gardner succeeded in recovering nearly every dollar of the amount.

It will be seen from what has already been written, that Mr. Gardner has become one of the most successful attorneys in the Hudson Valley. In the prosecution of a case he knows no such word as "fail." Every case is touched carefully from every point of view, and his conclusions almost invariably prove correct. Beginning at the lowest round of the ladder he has worked his way up step by step, until he has gained a most enviable reputation and a practice which he well deserves.

≪┼┼┼┼┼┼┼┼┼┼┼ ✹ ┼┼┼┼┼┼┼┼┼┼┼≫

DR. EDWIN R. VARCOE, one of the leading dentists of Orange County, located at Goshen, was born near Honesdale, Pa., November 4, 1850. His parents, Francis and Mary (Hocken) Varcoe, were natives of England and descendants of a long line of substantial English ancestry. Both were educated near Liskeard, in the county of Cornwall, where they grew to maturity and were married, in 1846. They came to America on their wedding tour and were so well pleased with the appearance of the country that they decided to remain. Settling near Honesdale, Pa., they engaged in farming pursuits, and remained there until their death, the father dying in 1895, and the mother in 1865. Both were devoted members of the Methodist Episcopal Church. Their eight children, three sons and five daughters, are all living.

The father of Francis Varcoe, Samuel Varcoe, was an English gentleman and a landed proprietor in the county of Cornwall. The maternal grandfather of Francis Varcoe was Rev. Charles Hicks, of the Church of England. One of Samuel's sons, Rev. R. Varcoe, came to this country and filled several important charges

in the Methodist Episcopal Church in Pennsylvania, where he died. The father of Mrs. Varcoe was Rev. Edward Hocken, a minister of the Church of England and a man of learning and eloquence. For fifty years he filled important pulpits in his native land, dying at an advanced age, revered for his many acts of kindness and his piety and benevolence. He reared a family of seven children, of whom Edward, Jr., became a clergyman under the celebrated John Wesley in the Methodist Church, during the pioneer era of that organization.

The great-grandfather of our subject on the maternal side was Rev. William Geake, of the Church of England, a learned man who ably filled parishes for many years in the county of Cornwall. It is a notable fact that the progenitors of the family were scholarly men, of sterling character and upright lives. Refinement and culture have always been characteristic of the race. The children of Francis and Mary Varcoe are as follows: Lavenia, wife of Isaiah Scudder, of Middletown, N. Y.; Sophia, widow of Ira S. Baxter and a resident of Jersey City; Edwin R.; Elizabeth, wife of Frank Sagendorph, of Jersey City; Selina, Mrs. T. Edson Harding, of Jersey City; William F., a practicing physician in New York City; Carrie, who married Herman Groffell, of Jersey City; and Charles W., a dentist of Walden, N. Y.

In 1875 Francis Varcoe married for his second wife Mrs. Elizabeth (Onger) Glenn, and they had one daughter, Kittie, now the wife of Charles Webb, of Bethany, Pa. Politically Mr. Varcoe was an old-line Whig originally, subsequently became a Republican, and was a stanch Union man during the Civil War. In religious belief he was identified with the Methodist Episcopal Church and held membership in that denomination until his death, which took place at the old homestead near Honesdale, Pa., September 6, 1895, aged eighty years.

The subject of this sketch, Dr. E. R. Varcoe, received his literary education in the schools of Wayne County and Wyoming Seminary at Kingston, Pa. At the age of twenty-one he began the study of his profession under Dr. J. W. Kesler, of Honesdale, Pa., with whom he remained for two years. He then practiced at different places in Orange County for five years. In 1880 he was graduated from the Philadelphia Dental College, carrying of the highest honors of his class and receiving the prize awarded, an S. S. White Dental Engine. In June, 1880, he established himself in practice in Goshen, where for the last fifteen years he has enjoyed an extensive and lucrative patronage. In all modern improvements and appliances pertaining to his profession he has kept abreast of the times, and is recognized as most skillful and successful. He is public-spirited and has ever been zealous in the promotion of the progressive interests of the town.

The Doctor is a member of the Presbyterian Church of Goshen. He is also a member of the Second District Dental Association, the order of Odd Fellows, Knights of Pythias and Encampment of Patriarchs. In politics he is a Republican. He has made a success not only in a professional way, but has also accumulated a comfortable competency and has found time during his vacations to make several trips to Europe, visiting Scotland, Ireland, England, France, Switzerland and Italy, besides traveling extensively through this country, Mexico, Cuba and the Sandwich Islands. For the benefit of the church and charitable interests he has frequently lectured on his travels in a most entertaining and eloquent manner.

J P. MANDIGO. Among the active business men of West Point is Mr. Mandigo, who is the proprietor of one of the finest livery stables in the county. He is successful in carrying on the same, and deserves honorable mention among the substantial and representative citizens of Orange County.

Mr. Mandigo was born at Highland Falls, April 16, 1846. For services rendered during the Revolutionary War, his paternal great-grandfather received a grant of land from the Govern-

ment, lying between Highland Falls and Ft. Montgomery. In the last-named place Grandfather Luke Mandigo and also Campbell, father of our subject, were born. For many years the latter followed farming with signal success; he is now eighty-two years of age and lives retired from work in Highland Falls. In religious affairs he is a devout Methodist. Our subject traces his ancestry back to the sunny land of Italy, where the name was spelled Mantahne.

Our subject's mother, who bore the maiden name of Jane Cox, was born in the North of Ireland, and came to America when a young lady. She was a member of the Episcopal Church, in the faith of which she died in 1885. Her two children were Charles, a builder of Highland, and J. P., of this sketch. The latter was reared in Highland Falls, and when a lad of sixteen years went to Cold Springs, where he was apprenticed to a horse-shoer and blacksmith, in order that he might learn the trade. He remained there for three years and on his return to Highland Falls followed his trade for two years as an apprentice, when he established in business for himself. He was successful in this industry and built up a large and paying business on the corner of Main Street and Park Avenue. This he abandoned in 1890, and, renting his shop, purchased the livery owned by Mr. Denton, since which time he has enlarged the buildings and made many valuable improvements. The stable is located on Government ground and is the only one in the place. Mr. Mandigo carries nothing but the fastest horses and finest turnouts, and has in his stables buggies, closed carriages, coupes, carts, etc. He runs four busses and derives a handsome income from his boarding stable. Although his business is located at West Point, his residence and family are at Highland Falls.

Mr. Mandigo was married in Cold Springs, in 1867, to Miss Sarah M. Smith, who was born in Hyde Park, Dutchess County, this state, and was the daughter of Stephen Smith, a grocer of that place and a well-to-do business man. The lady is now deceased, passing away in 1886. She became the mother of a daughter, Della, whose demise occurred when ten years of age. Mrs. Man-

ELI VAN INWEGEN.

digo was a believer in the doctrines advocated by the Presbyterian Church, to which she belonged.

Our subject has always been greatly interested in school matters, and for nine years was Trustee of the Board and three years served efficiently as its President. He was Collector of Highland for one year. In politics he is an influential supporter of Democratic principles, and has been Chairman of committees at the town, county and state conventions. He is a very pleasant gentleman and commands the respect and esteem of all all who know him.

ELI VAN INWEGEN, Vice-President of the First National Bank of Port Jervis, is a worthy representative of one of the old families of this state. He is a native of Orange County, born at Huguenot, April 23, 1816, and is a son of Benjamin and Charity (Cole) Van Inwegen. The family dates back to the first Holland emigration to this country. Gerardus Van Inwegen and his wife, Jane De Witt, were the first of the family to settle in New York. It is understood that they were married in this country, and their eldest son, Hermann Van Inwegen, wedded Margaret Cole. Hermann was Justice of the Peace for many years, and was the father of the following children: Gerardus, David, Cornelius, Jacob, Samuel, Jacob, Josias, Charlotte and Hannah.

The father of our subject was born at Huguenot, and removed across the line into Matamoras, Pa., on a farm opposite Port Jervis, where he died at the age of sixty-eight years. His wife was but twenty-four years of age at the time of her death, which occurred in 1816. Eli is the youngest of their three sons, the others being Lewis, a resident of Hastings, Minn.; and George, who died at the age of sixty years. The father was again married, his second union being with Phœbe Van Auken, and they had six children, four of whom are still living. Andrew J. lives at Matamoras, Pa.; Margaret is the wife of Luke S. Rosencrans, of Port Jervis; Hannah is the wife of Webb Cartwright, of Matamoras; and Ann, who is unmarried, lives in the same place.

On the death of his mother, Eli Van Inwegen, who was but a few weeks old, was sent to live with his maternal grandfather, Cornelius W. Cole, who was a son of Wilhelmus Cole. The latter's father, William Cole, or Cool, as the name was sometimes spelled, wedded Catherine Du Bois, and located at Machachemech, now the southern part of Port Jervis. His son Josias married Maria Kimmell about 1740, and their child was baptized in the Machachemech Church in 1743, as the records show. Our subject well remembers Wilhelmus Cole, who died at the age of about ninety years. His grandfather owned a large farm, and his house stood opposite to where Mr. Van Inwegen now stands, and the church stood on the main street near that place. Cornelius Cole died at the age of eighty-eight years, and his wife, whose maiden name was Hannah Gumaer, passed away four years previous. He spent his last years at the home of our subject, where his death occurred. His daughter, Margery, married Wilhelmus Westfall, and died at the age of sixty.

Mr. Van Inwegen remained upon his grandfather's farm until after he was married, when it was divided between him and his two brothers, but Lewis sold his share and removed to Minnesota. Eli received for his share one hundred acres, lying between the Delaware and Neversink Rivers, on which farm he has since made his home. He platted and laid out an addition to the village, which is now largely improved with first-class residences, and there he built his own home. When the Port Jervis Savings Bank was organized he became its Treasurer, and had full charge of the business for ten years, or during its entire existence. It was a success financially, but it was decided to close out, and all depositors and creditors were paid in full. He was one of the incorporators of the First National Bank in 1870, and has ever been one of its Directors, while he is now serving as Vice-President. He is an able financier, and the people have the utmost confidence in him.

On the 30th of December, 1841, Mr. Van Inwegen married Miss Elizabeth M. Bull, a daughter of Crissy and Catherine (Rosencrans) Bull, the former a grandson of William Bull, the first settler by that name in Orange County, who located near Goshen. Mr. Bull subsequently moved three miles below Matamoras, where he lived at the time Mr. and Mrs. Van Inwegen were married. By her union with our subject, Mrs. Van Inwegen became the mother of three children: Julia, who died in childhood; Cornelius, who studied civil-engineering in Union College at Schenectady, N. Y., and died at the age of twenty years; and Charles F., Cashier of the First National Bank of Port Jervis. Mrs. Van Inwegen is a member of the Reformed Church, and of it her husband is a liberal supporter. In political sentiment he is a Democrat, as was also his grandfather and most of his ancestors. He has held the offices of Justice of the Peace and Supervisor, and has ever been a prominent and leading citizen of Orange County.

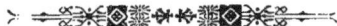

> ══╳══◈══✦══◈══╳══ <

JOHN FRANCIS DICKS, a Roadmaster on the Southern Division of the Ontario & Western Railroad, has had a very successful railroad career, having been Roadmaster since he was seventeen years of age. He was born at Howells Depot, January 21, 1858, and is a son of Lewis and Susan (Nichols) Dicks, both of whom were natives of the town of Wallkill, the latter being a daughter of J. D. Nichols, a teamster and farmer, and one of the earliest settlers of that locality. Lewis Dicks is of Scotch descent, and entered the employ of the Erie Railroad Company as foreman, 'and then became foreman of building on the old New York & Oswego Midland Railroad. He served as foreman of the Erie Railroad a period of twenty-seven years, since which time he has been with the Ontario & Western Railroad, being now employed as watchman. A present he resides in Middletown, at the age of sixty-seven years.

The subject of this sketch is second in the family of five children born to Lewis and Susan Dicks. The other members of the family are: Robert, in the employ of the Ontario & Western Railroad,

with headquarters at Middletown; William, an engineer on the Ontario & Western between Walton and Corning; Joseph, a section foreman; and Fannie, now Mrs. Hulslande, residing near Bloomingburg.

The childhood days of our subject were spent at Howells Depot, and his education was received in a district school. In 1868, when but ten years of age, he was employed as water-boy in the construction of the old Midland Railroad, his duties being the carrying of tools and water to the men employed. He continued in this work until the age of fourteen, when he was made a 'full hand on the section, and when sixteen was made section foreman. From October 1, 1875, to July 1, 1876, he was section foreman at Middletown. He was then made Roadmaster of the western district on the Middle Division of the Ontario & Western Railroad, which position he held until 1882, when he was put in charge of construction on the West Shore Railroad from Middletown to New York. In this work he had over three thousand men under him at different times, without having a man killed on his account. After the opening of the West Shore Railroad he returned as Roadmaster to Middletown, in the old Middle Division, and served there until 1885, when he was made Roadmaster of the Southern Division of the Ontario & Western between Middletown and New York. On the consolidation of the West Shore and New York Central Railways, he was made Division Roadmaster of the West Shore between Cornwall and New York. He continued there until 1887, when he returned to the Ontario & Western in his old position as Roadmaster of the Middle Division. In 1890 he had charge of the construction of the Scranton Division of the Ontario & Western Railroad, into the coal fields of Pennsylvania, in connection with his duties of Roadmaster at this point. He still has charge of the Middle Division as Roadmaster, and has under his supervision about one hundred miles, divided into eighteen regular sections.

On the 27th of November, 1878, Mr. Dicks was united in marriage, at Walton, Delaware County, with Miss Thirza D. Booth, who was born at Oxford Depot, Orange County. Her father, Nelson

FRANCIS GOULDY.

Booth. who was a native of Canada, and a ship carpenter by trade, was engaged in building in New York City, and later at Oxford, where he was accidentally killed by falling through a trestle. Her mother, Mary Miller, who was born near Utica, and was of Scotch descent, died in early life. In religious belief she was a Quaker. In their family were two children: Thirza D., the wife of our subject, and David, a farmer at Oxford Depot. Mrs. Dicks was reared and educated in New York City and in Walton Academy. To Mr. and Mrs. Dicks were born two children, Mary B. and Douglas.

In politics Mr. Dicks is a Democrat, and is a very active worker for the success of his party. While not an office-seeker, he has yet been honored by his fellow-citizens with local office. In 1890 he was elected Councilman from the First Ward, and served two years, during which time he was Chairman of the Street Committee. In 1893 he was elected Supervisor from the First Ward, and served a term of one year. While a member of this Board he was Chairman of the Coroner's Committee, and was a member of several other committees. Fraternally he is a member of Hoffman Lodge No. 412, F. & A. M., and of the Ancient Order of United Workmen. He is also a member of Excelsior Hook and Ladder Company No. 1.

Mr. Dicks is yet in the prime of life. Success has attended him in everything undertaken, and his long railroad service is proof of the fidelity with which he discharges every duty devolving upon him.

FRANCIS GOULDY, one of the old and most honored citizens of Newburgh, has made his home here for some thirty-three years, prior to which time he spent his summers here for several years. His birth occurred in London, England, April 19, 1812, and he was reared under the instruction of a devoted Christian mother. From boyhood he was trained in high and noble precepts, and in 1830 he became a member of the first Methodist Episcopal Church in New York

City, this being known as the John's Street church. He also attended the first Sunday-school of that denomination ever held in the metropolis, which assembled on Tryon Row. For several decades Mr. Gouldy has been one of the mainstays of the Trinity Methodist Episcopal Church of this city, and has been very liberal in his contributions to its maintenance. While in New York he was a member of the Board of Trustees, and when he transferred his membership to old Trinity he was given a like position on its board, and was soon made President, which office he still holds. He has always taken a great interest in educational and missionary work, and has done what was in his power to advance the same.

The father of the above gentleman, David Gouldy, was born in Edinburgh, Scotland, receiving a good education in the celebrated university of the city, and early became a local minister in the Methodist Episcopal Church, laboring in conjunction with John Wesley. For several years he was pastor of a London church, but in 1819 he decided to remove to New York, where his death occurred soon afterward. His wife, who was formerly Miss Mary Nichols, was born in England, and was a daughter of a prosperous farmer. After her husband's death she assumed the entire responsibility of rearing her children, and well did she perform her task. Our subject is the only survivor of the family, the others, David, Mary, Rachel and Elizabeth, all having died in New York City, where the mother was summoned to her final rest in 1840.

The first few years in the life of Francis Gouldy were passed in the city of his birth, while his education was mainly obtained in private schools in New York City. In his youth he took a position in a dry-goods store on Canal Street, running the business in partnership with his mother. Later he embarked in the lumber trade on the corner of West and LeRoy Streets, conducting a retail business for about a quarter of a century. From time to time he invested in real estate, which he bought and sold, and in 1855 he gave up his interest in the lumber business. In 1858 he met with a great misfortune in a paralytic stroke, but after a time partially recovered, and ultimately concluded to settle in Newburgh, where he could enjoy fresh air and an abundance of exercise.

In 1837, in New York City, occurred the first marriage of Mr. Gouldy, the lady of his choice being Eliza, daughter of William Mead, who was from Connecticut. Mrs. Gouldy was a native of New York, and died at the age of twenty-eight years, leaving three children, one of whom was summoned to the home beyond at the age of nineteen; the others are Mary E. and Nathaniel E. The daughter graduated from Mt. Holyoke Seminary, and was the first lady missionary in Japan. Becoming proficient in the language, she labored earnestly for the cause of Christianity for ten years, when she returned home. Nathaniel graduated from the Columbia Law School and is now living retired in New York City.

April 30, 1849, Mr. Gouldy married the lady who now bears his name. She was Miss Jane Disosway, a native of Staten Island, and daughter of Gabriel and granddaughter of Cornelius Disosway, both natives of the same island and the latter owner of large landed estates thereon. The family were originally French-Huguenots, who were obliged to flee to Holland on account of religious persecution, and, coming to New York about 1657, settled on Staten Island. The progenitor of one branch of the family in America was Marcus DuSanchy, who came from Picardy, France, by way of Holland, to this country, in company with two brothers. Mrs. Gouldy's father was a sea-captain and owner of a schooner engaged in trade along the Atlantic Coast. He died while in the prime of life, being but fifty-two years of age. His wife, Elizabeth, likewise a native of Staten Island, was a daughter of Capt. Barnett Sleight, who was born on the island, and who was also a captain on the high seas, being the proprietor of a fine schooner, which was engaged in the coasting trade. He was of the old Holland-Dutch Knickerbocker stock, and died when about fifty years of age. His wife died in 1849, aged fifty-six years.

Of the nine children born to Francis and Jane Gouldy, but three grew to maturity. Charles died in early manhood, and the others are Sarah E., wife of George A. Sanford, of Warwick; and Jennie A. The latter graduated from Vassar College and is living with her parents. She is very active in the Young Woman's Christian Association and is one of the Board of Managers for the Home of the Friendless. She has been Chairman of the Finance Committee of the latter organization, and is a most effective worker. In questions of political moment Mr. Gouldy is a true-blue Republican, and has made a special study of government and the great issues of the day.

GEORGE W. McELROY. The beautiful village of Warwick, Orange County, is the home of many prominent professional gentlemen, who have won for themselves both fame and fortune, but none merit more praise or are more highly esteemed than he whose history now claims attention, and who is one of the leading attorneys of the city.

Our subject is a native of this place, having been born February 22, 1859, to Henry and Julia A. (Lockwood) McElroy, and is the youngest in their family of five children. The parents were both natives of this state, spending their entire lives here. Henry McElroy was a carpenter by trade, and during the years which he followed this vocation was enabled to provide well for his family. He was well and favorably known throughout the county, and during his lifetime was the incumbent of several positions of honor and trust. In his death, which occurred July 6, 1881, the community lost one of its best citizens. His good wife survived him ten years, passing away January 4, 1891.

George W., of this sketch, graduated from the high school at Warwick, after which, in October, 1878, he began reading law with Hon. M. N. Kane, a noted attorney of Warwick. He continued under the latter's instruction until December, 1881, when he was admitted to the Bar as an attorney, and some six months later was admitted as a counselor. He at once opened an office for the practice of his profession, which he has successfully followed ever since.

Mr. McElroy was married, May 27, 1885, to Miss Agnes, daughter of William W. and Susan (McBride) Walling, natives, respectively, of the town of Warwick and Jersey City, N. J. Mrs. McElroy was born in Warwick in 1862, and by her union with our subject has become the mother of a son and daughter, G. Walling and Julia A. Although not members of any religious body, both attend services at the Presbyterian Church.

In politics Mr. McElroy is a true-blue Republican. He has served his fellow-townsmen in the capacity of Justice of the Peace and Police Magistrate, and at the present time is filling out his second term as Special Surrogate of Orange County. He is the efficient President of the Board of Education of Warwick, and through his influence the standard of scholarship has been greatly elevated. He is deservedly considered one of the substantial residents of the village, and to such men is Warwick indebted for its rapid growth and wonderful prosperity, which distinguish it as a desirable place of residence.

⸻ ❁❀❁ ⸻

HIRAM L. LEONARD, of Central Valley, Orange County, was born in Piscataquis County, Me., June 23, 1831. The family have long been residents of this country, three brothers coming from England in the "Mayflower," and locating in Massachusetts. To the one who settled in Boston our subject traces his ancestry. Lewis Leonard, the father of Hiram L., was born in Roxbury, a suburb of Boston, Mass., and received his education in a school of the latter place. From Boston he went to Maine, then a new country, to raise sheep. About the close of the War of 1812, the sheep industry became unprofitable, and he began manufacturing oars. In this he became so proficient that his fame spread first throughout this country, and then across the water. He was considered the best oar-maker in the world, and shipped his products to England and many other foreign countries.

He first began to manufacture oars at Bangor, but moved about wherever he could find ash, from which the best oars are made. In 1835 he went to Ellenville, Ulster County, N. Y., where he found timber for his product. This he used up in about three years, and then removed to Honesdale, Wayne County, Pa., where he plied his vocation until his death, which occurred shortly afterward. He was married in the town of Knox, Me., to Miss Hannah Blood, who is supposed to have been a native of New Hampshire.

When the subject of this sketch was four years old, the family removed to Ellenville, N. Y., where he first attended school. When nine years of age they moved to Pennsylvania, where he attended a district school until he was fifteen years of age. After that he studied civil-engineering without a teacher, becoming quite an expert engineer. For a time he had charge of the machinery department of the Pennsylvania Coal Company, but the work proving too hard, he went to Maine to recuperate. At Bangor he engaged in dealing in sporting goods, making trips to the north woods, supplying trappers and hunters with their supplies, and buying and trading in furs. He traveled over the north of Maine to Quebec. About this time, while in the region of Moosehead Lake, he met Thoreau, who speaks of Mr. Leonard in one of his books, though he does not use his name.

Mr. Leonard was married, September 28, 1858, at Bangor, Me., to Miss Elizabeth S. Head, a native of that city, and a daughter of Henry A. and Abbie (Harriman) Head, both of whom are also natives of Bangor. One child, Anna Cora, has been born to them.

Shortly after his marriage, Mr. Leonard suffered an illness which brought on lung trouble, and which threatened his life. He then again went to the woods, and for the next four years engaged in trapping and dealing in furs. He employed some twenty-seven men as trappers, covering territory of a hundred and fifty miles in length. Having again thoroughly regained his health, he returned to the city, but in two years again broke down. Again returning to the woods, he continued there until 1870. He was always quite expert with tools, and used to make his own guns and traps. Having seen a very fine fishing-rod, he concluded he would make one for himself, improving on the original. The Fish Commissioner of Maine, Mr. Stillman, seeing his rod, wanted one for himself, while Mr. Carlowe, a druggist of Bangor, also wanted one. He complied with their request, and those were the first rods made by him. A friend asked permission to send one to Boston to the largest dealer of shooting goods in that city. The firm was so well pleased with the rod, they at once sent an order for a large number, and from this beginning the business developed until Mr. Leonard is now the manufacturer of the finest rods in existance. The Boston firm asked if he could not make rods from bamboo, the rods at that time being made in four pieces. Mr. Leonard, thinking more pieces would be better, made them from six pieces, and sometimes from twelve pieces. The weight of rods, at that time, was ten to eleven ounces, but Mr. Leonard makes them as light as five ounces for a ten-foot rod, and two ounces for an eight-foot rod.

In 1881 Mr. Leonard left Bangor and came to Central Valley, where his factory is now located. He makes all the metal trimmings and everything used in the manufacture of rods. The Leonard rods are shipped to all parts of the world where fly-fishing is pursued. One of his rods he sent as a present to the King of Sweden, and two to English officers in India. He has always taken a first prize wherever his rod has been exhibited. He took the first prize at Berlin, at London, and at the Centennial Exposition at Philadelphia.

Mr. Leonard has devoted a good part of his time to studying the habits of fish. He succeeded in probating salmon, something that up to that time had never been accomplished. He built a hatchway at Lubeck Lake, but could get only few eggs. Under his management, however, eighty-five per cent. of the eggs were hatched. He afterward took eggs from the spawning ground and hatched all of them, something that had not been successfully done before.

Mrs. Leonard is a lady of more than ordinary ability, and has received a very thorough classical education, having a knowledge of Latin, Hebrew and French. She is of a poetical turn of mind, and many of her poems have appeared in the large city journals. She is a member of the Congregational Church of Bangor. Politically Mr. Leonard is a Republican, and socially he is a Mason, Odd Fellow, Knight of Pythias and a Red Man. He was first made a Mason in 1858, and is a charter member of Central Valley Lodge No. 502, I. O. O. F., and a member of Schunnemunk Lodge No. 276, K. of P., in which he has filled all the chairs. He is also a charter member of Wawa Lodge of Central Valley, a member of the Central Valley Literary Society, and of the Mechanics' Cornet Band.

FRANK S. McCOY, one of the enterprising young farmers of Orange County, was born on the homestead which he now operates, in the town of Goshen, in 1861. He devotes the greater part of his time and attention to dairy farming, although he does not neglect the raising of the various cereals. The growing of onions is a great industry in this section, and Mr. McCoy is not behind other farmers in this respect, and has eight acres planted in this vegetable.

In the family granted to William A. and Catherine B. (Case) McCoy, Frank S. was the third-born. The parents were both natives of this town, the father's birth occurring on the estate which is now owned by our subject. William A. worked for two years at his trade of a wagonmaker, but thereafter spent the active years of his life in agricultural pursuits, and became well known in this community for his progressive ideas and the success which invariably attended his efforts. He is now living retired from business of any kind in Goshen. His good wife departed this life in 1879, honored and respected by all who knew her.

After acquiring a good fund of useful information in the district school, Frank S. McCoy began working on the homestead, and has ever since made farming his occupation in life. His estate

JOHN W. SLAUSON.

is over one hundred acres in extent, and yields its owner a handsome income. As stated above, Mr. McCoy makes a specialty of dairy farming, having a number of the best breed of milch cows. His place is improved with all the buildings necessary in his business, and the residence is commodious and attractive in appearance. Although a comparatively young man, he is well known in the county and numbers his friends by the score.

The lady to whom our subject was married, in 1884, was Miss Ida, daughter of Jacob and Mary Moore, natives of Sullivan County, this state, which locality was also the birthplace of their daughter.

Our subject and his wife are not connected by membership with any denomination, although they attend services at the Methodist Episcopal Church. The former is a Democrat in politics, as the principles set forth by that party coincide with his views on almost all questions. Both himself and wife have a host of sincere friends, whom they have won by their upright and conscientious lives and by their genial and openhearted hospitality.

This sketch was prepared by W. T. Doty, editor of the *Orange County Farmer*, a long-time friend of Mr. Slauson, and who at various times has been connected with the *Press* editorial staff.

JOHN W. SLAUSON, now and for several years the senior editor of the *Orange County Press* and Middletown *Daily Press*, was born September 18, 1846, in the town of Greenville, on the family homestead, the farm which remained in the Slauson family for almost a century. He was the eldest of eight children, five of whom are still living (October 1, 1895). His father was David Slauson, the fifth of his name in an honored ancestry that came from Scotland and settled in Fairfield County, Conn., before removing to Orange County. His great-grandfather, David Slauson, second, who was a soldier in the War of the Revolution, was taken prisoner just after the burning of Danbury by General Tryon, in 1777, and with three others was taken to New York

and confined in an old coffee-house. After being imprisoned about three months he and one of his comrades made their escape, and after swimming the East River made their way home by circuitous routes. His mother was Antoinette Whiting, whose father, John Whiting, a member of a large and prominent Connecticut family, was the only one of the name who came to Orange County to make his home, the others settling in New York City and in parts of New England, where the name is a common one. The maternal grandmother of the subject of this sketch was Maria Penney, one of the noblest and best of women.

Mr. Slauson passed the early part of his life in the family of his maternal grandfather, John Whiting, in whose honor he was named, and who was one of the noted schoolteachers of his day in this section of the state. Many of the older residents of the town of Mt. Hope and of Middletown were his pupils. Mr. Whiting was a man of sturdy common-sense, with a well stored, cultivated mind, which was improved by almost constant reading and study. His stern sense of justice in the days of slavery agitation made him what was known as an Abolitionist, and he repeatedly voted for Gerritt Smith for President, though there was no organized Abolition party, and he had to write his ballot with a pen. The grandfather took charge of the grandson's instruction and laid the foundation of an education broad and thorough, as was characteristic of the man. This home instruction was supplemented by attendance at the Westtown Academy, at the Dolbear School for Young Men in New York City, and also by private instruction.

The time for leaving off systematic study found Mr. Slauson ready for grappling alone with the affairs of life, and he began teaching in the public schools at the age of twenty. In this work he met with pronounced success and was ranked among the foremost teachers of the county. In the autumn of 1870, while still at the teacher's work, Mr. Slauson was made candidate of his party for the office of School Commissioner in the Second Assembly District of Orange County, to fill the two-years vacancy occasioned by the death of the lamented Benjamin F. Hill. Although the district was then strongly Democratic, he was chosen to the office by a majority of four hundred and seventy-seven, the first Republican Commissioner ever elected in the district. During his term of office he adopted and extended the method of work inaugurated by Mr. Hill, of requiring written and uniform examinations for teachers, similar to the present admirable system, which was afterward introduced and made obligatory throughout the state by State Superintendent of Public Instruction Andrew S. Draper.

It was during the latter part of his term of office that Mr. Slauson purchased an interest in the *Press* establishment at Middletown, and the duties thus assumed prevented his accepting a renomination for School Commissioner, a fact regretted throughout the district. While this change terminated his active, or rather direct, connection with schoolroom work, Mr. Slauson was afterward for many years a member of the Middletown Board of Education and has always retained his interest in the noble profession of teaching, as well as in all educational matters.

In 1875 Mr. Slauson married Miss Olivia, daughter of Horatio R. Wilcox, Esq., of Middletown, and this union was one of "heart, of mind, and of interest." His wife and two sons, Harold Whiting and Kinsley Wilcox, aged twelve and ten years, respectively, constitute the family. Their first child, Horatio Wilcox, died in 1881, when but a year old.

Mr. Slauson is a member of Hoffman Lodge No. 412, F. & A. M., and was formerly a member of Neversink Chapter, R. A. M., and of Delaware Commandery, K. T., both of the latter of Port Jervis. He is also a member of Excelsior Hook and Ladder Company, and of the First Presbyterian Church of Middletown. For twenty years he has been a member of the New York State Press Association, having always taken an active part in its meetings, and was one of its Vice-Presidents in 1894. He is also an active member of the Republican Editorial Association of the state.

In politics Mr. Slauson has always been a Republican. His party allegiance is so strong, in fact, that he may be styled a partisan. This, however, has not prevented him from striving to be fair toward his political opponents. Indeed his love of justice, of fairness, of man's inalienable right to liberty and conscience, has ever made him most tolerant, liberal-minded and just in his treatment of others on all subjects. This reputation for fair dealing and steady adherence to the principles of the Golden Rule in all relations of life has earned him the merited esteem of his townsmen generally and the highest regard of those who know him best, a pleasure falling to the writer many years ago, and he cherishes the friendship thus formed as one of the pleasantest incidents in his life.

Mr. Slauson has been actively and continuously connected with the *Press* since his purchase of an interest in the concern in 1872, and with his pen and personality has done much to bring that able journal up to its present high standard. His aim, and that of his partners, has been to make it a clean, high-toned newspaper, one that could offend no elevated taste; while bright, readable and newsy, to make it honest, truthful and wholesome in its influence. This high aim has been attained in a degree rarely equalled in journalism.

Mr. Slauson is conceded to be one of Middletown's foremost and reliable business men, and he is identified with the business interests of the city in various ways. For several years past he has been the Vice-President of the Middletown Board of Trade. He never loses an opportunity to advocate and champion Middletown's interests, and he has done his part toward making the city the prosperous, attractive place that it is.

EMMET CRAWFORD has undoubtedly the largest stock of furniture, carpets and crockery in his five stores, located respectively at Middletown, Newburgh, Matteawan, Port Jervis and Goshen, of any one in the state of New York. He began at the foot of the ladder and has risen rapidly, now taking his place among the foremost merchants of the country. His fine establishment at No. 102 Water Street, Newburgh, was erected at a cost of $15,000 and is conducted under the title of the New York Furniture Company. It is four stories in height, well equipped with elevators and modern appliances, and is connected with a five-story building on Front Street.

Oliver Crawford, the grandfather of our subject, was born in the northern part of Ireland and was of Scotch ancestry. He was of strong Christian character and a devoted Presbyterian. At an early period in his history he came to America and settled on the farm near Goshen, later moving to the town of Wallkill. The old homestead, which bears his name, is situated two miles south of Middletown, and there his death occurred at the good old age of eighty-six years. He reared a family of eleven children. James B., the father of our subject, being the eldest. He was born in Goshen and received district-school advantages. Until 1855 he resided on a farm near Middletown, at that time moving to the farm of one hundred acres adjoining that city, now owned and occupied by C. E. Crawford. The latter's mother, Sarah M., was born in Middletown, being a daughter of Joshua McNish, of Scotch descent. She died about 1888, leaving three children. Her second son, Rev. O. C., is a minister in the Congregational Church of Syracuse; and J. W. is in business with our subject in Middletown. The father, now seventy-two years of age, is still an active man, and takes great interest in the prosperity of the Congregational Church, with which he has long been identified.

C. E. Crawford was born December 16, 1849, in Middletown, and received his higher education in Wallkill Academy, afterward preparing himself for his commercial career by a course of study at Eastman's Business College in Poughkeepsie. In 1870 he obtained a clerkship in a dry-goods store in Middletown, and two years later bought out the old furniture house of Hiram Brink. A year or two later he purchased the long-established crockery house of I. O. Beatty and combined the two concerns, which had occupied adjoining buildings at Nos. 44 and 46 North Street. It is now the largest business house in Middletown, and comprises twenty-five thousand square feet of storeroom. The building has a frontage of fifty feet, and is four stories in height and one hundred feet in depth. With the exception of stoves, everything in the line of house furnishings can be found in this immense establishment. For seven years Mr. Crawford conducted the business alone and then took in as a partner his brother, O. C. Crawford, who retired from the firm seven years later to devote himself to the ministry

In 1881 the brothers opened the Newburgh store, and in 1890 our subject started a branch in Matteawan, this also being known as the New York Furniture Company. The same year he sold a half-interest in the Middletown store to E. D. B. France, J. W. Crawford and Charles H. Mapes, the firm being known as the C. E. Crawford Furniture Company. In 1891 another store was started at Port Jervis, in connection with the Middletown partners, and in 1894 the one at Goshen, known as the C. E. Crawford Furniture Company, was also organized. Our subject is virtually the head of these various establishments, which have an immense trade. In connection with the Newburgh plant they have a factory on Front Street, where are manufactured parlor suites, lounges and mattresses. General upholstery work is also done here. The store at Matteawan is 25x75 feet, three stories in height; the one at Goshen 25x100 feet, four stories; and that at Port Jervis, 25x85 feet, also four stories, with a wing 20x60 feet.

Mr. Crawford owns the old homestead of one hundred and ten acres, a portion of which lies within the city limits of Middletown, and his residence is on Cottage Street. He makes a specialty of raising standard-bred horses. He is a member of the Newburgh Board of Trade, and also of the Middletown Board of Trade. Socially he belongs to the Newburgh and Matteawan City Clubs. In 1870 he married Alice, daughter of Rev. Dr. C. A. Harvey, now deceased, but formerly a minister of the Congregational Church of Middletown. Mr. and Mrs. Crawford have two children: A. H., who is in charge of the store at Goshen, and Mildred M. The family are members of the Congregational Church, and are liberal in their donations to religious activities. In his political faith Mr. Crawford is identified with the Republican party.

GEORGE HENRY DECKER, the subject of this sketch, was born in the town of Jerusalem, Yates County, N. Y., on the 23d of April, 1842. After attending the district school of the neighborhood he prepared for college at Genesee Wesleyan Seminary, at Lima, N. Y. He entered Genesee College, and at the expiration of the freshman year he entered Hamilton College at Clinton, N. Y., where he graduated in 1866, with the degree of A. B., and three years later the degree of A. M. was conferred upon him. With the following school year he began teaching as assistant in Wallkill Academy at Middletown. At the expiration of the year he returned to his native county and entered upon a course of law in the office of Franklin & Morris in Penn Yan. At the expiration of the year he was elected Principal of Wallkill Academy, where he had taught after leaving college, which position he accepted and retained for two years, when he resigned it to practice law, having been admitted to the Bar at the Poughkeepsie General Term, held in May, 1870.

Mr. Decker is a descendant in the fifth generation of his family in this country, the first having come hither from Holland and made settlement in Columbia County, N. Y. There the great-grandfather, the grandfather, Lawrence, and the father of our subject, William H., were born. The second of these removed in middle life to Yates County and settled on a farm near Branchport, where his remaining years were spent. He enlisted for service in the War of 1812 and held the rank of Lieutenant in a New York regiment.

At the time the family removed to Yates County, William H. Decker accompanied them, and the

remaining years of his life were spent on the home farm, where he died at the age of seventy-three. He was a member of the Methodist Episcopal Church, which was the religious belief of his ancestors for several generations. His wife, whose maiden name was Lucy C. Durham, was born in Yates County, and is still living at Branchport, being quite well and vigorous, notwithstanding her seventy-six years. She is a daughter of Benjamin Durham, a native of England, who came to the United States with several brothers, he settling in Yates County, where he took up a large tract of land, and was employed as a millwright. He erected the first gristmill built at Niagara Falls.

The family of which our subject is a member consisted, besides himself, of two children, namely: Ann Eliza, who died in 1865; and Charles D., who resides on the old homestead. For a time, after his admission to the Bar, Mr. Decker was alone; then he was in partnership with Henry M. McQuoid until the death of that gentleman, under the firm name of McQuoid & Decker. Later he was with T. N. Little for three years, the name of that firm being Decker & Little. Since that time he has practiced alone.

In addition to his professional labors, Mr. Decker has at various times held important local offices, and in these varied positions he has rendered efficient service in the interest of the people. He held the office of City Clerk of Middletown for three years, and he has also served at different times as City Attorney. For sixteen years he was a member of the Board of Education, a portion of the time serving as President. During that period several ward schoolhouses were built, the academy remodeled, and the free library founded. He introduced and secured the passage of the resolution that founded the library, now one of the best in the state.

At Middletown, December 31, 1872, Mr. Decker married Miss Frances Emily Horton, daughter of Charles Horton, a retired tanner, formerly of Callicoon, N. Y. Mrs. Decker was born in that village, and was the recipient of excellent educational advantages, being a graduate of Vassar College. They are the parents of four children,

HERBERT GEDNEY.

1510

namely: William Grant, who is a member of the Class of '96 of Wallkill Academy, preparing for college; Florence Louise, Clements Durham and Lucy Hortense. The family occupy an elegant residence on Highland Avenue, which was designed and built by Mr. Decker. He is a member of the Second Presbyterian Church. For a time he was President of Excelsior Hook and Ladder Company No. 1, and is now an honorary member of the organization. Socially he is identified with the Paughcaughmaughsinque Lodge of Red Men in this city. He is also a member of Clinton Lodge No. 169, F. & A. M., at Clinton; Midland Chapter No. 240, R. A. M.; Delaware Commandery No. 44, at Port Jervis, and of the Psi Chapter of the Psi Upsilon Fraternity.

HERBERT GEDNEY, attorney and counselor-at-law at Middletown, was born in Goshen, June 22, 1852. The Gedney family were originally from Kent, England, and the name, which is an old Saxon one, was originally spelled Gednaia. The first members of the family, who came from Pike Island, were of the landed gentry. The father of our subject, the late Judge David F. Gedney, was a son of Dr. Gedney, a prominent physician of Newburgh. His mother is the great-granddaughter of Lord Stirling, the famous Revolutionary General, whose daughter, Lady Katherine Alexander, married William Duer, Esq. The grandfather of the Doctor was the first of the family in America, and located in Newburgh. The father of our subject, D. F. Gedney, a native of Newburgh, was District Attorney of Orange County two terms, and County Judge the same length of time. After graduating from Union College, he studied law and was admitted to the Bar. Later he formed a partnership with Nathan Westcott, under the firm name of Gedney & Westcott, at Goshen, N. Y., this partnership continuing until the retirement of Mr. Westcott. Mr. Gedney continued alone until 1875, when he took his son Herbert into partnership, the firm becoming D. F. & H. Gedney.

During the war the Judge was instrumental in recruiting the One Hundred and Twenty-fourth New York Infantry. He was a man of good literary taste, a great linguist, and a musician of more than ordinary ability. He wrote a great deal of church music, and in church matters he always took a deep interest, for many years serving as Warden of St. James Episcopal Church at Goshen. As an attorney and jurist he was well known, and carried on an extensive practice. In politics he was a Republican, and for years was quite active in the councils of that party. He died in Goshen, July 9, 1888. His wife, Harriet Duer, was born in Goshen, and was a daughter of Alexander Duer, Jr., a prominent attorney in that place, whose brothers, John and William, were both Judges in the Superior Court of New York. Mrs. Harriet Gedney is still living at Goshen, N. Y. One of her sons, Alexander Duer Gedney, was lost at sea. He was in the United States navy, and when on a cruise off Cape Horn, was accidentally drowned. One daughter, Henrietta, yet remains at home.

The subject of this sketch was admitted to the Bar in February, 1875, and practiced law in Goshen until the death of his father in 1888. He opened an office in Middletown in 1893, and has since been connected with the Bar at this place. In many interesting and important cases he has acted as counsel, and has been very successful in the prosecution of cases in the various courts. In politics he is a Republican, and was a candidate for the office of District Attorney in 1882, but was defeated by Hon. Russell Headley, of Newburgh. He has decided literary taste, is well read in church history, and is greatly interested in church literature. He is a member of Grace Episcopal Church, and at present is connected with the choir.

Mr. Gedney was married, in Goshen, to Miss Eleanor B. Blauvelt, a native of Rockland County, and a daughter of Cornelius Blauvelt, now of Jersey City, who is interested in the Milk Exchange at that place. The Blauvelts were originally from Holland, and were old settlers in Rockland County. To Mr. and Mrs. Gedney have been born two children, Katharine and Minnie.

B VAN STEENBERGH is known not only in Goshen, where he resides, but throughout Orange County and the Hudson Valley, as a gentleman of large inventive skill, keen insight into affairs, and shrewd judgment. He was the builder, and is now the proprietor, of the New Paltz & Highland Electric Railroad, which is ten miles long, and was erected at a cost of $235,000. His office is at No. 53 Broadway, and he has an elegant residence on Golden Hill Avenue, where he and his family are surrounded by all the luxuries of life.

The history of the Van Steenbergh family in America extends back to an early period in the settlement of this country. Two brothers emigrated from Stefenhoffen, in Holland, and settled, one in Kingston, N. Y., and the other in the city of New York. The former, Abram Van Stefenhoffen (for in that way the family name was originally spelled), served on the Colonial side during the Revolution, and was a stanch patriot. His son, Thomas G., was born in Kingston, and was a carpenter, contractor and builder. He died in Kingston at the age of seventy-six.

The father of our subject, James E., a son of Thomas G., was born in Kingston, and was for a time teller in the Quassaick Bank, but later became Cashier of a bank in Fishkill. He had charge of the gas works at Fishkill and Cold Springs. At the age of forty-four he was killed in a train accident. For some time he was Superintendent of the Sunday-school and Deacon in the Dutch Reformed Church at Fishkill, where the congregation worshiped in a building that had been erected during the Revolution, and had been, during that conflict, temporarily converted into a hospital for the wounded soldiers.

The marriage of James E. Van Steenbergh united him with Miss Abigail Halstead, a native of Newburgh, and now a resident of New York City. Her father was one of the prominent Hudson River captains, and at different times had charge of a sloop, schooner and barge. Our subject is the eldest of four children, and was born in Newburgh, August 23, 1849. He was reared in Fishkill, where he attended the academy. Later he was a student in the Dutchess County

Academy at Poughkeepsie, and at the age of nineteen years completed a course at Warring's Military School at Poughkeepsie, in which he was Lieutenant. In 1868 he was employed in building the gas works at Fishkill, which he afterward owned. On selling the plant, he projected the Fishkill Landing gas works, which he sold upon completion. Later he built the gas works at Rhinebeck, N. Y., Coshocton and Barnesville, Ohio, and organized the gas works at London, Ohio, all of which he sold.

Coming to Goshen in 1880, Mr. Van Steenbergh organized the Gas-light Company and built the works, of which he later disposed. His next step was the organization of the Goshen Foundry and Gas-machinery Company, for which he built a plant, and of which he was President and general manager. While thus engaged he invented the water-gas process, for which he built the necessary machinery and procured patents. Subsequently he was given other letters-patent. His original and valuable ideas on the subject brought him into prominence throughout the country, and he was called to other cities to introduce the gas plant. He built the works at Somerville, N. J., and introduced the machinery for this process. Later he put in the plant for the Singer Manufacturing Company of Elizabeth, N. J., and afterward built the gas works at Delhi, Waterville, Herkimer and Onoville, N. Y.; Austin and Corsicana, Tex.; Macon, Ga.; and Rutherford, N. J. On his return to New York he erected the water works and the electric-light plant at New Paltz. He aided in the incorporation of the New Paltz & Highland Electric Railroad Company, which has a capital stock of $235,000. He owns the works at this place, and has been inseparably connected with the progress of this most important enterprise.

It is scarcely necessary to state to any one acquainted with Mr. Van Steenbergh, that he is a firm Republican, actively interested in the success of the party. In all public matters he takes a commendable interest, and he is both progressive and public-spirited. Since coming to Goshen he has established domestic ties, having been united with Miss Ida, daughter of John Decker, a stock-raiser of this place. Three children bless the union. Edward S., Marguerite and Henry P. Mrs. Van Steenbergh is identified with the Episcopal Church, and with her husband is a member of the best society of the place.

<<++++++++++++++✿++++++++++++++>>

STEELE HARRISON, one of the reliable and successful contractors and builders of Newburgh, has constructed upwards of a dozen residences on his own account and disposed of them to good advantage. During the twenty years of his employment in this line of work in the city he has been constantly employed in building residences, stores and public structures, and has given general satisfaction to those with whom he has had business dealings. At present he is the owner of three residences at the corner of Third and Dubois Streets and four others on Liberty Street, Washington Heights.

The paternal grandfather of our subject was born in England. His father, Steele Harrison, Sr., was born in County Antrim, Ireland, and was the owner of a valuable farm. He was a member of the Church of England, and at the time of his death, which occurred in 1890, was over eighty years of age. His wife, Jane, was a Miss Bamford before their marriage, and likewise a native of County Antrim. Her death occurred in the Emerald Isle in 1891, at the ripe old age of seventy-five years. They were the parents of five children, two of whom are deceased, and three of the number are now in America.

The birth of Steele Harrison, of this sketch, occurred near Ballymena, County Antrim, June 1, 1840. He was the eldest in the family, and was given a good education in the national schools of Ireland. In 1863 he went to Londonderry, where he took passage in the steamer "Nova Scotia," bound for America. After a fourteen-days voyage the vessel arrived in Portland, from which city Mr. Harrison proceeded direct to Newburgh. Here for a time he was employed in a foundry at the corner of Washington and Highland Streets, and two years later commenced serv-

ing an apprenticeship to the mason's trade under a Mr. Dobbins. Afterwards he was employed by John and Robert Kernahan, and then worked as a journeyman both here and in New York City for a few years. About 1874 he started in business in partnership with John McNeal. This connection existed for about five or six years, when it was dissolved by mutual consent, since which time Mr. Harrison has been alone. He built two residences for Colonel Dickey on the Heights, two for Mr. Chadborn, one for Mrs. Ross, another for Mrs. Ford, two residences for Frank Estabrook; the home of Mrs. Cavanagh, at the corner of Third and Lander Streets; the homes of Messrs. Jones and Steward, and scores of others. He erected Ryan's Building on Broadway, St. James' Catholic Church at Middletown, four buildings in Warwick, besides others. He is financially interested in the Palatine Hotel Company, and is a charter member of the Board of Trade.

In 1861 Mr. Harrison was married, in Ireland, to Mary J. Leech. She was born in the same locality as her husband, and, like him, received a good education. They are both members of the Reformed Presbyterian Church, and are active in all good works of benefit to the public. Politically Mr. Harrison is a Republican of the most loyal type, and is respected by all who have any dealings with him, whether in a business or social way.

THOMAS FULTON. Both in Washingtonville and the town of Blooming Grove the firm of Fulton & Co. is known as a reliable business concern, entirely worthy of the confidence of the people. Its prosperous condition is largely due to the energy and perseverance of Thomas Fulton, who gained a thorough knowledge of the business under his father's guidance. For a time he filled the position of bookkeeper, but on the 1st of January, 1892, he succeeded his father in the business, which he has since conducted judiciously and with success. In his store he carries a full line of lumber, together with coal, feed and building supplies generally.

The father of our subject, who was also named Thomas, was a native of Orange County, and was born at Bethlehem. In early life he removed to Ulster, and for a time resided at Wallkill, where he owned and operated a mill. About eighteen years ago he came to Washingtonville and embarked in the feed business, which he carried on continuously until 1892. In many respects he was a remarkable man, and it is safe to say that no one in the town of Blooming Grove was more highly esteemed than he. His death, which occurred September 3, 1892, at the age of eighty-three years, was mourned as a public loss. His political affiliations were with the Democratic party, and he was one of the most faithful and influential "wheel-horses" of that organization. For two terms he represented his town upon the County Board of Supervisors, and he was also a member of the Assembly from Orange County. His advice was often sought in party councils, and the greatest reliance was placed on his sagacity and judgment.

Thomas Fulton, Sr., was twice married, his first wife dying at the age of fifty-five. Afterward he was united with Miss Jennie McClung, of Newburgh, who passed away in April, 1892, shortly before his death. Their four children were Annie, widow of John O. Birdsall, of Brooklyn; Maggie, a trained nurse living in Newark, N. J.; Thomas and Carrie. The only son, our subject, was born in Wallkill, Ulster County, N. Y., June 5, 1871. At the age of six years he was brought by his parents to Washingtonville, where he has since resided. Attending the common schools, he laid the foundation of the extensive knowledge which he has since gained by observation and systematic reading. From an early age he has been active and ambitious, and his natural talents seemed to fit him for a business life. After keeping the books for his father, he succeeded to the business January 1, 1892. Since that time he has purchased the lumber and coal business of Charles Cooper, which has doubled his trade. He is qualified to do an extensive business, and his transactions are of such an hon-

orable nature that the people repose the greatest confidence in his ability. By his marriage with Miss Mamie C. Winans, of Brooklyn, he has one child, Miriam.

Following in the footsteps of his father, our subject takes a warm interest in political matters, and gives his support to the Democratic party. At present he is a member of the Democratic Central Committee, and without doubt his executive ability and good judgment will be recognized to an ever increasing extent by the members of his party. All public-spirited and progressive measures receive his cordial support, and Washingtonville has in him one of its most stirring citizens. In religious belief he is a member of the Presbyterian Church.

JOHN SMITH, one of the honored and respected citizens of Orange County, is now living retired in the city of Newburgh. He is a native of England, born in Manchester, February 9, 1853, and is a son of William and Louisa (Drinkwater) Smith. The father was also born in that city, where for many years he was engaged as a bleacher and dyer of cotton goods, in connection with his brother John.

John Smith, whose name heads this sketch, is the sixth in a family of eight children, three sons and five daughters. His early life was passed in Manchester, where he attended the grammar school, one of the largest and best schools in the north of England, and on completing the course was graduated therefrom. At the age of sixteen he obtained a position as salesman in a wholesale dry-goods house of Manchester, remaining with that firm until coming to America in 1871, when he entered the Boiling Springs Bleaching establishment of Chadwick Brothers, near Passaic, N. J., later becoming superintendent of their works. He held that position until 1878, when the business was consolidated and he became superintendent of the Newburgh Bleaching Works, where he remained until June, 1893, when he resigned and

FRANCIS A. WILLARD.

has since lived retired at his pleasant home on Montgomery Street. His long retention in that position indicates his faithfulness to his employers' interests, and the high regard in which he was held by them.

In Newburgh, in 1886, Mr. Smith married Miss Anna L. Quackenbush, who is a native of that city, and a daughter of T. S. Quackenbush, who was born in Albany County, N. Y. They have become the parents of three sons: Geoffrey Q., William Alfred and John Roland. In 1877 Mr. Smith visited his old home in England, and during his absence traveled some on the Continent, while in 1893 he made another trip across the Atlantic with his family, remaining three months, and visiting many places of interest.

In March, 1894, Mr. Smith was nominated on the Republican ticket as a member of the Board of Education, and on his election was made Chairman of the Committee on Laws and Conference with the Common Council, and a member of the Committees on Finance and Textbooks and Supplies. As he is deeply interested in educational affairs, he makes an efficient and active member of the board. He is a member of the County Republican Central Committee from the Fourth Ward, and from the second district of the same ward was elected a member of the Republican City Committee. Socially he belongs to the City Club of Newburgh, and is a Director and Treasurer of the Powelton Club, in which organizations he takes an active part. Himself and excellent wife hold membership with St. George's Episcopal Church.

⸻ ❀❀❀ ⸻

FRANCIS A. WILLARD, editor and proprietor of the *Register*, was born in Midway, Ky., August 23, 1856. His education was obtained in the public schools and academy at Boonville, and in the Whitestown Seminary. In 1878–79 he was clerk of the village of Boonville. In 1880 he was telegraph editor of the Watertown *Morning Dispatch*, and the following year served as its managing editor. In September, 1882, he became a member of the firm of Willard & Sons,

editors of the Boonville *Herald*. During the first year of the publication of the Utica *Daily Press*, in the campaign of 1882, he had charge of its editorial columns.

In 1884 Mr. Willard was elected Supervisor of the town of Boonville, and it is worthy of note that he was the first Democrat elected to that office on the regular party ticket since the war. In the session of 1885, though one of the youngest members of the Board, he was leader of the Democratic minority. In 1885 his party nominated him for Member of Assembly, representing the Third Oneida District, but he positively declined to accept. In August, 1886, he was appointed Postmaster at Boonville, being the unanimous choice of the people of that place. Had he so desired, he would have been tendered the nomination for Congress in 1888 and 1890 from the Twenty-third Congressional District.

In 1891 Mr. Willard disposed of his interest in the Boonville *Herald* to his brother, and then set about finding a plant located nearer the metropolis. The Newburgh *Register* was in the market; it belonged to John A. Mason, who had been absent from the city as Deputy Collector connected with the United States Custom House at New York City for several years, leaving the paper in the hands of others to conduct. The result was that the influence and value of the sheet, both as a newspaper and an advertising medium, had greatly deteriorated. Mr. Willard, recognizing that the task of bringing the *Register* to the front rank (the only place he would be content to have it) meant arduous and unceasing labor, hesitated about making the effort. Finally, May 9, 1891, he closed the contract, the *Daily* and *Weekly Register* passed into his hands, and since that time the improvements have been so numerous as to entirely change its position, as well as appearance, in the ranks of newspaperdom. The *Weekly* became a semi-weekly, the system of newsgathering was modernized by the employment of a city editor to manage the local department and a corps of reporters to gather the facts. Correspondents were secured in all neighboring towns and villages, in order that every happening of importance might be chronicled on the day of its occurrence. A soliciting agent was employed to keep the advertising standard at the top notch—being the first publisher on the Hudson River who considered this important feature worthy of consideration. To the editorial department he gave, and still gives, his personal attention, in addition to a general supervision of every branch and department of the vast establishment. The editorial utterances in behalf of the cause of Democracy have so much of snap in them that they are considered worthy of reproduction in the columns of the foremost party papers of the Empire State.

From an inconvenient and antiquated structure the *Register* was moved into a commodious, modern, four-story and basement building on the main thoroughfare of the city, greatly to the surprise of the old-time-idea newspaper men, who predicted that only ruin and disaster could follow such a radical change, owing to the expense attending the occupancy of such a model edifice. The wisdom of his choice has been evident from the outset, and No. 30 Water Street is visited weekly by hundreds of merchants, manufacturers and citizens who had never before crossed its threshhold.

Finally, as a crowning endeavor to bring the *Register* a trifle ahead of all its competitors, Mr. Willard added improved machinery to his plant, reduced the price of the paper to one cent, changed it from a nine-column 28x44 ½ folio to six pages, 23½x40, and made it the best local and general newspaper on the Hudson River. The change proved a popular one, and in two months time the *bona fide* circulation had more than doubled, and on October 1 more than three times as many papers were being printed as when he first took control; its advertising columns were crowded so they encroached on the reading matter, and the rates for advertising had been made to correspond with its increased value. The *Register* is all that is claimed for it, Mr. Willard considering this to be one of the secrets of success: "Always deal fair with patrons and never misrepresent anything."

Since coming to Newburgh Mr. Willard has become one of the leading citizens. When here

less than two years he was selected, in one of the longest and hardest contested conventions ever known in the city, as Chairman of the Democratic City Committee, a position that was coveted by life-long citizens. For two years he has held the position of Statistician in the Bureau of Labor Statistics at Albany. He is powerful in the councils of his party, and his views are respected and advice sought for. Mr. Willard has a strong love for home, and when office duties are over he may be found at his fireside, enjoying the companionship of his wife and daughter, and doing all that he can to make their lives happy and his home a pleasant one.

GEORGE CRAWFORD, for many years one of the influential and enterprising business men of Middletown, is now living retired at his beautiful home in this city. He has shown marked ability as a business man, and has been very successful in all that he has undertaken.

Our subject was born September 10, 1816, in the town of Crawford, which was named in honor of his grandfather, who located here many years ago. The parental family included eleven children, of whom we make the following mention: Emeline, who never married, died when eighty years of age; Leander at the time of his death was in his seventy-third year; Millicent was sixty-five years at the time of her death; John A. lived to be eighty-one; Albert was sixty-three years old when he died; George, of this sketch, was the next-born; Sarah E. is deceased, as is also Esther; Theron is one of the most prominent agriculturists of this section, and occupies the old home farm; Robert is a substantial farmer of the town of Crawford; and Angeline is also living in the town of Crawford.

The father of our subject, Robert I. Crawford, was born in Sullivan County, N. Y., and when young was taken to the town of Crawford, where he was reared to mature years, and where he led an honorable and useful life. He was a very prominent man in the affairs of his locality, and in settling up estates there was none better. Honorable and upright in all his dealings, he won many friends, who held him in high esteem.

The mother of our subject, Deborah (Dickerson) Crawford, was a native of the town of Crawford, and was the daughter of Benjamin and Esther (Ogden) Dickerson, who were born in Dutchess County. She belonged to the Hopewell Presbyterian Church, with which denomination her husband was also connected, and of which he was an Elder for many years.

Our subject passed the first thirty years of his life on the old homestead, in the meantime acquiring a good education. On starting out for himself, he purchased a farm in the town of Montgomery, which he operated with success for ten years. At the end of that time he rented his estate, and, moving into Middletown, engaged in the crockery and woodenware business. Several years later he opened up a grocery store, and for four years conducted a thriving trade among the best people of the locality. He is now living retired, giving his attention to looking after his real-estate interests.

November 5, 1846, Mr. Crawford married Miss Mary E. Crawford, a native of Orange County, and to them have been born two children: Emma, at home; and Frank, a merchant of Middletown. Mr. Crawford owns three residences in this place, which he rents, and in this way derives a good income. He is a stanch Republican in politics, and is actively interested in the success of his party. Like the other members of his family, he belongs to the Presbyterian Church.

COL. DANIEL C. DUSENBERRY, who is the oldest merchant by many years in Middletown, came to this place in 1838, and purchased the first jewelry store established here. He was born near Amity, town of Warwick, March 3, 1818, and is a son of Isaac and Anna (Knapp) Dusenberry, also natives of that town. The paternal grandfather, a native of Holland, emigrated to the United States, and after a short

sojourn on Long Island made settlement in Orange County. The maternal grandfather, William Knapp, was born at Pine Island, and spent his life principally in the town of Warwick. Isaac Dusenberry, who was a farmer by occupation, resided near the village of Amityville, where he died at the age of seventy; his wife passed away when eighty-two years old.

Of the family of five children born to Isaac and Anna Dusenberry, Daniel C. is the sole survivor. He remained at home until sixteen years of age. When he was twelve, the family moved to Goshen, and there he attended Farmer School. At the age of sixteen he was apprenticed to learn the watchmaker's trade, under Jonah K. Payne, of Goshen, with whom he remained for two years, completing the trade with Daniel Warden. He then came to Middletown, which at that time had less than three hundred inhabitants. As stated, he purchased the first jewelry store in the village, it being situated on the corner of North and Main Streets. After two years spent there, he removed to West Main Street, and two years later opened a store on East Main Street.

At the expiration of two years, Mr. Dusenberry purchased his present site and erected a building which he occupied many years. It was afterward replaced by the three-story brick structure at No. 14 North Street. In 1893 he admitted his son D. W. into the firm, and the business is continued under the firm name of D. C. Dusenberry & Son. They make a specialty of diamonds, sterling-silver tableware and fancy articles of every description suitable to the jewelry trade. Their assortment of diamonds and silverware is the largest in the county.

In 1862 Mr. Dusenberry was commissioned Colonel in the New York National Guards by Governor Seymour, and recruited the Ninety-first Regiment, composed of one thousand men, taken from the different towns in Sullivan and Orange Counties. After holding the commission a short time he resigned. During the '40s he assisted in the organization of a military company in Middletown, which was known as the Middletown Light Guards, of which he was commissioned First Lieutenant.

Colonel Dusenberry has been an active man in all the business relations of life. In 1869 he assisted in the organization of the Middletown Savings Bank, and was a member of the Finance Committee, then Trustee, and subsequently Vice-President, which position he held until his resignation, some years ago. He was instrumental in building the North Plank Road, the charter of which is still in existence. It is now, however, a turnpike. He also assisted in the building of the South Plank Road, which is now given up as a public road. In the location of the Middletown State Hospital he took an active part, contributing towards the purchase of the site, and was one of the committee to work for its location in Middletown. The cause of education has had in him a friend, and he contributed liberally to the Wallkill Academy, and has done everything in his power to make it a success. He was instrumental in building the railroad from Goshen to Middletown, after the Erie had partially graded it between the two places, and was one of a committee to raise the sum of $80,000 for its completion, with the understanding that the Erie Company should pay the money back, which was subsequently done. Stacey Beakes was Chairman of the committee.

In 1850 Colonel Dusenberry married, in this city, Miss Mary Bennett, a native of the town of Wallkill, and a daughter of Bedford Bennett, a farmer and representative of an old family who settled on the site of Middletown. She was educated at Goshen Academy. Of their family of four children, three are now living. Emma, a graduate of Port Jervis Academy, married a Mr. Thompson, and died in Middletown; Hattie married a Mr. Towner, a graduate of Monticello Academy and a merchant of Middletown; Clara, who was educated at Wallkill Academy, is yet at home; D. W., who is a graduate of Siglar's Preparatory Academy of Newburgh, is now engaged with his father in business. The mother of these children died in 1893.

Colonel Dusenberry was one of the charter members of both Hoffman and Goshen Lodges, F. & A. M. At Port Jervis he was made a Mason, but withdrew from the lodge there to assist in starting Hoffman Lodge No. 412 at Middletown. He later withdrew from the latter to start Goshen Lodge, and then returned to Hoffman Lodge. He was also one of the organizers of the old Pioneer Fire Company, which was the first in Middletown. In politics he is a Democrat, and has served on both the City and County Central Committees. He was Chairman of the County Central Committee several years, and has often represented his district in state conventions. He was a member of the state convention which nominated Seymour for Governor, and also of those which nominated Hoffman and Tilden, the latter of whom was a personal friend. Of late years he has not taken as active a part as formerly. In local politics he was very active in former years, and was one of the first Trustees on the incorporation of the village. He is a member of the Board of Trade, and was its President for several years.

———————✦✧✦———————

JOSEPH A. STEWART, storekeeper for the New York, Ontario & Western Railroad at the main distributing point, Middletown, was born in New York City, August 31, 1866. He was brought to Middletown when but two years of age, and has since continued to reside. His primary education was received at the public schools and was finished in the academy. When sixteen years of age he entered the employ of the New York, Ontario & Western Railway in the paint-shops, where he continued for about three years. The business not agreeing with his health, he was compelled to resign, and was appointed storekeeper for the company at this place, to which he devotes his entire time.

Mr. Stewart was united in marriage at Newark, N. J., with Miss Tillie Lemon, who was born in Circleville, and who is the daughter of Henry A Lemon, a farmer residing in that vicinity. They have one child, Selden H., and the family resides at Nos. 40 and 42 Hanford Street. Fraternally Mr. Stewart is a member of

JONATHAN M.

HAMILTON MORRISON
(FATHER)

DAVID A.

GEORGE H.

JOHN G.

WILLIAM H.H.

HAMILTON MORRISON AND SONS.

Hoffman Lodge No. 412, F. & A. M.; Midland Chapter No. 123, R. A. M.; and the Union Consistory of Middletown. Politically he is a Republican.

⸺◠⸻✴⸻◠⸺

HAMILTON MORRISON was born August 24, 1804, on the old homestead which is now occupied by his sons, George H. and John G. This property has been handed down in the family from father to son for over one hundred and fifty years. It contains two hundred and sixty acres, and is one of the best improved estates in the town of Montgomery. The parental family included eight children, of whom our subject was the youngest but one. His parents were Hamilton and Lydia (Beemer) Morrison, the former of whom was a native of Ireland, whence he crossed the Atlantic and landed on American shores when a lad of sixteen years, being accompanied by his father, John. The latter, who took up the land which is still held in the Morrison family, was then advanced in years, and only lived a short time after reaching his new home.

The parental family included the following children: Bathsheba, whose birth occurred August 20, 1790; Lydia, December 10, 1791; Prudence, who died in childhood; John Adam, who was born February 23, 1797; Elizabeth, who was born September 9, 1799, and died in childhood; Prudence, who was born November 1, 1802; Hamilton, August 24, 1804; Eliza, September 21, 1807. Hamilton passed his entire life on the home farm in the town of Montgomery, and died October 25, 1881. He was very successful in all his undertakings, and was highly regarded by all who knew him. The progress and development of the material resources of this section were due in a measure to his untiring efforts, and to him was given the credit of founding the Orange County Agricultural Society.

The father of our subject, Hamilton Morrison, was a tanner by trade. He was born in Ballynahinch, in the North of Ireland, but was of Scotch extraction. He was married, some years after coming to America, to Miss Beemer, who was born in New Jersey, on the banks of the Delaware

River, and who was a daughter of Adam and Deborah Beemer. She lived to the remarkable age of one hundred and three years, passing away January 24, 1868. She was twice married, and after the death of Mr. Morrison married George Morrow, by whom she had a son, George, Jr., whose sketch the reader will find elsewhere in this book. The Beemers were of Holland extraction, and Mrs. Morrison's father participated in the Revolutionary War.

The lady to whom our subject was married, January 15, 1827, was Miss Maria, daughter of Jonathan and Elizabeth (Mould) Mould. Her death occurred March 26, 1868. To our subject and his wife seven children were born, namely: Jonathan M., who is a resident of Montgomery, and who married Margaret Winfield; David A., whose sketch will be found on another page in this volume; George H.; Mary J., the widow of Elijah C. Thayer, of Hamptonburgh; John G.; William H. H., a farmer of this locality, who married Agnes Horton; and Elizabeth, the wife of William Hart, of Walden. George H. and John G. are unmarried and reside on the homestead, which they personally superintend. They carry on general farming, but make a specialty of dairying, selling the product to the creameries, there being quite a number in this county. The sons are progressive and influential citizens, and, with the exception of David A., none would ever accept office, finding they had all they could do to look after their property. They are Democratic in politics, as was also their father. Both our subject and wife were members of the Reformed Church, and were honored citizens of the county.

⸺◦⸻⸺⸻◦⸺

DAVID A. MORRISON belongs to one of the old and representative families of Orange County, where his entire life has been passed. He is of Scotch-Irish and Dutch ancestry.

His paternal ancestors emigrated from Scotland to the North of Ireland during the seventeenth century. His great-great-grandfather,

John Morrison, was born near Belfast, Ireland, in the year 1700, and came to this country prior to the Revolutionary War. He died in 1783. His son John, the founder of the family in America, had preceded him several years, and settled on what is now known as the Morrison Homestead in the town of Montgomery. He married Elizabeth Scott and had nine children: John, Joseph, Jane, James, Hamilton, William, Robert, Gwyn and Prudence, all born in Ireland except Prudence.

Hamilton, the grandfather of the subject of this sketch, was born near Belfast, Ireland, November 4, 1759, and accompanied his father to the New World. Arriving at manhood, he married Lydia Beemer, whose ancestors were of Dutch descent and came from Beemerville, N. J. He occupied the homestead farm and engaged in agricultural pursuits and tanning. He was one of the projectors of the Newburgh & Cochecton Turnpike, and was Justice of the Peace for several years. Diligent in business, he accumulated property rapidly. and, although he died in the prime of life, owned several farms at the time of his death, which occurred in 1808. His widow lived to the advanced age of one hundred and three years. They had eight children: Bathsheba, who died unmarried; Lydia, who married William Stewart, of Newburgh; Prudence, who died in infancy; John A., who became a prominent physician and large land-holder of Wurtsboro, N. Y.; Prudence, who married Hon. Stephen Rapalje. of Walden, N Y.; Elizabeth, who died young; Hamilton: and Eliza, the wife of the late Dr. Andrew King.

Hamilton Morrison, the father of David, was born August 24, 1804, and inherited the old homestead, on which he was reared. His education was obtained in the Montgomery Academy, after which he taught school for some time, but later gave his entire attention to the management of his farm, which comprised nearly three hundred acres. He was a prominent man and a leading agriculturist, and one of the original founders of the Orange County Agricultural Society, of which he was ever an active member. For many years he was a member of the Board

of Directors, twice served as President, and for a quarter of a century was Vice-President. With the Reformed (Dutch) Church he held membership. In politics he was first a Whig, and later a supporter of the Democratic party. Prudent in investments, he amassed a large fortune, and died in 1881, at the age of seventy-seven. In 1827 he married Maria Mould, the mother of our subject, and a most estimable woman, who departed this life in 1868, at the age of sixty-two years. She was the daughter of Jonathan Mould, an influential farmer of the town of Montgomery, and a pillar in the Dutch Reformed Church. His father, Johannes, and grandfather, Christopher Mould, were both born in Orange County, where they followed the occupation of farming. The latter was a son of Christoffel Mould, one of the earliest Dutch settlers in the Wallkill Valley.

David A. Morrison is the second in a family of seven children. Jonathan M., who married Margaret Winfield, is engaged in the insurance business, and is also a civil engineer in the village of Montgomery; he is an amateur florist, and takes an active interest in church work. David A. is the next; George H., who is a prominent farmer, resides on the old homestead; Mary J. is the widow of Elijah C. Thayer, and is a resident of the town of Hamptonburgh; John G., an intelligent agriculturist, is part owner of the home farm, on which he resides; William H. H., who is a successful and progressive farmer, married Miss Agnes Horton, and lives on a farm adjoining the old homestead; and Elizabeth M. is the wife of William C. Hart, who resides near Walden, this county.

On leaving the district schools Mr. Morrison entered the Montgomery Academy, and at the age of seventeen began teaching, being thus employed during the winter, while in the summer months he assisted his father in the labors of the farm. For about thirty terms he followed the profession of teaching, being Principal of the schools in Walden and Montgomery; also taught in district schools in the towns of Montgomery, Hamptonburgh and Blooming Grove.

Mr. Morrison has ever taken an active part in educational affairs, being elected School Commissioner for the First District of Orange County in 1867, and re-elected in 1881, 1884, 1887 and 1890, serving until 1894, in all five terms, or fifteen years, an event without parallel in the state. The last four times the election was in a district where the Republicans usually had a majority of from eight hundred to one thousand, but each time he was elected on the Democratic ticket with an increasing majority, thus showing his popularity. During his term of office educational progress was marked. He resurrected several school districts and placed them in a good condition. The following shows the advancement in the schools in his district between the first and last terms: Increase in number of teachers employed, sixty-eight per cent.; in average length of school terms, thirteen per cent.; number of children of school age, twelve per cent.; average daily attendance, fifty-three per cent.; aggregate number of days' attendance, fifty-seven per cent.; value of schoolhouses and sites, three hundred and sixteen per cent.; assessed valuation of districts, forty-five per cent.; amount of public money received, one hundred and twenty-two per cent.; and amount of teachers' wages, one hundred and fifteen per cent. In his reports Mr. Morrison made many useful suggestions, which have been embodied in the school laws of the state.

In 1880 Mr. Morrison was married to Miss Mary R. Lipsett, who was born in the town of Montgomery, and is a daughter of Robert Lipsett, who was one of its leading farmers, and a great-granddaughter of Col. William Faulkner, of Revolutionary fame. For many years Mr. Morrison continued to live on the old homestead, but in 1893 located in Newburgh, where he now makes his home.

Since 1858 he has been Secretary of the Orange County Agricultural Society. He has attended every fair held by the society since its organization in 1841, and is one of its mainstays. He is a painstaking and tireless worker, gentle yet firm, and a man of education and ability. His long continuance in the office of School Commissioner and Secretary of the Agricultural Society is sufficient evidence of his qualifications therefor. In politics, originally a Whig, he joined the Re-

publican party at its organization in 1856, and was an active supporter of the Union cause, but during Grant's second term he became identified with the Democratic party, of which he has since been an honored member.

JOHN E. SMITH GARDNER, now deceased, was born July 16, 1815, in Florida, Orange County N. Y. His father was Ira Gardner, after whom the village of Gardnerville was named, and who died many years ago. Our subject was the eldest of nine children, five of whom are now living, namely: Ann, wife of Gabriel Seeley, of the town of Chester; Virginia, wife of Benjamin Noyes, of New Haven, Conn.; Mrs. Sarah Coleman, proprietress of the Coleman House of Asbury Park; Harriet, who is unmarried; and Floyd, formerly a merchant of New Hampton, but who now lives in New York City. Three of the sisters who died a number of years ago in Middletown were Frances, widow of Capt. John M. Cash, and who afterwards was the wife of Herman B. Young; Caroline, wife of John S. Conkling; and Antoinette, wife of Menson Finch. Mr. Gardner married Phœbe Millicent Cash, who died in 1875, and who was the youngest daughter of Reuben Cash, and granddaughter of Daniel Cash, who narrowly escaped a massacre at Wyoming by the Indians under Brandt. Mrs. Gardner was a sister of Dr. Merritt H. Cash, a wealthy resident of Wawayanda, who died a number of years ago. At his death Dr. Cash left the use of his farm, known as the Rutger's Place, to Mrs. Gardner until her son Merritt should reach twenty-one, when the title passed to him. Mr. Gardner was a good citizen and a kind and accommodating neighbor. He lived for many years on the farm five miles north of Middletown, on the Bloomingburg Plank Road, for which he helped to secure the charter and donated the right of way through his farm, a distance of three-quarters of a mile. While a young man he united with the Westtown Presbyterian Church, of which he was a member at the time of his death.

Daniel Cash was born in New England, but

the date of his death is not known exactly. He and his wife, Mary Tracy, joined the Baptist Church in the year 1776. They were members of the Baptist Church at Pittston, Pa., to which place they went during the troublesome times in the Wyoming Valley, when the settlers were often threatened with destruction by the Indians. Previous to one of their incursions, the officers in command of the fort, which probably numbered forty, sent out a scout for information and to get reinforcements, but he was cut off by the Indians and never returned. A second one was sent out and met with the same fate. The commander of the fort then called for a volunteer to make the perilous trip to Connecticut for help and reinforcements. Daniel Cash stepped forward and volunteered to go. During his absence the massacre of Wyoming occurred, one of the most terrible in our history. He reached Connecticut safely, and on his return on horseback, after crossing the Delaware River, he met the fleeing fugitives from the valley returning to their old homes in Orange and adjoining counties. Among them were his wife and children, whom he met in the woods, each of the little ones carrying a little bundle of goods. He turned back with them, realizing for the first time that his lonely, perilous journey to Connecticut was the means of saving his life. He settled again in Orange County, in the town of Minisink, and occupied the farm now owned by Dorothea Brown, near Millsburg. He and his wife died in 1789, and were buried on the old burying-ground on the farm of David Slaison, a few rods distant from the present Cash Cemetery. There were but ten days between their deaths. Several of the Cash family were inhumanly butchered by the Mexicans during the Mexican War. George W. Cash was living in Texas during the struggle, and he joined the command under Colonel Fannin, who, after being closely besieged, surrendered to General Santa Anna, under the solemn assurances of quarter. The pledges were instantly violated, and nearly the whole command was inhumanly butchered. John S. Cash, a brother, hearing of the fate of George, enlisted to avenge his brother's death. He joined the expedition under command of T. J.

Green, known in history as the Meir Expedition. They captured the city of Meir, but under the false representation of the Mexican officers that they were besieged and surrounded by an overwhelming force, they were induced to surrender the city to the Mexicans. They were then marched off as prisoners toward the city of Mexico, and on the way were met by an order from Santa Anna to shoot every tenth man. They were marched up to a pot containing white and black beans. Those who drew black beans were to be shot. John drew a black one, and with the other ill-fated ones was massacred at nightfall.

Dr. Merritt H. Cash was born in the town of Wawayanda, July 20, 1802. He was the eldest son of Reuben Cash, who came to the town the latter part of the last century, and there made his home until the time of his death, experiencing many of the hardships incident to the life of pioneer settlers. Although quite young during our country's struggle for independence, he was an eye-witness of some of the exciting revolutionary scenes. He was one of the number allowed by the Indian leader Brandt to escape the Wyoming Massacre, and was often wont to speak of the white rag on his hatband that saved him from the upifted tomahawk and glittering scalping knife of the savages. He lived for over fifty years on his father's homestead and in a house that was built during the second year of the War for Independence. He was reared on a farm, and what little education he received was obtained in the district school for a few months during the winter season. But with these advantages and self-instruction he acquired a fair elementary education, at least enough to qualify him for teaching. On leaving the farm he turned his attention to teaching, in which occupation he was very successful. It was not until he had reached his majority that he fully decided to enter the medical profession. As soon as he formed this determination he relinquished his school and entered a neighboring academy, where he finished all the regular schooling that he ever had, with the exception of a few months' attendance at a select school kept by a man preparing for the ministry. It was while with him that he received his first religious awakening, and laid the foundation on which was built his pure, Christian character. He studied medicine in the office of Dr. James P. Youngs, of Edenville, one year, and in the office of Dr. James Huron, of Warwick, one year. His next preceptors were Dr. Thomas Royce and Dr. Benjamin B. Newkirk, all eminent practitioners of Orange County. In the fall and winter of 1824-25 he attended a course of lectures at the College of Physicians and Surgeons in New York. At the close of the lectures he passed an examination and obtained a diploma to practice medicine. This diploma bears the honored signature of Prof. David Hasack, President of the County Medical Society. The Doctor now turned his attention to a suitable field in which to practice his profession. After casting about for a time, he concluded to settle in the neighborhood where he was born and reared. He was not long without patients, and they began to multiply far beyond his ability to answer their requirements. He was honorably esteemed by neighboring physicians as a sound counselor, in which capacity he chiefly acted during the closing years of his practice. He was several times President of the County Medical Society, twice a delegate to the State Medical Society, and once or twice its delegate to the American Medical Association. He was elected a permanent member of the State Medical Society in 1859, on the recommendation of the society. The Regents of the University conferred on him the honorary degree of Doctor of Medicine. He was widely known as a politician as well as a physician, filling important offices at various times. He represented his town as Supervisor for several terms, and his assembly district three terms in the Legislature. He was in the House during the pendency of the bills incorporating the Albany Medical College and the Young Men's Association for the Mutual Improvement of the City of Albany, in both of which he took a great interest.

Dr. Çash did not marry until he reached his fortieth year, when he was united with Hannah Davis, a daughter of Hon. Joseph Davis. The marriage was a happy one, but of short duration,

as Mrs. Cash was soon called to that upper and better world. She left no children. The later years of the Doctor's life were devoted to his farm rather than to medicine. He owned at the time of his death several tracts of valuable land, principally in the western part of Orange County. Rutger's Place, his residence, so called by him after a tribe of Indians, is where Dr. Gardner now lives. At the time of his death he was the possessor of a handsome fortune. He bequeathed $4,000 to the Supervisors of Orange County to be expended in the erection of a monument to the memory of the patriots who fell in the battle of Minisink, the bones of whom were collected on the battleground and buried at Goshen.

JAMES FREDERICK SMITH, pilot on the steamer "William F. Hart," was born in Rhinebeck, Dutchess County, N. Y., July 23, 1861. His father, Frederick Smith, is a native of Germany, born in Ulm, Wurtemberg, and when a mere boy came to America and located at Rhinebeck, where he engaged as a teamster. He there married Catherine M. Dittes, also a native of Germany. She had been previously married, and has two living children by her first husband. In 1865 the family removed to Rondout, where the father engaged in the truck and express-transfer business, where he still continues, being superintendent of the company. He is a member of the Lutheran Church. and is greatly esteemed in the city where he has so long resided.

The subject of this sketch grew to manhood in Rondout, and was educated in the private schools of that city, taking a course in both English and German. When twelve years of age he commenced his river life as a cabin-boy on the schooner "Minnie C. Post," where he was employed for two seasons. During his last season he had his right arm split from the elbow down to the wrist, being hit by a boat while coming around Hell Gate. On his recovery from this wound he commenced work for George B. Hibbard, a coal dealer, and was engaged with him as clerk for two seasons. He then served as deck hand on the "Mary Powell" for four seasons, between Kingston and New York City. For the six seasons following he was mate on the "Jacob Tremper," assisting Capt. Ezra Hunter. In 1887 he was licensed as a first-class pilot on the Hudson River, and continued on the "Tremper" until April 1, 1892. He was then made pilot on the "William F. Hart," where he has since remained.

Mr. Smith was united in marriage at Rondout, N. Y., to Annie Myer, a daughter of William Myer, and a native of Hyde Park, N. Y. Three children have blessed their union, Tillie M., J. Frederick and J. Oliver. The family resides at No. 97 Smith Street. The parents are members of the German Lutheran Church. Socially he is a member of the Knights of Pythias fraternity. Mr. Smith is yet a young man, but understands the river throughout its entire length, and since serving as pilot has never yet met with an accident.

WILLIAM B. BEAKES is numbered among the successful and well-to-do citizens of Newburgh, where he has made his home for the past nine years. Formerly he owned a stock and dairy farm at Cornwall, Orange County, the place comprising some three hundred acres. For six years he made a business of supplying dairy products to customers in New York City, and on the Cornwall Stock Farm, as his homestead was termed, he usually kept from sixty to eighty cows. In 1886 he sold out his business to his brother, C. H. C. Beakes, and since then has been engaged in the retail trade in Newburgh, his headquarters being on the corner of North Street and Gidney Avenue. His supplies are obtained from his brother's farm, and his two delivery wagons are kept in constant service.

Our subject was born in Middletown, November 8, 1850, in which place his father and grandfather, Joseph, had also been born. The latter was a farmer by occupation and a son of Stacey Beakes, a native of Wallkill Town. The latter's

father, who bore the same Christian name, was the first of the family to settle in Orange County, and from that time till the present his descendants have been closely associated with the progress of this region. Stacey, Jr., father of our subject, was reared in Middletown, and owned a farm adjoining that place. This homestead, comprising one hundred and sixty acres, he continued to conduct until he retired from active cares. His last years were passed at the home of his son, C. H. C., near Cornwall, his death occurring when in his seventy-fifth year. He was a member of the old-school Baptist Church, and possessed the respect and high regard of all with whom he was acquainted. After the organization of the Republican party he became one of its loyal adherents. His wife, Emeline, was a daughter of William Carpenter, a farmer of Wallkill. She died in Middletown, leaving a family of ten children, one having previously died.

William B. Beakes is the fifth in his parents' family, and is one of six sons. Two of his brothers were soldiers in the Civil War. He was brought up to farm life, and his primary education was such as was afforded by the district schools. Subsequently it was his privilege to attend Wallkill Academy at Middletown for one term. He continued under the parental roof until eighteen years of age, when he went to New York City and, entering the employ of Brown & Bailey, delivered milk to their customers until his brother, C. H. C., bought them out. He was in his employ for six years, thus making a total of twelve years in the same occupation. He was thrifty as well as industrious, and each year managed to lay aside a goodly sum. With this capital he bought the farm in Cornwall, previously mentioned, in 1880. Owing to his good business methods and perseverance in his undertakings, he is now in the enjoyment of a substantial income and is on the high road to success.

November 15, 1877, Mr. Beakes was married, in New York City, to Clara Embler, who was born in Monticello, Sullivan County, N. Y., and is the daughter of W. T. Embler. This worthy couple have six children, two sons and four daughters, who in order of their birth are named as follows:

Clara, William, Florence, Sadie, Henry and Katie. Our subject follows his father's example in the matter of politics and is an ardent Republican.

> ⸺ ❖⊹⊹ ❖⸺ <

JOHN FERGUSON, a very successful real-estate and insurance broker of Middletown, has his office in the Central Building, on North Street. He is a native of Mt. Salem, Sussex County, N. J., born November 11, 1859, and is of Scotch descent, his grandfather, James Ferguson, having been born in Scotland. With two brothers, he was a refugee from Scotland to the North of Ireland, where they remained for a short time, and then came to America, the grandfather locating in the town of Minisink, where he purchased a tract of land and was engaged in farming until his death. In early life John Ferguson, the father of our subject, learned the trade of a shoemaker, and first engaged in business on his father's farm. Later he located in Mt. Salem, from which place he moved to Greenville, and later to Port Jervis, continuing to work at his trade until old age compelled him to retire. In 1887 he came to Middletown with our subject, and here died June 21, 1892, at the age of seventy-seven years. His wife, Eliza Young, the mother of our subject, was born in Mt. Hope, and was a daughter of Samuel Young, a native of Scotland, and a large farmer in the town of Mt. Hope. She died here December 1, 1893, in the faith of the Baptist Church, of which she had been a member for many years. Of their twelve children, seven grew to maturity, and six are now living.

John Ferguson, our subject, was tenth in the parental family. In childhood he removed with his parents to Port Jervis, where he grew to manhood and received his education in the public schools. When fourteen years of age he began work on a farm in the town of Deerpark, and for three seasons continued to work as a farm hand in that town and also in Minisink. He then returned to his father's house in Port Jervis, and soon afterward entered the employ of the Erie Railway, remaining as a locomotive fireman on a freight train between Port Jervis and Jersey City for two years. Later he was transferred to a passenger train, where he remained three years. In 1882 our subject left the employ of the railroad company and engaged as traveling salesman for the Scottford Manufacturing Company, of New York City, manufacturers of stamps and stencils. He traveled through New England and New York, and subsequently went west to the Missouri River. For nearly three years he was in the West, traveling through Missouri, Nebraska, Kansas, Minnesota and Kentucky. In this business he was very successful, but as he did not care to remain away from home, in September, 1886, he located in Middletown, where he engaged in the real-estate and insurance business, under the firm name of Ferguson & Corey. For two years they were located over Bull & Youngblood's, and then took Edward M. Madden in partnership, he remaining with them one year, during which time business was conducted under the firm name of Ferguson, Corey & Madden. On the retirement of Mr. Madden, the name of Ferguson & Corey was resumed, and the business was continued until 1890, when our subject withdrew from the firm.

With Mr. Corey our subject conducted an art and music store for one year, when the firm was dissolved, Mr. Ferguson again engaging in the real-estate and insurance business. In 1893 he organized the Central Building Association, and erected the Central Building at a cost of $30,000, he being one of the general overseers. The Central is one of the finest buildings in this city, and Mr. Ferguson was the first man to erect a business building north of the Erie Railroad. Recently he organized a stock company, entitled The Mechanics' Building Association, and they are erecting the Mechanics' Building, a magnificent structure on North Street. Many of the buildings in the north end were erected by them, nearly all the real estate sold was through their agency, and the Senator Low Tract was handled by them exclusively. With F. G. Kain, he is interested in fifty lots between Highland and Linden Avenues, near Wisner Avenue. These are among the finest building lots in the city, and are rapidly being disposed of. In addition to his real-estate business, Mr. Ferguson also acts as a loan and stock broker, and is appraiser of the New York Building Bank at this place.

In 1887 Mr. Ferguson was married, in Middletown, to Miss Mina C. Brooks, a native of Orange County, born near Tuxedo Park, where her father was engaged in merchandising. They have one child, Clinton B. In politics Mr. Ferguson is a Prohibitionist, and has been an advocate of the principles of that party for many years. He has been a candidate of his party for Assemblyman, running far ahead of his ticket, and has been a delegate to the state and national conventions, attending the convention at Pittsburg which nominated John P. St. John for President. For many years he has been an active member of the Independent Order of Good Templars, and is now Past Worthy Chief Templar of Middletown Lodge, and is the County Chief Templar. He was Lodge Deputy for several years, and has been a representative to the grand lodge of the state. He is a member of the Middletown Board of Trade, and religiously is a pronounced Methodist.

JOSEPH W. CONKLIN resides in the town of Tuxedo, and owns a farm lying on the banks of Little Long Pond, near the Rockland County line. The greater portion of his life has been spent in the forests of the Highland Mountains, and few are better judges of the land in this locality than is he. A native of the adjoining county of Rockland, his birth occurred in the town of Johnsontown, March 14, 1828. He was reared to maturity there, remaining with his father until the age of twenty-one. For a number of years he worked as a laborer in the mountains, and in the spring of 1867 purchased one hundred and eighty acres in the town of Tuxedo, to which he has since added from time to time. He spent a short time in Virginia, near Fairfax and Bull Run, getting out timber for shipbuilding, and has always given prominent attention to wood products.

The first marriage of Mr. Conklin was to Miss Irene Hill, a native of this county, and daughter of Andrew Hill, who was a cooper by trade. Five children were born unto this union, of whom we note the following: Margaret married Peter Bush, of Albany, N. Y.; David E., who married Louisa Conklin, makes his home with his father, and for seven years has been in the employ of Pierre Lorillard at Tuxedo Park; Georgiana married Isaac Wanamaker, of Rahway, N. J.; Ella is the wife of Jacob Taylor, of Spring Valley, Rockland County; and Irene is deceased.

The present wife of Mr. Conklin was Miss Elizabeth McKee, who was born near Warwick, and is a daughter of John and Elizabeth (Conklin) McKee. Her father, who was a hatter and merchant by occupation, went to New York on business and was never heard of afterward, but it was supposed that he was murdered for the money he carried with him. By his second marriage Mr. Conklin is the father of five children, namely: Albert, who married Isabel Odell, and lives at Haverstraw; James L., who for six years has been employed as a gardener at Tuxedo Park; Reuben B. and Aaron, who assist their father in the management of the home farm; and Bertha Mary, who resides with her parents.

The father of our subject, Walter, was a son of Joseph and Sarah Conklin, and the mother, whose maiden name was Adeline Jones, was a daughter of Abraham and Nancy (Pitt) Jones. Nancy Pitt was a daughter of Richard, brother of the illustrious William Pitt, of England. The former came to America and espoused the cause of the Revolution, remaining a loyal citizen of our Government until his death, which occurred on land now owned by our subject. Joseph Conklin was a soldier in the War of 1812, and his wife, Sarah, from the mountain-top saw the capture of Stony Point by the British fleet.

Since the division of the old town of Monroe, our subject has been one of the Assessors of Tuxedo. He has also served as School Trustee and Collector, and has been elected to other local offices. By principle he is a Republican, but is liberal in his views, and gives to others the freedom of thought and opinion which he demands as his own due. With his wife he holds membership in the Methodist Episcopal Church at Johnsontown. He is a man of sound judgment and great perseverance, and deserves all the prosperity he has attained.

JAMES J. McNALLY, editor and publisher of the Goshen *News* and *The Monroe Herald*, served his apprenticeship in the office of the *Signs of the Times*, published by Elder Gilbert Beebe, at New Vernon, Orange County. In 1845, having finished his apprenticeship, he went to New York City and worked for several months in J. W. Oliver's job-printing office, at that time located in the second story of *The Sun* building, corner of Fulton and Nassau Streets. Then, at the desire of Mr. and Mrs. Beebe, he returned to New Vernon and took charge of the office of the *Signs of the Times* until after his marriage, in February, 1846, to Phebe Adaline, youngest daughter of Elder Thomas P. and Charlotte Terry, of New Vernon. By this marriage there were three children: Willie, the present owner and publisher of the Ellenville *Press*; Mrs. Mallett, of New York City; and Victor Irving, deceased.

Soon after his marriage Mr. McNally moved to Newton, N. J., and became foreman in the office of the *New Jersey Herald*, then published by V. M. Drake, his brother-in-law, they having married sisters. He remained in this position until 1849, when he left for Milford, Pa., and established the *Pike County Democrat* (afterwards changed to the Milford *Herald*). This he published for several years and then sold out to John M. Heller, then of Milford, afterwards a prominent citizen of Port Jervis.

Mr. McNally then purchased the *Independent Republican* at Goshen and took possession in May, 1853. He was unacquainted with the political leaders of his party at that time, and as he had not consulted any of them nor asked their advice as to the purchase of the *Republican* office, they determined that he should not obtain possession, and the then Congressman from this dis-

trict, Hon. William Murray, sent special word to him from Washington that he should never have possession of the office; and to prevent his getting it Mr. Murray and his friends, among whom were included Hon. Charles H. Winfield, District Attorney; Hon. John G. Wilkin, County Judge; Walker Fowler, Surrogate; E. M. Madden, and others throughout the county equally influential, induced John S. Clark, one of the owners of the office, to refuse to sell or to accept him as a partner in place of I. V. Montanye, whose interest he had purchased.

Mr. McNally at once commenced proceedings to secure his right, which finally led to a surrender by Mr. Clark and the purchase of his half of the office by Mr. McNally, but at an increased price. He had hardly become accustomed to his new position, when the Democratic party was divided into two parts, between the "Hunkers" and the "Soft-shells," and the fight was very bitter. A day or two after the state nominations had been made, Wilkin, Winfield, Madden and Fowler, as a committee of the "Soft-shells," sent word to Mr. McNally that they desired to see him at the Surrogate's office. He there met them, and it transpired that their purpose was to dictate as to the course he was to pursue in the campaign. "Which ticket do you intend to place at the head of your editorial columns?" was demanded. "While I publish it, the *Republican* will be a Democratic paper, and nothing else," was Mr. McNally's reply, and Judge Wilkin responded, threateningly: "If you do not raise our ticket (the Soft-shell), we will bury you and your paper so deep that the hand of resurrection will never reach either you or your paper." "Thank you, gentlemen, for your courtesy," said Mr. McNally, and then added, "If the ticket I shall raise at the head of my columns does not suit you, then go on with your funeral, and we will see who furnishes the corpse."

Mr. McNally then left, and the fight went on, for he raised the "Hunker" (or Hard-shell) ticket, and this led to the starting of the *Democratic Recorder*, Soft-shell, in opposition to the *Republican*, with C. H. Winfield, one of the ablest writers in the state, as editor. It was, however, short-lived. Mr. McNally kept pouring into their ranks broadside upon broadside, and at the end of a year or so a truce was asked for and granted, which resulted in the transfer of the *Recorder* to Mr. McNally, and it was discontinued.

Then came the Anti-Lecompton (or Anti-Slavery) issue, and the introduction in Congress by Mr. Douglas of a bill for the repeal of the Missouri Compromise. These measures again disrupted the Democratic party (which had become united), and the fight here, as elsewhere, was very bitter, resulting in many of the local Democratic leaders going over to the Republicans. Among these were Murray, Wilkin, Madden, Fowler and many others. Winfield at one time was at the edge of the precipice, but he did not take the final step, and remained with the Democratic party.

In these contests, Mr. McNally kept the *Republican* up to the highest standard of journalism, and under his guidance it can truthfully be said it was a political power in the land. During all these political differences the social relations between the leaders and Mr. McNally were not strained; in fact, with some of them he was especially friendly, and they were daily associates. He came to be regarded by them as a safe and conservative politician, though positive in his ideas and always ready to maintain the right, as he regarded it, without fear or favor. For several years he was Chairman of the Democratic County Committee and served his party satisfactorily in that position.

When Mr. McNally first purchased the *Republican* office, the paper was printed on an old Tuft Platen Press, similar to the Adams Book Press, which was driven by horse-power, on an endless-chain threshing-machine, located in the rear of the office building. This necessitated the keeping of a horse, and on this machine Mr. McNally first indicated his liking for trotting-horses, as he purchased and used a trotter as motive-power for running the press, and would frequently go out with the boys and have a brush on the road.

From this Mr. McNally became more deeply interested, and eventually came to be widely known as the owner and driver of some of the best trotters in Orange County in those days. He was one of the original six gentlemen who established the Goshen trotting-track on the "Elliott Meadow," now included within the grounds of the Goshen Driving Park. The track was first started on the sod, and by constant driving and trotting it eventually became quite good, and required comparatively little work in grading and draining by outside ditches to make it noted, as it afterward became.

On this track the then popular "Orange County Society for the Improvement of Horses" gave its annual exhibitions, which were known and attended by horsemen from almost all sections of the Union, who came not only to see and enjoy the sport, but also to purchase the very promising young trotting stock, which they were sure to find here contending in the speed classes for supremacy, and also in the show classes for superiority, as all-round road and family horses. In this way much of the very best trotting stock of the Hambletonian, Star and Clay strains was taken from Orange County to Kentucky, California and other states, and served as the starters for the growth of the trotting interests there that have since become so prominent; in fact, have even overshadowed Orange County.

For fourteen years Mr. McNally acted as Secretary of this society, and was the active worker in making up the programs for meetings, arranging purses, speed and show classes, etc., etc. The society lasted only one year after he left Goshen and became a resident of Newburgh.

In 1858 Mr. McNally went to Newton, N. J., and became editor and publisher of the *New Jersey Herald*. Here he made the fight against Martin Ryerson on the Lecompton issue, which carried that great leader into the Republican party. He conducted the *Herald* until the fall of 1861, and in July, 1862, returned to Goshen and repurchased the *Independent Republican*. In 1869 he purchased the *Daily Press* office at Newburgh from A. A. Bensel, and published it from 1869 to 1874 as the *Daily and Weekly Telegraph*. He sold the plant to Dr. Cooper, of Warwick, for $10, 500, and after living at Middletown for a short time he purchased the *Carmel Courier*, of Putnam County, N. Y., and conducted that paper for several years. He then returned to Orange County, and for the past thirteen years has published the Monroe *Herald* and for eight years the Goshen *News*.

Mr. McNally was born in Paterson, N. J., in 1824, and is the son of James McNally and Elizabeth Bushforth. He is the youngest in a family of four children, and the only son. His father was the pioneer in a stage line which he established to run between Jersey City and Paterson, and at one time employed more than a hundred horses in the business. This was before there was railroad communications between the two places. He was also the owner of the largest hotel property in Paterson, which included the property now known as Congress Hall. In 1824, General La Fayette while on his visit to the United States, was a guest at Mr. McNally's hostelry.

For his second wife James J. McNally married Phebe Ann, the youngest daughter of Gilbert and Phebe Ann Beebe, of Middletown. They have no children.

———※———

THOMAS DOUGHERTY, one of the most successful business men of Newburgh, and one of her best citizens, is engaged in the wholesale manufacture of cider and cider vinegar, having the largest trade of the kind, not only in this immediate locality, but perhaps anywhere in the state. He embarked in this occupation in 1876, in a small way, and year by year has had to increase his facilities for meeting the demand. While his sales are principally in Newburgh, he has large orders from New York City, many points along the Hudson and inland, and has also sent consignments to Leadville, Colo., in the West; to Georgia in the South, and has even had sales in China.

Some seven generations ago, our subject's surname was spelled McDarrah, and the lineage has been faithfully kept. Members of the family emigrated from Scotland two or more centuries

ago, settling in County Antrim, Ireland, where our subject's grandfather, Harvey, was born. He was superintendent of a factory at Killwater, where flax was extensively manufactured. At an early day he emigrated to America, settling in Sullivan County, near the town of Pike Pond. He lived to reach the extreme old age of nearly ninety years, while his wife, Susannah, was in her eighty-sixth year at the time of her death. Our subject's father, William, was born in Killwater, County Antrim, Ireland, and learned the carpenter's trade. He was brought up as a Protestant and has long inclined toward the Presbyterian faith. He is now nearly seventy-two years of age, and resides on a small place near Monticello, N. Y. His wife, Elizabeth, was a daughter of Thomas Logan, and both were born in County Antrim. Mr. Logan was a farmer, and was also a fancy weaver, operating four looms. Mrs. Elizabeth Dougherty died in Monticello, in August, 1866. Of her ten children, all but two lived to manhood and womanhood, and these are still living. Thomas, the eldest, and his sisters, Mrs. Swan and Mrs. Burgher, reside in Newburgh; another sister resides in Yonkers, N. Y.; Harvey lives in Paterson, N. J.; William is a farmer of Schuyler County, N. Y.; and John and Samuel are engaged in cigar manufacturing in Binghamton, N. Y.

The birth of Thomas Dougherty occurred in the village of Broughshane, County Antrim, October 28, 1846. From the time he was nine years of age he attended the district schools of Monticello, and December 1, 1866, came to Newburgh with George Bennett, in whose employ he remained until the latter's death in 1876. The same year Mr. Dougherty embarked in his present business, and in 1888 rented the building which he now occupies, and which has a capacity of thirty thousand gallons in barrels. Two delivery wagons are kept in constant use, and the proprietor attends to every department and detail of the work. Such cider as he does not dispose of he converts into vinegar by nature's process. It is therefore in great demand by lovers of the pure article, and by housewifes who have a just regard for the health and welfare of their families.

For two years he was engaged in the wholesale grocery business on South Street, but now gives his entire time to his present occupation. He erected the fine three-story and basement brick building at No. 233 Dubois Street, on the corner of Gidney Avenue.

Our subject was first married, in this city, to Catherine J. Kennedy, who was born in County Roscommon, Ireland, but who is now deceased. The only child of this marriage, Mary E., graduated from the Newburgh Academy, and is now engaged in teaching school. The lady who now bears our subject's name was formerly Miss Mary J. Ray, and she too is a native of Ireland, having been born in County Donegal. Mrs. Dougherty and her daughter Mary are members of St. John's Methodist Episcopal Church. Politically our subject is a loyal supporter of the Republican party, and takes great interest not only in national affairs, but in everything tending toward the upbuilding and beautifying of Newburgh.

ENRY YOUNGS. Farming and dairying have formed the chief occupation of this prominent young citizen of Orange County, and the progressive manner in which he has taken advantage of every method and idea tending toward enhancing the value of his property has had considerable to do with his success in life. Through thrift and enterprise he has succeeded in making the old homestead farm, which he inherited upon the death of his father in 1885, one of the best dairy farms in the township. A visitor to the estate can here see the work of three generations of men distinctly marked out and added one to the other, the work of the three last Henry Youngses, while the modern machinery and the finishing touches are plainly the handiwork of the last, our subject.

Mr. Youngs was born in Brooklyn, N. Y., in 1866, and was the eldest member and only son of the family of Henry and Annie (Jackson) Youngs. He is the sixth Henry Youngs to own the farm on which he at present resides, and represents the ninth generation of Youngses in America.

His father, who was the fifth of the name, was born in New York City, where he passed the greater portion of his life. In 1869, upon the death of his uncle, Henry Youngs (fourth), he came to Orange County, where he lived until called from earth. While a resident of the metropolis he was engaged in the produce business, and was one of the founders, and up to the time of his death a member, of the Produce Exchange of that city. After coming to Orange County he lived retired from business of any kind, and died September 9, 1885, at the age of sixty-four years. His wife, who was a native of Brooklyn, has just died, October 4, 1895. Their family consisted of four daughters and one son, all of whom are living at the present writing.

The original of this sketch received his education in the Polytechnic Institute of Brooklyn. He has resided on his present beautiful farm for the past ten years, and in the carrying on of his labors is meeting with untold success. His place, besides being one of the largest in the township, ranks among the best in point of improvement. Mr. Youngs is one of the progressive and energetic young business men of the county, and his success is well deserved. He is a member of St. James' Episcopal Church, in which he is a Vestryman. In politics he is an ardent Republican, and takes great interest in the success of his party. Honorable and upright in his dealings with all, he has many warm friends throughout the county who hold him in high esteem.

The Youngs family is an old and time-honored one in this section. The founder of the family in America was Rev. John Youngs, a Puritan minister, who, with thirteen of his congregation emigrated from Hingham, England, and in 1637 landed on the shores of Connecticut at the then village of New Haven. He was the son of Rev. Christopher Youngs, the vicar of Southwold, Suffolk County, England. After a short stay there they crossed over to Long Island and settled the village of Southold. He built the first church there, which is still standing, and was the first pastor there, holding the office for many years. Here the family dwelt for many years, and is still well represented.

In 1732 four of the descendants, Reuben, Silas, Abimel and Henry, all brothers, left Long Island and came up the Hudson as far as Newburgh; thence striking across the country, they settled the territory between Washingtonville and Goshen. Henry settled where the present Henry, his sixth lineal descendant, now lives. The main farm of two hundred and twenty-two acres which the present Henry inherited through his father, Henry Youngs (fifth), from his great-uncle, Henry Youngs (fourth), has never been out of the possession of the Youngses. H. Youngs (fifth) added some seventy-eight acres, making a total of three hundred acres in all.

Two of the sons of H. Youngs (third) very early in the present century left their Orange County home for New York City, and engaged in the dry-goods business, later becoming very successful merchants. These sons were Henry Youngs (fourth) and Hiram. Upon the death of his mother, Henry Youngs (fourth) returned to Goshen, where he died, childless, in November, 1869, leaving the bulk of his property, and in particular the homestead farm, which he dearly loved, to his nephew, Henry Youngs (fifth), eldest son of his brother Hiram, for life, and upon his death, in fee to his son, H. Youngs (sixth), then a child three years old.

G EORGE N. CLEMSON. The history of Middletown is that of its successful business men, those who have developed its commercial activities, promoted its manufacturing interests and enlarged its material resources. Such a one is George N. Clemson, President of the National Saw Company, President of the Middletown Trust and Safety Deposit Company, Vice-President of the Hogan Boiler Works, Vice-President of the Middletown Glass Works, and member of the firm of Clemson Brothers. Though in achieving his present position he had the prestige of wealth and the influence of his father's name, it is but justice to him to say that, had he been obliged to begin the battle of life unaided, he would nevertheless have gained success, for he pos-

sesses those traits of character that almost invariably bring prosperity and prominence.

A native of Massachusetts, George N. is the son of William Clemson, a successful saw manufacturer, concerning whom mention is elsewhere made. He accompanied his father to Middletown, arriving in this city May 4, 1860. In childhood he gained a thorough knowledge of every detail connected with the manufacture of saws, and at an early age he began making bracket-saws in a building on his father's place, that he had fitted up for the purpose. So well did he succeed, that he soon enlarged the shop, and after a time moved to larger quarters. Like his father and grandfather, he possesses inventive genius and his patents have wrought a marvelous improvement in the saw business, increasing the speed of manufacture as well as the quality of the product.

The firm of Clemson Brothers, in which George N. and his brother Richard are interested, is one of the most complete manufacturing establishments in the country. In 1890 the firm built a large brick structure on Cottage Street, opposite the National Saw Works. This is a substantial building, with granite front and all modern conveniences for the manufacture of butchers' brackets and lock-saws. Prior to his father's death he and his brother Richard purchased his interest in the saw works of Wheeler, Madden & Clemson, and since that time he has become more largely interested in them. In 1891 he was one of the incorporators of the National Saw Company, into which the other concern was merged, and of which he has since been President. It is a very large corporation, having, besides the works at Middletown, manufacturing establishments in Cincinnati, Philadelphia and Brooklyn.

The home of Mr. Clemson on Highland Avenue is one of the finest residences in the city and is surrounded by beautiful and well kept grounds, the whole presenting a most inviting appearance to the passer-by. Mr. Clemson and his wife have two children now living. For some time he was Vice-President of the Middletown Trust and Safety Deposit Company, and in May, 1895, was elected its President, to succeed the late Hon. M. D. Stivers. In the organization of the Hogan

Boiler Works he was an active factor and is now its Vice-President. He is also Vice-President of the Middletown Glass Company. No man takes a deeper interest in the progress and prosperity of Middletown than does he, and every public-spirited enterprise receives his support and substantial aid. While his business duties are heavy and engrossing, he does not allow them to consume his entire time, but is fond of a drive behind a team of his fine horses, and a hunt with his hounds, that are the finest for miles around. In business and in society, at his office and in his home, he is ever the same tactful, courteous and affable gentleman, one with whom it is a pleasure to meet and associate.

···=⟶≪◫❀◻≫ᚴ≔··

MOSES V. SHUMAKER. If by success in life we mean securing a comfortable home and the means for a good support, then is our subject one of the most successful men in Orange County. He owns and occupies a fine estate in the town of Goshen, which is devoted to the raising of fruits and vegetables in great variety, and also to dairy farming, which he finds to be very profitable.

Our subject was born in Monroe County, Pa., in 1839, and is the second of the family born to John and Sarah (Van Campen) Shumaker, natives of New Jersey, within whose borders they were reared. John Shumaker was a well-to-do farmer during his lifetime and at the time of his decease, in 1893, was the possessor of a good estate. His wife preceded him to the land beyond by many years, her death occurring in 1860.

Although he attended the common schools, Moses V. received special training in farm work. It was not strange, then, that when ready to embark in life for himself, he should choose that vocation. Since his twenty-fifth year he has been carrying on farm pursuits. In October, 1891, he located on his present estate, and, as before stated, he gives his attention to raising fruits and vegetables and to dairying.

Mr. Shumaker was married, in 1870, to Miss Martha, daughter of John W. and Eleanor (Phil-

lips) Beemer, all of whom were natives of Sussex County, N. J. By her marriage with our subject, Mrs. Shumaker became the mother of eight children, one of whom is now deceased. Those living are: Lillie A., the wife of Frederick Northup, of Newburgh; Fannie O., Charles W., Albert L., Willard J., Lizzie M. and Florence L. Although not members of any religious body, both our subject and his wife are inclined toward the faith of the Presbyterian Church, which they attend. In politics he has abiding faith in the teachings of the Republican party, whose candidates always receive his vote and influence.

When the tocsin of war was sounded throughout the country in 1861, Mr. Shumaker donned the blue, enlisting in Company D, Thirtieth New Jersey Infantry, being mustered in at Flemington, that state. He was in active service for ten months, participating in all of the engagements in which his regiment was engaged, and was mustered out as Corporal of his company. He is now a member of Chaplain Haines Post, G. A. R., at Deckertown, N. J.

≪++++++++++++❀++++++++++++≫

DANIEL THOMPSON. Among the many fine farms that attract the stranger's eye in this part of Orange County, the one belonging to the subject of this sketch deserves special mention. The owner of this valuable piece of ground was born in the town of Crawford, this county, October 8, 1819. He was the seventh in order of birth in a family of ten children comprising the household of Alexander and Hannah (Bull) Thompson.

The following is a brief mention of the brothers and sisters of our subject: Jane married Archibald P. Nevins, of Monticello, and died when about seventy-four years of age. Catherine became the wife of John Moore, and in his death married A. W. Jackson, of Middletown; she died when in her eighty-ninth year. Albert was a physician of Ontario, N. Y., and died after reaching his seventy-fourth year. Mary became the wife of Hiram Phillips, and died when about thirty-eight years old. Sarah, Mrs. E. Sherman, was eighty-three years of age at the time of her death. Harriet married William H. Smith, and died in New York City when sixty-eight years old. Augustus was a farmer in this town, and died at the age of sixty-seven years. Martha married Samuel C. Brush, and her death occurred when in her sixty-eighth year; and John A. is a resident of Middletown.

The father of this family was born in the town of Crawford, where he spent his entire life, successfully engaged in farm pursuits. He lived to be eighty-six years old. For a period of nine years he was Supervisor, and during that time gave satisfaction to all concerned. In religious affairs he was a prominent member of the Presbyterian Church. He was in turn the son of Alexander and Jane Thompson, natives of County Longford, Ireland. The former came to America many years ago, in company with two of his brothers, Robert and Andrew. They were among the very earliest settlers of this town, where they took up Government land, which is still in the possession of the family.

The subject of this sketch lived with his parents until his marriage. He then located on his present place, which property was given him by his honored father, and here he has made his home ever since. The tract comprises one hundred and thirty acres, finely improved in every particular and cultivated in such a manner that it yields its owner a handsome income.

The marriage of Mr. Thompson with Miss Mary E. Hunter occurred October 3, 1850. The lady was born in this town January 7, 1830, and is the daughter of George and Sarah (Crawford) Hunter. Her father was born in the town of Montgomery, and was a well-to-do physician. He went to Searsville in 1823, when a young man, and was there engaged in a lucrative practice until the time of his death, in 1870, when threescore and ten years of age.

Four children have been born to Mr. and Mrs. Thompson. Frank H., born February 8, 1853, is now engaged as an engineer at Akron, Ohio; Anna, born March 21, 1856, is at home; George, who was born August 14, 1858, died August 4, 1893; and the fourth child died in infancy.

Our subject is an old-time Democrat in his political views. For twenty-seven years he held the office of Supervisor, for a number of terms was Commissioner of Highways, at one time was President of the Middletown and Pine Bush Railroad Company, and from 1876 to 1882 was Superintendent of the same.

Socially Mr. Thompson is a Mason of high standing, belonging to Hoffman Lodge No. 112 of Middletown. With his wife he is a devoted member of the Presbyterian Church, to the support of which they give liberally, and are always ready to lend a helping hand to the needy. Although Mr. Thompson is well advanced in years, he is hale and hearty and is still able to personally superintend his excellent farm. He is one of the leading citizens of the county, and as such we are pleased to be able to place this brief outline of his life before our readers.

WILLIAM E. DOUGLAS, M. D., began practice in Middletown in 1881. He was born in Franklin, Delaware County, N. Y., July 14, 1853, and is of good old Revolutionary stock, his great-grandfather, Asa Douglas, serving as Captain during that struggle. For his services he was granted a tract of land, supposed to have been in Massachusetts, but on surveying it was found between the two states, now in Rensselaer County, N. Y. He was born in Franklin, Delaware County. Judge Amos Douglas, the grandfather, was born in Stephentown, in Rensselaer County, and in early life moved to Franklin, Delaware County, where he was one of the first attorneys. He was subsequently County Judge there, which office he held for many years. The father of our subject, who was also named Amos, was a native of Franklin, and for twenty-five years was engaged in the mercantile business, and later in the banking business. He was one of the organizers of the First National Bank of Franklin, and was President of the same for more than twenty-five years. He married Miss Marriette Hine, who was also a native of Franklin, and was a daughter of William Hine, a native of Woodbridge, now New Milford, Conn. He was, however, an early settler in Franklin, and was by occupation a farmer. His grandfather, the great-grandfather of Mrs. Douglas, who was named Stephen Hine, served in the Revolutionary War, and died in Connecticut. Her father was a Deacon in the Congregational Church for many years. Amos Douglas, the father of our subject, was a strong Republican, but one who never aspired to official position. He was Clerk in the Congregational Church for many years, or until he gave it up on account of ill-health. He died in Franklin in 1888, and his wife died in 1886. They were the parents of four children, three of whom grew to maturity, and two are yet living: Amos Stanley, who resides in Middletown, and who is a special insurance adjustor; and Dr. William E., the subject of this sketch. Charles A. grew to manhood and was Cashier of the First National Bank of Middletown, but resigned, and has since died.

The subject of this notice was reared in Franklin, and received his education in the literary institute at that place, from which he graduated. At the age of sixteen he began reading medicine in the office of Dr. Ira Wilcox, and subsequently entered Bellevue Hospital Medical College, New York City, where he remained four and a-half years, taking his degree of M. D. in 1876. On graduating, he removed to Lisle, Broome County, where he opened an office and commenced the practice of his profession. He remained there until 1881, when, as already stated, he located in Middletown, where he has since resided, and where he has built up an extensive practice, being recognized as one of the leading physicians of the county. Since the institution was started he has been on the medical staff of Thrall Hospital. He is a member of the State Medical Society, is ex-President of the Orange County Medical Society, and is Examiner for several life-insurance companies, besides being a Director of the First National Bank of Middletown, and a member of the Board of Water Commissioners.

Dr. Douglas was married, in Broome County, to Miss Katharine Whitney, a native of that county, and they have one child, Amos Stanley,

Jr. Fraternally the Doctor holds membership with the Odd Fellows and the Knights of Pythias, and politically is a Republican. He is a member of the Congregational Church of Middletown, and is Chairman of its Board of Trustees. Personally he is very popular, and is held in high esteem by those who know him.

JOHN H. CHAPMAN. While this gentleman has gained success in business, his attention has not been so engrossed by personal affairs as to exclude participation in matters of public importance. At the present time he is rendering efficient service as a member of the Board of Health of Newburgh, and at different times he has held other responsible positions. In Masonry he has attained a high rank, and is well known among the members of that order in the Hudson River Valley.

The Chapman family is one of the oldest and most honorable in Orange County. The father of our subject, Isaac C. Chapman, is the well known wholesale and retail druggist of Newburgh, and to his sketch on another page the reader is referred for particulars concerning the family history. John H. was born in this city February 1, 1860, being an only son. He was reared in the home of his parents, and under their wise guidance was prepared for a useful and honorable career in the business world. After having graduated from the grammar school, he entered the free academy, and completed the course there in 1877. He then went to New York City, where he entered the New York College of Pharmacy, and for a time was connected with the wholesale drug house of R. W. Robinson & Son.

After about two years in New York, Mr. Chapman returned to Newburgh, establishing in business with his father, with whom he remained until 1890, when he took the stand formerly occupied by F. W. Reuter. This he has since conducted, and has met with the most flattering success in the enterprise. His location first was on the corner of South and Liberty Streets, but in May, 1895, he removed to South and Chambers Streets, where he occupies a new building, and has a large and well equipped pharmacy.

In addition to his business interests, Mr. Chapman is agent for the Northwestern Masonic Aid Association, which has its headquarters in Chicago, Ill. In 1893, under the administration of Mayor Lawson, he was appointed a member of the City Board of Health, and in 1895 he was again appointed to that position by Mayor Odell. He occupies a pleasant residence at No. 164 Grand Street.

Socially Mr. Chapman is identified with Hudson River Lodge No. 607, F. & A. M.; Highland Chapter No. 52, R. A. M.; and Hudson River Commandery No. 35, K. T., in which he has been Generalissimo, and since May, 1895, has held the rank of Commander. He also belongs to Mecca Temple, New York City, and the Noble and Mystic Shrine. He is an honorary member of the Newburgh Fire Department, and served for six years in the Ringgold Hose Company. With the City Club, of which he was a charter member, he is still actively connected. He is connected with the Veterans' Association of the Tenth Separate Company, National Guard of New York, and for six years served as Corporal of the old Tenth Separate Company. In politics he is active and enthusiastic in support of Democratic principles, and never fails to cast his ballot for the candidates of that party.

———⊙⋇⊙———

ALFRED BRIDGEMAN. While his business interests have required his presence in New York City at intervals for many years, Mr. Bridgeman has gained a large acquaintance in Orange County, especially in the city and town of Newburgh, where he has made his home for a long time. The enterprise with which he has been connected throughout his entire active life is one of the oldest of the kind in the metropolis, having been established in 1824. The first location of the house was at No. 876 Broadway, from

which place it was removed, in 1872, to No. 37 East Nineteenth Street, near Broadway. Here a large and remunerative business is carried on both in the importing and sale of vegetable, farm and flower seeds, etc. The premises occupied are of modern and substantial construction, and are finished artistically and in a most pleasing manner. The trade is large, not being limited to the city or state, but extending throughout the entire country, and from all points are received orders for the many varieties of goods carried.

The Bridgeman family originated in England, where the parents of our subject, Thomas and Hannah (Eastmond) Bridgeman, were born, the former in Abingdon, March 29, 1786, and the latter in Kintbury, May 16, 1787. Of their marriage, which took place in their native land May 23, 1807, nine children were born, of whom Alfred and two sisters are the sole survivors. The father, who was a horticulturist, seed-merchant and horticultural writer, brought his family to America and settled in New York City, where he engaged in business until his death, at the age of sixty-four. He was a man of industrious, persevering disposition, and held many positions of honor.

During the residence of his parents in Newbury, England, the subject of this sketch was born, June 6, 1818. He was brought by his father to America, where he completed his education in the Lafayette Institute of New York City. Possessing an aptitude for the business in which he is now engaged, he early turned his attention to it, gaining a familiarity with every department of the work. To it he has given his entire active life, and by managing his affairs in a systematic and business-like manner he has built up the reputation of the house. In addition to the business in New York City, he is proprietor of a nursery at Astoria, now Long Island City, N. Y.

In Brooklyn, N. Y., February 25, 1846, Mr. Bridgeman married Martha M. King, whose father, Gamaliel King, a noted architect of Brooklyn, was at one time a member of the State Legislature, and often held positions of public trust and honor. Five children comprised their family, but two have been called from earth, the survivors being Alfred T., Catherine H. and Ella M. Alfred T. married Jennie Adams, and they have one son. Catherine H. is the wife of Munson G. Muir, and the mother of a son and daughter. Ella M. is the wife of Augustus W. Bell, of Morristown, N. J., and is also the mother of one son and one daughter.

Mr. Bridgeman has been an extensive traveler through this country, and he has also visited Europe four times, having in that way gained familiarity with the customs of the people in this and other lands. To his children he gave the best educational advantages, both at home and abroad, and fitted them for positions of honor in social or business circles. February 4, 1850, he received from William H. Seward, Governor of the state of New York, the appointment of Second Lieutenant of the Third Regiment of Artillery, and he served as a commissioned officer in the same upwards of six years.

DEWITT C. DOMINICK is the energetic and progressive Superintendent of the public schools of Walden, N. Y. Himself a man of finished education, he is able to appreciate the benefits to be derived from a thorough knowledge of men and things, and has ever striven to instill into the young people under his charge a love for learning and perseverance in the pursuit of that knowledge which is power. His life has been devoted to school work, and in every position to which he has been called he has shown his executive ability in organization and his power to present puzzling and intricate truths in a simple and lucid manner.

The birth of Mr. Dominick occurred in Gallupville, Schoharie County, N. Y., on the 19th of September, 1851, and he was the son of Weidman Dominick, a native of Herkimer County. He is still living, making his home in his native county, where he is a prominent attorney. He has always been a very popular man and has been called to fill many positions of honor and public trust, performing the duties devolving upon him with ability and faithfulness.

Professor Dominick received the rudiments of his education in the public schools, and from the age of eighteen until twenty-one years of age was in the employ of his father. At that time he entered the Delaware City Institute, and later became a student at the Albany State Normal, from which he graduated in January, 1876. He spent the following year teaching in the public school of his native town, and during the summer was instructor in the Schoharie Academy, in his spare moments studying languages under the Superintendent of the academy.

In the year 1877 our subject entered Cornell University at Ithaca, N. Y., taking the scientific course, and graduated in 1881, although during his junior year he was obliged to teach for six months to defray his expenses. He paid his own way through college, and upon the completion of his course received the degree of Bachelor of Sciences. He was always very active in his class work, maintaining a high standing as a student and being a leader in his class. To perhaps unusual ability he added a genius for study and close application, and in the success which has come to him he has no cause for regret for the hard struggles of his early life.

In the autumn of 1881 he accepted the Principalship of the schools at Schaghticoke, N. Y., remaining there two years. He had engaged for a third year, but being released he accepted a more lucrative position at Greenport, L. I., which he held for two years. He then went to Gallupville, where for a similar length of time he dealt in hardware and drugs. For the succeeding two years he was employed as traveling salesman for the firm of E. L. Kellogg & Co., publishers of New York, canvassing teachers' institutes in New York and Illinois.

The Professor next came to Walden, where he has been connected with the schools for six years. During this time the educational interests of this locality have made great strides. The enrollment and average attendance have increased fifty per cent. and the corps of teachers has been advanced in number from six to ten. The school has been placed under the supervision of the Regents of the State University and carries a regular high-school course. The school ranks among the first in the county, and in several competitive examinations has taken first place. Its pupils took examinations with those of the Newburgh High School and the New Paltz State Normal, and in both cases carried off honors.

In county-institute work our subject has served two years as instructor, and is prominently identified with all educational associations, both state and national, and has been President of the county association. in which he is very active and influential. He is a Republican in politics, and is in demand as a public speaker. He is also one of the proprietors of the Walden *Citizen*, and assists in its management, although not on its editorial staff.

December 26, 1883, our subject married Miss Mabel F. Field. She is also a native of New York, and was born in Mt. Vision, Otsego County. To this union were born three children, two of whom survive, namely: Dewitt C., Jr., and Elma C. Field H. died aged five years. Mr. and Mrs. Rake are valued members of the Methodist Episcopal Church, and the former has been Superintendent of the Sunday-school for two years. He is a Steward in the congregation and was Secretary of the Building Committee which had in charge the erection of the new church, completed in 1894. Socially he is a Mason, having belonged to that fraternity since 1882. Judicious and enterprising in public affairs, progressive and interesting in the schoolroom, and genial and hospitable in his home, he is a man whom to know is to honor.

JOSEPH RAKE occupies a prominent place among the substantial and progressive business men of Turner, and is at present carrying on an extensive trade in the lumber and coal business, handling also lime, cement, etc. He is a native of Orange County and was born in the town of Monroe December 27, 1830. He attended the district schools until eighteen years of age, when he left home and apprenticed himself to a

carpenter in order to become fully acquainted with the trade. He worked for three years under Peter Rose, of Chester, and after completing his trade was in the employ of a Mr. Thompson, of that place, for seven or eight years. Later he began contracting, which he still follows to some extent in conjunction with his other business.

In the year 1868 our subject purchased the interest of Isaac Thompson, of the firm of Brown & Thompson, in his present business, and four years later Mr. Brown withdrew, leaving him the sole proprietor of the business. He has had the assistance of his son William ever since the latter was old enough, and together they manage an extensive enterprise, dealing in the various building materials and coal.

Our subject is a son of John and Mary Ann (Brooks) Rake, natives of London, England. Prior to his emigration to America, in 1828, the father was a teacher, but after making his home in the New World he gave his attention to farm pursuits. He died in 1863.

The parental household included ten sons and daughters, of whom three died in infancy. Those who grew to mature years were Jane; George, living in Monroe; Joseph, of this sketch; Rachel, who is the widow of Josiah Bull and makes her home in Oxford, this county; Elizabeth, who married John E. Ewery, of Monroe; William, who was killed in the battle of the Wilderness in the late war; and Agnes.

Our subject was married, December 23, 1856, to Miss Hannah Case, who was born in the town of Monroe and who was the daughter of Benjamin W. and Mary (Solomon) Case, natives of this county, although the family came originally from Long Island. They were the parents of eight children. Mr. and Mrs. Rake had a family of six sons and daughters, of whom four survive, namely: Carrie, who married Arthur P. Carey, of Newburgh; William, who is in business with his father, and who married Miss Bertha Coffee; Mary, the wife of Frank Griffin, of the village of Monroe; and Hannah, Mrs. William L. Dolly, of Jersey City. Mrs. Rake is a consistent member of the Methodist Episcopal Church. In politics our subject is a Republican, having always voted that ticket. He was first elected Justice of the Peace in the spring of 1875, and has continued to hold that position since, a period of twenty years. His interest in schools has led him to be placed on the Board of Trustees, and he has also been Supervisor of the town of Monroe and Justice of Sessions. Socially he belongs to Standard League No. 711, of Monroe, and is a Chapter and Commandery Mason. He is a member of Central Valley Lodge No. 502, I. O. O. F., and takes great interest in the work of these various orders.

SURNAME INDEX

1546

GURNEE, 454 455 820 929
GURNEY, 862
GWYER, (bio) 484 485
HACKH, 1397
HADAWAY, 610
HADDEN, 694 985 (bio) 1122 1125
HAFNER, (bio) 1132 1133
HAGAMAN, 1327
HAGERTY, 574 (bio) 829
HAIGHT, 421 1386 (bio) 1054 1055
HAINEN, (bio) 1092 1095
HAINES, 243 252 295 331
HAIT, 1403
HALCOTT, 659
HALE, 119 649
HALGIN, 551
HALL, 141 194 302 312 639 736 778
    1127 1152 1199 1481 (bio) 464 465
    823-825 937 938
HALLECK, 484
HALLENBECK, 681
HALLET, 795
HALLETT, 595
HALLIDAY, 165
HALLOCK, 161 292 415 641 797 827
    858 968 1355 1373 (bio) 316 319
    848 849 909 910 928 1185 Portrait
    908 1184
HALPIN, 381 414
HALSEY, 299 884 1054 1406
HALSTEAD, 213 459 475 1512 (bio)
    783 784
HALSTED, 463
HAMBLET, 564
HAMILTON, 341 371 521 522 601 644
    664 683 975 1199 (bio) 730 731
    1446
HAMMELL, 695
HAMMER, 530
HAMMERSTEIN, 1397 (bio) 203 204
HAMMOND, 494 923 (bio) 1090 1091
HAMPSON, 154
HAMPTON, 642
HANCOCK, 182 370
HANCON, 609
HANDERHAN, (bio) 255 256
HANFORD, 264 1355 1373
HANLON, 613
HANLY, 124
HANMORE, (bio) 323 324
HANNAH, 921
HANRETTY, (bio) 501 502
HANSFORD, 1447
HARCOURT, 459 606
HARDEN, (bio) 970 973
HARDENBERGH, 246 1445 1459 (bio)
    915 916 1271 1272 Portrait 914
HARDENBURG, 125
HARDESTY, 695
HARDING, 973 1001 1092 1162 1339
    1355 1442 1475 1491 (bio) 640 641

HARDY, 1035
HARFORD, 951
HARGNMALOR, 165
HARGRAVE, 1212
HARLOW, 626 632 743 976
HARMAN, 705 1393
HARMER, 899
HARMON, 973
HAROLD, King Of England 871
HARPER, 569
HARRIMAN, 1501
HARRINGTON, 401 710
HARRIS, 204 334 375 451 463 969 (bio)
    519 520 543 544 Portrait 518
HARRISON, 184 244 301 324 394 483
    500 566 629 701 782 785 1008 1017
    1073 1167 1251 1278 1364 1369
    1391 (bio) 191 192 490 491 1513
HART, 1362 1523 1524 (bio) 1442
HARTFORD, 1049
HARTIG, 525
HARTLEY, 311
HARTWICK, 513
HARVEY, 232 824 1507
HARWOOD, 436
HASACK, 1527
HASBROOK, 370 599 686
HASBROUCK, 513 690 691 1047 1251
    1368 1374 1393
HASBROUK, 291
HASBRUK, 1054
HASKINS, 138
HASTINGS, (bio) 390 391
HATCH, 301
HATFIELD, 1284
HATHAWAY, 299 710 (bio) 384 385
HATHORN, 1084 1137
HAUBER, 1404 1405
HAVELOCK, 140 531
HAVEMEYER, 495 504 1433
HAVENS, 970
HAVILAND, 416
HAWKES, 636
HAWKINS, 138 232 234 245 246 254
    620 623 734 835 1448 (bio) 905 906
HAWXHURST, 691
HAYDEN, 1061
HAYES, 201 660 (bio) 126 127 1042
    1043
HAYNE, 199 (bio) 1462 1465
HAYNES, 245 758 813
HAYT, 143 511 550
HAYTHORN, 296
HAYWARD, 1114
HAZARD, 774 810 869
HAZEN, 471 661
HAZZARD, 450 1096
HEAD, 1501
HEADLEY, 321 1511 (bio) 139-141
HEALY, 473 495
HEARD, 512 526 1038 1424 (bio) 366

MASSIE, 839
MASTEN, 360
MASTERS, 956
MASTERSON, 136 (bio) 940
MASTON, 385
MATHER, 785 838 1321 1370
MATHERSON, 526
MATHEWS, 211 249 250 480 (bio) 430
MATTHEWS, 146 192 346 401 945 (bio)
    482 483 1212 1215 1283 1284
    Portrait 1282
MAUBEY, 613
MAWHINNEY, 470
MAY, 793 861 862
MAYBEE, 775
MAYNARD, 214 1252
MCALLISTER, 460 1417
MCALOON, 1204
MCALPINE, 656
MCAULAY, 343
MCBAIN, 896
MCBRAIR, 1043 (bio) 660
MCBRIDE, 293 1501 (bio) 300 301
MCBURNEY, 264
MCCABE, 405 410 886 1032
MCCAIN, 163 284 879 880 1138 (bio)
    880 881 Portrait 875 878
MCCALLUM, 994
MCCAMLY, 544 879 1140 (bio) 1137
    1138 Portrait 1136
MCCARDLE, 882
MCCARRELL, 370
MCCARTER, 951
MCCARTNEY, 430 453
MCCLELLAN, 1391
MCCLELLAND, 306
MCCLENNAN, 452
MCCLEVE, 119
MCCLINTOCK, 1423
MCCLOSKEY, 286 1331
MCCLOUGHAN, 1103
MCCLOY, 138 372
MCCLUGAN, 386
MCCLUGHAM, 393
MCCLUNG, 141 345 431 445 1514 (bio)
    321 322 460 461
MCCLURE, 880
MCCLURG, 1011
MCCOBB, 903
MCCOMBER, 839
MCCONNELL, 980 1103
MCCONVILLE, (bio) 962
MCCOON, 1391
MCCORD, 480
MCCORMICK, 244 356 1292 (bio) 679
    680 Portrait 678
MCCORNELL, 1168
MCCORTNEY, 612
MCCOUN, 182 183 346
MCCOY, 533 904 957 (bio) 1502 1505
MCCREA, 433

MCCRORY, 151
MCCROSKERY, 531 562 (bio) 342 343
    814 815
MCCULLOUGH, 845
MCCUNE, 691
MCCURDY, 510 722 1257
MCCUTCHEON, 562
MCDARRAH, 1533
MCDONALD, 511 1103 1168 1302
MCDOUGAL, 436
MCDOUGALL, 626
MCDOWELL, 313 373 896 909
MCELHONE, 672
MCELROY, 755 768 955 (bio) 464 1500
    1501
MCENANY, (bio) 531 532
MCEWEN, 356 396 (bio) 314 315 690-
    691
MCFARLAN, 1403
MCFARLAND, 823
MCGARTH, 386
MCGEE, 172
MCGILL, 967
MCGINNIS, 356 601
MCGIVNEY, (bio) 136
MCGOVERN, 1260
MCGOWAN, (bio) 1382 1385
MCGREADY, 1187
MCGREGGOR, 382
MCGREGOR, 155 593 (bio) 371 372
MCGROTY, 935
MCGUIGAN, (bio) 532 533
MCGUIRE, 121 137 195 470 633
MCGUNN, 663
MCHALE, 1212
MCINNES, (bio) 938
MCINTOSH, 133
MCINTYRE, 970
MCKEAG, 830
MCKEE, 396 403 731 1381 1530
MCKEEBY, 987
MCKEEL, 481
MCKELVEY, 753 836 845 869 1096
MCKENNY, 1110
MCKENZIE, 1077 (bio) 386 389
MCKEY, 522
MCKIBBEN, 1182
MCKINLEY, 611 734
MCKINNEY, 266 664 1090 1186 (bio)
    930 933
MCKINSTRY, 1228
MCKISSOCK, 370
MCLAIN, 885
MCLAUGHLIN, 817 882 1060 1434
MCLERNON, 473 (bio) 385
MCMANNUS, 459
MCMEEKIN, 494
MCMILLAN, 324 573
MCMONAGLE, (bio) 1006 1007
MCMULLEN, 546
MCNALLY, (bio) 1531-1533

1570

VALENTINE, 646 794 805 874 (bio)
  262 263 469 470 Portrait 468
VANAIKEN, 1385
VANALEN, 771 772
VANALST, 291 611 723 (bio) 232 233
  256 715
VANAMBERG, 364
VANAMBERGH, 354
VANAMEE, 804 (bio) 1251 1252 Portrait
  1250
VANARSDALL, 800
VANAUKEN, 884 910 988 1170 1495
VANBENSCHOTEN, 855
VANBORSUM, 895
VANBUREN, 199 702 1133 (bio) 489
  Portrait 488
VANBUSKIRK, 291
VANCAMPEN, 1536
VANCE, 849
VANCLEFT, 184 1290 1295 1424 (bio)
  124-126
VANDALFSEN, 479 480
VANDERBILT, 629 817 916 937 1325
VANDERLYN, 1276
VANDERMARK, 512
VANDERMULIN, 845
VANDEROEF, 240 729 (bio) 691 692
  1191 1192 Portrait 1190
VANDERPOLE, 579
VANDERSHINES, 820
VANDERTHAAR, 1435
VANDERVORT, 1200
VANDEUSEN, 153
VANDEWATER, (bio) 969 970
VANDINE, 240
VANDUSER, 740 1316
VANDUZER, 272 594 766 772 773 810
  828 1186 1292 1340 (bio) 290 291
  304 305
VANETTEN, 635 856 870 883 884 893
  895 917 927 981 996 999 1014
  1150 1151 1185 1421 1439 1465
  (bio) 890 891 910 911 988 993
VANEVERA, 1101
VANFLEET, 293 785 858 968 996 1150
  1264 1421 1459 1462 1465 1487
  (bio) 765 766 895 896 921 922
  1024 1025
VANFREDENBERG, 881
VANGORDEN, 746
VANGORDON, 1150 1421
VANHAGEN, 550
VANHELTON, 234
VANHORN, 806 1116 1119 1187
VANHOUTEN, 282 1113
VANINWEGEN, 670 981 996 999 1068
  1149 1151 1264 1421 1439 1440
  1465 (bio) 893 894 1014 1017 1495
  1496 Portrait 1494
VANKEUREN, 212 431 664 935 1128
  1269 1421 (bio) 529 530 672 673

VANKEUREN (cont.)
  903 Portrait 528
VANNESS, 967 1309 (bio) 985 986
  Portrait 984
VANNEST, 213 1327
VANNORMAN, 1212
VANNORT, 131 323
VANNOSTRAND, 1227
VANNOY, 1303
VANORDEN, 1019 1037
VANOSTRAND, 693
VANOSTROM, 450 451
VANPLANCK, 521
VANSAUN, (bio) 281 282
VANSCHAKE, 1050
VANSCIVER, 1119
VANSICKLE, (bio) 602 603
VANSLYCK, 1441
VANSTEENBERGH, (bio) 1512 1513
VANSTEFENHOFFEN, 1512
VANSTEINBERG, 751
VANTASSEL, 573 944
VANTASSELL, 481 788
VANTYLE, 858
VANVAETER, 827
VANVAILER, 1019
VANVLACK, 1476
VANVLEET, 870
VANVLIET, 221 895 (bio) 1343 1344
  Portrait 1342
VANVOORHEES, 325
VANVORIS, 646
VANWART, 745
VANWINKLE, 820
VANWORMER, (bio) 671 936 937
VANWYCK, 590 995 1259 1263 1373
  1397
VANZYLE, 576
VARCOE, 1487 (bio) 1491 1492 Portrait
  1490
VATABLE, 442
VAUGHN, 1251
VELIE, 459 599 709
VENNEMA, (bio) 1435 1436
VERNON, 265 910
VILAS, 276
VINEER, 470
VINES, 143
VOAK, 632
VOGEL, (bio) 1104 1107
VOLCKMER, 530
VONMILTZBOCK, 714
VONSPIEGEL, 1192
VONSTUBEN, 751
VOSBURGH, 808
VOUGHT, 744 787 788
VREDENBURGH, 1216
VROOM, 420 421
VROOMAN, 209
WADDINGTON, (bio) 396 399
WADE, 371 630 644 (bio) 704 705 724

WADE (cont.)
725
WADSWORTH, 371 621 1144
WAGER, 1440 (bio) 1204 1205
WAGNER, 555 886
WAIT, 215 241 1245 1461 1487 (bio)
733 734
WAKEMAN, 693 1428
WALDRAM, 742
WALKER, 121 196 235 249 265 349
502 585 675 899 900 1138 1265
1285 1370 (bio) 549 550 891 892
Portrait 548
WALLACE, 264 512 663 664 725 995
1110 1192 1210 1308 1374 1487
(bio) 664 683 684 772 773 1380-
1382
WALLEN, 1091
WALLING, 1501
WALLIS, 653
WALSH, 162 193 346 516 521 535 554
569 783 819 (bio) 787
WALTERS, 879
WALTON, 949
WANAMAKER, 1530
WANDS, (bio) 133 134
WARD, 141 159 284 330 332 406 409
430 432 433 490 515 564 579 592
656 665 739 803 1007 1277 1331
1403 (bio) 138 139 551 552 601 602
995 996
WARDEN, 394 604 1519
WARFORD, (bio) 225 226
WARING, 424 501 605 869 1209 1397
(bio) 1349 1350 Portrait 1348
WARNER, 244 426 912 1175 1242
WARREN, 355 546 869 975 1012 1215
WARRING, 346
WARVEL, 585
WARWICK, (bio) 506
WASHBURN, 350 365 911
WASHINGTON, 117 140 263 381 384
646 670 686 752 755 756 763 772
794 819 826 827 915 933 949 958
975 1084 1090 1139 1187 1199
1259 1319 1345 1481 (bio) 899 900
Portrait 898
WASNICK, (bio) 731
WATERBURY, 294 806 1319 1364
WATERS, 752 1283 1284
WATKINS, 231 767
WATTS, 659
WAYNE, 355 1411
WEAR, 231
WEAVER, 786
WEBB, 266 275 579 825 827 938 1026
1062 1289 1422 1491 (bio) 221
WEBBER, 621 1338
WEBER, 383
WEBSTER, 652 653 979 1132 1217
1333 1427

WEED, 196 206 271 461 656 819 928
1084 1155 1174 1290 (bio) 163-165
452 453 1295 1296 Portrait 1294
WEEDEN, 1453
WEEKS, 646 744 798 806 1042 1134
1223 (bio) 766 767
WEESNER, 279
WEHNER, 848
WEIGAND, 179 180
WEILAND, 184
WEIR, 1400
WEISNER, 751 879 1191
WEITZEL, 976
WEITZER, 1035
WELCH, 685 733 969 1436
WELLER, 235 264 359 511 716 722
957 1056 1349 1350 1363 (bio) 346
349 375 376 721
WELLING, 272 280 282 295 305 540
740 1053 1357
WELLS, 333 392 574 604 686 754 1007
1038 1041 1101 1128 1224 1257
1411 (bio) 624 625 1263 1264 Por-
trait 1262
WELSH, 229
WENDOM, 273
WENDT, 1240
WENZEL, 480
WERK, 1236
WESER, 175
WESLEY, 1491 1499
WESSELS, 1155
WEST, 325 356 426 655 (bio) 999 1000
1440 1441 Portrait 998
WESTBROOK, 224 624 630 847 870
884 890 902 910 968 988 996 1150
1151 1417 1421 1465 1466
WESTCOTT, 273 274 1511
WESTERVELT, 490
WESTFALL, 870 922 968 988 996 1026
1029 1150 1151 1421 1465 1495
WESTLAKE, 1295
WESTON, 432 560 596 609 (bio) 446
449
WETEL, 1206
WETJEN, 479
WEYANT, 292 293 306 777 782 788
869 1096 (bio) 576 741 742 744 745
756 757
WEYGANT, 119 126 346 424 536 592
784 795 806 808 810 823 835 836
933 1115 1479 (bio) 179-183 797
798 Portrait 178
WEYMER, 858
WHALEN, 133 1019 1032
WHEAT, 636
WHEELER, 279 685 773 1013 1050
1073 1121 1137 1138 1191 1206
1241 1266 1320 1321 1398 1421
1466 1535 (bio) 481 1074 1332 1334
1447

WRITER, 896 (bio) 987 988
WURTS, 1418
WUST, 426
WYATT, 869
WYCKEHAM, 654
WYCKOFF, 838
WYKER, (bio) 274 275
WYLIE, 229 1272
WYMAN, 119
WYNCOOK, 681
WYNKOOP, 670 996
YACKEL, 361
YARAH, 819
YARD, 1339
YOERG, 1037
YORK, 474
YOUEY, 632

YOUMANS, (bio) 807 808
YOUNG, 117 193 194 255 343 486 514
654 671 683 696 767 775 781 808
809 857 858 863 944 1038 1164
1525 1529 (bio) 456 459 660 661
YOUNGBLOOD, 589 590 1061 1077
1529
YOUNGHANS, 786
YOUNGLOVE, 1283
YOUNGS, 706 830 936 1527 (bio) 1534
1535
ZEARBOSS, 1068
ZEARFOSS, 1430
ZELL, 1170
ZIEGLER, 324
ZINT, 413 (bio) 471 472

www.ingramcontent.com/pod-product-compliance
Lightning Source LLC
Chambersburg PA
CBHW071824270326
41929CB00013B/1894